The
Intellectuals

The
Intellectuals

A Controversial Portrait

Edited with an Introduction and Overviews by

George B. de Huszar

The Free Press of Glencoe, Illinois

Printed in the United States of America

Contents

(v)

Contents

Contents

PART VI
Intellectuals in Various Countries

The
Intellectuals

INTRODUCTION

BERTRAND DE JOUVENEL has pointed out that as against the attention devoted to various social groups such as workers and the bourgeoisie, "very little has been devoted to the intellectuals as such, even though their influence is unquestionable and a formidable advance in their numbers has occurred with the advent of universal education and universal information." Raymond Aron also made essentially the same point when he recently called attention to the absence of "a fully worked out sociology of the intelligentsia." These statements confirm the views expressed some years ago by Karl Mannheim: "The problem of a sociology of the intelligentsia is, in spite of the fact that much energy has been devoted to it, still in a preliminary stage. . . . There is an extensive literature in several countries on elites and intellectuals . . . the subject is a very complex one and the literature very vast. . . . There are, however, no systematic and comprehensive works on the subject."

The present work does not pretend to be a systematic treatise but its form provides two advantages:

1. There are books and many articles about intellectuals but none of them is comprehensive. This volume attempts to meet the need for a comprehensive treatment by bringing together essays which hitherto had to be sought in scattered books and journals. Because of the complexity of the subject it would be difficult for one person to discuss with comprehensive knowledge its manifold phases. Essays by numerous authors insures that each of them will devote attention to some particular phase and discuss it with some authority.

2. This multiple authorship, by bringing together contributors of varied backgrounds and views, also makes possible a diversity of viewpoints and interpretations. The central theme is approached from as many points of view as possible. These diverse and conflicting sources should stimulate the thinking of the reader. All controversial matters, not only the political, receive a balanced treatment. The diversity is further enhanced by the fact that the contributors vary not only by the period and place in which they lived, but also by their backgrounds. The arts, the humanities, and the social and natural sciences are represented; historians, sociologists, political scientists, economists, philosophers, poets, writers, and so on are represented.

The disadvantages of an anthology are threefold:

1. It is obvious that it cannot have the unity of a volume written by a single

(3)

individual. But in the absence of a systematic treatise by one author which may yet develop a comprehensive theory of the intellectuals, this volume may help fill a gap. It is hoped that it possesses unity in terms of the themes of its various parts. The Overviews, written by the Editor, may also be of some help.

2. An inevitable result of anthologies is unevenness of quality, tone, and style. More uniformity in these respects would have led to the exclusion of many pieces, which would have made for less comprehensiveness and balance. It may be objected that some of the contributors do not deserve to be ranked with Kierkegaard, Nietzsche, and Dostoevsky. This is obviously true but the purpose of this work is to include the *best* essays which are most *representative* from a historical and contemporary point of view.

3. In order to present essays representing the greatest possible diversity of interpretation and stance the Editor had to include some essays which he knows to be full of falsehood, and of which he disapproves.

Perhaps the best way to explain the nature of this volume is to compare it with the daily newspaper, with which we are so familiar. In fact, we rarely stop to reflect on its encyclopedic nature and variety. It includes diversity in virtually every sense of the word: tone, style, length, as well as subject matter. This book contains numerous pieces which are like editorials, news reports, and analyses. It even includes amusements like the piece by Mencken; and also crime reporting as represented in the piece by Gorky. The fact that a newspaper editor prints something does not necessarily mean that he agrees with it. He prints as news many political views to which he is strongly opposed, and crime news, the subject of which he deplores. The Editor of this book is in a similar predicament. The analogy with newspapers only fails in that this book does not include any advertisements.

Dr. Johnson has remarked that "A man will turn over half a library to make one book." It depends, of course, on the size of the library Dr. Johnson had in mind whether half a library has in fact been read or surveyed in the production of this volume. To create a comprehensive work the Editor has surveyed a great many books and articles to find candidates for inclusion. Because of the vastness of the literature, the Editor has undoubtedly missed some important items despite diligent search. Over two hundred candidates were located from which sixty-eight were finally selected. Some valuable essays were not included simply because of space limitations; other interesting pieces were excluded because they were not sufficiently relevant to the subject; pieces of timely interest only were also excluded. It is inevitable that in making the final selection from the available candidates another editor may have arrived at different results. The structure of the book and the arrangement of the pieces within each part are likewise subject to disagreements: overlappings between various essays could not be avoided. The Editor has tried to accomodate numerous complete essays but has had to cut some of them because of space limitations.

To allow the inclusion of a variety of essays, the term "intellectuals" was conceived of in a relatively broad sense. However, despite the ambitious aim of comprehensiveness, a major limitation has been observed in order to prevent the book from becoming substantially larger than it is: The modern intellectual is seen to have emerged around the time of the French Revolution. Authors who wrote prior to that event are not included, nor are discussions of intellectuals before that date written by recent authors. The emphasis has been on essays about intellectuals in the twentieth century. This limitation necessitated the exclusion of classical pieces such as Plato's theory of the philosopher-king; selections from non-Western figures such as Ibn Khaldun's essay on scholars, pieces from the Middle Ages and the Renaissance, such as Petrarch's essay on the man of letters, Leonardo da Vinci on the artist, Montaigne on pedantry, Cervantes' discourse on arms and letters, and Francis Bacon on learning; and many pieces written in the seventeenth and eighteenth centuries. Moreover, with some exceptions the emphasis has been on the selection of essays and not novels or plays.

Each author is obviously responsible only for the content of his own essay. The Editor is responsible for the inclusion or deletion of essays, their arrangement, and cutting them. The Editor is also responsible for the Overviews which are mostly summaries of the views expressed and do not express his attitude about the essays, whether it be approval or disapproval. The biographical information is also intended to be short and factual. If a reader wishes to have further information he can easily consult standard biographical reference works. The numbering of footnotes has been changed when necessary. Some footnotes in some essays, which were not essential to the understanding of the essays themselves, or were not intrinsically valuable, have been deleted. The essays have been reprinted in the original manner of publication, without changing punctuation, capitalization or style.

Thanks are due to the various publishers and authors who have given permission to reprint essays. The Editor also wishes to express his appreciation for valuable criticism and suggestions to Richard S. Barnes, Frank R. Barnett, James Burnham, David M. Cox, Hugh D. Duncan, Bertrand de Jouvenel, Professor M. M. Postan of Cambridge University, Professor Albert Salomon of the Graduate Faculty of the New School for Social Research, Professor Hugh Seton-Watson of London University, and particularly to Richard C. Cornuelle. The Editor also wishes to express his thanks to Jeremiah Kaplan whose cooperation and helpfulness went beyond the usual courtesies extended by a publisher; and also to Martha Roess of The Free Press. Thanks are due to Ben C. Bowman and staff members of The Newberry Library for numerous courtesies extended. Special appreciation is due to the late Loren B. Miller, and other Trustees of the Relm Foundation whose grant enabled the Editor to devote part of the time needed to complete this project. Finally it should be stated that without Barbara de Huszar's interest and assistance this volume would not have come into being.

Chicago, Illinois   *George B. de Huszar*

Part I

EMERGENCE
OF MODERN
INTELLECTUALS

OVERVIEW

JEAN COCTEAU has remarked regarding Alexander the Great: "All that remains of his success is a profile on a coin which Barrès gave me. The other side bears a wise man, seated. Everyone knows that the two sides of a coin have little chance of ever meeting." Yet many modern intellectuals have tried to attain power and tried in some measure to realize Plato's ideal of the philosopher-king. Part I contains some essays which show that modern intellectuals have tried not only to describe and understand historical developments but to grasp and change them. The significance of intellectuals to the French, American, and Russian Revolutions is emphasized: In the American Revolution and in England, intellectuals were successful in combining thought and power; their achievement in the French and Russian Revolutions is controversial. Attention is also paid in this Part to the predicament of literary men during the eighteenth and nineteenth centuries. It should be emphasized that Part I presents essays dealing with the history of intellectuals up to the twentieth century; the subsequent parts are organized topically until Part VI when the historical material is brought up to date for various countries.

Tocqueville asserts that never before the middle of the eighteenth century had the entire political education of a great nation been the work of men of letters (who are the prototype of modern intellectuals). French men of letters became the leading political figures since they spoke with authority, despite the fact that they did not hold the reins of government. Specifically Tocqueville make two points: (1) The aristocracy was declining and their place was taken by the men of letters. This decadent aristocracy in fact made much of the men of letters and did not fear their doctrines, which were hostile to them; the aristocracy was blind and compassed its own downfall. In connection with this it is worth recalling an observation of Stendhal that "Hitherto all our authors who have made themselves famous have been men paid by the government or the religion that they sought to undermine." (2) Unlike in England, precept and practice were in the hands of two different groups. The men of letters of eighteenth century France being out of touch with practical politics indulged in abstract political theories and vague generalizations. But they had great confidence in them and thought that under the rule of reason a sudden and radical transformation of a complex society was possible; the Revolution was conducted in these terms. Their vision of an ideal society appealed to the imagination of the masses, with disastrous results. A later French writer said that royal authority was not displaced by the sovereignty of the people but that the successors of the Bourbons were the men of letters: "Letters became king."

Salomon draws attention to the rise of a particular type of man of letters in the eighteenth century: the bohemian to whom the coffeehouse was the salon. The bohemian was to become a significant type, in what Salomon calls the age of total revolutions, the true epoch of the intellectuals. Messianic bohemians became prominent in the years after the French Revolution. Conspicuous were Saint-Simon and Comte, both uprooted men, out of sympathy with their time, unable to organize their own lives but believing that they had discovered a way to end the chaos of all history. They took over from Christian eschatology the idea of the establishment of the Kingdom of God on earth, with the addition that this would be attained at some specific date in history. In connection with this thought attention should also be paid to the article by Hook in Part V. The messianism of the positivist intellectuals acknowledged no alternative to its vision. The intellectuals in the years after the French Revolution differed from those prior to it mainly because of the tremendous development of science and the deification of Reason. The alliance between science and secular religion gave intellectuals the opportunity of playing the role of both "scientist" and "priest."

In contrast to the French men of letters of the eighteenth century as described by Tocqueville, and the messianic bohemians as depicted by Salomon, many intellectuals succeeded in combining theory and practice, thus attaining constructive and durable results. Tocqueville draws attention to the fact that English writers took an active part in public affairs and that there was no split between those who wrote on the theory of government and those who governed. Curti shows that similarly the gulf between theory and action was reduced in colonial, Revolutionary, and post-Revolutionary America. Many of the Patriot intellectuals did not limit themselves to the written and spoken word, but joined the rank and file in the practical work of the Revolution. Many of the members of the Constitutional Convention were intellectuals who were most successful in combining theory with practical statesmanship. The faith in the desirability and feasibility of applying knowledge to political action survived into the early years of the Republic.

Schücking also deals with the intellectuals of the eighteenth and nineteenth centuries but he concentrates on the literary artist rather than the political philosopher. He points out that for a long time to live by the pen was not considered respectable; many writers preferred to be known as gentlemen rather than as authors. With the rise of the middle class a change occurred and the prestige of authors grew. In the second half of the nineteenth century the artist gradually attains a position which in earlier centuries would have been impossible. Art began to be viewed as divine service and the artist was guided solely by his own taste and conviction. It was assumed that any connection with the public interfered with the priest in his service to beauty and thus the great public was viewed with hostility. Schücking's analysis appears to be more correct than the usual Marxist stress on the split between the bourgeoisie and the intelligentsia which was supposed to have taken place after 1848. Such a split occurred for aesthetic reasons and not because the intelligentsia became the champion of the working classes. For example, it has been said that Baudelaire saw in the revolution of 1848 merely a splendid opportunity to set fire to the house of his stepfather.

As in the French Revolution, the Russian intelligentsia also played an outstanding role in bringing about the Bolshevik Revolution. Seton-Watson says that it is important to distinguish between those aspects of the Russian intelligentsia which are specifically Russian and those which are not. Nationalism, liberalism, and socialism, reached Russia in the mid-nineteenth century through the intelligentsia. It imported, ready made from the West, ideas related to the reality of the West but not to that of Russia. The intelligentsia contained both admirers and critics of the West, both reformers and revolutionists. The reformers wanted to be constructive in contrast to those who clung to the desire for cataclysmic upheaval followed by utopia. The condition of alienation provided a favorable mental climate first for radical ideas and then for revolutionary movements. The intelligentsia's anti-bourgeois outlook and lack of respect for law prepared the ground in Russia for Marx. In this connection it should be noted that the combination of Russia's sense of mission, keenly felt by its intellectuals, with apocalyptic Marxism, resulted in a more dynamic messianism than the one previously described by Salomon with respect to French positivism. Seton-Watson also points out that the intelligentsia, separated from the political and social regime, had no experience in the management of government. Isolated from the Russian masses and the machinery of government, the radical intelligentsia lived in an abstract world of ideas. Recalling Tocqueville's and Curti's essays it is clear that in France and Russia, unlike in England and America, a split existed between the theorists and the actual rulers, which contributed to making the revolutionists of France and Russia committed to theoretical and abstract patterns. The Russian revolutionaries, like the French, out of touch with political realities, had great confidence in political theories which they thought could be translated into reality. The judgment of a former Russian revolutionary, Bakhtiarov, who committed suicide while imprisoned by the victorious Bolsheviks, makes the responsibility of an unrealistic and utopian intelligentsia clear. A former fellow prisoner reported: "Bakhtiarov . . . thought the Russian intelligentsia had done more than anything else to bring the country under Bolshevist domination. . . . The intelligentsia was the brains of the people. . . . It never gave a thought to what was going to follow the Tsar's regime. It did not understand the basic character of the Russian people. It had no notion how to govern them. It idealized the people and lived in a world of dreams."

HOW TOWARDS THE MIDDLE OF THE EIGHTEENTH CENTURY MEN OF LETTERS TOOK THE LEAD IN POLITICS AND THE CONSEQUENCES OF THIS NEW DEVELOPMENT

Alexis de Tocqueville

I NOW LEAVE BEHIND the circumstances remote in time and of a general order which prepared the way for the great revolution, and come to the particular, more recent events which finally determined its place of origin, its outbreak, and the form it took.

For a long while the French had been the most literary-minded of all the nations of Europe, but so far our writers had not displayed that intellectual brilliance which won them world-wide fame toward the middle of the eighteenth century. True, they did not play an active part in public affairs, as English writers did; on the contrary, never had they kept so steadily aloof from the political arena. In a nation teeming with officials none of the men of letters held posts of any kind, none was invested with authority.

Nevertheless, they did not (like most of their German contemporaries) resolutely turn their backs on politics and retire to a world apart, of *belles lettres* and pure philosophy. On the contrary, they were keenly interested in all that concerned the government of nations; this, one might almost say, was an obsession with them. Questions such as the origin of human society, its earliest forms, the original rights of citizens and of authority, the "natural" and the "artificial" relations between men, of the legitimacy of custom, and even the whole conception of law—all these bulked large in the literature of the day. As a result of this incessant probing into the bases of the society in which they lived, they were led both to examine its structure in detail and to criticize its general plan. Not all our writers, it is true, made these vast problems their exclusive study; indeed, the great majority dealt with them casually, even, one might say, toyed with them. But all took notice of them in one way or another. This kind of abstract, literary politics found its way, in varying proportions, into all the writings of the day, and there was none, from the most ponderous treatise to the lightest lyric, that had not at least a grain of it.

The political programs advocated by our eighteenth-century writers varied so much that any attempt to synthesize them or deduce a single coherent theory of government from them would be labor lost. Nonetheless if, disregarding details, we look to the directive ideas, we find that all these various systems stemmed from a single concept of a highly general order, their common source, and that our authors took this as their premise before venturing on their personal, often somewhat eccentric solutions of the problem of good government. Thus, though their ways diverged in the course of their researches, their starting point was the same in all cases; and this was the belief that what was wanted was to replace the complex of traditional customs governing the social order of the day by simple, elementary rules deriving from the exercise of the human reason and natural law.

When we look closely into it we find that the political philosophy of these writers consists to all intents and purposes in ringing the changes on this one idea. It was no new one; it had haunted men's imaginations off and on for three millennia, but never until now had it succeeded in making itself accepted as a basic principle. How was it that at this particular point of time it could root itself so firmly in the minds of the writers of the day? Why, instead of remaining as in the past the purely intellectual concept of a few advanced thinkers, did it find a welcome among the masses and acquire the driving force of a political passion to such effect that general and abstract theories of the nature of human society not only became daily topics of conversation among the leisure class but fired the imagination even of women and peasants? And why was it that men of letters, men without wealth, social eminence, responsibilities, or official status, became in practice the leading politicians of the age, since despite the fact that others held the reins of government, they alone spoke with accents of authority? These questions I shall now try to answer, and at the same time I shall draw attention to the remarkable, not to say formidable, influence these men's writings (which at first sight might seem to concern the history of our literature alone) had on the Revolution, and, indeed, still have today.

It was not by mere chance that our eighteenth-century thinkers as a body enounced theories so strongly opposed to those that were still regarded as basic to the social order; they could hardly be expected to do otherwise when they contemplated the world around them. The sight of so many absurd and unjust privileges, whose evil effects were increasingly felt on every hand though their true causes were less and less understood, urged or, rather, forced them towards a concept of the natural equality of all men irrespective of social rank. When they saw so many ridiculous, ramshackle institutions, survivals of an earlier age, which no one had attempted to co-ordinate or to adjust to modern conditions and which seemed destined to live on despite the fact that they had ceased to have any present value, it was natural enough that thinkers of the day should come to loathe everything that savored of the past and should desire to remold society on entirely new lines, traced by each thinker in the sole light of reason.[1]

Their very way of living led these writers to indulge in abstract theories and generalizations regarding the nature of government, and to place a blind confidence in these. For living as they did, quite out of touch with practical politics, they lacked the experience which might have tempered their enthusiasms. Thus they completely failed to perceive the very real obstacles in the way of even the most praiseworthy reforms, and to gauge the perils involved in even the most salutary revolutions. That they should not have had the least presentiment of these dangers was only to be expected, since as a result of the total absence of any political freedom, they had little acquaintance with the realities of public life, which, indeed, was *terra incognita* to them. Taking no personal part in it and unable to see what was being done by others in that field, they lacked even the superficial acquaintance with such matters which comes to those who live under a free régime, can see what is happening, and hear the voice of public opinion even though they themselves take no part whatever in the government of the country. As a result, our literary men became much bolder in their speculations, more addicted to general ideas and systems, more contemptuous of the wisdom of the ages, and even more inclined to trust their individual reason than most of those who have written books on politics from a philosophic angle.

When it came to making themselves heard by the masses and appealing to their emotions, this very ignorance served them in good stead. If the French people had still played an active part in politics (through the Estates-General) or even if they had merely continued to concern themselves with the day-to-day administration of affairs through the provincial assemblies, we may be

---

1. It has been said that the character of the philosophy of the eighteenth century was a sort of adoration of human intellect, an unlimited confidence in its power to transform at will laws, institutions, customs. To be accurate, it must be said that the human intellect which some of these philosophers adored was simply their own. They showed, in fact, an uncommon want of faith in the wisdom of the masses. I could mention several who despised the public almost as heartily as they despised the Deity. Toward the latter they evinced the pride of rivals—the former they treated with the pride of parvenus. They were as far from real and respectful submission to the will of the majority as from submission to the will of God. Nearly all subsequent revolutionaries have borne the same character. Very different from this is the respect shown by Englishmen and Americans for the sentiments of the majority of their fellow citizens. Their intellect is proud and self-reliant, but never insolent; and it has led to liberty, while ours has done little but invent new forms of servitude.

sure that they would not have let themselves be carried away so easily by the ideas of the writers of the day; any experience, however slight, of public affairs would have made them chary of accepting the opinions of mere theoreticians.

Similarly if, like the English, they had succeeded in gradually modifying the spirit of their ancient institutions without destroying them, perhaps they would not have been so prompt to clamor for a new order. As it was, however, every Frenchman felt he was being victimized; his personal freedom, his money, his self-respect, and the amenities of his daily life were constantly being tampered with on the strength of some ancient law, some medieval usage, or the remnants of some antiquated servitude. Nor did he see any constitutional remedy for this state of affairs; it seemed as if the choice lay between meekly accepting everything or destroying the whole system.

Nevertheless, in the nation-wide debacle of freedom we had preserved one form of it; we could indulge, almost without restriction, in learned discussions on the origins of society, the nature of government, and the essential rights of man. All who were chafing under the yoke of the administration enjoyed these literary excursions into politics; indeed, the taste for them spread even into sections of the community whose temperaments or upbringing would have normally discouraged them from abstract speculations. But there was no taxpayer aggrieved by the injustices of the *taille* who did not welcome the idea that all men should be equal; no farmer whose land was devastated by a noble neighbor's rabbits who did not rejoice at hearing it declared that privilege of any kind whatever was condemned by the voice of reason. Thus the philosopher's cloak provided safe cover for the passions of the day and the political ferment was canalized into literature, the result being that our writers now became the leaders of public opinion and played for a while the part which normally, in free countries, falls to the professional politician. And as things were, no one was in a position to dispute their right to leadership.

A powerful aristocracy does not merely shape the course of public affairs, it also guides opinion, sets the tone for writers, and lends authority to new ideas. By the eighteenth century the French nobility had wholly lost this form of ascendancy, its prestige had dwindled with its power, and since the place it had occupied in the direction of public opinion was vacant, writers could usurp it with the greatest ease and keep it without fear of being dislodged.

Still more remarkable was the fact that this very aristocracy whose place the writers had taken made much of them. So completely had our nobility forgotten that new political theories, once they are generally accepted, inevitably rouse popular passions and bear fruit in deeds, that they regarded even the doctrines most hostile to their prerogatives, and in fact to their very existence, as mere flights of fancy, entertaining *jeux d'esprit*. So they, too, took a hand in the new, delightful game and, while clinging to their immunities and privileges, talked lightheartedly of the "absurdity" of all the old French customs.

Astonishment has often been expressed at this singular blindness of the upper classes of the old régime and the way they compassed their own downfall. Yet how could they have known better? Political freedom is no less indispensable to the ruling classes to enable them to realize their perils than to the rank and file to enable them to safeguard their rights. More than a century had elapsed since the last traces of free public life had disappeared in France, and those most directly interested in the maintenance of the old constitution had not been forewarned by any sound or sign of an impending breakdown. Since outwardly nothing had changed, they had no fears for its stability. In a word, their point of view was that of their fathers, they could not move with the times. In the 1789 *cahiers* we find the nobility still harping as much on the "encroachments" of the royal power as if they were living in the fifteenth century. And that ill-starred King, Louis XVI, at the very moment when he was about to be engulfed by the flood tide of democracy, continued (as Burke has aptly pointed out) to regard the aristocracy as the chief danger to the throne and mistrusted it as much as if he were back in the days of the "Fronde." On the other hand, he, like his ancestors, saw in the middle class and the people the staunchest supporters of the Crown.

But what must seem still more extraordinary to us, given our experience of the aftermath of so many revolutions, is that the possibility of a violent upheaval never crossed our parents' minds. No one breathed a word of it, no one even dreamed of it. The small disturbances which, when there is political freedom, inevitably take place from time to time in even the most stable social systems are a constant reminder of the risk of large-scale cataclysms and keep the authorities on the *qui vive*. But in the eighteenth century, on the very eve of the Revolution, there had been as yet no warning that the ancient edifice was tottering.

I have closely studied the *cahiers* drawn up by the three Orders before the meeting of the Estates-General—by all three Orders, be it noted—nobility and clergy as well as the Third Estate. In the course of plowing my way through these voluminous documents I made many notes: here was a request for the amendment of a law, here for the suppression of a custom, and so forth. When I had reached the end of my labors and made a list of these various proposals I realized with something like consternation that what was being asked for was nothing short of the systematic, simultaneous abolition of *all* existing French laws and customs. There was no blinking the fact that what the authors of these *cahiers* jointly sponsored was one of the vastest, most catastrophic revolutions the world had ever known. Yet the men who were to be its victims had not the least presentiment of this; they nursed the foolish hope that a sudden, radical transformation of a very ancient, highly intricate social system could be effected almost painlessly, under the auspices of reason and by its efficacy alone. Theirs was a rude awakening! They would have done better to recall an ancient dictum formulated by their ancestors, four centuries before, in the rather crabbed language of the day: "Claim too great freedom, too much license, and too great subjection shall befall you!"

Given their long exclusion from any form of public life, it is not surprising that the nobility and bourgeoisie should have developed this singular obtuseness. But it is decidedly surprising that those who were at the helm of public affairs—statesmen, Intendants, the magistrates—should have displayed little more foresight. No doubt many of these men had proved themselves highly competent in the exercise of their functions and had a good grasp of all the details of public administration; yet, as for true statecraft—that is to say clear perception of the way society is evolving, an awareness of the trends of mass opinion and an ability to forecast the future—they were as much at sea as any ordinary citizen. For it is only in an atmosphere of freedom that the qualities of mind indispensable to true statesmanship can mature and fructify.

In this context a memorandum submitted by Turgot to the King in 1775 is enlightening. In it he advises the King, amongst other things, to convoke yearly a "representative assembly" for a six-week session at which he (the King) would be present; but at the same time he counsels him against granting the assembly any effective power. It was to be concerned with administration, not with government, its business would be to make suggestions rather than to legislate, and its function that of discussing laws, not making them. "Thus Your Majesty will be kept posted as to popular feeling without being trammeled by it, and public opinion satisfied without any peril to the State. For these assemblies will have no right to vote against necessary measures, and, even should they overstep their powers, Your Majesty will always have the last word." This blindness to the certain consequences of such a measure and this incomprehension of the spirit of the age are singularly revealing. Often, towards the close of revolutions it has been possible to do what Turgot proposed; that is to say to give the people the shadow of liberty without its substance. The Emperor Augustus brought this off successfully. A nation that is weary of internecine conflict is quite ready to be duped provided it is given peace, and history tells us that at such times all that is needed to satisfy public opinion is to gather together from all parts of the country a number of obscure or pliable men and to have them play the part of a national assembly at a fixed salary. There have been several instances of this. But at the early stage of a revolution such methods always fail; all they do is to whet the appetite of the masses, and nobody is satisfied. This is known to even the humblest citizen of a free country; but, great administrator though he was, Turgot was unaware of it.

When we remember also that the French nation, excluded as it was from the conduct of its own affairs, lacking in political experience, shackled by ancient institutions and powerless to reform them—when we remember that this was the most literary-minded of all nations and intellectually quickest in the uptake, it is easy to understand why our authors became a power in the land and ended up as its political leaders.

In England writers on the theory of government and those who actually governed co-operated with each other, the former setting forth their new theories, the latter amending or circumscribing these in the light of practical experience. In France, however, precept and practice were kept quite distinct and remained in the hands of two quite independent groups. One of these carried on the actual administration while the other set forth the abstract principles on which good government should, they said, be based; one took the routine measures appropriate to the needs of the moment, the other propounded general laws without a thought for their practical application; one group shaped the course of public affairs, the other that of public opinion.

Thus alongside the traditional and confused, not to say chaotic, social system of the day there was gradually built up in men's minds an imaginary ideal society in which all was simple, uniform, coherent, equitable, and rational in the full sense of the term. It was this vision of the perfect State that fired the imagination of the masses and little by little estranged them from the here-and-now. Turning away from the real world around them, they indulged in dreams of a far better one and ended up by living, spiritually, in the ideal world thought up by the writers.

The French Revolution has often been regarded as a consequence of the American and there is no denying that the latter had considerable influence on it. But it was due less to what actually took place in the United States than to ideas then prevalent in France. To the rest of Europe the American Revolution seemed merely a novel and remarkable historical event; whereas the French saw in it a brilliant confirmation of theories already familiar to them. Elsewhere it merely shocked and startled; for the French it was conclusive proof that they were in the right. Indeed, the Americans seemed only to be putting into practice ideas which had been sponsored by our writers, and to be making our dreams their realities. It is as if Fénelon had suddenly found himself in Salente. Never before had the entire political education of a great nation been the work of its men of letters and it was this peculiarity that perhaps did most to give the French Revolution its exceptional character and the régime that followed it the form we are familiar with.

Our men of letters did not merely impart their revolutionary ideas to the French nation; they also shaped the national temperament and outlook on life. In the long process of molding men's minds to their ideal pattern their task was all the easier since the French had had no training in the field of politics, and they thus had a clear field. The result was that our writers ended up by giving the Frenchman the instincts, the turn of mind, the tastes, and even the eccentricities characteristic of the literary man. And when the time came for action, these literary propensities were imported into the political arena.

When we closely study the French Revolution we find that it was conducted in precisely the same spirit as that which gave rise to so many books expounding theories of government in the abstract. Our revolutionaries had the same fondness for broad generalizations, cut-and-dried legislative systems, and a pedantic symmetry; the same contempt for hard facts; the same taste for reshaping institutions on novel, ingenious, original lines; the same desire to reconstruct the entire constitution according to the rules of logic and a preconceived system instead of trying to rectify its faulty parts. The result was nothing short of disastrous; for what is a merit in the writer may well be a vice in the statesman and the very qualities which go to make great literature can lead to catastrophic revolutions.

Even the politicians' phraseology was borrowed largely from the books they read; it was cluttered up with abstract words, gaudy flowers of speech, sonorous clichés, and literary turns of phrase. Fostered by the political passions that it voiced, this style made its way into all classes, being adopted with remarkable facility even by the lowest. Long before the Revolution, King Louis XIV in his edicts had often spoken of natural law and the rights of man. I have found peasants calling their neighbors "fellow citizens" in their petitions, the Intendant "our honorable magistrate," the village priest "the guardian of our altars," and God "the Supreme Being." All they needed, in fact, to become literary men in a small way was a better knowledge of spelling.

These habits have become so much ingrained in the French character that, recent though they are and due solely to a very special type of education, many seem to regard them as inborn. I have heard it said that the penchant, not to say the passion, of our politicians during the last sixty years for general ideas, systems, and high-flown verbiage stems from a national trait, the so-called "French spirit"—the idea presumably being that this alleged propensity suddenly came to the fore at the end of the last century after lying dormant throughout the rest of our history!

What seems particularly odd is that while retaining habits thus derived from books, we have almost completely lost our former love of literature. In the course of my public career I have often been struck by the fact that those who reproduce most faithfully some of the chief defects of the literary style prevailing in the previous generation are men who rarely, if ever, read our eighteenth-century books or, for that matter, any books at all.

THE MESSIANIC BOHEMIANS

Albert Salomon

Wно were the intellectuals whose thinking was to dominate the twentieth century? How did they live? What was their relationship to the academy? Did they retreat, or did they move freely in their world? To understand sociology, we must first understand its creators. In any age, it is interesting to study the psychological elements which are at play in the lives of its seminal thinkers; but it is imperative in the case of these "moderns" for, in reconstructing the banalities of a life such as Saint-Simon's, we come closer to seeing that the type he represents was something quite new and different in the history of the European intellectual.

During the Middle Ages there was no problem of the intellectual as such. Since all theoretical discussion took place within the Church, the merest fragment of the feudal elite—that is, the men of law—concerned themselves professionally in testing the claims of the ecclesiastical powers. With the opening of the monasteries during the Renaissance, many philosophically minded ecclesiastics departed eagerly into the independence of the secular world. Nevertheless, a Petrarch's enthusiasm for the life that lay beyond the walls was apt to be short-lived, for the problem of earning a living forced many of these newly-emerged intellectuals into the service of the princes, whose willingness to support poets and thinkers exacted in return a surrender to a new ministry of thought. The philosophers were hired as propagandists, and their status derived solely from that of their royal employers. Rabelais spoke with painful longing of the Abbey of Thélème in *Gargantua and Pantagruel*. The secular monastery represented a refuge from the demands of the princes, among whom the contemplative life was no longer possible. The intellectuals —much like the sophists and rhetors in the Greek and Roman worlds—found that their livelihoods depended largely on their ability to function as counselors to the holders of power at the cost of their own integrity. One man alone, Erasmus, escaped the dilemma of the intellectual and then only because of a unique situation, the support which he received from his printers. The alliance between author and printer in the sixteenth century, when both stood dedicated to social as well as religious and moral convictions, made it possible

Reprinted from *The Tyranny of Progress* (1955), pp. 25-39, by permission of the author and publisher, The Noonday Press.

for the humanist philosopher to hold himself aloof. Froben and Amorbach, the great liberal Swiss printers, believed in Erasmus's ideas on Church reform and therefore were willing to maintain him, pay his rent, and make him a partner in the firm, as long as he stayed in Basel. But Erasmus's position was unique. It preceded the development of publishing as a business institution, subject to the logic of economics and the demands of a book-buying public. With the growing rationalization of the publishing industry, the intellectual without private income lay at the mercy of the businessman. The gentlemen-authors—the *grand seigneurs,* Montaigne, Lord Shaftesbury, Montesquieu, and Baron Holbach—could afford to be philosophers, but the free-lance writer found that there was no place for serious work. Instead, the demands of the uneducated grew louder and more insistent and created authors of entertainment, of pornography, and of horror stories. These writers, separated from any form of *Kulturtraeger* and living on their wits alone, learned by the beginning of the eighteenth century to prefer each other's company to that of a hostile world. They created, so to speak, their own life-pattern for they had become a class of white-collar intellectuals who kept alive by meeting the demands of their publishers and whose spare time was taken up with more serious efforts. If it is permissible to speak of a literary stratification of society, these intellectuals were a new social group, a cadre, whose center was not the court, nor the Church, but the coffeehouse. Montesquieu discovered the social function of the coffeehouse—the home of the homeless intellectual. He wrote:

> Coffee is very much used in Paris. Here are a good many houses where it may be had. In some of these they meet to gossip, in others to play at chess. There is one where the coffee is prepared in such a way that it makes those who drink it witty: at least, there is not a single one who, on quitting the house, does not believe himself four times wittier than when he entered it.
> But that which shocks me most in these geniuses, is, that they are quite useless to their country, and amuse their talents with puerilities. For example, when I arrived at Paris, I found them warm at dispute over the most trifling matter imaginable. It was all about an old Greek poet, whose birthplace and time of dying no one has known about for 2000 years. Both sides agreed that he was a most excellent poet. It was only a question of the degree of merit to be ascribed to him. Each wished to fix his rank; but among those apportioners of praise, some carried more weight than others. Here you have the whole dispute. It was a lively quarrel; for both sides abused each other most heartily with such gross aspersions, and such bitter raillery, that I admired the conduct of the quarrel as much as the subject of it. "If any one," I said to myself, "were fool enough to attack in the presence of the defenders of the Greek poet, the reputation of some honest citizen, he surely would find a warm reception; and, indeed, I believe that this extreme zeal for the reputation of the dead, would blaze up to some purpose in defense of the living. But, however this may be," added I, "God keep me from ever drawing on myself the enmity of these censors of this poet, who has not been saved from their implacable hate, even after having lain

2000 years in his grave! At present they fight the air; but how would it be, if their rage were animated by the presence of an enemy"?

Ideally, coffeehouse intellectuals are bohemians—that special brand of learned men who have not submitted to the rules of social and professional careers which the society around them takes for granted. Above all, they are men who are utterly indifferent to the sources of their income. Whether they are married or not, their responsibilities may be sloughed off, and they do not care to pursue the organized channels of literary or academic advancement. It is the beauty of the café that one can sit there all day and all night, surrounded by poets, astronomers, military tacticians, revolutionaries, cardplayers, and philologists, and never be touched at all, for the coffeehouse offers a genuine guarantee against reality. It is the only spatial zone where talk constitutes truth, where giant plans and blueprints, utopian dreams, and anarchist plots, may be assumed to have taken place without one's ever leaving one's seat. (We hasten to add that revolutions are prepared in cafés as well. In 1916 Emil Lederer met with Rudi Hilferding in a Viennese café and discussed the problems of a Russian Revolution. Lederer was convinced of the impending revolution while Hilferding, the sceptical theoretician, answered, "Who will make the revolution? Mr. Trotsky, perhaps, of the Central Café?" But Mr. Trotsky stepped out of the café and made the revolution.)

The coffeehouse belongs to the bohemians. It is the salon of homeless thinkers, poets, and scientists, the drawing room of underpaid writers, their means of escape from the abysmal physical conditions under which they live. Poverty has always been the supreme condition of the bohemian, the disaster from which he flees to the comparative warmth of the coffeehouse. Obviously the inescapable fact of poverty has brought with it a set of defenses which have become, since the eighteenth century, standard procedure for nonconformists: the anarchical attitude towards the established goods of social conduct; the refusal to accept the normative requirements of manners, fashions, and conventions. True, there have been intellectuals who have made genuine contributions to intellectual independence in the very act of conforming. Goethe, for example, knew that true freedom itself consisted of possessing the flexibility to conform to the standards of the social group to which one aspired. Nevertheless, the routine requirements of society have often forced men with a specific spiritual destination—Baudelaire, for instance—to escape into Bohemia.

Montesquieu was deeply sensitive to the precariousness of the bohemian situation, and to the marginality of the bohemian himself, who frequently will remain forever a stranger. It is characteristic of Montesquieu's thinking that he was aware of the ambiguity in the bohemian phenomenon, that it contains both a positive and a negative function: positive, in that it chooses social distance in order to construct true standards; negative, in that it withdraws from social responsibility for selfish reasons. If the bohemian alone possesses knowledge of what constitutes a just world, then the true thinker must be forever at a distance from his own nation, his own people, his own culture. If it is the occupation of the intellectual to present perpetually to the world the difference between perfection and reality, then the intellectual is forced outside reality itself.

There are cases in the history of philosophy and literature which present almost ideal types of the bohemian pattern. Among others, the life and work of Diderot present an image which is the living representation of the bohemian paradox. He escaped from the theological and legal professions in order to dedicate himself to the life of a free moralist and thinker. As an independent writer, he lived for some time on the margins of Bohemia, in debt to his grocer, engaged in a fantastic charade with monks from whom he received money on the strength of spurious promises to join their orders. He wrote sermons for lazy and incompetent priests and earned his living tutoring on subjects with which he was not acquainted. His Parisian life was lived among the actors of the Café Procope in front of the Comédie Française and among the chess players of the Café Regence. In the gardens of the Palais Royale, he was surrounded by journalists, by idle intellectuals who invent rumors and spread them, and by free intellectual clowns who make fun of everything. The frontiers of his Bohemia were the bookstalls along the Seine where his companions were the bands of irresponsible writers who lived on their literary skill, their cynicism, and their absence of moral principles.

His way of life did not prevent him from working. One can only marvel at the concentration which produced one of the greatest summaries of the scientific mind, the *Encyclopédie,* which he managed to finish only after twenty years of constant and bitter conflict with ecclesiastical and political powers. His condition of life seemed even to help his work. Neither an unhappy marriage nor the demands of his friendships could break his working habits. It would seem that the specific social situation of the bohemian creates the only pattern by which a certain type of intellectual can accomplish his task.

Diderot originated the pattern of bohemianism which was to emerge in the age of total revolution, the true epoch of the intellectuals. Saint-Simon, who was born in 1760 under the regime of Louis XV, first exhibited a certain anti-social tendency at thirteen when he refused to make his first communion and was sent to jail, from which he later escaped. His august parents thought the best remedy might be a comprehensive education and thrust the impressionable boy into the hands of D'Alembert, the co-author of the *Encyclopédie.* Saint-Simon made some effort to conform to the traditions of his family by entering the army as a soldier. He served in the American Revolution and was taken prisoner. After his release, however, he returned to France, which was at the point of making its own revolution. Swept away by revolutionary ideas, full of enthusiasm, Saint-Simon decided that members of the old aristocracy, meaning himself, should not and could not participate in the coming struggle. Thus he decided to wage a private war. He would be active in the revolution only as a profiteer—a wise decision. He made a fortune in speculation in the revolution, buying and selling "national goods." When the revolution came to an untimely end, the profiteer turned *grand seigneur,* and, in the midst of luxury, devoted himself to the judicious advancement of learning. He surrounded himself with the greatest scholars of the age, listened in rapture to their conversation, and noted down much that they said. It should be added that Saint-Simon was a far from selfish pupil. He promoted with great energy the careers of future mathematicians, technologists, and scientists. The conversations of these great scientists actually were to provide him later with his deepest conviction: that science was the savior of society. In 1805, his life as patron ended abruptly. His money had run out. For the next twenty years, he worked in an office, constantly on the edge of poverty. This distant relative of the Duc of Saint-Simon (the author of the *Recollections*), this son of one of France's great families, for some years had to take a job as a clerk in a pawnshop at a thousand francs a year, doing all his writing at night. For a short time, he lived solely on the generosity of a man who had once been his butler, and who gave him the financial support he needed to finish his first great essay, *Introduction aux Travaux Scientifiques du XIX Siècle*. Unfortunately, this benefactor died before Saint-Simon could go on to other work.

Finally, his family tired of the impecuniousness of their black sheep. In 1814, they gave him a pension on which he lived modestly for a number of years. He surrounded himself with engineers and mathematicians, the elite of the *École Normale Polytechnique,* with disillusioned members of the innumerable revolutionary splinter groups, as well as with young bankers and industrialists. Augustin Thierry, the great historian, was for a time his secretary. And later Comte, himself, worked for him, although Comte betrayed this debt by turning viciously against Saint-Simon. For a time, he attracted the attention of several members of old aristocratic families who were as critical of the new bourgeois elite as were the classes whom this elite exploited. But Saint-Simon's radicalism was ultimately too shocking for them, and they withdrew their support. Since, in the meantime, his family had stopped his pension, once again he was thrust unprotected into the world. Utterly desperate, he tried to kill himself. But, in the last two years of his life, from 1823 to 1825, those ardent disciples, who considered him the world's only philosopher of history, took care of him. More than that, they worshipped him as a saint. If such a relationship constitutes happiness, he may be said to have died happy. His loving admirers must have gathered around his bedside to hear these last words that his closest disciple reports: "Religion cannot disappear; it can only be transformed. Rodriquez, do not forget this, and also remember that one must be dedicated with one's whole heart and might when one desires to accomplish great things."

Saint-Simon's life is a fascinating picture of the bohemian intellectual at home, but Auguste Comte's sounds like the purest fiction. It is even clearer in Comte's case that it is uprooted men, men who are absolutely out of sympathy with their time, who come to believe that they have discovered a way to end the chaos of all history—a way that is actually a vast projection of their own personalities onto the social scene. Later, we will speak of the anarchy that Comte and Saint-Simon saw all around them. At this point, it is enough to say that only a man as personally anarchical as Comte could have constructed the most organized, the most totalitarian, scheme of thought yet to appear in Western intellectual history.

Comte's life climaxed the development of the bohemian intellectual. A child prodigy, he was adored at home, and yet he always felt alienated from his family. He was a brilliant instructor of mathematics, and yet he always failed abysmally in this field because of his terrible temper. He would have enjoyed a successful career at the École Polytechnique, if he hadn't systematically ruined all his opportunities. He simply could not conform to the rules which make it possible for men to work together. Isolated from the organized academic life, he had to depend on whatever patron would send him students while making a precarious living from tutoring.

There is one great difference between Saint-Simon's bohemianism and Comte's—the former managed to get along without women; the latter could not. What's more, this possessor of a distinguished scientific mind, this man to whom philosophers, statesmen, theologians, and business men would listen, exhibited sexual patterns that were far from normal. There is some indication that he had an early affair with a married woman who bore him a child; later she vanishes from the record. Two other attachments followed. The first was to a mistress of his who had been a common prostitute (her name was on the police rolls); one day he suddenly married her—a decision that today we would describe as neurotic. On the one hand, he felt himself so unattractive that no decent woman could want to marry him, that he would have to take what he could get; on the other hand, he considered himself extremely magnanimous to have raised a fallen woman by marrying her. Another motive for his decision was a conviction that he owed it to his prestige to appear before his benefactors as a married man. Naturally, his marriage to this Caroline Massin was a complete failure, somewhat complicated by the presence of Caroline's first lover who refused to leave the Comte household and even made frequent contributions to its support. Occasionally, if finances sank too low at home, Mme. Comte would return to her "profession." This situation may well have contributed to Comte's mental collapse, the exact character of which is still a subject of dispute among psychiatrists. Between 1826 and 1828, he made two attempts at suicide. But in 1842, despite a succession of separations and reconciliations with Caroline, he managed to publish the last volume of the *Positive Philosophy*. Still there was no money. He gave some popular courses on astronomy, and he lived for a time on the generosity of John Stuart Mill and Mill's friends; but it was not a life that made for any inner satisfaction. His English acquaintances totally misunderstood his philosophic attitudes, and he had neither disciples nor friends. In 1844, he met the woman who was to provide him with the strangest relationship of all, Mme. Clothilde de Vaux, who was already dying of tuberculosis. M. de Vaux had been forced to flee from France to Brussels because of financial trouble, but his wife remained in her Paris apartment, writing mediocre short stories and, occasionally, poetry. Comte, fifteen years her senior, fell madly in love. Yet, always the scientist, he did not hesitate to remind his beloved that his feelings for her were of a certain systematic value:

Je suis d'ailleurs très convaincu que les diverses conditions de cette nouvelle existence ne tarderont pas à se ponderer et coordiner spontanément au common profit de mon travail, de mon bonheur, et même de santé physique.

Actually, the relationship with Clothilde cannot properly be classified as an erotic affair. She refused to have intimate relations with him, and so they conducted their affair on the plane of pure spirit and felt themselves superior to those less disembodied attachments they saw going on around them in society. In truth, it might be said that Comte's relationship with the dying Clothilde influenced him deeply during the development of his religion of humanity. He seems to have gained from the encounter the view that love is possible on a non-physical, ideal plane. After Clothilde's death, Comte devoted the rest of his life to the development of his position that the method of Positivism should be subjective rather than objective.

Although both Comte and Diderot were bohemians, Diderot had used his bohemian existence to develop his utopian ideas in the tradition of rationalist philosophers. Like Plato's *Republic* and More's *Utopia*, Diderot's heavenly city was really "nowhere." Its existence—if it could be said to have one—was in the realm of theoretical concepts, outside of the space-time continuum. With the French Revolution, however, there was a fundamental change in political philosophy. These later thinkers took over from Christian eschatology the idea of the establishment of The Kingdom of God on earth, with the addition that this would be achieved at some specific date in history. As we shall see, when Saint-Simon professed to know the inner meaning of history, he was thinking in terms of concrete time. He thought of himself as a prophet of a coming age rather than as a designer of utopian cities. His messianism, he believed, revealed the final truth of history—the end of time and the beginning. These ideas distinguish him from his eighteenth century predecessors.

The intellectuals who burst upon the scene in the years after the Revolution were genuinely different from those who had preceded it. Two historical experiences had preceded the full development of the type. The first was the tremendous advance that took place in the sciences between the years 1793 and 1799. Lagrange had published *The Theory of Analytic Functions;* Monge his *Descriptive Geometry;* Laplace his *Essay on Celestial Mechanics;* Richet his *Treatise on Surgery;* and Carnot his *Research on the Infinitesimal Calculus*. The second historical event of which we must take note was the creation of the Cult of Reason. It will be remembered that the revolutionaries had defied Reason, crowning her as a goddess. The alliance between this secularized religion and ascendant science gave impetus to the creation of a new type of intellectual. The first sociologists held the conviction that life was historical because the mind of man unfolded itself in the process of time. The implications of this were that the historical past was collective and that, at the same time, history had a specific goal. It was this goal that added an element of eschatological finality to eighteenth century rationalism. The merging of these two ideas—which previously in Western history had been conspicuously separate—gave the intellectuals the opportunity of being both scientists and priests.

It casts an interesting light upon the symbolic character of the new discipline itself that its intellectuals had a new part to play. For leadership in this new group what was needed were men who recognized the new telos of history, and who possessed the ability to develop ways of bringing it about; who combined a love of philosophy with moral enthusiasm, and who could bear the awful weight of guiding the destiny of the coming age. Such men might appear in any class—not solely among the proletariat, or the petit-bourgeoisie. The French intellectuals welcomed the idea that philosophers might arise in all classes, unrestricted by false class-consciousness. As a matter of fact, most of the Saint-Simonians were members of the bourgeoisie, but the class-label does not carry much weight. To qualify as a disciple of this prophet of industrial mankind, all one had to do was to accept his vision of a new context of socio-political meaning. Turgot and Condorcet, for instance, to whom the sociologists owed so much, were uprooted noblemen, aristocrats but voluntary "déclassés," who set the pattern for intellectuals to serve the truth of progress by renouncing their class-allegiance—a phenomenon that is characteristic of those chaotic ages in which radical analyses of fundamental societal relations tend to appear. Louis de Bonald, who later had a great influence on Saint-Simon, emigrated as a refuge from the Revolution, joined the army of the Prince de Condé, and finally settled in Germany to write his *Theorie du Pouvoir,* which was condemned by the Directory in 1796. Some American social scientists, with their naive belief that social thinking arises only in liberal and democratic context, may find it shocking that Saint-Simon's extraordinary sympathy for Bonald was based on this man's reputation as one of the foremost philosophers of the counter-revolutionary movement, an advocate of order and discipline. Saint-Simon was delighted to find a "reactionary" who had given up all traditionalist patterns and who declared that the ancient controversies were now done with forever and that men must start all over again as though from the beginning of human existence. Bonald, the aristocrat, taught Saint-Simon a great lesson: that traditionalism in itself could no longer persuade men and that philosophers must discover new verities which would make possible the reestablishment of order, hierarchy, and authority. Thus, it did not matter whether the intellectuals were members of this class or that. Progressives and reactionaries become indistinguishable from one another when the goal is to unite progress with order.

The lives of these new intellectuals give us a key to the content of sociology itself while, at the same time, they establish the pattern by which intellectuals may become the elite of a world in revolution. Messianic bohemianism is symbolic of the vision of total revolution: it is a life-style so unheralded in the general trend of European intellectual experience that by its very nature it illumines more fully the revolutionary character of the philosophy behind it. The "faith" of the positivist philosophers in the world-to-come reminds one of the providential teleology of the philosophers of the middle ages. Messianism, in both cases, acknowledged no alternatives to its vision. These sociologists were also *religieux* for they held that their position in regard to the future of man was absolute. This type of messianic intellectual, born in the years after the revolution, was to become a general phenomenon in a world that longed for order.

INTELLECTUALS AND THE FOUNDING FATHERS

Merle Curti

... V ERY EARLY American conditions began to modify the traditional distinction between theory and practice. We might say the modification started on the very day that Captain John Smith decreed that no one would be allowed to eat who did not work. Generally speaking, America did not nourish a separate intellectual class, as did China, India, and Europe. In America even the chief guardians of learning, the clergy, were not a class apart from the rest of the people. In early New England, for example, they assisted the magistrate in the conduct of public affairs. Since it was impossible in the New World to sustain specialized functions common in the Old, the clergy acted not only as preachers and teachers, but also as physicians, lawyers, farmers, and agricultural experts. In the eighteenth century the clergy also shared specialized intellectual functions with the rising newspaper publishers and with the increasingly influential lawyers. And all these men lived in close touch with the merchants and planters who carried weight in public affairs. The conditions of colonial society demanded this active participation of intellectuals in the common affairs of life.

Colonial conditions also discouraged the Old World patronage of scholars and writers as a class apart. There were some exceptions, but as a rule, those with special intellectual interests had to make their own way. This they did by becoming clergymen, by practicing law or medicine, by operating a farm or plantation or business, or even by following a craft, as Thomas Godfrey and David Rittenhouse did in Philadelphia.

Conditions in the colonies not only stimulated intellectuals to take up practical pursuits, but also stimulated practical men to cultivate intellectual interests. Many colonial planters investigated the world of nature, partly out of curiosity and partly in the hope of making practical use of what they learned about the unfamiliar birds, animals, plants, and flowers about them. They studied various types of soils, in the hope of discovering metal deposits

Reprinted from *American Paradox: the Conflict of Thought and Action* (1956), pp. 9-18, by permission of the author and the publisher, Rutgers University Press. Title supplied by the Editor.

and also in order to learn how to improve their crops through the use of fertilizers. Thus William Byrd II applied in his daily routine as a great land-owner and man of affairs not only his legal learning but his self-acquired knowledge of medicine, surveying, architecture, and horticulture. And even to a greater degree than his European counterpart, the merchant cherished those branches of knowledge functional to his own problems—navigation and astronomy, mathematics, geography and political economy, and the modern languages spoken by the peoples with whom his schooners traded.

The traditional line between knowledge and action was still further blurred in the seacoast towns along the Atlantic. In the eighteenth century, evening schools, libraries, and discussion groups were organized by and for enterprising young tradesmen and artisans, to supplement the meager oppor-tunities available in the schools. Eager to get ahead, poor but ambitious young artisans added book knowledge to what they had learned empirically about their craft. In some cases intellectual curiosity led them to explore fields of knowledge not immediately related to their occupations. The most famous example is Benjamin Franklin, whose self-education played an important part in his rise from apprentice printer to successful publisher and distinguished scientist. Franklin united theory and practice, using the one to check the other. Characteristically, he made original contributions to the theory of electricity, and also invented the lightning rod. In so doing he helped break down the ancient barrier between knowledge and action.

Many other colonials besides Franklin believed that knowledge should be used to improve man's estate. Take Jared Eliot, for example. From the time that he was called to a Connecticut parish in 1703 until his death more than forty years later, he did not miss preaching at least once each Sunday. But as one of the most famous medical practitioners in New England, he also went all over the countryside ministering to the sick. In the course of his journeys he discovered a substance in certain black earth deposits that led to the development of Connecticut's iron industry. Nor did his efforts in putting his knowledge to work stop with this, for he devoted himself also to the study of scientific agriculture. His practical *Essay on Field Husbandry* was widely used over a long period of time. Jared Eliot was only one of a goodly company whose scientific interests were directed to the improvement of man's well-being.

In eighteenth-century America, men of knowledge were interested also in the improvement of human relations. In so doing they were exemplifying one of the main tenets of the Enlightenment—the use of knowledge to free man from the ignorance and prejudice that militated against his happiness. Franklin's friend, Dr. Benjamin Rush, pioneered in the study of the nature and causes of insanity. He applied the knowledge he acquired by working to temper the cruel and inhuman treatment inflicted by custom on the victims of mental illness. Samuel Stanhope Smith, an intellectually curious Presbyterian minister, investigated the cause of color pigmentation and concluded that color differences are the result of varying physical environments, thus opening the way for a new attitude toward Negroes. It was no longer necessary to regard them, in the traditional fashion, as separately created beings inferior to white men. And it was no longer necessary to view color as an inherent badge of subordination and as a penalty for the sins of a common forefather, the Lot of Biblical lore.

The philosophy of the Enlightenment, so readily adopted and applied in America, also included the doctrine of natural rights, which provided a basis for resisting governmental authority when that authority violated man's natural rights to life, liberty, and property. This theory was developed first in Europe, and played an important role in resistance to Old World tyranny. Americans also made use of it in concrete political struggles. Thus in the late seventeenth and early eighteenth centuries the Reverend John Wise of Ipswich invoked it in leading resistance to the unpopular and autocratic Governor Andros and, later, to the local ecclesiastical authorities who set themselves against the traditional system of church government in Massachusetts.

Later, the Revolutionary struggle still further reduced the distance between theory and action, among Tories as well as among Patriots. The Reverend Jonathan Boucher, an outspoken Tory, defiantly continued to preach the religious duty of submission to authority after being warned by armed citizens not to enter his pulpit. But he preached with two pistols lying on the pulpit cushion! On the Patriot side, editors, lawyers, ministers, and other intellectuals did not limit themselves to the spoken and written word, but jointed the rank and file in the practical work of revolution. To cite one example, David Rittenhouse set aside his work at the Philadelphia observatory in order to supervise the casting of cannon and the making of saltpeter. He experimented with rifling cannon and musket balls, and devised chain defenses for the harbor at Philadelphia. He did not stop even with these technical services, for he also took part in the activities of the Committee of Safety, the General Assembly, and the Pennsylvania Constitutional Convention.

In view of the suspicion in our time of intellectuals in government, it is well to remember that many founders of the Republic combined scholarship with action. In fact, the Constitutional Convention of 1787 has been called the first American brain trust. At least thirty-one of the fifty-five members had been educated at colonial colleges or at similar institutions abroad. Many, including Franklin, had become first-rate scholars and scientists by their own efforts. Two university presidents and three college professors sat in Independence Hall during that hot and discouraging summer of 1787. Many others had been schoolmasters. James Madison, one of the most influential delegates, gave his colleagues the results of his study of ancient and modern confederacies so that the Convention might profit from knowledge of previous experiments in federal union. In creating a distinctive system of checks and balances the founding fathers framed a Constitution that reflected Newton's view of the universe as a harmonious, balanced, and self-regulating mechanism.

Faith in the desirability and feasibility of applying knowledge to political action survived into the early years of the Republic. At no time in our later history were intellectual training and action so happily united in our political leadership as in the last decades of the eighteenth century and the first decades of the nineteenth. Both the Federalist and Republican parties boasted leaders who were accomplished in scholarship as in politics.

Two examples can illustrate the point on the Federalist side. John Adams was a thorough classical scholar and a profound political theorist—his *Defense of the Constitution* served an immediate practical need and has remained a classic in political thought. A fellow New Englander, Josiah Quincy, won his reputation for learning through his pungent political satires, his support of the Massachusetts Historical Society, and his connection with the American Academy of Arts and Sciences. But as a farmer he also proved the efficacy of scientific agriculture. As mayor of Boston from 1823 to 1827 he made an enlightened attack on gambling, crime, and prostitution and inaugurated slum clearance, modern fire protection, a sewage system, and a municipal water supply.

The Jeffersonian party also had enlightened intellectuals as leaders. President Jefferson was a scholar in the classics, common law, and Anglo-Saxon, a student of musicology, archaeology, and ethnology. He carried on fruitful researches in scientific farming. Jefferson's Secretary of the Treasury, Albert Gallatin, often called the "father of American ethnology," was also a master of the theory and practice of political economy. Edward Livingston, an associate of Jefferson and Gallatin, was a great scholar in jurisprudence. His original work in this field led the distinguished French historian, François Mignet, to write in an obituary: "By the death of Mr. Livingston, America has lost her most powerful intellect, the Academy one of its most illustrious members, and Humanity one of her most zealous benefactors." Long after this Sir Henry Maine praised Livingston's code as the fruit of "the first legal genius in modern times." During his service as mayor of New York, member of Congress, and Minister to France, Livingston turned his learning to practical account.

SHIFTING OF THE SOCIOLOGICAL
POSITION OF THE ARTIST

Levin L. Schücking

IF WE now turn away from the conditions of past centuries and consider more recent times and particularly our own day, again looking for the determining factors, at first sight everything seems to be changed. In earlier times the sociological soil is mostly plain to see, the influence of particular people of social eminence is manifest, and there are only a few obvious centres from which the sustenance of the arts proceeds. To-day there are clearly many sources—numbers of theatres, publishing houses, associations, a public of varied tastes, and, in brief, theoretically a thousand opportunities. Social dependence has also clearly gone: remember, for instance, how lamentably Emperor William II failed in his attempt to introduce a taste into Germany from above, by means of a court art. This failure gave many people the pleasant feeling that social power can no longer influence the course of true artistic taste in our day. The only question is whether here, as in other fields, the effective influence has not shifted to another social force.

For this various circumstances are responsible. One of the principal ones is the change in the social standing of the artist. In past centuries the position of the artist in society was never particularly good. Those, of course, who had reached the peaks of Parnassus always found ready and honoured acceptance in the highest circles of society. Lord Chesterfield, who may be taken as an embodiment of the aristocratic culture of the eighteenth century in its highest manifestation, expressly states somewhere that he always felt it a distinction to be in the company of such men as Pope or Addison. It strikes us to-day, however, as odd when we hear that in 1723 a comedy of Steele's enjoyed great popularity because the author was reputed to have an income of a thousand a year. Clearly there was nothing much in being a mere artist.

For a long time the son of a "good family" was considered in some way to have lost caste if he became a professional writer or painter, and still more if he became an actor. To live by the pen was not very respectable. When Congreve, who had become the most famous of English dramatists, crossed

Reprinted from *The Sociology of Literary Taste* (1944), pp. 16-25, by permission of the publisher, Routledge & Kegan Paul, Ltd.

the Channel, Voltaire called to pay his respects to him, and mentioned that it was Congreve's fame as a writer that had inspired the visit. Congreve astonished Voltaire by replying that he was primarily not an author but a gentleman. Voltaire at once retorted that he would not have sought the acquaintance of Congreve the mere gentleman.

This social outlook changed only very gradually. It is significant that, for instance, Lady Bradshaugh, an aristocratic admirer of Samuel Richardson, was so afraid of what her Lancashire friends would say of her corresponding with "an author" that she kept the correspondence a secret as long as she could. When he sent her his portrait she altered his signature to Dickenson, to prevent the acquaintance from coming to light. Thomas Gray left a small fortune in the possession of the publisher of his *Elegy,* considering that it was beneath the dignity of a gentleman to take money from a publisher for his "inventions". Scott always preferred to be known as a landed gentleman rather than as an author. At the outset of his career Byron indulged in some magnanimous gestures to his publisher, though later these did not prevent him from extracting more money from the publisher for his works than any other poet of the nineteenth century.

In this respect the circumstances have probably never been the same all over Europe. This is, indeed, actually one of the criteria by which the national cultures may be distinguished. Thus, even in the twentieth century the social valuation of the artist has been rather different in Germany, rather higher, than in the Anglo-Saxon countries. If, however, one has regard to the great phases of development, these differences appear as no more than nuances. In the matter of the social standing of the artist it is very significant, for example, that in Germany at the beginning of the century, and for a long time after it, many aristocrats who engaged in literary work felt it necessary to assume middle-class pen-names—Anastasius Grün, for instance (Count von Auersperg), and Nikolaus Lenau (Niembsch, Edler von Strehlenau: an "Edler" corresponds roughly to a Baronet), and Halm (Baron von Münch-Bellinghausen). How the family of Annette Droste looked askance at her literary activities! How reluctant the Kleist family was to talk about its son of genius! In his wonderful description of the 'thirties of the last century in *The Newcomes,* Thackeray shows Lady Kew, genteel to the bone, rooted in the ideas of the eighteenth century, exclaiming with indignation at the news that a painter has asked for the hand of her granddaughter:

"An artist propose for Ethel! One of her footmen might propose next, and she supposed Barnes would bring the message. 'The father came and proposed for this young painter, and you didn't order him out of the room!' "

Gradually a complete change set in. It was the natural consequence of the changed outlook on life associated with the rise of the middle class. Here again the way was led by England, where the political revolutions of the seventeenth century had begun to make great changes in the relative power of the classes, which had remained unaltered through many centuries. Since the "glorious revolution" of 1688 it had been necessary for the Government to reckon with the factor of public opinion. Consequently writers who could influence public opinion were taken very seriously by the leaders of the State. They were granted sinecures and flattered. Subsequently the writers suffered some change for the worse for a while, but during the eighteenth century the belief grew in the power of the printed word. In France, too, the prestige of literature grew steadily up to the end of the century.

Gradually, too, the ideal of personality changed. The ideal cavalier of the eighteenth century was the man of society with exquisite manners. The upper middle class brought art and science into the place of honour; it regarded the deepening of the intellectual life and the artistic elevation of spiritual life as important objects of existence. Art had played in the life of the aristocracy the part of a decorative element; in the life of the independent-minded middle class it had the more exalted task of serving as herald and prophet of the highest and the profoundest thought of mankind. Under these circumstances its representatives also were accorded a higher place than formerly.

Byron, who with his aristocratic origin and interests sympathized in many things with the past, himself records the change, with some surprise. He writes in his diary on November 24, 1813:

"I do think the preference of writers to agents—the mighty stir made about scribbling and scribes, by themselves and others—a sign of effeminacy, degeneracy, and weakness. Who would write, who had anything better to do? 'Action—action—action,'—said Demosthenes: 'Actions—actions,' I say, and not writing,—least of all, rhyme."

In this there is a good deal of the earlier outlook. But now figures like Byron's, seen in the Bengal light of romance, served to give the poet a higher standing. The poetic activity of a man who moved among the highest peaks of society elevated, so to speak, the whole craft. Anyone who assumed Byron's air of world-weariness, and adopted his way of tying his cravat, gained, as he sought to gain, a portion of the interest and the admiration felt for the poet-lord.

Goethe's social position also exerted a powerful influence. In literature itself the signs of the changed social standing of the writer made their appearance. It is particularly instructive to see how late the artist is in appearing in literature as an attractive figure. The hero in the romances of earlier centuries is a knight, a prince, a cavalier, an officer; sometimes in the eighteenth century a clergyman. When from 1709 on, Addison and Steele began publishing the so-called "moral journals," the *Tatler* and the *Spectator,* which quickly found eager readers and imitators all over Europe, they represented themselves to the public as a sort of editorial committee, but in doing so they assumed the guise of a landed gentleman, a jurist, a great merchant, a half-pay officer, and an "elegant" from the world of gallantry. A writer or an artist would not yet have been considered dignified enough.

A hundred years later all this was changed. Interest centred, for the first time, in the artist. In Goethe's *Wilhelm Meister* the hero, characteristically, is something of an artist, and the greatest English novelist of the nineteenth century, Thackeray, in *The Newcomes* (1853), in many respects of all the novels the best documents of the 'thirties, also makes his hero an artist. The two novels had many successors, in which the newly revealed predilection of the dominant class is reflected. For this middle class, though originally it established its dominance on the ideas of common sense and naturalness, had fallen victim to all sorts of affectation, had become aristocratized and narrowed by a thousand conventions. Half conscious of this inner discordance, it nurtured a secret affection for the untrammelled existence, as it saw it, of the artist. He was the embodiment of the human freedom for which it longed but which it scarcely dared to approve openly, still less to practise. He was almost a higher type of human being.

In the second half of the nineteenth century the artist is gradually accorded a position of which no earlier century would have dreamed. Age-old aristocratic prejudices fail to withstand this development. Pen-names are thrown aside and the aristocracy now devotes itself openly to art, rejoicing if it is mentioned in connexion with artistic achievements. There was a poet who lived in princely palaces and took a valet with him on his travels; from the end of the century he appeared in Germany and gave public recitals of his works, charging for admission—happy to be able to describe himself as an artist.

Naturally this process was accompanied by a great increase in the artist's self-confidence. It is not difficult to produce instances from earlier times in which witness is borne to artists' pride. But this witness now took on a special character. It would be easy to compile a great garland of such statements from the time of the romanticists onward. "The man who stands above all others, the poet," declared the young Levin Schücking in an essay, as though it were a self-evident truth, and his friend Freiligrath claimed for the poet that he "goes about the world in solitude with flaming brow." Very similar views were heard at the same time in the rest of Europe. Tennyson, for instance, whose lyric diamonds were extracted from no great depth below the surface, advised the common man with priestly solemnity to give up the attempt to probe the poet's unfathomable mind with his "shallow wit". This attitude visibly gathered strength as the century proceeded. It was plainly visible at its extremest in France, very noticeable in England, faintest at first in Germany. In an age that levelled all external

differences, the poet marked himself off from the common man even in his
clothes. Velvet coat, a flowing mane, and if possible special headgear, served
to set apart many of these elect, especially the artists. Even in England, so
exceptionally correct in externals, traces of this habit were to be found,
though they did not succeed in effectively establishing themselves in face of
convention.[1]

Thus the picture slowly changed. In the eighteenth century the wise
Shaftesbury had expected almost a new flowering of literature from an
increased "personal dignity" in the status of the poet. His phrase proved
prophetic. The sense of bearing "the dignity of humanity", as Schiller said,
in his hands made the artist capable of the greatest achievements. But gradually the artist's position shifted. He began to be enthroned above men,
as the priest is enthroned above the faithful in church, and already intelligent people began to ask themselves, as happened as early as 1872 in a
very acute article in the *Quarterly Review,* what effect this exaggerated
artists' assessment of their function, this separation of their intellectual
sphere from that of the ordinary man, would be bound to have in the end
on art itself, how it would ultimately lead of necessity to a false relation
between human and artistic values in the life of art, and in a different form
would result of necessity in producing the artificiality and the estrangement
from the natural and the popular which it was supposed had been happily
overcome in the romantic movement.

At first, it is true, there was not much sign of this in the ruling art.
Tennyson set his hat but not his head against popular opinion. As his
biographers almost unanimously relate, he always adjusted his own inner
development—often almost by force—to the conception of what should be
the nature of a poet who wants to give his people the bread of life in his
art. Things were similar in France, where Victor Hugo altered the ending
of his tragedy *Marion de Lorme* at the desire of the public and under the
influence of Prosper Mérimée and Dumas.

How far from sovereign was the artist originally in Germany may
be seen from many examples. How patiently in the literary society of the
Tunnel the criticism of dillettantes was endured! The educated public had
here immense power in its hands, and it would certainly be wrong to say
that it always made wise use of it. This applies especially to its resistance
to the entry of new ideas in the sphere of the drama. It seems to us to-day
almost incredible that at the first production in Berlin of Ibsen's *Doll's
House* the concession was made to the public of bringing Nora back into

---

1. It is significant that on the morning of the day on which Tennyson was to make
his first entry into the House of Lords after the peerage granted to him as poet
laureate, a friend called on him to urge him on this occasion at least to discard his
customary poet's sombrero for the only correct wear, a top hat.

the doll's house at the end. It is difficult to say what is the more astonishing in this incident, the public aversion from new ideas or the deference to it of so furious a defender of all individual rights as Ibsen, who in permitting the change allowed the point of his problem play to be blunted.

The artist's attitude to the public. Art as divine service. The new conception of art that came with the fall of the aristocratic world radically changed the attitude of the artist to his times. It has at all times been natural to the artistic temperament to get rid of the uncomfortable sense of failure by simply throwing the blame on others, charging them with bad taste. In taking comfort from the thought that the work was too good, that, in Shakespeare's phrase, it was "caviare to the general", the self-confidence so essential to creative work was maintained, and the author was preserved from torturing, galling, incapacitating doubts.

Thus it would be easy to collect instances from the sixteenth century onwards, and perhaps even from earlier times, of expressions of dissatisfaction from artists in which the public and the critics are charged with lack of understanding. Especially they are set down as uneducated. But what now came was something different, a conception of artistic creative work in which no regard was paid to the existing public and the writer had in view only the ideal reader. He was guided now only by his own taste and conviction.

It is not always realized that past centuries did not hold such rigorous opinions on the subject. Alexander Pope, for instance, was regarded in England almost throughout the eighteenth century as a poet of the very first rank. Yet when he had completed his chief work, the translation of Homer, a real marvel in the opinion of his contemporaries, he read it to his patron, Lord Halifax, in the presence of a large assembly; and, says Samuel Johnson, the noble lord interrupted him now and then to propose improvements. Such proceedings had been allowed for centuries without protest by the artists. Chaucer's famous disciple Lydgate evidently regarded it as entirely natural when his patron Duke Humphrey of Gloucester, brother of Henry V, "corrected" his manuscript; and we know of exact parallels to this in the life of Spenser, who was contemporary with Shakespeare.

In France the conditions were similar to this even in the eighteenth century. Voltaire himself was essentially a writer for society, producing his works for a particular environment and accepting directives from it. He read his *Oedipus* at Sceaux in the entourage of the Duchess of Maine, and had no hesitation in paying a good deal of attention to the criticism and advice tendered to him in that circle.

This social pressure was not yet challenged, but it is easy to understand what a burden it must have been for the artist. Voltaire learned from Pope, who in material respects was fairly independent, of the more tolerable character, at all events, of the similar slavery to taste in England; and he inferred very logically that the principal thing was to get together some capital. We know how he accordingly entered into financial speculations, not all of a very admirable character. But we see also that Voltaire was only able to give play to his real nature and talents when he had established himself on his own estate near Geneva.

At this time conditions were changing, through the development of publishing, and a few generations later there were no more naïve attempts by aristocrats to improve the work of the foremost writers of their time. The artist emancipated himself more and more effectively from his environment.

With surprising speed the artist now proceeded toward the goal of entire autonomy, no longer paying any attention to his public. Shelley declared at the beginning of the nineteenth century as an obvious principle and nothing new:

"Write nothing, unless your conviction of its truth compels you to the writing. Give wise counsel, and accept no counsel from the simple-minded. Time reverses the judgment of the foolish crowd. Contemporary criticism is no more than the sum of the folly with which genius has to wrestle" (Retranslated from the German version).

The measure of hostility to the great public that may be detected in this statement from a passionate political democrat could be paralleled by earlier examples; it now became the accepted belief of an important literary movement, which later spread throughout Europe, the "aesthetic movement." The springing up of this movement all over Europe was a natural result of a certain specialization in every field and of the increased respect for art in certain groups. Their interest in art led them to occupy themselves with the elements of art on which its appeal depends. Its effect, they considered, on an educated taste cannot lie in things outside art, such as a morally uplifting or a stimulating subject. From this view came the cult of things that in the view of earlier generations were only the media of art—form, rhythm, tone, allusion, and so on. In earlier times these things had not been ignored, for poetry was not invented in the nineteenth century, but however highly they had been appreciated they had been considered only in conjunction with other factors that had been valued more highly. But for this new group, concerned only with cultured appreciation, there were no higher elements than these.

One of the first men in Europe to spread this view with any great success was Leigh Hunt. In the early part of the nineteenth century he continually expounded to his fellow-countrymen in learned periodicals the elements of the poetic achievement of such men as Marlowe, Spenser, or Milton. He had beyond question a keen eye for poetic beauties, but the things to which he pointed were largely elements of their art which Marlowe and Spenser and Milton would not themselves have regarded as the essence of their achievement.

In France this cult of the media of art was called *l'art pour l'art*—art for art's sake. It divorced art from all influence over life except the purely aesthetic, and so confined it within a sacred grove whose priests were the artists. Artist-priests performed their offices, often, like Gautier and later his emulator Oscar Wilde, entirely removed from the common herd by the extravagances in which they indulged at times. The ordinary man could not follow them, could not conceive why any sensible man should spend a whole day in the pursuit of the only right adjective or in the attuning of a couple of vowels.

The issue between these groups and the public was not hushed up but proclaimed. Another group, with Rossetti enthroned at its centre, came into existence in England with the aim of protecting the arcana of its art from the profane. Rossetti himself once drew a clear distinction between himself and Tennyson, who, he said, was always endeavouring to keep within "the realm of the public". All connexion with the public, it was assumed, weakens the priest for his service to beauty. The story is familiar of the opposition to the prevalent opinion into which the further development of this point of view drove Oscar Wilde, in whom, as Friedrich Brie wrote in his *Aesthetische Weltanschauung* (1921), "the idea that the beautiful contains a higher morality in itself became the idea that beauty and art sanctify whatever is done in their name, so that the artist can do no wrong."

The similar German movement, which came late on the scene, shows the same divorce on principle from the *"Bildungspöbel"* ("cultural mob"). The French talked of "the five of us", to mark the narrow circle of the truly cultured; Rossetti shut himself off even as a painter by refraining absolutely, on principle, from holding an exhibition, and wove about his whole existence a veil that to his contemporaries seemed mysterious and romantic; and similarly the group around Stefan George long seemed to the curious to be wreathed in a cloud—a more or less merciful one, perhaps.

This segregation from the public did not in all these cases mean a cessation of dependence on the public. Even the priest, high as he stands above the crowd, needs the crowd if only as the *"misera plebs contribuens"*. Not only that; recognition and admiration give wings to the artistic imagination, and so it may not seldom be observed how, from the most intimate of needs, the public so proudly driven from the front door by Their Magnificences was cordially admitted by the back door.

Contact with the public was maintained through the critic. But the only recognized critics were those who had the entry to the arcana and had been initiated—persons, that is to say, who had been more or less won over to the group's aesthetic outlook. Such critics proceeded from the circles of the aesthetes with the same inevitability as from any other logically developed system. It follows also that each of these esoteric groups grew into a sort of mutual admiration society. The contemporary world wondered why the critics, who had usually represented a conservative taste, suddenly threw themselves into the arms of the practitioners of a new art. But it failed to take account of sociological processes.

THE RUSSIAN INTELLECTUALS

Hugh Seton-Watson

THE WORD "intelligentsia" is Russian, and it was in Russia that the phenomenon itself first appeared. Most people in the West who regard themselves as reasonably well-educated have at least vaguely heard of the frustrated revolutionary intelligentsia of Russia, and when they think of it, it is as something uniquely Russian, a bizarre feature of the outlandish country that produced such people as Dostoevsky. Yet it is important to distinguish between those aspects of the Russian intelligentsia which are specifically Russian and those which are not. The great personalities of Russian intellectual history, like all great personalities, are unique. Some of the ideas, and perhaps still more the approach to ideas—the mental framework—of the Russian intelligentsia, can be traced to the specific influence of Russian history. But the social predicament was not and is not unique. The conditions which produced in 19th century Russia a frustrated and, in part, revolutionary intelligentsia, have repeated and are repeating themselves in one country after another in Eastern Europe, Asia, the Middle East, and Africa. The conditions in which the intelligentsia of Communist Russia live are likely to repeat themselves, and indeed are already repeating themselves, in other countries subjected to totalitarian rule. Neither predicament—pre-revolutionary or post-totalitarian—has any close parallel in Western societies, at least in the last two centuries. But because this is so, it is all the more necessary that Westerners should make an effort of imagination to understand them. Otherwise the West cannot hope to understand the social forces which are today profoundly affecting almost the whole world outside the "north-west corner" of Europe and North America.

The Russian intelligentsia is derived from the secular intellectual élite which grew up in Western Europe after the Reformation. Many generations of West European secular thought produced the radical political ideas of 18th century France, which determined the political development of 19th century Europe. Their offspring—liberalism, nationalism, and socialism—reached Russia in the mid-19th century, through the educated élite or

---

Reprinted from *Encounter* (September, 1955), pp. 43-50, by permission of the author and the periodical.

intelligentsia. One might say that the French *philosophes* were an intelligent-sia, a separate social category whose business was thought and culture, not administration or production, and who observed, disliked, and brilliantly criticised the social and political order around them. In this they resembled their Russian disciples. But there is also a basic difference. Voltaire and the illiterate French agricultural labourer were not much alike; Voltaire lived better, and knew more, than the labourer; yet both belonged to the same culture. Voltaire's ideas derived from a cultural tradition which had arisen on French soil, from French roots. Voltaire criticised an image, distorted perhaps, yet recognisable, of French reality. But the Russian intellectuals of the mid-19th century imported, ready-made from the West, ideas related to the reality of the West, not to the reality of Russia. Chernyshevsky and the Russian *muzhik* belonged to different cultures: their relationship was different in kind from that between Voltaire and the French peasant. This situation is without parallel in the West. It existed in the late 19th century in the Balkans, in the early 20th in Japan and Turkey. It exists today in India and Egypt and West Africa.

Modern secular education was introduced into Russia by Peter the Great, who sent young men abroad to learn military, naval, and industrial skills. Under Elizabeth and Catherine II, French social graces became popular at the Russian court, Russian landowners engaged Frenchmen as tutors to their children, and Russian noblemen went to Paris to enjoy themselves. By the end of the 18th century, Western learning was beginning to be taken seri-ously in St. Petersburg and Moscow, and Western radicalism was finding its first Russian pupils. Alexander I laid the foundations of a system of state education, and this was extended under his successor. By the middle of the 19th century, two important new developments had taken place.

The first was the appearance of a considerable number of persons, pos-sessing a modern education, who were not government officials. For several decades after Peter, education had been regarded as a means of improving the efficiency of generals, admirals, diplomats, and governors. It was at the summit of these professions that one could find the best-educated Russians. By the 1820's a large part of the nobility were seeking a modern education for their children, whether or not they intended to make a career in State service, while economic development also created a demand for new pro-fessions—teaching, the law, medicine. Thus, there appeared social groups which corresponded to the "free professions" of Western society.

The second development was the attainment of modern education by children of non-noble parents (*raznochintsy*). It is true that the Ministers of Education under Nicholas I attempted to restrict access to higher education, and this remained, indeed, a feature of Russian educational policy right up to 1905, even to 1917. Financial obstacles were supplemented by periodic changes in the curriculum of schools designed to make things hard for plebeian children. But these measures were ineffective: they delayed but did not prevent the spread of secondary and university education. Higher education advanced faster than primary education: the numbers of university graduates grew rapidly, but village schools lagged behind. This is of course no specifically Russian phenomenon. It has repeated itself in the Balkans, China, the Ottoman Empire, and most European colonial empires.

The Russian university graduate of 1870 was the cultural equal and cultural contemporary of his colleague in France or Britain or Germany, while the great majority of his compatriots still lived in the Muscovite past. If he was himself of plebeian origin, he was more painfully aware of the contrast than if he was a son of the nobility. If he was not an official but a member of the "free professions," he was isolated not only from the masses but also from the machinery of government, and he could the more easily preserve the purity of the revolutionary ideas which he had acquired in his university years—a purity uncontaminated by any experience of the prosaic business of government. He could not fail to be appalled by the backwardness and misery of the Russian village and the new industrial slums; but he soon discovered that to protest against these conditions would bring down on his head the heavy hand of the Tsar's policemen. More narrowly personal and material causes of frustration were also not lacking. His education and skill would not necessarily give him an attractive career, still less the respect of the bureaucrats. If he was a member of a religious minority (dissenter, sectarian, or Jew) or of a non-Russian nation (Pole, Georgian, or Tartar), the obstacles to his ambition were still greater.

In these conditions it is not surprising that the whole non-official educated class of Russia was profoundly alienated from the political and social régime. The word *intelligentsia,* which essentially denotes the "free professions," soon acquired an undertone of opposition to the régime. No member of the intelligentsia could be a supporter of the régime, and no convinced supporter of the régime could be considered a member of the intelligentsia. This does not, of course, mean that no bureaucrat could be so considered, for there were bureaucrats who detested the régime they served. Still less is this true of government employees in the wide sense, which included university professors, schoolmasters, and many doctors.

The intelligentsia, oppositional by its very nature, contained both admirers and critics of the West, both revolutionaries and reformers.

The famous controversy between "Westernisers" and "Slavophiles" was the main intellectual issue of the 1830's and 1840's. The distinction was not as clear as is often supposed. Even the extreme Westerniser, Chaadaev, believed in a great and independent destiny for Russia. Herzen himself at times showed signs of pan-Slav romanticism. On the other hand the earlier

Slavophiles denounced bureaucratic rule and wished to abolish serfdom: Kireevsky even admired English liberalism. The difference was one not so much of precise ideas or policies as of mental attitudes. The Westernisers were predisposed, on principle, to favour at least the more recent and "progressive" Western ideas and movements. The Slavophiles were inclined to idealise the Russian past, to exaggerate or even to imagine special virtues in the ancient rulers and subjects of Moscow; they liked to persuade themselves that all that the West had done Russia could do better, and in her own way. These two contrasted attitudes are not confined to Russia—parallels can be found in the history of Japan, Turkey, and the Arab world in the last hundred years. In Russia the division continued long after the original Westerniser-Slavophile controversy had become stale. It is clearly recognisable in the disputes between Marxist and Populist Socialists in the 1890's, between Mensheviks and Bolsheviks from 1906 to 1917, and even in the struggle between Trotsky and Stalin.

The general alienation of the intelligentsia from the régime, from at least the mid-1860's on, provided a favourable mental climate, first for radical ideas, and then for revolutionary movements. It was not enough to accept the new doctrines. It was felt to be the duty of the intellectual to place his knowledge at the service of the people, to devote his life to the task of liberating the masses, to lead them to social revolution. The small discussion groups and tiny conspiratorial factions of the sixties were followed by the "Going to the People" of the 1870's. University students, both men and girls, went to the village, first naïvely haranguing the uncomprehending peasants, then settling in their midst and seeking their confidence by becoming craftsmen or medical orderlies or midwives, or even learning to be professional sectarian preachers. But arrests, banishment, and imprisonment forced the revolutionaries to create a disciplined underground party. The first efficient conspiracy, the People's Will of 1879-1881, had few members but successfully carried out a series of assassinations, culminating in that of Tsar Alexander II himself. The police, which had failed to save its master, managed to break up the organisation after his death. But the example of People's Will was copied at the turn of the century by other revolutionaries, including Lenin, who in his *What is to be done* (1902) called for systematic training of "professional revolutionaries."

It is a serious error to confuse the intelligentsia as a whole with the professional revolutionaries—whether Bolshevik or Socialist Revolutionary ("SR"). The professionals were only a small minority—but it was from the intelligentsia that they were recruited. The intelligentsia as a whole regarded the régime as its enemy. It felt no loyalty towards it, recognised no obligation to defend it. Though most Russian intellectuals were not themselves active revolutionaries, and did not even agree with the revolutionaries' ideas, in the last resort they disliked the revolutionaries less than they disliked the Tsar and his bureaucrats. Certain plants grow only in certain soils. If such had not been the mental climate of the whole intelligentsia, the professional revolutionaries would not have become a serious force in Russia.

The alienation of the intelligentsia from the régime is not a peculiarly Russian phenomenon. The same general situation can be found in China at the beginning of this century, or in Hungary in the 1930's, and at various periods in the history of modern Spain. Nor is the "Going to the People" specifically Russian. Very similar attitudes can be found, for example, in the 1930's among such diverse groups of people as the Serbian Communist students, the Roumanian Iron Guardists, and the Hungarian "village explorer" writers. In the field of conspiratorial party organisation it must be admitted that the Russians were pioneers, followed in other lands by both Communist and other revolutionaries. In this field both People's Will and Bolsheviks can claim to have made original contributions.

Though the social predicament of the 19th century Russian intelligentsia differed radically from that of the 18th century French, its general approach to ideas was rather similar. The French intellectuals' long struggle against the alliance of absolute monarchy and Catholic Church had brought many of them into irreconcilable conflict with Christianity. Some were content to be sceptics, to do without a religion. But many required another faith to replace that which they had lost. Political doctrines had to satisfy not only political but also spiritual needs. They repudiated the Kingdom of Heaven in the life after death: instead they would instal the Reign of Virtue in this life. This was within the power of human reason, and it was the bounden duty of humane and rational men to do it, at whatever cost. Those misguided persons who resisted the rule of reason and virtue were enemies of the human race, and must take the consequences.

In France this conception of human affairs did not prevail for long. It met with resistance not only from the ancient institutions—church, army, and bureaucracy—but also from strong social forces—the rising bourgeoisie and an increasingly self-reliant peasantry—and from a deeply-rooted secular culture marked by the spirit of scepticism and inquiry. The development of France in the 19th century did not favour maximalist utopians. But there were other parts of Europe where the attractions of a secular religion to the embittered intelligentsia were not thus matched by institutional or social or cultural counter-forces. Such were the three regions which had been for several centuries forcibly removed from the prevalent civilisation of Europe —Spain, the Balkans, and Russia. The similarities between these three regions should not, of course, be exaggerated. There is an obvious distinction between the maritime, commercial-minded nations (Catalans and Greeks) and the land-locked, almost exclusively peasant nations (Castilians, South

Slavs, and Roumanians).[1] The Russians remained essentially a land-locked nation even many decades after Peter the Great's death. The similarities between Spanish and Russian history have often been pointed out—the strength of the monarchical power, the absence of an influential social élite, the savage patriotism of the peasant masses in the face of Napoleon's armies.[2] On the level of ideas, Spanish anarchism and Russian nihilism are alike in this, that their exponents sought at once political and spiritual goals. The Balkan peoples, re-entering European culture at a still later date, were similarly affected.

The high proportion of sons of priests among the first generations of non-noble Russian intelligentsia is a special factor that deserves emphasis. This factor was also important in the Orthodox Balkan countries in the 20th century. A substantial number of Serbian Communist and Roumanian fascist revolutionaries came from priestly families. In Imperial Russia, the desire to find in politics a spiritual substitute for religion was likely to be especially strong in children of priests and pupils of seminaries.[3] It is probable that the history both of official Orthodoxy and of the schismatic and sectarian communities contains valuable clues to the mentality of the Russian intelligentsia. This is a subject that Soviet scholars are obviously unable to explore, but to which Western historians may some day make useful contributions.

An "all-or-nothing" outlook characterised the Russian intelligentsia, yet was not specifically Russian. Perhaps more specific was the ruthless logic with which Russian intellectuals pursued their thoughts to their final conclusion, oblivious to anything outside their own narrow mental groove.

---

1. Catalans and Greeks in the 19th century were in their great majority peasants too. But the seafaring, commercial-minded element was numerous, and made an enormous contribution to these nations' culture, not least by bringing them into contact with north-western Europe. I am also aware that the Croats of the Adriatic coast had a seafaring and commercial tradition. But the great majority of South Slavs were untouched by such influences. A similar, though not identical, distinction could be drawn between North-Central and South Italy. Poland and Hungary were essentially land-locked states, with little commercial tradition, but the culture of their educated class had been that of Europe at least since the late Middle Ages.

2. The differences are of course also obvious. Spain had been part of Catholic Europe since the 15th century, and most of it for several centuries longer than this. Moreover, peasants and noblemen from land-locked Castile had crossed the Atlantic in their thousands to found a New World there. The colonisation of Siberia by Russian peasants or of the Don and Kuban steppes by Russian and Ukrainian Cossacks is not very comparable. Yet the similarities remain, and call for explanation. They have yet to be thoroughly investigated.

3. Not all seminarists were children of priests, though the latter enjoyed the hereditary privilege of free education in seminaries. Nor were all seminaries necessarily religious-minded. This can hardly be said to be a dominant characteristic of the Tiflis seminarist, Joseph Vissarionovich Djugashvili.

Ruthless logic is widely believed to be a French quality. The Russian intelligentsia learned both its earliest ideas and its habits of thought from the French, but its *jusqu' auboutisme* puts its masters to shame. This may well be due to purely Russian traditions, and here again it is to the history of church and sects that one should turn for enlightenment. But it was certainly reinforced by the social and political status of the intelligentsia. Isolated almost equally from the Russian masses and from the machinery of government, the radical intellectuals could live in the abstract world of their ideas. All political doctrines, conceived in opposition, have to be modified in practice as their bearers acquire experience of government. But in 19th century Russia the intellectuals had no power and no responsibility. Uncontaminated by sordid political realities, they could preserve their revolutionary purity.

As direct criticism of the political system of 19th century Russia was prevented by censorship, new political ideas could only find indirect expression in literary criticism. The pioneer in this field was V. G. Belinsky (1810-48), a convinced democrat, social radical, and anti-clerical, who exercised an enormous influence on the Russian intelligentsia up to 1917, and is even venerated as a minor patron saint by the present leaders of the Soviet Union. His successors carried even further the use of literary criticism for political purposes. The priest's son, N. A. Dobrolyubov (1836-61), a grimly high-minded young man, established the doctrine of revolutionary utilitarianism in cultural matters, which was expressed even more sharply by D. I. Pisarev (1840-68), the prototype of the "Nihilist." Literature and art were of value only in so far as they contributed to the radical cause; they were to be judged, not by their inherent merit, but by their social purpose. Russia's greatest poet, Pushkin, had died long before this doctrine became respectable, and such great prose writers as Tolstoy and Dostoevsky never conformed to it. Pisarev's most extreme judgments did not find much support, but the substance of the revolutionary utilitarian creed was sufficiently accepted by the intelligentsia to have lasting effects. It was no less harmful to Russian culture than were the activities of the notorious Supreme Procurator of the Holy Synod, the reactionary counsellor of the last two Tsars, Konstantin Pobedonostsev. Russian intellectual life in fact suffered from two separate obscurantisms, whose parallel streams at last merged in the Soviet era. Pobedonostsev and Dobrolyubrov were the two spiritual grandfathers of the late A. A. Zhdanov.

Even the Westernisers in most cases rejected the social forces and institutions in the West from which their ideas had been derived. Belinsky recognised that the bourgeoisie was a constructive force in Western society. His contemporary Herzen, however, was rapidly disgusted with the French bourgeoisie, and nearly thirty years of residence in Western Europe did not enable him to see Western society otherwise than through Russian eyes.

The hatred displayed by Russian intellectuals—from the 1850's onwards—for the bourgeoisie is difficult for a Western student of history to understand. Neither the misery of the peasants, which aroused the just indignation of the intellectuals, nor the unjust tyranny of Tsardom, which deprived educated persons of free speech, were caused by the bourgeoisie. The denunciation by Western socialists of Western capitalists was based on real facts, but had little relevance to Russian society. Russian radical intellectuals imported socialist doctrines from the West ready-made, but hatred of the bourgeois was not due only to socialist doctrine. The whole bourgeois ethos, the notions of compromise and of quantitative measurement, were repugnant to them. Not more trade and more prosperity, but the reign of virtue on earth was their aim.

The notion of law also had little meaning for them. They could not conceive that the principle of the rule of law could be important. That even those things which they most admired in the West had been made possible only by the growth of the rule of law, did not occur to them. Laws meant to them either decrees of autocrats or machinations of narrow-minded merchants. Nor did they understand the principle of choice in government. Tsardom in Russia was wrong because it was reactionary. It would be replaced by a government of the people, which would reflect the people's will. Then the reign of virtue would begin. That it was important to provide a machinery that would enable the people to choose between different aspirants to power, did not occur to them. Constitutions were sordid tricks of bourgeois lawyers.

These attitudes were widespread among the Russian intelligentsia long before Marx's doctrines were known, and still longer before any Marxist organisations existed on Russian soil.[4] But this mental climate was of course extremely favourable for Marxism. The Marxist baby-and-bathwater doctrine that, because bourgeois judges are influenced by class prejudice (which of course is often true), therefore the principle that law is above class and above persons must be rejected, found quick and enthusiastic support among Russian revolutionary intellectuals. So did Marxist contempt for "bourgeois constitutions." In a sense Soviet spokesmen are right in depicting Belinsky and Dobrolyubov as forerunners of Lenin. If they were more generous they would add the names of Karamzin and Pobedonostsev.

But it would be wrong to imagine that liberal values made no appeal to the Russian intelligentsia. Side by side with the two parallel obscurantisms there grew up, from the 1860's on, a liberal tradition. One of its strongholds

---

4. Marx's *Kapital* was published in Russian translation in 1872. Small discussion groups of Marxist intellectuals existed in the 1880's, Marxist workers' groups in the late 1890's. The Russian Social Democratic Workers' Party was founded in 1898, but it did not become a serious political force inside Russia until 1905.

was the legal profession. Alexander II's judicial reform of 1864 gave Russia a modern system of justice, and during the fifty years of its operation it achieved very high standards. Russian judges and barristers were equal in learning and integrity to their British or French colleagues. The other main stronghold was local government. The provincial and district zemstvos, and some municipalities, achieved much for good government, welfare, and education in the broadest sense. Change was especially rapid in the ten years following the abortive revolution of 1905. It is true that these were years of political reaction. The first, truly representative Dumas (parliaments) of 1906 and 1907 were followed by assemblies elected on a restricted franchise, and the government was never made responsible to the Duma. But there was a free press, free publication of political literature, and freedom to organise political parties and meetings.[5] All major issues of policy were publicly discussed, both inside and outside the Duma. Industry made extraordinary progress. Both the business class and the working class were growing in numbers, skill, social influence, and independence of mind. Both were approaching the level of the equivalent classes in Central Europe. Of the peasants, a large minority benefited directly from Stolypin's reforms, while the majority were at last obtaining a primary education.

In this greatly changed political and social climate the attitudes of the intelligentsia were also changing. Revolutionary utilitarianism was losing ground. This was a period of experiments in Russian literature. Philosophy and history were treated as serious subjects of study, rather than raw material for revolutionary slogans. The meaning of law, and the value of sound political institutions, were more widely recognised than ever before. As in the past, almost all educated Russians who were not senior bureaucrats—and even some who were—rejected the political system as it was, but there was much less desire for a cataclysmic upheaval followed by utopia. The intelligentsia was now divided between the progressives who wished to build, on social and cultural foundations that were already strong, a free Russia that would take its place in a free Europe, and the maximalist obscurantists who clung to the anachronism of "all-or-nothing." This division was different from the old cleavage between Westerners and Slavophiles, which had been an argument about ideas, neither group having had much contact with reality. In 1914 both the legal and social progress pursued by the

5. The nature of this period has been grossly distorted by those Western writers who take their information mainly from Lenin or other revolutionaries who lived in exile abroad after 1906. It is true that there was brutal repression in areas of armed revolt in 1906. It is true that the police retained large powers, and that some provincial governors showed little respect for the law even after 1907. It is also true that issues of newspapers which incited to armed rebellion were liable to be suppressed. But when all this has been said it remains true that the years 1907–14 were the period of greatest civil liberty in the entire history of Russia.

progressives, and the revolutionary movements cherished by the obscurantists, were realities. The progressives did not deny the backwardness of Russia
or the lack of political consciousness of the Russian peasants, nor did they
reject in principle the use of force against the autocracy. But they looked to
the future, and time seemed to be working in their favour.[6]

But time ran out. The chief victim of World War I was Russia. After
three years of heroic effort, the Russian armies succumbed to the combined
effects of the German onslaught and Nicholas II's leadership, surely the
most ignoble that a great nation has ever endured. Tsardom was overthrown
and in the following months the Russian state machine disintegrated. In
the chaos that spread throughout the country, despair combined with utopian
maximalist longings. The progressive part of the intelligentsia came apparently to power, but the new rulers lacked political experience and were
deprived of the apparatus of law and government to carry out their orders.
Placed between a ruthless invader and hard-pressed, exacting allies, they
could neither continue the war nor make peace. This was the opportunity
for the maximalists. In 1913 they were an anachronism, but 1917 was their
historic hour. Of the two groups of maximalists, the extreme wing of the
Socialist Revolutionaries or the Bolsheviks, the second were far superior in
leadership and discipline. Lenin made good use of most of his chances. Not
the ineluctable progress of history, but a fortuitous combination of exceptionally favourable internal and international forces raised him to supreme
power.

---

6. The outlook to which I refer could be found in some Populist and Marxist
socialists, as well as among the liberals in the political sense—the Constitutional
Democratic or "Kadet" Party. The labour movement within Russia was largely moving in this direction, to the rage of Lenin, who denounced its leaders as "Liquidators."
Perhaps the most striking expression of the search of the intelligentsia for new paths
was the symposium *Landmarks,* published in 1909, with contributions from the
former Marxists Struve, Berdyaev, and Bulgakov, who not only rejected revolutionary
utilitarianism but challenged the whole radical approach, sanctified by Belinsky,
towards Christianity.

Part II

NATURE OF

INTELLECTUALS

OVERVIEW

Democritus said that he would rather discover a single demonstration than win the throne of Persia. To this view of the pure intellectual there can be contrasted the counterfeit intellectual, who is best characterized by Georg Lichtenberg's comments on a would-be "great mind": "The attributes of the greatest men were all united in himself. Like Alexander, his head was tilted to one side; like Caesar, he always had something in his hair. He could drink coffee like Leibniz, and once settled in his armchair, he forgot eating and drinking like Newton, and like him, had to be awakened. He wore a wig like Dr. Johnson, and like Cervantes, the fly of his trousers was always open." It is obvious from these two contrasting views that the nature of intellectuals is complex and therefore it is difficult to define the "intellectual." Since the Introduction stated that this anthology conceives the "intellectual" in a relatively broad sense, this Part and the next one include a variety of essays on a variety of types of intellectuals. Two kinds of essays are included in this Part: The first four are systematic analyses of the nature of intellectuals, and the last three are unsystematic meditations.

Shils distinguishes five traditions of intellectuals: The tradition of scientism denies the validity of tradition as such and insists on testing everything. (A different view of scientism is presented by Wilson and Hayek in Part V.) The romantic tradition stresses the spontaneous manifestation of concrete individuality. The revolutionary tradition draws on scientism and romanticism but essentially rests on a much older one—the apocalyptic tradition to which reference has already been made in connection with the essays by Salomon and Seton-Watson in Part I. The populist tradition believes in the creativity and superior worth of the ordinary people; a variation of this tradition is presented by Dostoevsky and Berdyaev in Part III. The anti-intellectual tradition of order is best known in the West in the form of French positivism which has been analyzed in Salomon's essay, but has its roots in the ancient belief that excessive intellectual analysis disrupts the foundations of order.

While Shils discusses intellectuals in terms of traditions, Mannheim and Schumpeter discuss them in terms of class. Neither believe that intellectuals form a class, which is a problem also discussed by several essays in Parts V and VI. Mannheim maintains that unlike in the past, intellectual activity is not carried on exclusively by a rigidly defined social group. He stresses the heterogeneity of intellectuals which makes it impossible to conceive of them as a class, although their education binds them together. He says that a sociology oriented only by terms of class probably only slightly comprehends intellectuals. It may be noted in passing that this is the reason why Marxists have so much trouble in fitting the intelligentsia into their class-scheme. With regard to the possible roles of intellectuals Mannheim indicates two alternatives. Intellectuals may affiliate with one or the other of the antagonistic classes; in this connection he observes that both the workers and the bourgeois distrust intellectuals. Or they can try to become detached from classes and find their destiny as intellectuals by becoming aware of their own social position and the mission implicit in it, and create a forum outside party groups.

Schumpeter also argues that intellectuals are not a class in the sense in which peasants and industrial laborers are, yet they develop group attitudes and group interests. An important distinguishing feature of intellectuals is their absence of direct responsibility for practical affairs and absence of first hand knowledge about them. This is stated with respect to specific historical situations by Tocqueville and Seton-Watson in Part I; although it overlooks such exceptional situations as that discussed by Curti. Schumpeter shows that a by-product of capitalism was the emergence, as a collective patron, of the bourgeois public which gave recognition to the free lance intellectual. But the capitalist order is unwilling and unable to control its intellectual sector effectively. In defending the intellectuals as a group the bourgeoisie defended itself and its scheme of life. Only a socialist or fascist government is strong enough to discipline intellectuals. At the later stages of capitalism several factors have increased the number of intellectuals and also led to their discontent and resentment, a point of view which is also emphasized by many essays in Part V. Thus intellectuals supplied the theories and slogans of the labor movement and have also radicalized it.

Coser provides still another point of view—the relations of intellectuals to men of power. He provides two case studies to examine this relationship which is essentially a variation of the philosopher-king theme to which reference has been made in the previous Part. His discussion of Napolean and the Idéologues shows Napolean first courting the Idéologues, but gradually supressing them when he came to power. Similarly Gomulka in Poland, who was substantially helped into power by intellectuals who wanted to revise and criticize Marxist-Leninist dogma, finally suppressed them. Some Polish intellectuals resigned from the party while others found it necessary to accommodate themselves to restored party discipline.

Dostoevsky's observations are from the non-narrative part of *Notes from Underground;* selection was necessary in order to present only those portions which are particularly relevant to the psychology of the man of reflection versus that of the man of action. This profound and persistent issue has preoccupied many thinkers; it is central in *Don Quixote* and *Hamlet*. According to Dostoevsky, consciousness is a disease. The antithesis of the man of acute consciousness is the normal person, the man of action. It is necessary to be stupid and limited to be able to act; the man of action has his mind at rest, free from doubt, and clearly sees the righteousness of the end of action. Consciousness and reflection preclude the conditions necessary in order to act.

Montherlant's satiric letter is from a novel. It is received by the main character who remarks that some of those who signed the letter are thirty years old. Valéry's meditations on the nature and variety of intellectuals are an appropriate ending for this Part.

THE TRADITIONS OF INTELLECTUALS

Edward A. Shils

INTELLECTUAL WORK is sustained by and transmits a complex tradition which persists through changes in the structure of the intellectual class. In these traditions, the most vital ones are the standards and rules in the light of which achievement is striven for and assessed and the substantive beliefs and symbols which constitute the heritage of valid achievement. It is by the participation in these traditions of perception, appreciation, and expression, and the affirmation of the importance of performing in the modes accredited by these traditions, that the intellectual is defined. One could almost say that if these traditions did not confront the intellectual as an ineluctable inheritance, they would be created anew in each generation by the passionate disposition of the "natural" intellectual to be in contact, by perception, ratiocination or expression, with symbols of general scope. They are traditions which are so to speak given by the nature of intellectual work. They are the immanent traditions of intellectual performance, the accepted body of rules of procedure, standards of judgment, criteria for the selection of subject-matters and problems, modes of presentation, canons for the assessment of excellence, models of previous achievement and prospective emulation. Every field of intellectual performance, more than any other craft or profession, possessing a long and acknowledged accumulation of achievements, has such a cultural tradition, always—though at varying rates—being added to and modified. What is called scientific method in each particular field of science or scholarship and the techniques of literary creation and of work in the plastic and other arts, each possess such a tradition, and without that tradition even the greatest and most creative geniuses who seek to discover and create in that domain could not be effective. Colleges and universities, scientific, scholarly, and artistic journals, museums, galleries —in short the whole system of intellectual institutions—exist to select those who are qualified to work within these traditions, and to train them in their appreciation, application and development. Even the most creative and

Reprinted from "The Intellectuals and the Powers: Some Perspectives for Comparative Analysis," in *Comparative Studies in Society and History* (October, 1958), pp. 15-21, by permission of the author and the journal, and forming part of a larger work on the intellectuals to be published by The Free Press of Glencoe, Illinois.

rapidly developing domains of intellectual performance could disregard them only with very great loss.

These traditions, though they make neither direct nor logically implicit reference to the position of their adherents in relation to the surrounding society and the authorities which rule it, seem from their very structure to entail a measure of tension between themselves and the laity. The very intensity and concentration of commitment of these values, which are remote from the executive routines of daily life in family, firm, office, factory, church and civil service, from the pleasures of the ordinary man, and the obligations, compromises, and corruptions of those who exercise commanding authority in church, state, business, and army, entail an at least incipient sense, on each side, of the distance which separates these two trends of value-orientation.

Intellectual work arose from religious preoccupations. In the early history of the human race, it tended, in its concern with the ultimate or at least with what lies beyond the immediate concrete experience, to think with religious symbols. It continues to share with genuine religious experience the fascination with the sacred or the ultimate ground of thought and experience, and the aspiration to enter into intimate contact with it. In secular intellectual work, this involves the search for the truth, for the principles embedded in events and actions or for the establishment of a relationship between the self and the essential, whether the relationship be cognitive, appreciative, or expressive. The deeper religious attitude, the striving for contact and communion with the symbols of the ultimate powers which dominate human life, has a very intimate affinity with the profoundest scientific orientations, which seek to discern the most general and comprehensive laws of universal and human existence. Differently disciplined, both the religious and the scientific dispositions at their most creative, have in common the striving for contact with the most decisive and significant symbols and the realities underlying those symbols. It is therefore no stretching of the term to say that science and philosophy, even when they are not religious in a conventional sense, are as concerned with the sacred as religion itself. In consequence of this, in our enumeration of the traditions under which intellectual pursuits are carried on, we should say that the tradition of awesome respect and of serious striving for contact with the sacred, is perhaps the first, the most comprehensive and the most important of all the traditions of the intellectuals. In the great religious cultures of Islam, Buddhism, Taoism, and Hinduism, prior to the emergence of a differentiated modern intellectual class, the care of the sacred through the mastery, interpretation, and exposition of sacred writings, and the cultivation of the appropriate mental states or qualities were the first interests of the intellectuals. (In China, the development of a class of Confucian intellectual-civil servants produced its own tradition, more civil and aesthetic than religious in the conventional meaning.) In the West too, in antiquity, a substantial section of the philosophical intelligentsia bore this tradition, and on the higher reaches, even those who cut themselves off from the tribal and territorial religions, continued to be impelled by such considerations (e.g. Pythagoras, Euclid, Ptolemy, Aristotle, Plato, Socrates, Lucretius, Seneca). In modern times, although attracting a diminishing share of the creative capacities of the oncoming intellectual elite, religious orientations still remain a major preoccupation of a substantial fraction of the educated classes and not less of the most creative minds.

With this striving for contact with the ultimately important comes the self-esteem which always accompanies the performance of important activities. Any effort to understand the traditions of the intellectuals and their relations with the authorities who rule the other sections of society at any given time, must bear in mind the crucial significance of the self-regard which comes from preoccupation and contact with the most vital facts of human and cosmic existence, and the implied attitude of derogation towards those who act in more mundane or more routine capacities.[1]

When intellectuals ceased to be solely bearers of religiosity, the very act of separation, however gradual and unwitting and undeliberate, sets up a tension between the intellectuals and the religious authority of their society. Insofar as they were not merely civil servants and counsellors to princes—itself an unsettling, tension-generating relationship—there was created a tension between the public authorities and the intellectuals. Ecclesiastical and exemplary religious authority became an object of the distrust of intellectuals, and insofar as the authority of the government of earthly affairs associated itself with the religious powers, it too shared in that skepticism. The attitude is by no means universal nor need the distrust be aggressive. Confucian civil servants, disdainful towards Taoism or Buddhism, did not become rebels against their sovereigns as long as they themselves were treated respectfully. In the West where the separation of religious and other intellectual activities has become most pronounced, a more general feeling of distance from authority has been engendered and has become one of the strongest of the traditions of the intellectuals. First in the West, and then in the past half-century in Africa and Asia among intellectuals who have come under the Western traditions, the tradition of distrust of secular and ecclesiastical authority, and with these, of familial and communal authority, and in fact of tradition as such—has become the chief secondary tradition of the intellect-

---

1. Naturally this sentiment is not equally shared by all intellectuals. Not all are equally involved in these "vital facts"—and therefore not all have the same feeling of the dignity of their activities. Intellectuals vary greatly in their sensitivity to their traditions—just as do the laity with respect to their traditions—but even in those who are relatively insensitive, there remains a considerable unconscious assimilation of many elements of these central traditions.

uals. As such, it is nurtured by many of the subsidiary traditions such as scientism, revolutionism, progressivism, etc., which we shall treat below.

The tension between the intellectuals and the powers—their urge to submit to authority as the bearer of the highest good—whether it be order or progress or some other value—and to resist or condemn authority as a betrayer of the highest values, comes ultimately from the constitutive orientation of the intellectuals towards the sacred. Practically all the more concrete traditions in the light and shadows of which intellectuals have lived express this tension. We shall note, in brief, some of these traditions which, however diverse in their age and origins, have played a great part in forming the relations of the modern intellectuals to authority. They are a) the tradition of scientism, b) the romantic tradition, c) the apocalyptic tradition, d) the populistic tradition, and e) the tradition of anti-intellectual order.

All of these traditions are in conflict with other traditions of deference towards ecclesiastical and temporal authorities and the expectation of a career in their service. Even in those modern cultures where the traditions of the intellectuals' acceptance of authority are strongest, in modern Britain and modern Germany, they have by no means had the field to themselves. Similarly in modern Asia where variants of the traditions of devotion to the religiously sacred values and the service of temporal authority have, in ancient as well as modern times, had a powerful hold, anti-authoritarian and anti-civil traditions, diffused from the West and nurtured by related traditions derived from Taoism, Buddhism, and Hinduism, have found an eager and widespread reception.

The *tradition of scientism* is the tradition which denies the validity of tradition as such; it insists on the testing of everything which is received and on its rejection, if it does not correspond with the "facts of experience". It is the tradition which demands the avoidance of every extraneous impediment to the precise perception of reality, regardless of whether that impediment comes from tradition, from institutional authority, or internal passion or impulse. It is critical of the arbitrary and the irrational. In its emphasis on the indispensability of first-hand and direct experience, it sets itself in opposition to everything which comes between the mind of the knowing individual and "reality". It is easy to see how social convention and the traditional authority associated with institutions would fall prey to the ravages of this powerfully persuasive and corrosive tradition.

The *romantic tradition* appears at first sight to be in irreconcilable opposition to the tradition of scientism. At certain points, such as the estimation of the value of impulse and passion, there is a real and unbridgeable antagonism. In many important respects however they share fundamental features. Romanticism starts with the appreciation of the spontaneous manifestations of the essence of concrete individuality. Hence it values originality, i.e. the novel, that which is produced from the "genius" of the individual (or the folk), in contrast with the stereotyped and traditional actions of the philistine. Since ratiocination and detachment obstruct spontaneous expression, they are thought to be life-destroying. Institutions which have rules and which prescribe the conduct of the individual members by conventions and commands are likewise viewed as life-destroying. The bourgeois family, mercantile activity, the market, indeed civil society in general, with its curb on enthusiasm and its sober acceptance of obligation, are repugnant to the romantic tradition—all are the enemies of spontaneity and genuineness, they impose a role on the individual and do not permit him to be himself. They kill what is living in the folk. Civil society has no place for the intellectual who is afflicted with a sense of his moral solitude within it. The affinities of the romantic tradition to the revolutionary criticism of the established order and to the bohemian refusal to have more part in it than is absolutely necessary are obvious. It too is one of the most explosively anti-authoritarian, and even anti-civil, powers of modern intellectual life.

The revolutionary tradition which has found so many of its leading recipients and exponents among intellectuals, draws much from scientism and romanticism, but essentially it rests on one much older, namely the *apocalyptic* or millenarian tradition. The belief that the evil world as we know it, so full of temptation and corruption, will come to an end one day and will be replaced by a purer and better world, originates in the apocalyptic outlook of the prophets of the Old Testament. It is promulgated in the Christian idea of the Kingdom of God, which the earlier Christians expected in their own time, and it lingers as a passionately turbulent stream, dammed up and hidden by the efforts of the Church, but recurrently appearing on the surface of history through the teaching and action of heretical sects. It received a powerful impetus from Manicheanism. In the Donatists, in the Bogomils, in the Albigensians and Waldensians, in the Hussites and Lollards, in the Anabaptists and in the Fifth Monarchy Men, in the belief that the evil world, the world of the Children of Darkness, would be destroyed and supplanted by the world of the Children of Light after a decisive judgment by the Sovereign of the universe, this tradition has lived on. It has come down to our own times in a transmuted form. Although it still exists in its religious form among numerous Christian and quasi-Christian sects in Europe, America, and Africa, its true recipients are the modern revolutionary movements and above all the Marxian movements. Marxian writers of the early part of this century acknowledged the Anabaptists, the Fifth Monarchy Men, the Levellers and the Diggers, as their forerunners, and although the Bolsheviks have been less willing to admit Russian sectarianism as an antecedent, there can be little doubt that the Russian sectarian image of the world and its cataclysmic history made it easier for the Marxian conception of society and its historical destiny to find acceptance in Russia. The disposition to distinguish sharply between good and evil and to refuse to admit the permissibility of any admixture, the insistence that justice be done though the heavens fall, the obstinate refusal to compromise or to tolerate compromise—all the features of doctrinaire politics, or the politics of the ideal— which are so common among modern intellectuals must be attributed in some measure at least to this tradition.

Another of the traditions which has everywhere in the world moved intellectuals in the last century and a half is the *populistic tradition.* Populism is a belief in the creativity and in the superior moral worth of the ordinary people, of the uneducated and unintellectual; it perceives their virtue in their actual qualities or in their potentialities. In the simplicity and wisdom of their ways, the populist tradition alleges that it has discerned virtues which are morally superior to those found in the educated and in the higher social classes. Even where, as in Marxism, the actual state of the lower classes is not esteemed, they are alleged to be by destiny fitted to become the salvationary nucleus of their whole society. Romanticism with its distrust of the rational and calculating elements in bourgeois society, revolutionism with its hatred of the upper classes as the agents of wicked authority, the apocalyptic attitude which sees the last coming first and which alleges that official learning (religious and secular) has falsified the truths which the last judgment and the leap into freedom will validate—all these manifest a populistic disposition. German historical and philological scholarship in the 19th century, imbued with the romantic hatred of the rational, the economic, the analytic spirit, which it castigated as the source and product of the whole revolutionary, rationalistic trend of Western European culture, discovered in the nameless masses, the folk, the fountain of linguistic and cultural creativity. French socialism went a step further and Marxism elevated this essentially romantic outlook into a systematic "scientific" theory.

In all countries peripheral to the most creative centers of Western culture at the height of its hegemony over the modern mind, intellectuals were both fascinated and rendered uneasy by the culture of Western Europe. Not only in early 19th century Germany, but in Russia of the 50's, in the 20th century Middlewestern United States, in Brazil (in the doctrine of "Indianism"), in the resentful and embittered Weimar Republic, in India since the ascendancy of Gandhi and in the emerging intelligentsia of the new countries of Africa, populistic tendencies are massively at work. In all these countries the intellectuals have been or were educated either in foreign countries or in institutions within their own countries modelled on those at the center of the culture they sought or seek to emulate. In all these countries the intellectuals have developed anxiety about whether they have not allowed themselves to be corrupted by excessive permeation with the admired foreign culture.

To identify themselves with the people, to praise the culture of the ordinary people as richer, truer, wiser and more relevant than the foreign culture in which they had themselves been educated, has been a way out of this distress. In most of these cases it is a protest against the "official" culture, the culture of the higher civil servants, of the universities and of the culture, political, literary, and philosophical, which has come out of them. As such it has fused easily with the other traditions of hostility to civil institutions and civil authority.

There is another tradition, closely connected with all of these and yet apparently their negation, which merits mention. This is the *anti-intellectual tradition of order*. Best known in the West in the form of French positivism (St. Simon and Comte), it has its roots in antiquity and in the belief that excessive intellectual analysis and discussion can disrupt the foundations of order. Plato's attitude towards poets had its parallel in the burning of the books by the former Confucian, Li-Ssu, at the origin of the Ch'in Dynasty; Hobbes' analysis of the role of intellectuals in bringing about the English civil war, Taine's interpretation of the significance of the *philosophes* in bringing on the French Revolution of 1789, and the ideas of Joseph de Maistre, all testify to the ambivalence in the traditional anti-authoritarianism of intellectuals.

THE SOCIOLOGICAL PROBLEM OF
THE "INTELLIGENTSIA"

Karl Mannheim

THIS UNANCHORED, *relatively* classless stratum is, to use Alfred Weber's terminology, the "socially unattached intelligentsia" (*freischwebende Intelligenz*). It is impossible in this connection to give even the sketchiest outline of the difficult sociological problem raised by the existence of the intellectual. But the problems we are considering could not be adequately formulated, much less solved, without touching upon certain phases of the position of the intellectuals. A sociology which is oriented only with reference to social-economic classes will never adequately understand this phenomenon. According to this theory, the intellectuals constitute either a class or at least an appendage to a class. Thus it might describe correctly certain determinants and components of this unattached social body, but never the essential quality of the whole. It is, of course, true that a large body of our intellectuals come from *rentier* strata, whose income is derived directly or indirectly from rents and interest on investments. But for that matter certain groups of the officials and the so-called liberal professions are also members of the intelligentsia. A closer examination, however, of the social basis of these strata will show them to be less clearly identified with one class than those who participate more directly in the economic process.

If this sociological cross-section is completed by an historical view, further heterogeneity among the intellectuals will be disclosed. Changes in class relationships at different times affect some of these groups favourably, others unfavourably. Consequently it cannot be maintained that they are homogeneously determined. Although they are too differentiated to be regarded as a single class, there is, however, one unifying sociological bond between all groups of intellectuals, namely, education, which binds them together in a striking way. Participation in a common educational heritage progressively tends to suppress differences of birth, status, profession, and wealth, and to unite the individual educated people on the basis of the education they have received.

From *Ideology and Utopia,* by Karl Mannheim, pp. 155-162. Reprinted by permission of the publisher, A Harvest Book, Harcourt, Brace and Company, Inc. Translated by Louis Wirth and Edward A. Shils.

In my opinion nothing could be more wrong than to misinterpret this view and maintain that the class and status ties of the individual disappear completely by virtue of this. It is, however, peculiarly characteristic of this new basis of association that it preserves the multiplicity of the component elements in all their variety by creating a homogeneous medium within which the conflicting parties can measure their strength. Modern education from its inception is a living struggle, a replica, on a small scale of the conflicting purposes and tendencies which rage in society at large. Accordingly the educated man, as concerns his intellectual horizon, is determined in a variety of ways. This acquired educational heritage subjects him to the influence of opposing tendencies in social reality, while the person who is not oriented toward the whole through his education, but rather participates directly in the social process of production, merely tends to absorb the *Weltanschauung* of that particular group and to act exclusively under the influence of the conditions imposed by his immediate social situation.

One of the most impressive facts about modern life is that in it, unlike preceding cultures, intellectual activity is not carried on exclusively by a socially rigidly defined class, such as a priesthood, but rather by a social stratum which is to a large degree unattached to any social class and which is recruited from an increasingly inclusive area of social life. This sociological fact determines essentially the uniqueness of the modern mind, which is characteristically not based upon the authority of a priesthood, which is not closed and finished, but which is rather dynamic, elastic, in a constant state of flux, and perpetually confronted by new problems. Even humanism was already largely the expression of such a more or less socially emancipated stratum, and where the nobility became the bearer of culture it broke through the fixedness of a class-bound mentality in many respects. But not until we come to the period of bourgeois ascendancy does the level of cultural life become increasingly detached from a given class.

The modern bourgeoisie had from the beginning a twofold social root—on the one hand the owners of capital, on the other those individuals whose only capital consisted in their education. It was common therefore to speak of the propertied and educated class, the educated element being, however, by no means ideologically in agreement with the property-owning element.

There arises, then, in the midst of this society, which is being deeply divided by class cleavages, a stratum, which a sociology oriented solely in terms of class probably can only slightly comprehend. Nevertheless, the specific social position of this stratum can be quite adequately characterized. Although situated between classes it does not form a middle class. Not, of course, that it is suspended in a vacuum into which social interests do not penetrate; on the contrary, it subsumes in itself all those interests with which social life is permeated. With the increase in the number and variety of the classes and strata from which the individual groups of intellectuals are recruited, there comes greater multiformity and contrast in the tendencies operating on the intellectual level which ties them to one another. The individual, then, more or less takes a part in the mass of mutually conflicting tendencies.

While those who participate directly in the process of production—the worker and the entrepreneur—being bound to a particular class and mode of life, have their outlooks and activities directly and exclusively determined by their specific social situations, the intellectuals, besides undoubtedly bearing the imprint of their specific class affinity, are also determined in their outlook by this intellectual medium which contains all those contradictory points of view. This social situation always provided the potential energy which enabled the more outstanding intellectuals to develop the social sensibility that was essential for becoming attuned to the dynamically conflicting forces. Every point of view was examined constantly as to its relevance to the present situation. Furthermore, precisely through the cultural attachments of this group, there was achieved such an intimate grasp of the total situation, that the tendency towards a dynamic synthesis constantly reappeared, despite the temporary distortions with which we have yet to deal.

Hitherto, the negative side of the "unattachedness" of the intellectuals, their social instability, and the predominantly deliberate character of their mentality has been emphasized almost exclusively. It was especially the politically extreme groups who, demanding a definite declaration of sympathies, branded this as "characterlessness." It remains to be asked, however, whether in the political sphere, a decision in favour of a dynamic mediation may not be just as much a decision as the ruthless espousal of yesterday's theories or the one-sided emphasis on to-morrow's.

There are two courses of action which the unattached intellectuals have actually taken as ways out of this middle-of-the-road position: first, what amounts to a largely voluntary affiliation with one or the other of the various antagonistic classes; second, scrutiny of their own social moorings and the quest for the fulfilment of their mission as the predestined advocate of the intellectual interests of the whole.

As regards the first way out, unattached intellectuals are to be found in the course of history in all camps. Thus they always furnished the theorists for the conservatives who themselves because of their own social stability could only with difficulty be brought to theoretical self-consciousness. They likewise furnished the theorists for the proletariat which, because of its social conditions, lacked the prerequisites for the acquisition of the knowledge necessary for modern political conflict. Their affiliation with the liberal bourgeoisie has already been discussed.

This ability to attach themselves to classes to which they originally did not belong, was possible for intellectuals because they could adapt themselves to any viewpoint and because they and they alone were in a position to choose their affiliation, while those who were immediately bound by class affiliations were only in rare exceptions able to transcend the boundaries of their class outlook. This voluntary decision to join in the political struggles of a certain class did indeed unite them with the particular class during the struggle, but it did not free them from the distrust of the original members of that class. This distrust is only a symptom of the sociological fact that the assimilability of intellectuals into an outside class is limited by the psychic and social characteristics of their own. Sociologically this peculiarity of belonging to the intelligentsia accounts for the fact that a proletarian who becomes an intellectual is likely to change his social personality. A detailed case-study of the path taken by the intellectual confronted by this distrust would not be in place here. We wish merely to point out that the fanaticism of radicalized intellectuals should be understood in this light. It bespeaks a psychic compensation for the lack of a more fundamental integration into a class and the necessity of overcoming their own distrust as well as that of others.

One could of course condemn the path taken by individual intellectuals and their endless wavering, but our sole concern here is to explain this behaviour by means of the position of intellectuals in the whole social structure. Such social dereliction and transgression may be regarded as no more than a negative misuse of a peculiar social position. The individual, instead of focussing his energies on the positive potentialities of the situation, falls victim to the temptations potential in the situation. Nothing would be more incorrect than to base one's judgment of the function of a social stratum on the apostatic behaviour of some of its members and to fail to see that the frequent "lack of conviction" of the intellectuals is merely the reverse side of the fact that they alone are in a position to have intellectual convictions. In the long run, history can be viewed as a series of trial and error experiments in which even the failings of men have a tentative value and in the course of which the intellectuals were those who through their homelessness in our society were the most exposed to failure. The repeated attempts to identify themselves with, as well as the continual rebuffs received from, other classes must lead eventually to a clearer conception on the part of the intellectuals of the meaning and the value of their own position in the social order.

The first way, then, out of the predicament of the intellectuals, namely, the direct affiliation with classes and parties, shows a tendency, even though it is unconscious, towards a dynamic synthesis. It was usually the class in need of intellectual development which received their support. It was primarily the conflict of intellectuals which transformed the conflict of interests into a conflict of ideas. This attempt to lift the conflict of interests to a spiritual plane has two aspects: on the one hand it meant the empty glorification of naked interests by means of the tissues of lies spun by apologists; on the other hand, in a more positive sense, it meant the infusion of certain intellectual demands into practical politics. In return for their collaboration with parties and classes, the intellectuals were able to leave this imprint upon them. If they had no other achievement to their credit, this alone would have been a significant accomplishment. Their function is to penetrate into the ranks of the conflicting parties in order to compel them to accept their demands. This activity, viewed historically, has amply shown wherein the sociological pecularity and the mission of this unattached social stratum lie.

The second way out of the dilemma of the intellectuals consists precisely in becoming aware of their own social position and the mission implicit in it. When this is achieved, political affiliation or opposition will be decided on the basis of a conscious orientation in society and in accordance with the demands of the intellectual life.

One of the basic tendencies in the contemporary world is the gradual awakening of class-consciousness in all classes. If this is so, it follows that even the intellectuals will arrive at a consciousness—though not a class-consciousness—of their own general social position and the problems and opportunities it involves. This attempt to comprehend the sociological phenomenon of the intellectuals, and the attempt, on the basis of this, to take an attitude towards politics have traditions of their own quite as much as has the tendency to become assimilated into other parties.

We are not concerned here with examining the possibilities of a politics exclusively suited to intellectuals. Such an examination would probably show that the intellectuals in the present period could not become independently politically active. In an epoch like our own, where class interests and positions are becoming more sharply defined and derive their force and direction from mass action, political conduct which seeks other means of support would scarcely be possible. This does not imply, however, that their particular position prevents them from achieving things which are of indispensable significance for the whole social process. Most important among these would be the discovery of the position from which a total perspective would be possible. Thus they might play the part of watchmen in what otherwise would be a pitch-black night. It is questionable whether it is desirable to throw overboard all of the opportunities which arise out of their peculiar situation.

A group whose class position is more or less definitely fixed already has its political viewpoint decided for it. Where this is not so, as with the intellectuals, there is a wider area of choice and a corresponding need for total orientation and synthesis. This latter tendency which arises out of the position of the intellectuals exists even though the relation between the various groups does not lead to the formation of an integrated party. Similarly, the intellectuals are still able to arrive at a total orientation even when they have joined a party. Should the capacity to acquire a broader point of view be considered merely as a liability? Does it not rather present a mission? Only he who really has the choice has an interest in seeing the whole of the social and political structure. Only in that period of time and that stage of investigation which is dedicated to deliberation is the sociological and logical locus of the development of a synthetic perspective to be sought. The formation of a decision is truly possible only under conditions of freedom based on the possibility of choice which continues to exist even after the decision has been made. We owe the possibility of mutual interpenetration and understanding of existent currents of thought to the presence of such a relatively unattached middle stratum which is open to the constant influx of individuals from the most diverse social classes and groups with all possible points of view. Only under such conditions can the incessantly fresh and broadening synthesis, to which we have referred, arise.

Even Romanticism, because of its social position, had already included in its programme the demand for a broad, dynamic mediation *(dynamische Vermittlung)* of conflicting points of view. In the nature of the case, this demand led to a conservative perspective. The generation that followed Romanticism, however, supplanted this conservative view with a revolutionary one as being in accord with the needs of the time. The essential thing in this connection is that only in this line of development did there persist the attempt to make this mediation a living one, and to connect political decisions with a prior total orientation. To-day more than ever it is expected of such a dynamic middle group that it will strive to create a forum outside the party schools in which the perspective of and the interest in the whole is safeguarded.

It is precisely to these latent tendencies that we owe our present realization that all political interest and knowledge are necessarily partisan and particular. It is only to-day, when we have become aware of all the currents and are able to understand the whole process by which political interests and *Weltanschauungen* come into being in the light of a sociologically intelligible process, that we see the possibility of politics as science. Since it is likely, in accord with the spirit of the age, that more and more party schools will arise, it is all the more desirable that an actual forum be established whether it be in the universities or in specialized higher institutions of learning, which shall serve the pursuit of this advanced form of political science. If the party schools address themselves exclusively to those whose political decisions have been made in advance by parties, this mode of study will appeal to those whose decision remains yet to be made. Nothing is more desirable than that those intellectuals who have a background of pronounced class interests should, especially in their youth, assimilate this point of view and conception of the whole.

Even in such a school it is not to be assumed that the teachers should be partyless. It is not the object of such a school to avoid arriving at political decisions. But there is a profound difference between a teacher who, after careful deliberation, addresses his students, whose minds are not yet made up, from a point of view which has been attained by careful thinking leading to a comprehension of the total situation and a teacher who is exclusively concerned with inculcating a party outlook already firmly established.

THE SOCIOLOGY OF THE INTELLECTUALS

Joseph A. Schumpeter

... NEITHER the opportunity of attack nor real or fancied grievances are in themselves sufficient to produce, however strongly they may favor, the emergence of active hostility against a social order. For such an atmosphere to develop it is necessary that there be groups to whose interest it is to work up and organize resentment, to nurse it, to voice it and to lead it. As will be shown in Part IV, the mass of people never develops definite opinions on its own initiative. Still less is it able to articulate them and to turn them into consistent attitudes and actions. All it can do is to follow or refuse to follow such group leadership as may offer itself. Until we have discovered social groups that will qualify for that role our theory of the atmosphere of hostility to capitalism is incomplete.

Broadly speaking, conditions favorable to general hostility to a social system or specific attack upon it will in any case tend to call forth groups that will exploit them. But in the case of capitalist society there is a further fact to be noted: unlike any other type of society, capitalism inevitably and by virtue of the very logic of its civilization creates, educates and subsidizes a vested interest in social unrest.[1] Explanation of this phenomenon, which is as curious as it is important, follows from our argument in Chapter XI, but may be made more telling by an excursion into the Sociology of the Intellectual.

1. This type is not easy to define. The difficulty is in fact symptomatic of the character of the species. Intellectuals are not a social class in the sense in which peasants or industrial laborers constitute social classes; they hail from all the corners of the social world, and a great part of their activities

---

From *Capitalism, Socialism and Democracy*, by Joseph A. Schumpeter, pp. 145-155. Copyright 1942, 1947, by Joseph A. Schumpeter. Reprinted by permission of the publisher, Harper & Brothers. Footnotes referring to other chapters have been deleted by the Editor.

1. Every social system is sensitive to revolt and in every social system stirring up revolt is a business that pays in case of success and hence always attracts both brain and brawn. It did in feudal times—very much so. But warrior nobles who revolted against their superiors attacked individual persons or positions. They did not attack the feudal system as such. And feudal society as a whole displayed no tendencies to encourage—intentionally or unintentionally—attacks upon its own social system as a whole.

consist in fighting each other and in forming the spearheads of class interests not their own. Yet they develop group attitudes and group interests sufficiently strong to make large numbers of them behave in the way that is usually associated with the concept of social classes. Again, they cannot be simply defined as the sum total of all the people who have had a higher education; that would obliterate the most important features of the type. Yet anyone who had—and, save exceptional cases, nobody who had not—is a potential intellectual; and the fact that their minds are all similarly furnished facilitates understanding between them and constitutes a bond. Nor would it serve our purpose to make the concept coextensive with the membership of the liberal professions; physicians or lawyers for instance are not intellectuals in the relevant sense unless they talk or write about subjects outside of their professional competence which no doubt they often do—particularly the lawyers. Yet there is a close connection between the intellectuals and the professions. For *some* professions—especially if we count in journalism—actually do belong almost wholly to the domain of the intellectual type; the members of *all* professions have the opportunity of becoming intellectuals; and many intellectuals take to some profession for a living. Finally, a definition by means of the contrast to manual labor would be much too wide.[2] Yet the Duke of Wellington's "scribbling set" seems to be too narrow.[3] So is the meaning of *hommes de lettres*.

But we might do worse than take our lead from the Iron Duke. Intellectuals are in fact people who wield the power of the spoken and the written word, and one of the touches that distinguish them from other people who do the same is the absence of direct responsibility for practical affairs. This touch in general accounts for another—the absence of that first-hand knowledge of them which only actual experience can give. The critical attitude, arising no less from the intellectual's situation as an onlooker—in most cases also as an outsider—than from the fact that his main chance of asserting himself lies in his actual or potential nuisance value, should add a third touch. The profession of the unprofessional? Professional dilettantism? The people who talk about everything because they understand nothing? Bernard Shaw's journalist in *The Doctor's Dilemma?* No, no. I have not said that and I do not mean that. That sort of thing would be still more untrue than it would be offensive. Let us give up trying to define by words and instead define "epideiktically": in the Greek museum we can

---

2. To my sorrow, I have found that the Oxford English Dictionary does not list the meaning I wish to attach to the term. It does give the turn of phrase "a dinner of intellectuals," but in connection with "superior powers of intellect" which points in a very different direction. I have been duly disconcerted, yet have not been able to discover another term that would serve my purpose equally well.

3. The Duke's phrase occurs in *The Croker Papers* (ed. L. J. Jennings, 1884).

see the object, nicely labeled. The sophists, philosophers and rhetors—however strongly they objected to being thrown together, they were all of the same genus—of the fifth and fourth centuries B.C. illustrate ideally what I mean. That practically all of them were teachers does not destroy the value of the illustration.

2. When analyzing the rationalist nature of capitalist civilization (Chapter XI) I pointed out that the development of rational thought of course precedes the rise of the capitalist order by thousands of years; all that capitalism did was to give a new impulse and a particular bend to the process. Similarly—leaving aside the Graeco-Roman world—we find intellectuals in thoroughly pre-capitalist conditions, for instance in the Kingdom of the Franks and in the countries into which it dissolved. But they were few in number; they were clergymen, mostly monks; and their written performance was accessible to only an infinitesimal part of the population. No doubt strong individuals were occasionally able to develop unorthodox views and even to convey them to popular audiences. This however in general implied antagonizing a very strictly organized environment—from which at the same time it was difficult to get away—and risking the lot of the heretic. Even so it was hardly possible without the support or connivance of some great lord or chieftain, as the tactics of missionaries suffice to show. On the whole, therefore, intellectuals were well in hand, and kicking over the traces was no joke, even in times of exceptional disorganization and license, such as during the Black Death (in and after 1348).

But if the monastery gave birth to the intellectual of the medieval world, it was capitalism that let him loose and presented him with the printing press. The slow evolution of the lay intellectual was merely an aspect of this process; the coincidence of the emergence of humanism with the emergence of capitalism is very striking. The humanists were primarily philologists but —excellently illustrating a point made above—they quickly expanded into the fields of manners, politics, religion and philosophy. This was not alone due to the contents of the classic works which they interpreted along with their grammar—from the criticism of a text to the criticism of a society, the way is shorter than it seems. Nevertheless, the typical intellectual did not relish the idea of the stake which still awaited the heretic. As a rule, honors and comfort suited him a great deal better. And these were after all to be had only from princes, temporal or spiritual, though the humanists were the first intellectuals to have a public in the modern sense. The critical attitude grew stronger every day. But *social* criticism—beyond what was implied in certain attacks on the Catholic Church and in particular its head—did not flourish under such conditions.

Honors and emoluments can however be had in more than one way. Flattery and subservience are often less remunerative than are their opposites.

This discovery was not made by the Aretino[4] but no mortal ever surpassed him in exploiting it. Charles V was a devoted husband but, during his campaigns which kept him from home for many months at a time, he lived the life of a gentleman of his time and class. Very well, the public—and what particularly mattered to Charles, his empress—need never know, provided arguments of the right kind and weight were duly handed to the great critic of politics and morals. Charles paid up. But the point is that this was not simple blackmail which in general benefits one party only and inflicts uncompensated loss on the other. Charles knew why he paid though doubtless it would have been possible to secure silence by cheaper if more drastic methods. He did not display resentment. On the contrary he even went out of his way to honor the man. Obviously he wanted more than silence and, as a matter of fact, he received full value for his gifts.

3. In a sense, therefore, the Aretino's pen was indeed stronger than the sword. But, perhaps through ignorance, I do not know of comparable instances of that type for the next hundred and fifty years,[5] during which intellectuals do not seem to have played any great role outside and independently of the established professions, mainly the law and the church. Now this setback roughly coincides with the setback in capitalist evolution which in most countries of continental Europe occurred in that troubled period. And the subsequent recovery of capitalist enterprise was similarly shared by the intellectuals. The cheaper book, the cheap newspaper or pamphlet, together with the widening of the public that was in part their product but partly an independent phenomenon due to the access of wealth and weight which came to the industrial bourgeoisie and to the incident increase in the political importance of an anonymous public opinion—all these boons, as well as increasing freedom from restraint, are by-products of the capitalist engine.

In the first three-quarters of the eighteenth century the individual patron was slow to lose the paramount importance in the intellectual's career that he had held at the beginning. But in the peak successes at least, we clearly discern the growing importance of the new element—the support of the collective patron, the bourgeois public. In this as in every other respect, Voltaire affords an invaluable instance. His very superficiality that made it possible for him to cover everything from religion to Newtonian optics, allied to indomitable vitality and an insatiable curiosity, a perfect absence of inhibitions, an unerring instinct for and a wholesale acceptance of the humors of his time, enabled that uncritical critic and mediocre poet and historian to fascinate—and to sell. He also speculated, cheated, accepted gifts and ap-

---

4. Pietro Aretino, 1492-1556.

5. In England, however, the scope and importance of pamphleteering increased greatly in the seventeenth century.

pointments, but there was always the independence founded on the solid base of his success with the public. Rousseau's case and type, though entirely different, would be still more instructive to discuss.

In the last decades of the eighteenth century a striking episode displayed the nature of the power of a free-lance intellectual who has nothing to work with but the socio-psychological mechanism called Public Opinion. This happened in England, the country that was then farthest advanced on the road of capitalist evolution. John Wilkes' attacks on the political system of England, it is true, were launched under uniquely favorable circumstances; moreover, it cannot be said that he actually upset the Earl of Bute's government which never had any chance and was bound to fall for a dozen other reasons; but Wilkes' *North Briton* was nevertheless the last straw that broke . . . Lord Bute's political back. No. 45 of the *North Briton* was the first discharge in a campaign that secured the abolition of general warrants and made a great stride toward the freedom of the press and of elections. This does not amount to making history or to creating the conditions for a change in social institutions, but it does amount to playing, say, the role of a midwife's assistant.[6] The inability of Wilkes' enemies to thwart him is the most significant fact about it all. They evidently had all the power of organized government at their command. Yet something drove them back.

In France, the years preceding the revolution and the revolution itself brought the rabble-raising tabloid (Marat, Desmoulins), which however did not, like ours, completely jettison style and grammar. But we must hurry on. The Terror and, more systematically, the First Empire put an end to this. Then followed a period, interrupted by the rule of the *roi bourgeois,* of more or less resolute repression that lasted until the Second Empire felt compelled to loosen the reins—about the middle sixties. In central and southern Europe this period also lasted about as long, and in England analogous conditions prevailed from the beginning of the revolutionary wars to Canning's accession to power.

4. How impossible it is to stem the tide within the framework of capitalist society is shown by the failure of the attempts—some of them prolonged and determined—made during that period by practically all European gov-

---

6. I do not fear that any historian of politics will find that I have exaggerated the importance of Wilkes' success. But I do fear objection to my calling him a free lance and to the implication that he owed everything to the collective, and nothing to any individual patron. In his beginnings he was no doubt encouraged by a *coterie.* On examination it will however be conceded, I think, that this was not of decisive importance and that all the support and all the money and honors he got afterwards were but a consequence of and tribute to previous success and to a position independently acquired with the public.

ernments to bring the intellectuals to heel. Their histories were nothing but so many different versions of Wilkes' exploits. In capitalist society—or in a society that contains a capitalist element of decisive importance—any attack on the intellectuals must run up against the private fortresses of bourgeois business which, or some of which, will shelter the quarry. Moreover such an attack must proceed according to bourgeois principles of legislative and administrative practice which no doubt may be stretched and bent but will checkmate prosecution beyond a certain point. Lawless violence the bourgeois stratum may accept or even applaud when thoroughly roused or frightened, but only temporarily. In a purely bourgeois regime like that of Louis Philippe, troops may fire on strikers, but the police cannot round up intellectuals or must release them forthwith; otherwise the bourgeois stratum, however strongly disapproving some of their doings, will rally behind them because the freedom it disapproves cannot be crushed without also crushing the freedom it approves.

Observe that I am not crediting the bourgeoisie with an unrealistic dose of generosity or idealism. Nor am I unduly stressing what people think and feel and want—on the importance of which I almost, though not quite, agree with Marx. In defending the intellectuals as a group—not of course every individual—the bourgeoisie defends itself and its scheme of life. Only a government of non-bourgeois nature and non-bourgeois creed—under modern circumstances only a socialist or fascist one—is strong enough to discipline them. In order to do that it would have to change typically bourgeois institutions and drastically reduce the individual freedom of *all* strata of the nation. And such a government is not likely—it would not even be able—to stop short of private enterprise.

From this follows both the unwillingness and the inability of the capitalist order to control its intellectual sector effectively. The unwillingness in question is unwillingness to use methods consistently that are uncongenial to the mentality shaped by the capitalist process; the inability is the inability to do so within the frame of institutions shaped by the capitalist process and without submitting to non-bourgeois rule. Thus, on the one hand, freedom of public discussion involving freedom to nibble at the foundations of capitalist society is inevitable in the long run. On the other hand, the intellectual group cannot help nibbling, because it lives on criticism and its whole position depends on criticism that stings; and criticism of persons and of current events will, in a situation in which nothing is sacrosanct, fatally issue in criticism of classes and institutions.

5. A few strokes will complete the modern picture. There are the increasing means. There is the increase in the standard of life and in the leisure of the masses that changed and is still changing the composition of

the collective patron for the tastes of whom the intellectuals have to provide. There was and is the further cheapening of the book and newspaper and the large-scale newspaper concern.[7] There is now the radio. And there was and is the tendency toward complete removal of restraints, steadily breaking down those short-run attempts at resistance by which bourgeois society proves itself so incompetent and occasionally so childish a disciplinarian.

There is, however, another factor. One of the most important features of the later stages of capitalist civilization is the vigorous expansion of the educational apparatus and particularly of the facilities for higher education. This development was and is no less inevitable than the development of the largest-scale industrial unit,[8] but, unlike the latter, it has been and is being

---

7. The emergence and the career up to date of the large-scale newspaper concern illustrate two points which I am anxious to stress: the manifold aspects, relations and effects of *every* concrete element of the social pattern that preclude simple and one-way propositions, and the importance of distinguishing short-run and long-run phenomena for which different, sometimes opposite, propositions hold true. The *large*-scale newspaper concern is in most cases simply a capitalist business enterprise. This does not *imply* that it espouses capitalist or any other class interests. It *may* do so, but only from one or more of the following motives, the limited importance of which is obvious: because it is subsidized by a capitalist group for the very purpose of advocating its interests or views—the larger the concern and its sales, the less important this element; because it intends to sell to a public of bourgeois tastes—this, very important until about 1914, now increasingly cuts the other way; because advertisers prefer to use a congenial medium—but mostly they take a very businesslike view of the matter; because the owners insist on a certain course irrespective of their interest in sales—to a certain extent, they do and especially did, but experience teaches that they do not hold out if the conflict with their pecuniary interest in sales is too severe. In other words, the large-scale newspaper concern is a most powerful tool for raising the position and increasing the influence of the intellectual group, but it is even now not completely in its control. It means employment and a wider public, but it also means "strings." These are mainly of importance in the short run; in fighting for greater freedom to do as he pleases, the individual journalist may easily meet defeat. But this short-run aspect—and the group's recollection of past conditions—are what enters the intellectual's mind and what determines the colors of the picture of slavery and martyrdom he draws for the public. In reality, it should be a picture of conquest. Conquest and victory are in this, as in so many other cases, a mosaic composed of defeats.

8. At present this development is viewed by most people from the standpoint of the ideal of making educational facilities of any type available to all who can be induced to use them. This ideal is so strongly held that any doubts about it are almost universally considered to be nothing short of indecent, a situation not improved by the comments, all too often flippant, of dissentients. Actually, we brush here against a set of extremely complex problems of the sociology of education and educational ideals which we cannot attack within the limits of this sketch. This is why I have confined the above paragraph to two incontestable and noncommittal trivialities that are all we want for the purpose in hand. But of course they do not dispose of the larger problems which must be left aside to testify to the incompleteness of my exposition.

fostered by public opinion and public authority so as to go much further than it would have done under its own steam. Whatever we may think of this from other standpoints and whatever the precise causation, there are several consequences that bear upon the size and attitude of the intellectual group.

First, inasmuch as higher education thus increases the supply of services in professional, quasi-professional and in the end all "white-collar" lines beyond the point determined by cost-return considerations, it may create a particularly important case of sectional unemployment.

Second, along with or in place of such unemployment, it creates unsatisfactory conditions of employment—employment in substandard work or at wages below those of the better-paid manual workers.

Third, it may create unemployability of a particularly disconcerting type. The man who has gone through a college or university easily becomes psychically unemployable in manual occupations without necessarily acquiring employability in, say, professional work. His failure to do so may be due either to lack of natural ability—perfectly compatible with passing academic tests—or to inadequate teaching; and both cases will, absolutely and relatively, occur more frequently as ever larger numbers are drafted into higher education and as the required amount of teaching increases irrespective of how many teachers and scholars nature chooses to turn out. The results of neglecting this and of acting on the theory that schools, colleges and universities are just a matter of money, are too obvious to insist upon. Cases in which among a dozen applicants for a job, all formally qualified, there is not one who can fill it satisfactorily, are known to everyone who has anything to do with appointments—to everyone, that is, who is himself qualified to judge.

All those who are unemployed or unsatisfactorily employed or unemployable drift into the vocations in which standards are least definite or in which aptitudes and acquirements of a different order count. They swell the host of intellectuals in the strict sense of the term whose numbers hence increase disproportionately. They enter it in a thoroughly discontented frame of mind. Discontent breeds resentment. And it often rationalizes itself into that social criticism which as we have seen before is in any case the intellectual spectator's typical attitude toward men, classes and institutions especially in a rationalist and utilitarian civilization. Well, here we have numbers; a well-defined group situation of proletarian hue; and a group interest shaping a group attitude that will much more realistically account for hostility to the capitalist order than could the theory—itself a rationalization in the psychological sense—according to which the intellectual's righteous indignation about the wrongs of capitalism simply represents the logical inference from outrageous facts and which is no better than the theory of lovers that their feelings represent nothing but the logical inference from the virtues of the beloved.[9] Moreover our theory also accounts for the fact that this hostility increases, instead of diminishing, with every achievement of capitalist evolution.

Of course, the hostility of the intellectual group—amounting to moral disapproval of the capitalist order—is one thing, and the general hostile atmosphere which surrounds the capitalist engine is another thing. The latter is the really significant phenomenon; and it is not simply the product of the former but flows partly from independent sources, some of which have been mentioned before; so far as it does, it is raw material for the intellectual group to work on. There are give-and-take relations between the two which it would require more space to unravel than I can spare. The general contours of such an analysis are however sufficiently obvious and I think it safe to repeat that the role of the intellectual group consists primarily in stimulating, energizing, verbalizing and organizing this material and only secondarily in adding to it. Some particular aspects will illustrate the principle.

6. Capitalist evolution produces a labor movement which obviously is not the creation of the intellectual group. But it is not surprising that such an opportunity and the intellectual demiurge should find each other. Labor never craved intellectual leadership but intellectuals invaded labor politics. They had an important contribution to make: they verbalized the movement, supplied theories and slogans for it—class war is an excellent example—made it conscious of itself and in doing so changed its meaning. In solving this task from their own standpoint, they naturally radicalized it, eventually imparting a revolutionary bias to the most bourgeois trade-union practices, a bias most of the non-intellectual leaders at first greatly resented. But there was another reason for this. Listening to the intellectual, the workman is almost invariably conscious of an impassable gulf if not of downright distrust. In order to get hold of him and to compete with non-intellectual leaders, the intellectual is driven to courses entirely unnecessary for the latter who can afford to frown. Having no genuine authority and feeling always in danger of being unceremoniously told to mind his own business, he must flatter, promise and incite, nurse left wings and scowling minorities, sponsor doubtful or submarginal cases, appeal to fringe ends, profess himself ready to obey—in short, behave toward the masses as his predecessors behaved first toward their ecclesiastical superiors, later toward princes and

9. The reader will observe that any such theories would be unrealistic even if the facts of capitalism or the virtues of the beloved were actually all that the social critic or the lover believes them to be. It is also important to note that in the overwhelming majority of cases both critics and lovers are obviously sincere; neither psycho-sociological nor psycho-physical mechanisms enter as a rule into the limelight of the Ego, except in the mask of sublimations.

other individual patrons, still later toward the collective master of bourgeois complexion. Thus, though intellectuals have not created the labor movement, they have yet worked it up into something that differs substantially from what it would be without them.

The social atmosphere, for the theory of which we have been gathering stones and mortar, explains why public policy grows more and more hostile to capitalist interests, eventually so much so as to refuse on principle to take account of the requirements of the capitalist engine and to become a serious impediment to its functioning. The intellectual group's activities have however a relation to anti-capitalist policies that is more direct than what is implied in their share in verbalizing them. Intellectuals rarely enter professional politics and still more rarely conquer responsible office. But they staff political bureaus, write party pamphlets and speeches, act as secretaries and advisers, make the individual politician's newspaper reputation which, though it is not everything, few men can afford to neglect. In doing these things they to some extent impress their mentality on almost everything that is being done.

The actual influence exerted varies greatly with the state of the political game from mere formulation to making a measure politically possible or impossible. But there is always plenty of scope for it. When we say that individual politicians and parties are exponents of class interests we are at best emphasizing one-half of the truth. The other half, just as important if not more so, comes into view when we consider that politics is a profession which evolves interests of its own—interests that may clash with as well as conform to the interests of the groups that a man or party "represents."[10] Individual and party opinion is, more than anything else, sensitive to those factors in the political situation that directly affect the career or the standing of the individual or party. Some of these are controlled by the intellectual group in much the same sense as is the moral code of an epoch that exalts the cause of some interests and puts the cause of others tacitly out of court.

Finally, that social atmosphere or code of values affects not only policies —the spirit of legislation—but also administrative practice. But again there is also a more direct relation between the intellectual group and bureaucracy. The bureaucracies of Europe are of pre- and extra-capitalist origin. However much they may have changed in composition as the centuries rolled on, they never identified themselves wholly with the bourgeoisie, its interests or its scheme of values, and never saw much more in it than an asset to be managed in the interest of the monarch or of the nation. Except for inhibitions due to professional training and experience, they are therefore open to

---

10. This of course is just as true of the intellectuals themselves with respect to the class from which they come or to which, economically and culturally, they belong.

conversion by the modern intellectual with whom, through a similar education, they have much in common, while the tinge of gentility that in many cases used to raise a barrier has been fading away from the modern civil servant during the last decades. Moreover, in times of rapid expansion of the sphere of public administration, much of the additional personnel required has to be taken directly from the intellectual group—witness this country.

INTELLECTUALS AND MEN OF POWER— TWO CASE HISTORIES

Lewis A. Coser

I. NAPOLEON AND THE IDÉOLOGUES

"It is to ideology", barked Napoleon in 1812, "this gloomy metaphysics which subtly looks for first causes upon which to base the legislation of people—that all the misfortune of our beautiful France must be attributed."[1] It was not the first time that he had vented his spleen on the men whom he called derisorily the "Idéologues." He had earlier spoken of a "dozen or fifteen metaphysicians who ought to be thrown into a pond. They are swarming like vermin around me."[2] He had referred to the Idéologues as "a band of imbeciles who sigh from the bottom of their souls for liberty of the press and of speech, and believe in the omnipotence of public opinion."[3]

But the same men against whom the Emperor spoke with so much venom had been a few years before his close friends and allies, he had sought their company and been honored by their attention.[4] By tracing the sources of this reversal we may throw some light on the more general problem of the relations between intellectuals and men of power.

What was "ideology"? The term had been coined in 1802 by Antoine Destutt de Tracy, the major philosopher of the school, to denote a philosophical discipline that set as its goal to observe and describe the operation of the human mind in the same strictly empirical manner as one describes an object

Printed by permission of the author. The piece is a shortened version of a chapter in a forthcoming book on *The Sociology of Intellectuals,* soon to be published by The Free Press of Glencoe, Illinois.

1. Quoted in Hippolyte Taine, *Les Origines de la France contemporaine,* Paris 1898, II, 219/20.

2. Quoted in Charles Hunter van Dunzer, *Contribution of the Idéologues to French Revolutionary Thought,* The Johns Hopkins Press, Baltimore 1935, p. 151.

3. Quoted in *Cambridge Modern History,* vol. 9, Cambridge 1906, p. 132.

4. I am heavily indebted for the account that follows to Dr. van Dunzer's seminal work. Hans Barth, *Wahrheit and Ideologie,* Zurich 1945, was also most helpful. Other important works for the understanding of the thought of the idéologues and for the milieu in which they functioned are: Francois Picavet, *Les Ideologues,* Paris 1891, and Antoine Guillois, *Le Salon de Madame Helvétius,* Paris 1894. For a full bibliography see van Dunzer's work.

of nature, a mineral or a plant. Continuing the tradition of Condillac, Destutt and his co-thinkers insisted that ideas must always be traced back to sensations. Analysis of the processes of the human mind in the formation of ideas would lead to a scientific discipline which would allow recognition of truth and detection of error in the world of ideas with as much accuracy as the physical sciences had attained in the study of natural phenomena.

But ideological doctrine was not limited to purely theoretical considerations. The Idéologues, true to the 18th century tradition of the enlightenment, taught that the systematic reduction of all ideas to their constituent sensations had immense practical importance for the reconstruction of political and social life. Only if the lawgiver is armed with a system which furnishes him with undubitable knowledge about men and ideas can he erect a just and reasonable social order. But there can be no reasonable legislation without enlightened citizens. The education of the citizen must be a matter of central concern. Hence ideology became a philosophical discipline and a pedagogical one as well. It can serve its purpose only if the whole educational system, until now dominated by religious training and instruction in the classics, is reconstituted according to rational and scientific principles.

Education, however, was so intimately connected with politics that the ideologists were inevitably drawn into the political battle. Since man can fully develop his faculties only in freedom, pedagogical freedom is deeply tied to freedom in the political and economic sphere.

Given these premises it is not surprising to find the ideologists from the onset of the Revolution playing a prominent role in the various legislative committees—especially in those devoted to educational and constitutional affairs. Many of them were members of the Constituent and later of the Legislative Assembly, many of them sat in the Convention. Moderate liberal bourgeois, deeply devoted to the rational ideals of the enlightenment, they were sympathetic first to Mirabeau and later the Girondins. Hence most of them incurred during the Terror the wrath of the Mountain. Not until Thermidor did the Idéologues again come into their own.

The Idéologues, it stands to reason, differed from each other in numerous detail, yet what strikes the observer is a remarkable cohesion among at least the central figures of the group. Such cohesion must be traced to three factors: a common tradition, an occasion for close and intimate contact with each other, and the availability of a magazine which could express the central lines of the doctrine and adapt it to the shifting events on the political scene.

It is important to note that these heirs of the eighteenth-century enlightenment developed their peculiar doctrine while still in intimate contact with some of the major figures of the older generation. The famous salon of Madame Helvétius where the ideological movement was born is of special importance in this respect. In 1772, after the death of her husband, the great sensationalist philosopher, Madame Helvétius moved from Paris to the suburb of Auteuil there to reopen the salon which during the lifetime of her husband had been a major nursery for the ideas of the encyclopedists and where Condillac, Diderot and d'Alembert had often gathered to discuss with passion the ideas which informed the philosophy of the enlightenment. Now old friends among the survivors again gathered at Auteuil, but a new group of younger intellectuals began to make their appearance. Morellet, Volney, Turgot, Condorcet, the elderly Benjamin Franklin, mixed with Pierre Cabanis, the young physiologist and moral philosopher, Destutt de Tracy, the former cavalry officer turned philosopher, and a whole group of young men in the process of developing that particular philosophical doctrine which in later years was to be named the ideological movement. This direct and immediate contact with their elders insured that the younger Idéologues remained strongly imbued with a consciousness of the continuity of the enlightenment tradition, even when they were intent on giving new twists to traditional assumptions. They did not see themselves as radical innovators but as inheritors of a tradition to be put to their own use.

Auteuil allowed the young intellectuals to form close and enduring contacts with each other and at the same time they remained conscious of the preeminence of their elders. This drawing together in Madame Helvétius' salon counterbalanced the dispersive tendencies of Parisian intellectual life and helped to give the doctrine the character of a collective enterprise. For many of the ideologists Auteuil became more than a salon to which one repaired from time to time. Cabanis lived there for many years, so did de Tracy. Condorcet stayed here before he was forced to go into hiding.

The considerable degree of cohesion derived from the Auteuil setting was further increased after the fall of the Jacobins. The ideologists now again reenacted common public roles. The constitution of the year III was written by the ideologist Daunou and was conceived as a kind of charter of the ideas of the ideologists. The transformation of the school system of France which the Convention undertook after Thermidor was to a very large extent the work of the ideologists. The *École Normale,* the *École Centrale,* the *École Polytechnique* were founded by men deeply imbued with ideologist doctrine. Under Lakanal's leadership the Convention left as its academic testament a complete system of public instruction based on the blueprints of the Idéologues.

The founding of a new learned society, the famous *Institut National* was likewise the achievement of the ideologists. The *Institut* was divided into three classes: physical and mathematical science, moral and political science, literature and the fine arts. The Second Class, to which most of the ideologists belonged soon became the forum where the important works of the school were debated, and its *Mémoires* published the more important contributions.

In the *École Normale* Cabanis taught hygiene, Volney history, Garat philosophy, Lagrange and Laplace mathematics. At the *Council for Public Instruction* the key position was occupied by another ideologist, Ginguené. The Idéologues seemed to be triumphant. They had a considerable voice in the place of power, they lived under a constitution written by one of them, they dominated legislative committees, the new school system was under their influence, the new learned society was to a large extent dominated by them.

In addition to Auteuil and the *Institut* the ideologists still had another meeting ground; the offices of the *Décade philosophique, litteraire et politique,* chief literary organ of the Idéologues. The magazine, published from 1794 to 1807, served the development and refinement of ideological thought and became the tribune from where they could make their critical comments on the political and intellectual scene.

Since Idéologues were the leaders of the intellectual and political life of the France of the Directory, it is hardly surprising that the young Bonaparte courted them assiduously. When he became commander of the Armies of Italy he stepped up his courtship. In turn the Idéologues joined in the widespread enthusiasm for the young general when he returned to Paris from his victorious campaign. Napoleon now frequented the ideologist circles and courted the intellectuals who determined public opinion. To be elected to the *Institut* seemed to him a most desirable goal. Such was the atmosphere of the time that successful generals needed the legitimation of the intellectual community. Napoleon's election campaign proved as successful as his recent Italian campaign: he was elected a member of the *Institut's* section on mechanics in December 1797. Bonaparte was exceedingly proud of his membership and attended the meetings of the *Institut* up to the time he left for his Egyptian campaign. During this campaign Napoleon behaved like an Idéologue on horseback. It is hardly surprising that he appeared to the intellectuals as an incarnation of all the virtues they attributed to the enlightened man of power. Napoleon was wont to sign his proclamations to the army in the name of "Bonaparte, *général en chef, membre de l'institut*" thus symbolizing, or so his Idéologue admirers believed, the union of power and intellect of which they had dreamed. And the Egyptian expedition far transcended the purely military sphere. Napoleon attempted to create in Egypt institutions which the Idéologues had been instrumental in creating in France. Scientists and other intellectuals were his companions and camp followers. He created an *École Centrale* in Malta, primary schools in Malta and Gozo, he organized an *Institut du Caire* patterned on the French model and designed to bring progress and enlightenment to Egypt. Finally Napoleon created a literary and philosophical journal *Décade Egyptienne,* a replica in title and general orientation of the ideologists' Parisian magazine. The ideologists saw in him their future philosopher-king.

When Napoleon returned to Paris he had conquered the major figures in the world of letters. It is hardly surprising that the Idéologues, moderate middle-class republicans for the most part, acclaimed the 18th Brumaire with enthusiasm. After Napoleon's coup even more than after the fall of the Jacobins, they believed that their hour had finally come. The aristocracy of learning and intellect was now, or so it seemed, to be the governing elite.

The Idéologues had written the liberal yet undemocratic constitution of the year III. They now helped write the illiberal and undemocratic constitution of the year VIII, and they acclaimed it with enthusiasm. The legislature under the new constitution included almost all major members of the ideological school. They were to be found everywhere, in the Senate, in the Council of State, in the Tribunate.

But it soon became apparent that Napoleon, despite his earlier professions of amity, profoundly disliked these "men with a system" who exhibited lack of sufficient flexibility in adapting themselves to the demands of the new regime. He preferred men "concerned with positive and exact facts" to ideological analysts and enlightened dreamers. The whole elaborate system of political bodies set up by the ideologist fathers of the constitution was soon converted into an instrument of dictatorship. Senate, Tribunate and Legislative Body soon played only a passive and ornamental role. Pragmatic power considerations took precedence over ideological preferences. The First Consul soon realized that it would be to his advantage to make his peace with Rome. Religion was a useful buttress of power, critical thought was not. Philosophy could at best be used as a minor *ancilla politicae.*

The Concordat marked Napoleon's final rejection of the dreams of the ideologists. He now turned from the enlightenment using religious sentiment to bolster temporal power. The *Décade* voiced indignant criticism, many Idéologues protested in public or in private, but without avail. The consolidated regime no longer needed the support of liberal intellectuals. When the Senate rejected a few of Napoleon's proposals he purged it of twenty of its more recalcitrant members, among them almost all the leading Idéologues. Those Idéologues or other intellectuals who clung to the anti-clericalism, the liberalism of an earlier day, were now dispersed and divided among themselves, they were no longer an effective force.

In 1797 Napoleon, the conqueror of Italy, had written to the *Institut*: "The only true conquests, the only ones which inspire no regret in me, are the conquests that are made over ignorance." But the honeymoon between the ideologists and the dictator had now come to an end. On January 23,

1803 Napoleon dissolved the second section of the *Institut,* the section devoted to moral and political sciences, to which most of the major ideologists belonged. New sections were given the innocuous tasks of writing a dictionary of the French language and of translating Greek, Latin and oriental authors.

The revolutionary educational system, that masterpiece of ideological long-range planning, was also abolished. Profoundly convinced of the need to impart authoritarian norms to the young so that his order could perpetuate itself, Napoleon abolished the *Écoles Centrales,* those nurseries of doubt, enlightenment and the inquiring and sceptical spirit. His educational reforms between 1802 and 1806 were designed to train imperial subjects, not liberal citizens. The ideologists were beaten on all fronts. It mattered little whether some accommodated themselves or whether others withdrew from the public arena and devoted themselves to private studies, whatever personal course they chose the ideological movement was beaten. The time for the analysis of ideas was gone, they had now to be accepted unanalyzed.

Daunou, the proud republican enemy of Napoleon's imperial ambitions, who had held out more than many others was finally reduced to write: "My intention is to publish nothing which might *displease* the government; I am hence disposed to make any changes that might be required in that respect."

Increasingly restrained by censorship, the *Décade* ceased to appear in 1807. Power had won over intellect.

It would be superficial to attribute the defeat of the Idéologues solely to Napoleon's successful consolidation of his authoritarian regime. The whole climate of ideas was no longer propitious to the Idéologues. The young men who began to flock to the schools were tired of philosophical discussion and ideological contentions. Careers seemed open to talent but a talent willing to engage in technical, military, administrative, or scientific pursuits. Students tended to neglect courses that dealt with cultural themes, but they flocked to the new polytechnical school. "The moral sciences are neglected," writes the *Décade,* "the study of the arts and letters is neglected, only mathematics are studied."[5]

The civic enthusiasm of the revolutionary years had subsided. Vocational goals seemed far more important than general cultivation. When self-advancement absorbed the energies of a young post-revolutionary generation, the receptivity for liberal ideas declined. The enlightened ideology was faced not only by the police measures of the men of power, but by the apathy of a society of self-interested, career-oriented subjects. The youth sought training rather than cultivation, a secure niche in the prevailing order rather than comprehensive ideas. As their audience slowly disappeared, the Idéo-

---

5. Quoted in Guillois, op. cit., p. 206.

logues were unable to resist the demands of the men of power. The alternatives were accommodation or withdrawal from the public scene. The age of ideology was over.

II. GOMULKA AND THE REVISIONISTS[6]

"If a Party member disagrees with Party policy; if he does not submit to the Party majority on questions of principle," barked Wladyslaw Gomulka six months after the October 1956 Polish Revolution, "if his world view prevents him from accepting the Party's ideological principle, either he leaves the ranks, gives up his Party card, or the Party must expel him." He then went on to attack "revisionism" which "crippled Marxist principles by introducing false theses that do not reflect social reality in Marxist teaching . . . Revisionism represents the ideology of capitulation because of the difficulties of building socialism." The main ideological spokesman of the Polish Communist Party, Adam Schaff followed Gomulka in the same style. The Party, he said, could not allow "a camouflaged struggle against the policy of socialism to be carried on under the cloak of an alleged struggle for the freedom of spiritual creativity . . . True freedom for science depends on a clear and effective cultural policy of the Party . . . The absence of such a policy is not democracy and only leads to anarchy."

The men against whom Gomulka spoke with such venom had been his close friends and allies a few months earlier. He had sought their support and had been strengthened by their adhesion to his cause. The dialectics of the intellectuals' support of and alienation from power which had stretched out over several years in the case of the Idéologues was now com-

---

6. The British journal *Soviet Survey* was especially helpful for documentation on the Polish events since 1955. The American *Problems of Communism* has also carried a number of helpful articles. Interesting documentation can be found in the magazine *East Europe* published in New York.

The following books reproduce translations from the writings of revisionist writers: *The Broken Mirror,* edited by Pawel Mayewski, Random House, New York, 1958 and *Bitter Harvest,* edited by Edmund Stillman, Frederick A. Praeger, New York, 1959. The special edition of *Les Temps Modernes* for February-March 1957 has additional translations into French.

I have relied very heavily on the following: K. A. Jelinski, "Revisionism, Pragmatism, Gomulkaism" in *Problems of Communism,* VII, 3, May-June 1958; L. Labedz, "The Polish Road to Socialism" in *Soviet Survey,* 11, January 1957; Leopold Labedz "Poland: The Evasion of Freedom" in *Dissent,* Spring 1958. The quotations from Polish sources, unless otherwise indicated, are from these three articles.

A number of journalistic accounts of events in Poland have appeared in recent years. The most recent, S. L. Shneiderman, *The Warsaw Heresy,* Horizon Press, New York, 1959 has some helpful information.

pressed into a much shorter span of time in the relations between Gomulka and the revisionists.

What was "revisionism?" The term came to designate the ideas of a wide and often quite heterogenous group of Polish intellectuals within the Communist Party and around its fringes who, in 1955, had begun to waken from their dogmatic slumbers and had become the ideological spokesmen for the October Revolution of 1956. The revisionist current had started as a protest against the Party's strangulation of cultural affairs, the regime of censorship, the enforced orthodoxy of a narrowly interpreted Marxism-Leninism, and generally against the absence of political and intellectual freedom. The first writer to present a revisionist thesis was the well-known sociologist Jozef Chalasinski. Writing in 1955 Chalasinski, who had previously found ways to accommodate himself to the Stalinist regime, advanced the thesis that it is not incumbent upon supporters of historical materialism to accept uncritically every assertion of the founders of Marxism. He denounced the stultifying effect of Marxist orthodoxies in the humanities and the sciences, the impersonal ritualistic style, the enforced unanimity, the absence of any real intellectual achievement in Communist Poland. This first attack gave the signal for similar assaults on the monopoly of the Party in the intellectual and literary field. In the Summer of 1955 appeared the by now famous poem by Adam Wazyk "A Poem for Adults." This poem summed up the disillusion of the postwar decade. "They drink sea water, crying: 'lemonade'! returning home secretly to vomit."

After the Twentieth Congress of the CPSU and the shattering revelations of Khrushchev, attacks against dogmatism swelled. The revisionists now engaged in a general assault against the tyranny of politics over science, art and literature. Leszek Kolakowski, once the most brilliant of the young philosophical defenders of orthodoxy and soon to become the major philosopher of revisionism, wrote in the theoretical journal of the Party in September 1956: "Every petrification of doctrine necessarily leads to its transformation into mythology, surrounded by a ritual cult, turned into an object of devotion, and safeguarded from criticism. In this situation embarrassing platitudes are proclaimed as theoretical achievements."

The main attacks of the revisionists were directed against the ideological distortions of truth involved in the official *Dialectical Materialism* (Diamat), Russian style, but given the intellectual climate the revisionist attack could not remain limited to purely theoretical concerns. The revisionist movement could no longer be contained within the scope of the official framework; it led to a general assault on orthodoxy in the sphere of political practice. The revisionists had been reared in an intellectual tradition in which the unity of theory and practice was considered axiomatic. The make-believe of the economic plans, the miserable conditions of the workers, the absence of any democracy, all were now attacked.

In March 1956, the Nineteenth Cultural Session of Polish Writers and Artists opened with a violent attack by the leading critic Jan Kott on party line socialist realism, entitled "Mythology and Truth." The debates which followed showed that the bulk of Polish writers had joined the revisionist camp, that it was no longer possible to contain criticism to the comparatively safe channels of purely theoretical debate.

Had the revisionists been isolated critics, their impact would have been less shattering. But soon all the leading cultural periodicals became strongholds of the heresy. The young heretics had at their disposal several magazines which could express the central lines of revisionist doctrine and where revisionism could be adopted to the shifting events of the day. And the writers' clubs and Warsaw cafes came to fulfill the same functions for revisionist intellectuals that the Parisian salons had performed for the men of letters of the enlightenment and "idéologie."

Had revisionism been limited in its impact to older intellectuals in or around the Party, it probably would not have had the effectiveness which it soon proved to have. But it became clear that the bulk of the students, especially at Warsaw University, stood behind the revisionists. This is why the student paper *Pro Postu* quickly became the main revisionist organ, reaching the unprecedented circulation of 150,000 copies.

In June 1956 riots broke out in one of the main factories of Poznan. This outbreak revealed that the workers were as discontented with the regime as were the intellectuals. When the defense of the accused rioters called upon one of the fathers of revisionism, Professor Chalasinski, to be a witness for the defense, this symbolized the emerging alliance between the discontented workers and the aroused intellectuals. The link was finally fully forged in the days of October 1956 that brought Gomulka to power. In these October days the elite of Warsaw students and Warsaw factory workers lined up behind Gomulka in his struggle against the Stalinist remnants of the Central Committee and against the Russians, headed by Khrushchev.

Gomulka had been in disgrace and in prison since 1948. His "national communist deviation," which on the face of it anticipated revisionism, earned him the hatred of the Stalinist diehards who ruled Poland until October. Now the scorned prophet of a special Polish road to socialism was called into power at a moment of supreme crisis. The writers and scientists, the students as well as the workers who had chafed under the Stalinist regime saw in Gomulka the man who would return Poland to the path of a more humane socialism, a more democratic regime.

For the bulk of the Polish population, Gomulka represented resistance to Russian demands and the end of the hated regime of thought control, secret police, censorship, and ideological conformism. When Gomulka, soon upon taking office, declared that "the only unalterable principle of socialism is the end of the exploitation of man by man," when he proceeded to engage in an unmerciful exposé of the errors as well as the crimes of the last ten years of the regime's history, when he seemed to move toward a wide democratization of political institutions and the extension of workers' control over industrial life, he became the hero of the intellectuals. Now at last the union of theory and practice, of power and intellect of which the founders of Marxism had dreamed could finally be enacted. The reign of terror of the bureaucratic pseudo-jacobins had come, as it seemed, to an end, the time for a humane socialist reconstruction under revisionist aegis seemed to have arrived.

Until the elections of January 1957, the revisionist intellectuals were the surest allies of Gomulka. He called many of them into the councils of government, he relied on them to uncover the crimes and errors of the past. They served as his mouthpieces. Their passionate appeals contributed a great deal to making the elections into a plebiscite for Gomulka. But soon after the elections, Gomulka, his power having been consolidated and the diehard Stalinists eliminated, began to turn against the revisionist intellectuals. He apparently thought that if he were to maintain the party apparatus at all, he had to appease the old party functionaries, the *apparatchiki*. The revisionists with their principled attack against the whole *apparat* became an obstacle. Furthermore, Moscow, sensing danger of contagion, launched a violent campaign against the revisionists, and Gomulka apparently felt that if gestures of appeasement toward Moscow were inevitable then attacks against the intellectuals would be the least costly. Though Gomulka was feeling his way toward a somewhat more liberal communist position, he was by no means prepared to condone the younger revisionists who were by now engaged in a generalized onslaught against any kind of dogmatism be it of the Stalinist or any other variety.

In the days of October, when the whole regime threatened to crumble, the ideological support for reform which the revisionists had voiced so passionately, had been invaluable to Gomulka. By attacking the past and reviving hopes in a fundamental revision of the regime's policies the young intellectuals had effectively labored for the legitimation of the regime. But a consolidated regime was no longer in need of the kind of legitimation which critical intellectuals were able to supply; continued support from the Church was of considerably greater importance in this respect.

The consolidated regime needed to appeal to a continuity of, rather than a break with, Party tradition. Thus the functionaries who had been serving their Stalinist masters and who had been frightened by the October events could be made to serve the new masters with devotion. This is why the official *Trybuna Luda* now attacked the revisionist *Pro Postu* writings as "a complete negation of the thirteen year achievements of the Polish Peoples Republic and an apologia for the capitalist West."

Not quite a year after October, *Pro Postu* was closed down and a number of members of its editorial board were expelled from the Party. Warsaw students rioted in street demonstrations, but to no avail. The workers were by now apathetic. Censorship again became rigorous. B. Werblan, a key Party official, announced that "in the future, neither time nor money would be wasted on the publication of demoralizing works which do not contribute to the socialist reconstruction of the state." In protest against these measures some of the most famous among Polish writers, Adam Wazyk and Jan Kott among them, resigned from the Party.

A number of revisionist intellectuals still maintained positions of influence within the Party and the governmental machine between 1957 and 1959, hoping against hope to influence it in a more liberal direction. But by 1959 a new tightening of Gomulka's grip resulted in the ouster of the last major revisionists.[7]

Gomulka had successfully consolidated his authoritarian regime. The revisionists were beaten on all fronts. It mattered little whether some accommodated themselves to the regime, serving it in various technical capacities, or whether others withdrew from the public arena and devoted themselves to university teaching and private studies. Whatever personal course they chose, the revisionist movement was beaten. The time for a critical evaluation of Marxist ideology and communist practice was gone. The free play of ideas which the revisionists demanded would undermine the pragmatist course of accommodation to the powerful Eastern neighbor which seemed to Gomulka the only possible course.

The political enthusiasm of the students and the younger intelligentsia has subsided, political apathy has taken its place. Those who had been enthused about Gomulka's emphasis on socialism as the end of the exploitation of man by man now told the bitter joke about the Party instructor who when asked to define capitalism replies "correctly" that capitalism means the exploitation of man by man and who then, when asked to define socialism, simply answers with "the other way around."

The students now are intent on vocational training rather than ideological discussion. Careers are open for technical training and administrative talent, and as self-advancement absorbs the energies of the younger generation, receptivity to revisionist ideas has declined. In May 1958 the Department of Sociology at the University of Warsaw made a survey of the political

---

7. *New York Times*, October 30, 1959.

and social attitudes of students. When asked about their activities in the October days, 45.5 per cent indicated that they had been "very active" or "rather active" participants. But when asked whether they now considered themselves Marxists, only 1.8 per cent answered "decidedly yes" and another 11.4 per cent answered "rather yes." Sixty-eight per cent of the student sample declared themselves "rather not" or "definitely not" Marxist. While a vast majority of students stated that they believed it very important to abolish the exploitation of some men by others, a majority also felt that wide ranges of salaries and wages did not constitute an indirect form of exploitation. Eighty per cent of the students in the sample considered that professions and jobs requiring a higher education ought to be paid much more than jobs not requiring a higher education . . .[8] The students in shedding whatever Marxist ideology they once had, now adapt to the realities of bureaucratic society and prepare themselves for privileged status. In today's Poland the bulk of the youth seeks training rather than cultivation, a secure niche in the prevailing order, rather than comprehensive ideas.

As their audience slowly disappeared, the revisionists were unable to resist the demands of the men of power. The alternatives were accommodation or withdrawal from the public scene. The age of revisionism was over.

*   *   *   *   *

Historical events never come to a stop. The seeds which grew under the snow of the age of Napoleon and the Restoration sprouted in 1830 and 1848. Only fools can believe that Gomulka can permanently extinguish that vital critical impulse which is the birthright of intellectuals, and which in his reign went under the name of revisionism.

---

8. Excerpts from the study of Warsaw students by Stefan Nowak and Anna Pawelczynska were printed in *Esprit* (Paris), XXVI, 11 (November 1958). More detailed data are found in Stefan Nowak "Factors determining egalitarian attitudes of Warsaw students" (mimeoed) in the possession of this writer. Other parts of the survey are translated into English in the monthly *Polish Perspectives* 3-4 and 7-8, Warsaw 1958.

THE MAN OF REFLECTION
vs. THE MAN OF ACTION

Feodor Dostoevsky

. . . I SWEAR, gentlemen, that to be too conscious is an illness —a real thoroughgoing illness. For man's everyday needs, it would have been quite enough to have the ordinary human consciousness, that is, half or a quarter of the amount which falls to the lot of a cultivated man of our unhappy nineteenth century, especially one who has the fatal ill-luck to inhabit Petersburg, the most theoretical and intentional town on the whole terrestrial globe. (There are intentional and unintentional towns.) It would have been quite enough, for instance, to have the consciousness by which all so-called direct persons and men of action live. I bet you think I am writing all this from affectation, to be witty at the expense of men of action; and what is more, that from ill-bred affectation, I am clanking a sword like my officer. But, gentlemen, whoever can pride himself on his diseases and even swagger over them? . . .

With people who know how to revenge themselves and to stand up for themselves in general, how is it done? Why, when they are possessed, let us suppose, by the feeling of revenge, then for the time there is nothing else but that feeling left in their whole being. Such a gentleman simply dashes straight for his object like an infuriated bull with its horns down, and nothing but a wall will stop him. (By the way: facing the wall, such gentlemen—that is, the "direct" persons and men of action—are genuinely nonplussed. For them a wall is not an evasion, as for us people who think and consequently do nothing; it is not an excuse for turning aside, an excuse for which we are always very glad, though we scarcely believe in it ourselves, as a rule. No, they are nonplussed in all sincerity. The wall has for them something tranquillizing, morally soothing, final—maybe even something mysterious . . . but of the wall later.)

Well, such a direct person I regard as the real normal man, as his tender mother Nature wished to see him when she graciously brought him into being on the earth. I envy such a man till I am green in the face. He is

Reprinted from *Notes from Underground,* selections from Part I, sections i, ii, and v, by permission of the publisher, The Macmillan Company. Translated by Constance Garnett. Title supplied by the Editor.

(92)

stupid. I am not disputing that, but perhaps the normal man should be stupid, how do you know? Perhaps it is very beautiful, in fact. And I am the more persuaded of that suspicion, if one can call it so, by the fact that if you take, for instance, the antithesis of the normal man, that is, the man of acute consciousness, who has come, of course, not out of the lap of Nature but out of a retort (this is almost mysticism, gentlemen, but I suspect this, too), this retort-made man is sometimes so nonplussed in the presence of his antithesis that with all his exaggerated consciousness he genuinely thinks of himself as a mouse and not a man. It may be an acutely conscious mouse, yet it is a mouse, while the other is a man, and therefore, et caetera, et caetera. And the worst of it is, he himself, his very own self, looks on himself as a mouse; no one asks him to do so; and that is an important point. Now let us look at this mouse in action. Let us suppose, for instance, that it feels insulted, too (and it almost always does feel insulted), and wants to revenge itself, too. There may even be a greater accumulation of spite in it than in *l'homme de la nature et de la vérité*. The base and nasty desire to vent that spite on its assailant rankles perhaps even more nastily in it than in *l'homme de la nature et de la vérité*. For through his innate stupidity the latter looks upon his revenge as justice pure and simple; while in consequence of his acute consciousness the mouse does not believe in the justice of it. To come at last to the deed itself, to the very act of revenge. Apart from the one fundamental nastiness the luckless mouse succeeds in creating around it so many other nastinesses in the form of doubts and questions, adds to the one question so many unsettled questions, that there inevitably works up around it a sort of fatal brew, a stinking mess, made up of its doubts, emotions, and of the contempt spat upon it by the direct men of action who stand solemnly about it as judges and arbitrators, laughing at it till their healthy sides ache. Of course the only thing left for it is to dismiss all that with a wave of its paw, and, with a smile of assumed contempt in which it does not even itself believe, creep ignominiously into its mouse-hole. There in its nasty, stinking, underground home our insulted, crushed and ridiculed mouse promtly becomes absorbed in cold, malignant and, above all, everlasting spite. . . .

You know the direct, legitimate fruit of consciousness is inertia, that is, conscious sitting-with-the-hands-folded. I have referred to this already. I repeat, I repeat with emphasis: all "direct" persons and men of action are active just because they are stupid and limited. How explain that? I will tell you: in consequence of their limitation they take immediate and secondary causes for primary ones, and in that way persuade themselves more quickly and easily than other people do that they have found an infallible foundation for their activity, and their minds are at ease and you know that is the chief thing. To begin to act, you know, you must first have your mind completely at ease and no trace of doubt left in it. Why, how am I, for example, to set my mind at rest? Where are the primary causes on which I am to build? Where are my foundations? Where am I to get them from? I exercise myself in reflection, and consequently with me every primary cause at once draws after itself another still more primary, and so on to infinity. That is just the essence of every sort of consciousness and reflection. It must be a case of the laws of nature again. What is the result of it in the end? Why, just the same. Remember I spoke just now of vengeance. (I am sure you did not take it in.) I said that a man revenges himself because he sees justice in it. Therefore he has found a primary cause, that is, justice. And so he is at rest on all sides, and consequently he carries out his revenge calmly and successfully, being persuaded that he is doing a just and honest thing. But I see no justice in it, I find no sort of virtue in it either, and consequently if I attempt to revenge myself, it is only out of spite. Spite, of course, might overcome everything, all my doubts, and so might serve quite successfully in place of a primary cause, precisely because it is not a cause. But what is to be done if I have not even spite (I began with that just now, you know)? In consequence again of those accursed laws of consciousness, anger in me is subject to chemical disintegration. You look into it, the object flies off into air, your reasons evaporate, the criminal is not to be found, the wrong becomes not a wrong but a phantom, something like the toothache, for which no one is to blame, and consequetnly there is only the same outlet left again—that is, to beat the wall as hard as you can. So you give it up with a wave of the hand because you have not found a fundamental cause. And try letting yourself be carried away by your feelings, blindly, without reflection, without a primary cause, repelling consciousness at least for a time; hate or love, if only not to sit with your hands folded. The day after to-morrow, at the latest, you will begin despising yourself for having knowingly deceived yourself. Result: a soap-bubble and inertia. Oh, gentlemen, do you know, perhaps I consider myself an intelligent man only because all my life I have been able neither to begin nor to finish anything. Granted I am a babbler, a harmless vexatious babbler, like all of us. But what is to be done if the direct and sole vocation of every intelligent man is babble, that is, the intentional pouring of water through a sieve?

SOME AMBITIOUS YOUNG INTELLECTUALS

Henry de Montherlant

D EAR MASTER:

You certainly must feel, like ourselves, that the hour has come to re-consider the Universe. Studio 27, the Youth Group, is assuming the most delicate of the necessary investigations: that of taking the measure of man. Our Council has therefore thought it necessary above all to open a vast debate on the most urgent of problems: God, the Revolution, Poetry. A Congress, to which the thinking Youth of the entire world will be fraternally invited, will be organized by us in March. At the end of these sessions, we will reach our conclusions, and we will suggest, and if necessary, we shall demand. . . .

A preliminary inquiry should furnish us with the necessary instruments for our work. We beg of you to answer the following three questions (N. B. Since Studio 27 is so far only able to appear on a limited number of pages, please do not give your answer in more than four typewritten pages).

Questions:

1. What is God?

2. Don't you think that God is the permanent message of revolution? If yes, what place does this thought occupy in your life?

3. The gratuitousness of God, and the gratuitousness of Revolution. Are they expressible in terms of each other?

4. The doctrine of Studio 27,—that God begins where poetry ends—is this of such nature as to modify your vocation as a European?

5. Reasons for your despair.

Please believe us, dear Master, etc.

P.S. We go to press at nine o'clock tonight. Can we hope to have your reply in time?

Reprinted from *Les Lépreuses* (1939), pp. 35-36, by permission of the publisher, Librarie Gallimard. Translated by the Editor. Title supplied by the Editor.

INTELLECTUAL?

Paul Valéry

So, I was in my own abyss—which for being my own was no less an abyss—so I was in my own abyss, unable to explain to a child, to a savage, to an archangel—to myself, this word, *Intellectual,* which gives nobody else any difficulty at all.

It wasn't that images failed me. On the contrary, every time this terrible word consulted my mind, the oracle responded with a different image. All were naïve. Not one of them precisely annulled the sensation of not understanding.

Tatters of dream came to me.

I formed figures which I called "Intellectuals." Men almost motionless, who caused great movement in the world. Or very animated men, by the lively action of whose hands and mouths, imperceptible powers and essentially invisible objects were made manifest. . . . Pardon me for telling you the truth. I saw what I saw.

Men of *thought,* Men of *letters,* Men of *science, Artists*—Causes, living causes, individuate causes, minimal causes, causes within causes and inexplicable to themselves—and causes whose effects were as vain, but at the same time as prodigiously important, *as I wished.* . . . The universe of these causes and their effects existed and did not exist. This system of strange acts, productions, and prodigies had the all-powerful and vacant reality of a game of cards. Inspirations, meditations, works, glory, talents, it took no more than a certain look to make these things nearly everything, and a certain other look to reduce them to nearly nothing.

Then, in an apocalyptic flash, I seemed to glimpse the disorder and ferment of a whole society of demons. There appeared, in some supernatural space, a sort of comedy of what happens in History. Struggles, factions, triumphs, solemn execrations, executions, riots, tragedies over power! In this Republic all rumors were of scandal, of colossal or collapsing fortunes, of plots and assaults. There were committee-room plebiscites, insignificant coronations, many assassinations *by word.* I do not even mention the pilfering. This whole population of "intellectuals" was like the

Reprinted from *Monsieur Teste* (1948), pp. 61-62, by permission of the publisher, Alfred A. Knopf, Inc. Translated by Jackson Mathews.

other. Among them were puritans, speculators, prostitutes, believers who seemed to be infidels and infidels who put on the face of believers; some posed as fools, some were fools; there were authorities, and anarchists, and even executioners whose blades inspired disgust for ink. Some believed themselves priests and pontiffs, others prophets, still others Cæsars, or even martyrs, or a little of each. Several, even in their acts, took themselves for children or women. The most ridiculous were those who made themselves, on their own authority, the judges and justices of the tribe. They did not seem in the least to suspect that our judgments judge us, and that nothing reveals us, exposes our weaknesses more ingenuously than the attitude of pronouncing upon our fellows. It is a dangerous art, one in which the slightest errors may always be attributed to our character.

Each of these demons looked at himself rather frequently in a paper mirror; there, he saw the highest or lowest of beings. . . .

I was vaguely seeking the laws of this empire. The necessity to amuse; the need to live; the desire to survive; the pleasure of surprising, shocking, rebuking, teaching, despising; the needle of jealousy, all drove, irritated, excited, and explained this Hell.

Part III

TYPES OF
INTELLECTUALS

OVERVIEW

IN RUSSIA in the 1840's it was common to carry on disputes throughout the night. At one time a controversy was raging at its height when someone suggested that the disputants have something to eat— whereupon the critic Belinsky shouted out, "We have not yet decided the question of the existence of God and you want to eat!" Because the Russian "intelligentsiya" has been somewhat unique, because Russians have been particularly concerned with the subject, and because the word itself is of Russian origin, special attention will be paid to it. While Mannheim, Schumpeter, and others concentrate on the relation of intellectuals to classes, Dostoevsky and Berdyaev are concerned with the relation of the "intelligentsiya" to the people, which was an idealized, mysterious force in some Russian circles.

Dostoevsky considers it a tragedy when intellectuals become detached from the people. In his famous speech on Pushkin, he delineates the uprooted intellectual who is detached from the soil and the people. For him Pushkin was the first to create and understand the wandering, rootless Russian intellectual. In the rest of the selection which is in reply to criticism, Dostoevsky further comments on this type. His concept of the alienated intellectual should be compared and contrasted with the popular Western concept which is mainly of Marxist origin and which is analyzed in some detail by Hook in Part VI.

Berdyaev further comments on Dostoevsky's view of the "intelligentsiya" which he says is particularly Russian. They idealized the people and were hostile to culture; it sought for truth outside rather than inside itself. For Dostoevsky and for other slavophiles the simple folk, particularly the peasants, were the guardians of the true faith from which intellectuals were separated. The greatest Russian geniuses were unable to bear the lyricism of the mountain top with its solitude and sought the truth in flat places among the people.

While one tradition indicated above juxtaposes the people and the intellectuals and proclaims the superiority of the people, another tradition stresses the opposition between original thinkers and scholars and affirms the superiority of the former. This opposition is an ancient one; in the Renaissance, among others, Giordano Bruno, Montaigne, Thomas Overbury, Cervantes, and Juan de Valdés expressed criticism of the scholar, which is summed up in the latter's statement that "Whilst a man studies merely in the books of other men, he becomes acquainted with the minds of their authors, but not with his own." In nineteenth century Germany this tradition appears in terms of the contrast between professors of philosophy and philosophers, a distinction which was formulated by Schopenhauer. Both Kierkegaard and Nietzsche are indebted to Schopenhauer's thought and all three of them delineate the type of independent passionate thinker who is vitally different from the professor, the scholar, and the specialist. This tradition can be compared to what Mann has to say in Part VI about intellectuals in Germany.

Schopenhauer states that most learned men seek erudition in alien thoughts rather than being concerned with their own; too much reading and learning is prejudicial to thinking for oneself. Moreover, for many learned men knowledge is a means and not an end and they therefore call those who pursue art or learning for itself "dilettanti." He also notes that between professors and independent men of learning there has always been antagonism. Finally he says that the specialist outside his field is as ignorant as the ordinary man. Kierkegaard's remarks are in the tradition of the Schopenhauerian distinction between professors of philosophy and philosophers, but are more forceful.

Nietzsche distinguishes between philosophers and scholars and notes that the latter want to dominate the former. Some who claim to be philosophers are just scholars and specialists. But philosophy reduced to science involves the end of philosophy; yet because of the increased prestige of science there is a danger that the philosopher will abandon his lofty aim, specialize and attach himself to the scientists. Thus philosophers must not be confused with the scientific man and the scholar, or with the religious man. The genuine philosopher lives imprudently and risks himself constantly. To such philosophers the scholar and scientist has something of the old maid about him. The scientist is the commonplace man, non-ruling, and non-authoritative. He is the objective man—just a mirror—and whatever "personality" he still possesses seems to him accidental and disturbing. He is a measuring instrument and a mirroring apparatus; he is nothing in himself. In contrast, the task of the genuine philosopher is to create values. Elsewhere Nietzsche is vitriolic against professors of philosophy: "nothing real escaped their grasp alive. When these honorable idolators of concepts worship something, they kill it and stuff it; they threaten the life of everything they worship."

Emerson's piece, although considerably milder than the previous three pieces, belongs to the same tradition despite the fact that it was done by an American. It was originally delivered as an oration and that accounts for its rhetorical tone. According to Emerson living is a total act, thinking a partial act. The real scholar is man thinking but in the degenerate state he tends to become a mere thinker or still worse, the parrot of other men's thinking. The past comes to him through books but he must not become a slave to them, for each generation must write its own books. Books must be guides and not tyrants. They should be written by man thinking and not by book-worms for the one thing in the world of value is the thinking soul. Emerson echoes the outlook of the Founding Fathers who combined thought with action. Experience is the raw material out of which the intellect molds its works. A scholar must have confidence in himself and should never defer to the popular cry. He should not think of himself as a member of a protected class nor should he shy away from controversial questions. His main enterprise should be the upbuilding of man.

While Emerson exhorts American scholars as to what they should be, Mencken satirizes some of them because of what they are. Mencken's essay, of course, has wider application than that of the particular "Great Thinker" he satirizes. Mencken is essentially talking about a type which is as prevalent today and as influential, if not more so, than at the time he wrote this piece. It exists in every nation despite Mencken's contention that some of its traits are particularly American. In spite of this contention the craze in "Great Thinkers" and the subservience of pedagogues to their "correct" thought is almost universal. Mencken finds most significant not the "Great Thinker" himself, or his notions and his language, but the gravity with which these are received. Important matters are discussed not by men seeking the truth but by "Great Thinkers" who are only trying to get "kudos" out of them. The remedy is to be concerned with ideas and not with crazes on which "Great Thinkers" thrive. In connection with the chatter and publications of counterfeit intellectuals in Academia and Bohemia one cannot help but sympathize with Flaubert's bitter statement: "If the Emperor were to abolish printing tomorrow, I'd crawl to Paris on my hands and knees and kiss his behind in gratitude."

In one Russian tradition all intellectuals are attacked in the name of the people and in the Schopenhauer-Kierkegaard-Nietzsche tradition scholars and professors of philosophy are criticized in the name of philosophers. In contrast to these two schools of thought, professors, scholars, scientists, and experts are viewed differently in Section C. Znaniecki distinguishes among the following kinds of men of knowledge: the discoverer of truth who if he finds followers becomes the initiator of a new school; the systematizer who has the most characteristic role in the history of scholarship—sometimes his role is combined with the discoverer of truth. The contributor is another variety and he is needed, for culture is changing and therefore a school of thought cannot rest. The rivalry between schools representing different systems of knowledge gave birth to a specific function and the fighter for truth who performs it aims to gain logical victory for the doctrine of one school over those of other schools. Still another variety of man of knowledge is the eclectic and the historian of knowledge. The social significance of the disseminator of knowledge—popularizers and educating teachers—has increased in modern times and their number is many times that of the productive man of knowledge. Hayek in Part V considers the dissemination of knowledge the most characteristic function of those intellectuals, whom he calls professional secondhand dealers in ideas. Among the scientific explorers, Znaniecki distinguishes between the discoverer of new facts and those whose function is to discover hitherto unforeseen theoretical problems and to solve them by new theories.

Aron maintains that every society in the past has had its scribes, men of letters, and experts. Today those who are called the "intelligentsia" are more numerous, more emancipated, and more influential. In a broader sense all non-manual workers belong to this group but a narrower definition would include men of letters and experts only. Aron refers to further differentiations among intellectuals and comes to the conclusion that a single definition of "intellectual" is not feasible.

Laski concentrates on the experts, who have become so prominent due to their outstanding success in medicine, engineering, and other fields, that it is commonly assumed that even in matters of social policy reliance should be placed on the expert. Indeed expert consultation is needed at every stage in policy making but the expert's judgment must not be final. This is so because the expert lacks the insight of common sense, is unable to accept new views, frequently fails to see problems in perspective, is unable to adapt rapidly, has a tendency to be immersed in specialization, and frequently lacks understanding of the plain man. The expert is an invaluable servant but an impossible master. The statesman at his best represents supreme common sense; he is the broker of ideas without whom no bridges can be built between the expert and plain men. The fact that plain men are ignorant of technical matters does not mean that experts should make the final decisions, for the plain man should be the ultimate judge.

The specialist is also criticized by Ortega but from a different point of view. He says that science demands specialization, not in itself, but in scientists because scientific work calls for narrow concentration. Experimental science has progressed mainly due to the work of mediocre men. The specialist knows his field but is ignorant of the rest of knowledge. He is a "learned ignoramus" which implies that he is a person who is ignorant, not in the fashion of the ignorant man, but with the petulance of one who is learned in his own special line. Outside his own field the specialist will adopt the attitude of the ignorant man and he will adopt it with forcefulness and self-sufficiency for paradoxically he will not admit specialists in fields outside his own. The result is that the specialists behave like mass-men.

Ortega says in effect that scientists and specialists outside their field are ignorant and this makes them limited creatures. Holton maintains the opposite; intellectuals are limited because they do not understand science. After outlining the seven current images of science, he argues that the prevalence of these false images is the main source of alienation between the scientific and non-scientific worlds. Many of the leading thinkers of the seventeenth and eighteenth centuries would have been horrified by the proposition that cultured persons could dispense with a good grasp of science. Yet today, for the first time in history, intellectuals are losing their hold of understanding upon the world.

Whatever the merits and limitations of experts may be, Molnar believes that the world is moving toward a society without conflicting groups and organized oppositions wherein the role of experts will increase and that of the ideologically committed intellectuals will decrease. Intellectuals possess weapons which are needed for ideological conflict and when the need for these decline their role likewise decreases in importance. Bureaucrats, experts, and social engineers will become more important for their task is not to exert ideological influence but to preserve equilibrium by making use of and further developing existing mechanisms of adjustment. Unlike the intellectuals whose tasks had been essentially destructive while serving the middle class and then the proletariat, social engineers are primarily conservative organizers and constitute the new elite. As for the future of intellectuals, they will be freed from ideological commitments and will gain in mobility that which they have lost in status.

Barzun concentrates upon three types of intellectuals who in his view are enemies of the intellect. Artists resemble engineers and physical scientists in that they follow modes of thought quite other than those of discursive intellect. Despite differences, science and art have reinforced each other's effect. From the symbolist period on, Western art has been based on the rejection of common speech, common language, and common knowledge. Through the increasing fantasy of its concepts and symbols, through its diverging technical tongues, science has also receded from the common world. Scientists have planted citadels throughout the realm of the mind, but have given no thought to means for intellectual exchange among them. "The House of Intellect" is lost somewhere in this no man's land. Barzun also shows the connections between modern art and science and philanthropy, which he calls the liberal doctrine of free and equal opportunity as applied to the things of the mind, which leads to the corruption of judgment and the products of the intellect themselves.

Tchekov strikes to the essence of the profession of writing by pointing out that a man of letters cannot enjoy experiences because virtually all of them become raw material to be transformed into writing on white sheets of paper. His concluding remarks regarding Tolstoy and Turgenev are also applicable to other writers with a critical sense, who feel disturbed because no matter how great they are they are not as good as Cervantes and Shakespeare; one wonders how these last two felt about their work—that is the mystery!

The selection from Mallarmé is a letter he wrote on May 17, 1867 to Eugene Lefébure. Because of his dedication to poetry and his martyrdom to beauty, André Gide wrote of "St. Mallarmé, the Esoteric." The following conversation between Degas and Mallarmé gives a clue to the latter's attitude toward poetry: "Yours is a hellish craft. I can't manage to say what I want, and yet I'm full of ideas. . . ." Mallarmé answered: "My dear Degas, one does not make poetry with ideas, but with *words*."

Degas' aphorisms about the artist have been selected because he was one of the most intellectual of modern painters. According to Valéry, he cogitated long and passionately on the problems of painting and was a "wonderful coiner of epigrams." The first two paragraphs were taken from an early notebook of Degas and are dated 1856-57; the others are undated and are from oral, but reliable, reports.

In contrast to the shorter aphoristic treatment the artists receive in this section, there is a more extended discussion of them in Part IV.

THE UPROOTED INTELLECTUAL

Feodor Dostoevsky

... PUSHKIN, with his profoundly perspicacious and ingenious mind and purely Russian heart, was the first to detect and record the principal pathological phenomenon of our educated society, historically detached from, and priding itself on, the people. He indicated and graphically set before us our negative type—the restless man, refusing to be reconciled, having no faith in his own soil and in the native forces, denying Russia and ultimately himself (*i.e.,* his own society, his educated stratum which grew up on our native soil), refusing to co-operate with others and sincerely suffering. Aleko and Onegin subsequently generated in our belles-lettres a number of related characters: they were followed by the Pechorins, the Tchitchikovs, the Rudins, the Lavretzkys, the Bolkonskys (in Leo Tolstoy's *War and Peace*), and many others whose very appearance bears witness to his immense intellect and genius, to the *truth of the idea originally conceived by Pushkin. To him belong the honor* and the glory, for having spotted the principal sore of the society which came into existence after Peter's great reform. It is to his ingenious diagnosis that we owe the knowledge of our disease, and he was also the first to comfort us, by giving us the great hope that this is not a mortal illness; that Russian society can be cured, reformed and resurrected if it embraces the people's truth. ...

In my childhood I saw once on a highway a state courier in uniform with flaps, wearing a three-cornered hat with a feather sticking in it, brutally with his fist beating the driver on his nape, while the latter madly whipped the steaming troika racing at full speed. Of course this courier was Russian by birth, but one so blinded, so alienated from the people that he did not know how to deal with a Russian otherwise than with his heavy fist in lieu of conversing with him in any manner whatsoever. And yet he spent all his life in the company of postboys and Russian commoners of every kind. However, the flaps of his uniform, his feathered hat, his polished Petersburg boots, to him were spiritually dearer not only than the Russian peasant, but perhaps than Russia *in toto,* which he crossed from one end

Reprinted from *The Diary of a Writer,* Volume Two (1949), pp. 959-960, 989-990, by permission of the publisher, Charles Scribner's Sons. Translated by Boris Brasol. Title supplied by the Editor.

to the other, in which, probably, he found nothing remarkable or worthy of note other than his own fist or the kick of his polished boot. The whole of Russia represented itself to him merely in the guise of his superiors, outside of whom virtually nothing was worthy of existence. How could such a fellow understand the people's essence and their soul! Although a Russian, he was a "European" Russian, only one who had embarked upon his Europeanism not with education but with debauchery, just in the same way as many others did. Yes, sir, this debauchery on many occasions was held in Russia to be the surest means of converting Russians into Europeans. Indeed, the son of that state-messenger might have become a professor, *i.e.,* a patented European.

And so, don't speak about their understanding of the people's essence. We had to have Pushkin, the Khomiakovs, the Samarins, the Aksakovs before we could begin to speak about the people's essence. (Although prior to them this subject used to be discussed but in a somewhat pseudo-classical and histrionic fashion.) And when they began to speak about "the people's truth," everybody looked upon them as epileptics and idiots whose ideal was "eating radishes and writing denunciations." At first their appearance and opinions surprised everybody to such an extent that liberals began to wonder: aren't these men about to start denouncing them?—It is up to you to decide whether or not our contemporary liberals have much advanced from that silly view on Slavophiles.

But let us turn to business. You state that Aleko fled to the Gypsies from Derjimorda. Let us concede that this is true. But the worst thing is that you, Mr. Gradovsky, with full conviction admit Aleko's right to such surliness. You imply: "He could not have failed to flee to the Gypsies because Derjimorda was too repulsive." But I assert that in a certain sense Aleko and Onegin were also Derjimordas, and perhaps even worse than these, with that difference only that I am not accusing them in the least, fully realizing the tragedy of their fate, whereas you are lauding them for their escape. "Such great"—you seem to imply—"such interesting men were unable to live on good terms with such monsters." You are awfully mistaken. You infer that Aleko and Onegin did not in the least alienate themselves from their native soil and did not deny the people's truth. Moreover, you seem to say: "they were by no means haughty!"—This is what you maintain. Well, in this case haughtiness is a logical and unavoidable consequence of their abstraction and their detachment from their own soil. Indeed, you cannot deny the fact that they did not know their soil, that they grew and were brought up as if in a convent. They acquired their knowledge of Russia in Petersburg, through bureaucratic channels, and their relations with the people were those of a master with his serf. Let us even admit that at times they lived in the country, in proximity to the peasant. My state messenger, all life long, rubbed shoulders with postilions, and admitted that they were worthy of nothing but his fist. Aleko and Onegin behaved in Russia haughtily and impatiently like all men who live in a small group segregated from the people, fully provided for, *i.e.,* supported by the peasant's labor and depending on European education, which they also received gratuitously. The very fact that our educated classes, as a result of historical preparation, virtually throughout our whole national existence have been converted into lazy creatures, explains their abstraction and alienation from their native soil. They perished not because of Derjimorda as such but because they were unable to explain to themselves the phenomenon of Derjimorda and its origin. For this they were too proud. But having failed to find the meaning of Derjimorda, they deemed it impossible to toil on their native soil, regarding those who believed in such a possibility as blockheads or as Derjimordas themselves.

THE PEOPLE vs. THE INTELLECTUALS

Nicholas Berdyaev

DOSTOIEVSKY was in his way a "populist" (*narodnik*), believing in a religious "populism." This particular sort of love for the people
is a phenomenon unknown in the West, for it is only in Russia that we
meet the everlasting opposition of the "*intelligentzia*" and "the people,"
with its idealization of "the masses" that goes to the length of bowing down
before them and looking for God and truth among them. Populism was
always a sign of the weakness of the cultural movement and the lack
of a healthy consciousness of its mission. When Russia was an immense
kingdom of peasants with the Tzar at their head it included a very limited
number of classes, with a relatively weak and small cultured *élite* and a
conservative machinery of government that was hopelessly swollen and
unwieldy. In such a social structure the intellectual class felt helpless in
face of the dark ocean of the people at large and in danger of being
drowned in it. The imperial power, which enjoyed a religious sanction in
popular consciousness, both safeguarded the educated class and persecuted
it. The state of mind of this class (which at a certain moment gave itself
the name of "the *intelligentzia*") was tragic during the nineteenth century,
completely pathological. There were no strong cultural traditions in Russian
history and there were no organic ties with any differentiated society of
classes proud and well-established in a glorious past, and this cultured
minority found itself caught between the tzarist authority and the life of the
people: it was in a cleft stick. So, by an instinct of spiritual self-preservation,
it began to idealize one or the other of these elements by turn, or even both
together, in an endeavour to find a *point d'appui*. Eventually it admitted a
number of the common people to its ranks (it was then that it took the
name of *intelligentzia*) and surrendered to the element that threatened to
swallow it. Henceforward "the people" represents for the *intelligentzia* a
mysterious and compelling force which holds the secret of life and is the
depository of some special truth; in the people the intellectuals found the
God they had lost.

The *intelligentzia* did not feel itself an organic part of Russian life, for

Reprinted from *Dostoievsky* (1934), pp. 163-169, by permission of the publisher,
Sheed and Ward, Inc. Translated by Donald Attwater. Title supplied by the Editor.

its roots and its unity were gone; its integrity had been handed over to the people, through whom alone it now lived and knew truth. This intellectual class did not have the courage to preach its message to the people and fulfil its duty of bringing light into their dark places; it was doubtful of its office of enlightener, it did not believe in itself, it questioned the intrinsic worth of culture. This is a bad state of mind for the discharge of culture's undeniable mission. The intellectuals came to cast suspicion on it from moral, religious, and social points-of-view alike: culture was a fruit of injustice, bought at too high a price, it signified a rupture with the people's life, a violation of its organic integrity: it was a crime against the people, a going-out from among them, a forgetfulness of them. This feeling of its guilt pursued the Russian *intelligentzia* throughout the nineteenth century and undermined its creative energy; and it was due, I must emphasize it, to the fact that the educated class was not sufficiently conscious of the absolute value of culture and even allowed a moral doubt about it.

This is very characteristic of Russian populism: truth is not to be looked for in culture and its objective aims but in "the people," a stream of organic life, wherein, too (and not in culture and the spirit), resides religious life. I am speaking here of the first principles of populism, independent of various tendencies and shades of opinion. Actually, there were two main tendencies, naturalistic and religious, and both forms were expressive of the same psychology. The extreme "right" and the extreme "left," slavophil populists and atheistic socialist populists, have notable points of resemblance: there is the same idealization of the people and reactionary hostility to culture, there is a similar inhibition of the personal principle and of the cultivation of personality, responsibility, and honour, a similar incapacity for spiritual autonomy, a similar intolerance, a similar seeking for truth outside rather than within oneself; the disease of the national soul is manifest at either pole. The absence of an age of chivalry in Russia has been disastrous for her moral culture. Her collectivism has shown more than once how insufficiently awakened the personal spirit is, the personality of men remaining absorbed in the natural current of the people's existence—and therefore that is where the populist theory looks for God and truth.

What exactly is "the people" for this theory? The answer even to that question is extremely uncertain and difficult. For most populists the people is not the nation, understanding by that term a whole organism, including all social classes and states, all historical generations, the "intellectual" and the nobleman as well as the peasant, the shopkeeper and the artisan as well as the labourer. The word "people" has not for them its ontological and defined meaning but carries a social and class signification, indicating principally peasants and "workers," the lower classes of society who live by their physical labour. The nobility, manufacturers and traders, scholars, men-of-letters, artists, are not an organic part of the people; they are, indeed, set up against them as the *bourgeoisie* or *intelligentzia*. It is, of course, this class conception that rules in revolutionary and materialist populism, but the curious thing is that it also predominated in religious populism and in Slavophilism, even though it was in flagrant contradiction with the principles of the slavophil conscience. For the slavophils—as for Dostoievsky —the people was above all the simple folk, particularly the peasants, from whose unity and truth the intellectual class was separated in their eyes. The *muzhik* was the guardian of the true faith. If I was a noble or a business-man, a scholar or a writer, an engineer or a physician, I could not feel myself as part of "the people"; I had to regard them as a mysterious energy opposed to myself, to which I must kneel as to a bearer of a higher truth. There was no possibility of an immanent relation for me with them; it could be only transcendent, for the people above all was the "not-I," opposed to myself, in whose presence I felt a sense of guilt. That is a purely slavish idea, excluding all freedom of spirit and consciousness of a personal spiritual liberty. This illusory populism was Dostoievsky's own, and it was in striking contrast with the words on the subject of the Russian nobility that he put into the mouth of Versilov: "I cannot but respect our nobility. During the course of centuries it has created a certain type of high culture like no other in the world, a culture which takes upon itself the sufferings of all. It is a Russian type and as it is rooted in the higher and more cultivated class of our people I am able to have the honour to partake of it. This group is guardian of the Russia of the future. It may number a thousand (perhaps more, perhaps less), but all Russia has existed solely to produce that thousand."

The greatest of Russian geniuses, even at the height of their spiritual life and creative powers, were unable to bear the lofty peaks and haughty free-dom of the spirit; they were afraid of solitude and hurled themselves down into the flat places of the life of the people, hoping by so doing to reach a higher truth. They had not the lyricism which belongs to the mountain-tops; they dreaded the loneliness, the forsakenness, the cold, and sought refuge in the lukewarm stream of the people's collective existence. Herein the Russian genius (*e.g.,* Dostoievsky) differs absolutely from the European genius (*e.g.,* Nietzsche), and the first to experience Russian consciousness, the slavophils, shared this national characteristic. They certainly held a very high position in European culture and were the most cultured of all Russians; they understood that culture cannot be only national and in that respect were nearer to the Western mind than the "westernizing" Russians themselves. But they surrendered to the peasants, not having the strength to defend their truth as a national truth common to everybody; and they also looked upon the people, "the folk," as in opposition to the cultured class—

a mistake which had dire consequences for the national consciousness. The irreligious "left" garnered the harvest of this identification of the people with a class. The gulf between *intelligentzia* and "people" was widened, a *national* consciousness became impossible, and only the notion of *populism* remained. All the time there were in the heart of Slavophilism seeds of a larger and more living understanding of the people, as a nation, as a mystical body; but the slavophils fell victims to the malady of the intellectuals, and so did Dostoievsky himself.

ON MEN OF LEARNING

Arthur Schopenhauer

Wᴴᴱɴ one sees the number and variety of institutions which exist for the purposes of education, and the vast throng of scholars and masters, one might fancy the human race to be very much concerned about truth and wisdom. But here, too, appearances are deceptive. The masters teach in order to gain money, and strive, not after wisdom, but the outward show and reputation of it; and the scholars learn, not for the sake of knowledge and insight, but to be able to chatter and give themselves airs. Every thirty years a new race comes into the world—a youngster that knows nothing about anything, and after summarily devouring in all haste the results of human knowledge as they have been accumulated for thousands of years, aspires to be thought cleverer than the whole of the past. For this purpose he goes to the University, and takes to reading books—new books, as being of his own age and standing. Everything he reads must be briefly put, must be new! he is new himself. Then he falls to and criticizes. And here I am not taking the slightest account of studies pursued for the sole object of making a living.

Students, and learned persons of all sorts and every age, aim as a rule at acquiring *information* rather than insight. They pique themselves upon knowing about everything—stones, plants, battles, experiments, and all the books in existence. It never occurs to them that information is only a means of insight, and in itself of little or no value; that it is his way of *thinking* that makes a man a philosopher. When I hear of these portents of learning and their imposing erudition, I sometimes say to myself: Ah, how little they must have had to think about, to have been able to read so much! And when I actually find it reported of the elder Pliny that he was continually reading or being read to, at table, on a journey, or in his bath, the question forces itself upon my mind, whether the man was so very lacking in thought of his own that he had to have alien thought incessantly instilled into him; as though he were a consumptive patient taking jellies to keep himself alive. And neither his undiscerning credulity nor his inexpressibly repulsive and barely intelligible style—which seems like that of a man taking notes, and

Reprinted from *Essays* (1951), "The Art of Literature," pp. 33-38, by permission of the publishers, George Allen and Unwin, Ltd. Translated by T. Bailey Saunders.

very economical of paper—are of a kind to give me a high opinion of his power of independent thought.

We have seen that much reading and learning is prejudicial to thinking for oneself; and, in the same way, through much writing and teaching, a man loses the habit of being quite clear, and therefore thorough, in regard to the things he knows and understands; simply because he has left himself no time to acquire clearness or thoroughness. And so, when clear knowledge fails him in his utterances, he is forced to fill out the gaps with words and phrases. It is this, and not the dryness of the subject-matter, that makes most books such tedious reading. There is a saying that a good cook can make a palatable dish even out of an old shoe; and a good writer can make the driest things interesting.

With by far the largest number of learned men, knowledge is a means, not an end. That is why they will never achieve any great work; because, to do that, he who pursues knowledge must pursue it as an end, and treat everything else, even existence itself, as only a means. For everything which a man fails to pursue for its own sake is but half-pursued; and true excellence, no matter in what sphere, can be attained only where the work has been produced for its own sake alone, and not as a means to further ends.

And so, too, no one will ever succeed in doing anything really great and original in the way of thought, who does not seek to acquire knowledge for himself, and, making this the immediate object of his studies, decline to trouble himself about the knowledge of others. But the average man of learning studies for the purpose of being able to teach and write. His head is like a stomach and intestines which let the food pass through them undigested. That is just why his teaching and writing is of so little use. For it is not upon undigested refuse that people can be nourished, but solely upon the milk which secretes from the very blood itself.

The wig is the appropriate symbol of the man of learning, pure and simple. It adorns the head with a copious quantity of false hair, in lack of one's own: just as erudition means endowing it with a great mass of alien thought. This, to be sure, does not clothe the head so well and naturally, nor is it so generally useful, nor so suited for all purposes, nor so firmly rooted; nor when alien thought is used up, can it be immediately replaced by more from the same source, as is the case with that which springs from soil of one's own. So we find Sterne, in his *Tristram Shandy,* boldly asserting that *an ounce of a man's own wit is worth a ton of other people's.*

And in fact the most profound erudition is no more akin to genius than a collection of dried plants is like Nature, with its constant flow of new life, ever fresh, ever young, ever changing. There are no two things more opposed than the childish naïveté of an ancient author and the learning of his commentator.

Dilettanti, dilettanti! This is the slighting way in which those who pursue any branch of art or learning for the love and enjoyment of the thing—*per il loro diletto,* are spoken of by those who have taken it up for the sake of gain, attracted solely by the prospect of money. This contempt of theirs comes from the base belief that no man will seriously devote himself to a subject, unless he is spurred on to it by want, hunger, or else some form of greed. The public is of the same way of thinking; and hence its general respect for professionals and its distrust of *dilettanti.* But the truth is that the *dilettante* treats his subject as an end, whereas the professional, pure and simple, treats it merely as a means. He alone will be really in earnest about a matter, who has a direct interest therein, takes to it because he likes it, and pursues it *con amore.* It is these, and not hirelings, that have always done the greatest work.

In the republic of letters it is as in other republics; favour is shown to the plain man—he who goes his way in silence and does not set up to be cleverer than others. But the abnormal man is looked upon as threatening danger; people band together against him, and have, oh! such a majority on their side.

The condition of this republic is much like that of a small State in America, where every man is intent only upon his own advantage, and seeks reputation and power for himself, quite heedless of the general weal, which then goes to ruin. So it is in the republic of letters; it is himself, and himself alone, that a man puts forward, because he wants to gain fame. The only things in which all agree is in trying to keep down a really eminent man, if he should chance to show himself, as one who would be a common peril. From this it is easy to see how it fares with knowledge as a whole.

Between professors and independent men of learning there has always been from of old a certain antagonism, which may perhaps be likened to that existing between dogs and wolves. In virtue of their position, professors enjoy great facilities for becoming known to their contemporaries. Contrarily, independent men of learning enjoy, by their position, great facilities for becoming known to posterity; to which it is necessary that, amongst other and much rarer gifts, a man should have a certain leisure and freedom. As mankind takes a long time in finding out on whom to bestow its attention, they may both work together side by side.

He who holds a professorship may be said to receive his food in the stall; and this is the best way with ruminant animals. But he who finds his food for himself at the hands of Nature is better off in the open field.

Of human knowledge as a whole and in every branch of it by far the largest part exists nowhere but on paper—I mean, in books, that paper memory of mankind. Only a small part of it is at any given period really active in the minds of particular persons. This is due, in the main, to the brevity and uncertainty of life; but it also comes from the fact that men are lazy and bent on pleasure. Every generation attains, on its hasty passage through existence, just so much of human knowledge as it needs, and then soon disappears. Most men of learning are very superficial. Then follows a new generation, full of hope, but ignorant, and with everything to learn from the beginning. It seizes, in its turn, just so much as it can grasp, or find useful on its brief journey, and then too goes its way. How badly it would fare with human knowledge if it were not for the art of writing and printing! This it is that makes libraries the only sure and lasting memory of the human race, for its individual members have all of them but a very limited and imperfect one. Hence most men of learning are as loth to have their knowledge examined as merchants to lay bare their books.

Human knowledge extends on all sides farther than the eye can reach; and of that which would be generally worth knowing, no one man can possess even the thousandth part.

All branches of learning have thus been so much enlarged that he who would "do something" has to pursue no more than one subject and disregard all others. In his own subject he will then, it is true, be superior to the vulgar; but in all else he will belong to it. If we add to this that neglect of the ancient languages, which is nowadays on the increase and is doing away with all general education in the humanities—for a mere smattering of Latin and Greek is of no use—we shall come to have men of learning who outside their own subject display an ignorance truly bovine.

An exclusive specialist of this kind stands on a par with a workman in a factory, whose whole life is spent in making one particular kind of screw, or catch, or handle, for some particular instrument or machine, in which, indeed, he attains incredible dexterity. The specialist may also be likened to a man who lives in his own house and never leaves it. There he is perfectly familiar with everything, every little step, corner, or board; much as Quasimodo in Victor Hugo's *Notre Dame* knows the cathedral; but outside it, all is strange and unknown.

For true culture in the humanities it is absolutely necessary that a man should be many-sided and take large views; and for a man of learning in the higher sense of the word, an extensive acquaintance with history is needful. He, however, who wishes to be a complete philosopher, must gather into his head the remotest ends of human knowledge: for where else could they ever come together?

It is precisely minds of the first order that will never be specialists. For their very nature is to make the whole of existence their problem; and this is a subject upon which they will every one of them in some form provide mankind with a new revelation. For he alone can deserve the name of genius who takes the All, the Essential, the Universal, for the theme of his achievements; not he who spends his life in explaining some special relation of things one to another.

THE PROFESSOR

Søren Kierkegaard

THANKS, Lichtenberg, thanks! for having said that there is nothing so feeble as the conversation of learned literary men who have never thought for themselves but know a thousand historical-literary facts.* 'It is almost like a reading from a cookery book when one is hungry.' ...

*Like Leporello they keep a list, but the point is what they lack; while Don Juan seduces girls and enjoys himself—Leporello notes down the time, the place and a description of the girl.

* * * * *

The same thing has happened in the scientific world as in the world of trade. First of all people bartered real goods, later money was invented. Nowadays the form of exchange in the scientific world is paper money, and nobody bothers about it except dons.

* * * * *

The Two ways: One is to suffer; the other is to become a professor of the fact that another suffered.

The first is 'the way'; the second goes round about (the proposition 'about' is so aptly used for lectures and sermons) and perhaps it ends by going down.

* * * * *

In one of the Pslams it is said of the rich man that he heaps up treasures with great toil "and knoweth not who shall inherit them." So I shall leave behind me, intellectually speaking, a capital by no means insignificant—and alas, I know full well who will be my heir. It is that figure so exceedingly distasteful to me, he that till now has inherited all that is best and will continue to do so: the Docent, the Professor.

The first three items are reprinted from *The Journals* (1938), pp. 49, 107, and 528, by permission of the publisher, Oxford University Press. Translated by Alexander Dru. The last item is reprinted from *A Kierkegaard Anthology* (1947), p. 432, by permission of the publisher, Princeton University Press and the editor of the anthology. Title supplied by the Editor.

Yet this also is a necessary part of my suffering—to know this and then go calmly on with my endeavor, which brings me toil and trouble and the profit of which, in one sense, the Professor will inherit. "In one sense"— for in another sense I take it with me.

Note. And even if the "Professor" should chance to read this, it will not give him pause, will not cause his conscience to smite him; no, this too will be made the subject of a lecture. And again this observation will not give him pause, if the Professor should chance to read it, no, this too will be made the subject of a lecture. For longer even than the tapeworm which recently was extracted from a woman . . . even longer is the Professor, and the man in whom the Professor is lodged cannot be rid of this by any human power, only God can do it, if the man himself is willing.

WE SCHOLARS

Friedrich Nietzsche

At THE RISK that moralising may also reveal itself here as that which it has always been—namely, resolutely *montrer ses plaies,* according to Balzac—I would venture to protest against an improper and injurious alteration of rank, which quite unnoticed, and as if with the best conscience, threatens nowadays to establish itself in the relations of science and philosophy. I mean to say that one must have the right out of one's own *experience* —experience, as it seems to me, always implies unfortunate experience?—to treat of such an important question of rank, so as not to speak of colour like the blind, or *against* science like women and artists ("Ah! this dreadful science!" sigh their instinct and their shame, "it always *finds things out!*"). The declaration of independence of the scientific man, his emancipation from philosophy, is one of the subtler after-effects of democratic organisation and disorganisation: the self-glorification and self-conceitedness of the learned man is now everywhere in full bloom, and in its best springtime—which does not mean to imply that in this case self-praise smells sweetly. Here also the instinct of the populace cries, "Freedom from all masters!" and after science has, with the happiest results, resisted theology, whose "handmaid" it had been too long, it now proposes in its wantonness and indiscretion to lay down laws for philosophy, and in its turn to play the "master"—what am I saying! to play the *philosopher* on its own account. My memory—the memory of a scientific man, if you please!—teems with the naïvetés of insolence which I have heard about philosophy and philosophers from young naturalists and old physicians (not to mention the most cultured and most conceited of all learned men, the philologists and schoolmasters, who are both the one and the other by profession). On one occasion it was the specialist and the Jack Horner who instinctively stood on the defensive against all synthetic tasks and capabilities; at another time it was the industrious worker who had got a scent of *otium* and refined luxuriousness in the internal economy of the philosopher, and felt himself aggrieved and belittled thereby. On another occasion it was the colour-blindness of the utilitarian, who sees nothing in philosophy but a series of *refuted* systems, and

Reprinted from *Beyond Good and Evil* (1911), pp.. 133-142, 151-152, by permission of the publisher, The Macmillan Company. Translated by Helen Zimmern.

an extravagant expenditure which "does nobody any good." At another time
the fear of disguised mysticism and of the boundary-adjustment of knowledge became conspicuous, at another time the disregard of individual philosophers, which had involuntarily extended to disregard of philosophy generally.
In fine, I found most frequently, behind the proud disdain of philosophy
in young scholars, the evil after-effect of some particular philosopher, to
whom on the whole obedience had been foresworn, without, however, the
spell of his scornful estimates of other philosophers having been got rid of—
the result being a general ill-will to all philosophy. (Such seems to me, for
instance, the after-effect of Schopenhauer on the most modern Germany: by
his unintelligent rage against Hegel, he has succeeded in severing the whole
of the last generation of Germans from its connection with German culture,
which culture, all things considered, has been an elevation and a divining
refinement of the *historical sense;* but precisely at this point Schopenhauer
himself was poor, irreceptive, and un-German to the extent of ingeniousness.)
On the whole, speaking generally, it may just have been the humanness,
all-too-humanness of the modern philosophers themselves, in short, their
contemptibleness, which has injured most radically the reverence for
philosophy and opened the doors to the instinct of the populace. Let it
but be acknowledged to what an extent our modern world diverges from the
whole style of the world of Heraclites, Plato, Empedocles, and whatever
else all the royal and magnificent anchorites of the spirit were called; and
with what justice an honest man of science *may* feel himself of a better family
and origin, in view of such representatives of philosophy, who, owing to the
fashion of the present day, are just as much aloft as they are down below—in
Germany, for instance, the two lions of Berlin, the anarchist Eugen Dühring
and the amalgamist Eduard von Hartmann. It is especially the sight of those
hotch-potch philosophers, who call themselves "realists," or "positivists,"
which is calculated to implant a dangerous distrust in the soul of a young and
ambitious scholar: those philosophers, at the best, are themselves but scholars
and specialists, that is very evident! All of them are persons who have been
vanquished and *brought back again* under the dominion of science, who at
one time or another claimed more from themselves, without having a right
to the "more" and its responsibility—and who now, creditably, rancorously
and vindictively, represent in word and deed, *disbelief* in the master-task and
supremacy of philosophy. After all, how could it be otherwise? Science
flourishes nowadays and has the good conscience clearly visible on its counte-
nance; while that to which the entire modern philosophy has gradually sunk,
the remnant of philosophy of the present day, excites distrust and dis-
pleasure, if not scorn and pity. Philosophy reduced to a "theory of knowledge," no more in fact than a diffident science of epochs and doctrine of
forbearance: a philosophy that never even gets beyond the threshold, and

rigorously *denies* itself the right to enter—that is philosophy in its last throes, an end, an agony, something that awakens pity. How could such a philosophy —*rule!*

* * * * *

The dangers that beset the evolution of the philosopher are, in fact, so manifold nowadays, that one might doubt whether this fruit could still come to maturity. The extent and towering structure of the sciences have increased enormously, and therewith also the probability that the philosopher will grow tired even as a learner, or will attach himself somewhere and "specialise": so that he will no longer attain to his elevation, that is to say, to his superspection, his circumspection, and his *despection.* Or he gets aloft too late, when the best of his maturity and strength is past; or when he is impaired, coarsened, and deteriorated, so that his view, his general estimate of things, is no longer of much importance. It is perhaps just the refinement of his intellectual conscience that makes him hesitate and linger on the way; he dreads the temptation to become a dilettante, a millepede, a milleantenna; he knows too well that as a discerner, one who has lost his self-respect no longer commands, no longer *leads;* unless he should aspire to become a great play-actor, a philosophical Cagliostro and spiritual rat-catcher —in short, a misleader. This is in the last instance a question of taste, if it has not really been a question of conscience. To double once more the philosopher's difficulties, there is also the fact that he demands from himself a verdict, a Yea or Nay, not concerning science, but concerning life and the worth of life—he learns unwillingly to believe that it is his right and even his duty to obtain this verdict, and he has to seek his way to the right and the belief only through the most extensive (perhaps disturbing and destroying) experiences, often hesitating, doubting, and dumbfounded. In fact, the philosopher has long been mistaken and confused by the multitude, either with the scientific man and ideal scholar, or with the religiously elevated, desensualised, desecularised visionary and God-intoxicated man; and even yet when one hears anybody praised, because he lives "wisely," or "as a philosopher," it hardly means anything more than "prudently and apart." Wisdom: that seems to the populace to be a kind of flight, a means and artifice for withdrawing successfully from a bad game; but the *genuine* philosopher—does it not seem so to *us,* my friends?—lives "unphilosophically" and "unwisely," above all, *imprudently,* and feels the obligation and burden of a hundred attempts and temptations of life—he risks *himself* constantly, he plays *this* bad game.

* * * * *

In relation to the genius, that is to say, a being who either *engenders* or *produces*—both words understood in their fullest sense—the man of learning, the scientific average man, has always something of the old maid about him; for, like her, he is not conversant with the two principal functions of man. To both, of course, to the scholar and to the old maid, one concedes respectability, as if by way of indemnification—in these cases one emphasises the respectability—and yet, in the compulsion of this concession, one has the same admixture of vexation. Let us examine more closely: what is the scientific man? Firstly, a commonplace type of man, with commonplace virtues: that is to say, a non-ruling, non-authoritative, and non-self-sufficient type of man; he possesses industry, patient adaptableness to rank and file, equability and moderation in capacity and requirement; he has the instinct for people like himself, and for that which they require—for instance: the portion of independence and green meadow without which there is no rest from labour, the claim to honour and consideration (which first and foremost presupposes recognition and recognisability), the sunshine of a good name, the perpetual ratification of his value and usefulness, with which the inward *distrust* which lies at the bottom of the heart of all dependent men and gregarious animals, has again and again to be overcome. The learned man, as is appropriate, has also maladies and faults of an ignoble kind: he is full of petty envy, and has a lynx-eye for the weak points in those natures to whose elevations he cannot attain. He is confiding, yet only as one who lets himself go, but does not *flow;* and precisely before the man of the great current he stands all the colder and more reserved—his eye is then like a smooth and irresponsive lake, which is no longer moved by rapture or sympathy. The worst and most dangerous thing of which a scholar is capable results from the instinct of mediocrity of his type, from the Jesuitism of mediocrity, which labours instinctively for the destruction of the exceptional man, and endeavours to break—or still better, to relax—every bent bow. To relax, of course, with consideration, and naturally with an indulgent hand—to *relax* with confiding sympathy: that is the real art of Jesuitism, which has always understood how to introduce itself as the religion of sympathy.

*　*　*　*　*

However gratefully one may welcome the *objective* spirit—and who has not been sick to death of all subjectivity and its confounded *ipsissimosity!*—in the end, however, one must learn caution even with regard to one's gratitude, and put a stop to the exaggeration with which the unselfing and depersonalising of the spirit has recently been celebrated, as if it were the goal in itself, as if it were salvation and glorification—as is especially accustomed to happen in the pessimist school, which has also in its turn good reasons for paying the highest honours to "disinterested knowledge." The objective man, who no longer curses and scolds like the pessimist, the *ideal* man of learning in whom the scientific instinct blossoms forth fully after a thousand complete and partial failures, is assuredly one of the most costly instruments that exist, but his place is in the hand of one who is more powerful. He is only an instrument; we may say, he is a *mirror*—he is no "purpose in himself." The objective man is in truth a mirror: accustomed to prostration before everything that wants to be known, with such desires only as knowing or "reflecting" imply—he waits until something comes, and then expands himself sensitively, so that even the light footsteps and gliding past of spiritual beings may not be lost on his surface and film. Whatever "personality" he still possesses seems to him accidental, arbitrary, or still oftener, disturbing; so much has he come to regard himself as the passage and reflection of outside forms and events. He calls up the recollection of "himself" with an effort, and not infrequently wrongly; he readily confounds himself with other persons, he makes mistakes with regard to his own needs, and here only is he unrefined and negligent. Perhaps he is troubled about the health, or the pettiness and confined atmosphere of wife and friend, or the lack of companions and society—indeed, he sets himself to reflect on his suffering, but in vain! His thoughts already rove away to the *more general* case, and to-morrow he knows as little as he knew yesterday how to help himself. He does not now take himself seriously and devote time to himself: he is serene, *not* from lack of trouble, but from lack of capacity for grasping and dealing with *his* trouble. The habitual complaisance with respect to all objects and experiences, the radiant and impartial hospitality with which he receives everything that comes his way, his habit of inconsiderate good-nature, of dangerous indifference as to Yea and Nay: alas! there are enough of cases in which he has to atone for these virtues of his!— and as man generally, he becomes far too easily the *caput mortuum* of such virtues. Should one wish love or hatred from him—I mean love and hatred as God, woman, and animal understand them—he will do what he can, and furnish what he can. But one must not be surprised if it should not be much —if he should show himself just at this point to be false, fragile, questionable, and deteriorated. His love is constrained, his hatred is artificial, and rather *un tour de force,* a slight ostentation and exaggeration. He is only genuine so far as he can be objective; only in his serene totality is he still "nature" and "natural." His mirroring and eternally self-polishing soul no longer knows how to affirm, no longer how to deny; he does not command; neither does he destroy. *"Je ne méprise presque rien"*—he says, with Leibnitz: let us not overlook nor undervalue the *presque!* Neither is he a model man; he does not go in advance of any one, nor after either; he places himself generally too far off to have any reason for espousing the cause of either

good or evil. If he has been so long confounded with the *philosopher,* with
the Cæsarean trainer and dictator of civilisation, he has had far too much
honour, and what is most essential in him has been overlooked—he is an
instrument, something of a slave, though certainly the sublimest sort of
slave, but nothing in himself—*presque rien!* The objective man is an instrument, a costly, easily injured, easily tarnished, measuring instrument and
mirroring apparatus, which is to be taken care of and respected; but he is
no goal, no outgoing nor upgoing, no complementary man in whom the
rest of existence justifies itself, no termination—and still less a commence-
ment, an engendering, or primary cause, nothing hardy, powerful, self-
centred, that wants to be master; but rather only a soft, inflated, delicate,
movable potter's-form, that must wait for some kind of content and frame to
"shape" itself thereto—for the most part a man without frame and content, a
"selfless" man. Consequently, also, nothing for women, *in parenthesi.* . . .

* * * *

I insist upon it that people finally cease confounding philosophical
workers, and in general scientific men, with philosophers—that precisely
here one should strictly give "each his own," and not give those far too much,
these far too little. It may be necessary for the education of the real
philosopher that he himself should have once stood upon all those steps upon
which his servants, the scientific workers of philosophy, remain standing,
and *must* remain standing: he himself must perhaps have been critic, and
dogmatist, and historian, and besides, poet, and collector, and traveller, and
riddle-reader, and moralist, and seer, and "free spirit," and almost everything,
in order to traverse the whole range of human values and estimations, and
that he may *be able* with a variety of eyes and consciences to look from a
height to any distance, from a depth up to any height, from a nook into
any expanse. But all these are only preliminary conditions for his task; this
task itself demands something else—it requires him *to create values.* The
philosophical workers, after the excellent pattern of Kant and Hegel, have to
fix and formalise some great existing body of valuations—that is to say,
former *determinations of value,* creations of value, which have become prevalent, and are for a time called "truths"—whether in the domain of the
logical, the *political* (moral), or the *artistic.* It is for these investigators to
make whatever has happened and been esteemed hitherto, conspicuous, conceivable, intelligible, and manageable, to shorten everything long, even
"time" itself, and to *subjugate* the entire past: an immense and wonderful
task, in the carrying out of which all refined pride, all tenacious will, can
surely find satisfaction. *The real philosophers, however, are commanders and
lawgivers;* they say: "Thus *shall* it be!" They determine first the Whither
and the Why of mankind, and thereby set aside the previous labour of all

philosophical workers, and all subjugators of the past—they grasp at the future with a creative hand, and whatever is and was, becomes for them thereby a means, an instrument, and a hammer. Their "knowing" is *creating,* their creating is a law-giving, their will to truth is—*Will to Power.*—Are there at present such philosophers? Have there ever been such philosophers? *Must* there not be such philosophers some day? . . .

THE AMERICAN SCHOLAR

Ralph Waldo Emerson

M R. PRESIDENT and Gentlemen, I greet you on the recommencement of our literary year. Our anniversary is one of hope, and, perhaps, not enough of labor. We do not meet for games of strength or skill, for the recitation of histories, tragedies, and odes, like the ancient Greeks; for parliaments of love and poesy, like the Troubadours; nor for the advancement of science, like our contemporaries in the British and European capitals. Thus far, our holiday has been simply a friendly sign of the survival of the love of letters amongst a people too busy to give to letters any more. As such it is precious as the sign of an indestructible instinct. Perhaps the time is already come when it ought to be, and will be, something else; when the sluggard intellect of this continent will look from under its iron lids and fill the postponed expectation of the world with something better than the exertions of mechanical skill. Our day of dependence, our long apprenticeship to the learning of other lands, draws to a close. The millions that around us are rushing into life, cannot always be fed on the sere remains of foreign harvests. Events, actions arise, that must be sung, that will sing themselves. Who can doubt that poetry will revive and lead in a new age, as the star in the constellation Harp, which now flames in our zenith, astronomers announce, shall one day be the pole-star for a thousand years?

In this hope I accept the topic which not only usage but the nature of our association seem to prescribe to this day—the AMERICAN SCHOLAR. Year by year we come up hither to read one more chapter of his biography. Let us inquire what light new days and events have thrown on his character and his hopes.

It is one of those fables which out of an unknown antiquity convey an unlooked-for wisdom, that the gods, in the beginning, divided Man into men, that he might be more helpful to himself; just as the hand was divided into fingers, the better to answer its end.

The old fable covers a doctrine ever new and sublime; that there is One Man—present to all particular men only partially, or through one faculty; and that you must take the whole society to find the whole man. Man is

An oration delivered before the Phi Beta Kappa Society at Cambridge, August 31, 1837.

not a farmer, or a professor, or an engineer, but he is all. Man is priest, and scholar, and statesman, and producer, and soldier. In the *divided* or social state these functions are parcelled out to individuals, each of whom aims to do his stint of the joint work, whilst each other performs his. The fable implies that the individual, to possess himself, must sometimes return from his own labor to embrace all the other laborers. But, unfortunately, this original unit, this fountain of power, has been so distributed to multitudes, has been so minutely subdivided and peddled out, that it is spilled into drops, and cannot be gathered. The state of society is one in which the members have suffered amputation from the trunk, and strut about so many walking monsters—a good finger, a neck, a stomach, an elbow, but never a man.

Man is thus metamorphosed into a thing, into many things. The planter, who is Man sent out into the field to gather food, is seldom cheered by any idea of the true dignity of his ministry. He sees his bushel and his cart, and nothing beyond, and sinks into the farmer, instead of Man on the farm. The tradesman scarcely ever gives an ideal worth to his work, but is ridden by the routine of his craft, and the soul is subject to dollars. The priest becomes a form; the attorney a statute-book; the mechanic a machine; the sailor a rope of the ship.

In this distribution of functions the scholar is the delegated intellect. In the right state he is *Man Thinking*. In the degenerate state, when the victim of society, he tends to become a mere thinker, or still worse, the parrot of other men's thinking.

In this view of him, as Man Thinking, the theory of his office is contained. Him Nature solicits with all her placid, all her monitory pictures; him the past instructs; him the future invites. Is not indeed every man a student, and do not all things exist for the student's behoof? And, finally, is not the true scholar the only true master? But the old oracle said, "All things have two handles: beware of the wrong one." In life, too often, the scholar errs with mankind and forfeits his privilege. Let us see him in his school, and consider him in reference to the main influences he receives.

The first in time and the first in importance of the influences upon the mind is that of nature. Every day, the sun; and, after sunset, Night and her stars. Ever the winds blow; ever the grass grows. Every day, men and women, conversing, beholding and beholden. The scholar is he of all men whom this spectacle most engages. He must settle its value in his mind. What is nature to him? There is never a beginning, there is never an end, to the inexplicable continuity of this web of God, but always circular power returning into itself. Therein it resembles his own spirit, whose beginning, whose ending, he never can find—so entire, so boundless. Far too as her splendors shine, system on system shooting like rays, upward, downward, without center, without circumference—in the mass and in the particle, Nature hastens to render account of herself to the mind. Classification begins. To the young mind every thing is individual, stands by itself. By and by, it finds how to join two things and see in them one nature; then three, then three thousand; and so, tyrannized over by its own unifying instinct, it goes on tying things together, diminishing anomalies, discovering roots running under ground whereby contrary and remote things cohere and flower out from one stem. It presently learns that since the dawn of history there has been a constant accumulation and classifying of facts. But what is classification but the perceiving that these objects are not chaotic, and are not foreign, but have a law which is also a law of the human mind? The astronomer discovers that geometry, a pure abstraction of the human mind, is the measure of planetary motion. The chemist finds proportions and intelligible method throughout matter; and science is nothing but the finding of analogy, identity, in the most remote parts. The ambitious soul sits down before each refractory fact; one after another reduces all strange constitutions, all new powers, to their class and their law, and goes on forever to animate the last fibre of organization, the outskirts of nature, by insight.

Thus to him, to this school-boy under the bending dome of day, is suggested that he and it proceed from one root; one is leaf and one is flower; relation, sympathy, stirring in every vein. And what is that root? Is not that the soul of his soul? A thought too bold; a dream too wild. Yet when this spiritual light shall have revealed the law of more earthly natures —when he has learned to worship the soul, and to see that the natural philosophy that now is, is only the first gropings of its gigantic hand, he shall look forward to an ever expanding knowledge as to a becoming creator. He shall see that nature is the opposite of the soul, answering to it part for part. One is seal and one is print. Its beauty is the beauty of his own mind. Its laws are the laws of his own mind. Nature then becomes to him the measure of his attainments. So much of nature as he is ignorant of, so much of his own mind does he not yet possess. And, in fine, the ancient precept, "Know thyself," and the modern precept, "Study nature," become at last one maxim.

The next great influence into the spirit of the scholar is the mind of the Past—in whatever form, whether of literature, of art, of institutions, that mind is inscribed. Books are the best type of the influence of the past, and perhaps we shall get at the truth—learn the amount of this influence more conveniently—by considering their value alone.

The theory of books is noble. The scholar of the first age received into him the world around; brooded thereon; gave it the new arrangement of his own mind, and uttered it again. It came into him life; it went out from him truth. It came to him short-lived actions; it went out from him immortal thoughts. It came to him business; it went from him poetry. It was dead fact; now, it is quick thought. It can stand, and it can go. It now endures, it now flies, it now inspires. Precisely in proportion to the depth of mind from which it issued, so high does it soar, so long does it sing.

Or, I might say, it depends on how far the process had gone, of transmuting life into truth. In proportion to the completeness of the distillation, so will the purity and imperishableness of the product be. But none is quite perfect. As no air-pump can by any means make a perfect vacuum, so neither can any artist entirely exclude the conventional, the local, the perishable from his book, or write a book of pure thought, that shall be as efficient, in all respects, to a remote posterity, as to contemporaries, or rather to the second age. Each age, it is found, must write its own books; or rather, each generation for the next succeeding. The books of an older period will not fit this.

Yet hence arises a grave mischief. The sacredness which attaches to the act of creation, the act of thought, is transferred to the record. The poet chanting was felt to be a divine man: henceforth the chant is divine also. The writer was a just and wise spirit: henceforward it is settled the book is perfect; as love of the hero corrupts into worship of his statue. Instantly the book becomes noxious: the guide is a tyrant. The sluggish and perverted mind of the multitude, slow to open to the incursions of Reason, having once so opened, having once received this book, stands upon it, and makes an outcry if it is disparaged. Colleges are built on it. Books are written on it by thinkers, not by Man Thinking; by men of talent, that is, who start wrong, who set out from accepted dogmas, not from their own sight of principles. Meek young men grow up in libraries, believing it their duty to accept the views which Cicero, which Locke, which Bacon, have given; forgetful that Cicero, Locke, and Bacon were only young men in libraries when they wrote these books.

Hence, instead of Man Thinking, we have the bookworm. Hence the book-learned class, who value books, as such; not as related to nature and the human constitution, but as making a sort of Third Estate with the world and the soul. Hence the restorers of readings, the emendators, the bibliomaniacs of all degrees.

Books are the best of things, well used; abused, among the worst. What is the right use? What is the one end which all means go to effect? They are for nothing but to inspire. I had better never see a book than to be warped by its attraction clean out of my own orbit, and made a satellite instead of a system. The one thing in the world, of value, is the active soul. This every man is entitled to; this every man contains within him, although in almost all men obstructed, and as yet unborn. The soul active sees absolute truth and utters truth, or creates. In this action it is genius; not the privilege of here and there a favorite, but the sound estate of every man. In its essence it is progressive. The book, the college, the school of art, the institution of any kind, stop with some past utterance of genius. This is good, say they,—let us hold by this. They pin me down. They look backward and not forward. But genius looks forward: the eyes of man are set in his forehead, not in his hindhead: man hopes: genius creates. Whatever talents may be, if the man create not, the pure efflux of the Deity is not his—cinders and smoke there may be, but not yet flame. There are creative manners, there are creative actions, and creative words; manners, actions, words, that is, indicative of no custom or authority, but springing spontaneous from the mind's own sense of good and fair.

On the other part, instead of being its own seer, let it receive from another mind its truth, though it were in torrents of light, without periods of solitude, inquest, and self-recovery, and a fatal disservice is done. Genius is always sufficiently the enemy of genius by over-influence. The literature of every nation bears me witness. The English dramatic poets have Shakespearized now for two hundred years.

Undoubtedly there is a right way of reading, so it be sternly subordinated. Man Thinking must not be subdued by his instruments. Books are for the scholar's idle times. When he can read God directly, the hour is too precious to be wasted in other men's transcripts of their readings. But when the intervals of darkness come, as come they must—when the sun is hid and the stars withdraw their shining—we repair to the lamps which were kindled by their ray, to guide our steps to the East again, where the dawn is. We hear, that we may speak. The Arabian proverb says, "A fig tree, looking on a fig tree, becometh fruitful."

It is remarkable, the character of the pleasure we derive from the best books. They impress us with the conviction that one nature wrote and the same reads. We read the verses of one of the great English poets, of Chaucer, of Marvell, of Dryden, with the most modern joy—with a pleasure, I mean, which is in great part caused by the abstraction of all *time* from their verses. There is some awe mixed with the joy of our surprise, when this poet, who lived in some past world, two or three hundred years ago, says that which lies close to my own soul, that which I also had well-nigh thought and said. But for the evidence thence afforded to the philosophical doctrine of the identity of all minds, we should suppose some pre-established harmony, some foresight of souls that were to be, and some preparation of stores for their future wants, like the fact observed in insects, who lay up food before death for the young grub they shall never see.

I would not be hurried by any love of system, by any exaggeration of instincts, to underrate the Book. We all know, that as the human body can be nourished on any food, though it were boiled grass and the broth of shoes, so the human mind can be fed by any knowledge. And great and heroic men have existed who had almost no other information than by the printed page. I only would say that it needs a strong head to bear that diet. One must be an inventor to read well. As the proverb says, "He that would bring home the wealth of the Indies, must carry out the wealth of the Indies." There is then creative reading as well as creative writing. When the mind is braced by labor and invention, the page of whatever book we read becomes luminous with manifold allusion. Every sentence is doubly significant, and the sense of our author is as broad as the world. We then see, what is always true, that as the seer's hour of vision is short and rare among heavy days and months, so is its record, perchance, the least part of his volume. The discerning will read, in his Plato or Shakespeare, only that least part—only the authentic utterances of the oracle—all the rest he rejects, were it never so many times Plato's and Shakespeare's.

Of course there is a portion of reading quite indispensable to a wise man. History and exact science he must learn by laborious reading. Colleges, in like manner, have their indispensable office—to teach elements. But they can only highly serve us when they aim not to drill, but to create; when they gather from far every ray of various genius to their hospitable halls, and by the concentrated fires, set the hearts of their youth on flame. Thought and knowledge are natures in which apparatus and pretension avail nothing. Gowns and pecuniary foundations, though of towns of gold, can never countervail the least sentence or syllable of wit. Forget this, and our American colleges will recede in their public importance, whilst they grow richer every year.

There goes in the world a notion that the scholar should be a recluse, a valetudinarian—as unfit for any handiwork or public labor as a penknife for an ax. The so-called "practical men" sneer at speculative men, as if, because they speculate or *see,* they could do nothing. I have heard it said that the clergy—who are always, more universally than any other class, the scholars of their day—are addressed as women; that the rough, spontaneous conversation of men they do not hear, but only a mincing and diluted speech. They are often virtually disfranchised; and indeed there are advocates for their celibacy. As far as this is true of the studious classes, it is not just and wise. Action is with the scholar subordinate, but it is essential. Without it he is not yet man. Without it thought can never ripen into truth. Whilst the world hangs before the eye as a cloud of beauty, we cannot even see its beauty. Inaction is cowardice, but there can be no scholar without the heroic mind. The preamble of thought, the transition through which it passes from the unconscious to the conscious, is action. Only so much do I know, as I have lived. Instantly we know whose words are loaded with life, and whose not.

The world—this shadow of the soul, or *other me*, lies wide around. Its attractions are the keys which unlock my thoughts and make me acquainted with myself. I run eagerly into this resounding tumult. I grasp the hands of those next me, and take my place in the ring to suffer and to work, taught by an instinct that so shall the dumb abyss be vocal with speech. I pierce its order; I dissipate its fear; I dispose of it within the circuit of my expanding life. So much only of life as I know by experience, so much of the wilderness have I vanquished and planted, or so far have I extended my being, my dominion. I do not see how any man can afford, for the sake of his nerves and his nap, to spare any action in which he can partake. It is pearls and rubies to his discourse. Drudgery, calamity, exasperation, want, are instructors in eloquence and wisdom. The true scholar grudges every opportunity of action past by, as a loss of power.

It is the raw material out of which the intellect molds her splendid products. A strange process too, this by which experience is converted into thought, as a mulberry leaf is converted into satin. The manufacture goes forward at all hours.

The actions and events of our childhood and youth are now matters of calmest observation. They lie like fair pictures in the air. Not so with our recent actions—with the business which we now have in hand. On this we are quite unable to speculate. Our affections as yet circulate through it. We no more feel or know it than we feel the feet, or the hand, or the brain of our body. The new deed is yet a part of life—remains for a time immersed in our unconscious life. In some contemplative hour it detaches itself from the life like a ripe fruit, to become a thought of the mind. Instantly it is raised, transfigured; the corruptible has put on incorruption. Henceforth it is an object of beauty, however base its origin and neighborhood. Observe too the impossibility of antedating this act. In its grub state, it cannot fly, it cannot shine, it is a dull grub. But suddenly, without observation, the self-same thing unfurls beautiful wings, and is an angel of wisdom. So is there no fact, no event, in our private history, which shall not, sooner or later, lose its adhesive, inert form, and astonish us by soaring from our body into the empyrean. Cradle and infancy, school and playground, the fear of boys, and dogs, and ferules, the love of little maids and berries, and many another fact that once filled the whole sky, are gone already; friend and relative, profession and party, town and country, nation and world, must also soar and sing.

Of course, he who has put forth his total strength in fit actions has the richest return of wisdom. I will not shut myself out of this globe of action, and transplant an oak into a flower-pot, there to hunger and pine; nor trust the revenue of some single faculty, and exhaust one vein of thought, much like those Savoyards, who, getting their livelihood by carving shepherds, shepherdesses, and smoking Dutchmen, for all Europe, went out one day to the mountain to find stock, and discovered that they had whittled up the last of their pine trees. Authors we have, in numbers, who have written out their vein, and who, moved by a commendable prudence, sail for Greece or Palestine, follow the trapper into the prairie, or ramble round Algiers, to replenish their merchantable stock.

If it were only for a vocabulary, the scholar would be covetous of action. Life is our dictionary. Years are well spent in country labors; in town; in the insight into trades and manufactures; in frank intercourse with many men and women; in science; in art; to the one end of mastering in all their facts a language by which to illustrate and embody our perceptions. I learn immediately from any speaker how much he has already lived, through the poverty or the splendor of his speech. Life lies behind us as the quarry from whence we get tiles and copestones for the masonry of today. This is the way to learn grammar. Colleges and books only copy the language which the field and the work-yard made.

But the final value of action, like that of books, and better than books, is that it is a resource. That great principle of Undulation in nature, that shows itself in the inspiring and expiring of the breath; in desire and satiety; in the ebb and flow of the sea; in day and night; in heat and cold; and, as yet more deeply ingrained in every atom and every fluid, is known to us under the name of Polarity—these "fits of easy transmission and reflection," as Newton called them—are the law of nature because they are the law of spirit.

The mind now thinks, now acts, and each fit reproduces the other. When the artist has exhausted his materials, when the fancy no longer paints, when thoughts are no longer apprehended and books are a weariness—he has always the resource *to live*. Character is higher than intellect. Thinking is the function. Living is the functionary. The stream retreats to its source. A great soul will be strong to live, as well as strong to think. Does he lack organ or medium to impart his truth? He can still fall back on this elemental force of living them. This is a total act. Thinking is a partial act. Let the grandeur of justice shine in his affairs. Let the beauty of affection cheer his lowly roof. Those "far from fame," who dwell and act with him, will feel the force of his constitution in the doings and passages of the day better than it can be measured by any public and designed display. Time shall teach him that the scholar loses no hour which the man lives. Herein he unfolds the sacred germ of his instinct, screened from influence. What is lost in seemliness is gained in strength. Not out of those on whom systems of education have exhausted their culture, comes the helpful giant to destroy the old or to build the new, but out of unhandselled savage nature; out of terrible Druids and Berserkers come at last Alfred and Shakespeare.

I hear therefore with joy whatever is beginning to be said of the dignity and necessity of labor to every citizen. There is virtue yet in the hoe and the spade, for learned as well as for unlearned hands. And labor is everywhere welcome; always we are invited to work; only be this limitation observed, that a man shall not for the sake of wider activity sacrifice any opinion to the popular judgments and modes of action.

I have now spoken of the education of the scholar by nature, by books, and by action. It remains to say somewhat of his duties.

They are such as become Man Thinking. They may all be comprised in self-trust. The office of the scholar is to cheer, to raise, and to guide men by showing them facts amidst appearances. He plies the slow, unhonored, and unpaid task of observation. Flamsteed and Herschel, in their glazed observatories, may catalogue the stars with the praise of all men, and the results being splendid and useful, honor is sure. But he, in his private observatory, cataloguing obscure and nebulous stars of the human mind, which as yet no man has thought of as such—watching days and months sometimes for a few facts; correcting still his old records—must relinquish display and immediate fame. In the long period of his preparation he must betray often an ignorance and shiftlessness in popular arts, incurring the disdain of the able who shoulder him aside. Long he must stammer in his speech; often forego the living for the dead. Worse yet, he must accept—how often! poverty and solitude. For the ease and pleasure of treading the old road, accepting the fashions, the education, the religion of society, he takes the cross of making his own, and, of course, the self-accusation, the faint heart, the frequent uncertainty and loss of time, which are the nettles and tangling vines in the way of the self-relying and self-directed; and the state of virtual hostility in which he seems to stand to society, and especially to educated society. For all this loss and scorn, what offset? He is to find consolation in exercising the highest functions of human nature. He is one who raises himself from private considerations and breathes and lives on public and illustrious thoughts. He is the world's eye. He is the world's heart. He is to resist the vulgar prosperity that retrogrades ever to barbarism, by preserving and communicating heroic sentiments, noble biographies, melodious verse, and the conclusions of history. Whatsoever oracles the human heart, in all emergencies, in all solemn hours, has uttered as its commentary on the world of actions—these he shall receive and impart. And whatsoever new verdict Reason from her inviolable seat pronounces on the passing men and events of today—this he shall hear and promulgate.

These being his functions, it becomes him to feel all confidence in himself, and to defer never to the popular cry. He and he only knows the world. The world of any moment is the merest appearance. Some great decorum, some fetish of a government, some ephemeral trade, or war, or man, is cried up by half mankind and cried down by the other half, as if all depended on this particular up or down. The odds are that the whole question is not worth the poorest thought which the scholar has lost in listening to the controversy. Let him not quit his belief that a popgun is a popgun, though the ancient and honorable of the earth affirm it to be the crack of doom. In silence, in steadiness, in severe abstraction, let him hold by himself; add observation to observation, patient of neglect, patient of reproach, and bide his own time—happy enough if he can satisfy himself alone that this day he has seen something truly. Success treads on every right step. For the instinct is sure, that prompts him to tell his brother what he thinks. He then learns that in going down into the secrets of his own mind he has descended into the secrets of all minds. He learns that he who has mastered any law in his private thoughts, is master to that extent of all men whose language he speaks, and of all into whose language his own can be translated. The poet, in utter solitude remembering his spontaneous thoughts and recording them, is found to have recorded that which men in crowded cities find true for them also. The orator distrusts at first the fitness of his frank confessions, his want of knowledge of the persons he addresses, until he finds that he is the complement of his hearers—that they drink his words because he fulfils for them their own nature; the deeper he dives into his privatest, secretest presentiment, to his wonder he finds this is the most acceptable, most public, and universally true. The people delight in it; the better part of every man feels, This is my music; this is myself.

In self-trust all the virtues are comprehended. Free should the scholar be —free and brave. Free even to the definition of freedom, "without any hindrance that does not arise out of his own constitution." Brave; for fear is a thing which a scholar by his very function puts behind him. Fear always springs from ignorance. It is a shame to him if his tranquility, amid dangerous times, arise from the presumption that like children and women his is a protected class; or if he seek a temporary peace by the diversion of his thoughts from politics or vexed questions, hiding his head like an ostrich in the flowering bushes, peeping into microscopes, and turning rhymes, as a boy whistles to keep his courage up. So is the danger a danger still; so is the fear worse. Manlike let him turn and face it. Let him look into its eye and search its nature, inspect its origin—see the whelping of this lion—which lies no great way back; he will then find in himself a perfect comprehension of its nature and extent; he will have made his hands meet on the other side, and can henceforth defy it and pass on superior. The world is his who can see through its pretension. What deafness, what stone-blind custom, what

overgrown error you behold is there only by sufferance—by your sufferance.
See it to be a lie, and you have already dealt it its mortal blow.

Yes, we are the cowed—we the trustless. It is a mischievous notion that
we are come late into nature; that the world was finished a long time ago. As
the world was plastic and fluid in the hands of God, so it is ever to so much
of his attributes as we bring to it. To ignorance and sin, it is flint. They
adapt themselves to it as they may; but in proportion as a man has anything
in him divine, the firmament flows before him and takes his signet and form.
Not he is great who can alter matter, but he who can alter my state of mind.
They are the kings of the world who give the color of their present thought
to all nature and all art, and persuade men by the cheerful serenity of their
carrying the matter, that this thing which they do is the apple which the
ages have desired to pluck, now at last ripe, and inviting nations to the
harvest. The great man makes the great thing. Wherever Macdonald sits,
there is the head of the table. Linnæus makes botany the most alluring of
studies, and wins it from the farmer and the herb-woman; Davy, chemistry;
and Cuvier, fossils. The day is always his who works in it with serenity and
great aims. The unstable estimates of men crowd to him whose mind is
filled with a truth, as the heaped waves of the Atlantic follow the moon.

For this self-trust, the reason is deeper than can be fathomed—darker
than can be enlightened. I might not carry with me the feeling of my audience in stating my own belief. But I have already shown the ground of my
hope, in adverting to the doctrine that man is one. I believe man has been
wronged; he has wronged himself. He has almost lost the light that can
lead him back to his prerogatives. Men are become of no account. Men in
history, men in the world of today, are bugs, are spawn, and are called "the
mass" and "the herd." In a century, in a millennium, one or two men; that is
to say, one or two approximations to the right state of every man. All the
rest behold in the hero or the poet their own green and crude being—
ripened; yes, and are content to be less, so *that* may attain to its full stature.
What a testimony, full of grandeur, full of pity, is borne to the demands of
his own nature, by the poor clansman, the poor partisan, who rejoices in
the glory of his chief. The poor and the low find some amends to their
immense moral capacity, for their acquiescence in a political and social
inferiority. They are content to be brushed like flies from the path of a great
person, so that justice shall be done by him to that common nature which
it is the dearest desire of all to see enlarged and glorified. They sun themselves in the great man's light, and feel it to be their own element. They cast
the dignity of man from their downtrod selves upon the shoulders of a hero,
and will perish to add one drop of blood to make that great heart beat,
those giant sinews combat and conquer. He lives for us, and we live in him.

Men such as they are, very naturally seek money or power; and power because it is as good as money—the "spoils," so called, "of office." And why not? for they aspire to the highest, and this, in their sleep-walking, they dream is highest. Wake them and they shall quit the false good and leap to the true, and leave governments to clerks and desks. This revolution is to be wrought by the gradual domestication of the idea of Culture. The main enterprise of the world for splendor, for extent, is the upbuilding of a man. Here are the materials strewn along the ground. The private life of one man shall be a more illustrious monarchy, more formidable to its enemy, more sweet and serene in its influence to its friend, than any kingdom in history. For a man, rightly viewed, comprehendeth the particular natures of all men. Each philosopher, each bard, each actor has only done for me, as by a delegate, what one day I can do for myself. The books which once we valued more than the apple of the eye, we have quite exhausted. What is that but saying that we have come up with the point of view which the universal mind took through the eyes of one scribe; we have been that man, and have passed on. First, one, then another, we drain all cisterns, and waxing greater by all these supplies, we crave a better and more abundant food. The man has never lived that can feed us ever. The human mind cannot be enshrined in a person who shall set a barrier on any one side to this unbounded, unboundable empire. It is one central fire, which, flaming now out of the lips of Etna, lightens the capes of Sicily, and now out of the throat of Vesuvius, illuminates the towers and vineyards of Naples. It is one light which beams out of a thousand stars. It is one soul which animates all men. . . .

. . . The scholar is that man who must take up into himself all the ability of the time, all the contributions of the past, all the hopes of the future. He must be an university of knowledges. If there be one lesson more than another which should pierce his ear, it is, The world is nothing, the man is all; in yourself is the law of all nature, and you know not yet how a globule of sap ascends; in yourself slumbers the whole of Reason; it is for you to know all; it is for you to dare all. Mr. President and Gentlemen, this confidence in the unsearched might of man belongs, by all motives, by all prophecy, by all preparation, to the American Scholar. We have listened too long to the courtly muses of Europe. The spirit of the American freeman is already suspected to be timid, imitative, tame. Public and private avarice make the air we breathe thick and fat. The scholar is decent, indolent, complaisant. See already the tragic consequence. The mind of this country, taught to aim at low objects, eats upon itself. There is no work for any but the decorous and the complaisant. Young men of the fairest promise, who begin life upon our shores, inflated by the mountain winds, shined upon by all the stars of God, find the earth below not in unison with these, but are hindered from action by the disgust which the principles on which business is managed inspire, and turn drudges, or die of disgust, some of them sui-cides. What is the remedy? They did not yet see, and thousands of young men as hopeful now crowding to the barriers for the career do not yet see, that if the single man plant himself indomitably on his instincts, and there abide, the huge world will come round to him. Patience—patience; with the shades of all the good and great for company; and for solace the perspective of your own infinite life; and for work the study and the communication of principles, the making those instincts prevalent, the conversion of the world. Is it not the chief disgrace in the world, not to be an unit—not to be reckoned one character—not to yield that peculiar fruit which each man was created to bear, but to be reckoned in the gross, in the hundred, or the thousand, of the party, the section, to which we belong; and our opinion predicted geographically, as the north, or the south? Not so, brothers and friends—please God, ours shall not be so. We will walk on our own feet; we will work with our own hands; we will speak our own minds. The study of letters shall be no longer a name for pity, for doubt, and for sensual indulgence. The dread of man and the love of man shall be a wall of de-fence and a wreath of joy around all. A nation of men will for the first time exist, because each believes himself inspired by the Divine Soul which also inspires all men.

"THE GREAT THINKER" IN AMERICA

H. L. Mencken

TEN or twelve years ago, being engaged in a bombastic discussion with what was then known as an intellectual Socialist (like the rest of the *intelligentsia,* he succumbed to the first fife-corps of the war, pulled down the red flag, damned Marx as a German spy, and began whooping for Elihu Root, Otto Kahn and Abraham Lincoln), I was greatly belabored and incommoded by his long quotations from a certain Prof. Dr. Thorstein Veblen, then quite unknown to me. My antagonist manifestly attached a great deal of importance to these borrowed sagacities, for he often heaved them at me in lengths of a column or two, and urged me to read every word of them. I tried hard enough, but found it impossible going. The more I read them, in fact, the less I could make of them, and so in the end, growing impatient and impolite, I denounced this Prof. Veblen as a geyser of pishposh, refused to waste any more time upon his incomprehensible syllogisms, and applied myself to the other Socialist witnesses in the case, seeking to set fire to their shirts.

That old debate, which took place by mail (for the Socialist lived like a munitions patriot on his country estate and I was a wage-slave attached to a city newspaper), was afterward embalmed in a dull book, and made the mild pother of a day. The book, by name, "Men vs. the Man," is now as completely forgotten as Baxter's "Saint's Rest" or the Constitution of the United States. I myself, perhaps the only man who remembers it at all, have not looked into it for six or eight years, and all I can recall of my opponent's argument (beyond the fact that it not only failed to convert me to the nascent Bolshevism of the time, but left me a bitter and incurable scoffer at democracy in all its forms) is his curious respect for the aforesaid Prof. Dr. Thorstein Veblen, and his delight in the learned gentleman's long, tortuous and (to me, at least) intolerably flapdoodlish phrases.

There was, indeed, a time when I forgot even this—when my mind was empty of the professor's very name. That was, say, from 1909 or thereabout to the middle of 1917. During those years, having lost all my old superior interest in Socialism, even as an amateur psychiatrist, I ceased to read its

Reprinted from *Prejudices; First Series* (1919), pp. 59-76, 78-82, by permission of the publisher, Alfred A. Knopf, Inc. Title supplied by the Editor.

literature, and thus lost track of its Great Thinkers. The periodicals that I then gave an eye to, setting aside newspapers, were chiefly the familiar American imitations of the English weeklies of opinion, and in these the dominant Great Thinker was, first, the late Prof. Dr. William James, and, after his decease, Prof. Dr. John Dewey. The reign of James, as the illuminated will recall, was long and glorious. For three or four years running he was mentioned in every one of those American *Spectators* and *Saturday Reviews* at least once a week, and often a dozen times. Among the less somber gazettes of the republic, to be sure, there were other heroes: Maeterlinck, Rabindranath Tagore, Judge Ben B. Lindsey, the late Major-General Roosevelt, Tom Lawson and so on. Still further down the literary and intellectual scale there were yet others: Hall Caine, Brieux and Jack Johnson among them, with paper-bag cookery and the twilight sleep to dispute their popularity. But on the majestic level of the old *Nation,* among the white and lavender peaks of professorial ratiocination, there was scarcely a serious rival to James. Now and then, perhaps, Jane Addams had a month of vogue, and during one winter there was a rage for Bergson, and for a short space the unspeakable Bernstorff tried to set up Eucken (now damned with Wagner, Nietzsche and Ludendorff), but taking one day with another James held his own against the field. His ideas, immediately they were stated, became the ideas of every pedagogue from Harvard to Leland Stanford, and the pedagogues, laboring furiously at space rates, rammed them into the skulls of the lesser *cerebelli.* To have called James an ass, during the year 1909, would have been as fatal as to have written a sentence like this one without having used so many *haves.* He died a bit later, but his ghost went marching on: it took three or four years to interpret and pigeon-hole his philosophical remains and to take down and redact his messages (via Sir Oliver Lodge, Little Brighteyes, Wah-Wah the Indian Chief, and other gifted psychics) from the spirit world. But then, gradually, he achieved the ultimate stupendous and irrevocable act of death, and there was a vacancy. To it Prof. Dr. Dewey was elected by the acclamation of all right-thinking and forward-looking men. He was an expert in pedagogics, metaphysics, psychology, ethics, logic, politics, pedagogical metaphysics, metaphysical psychology, psychological ethics, ethical logic, logical politics and political pedagogics. He was *Artium Magister, Philosophiæ Doctor* and twice *Legum Doctor.* He had written a book called "How to Think." He sat in a professor's chair and caned sophomores for blowing spit-balls. *Ergo,* he was the ideal candidate, and so he was nominated, elected and inaugurated, and for three years, more or less, he enjoyed a peaceful reign in the groves of sapience, and the inferior *umbilicarii* venerated him as they had once venerated James.

I myself greatly enjoyed and profited by the discourses of this Prof.

Dewey and was in hopes that he would last. Born so recently as 1859 and a man of the highest bearable sobriety, he seemed likely to peg along until 1935 or 1940, a gentle and charming volcano of correct thought. But it was not, alas, to be. Under cover of pragmatism, that serpent's metaphysic, there was unrest beneath the surface. Young professors in remote and obscure universities, apparently as harmless as so many convicts in the deathhouse, were secretly flirting with new and red-hot ideas. Whole regiments and brigades of them yielded in stealthy privacy to rebellious and often incomprehensible yearnings. Now and then, as if to reveal what was brewing, a hell fire blazed and a Prof. Dr. Scott Nearing went sky-hooting through its smoke. One heard whispers of strange heresies—economic, sociological, even political. Gossip had it that pedagogy was hatching vipers, nay, was already brought to bed. But not much of this got into the home-made *Saturday Reviews* and Yankee *Athenæums*—a hint or two maybe, but no more. In the main they kept to their old resolute demands for a pure civil-service, the budget system in Congress, the abolition of hazing at the Naval Academy, an honest primary and justice to the Filipinos, with extermination of the Prussian serpent added after August, 1914. And Dr. Dewey, on his remote Socratic Alp, pursued the calm reënforcement of the philosophical principles underlying these and all other lofty and indignant causes. . . .

Then, of a sudden, Siss! Boom! Ah! Then, overnight, the upspringing of the intellectual soviets, the headlong assault upon all the old axioms of pedagogical speculation, the nihilistic dethronement of Prof. Dewey—and rah, rah, rah for Prof. Dr. Thorstein Veblen! Veblen? Could it be—? Aye, it was! My old acquaintance! The *Doctor obscurus* of my half-forgotten bout with the so-called intellectual Socialist! The Great Thinker *redivivus!* Here, indeed, he was again, and in a few months—almost it seemed a few days—he was all over the *Nation,* the *Dial,* the *New Republic* and the rest of them, and his books and pamphlets began to pour from the presses, and the newspapers reported his every wink and whisper, and everybody who was anybody began gabbling about him. The spectacle, I do not hesitate to say, somewhat disconcerted me and even distressed me. On the one hand, I was sorry to see so learned and interesting a man as Dr. Dewey sent back to the insufferable dungeons of Columbia, there to lecture in imperfect Yiddish to classes of Grand Street Platos. And on the other hand, I shrunk supinely from the appalling job, newly rearing itself before me, of re-reading the whole canon of the singularly laborious and muggy, the incomparably tangled and unintelligible works of Prof. Dr. Thorstein Veblen. . . .

But if a sense of duty tortures a man, it also enables him to achieve prodigies, and so I managed to get through the whole infernal job. I read "The Theory of the Leisure Class," I read "The Theory of Business Enterprise," and then I read "The Instinct of Workmanship." An hiatus followed;

I was racked by a severe neuralgia, with delusions of persecution. On recovering I tackled "Imperial Germany and the Industrial Revolution." Malaria for a month, and then "The Nature of Peace and the Terms of Its Perpetuation." What ensued was never diagnosed; probably it was some low infection of the mesentery or spleen. When it passed off, leaving only an asthmatic cough, I read "The Higher Learning in America," and then went to Mt. Clemens to drink the Glauber's salts. Eureka! the business was done! It had strained me, but now it was over. Alas, a good part of the agony had been needless. What I found myself aware of, coming to the end, was that practically the whole system of Prof. Dr. Veblen was in his first book and his last—that is, in "The Theory of the Leisure Class," and "The Higher Learning in America." I pass on the good news. Read these two, and you won't have to read the others. And if even two daunt you, then read the first. Once through it, though you will have missed many a pearl and many a pain, you will have a fairly good general acquaintance with the gifted metaphysician's ideas.

For those ideas, in the main, are quite simple, and often anything but revolutionary in essence. What is genuinely remarkable about them is not their novelty, or their complexity, nor even the fact that a professor should harbor them; it is the astoundingly grandiose and rococo manner of their statement, the almost unbelievable tediousness and flatulence of the gifted headmaster's prose, his unprecedented talent for saying nothing in an august and heroic manner. There are tales of an actress of the last generation, probably Sarah Bernhardt, who could put pathos and even terror into a recitation of the multiplication table. The late Louis James did something of the sort; he introduced limericks into "Peer Gynt" and still held the yokelry agape. The same talent, raised to a high power, is in this Prof. Dr. Veblen. Tunnel under his great moraines and stalagmites of words, dig down into his vast kitchen-midden of discordant and raucous polysyllables, blow up the hard, thick shell of his almost theological manner, and what you will find in his discourse is chiefly a mass of platitudes—the self-evident made horrifying, the obvious in terms of the staggering. Marx, I daresay, said a good deal of it, and what Marx overlooked has been said over and over again by his heirs and assigns. But Marx, at this business, labored under a technical handicap: he wrote in German, a language he actually understood. Prof. Dr. Veblen submits himself to no such disadvantage. Though born, I believe, in These States, and resident here all his life, he achieves the effect, perhaps without employing the means, of thinking in some unearthly foreign language—say Swahili, Sumerian or Old Bulgarian—and then painfully clawing his thoughts into a copious but uncertain and book-learned English. The result is a style that affects the higher cerebral centers like a constant roll of subway expresses. The second result is a sort of bewildered numbness of the senses, as before some fabulous and unearthly marvel. And the third result, if I make no mistake, is the celebrity of the professor as a Great Thinker. In brief, he states his hollow nothings in such high, astounding terms that they must inevitably arrest and blister the right-thinking mind. He makes them mysterious. He makes them shocking. He makes them portentous. And so, flinging them at naïve and believing minds, he makes them stick and burn.

No doubt you think that I exaggerate—perhaps even that I lie. If so, then consider this specimen—the first paragraph of Chapter XIII of "The Theory of the Leisure Class":

In an increasing proportion as time goes on, the anthropomorphic cult, with its code of devout observances, suffers a progressive disintegration through the stress of economic exigencies and the decay of the system of status. As this disintegration proceeds, there come to be associated and blended with the devout attitude certain other motives and impulses that are not always of an anthropomorphic origin, nor traceable to the habit of personal subservience. Not all of these subsidiary impulses that blend with the bait of devoutness in the later devotional life are altogether congruous with the devout attitude or with the anthropomorphic apprehension of sequence of phenomena. Their origin being not the same, their action upon the scheme of devout life is also not in the same direction. In many ways they traverse the underlying norm of subservience or vicarious life to which the code of devout observances and the ecclesiastical and sacerdotal institutions are to be traced as their substantial basis. Through the presence of these alien motives the social and industrial régime of status gradually disintegrates, and the canon of personal subservience loses the support derived from an unbroken tradition. Extraneous habits and proclivities encroach upon the field of action occupied by this canon, and it presently comes about that the ecclesiastical and sacerdotal structures are partially converted to other uses, in some measure alien to the purposes of the scheme of devout life as it stood in the days of the most vigorous and characteristic development of the priesthood.

Well, what have we here? What does this appalling salvo of rhetorical artillery signify? What is the sweating professor trying to say? What is his Message now? Simply that in the course of time, the worship of God is commonly corrupted by other enterprises, and that the church, ceasing to be a mere temple of adoration, becomes the headquarters of these other enterprises. More simply still, that men sometimes vary serving God by serving other men, which means, of course, serving themselves. This bald platitude, which must be obvious to any child who has ever been to a church bazaar or a parish house, is here tortured, worried and run through rollers until it is spread out to 241 words, of which fully 200 are unnecessary. The next paragraph is even worse. In it the master undertakes to explain in his peculiar dialect the meaning of "that non-reverent sense of æsthetic congruity with the environment which is left as a residue of the latter-day act of worship after elimination of its anthropomorphic content." Just what does he mean by this "non-reverent sense of æsthetic congruity"? I have studied the whole paragraph for three days, halting only for prayer and sleep, and I have come to certain conclusions. I may be wrong, but nevertheless it is the best that I can do. What I conclude is this: he is trying to say that many people go to church, not because they are afraid of the devil but because they enjoy the music, and like to look at the stained glass, the potted lilies and the rev. pastor. To get this profound and highly original observation upon paper, he wastes, not merely 241, but more than 300 words! To say what might be said on a postage stamp he takes more than a page in his book! . . .

And so it goes, alas, alas, in all his other volumes—a cent's worth of information wrapped in a bale of polysyllables. In "The Higher Learning in America" the thing perhaps reaches its damnedest and worst. It is as if the practice of that incredibly obscure and malodorous style were a relentless disease, a sort of progressive intellectual diabetes, a leprosy of the horse sense. Words are flung upon words until all recollection that there must be a meaning in them, a ground and excuse for them, is lost. One wanders in a labyrinth of nouns, adjectives, verbs, pronouns, adverbs, prepositions, conjunctions and participles, most of them swollen and nearly all of them unable to walk. It is difficult to imagine worse English, within the limits of intelligible grammar. It is clumsy, affected, opaque, bombastic, windy, empty. It is without grace or distinction and it is often without the most elementary order. The learned professor gets himself enmeshed in his gnarled sentences like a bull trapped by barbed wire, and his efforts to extricate himself are quite as furious and quite as spectacular. He heaves, he leaps, he writhes; at times he seems to be at the point of yelling for the police. It is a picture to bemuse the vulgar and to give the judicious grief.

Worse, there is nothing at the bottom of all this strident wind-music— the ideas it is designed to set forth are, in the overwhelming main, poor ideas, and often they are ideas that are almost idiotic. One never gets the thrill of sharp and original thinking, dexterously put into phrases. The concepts underlying, say, "The Theory of the Leisure Class" are simply Socialism and water; the concepts underlying "The Higher Learning in America" are so childishly obvious that even the poor drudges who write editorials for newspapers have often voiced them. When, now and then, the professor tires of this emission of stale bosh and attempts flights of a more original character, he straightway comes tumbling down into absurdity. What the reader then has to struggle with is not only intolerably bad writing, but also loose, flabby, cocksure and preposterous thinking. . . . Again I take refuge in an example. It is from Chapter IV of "The Theory of the Leisure Class." The problem before the author here has to do with the social convention which frowns upon the consumption of alcohol by women—at least to the extent to which men may consume it decorously. Well, then, what is his explanation of this convention? Here, in brief, is his process of reasoning:

1. The leisure class, which is the predatory class of feudal times, reserves all luxuries for itself, and disapproves their use by members of the lower classes, for this use takes away their charm by taking away their exclusive possession.

2. Women are chattels in the possession of the leisure class, and hence subject to the rules made for inferiors. "The patriarchal tradition . . . says that the woman, being a chattel, should consume only what is necessary to her sustenance, except so far as her further consumption contributes to the comfort or the good repute of her master."

3. The consumption of alcohol contributes nothing to the comfort or good repute of the woman's master, but "detracts sensibly from the comfort or pleasure" of her master. *Ergo,* she is forbidden to drink.

This, I believe, is a fair specimen of the Veblenian ratiocination. Observe it well, for it is typical. That is to say, it starts off with a gratuitous and highly dubious assumption, proceeds to an equally dubious deduction, and then ends with a platitude which begs the whole question. What sound reason is there for believing that exclusive possession is the hall-mark of luxury? There is none that I can see. It may be true of a few luxuries, but it is certainly not true of the most familiar ones. Do I enjoy a decent bath because I know that John Smith cannot afford one—or because I delight in being clean? Do I admire Beethoven's Fifth Symphony because it is incomprehensible to Congressmen and Methodists—or because I genuinely love music? Do I prefer terrapin á la Maryland to fried liver because plowhands must put up with the liver—or because the terrapin is intrinsically a more charming dose? Do I prefer kissing a pretty girl to kissing a charwoman because even a janitor may kiss a charwoman—or because the pretty girl looks better, smells better and kisses better? Now and then, to be sure, the idea of exclusive possession enters into the concept of luxury. I may, if I am a bibliophile, esteem a book because it is a unique first edition. I may, if I am fond, esteem a woman because she smiles on no one else. But even here, save in a very small minority of cases, other attractions plainly enter into the matter. It pleases me to have a unique first edition, but I wouldn't care anything for a unique first edition of Robert W. Chambers or Elinor Glyn; the author must have my respect, the book must be intrinsically valuable, there must be much more to it than its mere uniqueness. And if, being fond, I glory in the exclusive smiles of a certain Miss —— or Mrs. ——, then surely my satisfaction depends chiefly upon the lady herself, and not upon my mere monopoly. Would I delight in the fidelity of the charwoman? Would it give me any joy to learn that, through a sense of duty to me, she had ceased to kiss the janitor?

Confronted by such considerations, it seems to me that there is little truth left in Prof. Dr. Veblen's theory of conspicuous consumption and conspicuous waste—that what remains of it, after it is practically applied a few times, is no more than a wraith of balderdash. In so far as it is true it is obvious. All the professor accomplishes with it is to take what every one knows and pump it up to such proportions that every one begins to doubt it. What could be plainer than his failure in the case just cited? He starts off with a platitude, and ends in absurdity. No one denies, I take it, that in a clearly limited sense, women occupy a place in the world—or, more accurately, aspire to a place in the world—that is a good deal like that of a chattel. Marriage, the goal of their only honest and permanent hopes, invades their individuality; a married woman becomes the function of another individuality. Thus the appearance she presents to the world is often the mirror of her husband's egoism. A rich man hangs his wife with expensive clothes and jewels for the same reason, among others, that he adorns his own head with a plug hat: to notify everybody that he can afford it—in brief, to excite the envy of Socialists. But he also does it, let us hope, for another and far better and more powerful reason, to wit, that she intrigues him, that he delights in her, that he loves her—and so wants to make her gaudy and happy. This reason may not appeal to Socialist sociologists. In Russia, according to an old scandal (officially endorsed by the British bureau for pulling Yankee noses) the Bolsheviki actually repudiated it as insane. Nevertheless, it continues to appeal very forcibly to the majority of normal husbands in the nations of the West, and I am convinced that it is a hundred times as potent as any other reason. The American husband, in particular, dresses his wife like a circus horse, not primarily because he wants to display his wealth upon her person, but because he is a soft and moony fellow and ever ready to yield to her desires, however preposterous. If any conception of her as a chattel were actively in him, even unconsciously, he would be a good deal less her slave. As it is, her vicarious practice of conspicuous waste commonly reaches such a development that her master himself is forced into renunciations—which brings Prof. Dr. Veblen's theory to self-destruction.

His final conclusion is as unsound as his premises. All it comes to is a plain begging of the question. Why does a man forbid his wife to drink all the alcohol she can hold? Because, he says, it "detracts sensibly from his comfort or pleasure." In other words, it detracts from his comfort and pleasure because it detracts from his comfort and pleasure. Meanwhile, the real answer is so plain that even a professor should know it. A man forbids his wife to drink too much because, deep in his secret archives, he has records of the behavior of other women who drank too much, and is eager to safeguard his wife's self-respect and his own dignity against what he knows to be certain invasion. In brief, it is a commonplace of observation, familiar to all males beyond the age of twenty-one, that once a woman is drunk the rest is a mere matter of time and place: the girl is already there. A husband, viewing this prospect, perhaps shrinks from having his chattel damaged. But let us be soft enough to think that he may also shrink from seeing humiliation, ridicule and bitter regret inflicted upon one who is under his protection, and one whose dignity and happiness are precious to him, and one whom he regards with deep and (I surely hope) lasting affection. A man's grandfather is surely not his chattel, even by the terms of the Veblen theory, and yet I am sure that no sane man would let the old gentleman go beyond a discreet cocktail or two if a bout of genuine bibbing were certain to be followed by the complete destruction of his dignity, his chastity and (if a Presbyterian) his immortal soul. . . .

So much, at least for the present, for this Prof. Dr. Thorstein Veblen, head Great Thinker to the parlor radicals, Socrates of the intellectual Greenwich Village, chief star (at least transiently) of the American *Athenæums*. I am tempted to crowd in mention of some of his other astounding theories— for example, the theory that the presence of pupils, the labor of teaching, a concern with pedagogy, is necessary to the highest functioning of a scientific investigator—a notion magnificently supported by the examples of Flexner, Ehrlich, Metchnikoff, Loeb and Carrel! I am tempted, too, to devote a thirdly to the astounding materialism, almost the downright hoggishness, of his whole system—its absolute exclusion of everything approaching an æsthetic motive. But I must leave all these fallacies and absurdities to your own inquiry. More important than any of them, more important as a phenomenon than the professor himself and all his works, is the gravity with which his muddled and highly dubious ideas have been received. At the moment, I daresay, he is in decline; such Great Thinkers have a way of going out as quickly as they come in. But a year or so ago he dominated the American scene. All the reviews were full of his ideas. A hundred lesser sages reflected them. Every one of intellectual pretensions read his books. Veblenism was shining in full brilliance. There were Veblenists, Veblen clubs, Veblen remedies for all the sorrows of the world. There were even, in Chicago, Veblen Girls—perhaps Gibson girls grown middle-aged and despairing.

The spectacle, unluckily, was not novel. Go back through the history of America since the early nineties, and you will find a long succession of just such violent and uncritical enthusiasms. James had his day; Dewey had his day; Ibsen had his day; Maeterlinck had his day. Almost every year sees another intellectual Munyon arise, with his infallible peruna for all the current malaises. Sometimes this Great Thinker is imported. Once he was Pastor Wagner; once he was Bergson; once he was Eucken; once he was Tolstoi; once he was a lady, by name Ellen Key; again he was another lady, Signorina Montessori. But more often he is of native growth, and full of the pervasive cocksureness and superficiality of the land. I do not rank Dr. Veblen among the worst of these haruspices, save perhaps as a stylist; I am actually convinced that he belongs among the best of them. But that best is surely depressing enough. What lies behind it is the besetting intellectual sin of the United States—the habit of turning intellectual concepts into emotional concepts, the vice of orgiastic and inflammatory thinking. There is, in America, no orderly and thorough working out of the fundamental problems of our society; there is only, as one Englishman has said, an eternal combat of crazes. The things of capital importance are habitually discussed, not by men soberly trying to get at the truth about them, but by brummagem Great Thinkers trying only to get *kudos* out of them. We are beset endlessly by quacks—and they are not the less quacks when they happen to be quite honest. In all fields, from politics to pedagogics and from theology to public hygiene, there is a constant emotional obscuration of the true issues, a violent combat of credulities, an inane debasement of scientific curiosity to the level of mob gaping.

The thing to blame, of course, is our lack of an intellectual aristocracy—sound in its information, skeptical in its habit of mind, and, above all, secure in its position and authority. Every other civilized country has such an aristocracy. It is the natural corrective of enthusiasms from below. It is hospitable to ideas, but as adamant against crazes. It stands against the pollution of logic by emotion, the sophistication of evidence to the glory of God. But in America there is nothing of the sort. On the one hand there is the populace—perhaps more powerful here, more capable of putting its idiotic ideas into execution, than anywhere else—and surely more eager to follow platitudinous messiahs. On the other hand there is the ruling plutocracy—ignorant, hostile to inquiry, tyrannical in the exercise of its power, suspicious of ideas of whatever sort. In the middle ground there is little save an indistinct herd of intellectual eunuchs, chiefly professors—often quite as stupid as the plutocracy and always in great fear of it. When it produces a stray rebel he goes over to the mob; there is no place for him within his own order. This feeble and vacillating class, unorganized and without authority, is responsible for what passes as the well-informed opinion of the country—for the sort of opinion that one encounters in the serious periodicals —for what later on leaks down, much diluted, into the few newspapers that are not frankly imbecile. Dr. Veblen has himself described it in "The Higher Learning in America"; he is one of its characteristic products, and he proves that he is thoroughly of it by the timorousness he shows in that book. It is, in the main, only half-educated. It lacks experience of the world, assurance, the consciousness of class solidarity and security. Of no definite position in our national life, exposed alike to the clamors of the mob and the discipline of the plutocracy, it gets no public respect and is deficient in self-respect.

Thus the better sort of men are not tempted to enter it. It recruits only men of feeble courage, men of small originality. Its sublimest flower is the American college president, well described by Dr. Veblen—a perambulating sycophant and platitudinarian, a gaudy mendicant and bounder, engaged all his life, not in the battle of ideas, the pursuit and dissemination of knowledge, but in the courting of rich donkeys and the entertainment of mobs. . . .

Nay, Veblen is not the worst. Veblen is almost the best. The worst is— but I begin to grow indignant, and indignation, as old Friedrich used to say, is foreign to my nature.

THE SOCIAL ROLE OF THE MAN OF KNOWLEDGE

Florian Znaniecki

... N OT ONLY does the role of the secular scholar differ essentially from that of the religious scholar but there are several distinct varieties within the general class of secular scholars. It will be best to consider each of these varieties separately, though of course some of them may be found combined in the life of the same individual.

THE DISCOVERER OF TRUTH. Every secular school of knowledge, whether it originates outside all sacred schools or branches off from a sacred school as a more or less independent outgrowth, begins with an individual discovery. A man discovers a truth or a complex of truths, hitherto unknown, which he claims to be absolute and fundamental to all knowledge in general or to a particular domain of knowledge. If he finds followers who accept his discovery and transmit it to others, he becomes the initiator of a new school. Perhaps the truths he has discovered, though regarded as absolute, will be found insufficient as a basis for the total knowledge of the school, in which case another discoverer supplements them. Aristotle is, of course, the greatest example in history of a discoverer of absolute truths who has been recognized as an initiator of schools in three different civilizations. Other familiar examples are: Pythagoras, Parmenides, Plato, Zeno the Stoic, Epicure, Occam, Descartes, Kant, and Hegel in general knowledge; Hippocrates and Galen in medicine; Ptolemy, Copernicus, and Kepler in astronomy; Galilei and Newton in physics; Lavoisier in chemistry; Buffon in zoölogy; Linnaeus in botany; Fechner and Freud in psychology.

A reservation must be made, however, when speaking of modern scientists. Many of them had no intention of becoming scholars; on the contrary, they started as rebels against the scholarly learning of their times. But they found no ready social pattern into which they could fit except that of secular scholarship. We shall see later how slow and difficult has been the development of a new pattern of scientists' roles and how little this pattern is

Reprinted from *The Social Role of the Man of Knowledge* (1940), pp. 116-120, 122-124, 127-130, 135-139, 148-151, 169-174, 178-180, 185-186, by permission of the publisher, Columbia University Press.

understood and recognized in wider social circles even now. Consequently, inasmuch as they did claim to have discovered fundamental and absolutely valid truths and did collect disciples who in turn transmitted by teaching the knowledge based on those truths, their status and function came to be regarded as essentially similar to those of earlier initiators of secular scholarship. The acceptance of a new theory for transmission in universities and other institutions of higher learning still remains the chief and final test of its social approval.

How could an individual's discovery be accepted as valid—especially in the early days of the secularization of scholarship—if it implicitly ignored or even explicitly opposed the claim of sacred schools that the knowledge of which they were the bearers, coming as it did from divine revelation or inspiration, was the only absolutely true knowledge? Neither the pragmatic usefulness of the technologist nor the socially prejudiced wisdom of the worldly sage could compare with this supreme standard of validity. That the secular discoverer's position was regarded as somewhat doubtful at first is shown by the frequent attempts of his disciples to raise his standing by proclaiming his original connection with some sacred school; thus, Thales, Pythagoras, and later Plato were said to have acquired their knowledge in the old sacred schools of the East.

Of course, the individual could claim that he had obtained his knowledge directly from the original divine source by exclusive revelation or personal inspiration. Some of the "discoverers of truth" did make such claims, among them Xenophanes, Parmenides, Socrates, Plotinus, at times even Plato. But such a claim alone would put the discoverer below the level of the sacred scholar, in the same line as the prophet whose revelation is accepted by the people not for theoretic reasons but only because of popular faith in his personal sanctity, his "mana," whereas the sacred school has risen far above such uncritical belief and will not accept anybody's alleged revelation without investigating its content and determining its significance from the point of view of its agreement with the entire body of established knowledge.

The discoverer of truth must find a new standard of theoretic validity, a standard that can successfully compete in social recognition not only with the popular prestige of the prophet but with the age-old authority of the sacred school as a social group of men who have specialized in the cultivation of absolute knowledge. It has to be a standard that makes possible the recognition of an isolated individual as a bearer of superindividual, objectively and uncontrovertibly certain truth, raised like sacred lore above technical applications and social currents. It must be a standard immanent in the truth itself and thus independent of all external, nonscientific support, accessible to everybody capable of understanding the truth.

Such a standard was evolved indeed by secular Greek scholars and has since been perfected. It is the standard of *evident rational certainty* or, briefly, of *rational evidence*. Perhaps the school of Elea was the first to apply it thoroughly and consistently and also to distinguish fully between rational evidence, as the ultimate objective criterion of absolutely certain truth, and empirical evidence which, however convincing it may seem, must be rejected if it conflicts with the former—as Zeno of Elea in his famous arguments rejects the empirical evidence which leads us to assume the reality of movement.

Rationally evident knowledge, according to scholarly epistemology, is absolutely objective, not only superindividual but supersocial. Every thinking being who has become aware of a rationally evident truth is compelled by inner necessity to recognize it as absolutely valid, even if his traditional beliefs condemn it, his social prejudices make him wish it were false, his practical interests cause it to seem irrelevant, and his senses suggest to him conflicting representations. Any opinion which disagrees with such a truth, however old and widely spread, must be erroneous, no matter what the personal prestige or the group authority of those who support it. . . .

THE SYSTEMATIZER. No secular school can be founded without a systematizer: his is the most characteristic role in the history of scholarship. Frequently the roles of discoverer and systematizer are combined in the same personality, and the men who have combined them are the best known historically. Here again Aristotle, as founder of the Peripatetic school, is the most prominent example; but to the Mohammedan and Christian Aristotelians the old master was rather a discoverer, whereas men like Avicenna and St. Thomas performed the roles of founders of schools by a new systematization of Aristotelian doctrines in relation to the existing knowledge of their own times. Newton in the physical sciences and Hegel, Spencer, and Wundt in synthetic philosophy are other instances of the two roles of discoverer and systematizer perfectly blended. Descartes achieved only a partial systematization of his all-inclusive philosophy, leaving much for his followers to do. Similarly, Zeno, as founder of the Stoic school, seems to have only partially systematized the doctrine, since long after him a man as prolific as Chrysippus spent his life developing its various parts and aspects.

The unification of the two roles of discoverer and systematizer is an advantage to the school; for the discoverer, before achieving the task of systematization, is apt to be carried away by his enthusiasm for unknown truths and to make later discoveries which cannot always be reconciled with his earlier ones. A man who wants to found a school must know when to stop: in his function, more than in any other, *principia non sunt multiplicanda praeter necessitatem*. The fact that Plato would not stop was certainly one of the factors in the curious lack of continuity we see in the history of the Academy. From the point of view of the consistency and durability of scholarly doctrines, it is perhaps best if a famous discoverer has followers in various institutions of higher learning who develop systematically his discoveries and transmit such systematized doctrines to their disciples.

The task of the systematizer is to test the total knowledge of his epoch and civilization or—in a special school—the total existing knowledge about a certain field of reality and to organize into a system the truths that stand the test. Testing and organizing are parallel and interdependent functions. The systematizer starts with the original, evidently certain truths that have been discovered by rational insight, accepting them as absolutely *self-evident first principles* of all true knowledge in general or of all true knowledge in a particular scientific domain. Only those and all those would-be truths are valid which conform with the first principles. For any truth, conformity with the first principles means that its validity is logically implied in the self-evident rational certainty of the latter. This can be proved only by deducing the truth in question from the principles or from other truths which have been deduced from the principles. . . .

THE CONTRIBUTOR. However self-evident the principles established by the discoverer may seem, however perfectly the systematizer may have performed his task of testing and organizing existing knowledge, the school cannot rest in the security of their achievements; for any culture within which secular schools are possible is a changing culture. New generalizations are apt to be introduced at any moment by technologists, sages, disinterested thinkers and observers, or borrowers of foreign ideas. A secular school can afford to ignore such innovations even less than a sacred school, for its influence and prestige in the wider society depend exclusively on the confidence which intellectually interested outsiders have in the certainty and completeness of the knowledge of which it is a bearer. New generalizations have to be tested and, if they stand the test, incorporated into the system of the school.

A school tends to deal differently with inductive generalizations and with new "discoveries" of would-be absolute truths claiming self-evident rational certainty. The latter, especially if made by outsiders, are apt to be treated as dangerous, because they may initiate the formation of a rival school of thought; the task of defending the school against such a danger belongs to the role of "fighter for truth," which we shall analyze presently. The former has no claim to theoretic validity comparable to that of the first principles of the school or that of the truths already deduced from those principles by proper logical methods. Taken by itself as a conclusion from empirical data and judged by scholarly standards, an inductive generalization can be at best "probable" or—to use a less ambiguous and more expressive term—

"verisimilar." The only way of proving that it is "verily true" consists in reducing it logically to some more general truths already proved valid by deduction from self-evident first principles. If such a reduction is successful, the new truth becomes a component of the deductive system from which it draws indirectly rational evidence otherwise unattainable; if unsuccessful, either the system must be adapted to the inductive conclusion or the latter must be made to accord with the system. And under scholarly standards the system has indubitable superiority over any and every inductive conclusion.

Of course, it is possible that the initiators and founders of the school—who were after all only men, not pure and perfect Minds—have either failed to discover some important self-evident truth without which the system is incomplete or have erred somewhere in their deduction and included in the doctrine of the school some generalizations which did not follow logically from its principles instead of some others which ought to have been incorporated into the system. But it would need a great agglomeration of inductive "verisimilitudes" to shake the faith of the school in the system built by scientists of recognized greatness and stabilized in the process of teaching. Whenever a new inductive generalization proves irreducible to the system, it seems much more sensible to assume that whoever formulated it erred either in observing facts or in drawing conclusions from them.

It behooves a scholar, then, to correct such a generalization: to uncover mistakes and imperfections in the observations already made, to observe more exactly the same or similar facts, to study different kinds of data for comparison, to give a more adequate interpretation of the facts, to criticize and improve the method of drawing inductive conclusions. Of course, the scholar who performs such a task from the point of view of the system and in the interest of the school usually reaches a satisfactory result and substitutes instead of the original generalization, irreducible to the system, an improved generalization also empirically "verisimilar" but capable of being rationally reduced to the established truths of the system and therefore, in the light of the standards of rational evidence, indubitably true.

Such a correction and reduction of inductive generalizations, clearly shown in Plato's dialogues and widely practiced in antiquity and the late Middle Ages, was probably the beginning of a regular function supplementing in every school that of the systematizer. This function developed fully when scholars—like that great master and model of all scholarship, Aristotle —not waiting for generalizations to be thrust upon them from the outside, initiated inductive research themselves along lines deductively indicated by the system and made their new verisimilar conclusions certainly true by the reductive method. This was and still is the function of the "contributor.". . .

THE FIGHTER FOR TRUTH. At every period in the history of secular scholarship, there has been rivalry between schools representing different systems of knowledge. The struggles between philosophic schools are best known, and justly so; for they have exercised the greatest influence upon the evolution of scientific thinking in general. But similar struggles have been carried on in every special scientific field. Even after modern methodological and epistemological reflection, accompanying the steady growth of inductive research, introduced a new conception of knowledge, under which there is no place for the old type of competition between rival doctrines, such "polemics" persist in many fields along with other components of the scholarly tradition. In biology, the fights about the theory of organic evolution raged violently until quite recently; there are still several partly competing schools in medicine; psychology is divided into a number of incompatible schools; in sociology, systems of "absolute truths" brought over from psychology, biology, anthropology, geography, and even physical science are used as foundations for largely conflicting doctrines; in history, religionistics, political science, and economics the fighting goes on as in the good old times.

The diversity of scholarly systems is difficult to explain, for its main factor must be sought in the individuality of the men who built them; but a certain gradation is noticeable in the differences between particular systems. Their "first principles" may differ radically, as, for example, between spiritualism and materialism; or while agreeing on their first principles, they may disagree as to certain conclusions deductively drawn from them; or disagreement may concern the validity of certain inductive generalizations as judged by the standards of the system. However, the intensity of struggles between schools does not seem to depend upon the degree of difference between the systems which they represent: disagreement upon minor points has often stirred as prolonged and violent disputes as fundamental opposition between leading conceptions. We may even venture the hypothesis that competition for prestige and influence has been a factor in making rival schools not only exaggerate the importance of whatever differences originally separated their systems but actually increase those differences by "discovering" that disagreement on some minor point implied a fundamental and hitherto unnoticed opposition of principles.

The rivalry of schools gave birth to a specific function which consists in struggling to gain a logical victory for the doctrine of one school over those of other schools. A scholar who performs such a function may be called a "fighter for truth," since to him the doctrine of his own school is presumably the only absolutely true system within the domain of reality to which it is applied. Though, strictly speaking, this function is not essential to the positive construction and development of the system, yet as a matter of fact it has had great historical significance. Most discoverers, systematizers, and contributors have assumed from time to time the role of fighters for truth to defend their own theories and to attack the theories of their opponents; some scholars even specialized in it during periods when scientific polemics were more intensive than now. The "logical" criteria of theoretic validity and of scientific systematization which we have inherited from the past and to which most of us still render homage in our good intentions, if not in our actual thinking, have been for the greater part developed and perfected, though not initiated, by fighters for truth.

The difference is clear between a fighter for truth who wants logical victory for a system which he believes absolutely true and the partisan sage who struggles for the social victory of those active tendencies which he shares with his group and which he tries to rationalize and justify by theoretic arguments. Problems of truth and error are for genuine scholars raised unconditionally above all practical conflicts, and absolute knowledge should not be lowered to serve as an instrument for partisan ends. Scholarly fights are waged not on the open forum of public opinion but in a closed arena where only those are admitted to whom truth is the highest value.

Of course, victory or defeat does have an influence upon the social standing of the school and its members, even upon their economic status. Other, nonscientific tendencies may therefore—and often do—influence the fighters for truth; but these can find expression only in ways conforming with the character of the school as a group of participants in a system of truths which they regard as unconditionally certain and essentially complete. Desires to raise one's personal status and to humiliate opponents, social loyalty to one's own group, and social prejudice against the other group may strengthen the fighter's conviction that only his school possesses a knowledge which is absolutely true and fundamentally sufficient about the world at large or about a certain part of it and may make him more eager to spread this conviction. But because other schools have similar claims, he must *convince* scholars who do not belong to his school that its claims are objectively valid, while the claims of any school with a different doctrine are invalid; and this can be done only in good faith by theoretic arguments of indisputable validity. . . .

THE ECLECTIC AND THE HISTORIAN OF KNOWLEDGE. The intellectual atmosphere of scholarly struggles favors the appearance of eclectics, men who see something true in every school but do not wish to be identified with any because of the attacks to which it is subjected from its opponents. The role the eclectic desires to play is that of impartial judge of scholarly claims. But no school with any vitality will recognize such a role, any more than a creative school of art will acknowledge the authority of an "impartial" critic.

There is, though, another function which eclectics often perform incidentally and which gains the appreciation of all schools. They must have erudition, information about the doctrines of various schools, present and past. Of course, every scholar must know the essentials about the doctrines of other schools besides his own, inasmuch as they bear upon his subject. But as scholarly knowledge agglomerates, collecting information about it becomes a long and arduous task, the utility of which is generally acknowledged. Thus grows the role of the historian of knowledge. Originally, he is a mere gatherer of the results of other people's thinking and observation, usually interspersing his information with "impartial" evaluative judgments. Eventually, however, the task of objectively determining the historical facts, of adequately reconstructing and interpreting the theories of the past and thus saving them from oblivion or misunderstanding, and finally of tracing and explaining the historical evolution of knowledge gives rise to specific theoretic problems; the historian, from a mere chronicler of other people's search for truth, becomes a searcher for truth in his own right, with a distinctive scientific domain of his own. This is a relatively recent development, though already represented by a long list of famous names on whose works we have freely drawn, such as Grote, Zeller, Gomperz, Überweg, Windelband, de Candolle, Compayré, Lynn Thorndike, Barry, Rey, Granet, and many others.

THE DISSEMINATOR OF KNOWLEDGE. The transmission of knowledge by older to younger generations of scholars has always been accompanied by a certain amount of its dissemination among nonscholarly groups. Sacred scholars spread esoteric elements of religious knowledge among the lay population, either directly or through the medium of active religious leaders who had been trained in the schools. Secular scholarship not only continued this custom with respect to nonreligious knowledge but developed, expanded, and institutionalized it to an unprecedented degree. For the status of secular schools in wider society, lacking the prestige of sacred authority based on divine revelation or inspiration, could be gained and maintained either by the support of rulers and other powerful individuals who happened to be interested in scholarship or by popular support. The latter has become more and more important with the progress of political and—more generally— social democratization; moreover, once obtained, it assures the scholars a relatively greater and more lasting independence in the pursuit of their scientific work than the uncertain favor of princes and plutocrats uncontrolled by public opinion. And the way to obtain it is to disseminate widely a minimum of understanding and appreciation of scholarship.

This is a function which absorbs much time and energy; but, while important socially, it is scientifically unproductive. Therefore, scholars who are active in any of the roles previously discussed are seldom expected to perform it. In older schools it was entrusted temporarily to persons who had not yet attained higher levels of scholarship or permanently to those who had no hope of ever adding anything significant to scholarly knowledge. Thus, special roles of disseminators of knowledge developed and, as in modern times their social significance increased, the number of disseminators grew until now it exceeds many times that of scientifically productive scholars.

There are two distinct classes of disseminators of knowledge: (A) *popularizers* who spread scientific information and tend to arouse theoretic interests among the adult population actually participating in organized society; (B) *educating teachers* who impart knowledge to the young in the course of a general educational process intended to prepare them for future membership in organized society. Recently, with the development of so-called adult education, a third, intermediary type of disseminator of knowledge has begun to evolve; but the pattern is as yet too indefinite for a separate analysis of it. . . .

THE DISCOVERER OF FACTS. The first stage in the development of scientific exploration is the search for new and unexpected facts, that is, for empirical data hitherto unknown to scientists and not anticipated in their theories. Many explorers do not go beyond this stage; they regard the discovery of new facts as the most important scientific achievement.

The term "fact-finder" could be used to designate them, if it had not a somewhat contemptuous connotation. The expression "discoverer of facts" is nonevaluative and has besides the advantage of denoting both an analogy and a contrast between this kind of scientific activity and the scholarly function of the "discoverer of truth."

In the history of every inductive science there have been periods of extensive search for unknown data, which were also periods of intellectual revolt against the stabilized technology of recognized leaders and experts, the self-assured wisdom of official sages, and doctrines taught by scholars as absolutely true.

Every one of these scientists desires "new" facts, facts he has not already observed, provided they are such as he expects them to be. Their essential character must be known to him in advance, for he wishes all the facts he has to deal with in the performance of his function to prove helpful for the achievement of his task; or, at least, he wants to be sure that none will interfere with this achievement.

The technological leader desires factual knowledge which he can utilize in making his plans and controlling their realization. If his plans were entirely undetermined, he might welcome any kind of new facts. But they are not: his social role gives a definite direction to his leadership and limits the range of his planning. His plans must follow certain patterns compatible with the social conditions under which he acts. The discovery of unforeseen facts within the range of his activity may show that the latter is not so rational as he and his followers believed it to be, that the means he chooses are wasteful, that his successes must be ascribed to favorable circumstances rather than to careful planning, or that the realization of his plans is followed by some undesirable and hitherto unsuspected aftereffects. Any such discovery is apt to undermine his status or be used by his rivals and competitors for planning more efficient than his own. As to technological experts, since their type of specialized research is determined by what men in power wish to know, it may be quite dangerous for their role to indulge in seeking for new data without knowing more or less what they will find: they may discover facts which from the point of view of men in power had better have remained unknown. Many an expert has been made to suffer for such unwelcome discoveries.

The sage, as we have seen, wants only facts that he expects to use in his arguments for his side in social conflicts or against the opposite side. Unexpected facts may, contrarywise, furnish material which his opponents will use in the arguments against his side. It is not so bad if the opponents themselves find such facts, for they are known to be partial, and their factual evidence can be invalidated on that ground. But facts discovered by impartial observers cannot be so easily swept away. Therefore, impartial seekers for unknown facts in the social field are viewed as unsafe people by both sides in a social conflict; and if either side be victorious, it bars free impartial observation almost as carefully as ideological opposition.

Scholars—especially secular scholars—are not averse to new and unexpected facts, so long as the system of the school is in the formative stage of discovery of new truths and fundamental systematization: new facts are even welcome to illustrate and exemplify new truths or to help disclose the errors of older schools; nor is there any danger that empirical evidence might prove an obstacle in building the system, for it will be interpreted in the light of rational evidence. We know, for instance, about the assiduous search for unknown biological facts which Aristotle carried on for years with the help of a large staff of assistants, who collected data in various countries. Albert the Great, the teacher of St. Thomas, was famous for his factual explorations; so was Descartes. The scientists of the nineteenth century who, even if they began as explorers, developed into founders of schools were eager for new facts, while they were building their systems: take the enormous mass of materials used by Wundt in psychology or by Herbert Spencer in sociology.

However, as the system becomes stabilized and extended by successive additions, the search for new and unexpected facts not only abates but becomes more and more unwelcome. Contributors, as we have seen, must take care that generalizations based on facts within the domain of the school's knowledge be reducible to the system. Inductive "verisimilitudes," if thus reduced, become accepted as certain truths, necessary and universal. Thus, the stabilization and progressive extension of the system means that the school is committing itself to uphold as absolutely true a growing number of generalizations about empirical facts. An unexpected new fact may disagree with such a generalization and thus invalidate it, since no exceptions are possible to a necessary and universal truth. It may be saved at the cost of necessity and universality: the judgment "Some S are P" may be substituted for "All S are P." But this means that the attempt to reduce it to the rationally evident truths of the deducive system was an error: and it breaks the chain of deductive reasoning, makes a further extension of the system in this direction impossible, whereas if the school assumes that the exception is only apparent and can be explained by some universal truth yet unknown, it risks the danger that this unknown truth, once discovered, will conflict with the system. Schools generally welcome factual exploration only if it upsets the theories of other schools.

It is thus obvious that a discoverer of facts, freely roaming in search of the unexpected, has no place in a milieu of scientists with well-regulated traditional roles. He may be a solitary, independent individual with no interest in professional traditions or else a rebel against established intellectual authority. Neither of these types is actuated merely by curiosity or by the desire for adventure. Curiosity alone does not make men search for facts objectively unknown, not yet observed by other investigators: on the contrary, it is rather stimulated by social communication in which the individual learns from other people about data unknown to him but known to them. As to the "spirit of adventure," it may indeed lead the individual into unexplored fields but in search not of objective facts to be recorded for scientific use but only of extraordinary personal experiences. Tourists, wild-game hunters, prospectors, pioneers, and colonists are not scientific explorers.

Other tendencies must be active in factual exploration. The solitary observer of nature, like Fabre or Thoreau, or of culture, like those archeologists and ethnologists who initiated intensive studies of various past or exotic civilizations, is animated by love for the factual domain which he investigates. He experiences aesthetic joy in contemplating every particular new phenomenon which his search discloses; and this joy alternates with a deeply thrilling consciousness of the inexhaustible wealth of his domain, the innumerable mysteries it conceals, and the possibilities of new discoveries which it provides. This kind of love can rise to a mystical enthusiasm, as with Giordano Bruno, who, though treated as a rebel, remained primarily a passionate lover of the infinite empirical world which to him offered marvels enough to contemplate through eternity.

Some of this aesthetic and intellectual thrill will probably be found in the lives of all discoverers of facts, though in the rebellious type social tendencies seem to predominate. The latter is mainly desirous to throw off the intellectual yoke of professional science. Often he is an unsuccessful technologist, sage, or scholar who could not or would not conform with traditional requirements, sometimes a rank outsider, a self-taught amateur. His rebellion, however, is not a mere personal problem of subjective misadaptation. It becomes depersonalized and objectified as a problem of the validity of the very knowledge cultivated in those scientific circles against which he revolts. He tries to undermine this validity by discovering facts hitherto unknown which will conflict with recognized generalizations. . . .

THE DISCOVERER OF PROBLEMS (INDUCTIVE THEORIST). The development of scientific exploration culminates in the social role of the scientist who, like the discoverer of facts, explores empirical reality but whose self-appointed function is not to find hitherto unknown empirical data but to discover new, hitherto unforeseen *theoretic problems* and to solve them by new theories. And new theoretic problems may concern data which have long been familiar to scientific observers as well as data which have never yet been observed.

We speak of "discovering," not of "raising," new problems. For a theoretic problem is an objective problem of science, not a subjective problem of an individual or a collectivity. Every theoretic problem originates in an application of an objective, rationally standardized theory to an objective, methodically standardized reality, and is solved by an objective modification of the original theory or by an entirely different theory, also rationally standardized.

The discoverer of problems is not a rebel against scientific rationalism as manifested in theoretic construction: what he rejects is scientific dogmatism, as expressed in the claim that a certain theory contains the only true knowledge about a certain object matter. He is opposed to every kind of dogmatism: the kind which the social milieu imposes upon the theoretic conceptions of technologists and of sages in the name of practical utility; the kind with which a sacred school maintains that its doctrine is the Truth because its source is divine; and the kind which the knowledge of secular scholars derives from the rational evidence of its ontological principles and the formal necessity of its logic. For a dogmatic theory tends to close within the field of its application the way to new theoretic possibilities, whereas the explorer sees new theoretic possibilities in every field he approaches.

Of course, scientific dogmatism can never altogether prevent new theoretic problems from arising: there always have been scientists whose thinking transgressed the limits imposed by a socially immobilized theory. The technologists who went beyond the demands of their social circles in setting new practical problems and risking hazardous solutions were often led to doubt old theoretic certainties on which they were supposed to rely in practice, and they applied instead new theoretic hypotheses of which this very application was to be a test. This has been one of the factors in the gradual disappearance of magical thinking and has resulted in an agglomeration of many specific inductive generalizations, descriptive and causal, concerning inorganic and organic nature which—as recent historians have amply shown —prepared the way for modern science. However, theoretic problematization is only incidental in the performance of the technologist's function and subsidiary to his practical task; if consistently pursued, it would lead him away from his role. Therefore, even such theoretic problems as arise in the course of technological planning and invention are nowadays mostly taken over by theoretic explorers. . . .

. . . Empirical reality gives the scientist inexhaustible materials for creative thinking; new theories are products of scientific creativeness. This involves a complete rejection of the deductive structure of science which in the scholarly conception of knowledge is essential to its validity. All science is inductive; deduction can serve only as an auxiliary method in raising problems for inductive research, never as the ruling method by which inductive solutions of those problems have to be validated. Inductive science is theoretic science, not mere agglomeration of facts; but its theories must be judged by its own standards of objective validity, which were unknown to scholars.

We may for this reason call the modern discoverer of new problems which he solves by new theories of empirical reality also an "inductive theorist." Nowadays, he is no longer (as his early predecessors were) socially dependent for his scientific status upon the recognition of scholars, who judged his theories by their criteria; he is a participant in a world-wide community of explorers with the same interest in untried theoretic possibilities as he has. He finds the problems he has discovered stimulating them to new research and is stimulated to new research by the problems which they discover.

HISTORICAL AND RECENT TYPES

Raymond Aron

EVERY society of the past has had its *scribes,* who made up the clerical staff of public or private administrations, its *artists* or *men of letters,* who handed on or perhaps enriched the heritage of culture, and its *experts,* either jurists who put their knowledge of the law and the art of disputation at the disposal of the rulers, or scientists who deciphered the secrets of Nature and taught men how to cure sickness or to win battles. None of these three species belongs strictly to our modern civilisation, but the latter has none-the-less its own special characteristics which affect the numbers and the status of the intellectuals.

The distribution of manpower among the different professions alters with the progress of economic development: the percentage of manpower employed in industry grows, the proportion employed in agriculture decreases, while the size of the so-called tertiary sector, which includes a multitude of professions of varying degrees of prestige—from the quill-driver in his office to the research worker in his laboratory—is enormously inflated. Modern industrial societies comprise a greater number of non-manual workers, absolutely and relatively, than any society of the past. Organisation, technique and administration increase in complexity as if to reduce to a perfect simplicity the motions of the manual worker.

The modern economy also requires proletarians who can read and write. As they become less impoverished, collectivities devote more and more money to the education of the young: secondary training lasts longer, and is extended to a wider section of every new generation.

The three categories of non-manual workers—*scribes, experts* and *men of letters*—develop simultaneously, if not at the same rate. Bureaucracies offer outlets to *scribes* with inferior qualifications; the management of labour and the organisation of industry require more and more specialised *experts;* schools, universities, the various mediums of entertainment or communication, employ *men of letters, artists,* or mere technicians of speech and writing, hacks and popularisers. Sometimes involvement in these enterprises degrades

From *The Opium of the Intellectuals,* by Raymond Aron, pp. 203-208. Copyright 1957, by Raymond Aron. Reprinted by permission of the publisher, Doubleday & Company, Inc. Translated by Terence Kilmartin. Title supplied by the Editor.

the scholar or man of letters into a second-rate expert: the writer becomes a 'rewriter'. Though its significance is not always fully recognised, the growth in the number of jobs remains a crucial fact which is evident to all.

Experts and *men of letters* did not always constitute quasi-republics, jealous of their independence. For centuries they were spiritually inseparable from the clergy, from those whose function it was to maintain or interpret the beliefs of the Church and the realm. Socially, they were dependent on those who provided them with their means of livelihood—the Church, the rich and powerful, and the State. The meaning of art, and not merely the situation of the artist, altered with the source of authority or the character-istics of the cultivated class. The arts produced *by* and *for* believers were very different from those patronised by secular rulers or merchant princes.

In our day, scientists possess an authority and prestige which shield them from the pressure of the Churches (the exceptions are rare and on the whole insignificant). Freedom of enquiry, even in matters which affect the dogma, is scarcely contested. As the public grows and patrons disappear, writers and artists gain in freedom what they risk losing in security—and even this is offset by the fact that many of them are able to earn their living in a profes-sion unconnected with their creative work. Of course, neither private em-ployers nor the State are liable to pay without demanding a *quid pro quo;* but film companies or universities, for example, do not impose their ortho-doxy outside the studios or the lecture rooms.

Finally, every political régime offers opportunities to those who possess the ability to manipulate words and ideas. It is no longer the military man, relying on courage or good luck, who accedes to the throne, but the orator, the man who knows how to convince the crowd or the electorate or parlia-ment, the doctrinaire who has elaborated a system of thought. There has never been any lack of scholars or writers to lend their talents to justifying a régime, but in our day governments need experts in the art of speech. The theorist and the propagandist meet in one man; the secretary-general of the party elaborates the doctrine at the same time as he guides the revolution.

More numerous, more emancipated, more influential, nearer the centre of power—such, in our day, does the social category which we vaguely desig-nate by the term 'intelligentsia' seem to have become. The variety of defini-tions applied to it are in certain respects revealing; they help to unravel the heterogeneous characteristics of the species.

In the widest sense it is made to cover all non-manual workers. In France or in England, no-one would call an office worker an intellectual, even if he has been to a university and obtained a degree. Integrated into a collective enterprise, reduced to the function of an operative, the university graduate is no more than a labourer whose tool is his typewriter. The qualifications re-quired in order to earn the title of intellectual grow higher as the number of non-manual workers increases—in other words, they are proportionate to economic development. In backward countries, any university graduate passes for an intellectual—and in a sense the term is not inaccurate: a young Arab who comes to study in France does in fact take up, vis-à-vis his own compatriots, attitudes which are typical of the man of letters: the 'ruritanian' ex-student resembles the Western writer.

A second and narrower definition would include *experts* and *men of letters* only. The frontier between 'scribes' and experts is somewhat vague: there is a continuous movement from one category to the other. Certain experts, such as doctors, remain independent—members of what are known as the liberal professions. The distinction between 'self-employed' and 'wage-earning', which sometimes influences ways of thinking, is nevertheless secondary: doctors who work for the State health services do not cease to be intellectuals (if they have ever been) simply because they receive a salary. Does the real distinction perhaps concern the nature of the non-manual work? The engineer or the doctor is at grips with inorganic nature or living phenomena, the writer or the artist with words or with a substance which he moulds in accordance with an idea. In this case, lawyers or administrators, who manipulate words or men, would belong to the same category as writers or artists, whereas in fact they approximate more closely to the experts, engineers or doctors.

These ambiguities arise from the conjunction, in the concept of the intellectual, of several characteristics which are not always simultaneously present. The best way of clarifying the notion is to start from the hard-and-fast cases and work outwards to the more peripheral ones.

Poets, novelists, painters, sculptors and philosophers form the inner circle: they live by and for the exercise of the intellect. If the value of the activity is taken as the criterion, one would gradually descend the ladder from Balzac to Eugène Sue, from Proust to the authors of 'human interest' stories in the daily papers. Artists who go on producing without developing new ideas or new forms, professors in their chairs, research workers in their laboratories, form the bulk of the community of knowledge and culture. Below them are the journalists of the press and the radio, who disseminate the ideas of others and are the communicating link between the big public and the elect. In this context, the nucleus of the category would be the creators, and its frontier would be the ill-defined zone where the popularisers cease to interpret and begin to mislead, where, bent only on success or money, slaves of the supposed tastes of their public, they become indifferent to the values they profess to serve.

The disadvantage of such an analysis is that it neglects two important considerations—on the one hand the social situation and source of income, and on the other the objective, theoretical or practical, of the professional activity.

It is permissible, after the event, to call Pascal or Descartes—the one a member of a 'parliamentary' bourgeois family, the other a knight—intellectuals. One would not have dreamed of putting them into that category in the seventeenth century, because they were amateurs. Amateurs are no less intellectuals than professionals if one judges by the quality of the mind or the nature of the activity involved, but they are not socially definable by that activity.[1] In modern societies, the number of professions grows, the number of amateurs decreases.

In another sense, the professor of law seems to deserve the title of intellectual more than the barrister or solicitor, and the professor of political economy more than the journalist who comments on the subject. Is this because the latter is usually a wage-earner working for a capitalist enterprise, and the former an official? It would appear not, since in the first example the barrister is a member of a liberal profession and the professor a functionary. The professor seems to us more of an intellectual because he has no other objective but the maintenance, the transmission or the extension of knowledge for its own sake.[2]

These analyses do not permit us to choose, dogmatically, a single definition; they merely show how many definitions are possible. Either one regards the number of experts as one of the prime characteristics of industrial societies and consequently baptises with the name 'intelligentsia' the category of individuals who have acquired, in universites or technical schools, the qualifications needed for the exercise of technobureaucratic functions. Or one places writers, scholars, scientists and creative artists on the top rung of the intellectual ladder, teachers or critics on the second, popularisers or journalists on the third, with the practitioners—doctors, lawyers, engineers—excluded from the category to the extent that they abandon themselves to the desire for practical achievement and lose interest in culture. In the Soviet Union, the tendency is towards the first definition: the technical intelligentsia is considered the true representative of the species and writers themselves are 'engineers of the soul'. In the West, the second definition would find more favour, though it would be narrowed further and in fact limited to those whose "principal occupation is to write, to teach, to preach, to appear on the stage or to practice art or letters."

---

1. In the France of the eighteenth century, the category of intellectuals is easily recognisable. Diderot, the Encyclopaedists, the 'philosophers', are intellectuals.

2. These last two criteria, without being contradictory, are visibly divergent. The intelligentsia have been more and more recruited into practical service, administrative or industrial. It is among the pure scientists or scholars that the amateur species has survived.

THE LIMITATIONS OF THE EXPERT

Harold J. Laski

THE DAY of the plain man has passed. No criticism of democracy is more fashionable in our time than that which lays emphasis upon his incompetence. This is, we are told, a big and complex world, about which we have to find our way at our peril. The plain man is too ignorant and too uninterested to be able to judge the adequacy of the answers suggested to our problems. As in medicine we go to a doctor, or in bridge-building to an engineer, so in matters of social policy we should go to an expert in social questions. He alone, we are told with increasing emphasis, can find his way about the labyrinthine intricacies of modern life. He alone knows how to find the facts and determine what they mean. The plain man is simply obsolete in a world he has never been trained to understand. Either we must trust the making of fundamental decisions to experts, or there will be a breakdown in the machinery of government.

Now much of this scepticism is a natural and justifiable reaction from the facile and romantic optimism of the nineteenth century. Jefferson in America, Bentham in England did too easily assume not only an inherent rightness in the opinions of the multitude but also an instinctive wisdom in its choices. They did tend to think that social problems could be easily understood and that public interest in their solution would be widespread and passionate. From their philosophy was born the dangerous inference that any man, without training in affairs, could hope usefully to control their operation. They did not see that merely to formulate rightly the nature of a social problem is far more difficult than to formulate rightly a problem in physics or chemistry. No one assumes that the plain man is entitled to an opinion about the ether or vitamins or the historicity of the Donation of Constantine. Why should it be assumed that he has competence about the rates of taxation, or the validity of tariff-schedules, or the principles of a penal code? Here, as in the fields of pure and applied science, his well-being, it is argued, depends essentially upon accepting the advice of the disinterested expert. The more elbow-room the latter possesses, the more likely we are to arrive at adequate decisions.

Reprinted from Fabian Tract No. 235, pp. 1-7, 9-12, 13-14, by permission of the Fabian Society and Mrs. Frida Laski.

No one, I think, could seriously deny to-day that in fact none of our social problems are capable of wise resolution without formulation of its content by an expert mind. A Congressman at Washington, a Member of Parliament at Westminster cannot hope to understand the policy necessary to a proper understanding of Soviet Russia merely by the light of nature. The facts must be gathered by men who have been trained to a special knowledge of the new Russia, and the possible inferences from those facts must be set out by them. The plain man cannot plan a town, or devise a drainage system, or decide upon the wisdom of compulsory vaccination without aid and knowledge at every turn from men who have specialised in those themes. He will make grave mistakes about them, possibly even fatal mistakes. He will not know what to look for; he may easily miss the significance of what he is told. That the contours of any subject must be defined by the expert before the plain man can see its full significance will, I believe, be obvious to anyone who has reflected upon the social process in the modern world.

But it is one thing to urge the need for expert consultation at every stage in making policy; it is another thing, and a very different thing, to insist that the expert's judgment must be final. For special knowledge and the highly trained mind produce their own limitations which, in the realm of statesmanship, are of decisive importance. *Expertise,* it may be argued, sacrifices the insight of common sense to intensity of experience. It breeds an inability to accept new views from the very depth of its preoccupation with its own conclusions. It too often fails to see round its subject. It sees its results out of perspective by making them the centre of relevance to which all other results must be related. Too often, also, it lacks humility; and this breeds in its possessors a failure in proportion which makes them fail to see the obvious which is before their very noses. It has, also, a certain caste-spirit about it, so that experts tend to neglect all evidence which does not come from those who belong to their own ranks. Above all, perhaps, and this most urgently where human problems are concerned, the expert fails to see that every judgment he makes not purely factual in nature brings with it a scheme of values which has no special validity about it. He tends to confuse the importance of his facts with the importance of what he proposes to do about them.

Each one of these views needs illustration, if we are to see the relation of *expertise* to statesmanship in proper perspective. The expert, I suggest, sacrifices the insight of common sense to the intensity of his experience. No one can read the writings of Mr. F. W. Taylor, the efficiency-engineer, without seeing that his concentration upon the problem of reaching the maximum output of pig-iron per man per day made him come to see the labourer simply as a machine for the production of pig-iron. He forgot the complexities of human nature, the fact that the subject of his experiments had a will of his own whose consent was essential to effective success. Business men prophesied the rapid breakdown of the Russian experiment because it had eliminated that profit-making motive which experience had taught them was at the root of Western civilization. But they failed to see that Russia might call into play new motives and new emotions not less powerful, even if different in their operation, from the old. The economic experts of the early nineteenth century were fairly unanimous in insisting that the limitation of the hours of labour must necessarily result in a decrease of prosperity. They lacked the common sense to see that a prohibition upon one avenue of profit would necessarily lead to so intense an exploration of others as to provide a more than adequate compensation for the effort they deplored.

The expert, again, dislikes the appearance of novel views. Here, perhaps, the experience of science is most suggestive since the possibility of proof in this realm avoids the chief difficulties of human material. Everyone knows of the difficulties encountered by Jenner in his effort to convince his medical contemporaries of the importance of vaccination. The Royal Society refused to print one of Joule's most seminal papers. The opposition of men like Sir Richard Owen and Adam Sedgwick to Darwin resembled nothing so much as that of Rome to Galileo. Not even so great a surgeon as Simpson could see merit in Lister's discovery of antiseptic treatment. The opposition to Pasteur among medical men was so vehement that he declared regretfully that he did not know he had so many enemies. Lacroix and Poisson reported to the French Academy of Sciences that Galois' work on the theory of groups, which Cayley later put among the great mathematical achievements of the nineteenth century, was quite unintelligible. Everyone knows how biologists and physicists failed to perceive for long years the significance of Gregor Mendel and Willard Gibbs.

These are instances from realms where, in almost every case, measurable proof of truth was immediately obtainable; and, in each case, novelty of outlook was fatal to a perception of its importance. In social matters, where the problem of measurement is infinitely more difficult, the expert is entitled to far less assurance. He can hardly claim that any of his fundamental questions have been so formulated that he can be sure that the answer is capable of a certainly right interpretation. The student of race, for instance, is wise only if he admits that his knowledge of his subject is mainly a measure of his ignorance of its boundaries. The student of eugenics can do little more than insist that certain hereditary traits, deaf-mutism, for example, or hæmophilia, make breeding from the stocks tainted by them undesirable; he cannot tell us what fitness means nor show us how to breed the qualities upon which racial adequacy depends. It would be folly to say that we are destined never to know the laws which govern life; but, equally certainly, it would be folly to argue that our knowledge is sufficient to justify any expert, in any realm of social importance, claiming finality for his outlook.

He too often, also, fails to see his results in their proper perspective. Anyone who examines the conclusions built, for example, upon the use of intelligence tests will see that this is the case. For until we know exactly how much of the ability to answer the questions used as their foundation is related to differentiated home environment, how effectively, that is, the experiment is really pure, they cannot tell us anything. Yet the psychologists who accept their results have built upon them vast and glittering generalisations as, for instance, about the inferior mental quality of the Italian immigrant in America; as though a little common sense would not make us suspect conclusions indicating mental inferiority in the people which produced Dante and Petrarch, Vico and Machiavelli. Generalisations of this kind are merely arrogant; and their failure to see, as experts, the *a priori* dubiety of their results, obviously raises grave issues about their competence to pronounce upon policy.

Vital, too, and dangerous, is the expert's caste-spirit. The inability of doctors to see light from without is notorious; and a reforming lawyer is at least as strange a spectacle as one prepared to welcome criticism of his profession from men who do not practice it. There is, in fact, no expert group which does not tend to deny that truth may possibly be found outside the boundary of its private Pyrenees. Yet, clearly enough, to accept its dicta as final, without examination of their implications, would be to accept grave error as truth in almost every department of social effort. Every expert's conclusion is a philosophy of the second best until it has been examined in terms of a scheme of values not special to the subject matter of which he is an exponent.

Everyone knows, for example, that admirals invariably fail to judge naval policy in adequate terms; and in Great Britain, at any rate, the great military organisers, men like Cardwell and Haldane, have had to pursue their task in face of organised opposition from the professional soldier. The Duke of Wellington was never brought to see the advantage of the breech-loading rifle, and the history of the tank in the last war is largely a history of civilian enterprise the value of which the professional soldier was brought to see only with difficulty.

The expert, in fact, simply by reason of his immersion in a routine, tends to lack flexibility of mind once he approaches the margins of his special theme. He is incapable of rapid adaptation to novel situations. He unduly discounts experience which does not tally with his own. He is hostile to views which are not set out in terms he has been accustomed to handle. No man is so adept at realising difficulties within the field that he knows; but, also, few are so incapable of meeting situations outside that field. Specialism seems to breed a horror of unwonted experiment, a weakness is achieving adaptability, both of which make the expert of dubious value when he is in supreme command of a situation.

This is, perhaps, above all because the expert rarely understands the plain man. What he knows, he knows so thoroughly that he is impatient with men to whom it has to be explained. Because he practices a mystery, he tends to assume that, within his allotted field, men must accept without question the conclusions at which he has arrived. He too often lacks that emollient quality which makes him see that conclusions to which men assent are far better than conclusions which they are bidden, without persuasion, to decline at their peril. Everyone knows how easily human personality becomes a unit in a statistical table for the bureaucrat; and there must be few who have not sometimes sympathised with the poor man's indignation at the social worker. People like Jane Addams, who can retain, amid their labours, a sense of the permanent humanity of the poor are rare enough to become notable figures in contemporary life. . . .

My point may, perhaps, be made by saying that *expertise* consists in such an analytic comprehension of a special realm of facts that the power to see that realm in the perspective of totality is lost. Such analytic comprehension is purchased at the cost of the kind of wisdom essential to the conduct of affairs. The doctor tends to think of men as patients; the teacher sees them as pupils; the statistician as units in a table. Bankers too often fail to realise that there is humanity even in men who have no cheque-books; Marxian socialists see sinister economic motive in the simplest expressions of the universal appetite for power. To live differently is to think differently; and to live as an expert in a small division of human knowledge is to make its principles commensurate with the ultimate deposit of historic experience. Not in that way does wisdom come.

Because a man is an expert on medieval French history, that does not make him the best judge of the disposition of the Saar Valley in 1919. Because a man is a brilliant prison doctor, that does not make him the person who ought to determine the principles of a penal code. The skill of the great soldier does not entitle him to decide upon the scale of military armament; just as no anthropologist, simply as an anthropologist, would be a fitting governor for a colonial territory peopled by native races. To decide wisely, problems must be looked at from an eminence. Intensity of vision destroys the sense of proportion. There is no illusion quite so fatal to good government as that of the man who makes his expert insight the measure of social need. We do not get progress in naval disarmament when admirals confer. We do not get legal progress from meetings of Bar associations. Congresses of teachers seem rarely to provide the means of educational advance. The knowledge of what can be done with the results obtained in special disciplines seems to require a type of co-ordinating mind to which the expert, as such, is simply irrelevant.

This may be looked at from two points of view. "Political heads of departments are necessary," said Sir William Harcourt, "to tell the civil service what the public will not stand." That is, indeed, an essential picture of the place of the expert in public affairs. He is an invaluable servant and an impossible master. He can explain the consequences of a proposed policy, indicate its wisdom, measure its danger. He can point out possibilities in a proposed line of action. But it is of the essence of public wisdom to take the final initiative out of his hands.

For any political system in which a wide initiative belongs to the expert is bound to develop the vices of bureaucracy. It will lack insight into the movement and temper of the public mind. It will push its private nostrums in disregard of public wants. It will become self-satisfied and self-complacent. It will mistake its technical results for social wisdom, and it will fail to see the limits within which its measures are capable of effective application. For the expert, by definition, lacks contact with the plain man. He not only does not know what the plain man is thinking; he rarely knows how to discover his thoughts. He has dwelt so austerely in his laboratory or his study that the content of the average mind is a closed book to him. He is at a loss how to manipulate the opinions and prejudices which he encounters. He has never learned the art of persuading men into acceptance of a thing they only half understand. He is remote from the substance of their lives. Their interests and hopes and fears have never been the counters with which he has played. He does not realise that, for them, his technical formulæ do not carry conviction because they are, as formulæ, incapable of translation into terms of popular speech. For the plain man, he is remote, abstract, alien. It is only the juxtaposition of the statesman between the expert and the public which makes specialist conclusions capable of application.

That, indeed, is the statesman's basic task. He represents, at his best, supreme common sense in relation to *expertise*. He indicates the limits of the possible. He measures what can be done in terms of the material at his disposal. A man who has been for long years in public affairs learns the art of handling men so as to utilise their talents without participating in their experience. He discovers how to persuade antagonistic views. He finds how to make decisions without giving reasons for them. He can judge almost by intuition the probable results of giving legislative effect to a principle. He comes to office able to coordinate varied aspects of *expertise* into something which looks like a coherent programme. He learns to take risks, to trust to sub-conscious insight instead of remaining dependent upon reasoned analysis. The expert's training is, as a rule, fatal to these habits which are essential to the leadership of a multitude. That is why, for example, the teacher and the scholar are rarely a success in politics. For they have little experience of the need for rapid decision; and their type of mental discipline leads them to consider truth in general rather than the truth of popular discussion. They have not been trained to the business of convincing the plain man, and modern government is impossible to those who do not possess this art.

Nothing, indeed, is more remarkable in a great public department than to watch a really first-rate public man drive his team of expert officials. He knows far less than they do of the affairs of the Department. He has to guess at every stage the validity of their conclusions. On occasion, he must either choose between alternatives which seem equally balanced or decide upon a policy of which his officials disapprove. Not seldom, he must quicken their doubts into certainties; not seldom, also, he must persuade them into paths they have thus far refused to tread. The whole difference between a great Minister and a poor one lies in his ability to utilise his officials as instruments. His success depends upon weaving a policy from the discrete threads of their *expertise*. He must discover certain large principles of policy and employ them in finding the conditions of its successful operation. He must have the power to see things in a big way, to simplify, to co-ordinate, to generalise. Anyone who knows the work of Lord Haldane at the British War Office from 1906 to 1911, or of Mr. Arthur Henderson as Foreign Secretary in the last eighteen months, can understand the relation between the statesman and his expert which makes, and which alone can make, for successful administration.

Its essence, as a relation, is that the ultimate decisions are made by the amateur and not by the specialist. It is that fact which gives them coherence and proportion. A cabinet of experts would never devise a great policy. Either their competing specialisms would clash, if their *expertise* was various in kind, or its perspective would be futile because it was similar. The amateur brings to them the relevance of the outer world and the knowledge of men. He disposes of private idiosyncrasy and technical prejudice. In convincing the non-specialist Minister that a policy propounded is either right or wrong, the expert is already half-way to convincing the public of his plans; and if he fails in that effort to convince, the chances are that his plans are, for the environment he seeks to control, inadequate or mistaken. For politics by its nature is not a philosophy of technical ideals, but an art of the immediately practical. And the statesman is pivotal to its organisation because he acts as the broker of ideas without whom no bridges can be built between the expert and the multitude. It is no accident, but an inherent quality of his character, that the expert distrusts his fellow specialist when the latter can reach that multitude. For him the gift of popular explanation is a proof of failure in the grasp of the discipline. His intensity of gaze makes him suspect the man who can state the elements of his mystery in general terms. He knows too much of minutiæ to be comfortable upon the heights of generalisation.

Nor must we neglect the other aspect of the matter. "The guest," said Aristotle with his homely wisdom, "will judge better of a feast than the cook." However much we may rely upon the expert in formulating the materials for decision, what ultimately matters is the judgment passed upon the results of policy by those who are to live by them. Things done by government must not only appear right to the expert; their consequences must seem right to the plain and average man. And there is no way known of discovering his judgment save by deliberately seeking it. This, after all, is the really final test of government; for, at least over any considerable period, we cannot maintain a social policy which runs counter to the wishes of the multitude.

It is not the least of our dangers that we tend, from our sense of the complexity of affairs, to underestimate both the relevance and the significance of those wishes. We are so impressed by the plain man's ignorance that we tend to think his views may be put aside as unimportant. Not a little of the literature upon the art of government to-day is built upon the supposition that the plain man has no longer any place in social economy. We know, for example, that he does not understand the technicalities of the gold standard. It is clear that it would be folly to consult him upon matters like the proper area for the generation of electricity supply, or the amount that it is wise for a government to spend in testing the action of pavements under changing temperatures and variations of load. But the inference from a knowledge that the plain man is ignorant of technical detail and, broadly speaking, uninterested in the methods by which its results are attained, is certainly not the conclusion that the expert can be left to make his own decisions. . . .

The importance of the plain man's judgment is, in short, the foundation upon which the expert, if he is to be successful, must seek to build. It is out of that judgment, in its massive totality, that every society forms its schemes of values. The limits of possible action in society are always set by that scheme. What can be done is not what the expert thinks ought to be done. What can be done is what the plain man's scheme of values permits him to consider as just. His likes and dislikes, his indifference and his inertia, circumscribe at every stage the possibilities of administration. That is why a great expert like Sir Arthur Salter has always insisted upon the importance of advisory committees in the process of government. He has seen that the more closely the public is related to the work of *expertise,* the more likely is that work to be successful. For the relation of proximity of itself produces conviction. The public learns confidence, on the one hand, and the expert learns proportion on the other. Confidence in government is the secret of stability, and a sense of proportion in the expert is the safeguard against bureaucracy.

At no time in modern history was it more important than now that we should scrutinise the claims of the expert more critically; at no time, also, was it more important that he himself should be sceptical about his claims. Scientific invention has given us a material power of which the possible malignancy is at least as great as its contingent benefits. The danger which confronts us is the quite fatal one that, by the increase of complexity in civilisation, we may come to forget the humanity of men. A mental climate so perverted as this would demonstrate at a stroke the fragility of our social institutions. For it would reveal an abyss between rulers and subjects which no amount of technical ingenuity could bridge. The material power that our experts multiply brings with it no system of values. It can only be given a system related to the lives of ordinary people to the degree that they are associated with its use. To exclude them from a share in its direction is quite certainly to exclude them also from a share in its benefits; for no men have been able in the history of past societies exclusively to exercise its authority without employing it ultimately for their own ends. Government by experts would, however ardent their original zeal for the public welfare, mean after a time government in the interest of experts. Of that the outcome would be either stagnation, on the one hand, or social antagonism, upon the other.

THE BARBARISM OF "SPECIALISATION"

José Ortega y Gasset

W HO IS IT that exercises social power to-day? Who imposes the forms of his own mind on the period? Without a doubt, the man of the middle class. Which group, within that middle class, is considered the superior, the aristocracy of the present? Without a doubt, the technician: engineer, doctor, financier, teacher, and so on. Who, inside the group of technicians, represents it at its best and purest? Again, without a doubt, the man of science. If an astral personage were to visit Europe to-day and, for the purpose of forming judgment on it, inquire as to the type of man by which it would prefer to be judged, there is no doubt that Europe, pleasantly assured of a favourable judgment, would point to her men of science. Of course, our astral personage would not inquire for exceptional individuals, but would seek the generic type of "man of science," the high-point of European humanity.

And now it turns out that the actual scientific man is the prototype of the mass-man. Not by chance, not through the individual failings of each particular man of science, but because science itself—the root of our civilisa-tion—automatically converts him into mass-man, makes of him a primitive, a modern barbarian. The fact is well known; it has made itself clear over and over again; but only when fitted into its place in the organism of this thesis does it take on its full meaning and its evident seriousness.

Experimental science is initiated towards the end of the XVIth Century (Galileo), it is definitely constituted at the close of the XVIIth (Newton), and it begins to develop in the middle of the XVIIIth. The development of anything is not the same as its constitution; it is subject to different condi-tions. Thus, the constitution of physics, the collective name of the experi-mental sciences, rendered necessary an effort towards unification. Such was the work of Newton and other men of his time. But the development of physics introduced a task opposite in character to unification. In order to progress, science demanded specialisation, not in herself, but in men of science. Science is not specialist. If it were, it would *ipso facto* cease to be true. Not even empirical science, taken in its integrity, can be true if separated

Reprinted from *The Revolt of the Masses* (1932), pp. 120-126, by permission of the publisher, W. W. Norton & Company, Inc.

from mathematics, from logic, from philosophy. But scientific work does, necessarily, require to be specialised.

It would be of great interest, and of greater utility than at first sight appears, to draw up the history of physical and biological sciences, indicating the process of increasing specialisation in the work of investigators. It would then be seen how, generation after generation, the scientist has been gradually restricted and confined into narrower fields of mental occupation. But this is not the important point that such a history would show, but rather the reverse side of the matter: how in each generation the scientist, through having to reduce the sphere of his labour, was progressively losing contact with other branches of science, with that integral interpretation of the universe which is the only thing deserving the names of science, culture, European civilisation.

Specialisation commences precisely at a period which gives to civilised man the title "encyclopaedic." The XIXth Century starts on its course under the direction of beings who lived "encyclopaedically," though their production has already some tinge of specialism. In the following generation, the balance is upset and specialism begins to dislodge culture from the individual scientist. When by 1890 a third generation assumes intellectual command in Europe we meet with a type of scientist unparalleled in history. He is one who, out of all that has to be known in order to be a man of judgment, is only acquainted with one science, and even of that one only knows the small corner in which he is an active investigator. He even proclaims it as a virtue that he takes no cognisance of what lies outside the narrow territory specially cultivated by himself, and gives the name of "dilettantism" to any curiosity for the general scheme of knowledge.

What happens is that, enclosed within the narrow limits of his visual field, he does actually succeed in discovering new facts and advancing the progress of the science which he hardly knows, and incidentally the encyclopedia of thought of which he is conscientiously ignorant. How has such a thing been possible, how is it still possible? For it is necessary to insist upon this extraordinary but undeniable fact: experimental science has progressed thanks in great part to the work of men astoundingly mediocre, and even less than mediocre. That is to say, modern science, the root and symbol of our actual civilisation, finds a place for the intellectually commonplace man and allows him to work therein with success. The reason of this lies in what is at the same time the great advantage and the gravest peril of the new science, and of the civilisation directed and represented by it, namely, mechanisation. A fair amount of the things that have to be done in physics or in biology is mechanical work of the mind which can be done by anyone, or almost anyone. For the purpose of innumerable investigations it is possible to divide science into small sections, to enclose oneself in one of

these, and to leave out of consideration all the rest. The solidity and exacti-
tude of the methods allow of this temporary but quite real disarticulation of
knowledge. The work is done under one of these methods as with a machine,
and in order to obtain quite abundant results it is not even necessary to have
rigorous notions of their meaning and foundations. In this way the majority
of scientists help the general advance of science while shut up in the narrow
cell of their laboratory, like the bee in the cell of its hive, or the turnspit in
its wheel.

But this creates an extraordinarily strange type of man. The investigator
who has discovered a new fact of Nature must necessarily experience a
feeling of power and self-assurance. With a certain apparent justice he will
look upon himself as "a man who knows." And in fact there is in him a
portion of something which, added to many other portions not existing in
him, does really constitute knowledge. This is the true inner nature of the
specialist, who in the first years of this century has reached the wildest
stage of exaggeration. The specialist "knows" very well his own tiny corner
of the universe; he is radically ignorant of all the rest.

Here we have a precise example of this strange new man, whom I have
attempted to define, from both of his two opposite aspects. I have said that
he was a human product unparalleled in history. The specialist serves as a
striking concrete example of the species, making clear to us the radical nature
of the novelty. For, previously, men could be divided simply into the learned
and the ignorant, those more or less the one, and those more or less the
other. But your specialist cannot be brought in under either of these two
categories. He is not learned, for he is formally ignorant of all that does not
enter into his speciality; but neither is he ignorant, because he is "a scientist,"
and "knows" very well his own tiny portion of the universe. We shall have
to say that he is a learned ignoramus, which is a very serious matter, as it
implies that he is a person who is ignorant, not in the fashion of the
ignorant man, but with all the petulance of one who is learned in his own
special line.

And such in fact is the behaviour of the specialist. In politics, in art, in
social usages, in the other sciences, he will adopt the attitude of primitive,
ignorant man; but he will adopt them forcefully and with self-sufficiency,
and will not admit of—this is the paradox—specialists in those matters. By
specialising him, civilisation has made him hermetic and self-satisfied within
his limitations; but this very inner feeling of dominance and worth will
induce him to wish to predominate outside his specialty. The result is that
even in this case, representing a maximum of qualification in man—specialisation—and therefore the thing most opposed to the mass-man, the result
is that he will behave in almost all spheres of life as does the unqualified,
the mass-man.

This is no mere wild statement. Anyone who wishes can observe the stupidity of thought, judgment, and action shown to-day in politics, art, religion, and the general problems of life and the world by the "men of science," and of course, behind them, the doctors, engineers, financiers, teachers, and so on. That state of "not listening," of not submitting to higher courts of appeal which I have repeatedly put forward as characteristic of the mass-man, reaches its height precisely in these partially qualified men. They symbolise, and to a great extent constitute, the actual dominion of the masses, and their barbarism is the most immediate cause of European demoralisation. Furthermore, they afford the clearest, most striking example of how the civilisation of the last century, *abandoned to its own devices,* has brought about this rebirth of primitivism and barbarism.

The most immediate result of this *unbalanced* specialisation has been that to-day, when there are more "scientists" than ever, there are much less "cultured" men than, for example, about 1750. And the worst is that with these turnspits of science not even the real progress of science itself is assured. For science needs from time to time, as a necessary regulator of its own advance, a labour of reconstruction, and, as I have said, this demands an effort towards unification, which grows more and more difficult, involving, as it does, ever-vaster regions of the world of knowledge. Newton was able to found his system of physics without knowing much philosophy, but Einstein needed to saturate himself with Kant and Mach before he could reach his own keen synthesis. Kant and Mach—the names are mere symbols of the enormous mass of philosophic and psychological thought which has influenced Einstein—have served to *liberate* the mind of the latter and leave the way open for his innovation. But Einstein is not sufficient. Physics is entering on the gravest crisis of its history, and can only be saved by a new "Encyclopaedia" more systematic than the first.

The specialization, then, that has made possible the progress of experimental science during a century, is approaching a stage where it can no longer continue its advance unless a new generation undertakes to provide it with a more powerful form of turnspit.

But if the specialist is ignorant of the inner philosophy of the science he cultivates, he is much more radically ignorant of the historical conditions requisite for its continuation; that is to say: how society and the heart of man are to be organised in order that there may continue to be investigators. The decrease in scientific vocations noted in recent years, to which I have alluded, is an anxious symptom for anyone who has a clear idea of what civilisation is, an idea generally lacking to the typical "scientist," the highpoint of our present civilisation. He also believes that civilisation *is there* in just the same way as the earth's crust and the forest primeval.

MODERN SCIENCE AND THE INTEL-
LECTUAL TRADITION

Gerald Holton

WHEN future generations look back to our day, they will envy us for having lived at a time of brilliant achievement in many fields, and not least in science and technology. We are at the threshold of basic knowledge concerning the origins of life, the chemical elements, and the galaxies. We are near an understanding of the fundamental constituents of matter, of the process by which the brain works, and of the factors governing behavior. We have launched the physical exploration of space, and have begun to see how to conquer hunger and disease on a large scale. With current technical ingenuity one can at last hope to implement most utopian dreams of the past. There seems to be no inherent limitation to what is possible within the compass of scientific thought.

Hand in hand with the quality of excitement in scientific work today goes an astonishing quantity. The world-wide output is vast. There are now over 50,000 scientific and technical journals, publishing annually about 1,200,000 articles of significance for some branch of research and engineering in the physical and live sciences. Each year there are about 60,000 new science books and 100,000 research reports[1]. And the amount of scientific work being done is increasing at a rapid rate, doubling approximately every twenty years. Every phase of daily and national life is being penetrated by some aspect of this exponentially growing activity.

It is appropriate, therefore, that searching questions are now being asked about the function and place of this lusty giant. Just as a man's vigorously pink complexion may alert the trained eye to a grave disease of the circulatory system, so too may the spectacular success and growth of science and technology turn out, on more thorough study, to mask a deep affliction of our culture. And indeed, anyone committed to the view that science should be a basic part of our intellectual tradition will soon find grounds for serious concern.

Some of the major symptoms of the precariously narrow place science

1. *Improving the Availability of Scientific and Technical Information in the United States,* President's Science Advisory Committee (1958).

has in the total landscape are quantitative. For example, while the total annual expenditure for scientific research and development in this country is now at the high level of $10,000,000,000, basic research—the main roots of the tree furnishing scientific knowledge and the fruits of technology—has a share of less than 8% at best[2]. Correspondingly, a recent manpower study showed that of the 750,000 trained scientists and engineers only 15,000 are responsible for the major part of creative work being done in basic research[3]. Another nationwide survey found that in 1958 nearly forty percent of the men and women who had attended college in the U.S.A. confessed to have taken not a single course in the physical and biological sciences[4]. Similarly, in contrast to the overwhelming amount of and concern with science and technology today, the mass media pay only negligible attention to it: the newspapers have been found to give less than five percent of their space to factual presentations of science, medicine and technology, and TV stations only about 0.3 percent of their time[5]. In short, all our voracious consumption of technological devices, all our talk about the threats or beauties of science, and all our money spent on engineering development merely draw attention from the fact that the pursuit of scientific knowledge itself is not a strong component of the operative system of values.

THE ATOMIZATION OF LOYALTIES. In the qualitative sense, and particularly among intellectuals, the symptoms are no better. One hears talk of the hope that the forces of science may be tamed and harnessed to the general advance of ideas, that the gap between the scientists and the humanists may be bridged. But the truth is that both the hopes and the bridges are illusory. The separation—which I shall examine further—between the work of the scientist on the one hand and that of the intellectual outside science on the other is steadily increasing, and the genuine acceptance of science as a valid part of culture is becoming less rather than more likely.

Moreover, there appears at present no force in our cultural dynamics strong enough to change this trend. This is due mainly to the atrophy of two mechanisms by which the schism was averted in the past: first, the wide range of their interests was apt to bring scholars and scientists together at some level where there could be mutual communication on the subjects of their individual loyalties; and second, the concepts and attitudes of contemporary science were made a part of the general humanistic con-

---

2. National Science Foundation Report No. 15, *Reviews of Data on Research and Development.* (1959)

3. Naval Research Advisory Committee Report on Basic Research in the Navy, June 1, 1959, v I, 29; v II, 34.

4. *The Public Impact of Science in the Mass Media* (University of Michigan, 1958), 150.

5. *Ibid.*

cerns of the time. In this way a reasonable equilibrium of compatible interpretations was felt to exist during the last century between the concepts and problems of science on the one hand, and of intelligent common sense on the other; this was also true with respect to the scientific and the non-scientific aspects in the training of intellectuals. Specialists, of course, have always complained of being inadequately appreciated; what is more, they are usually right. But although there were some large blind spots and some bitter quarrels, the two sides were not separated, as they have come to be, by a gulf of ignorance and indifference.

The present separation is to a large extent merely one aspect of the more general atomization of loyalties among intellectual leaders. The writer, the scholar, the scientist, the engineer, the teacher, the lawyer, the politician, the physician—each regards himself first of all as a member of a separate, special group of fellow professionals to which he gives almost all his allegiance and intellectual energy; these professionals do not feel a strong sense of responsibility toward or of belonging to a larger intellectual community. This loss of cohesion is perhaps the most relevant symptom of the disease of our culture, for it points directly to a specific cause of it. As in other cases of this sort, it is a failure of image.

PURE THOUGHT AND PRACTICAL POWER. Each person's image of the role of science may differ in detail from that of the next, but all public images are in the main based on one or more of seven positions. The first of these goes back to Plato and portrays science as an activity with double benefits—science as pure thought helps the mind find truth, and science as power provides the tools for effective action. The main flaw in this image is that it omits a third vital aspect. Pure science allows us to understand the physical world and, through its applications, allows us to control and change that world. But science also has had a mythopoeic function; that is, it generates an important part of our symbolic vocabulary and provides some of the metaphysical bases and philosophical orientations of our ideology.

As a consequence the methods of argument of science, its conceptions and its models, have permeated first the intellectual life of the time, then the tenets and usages of everyday life. Our language of ideas, for example, owes a great debt to statics, hydraulics, and the model of the solar system. These have furnished powerful analogies in many fields of study. Guiding ideas—such as conditions of equilibrium, centrifugal and centripetal forces, conservation laws, the energy budget, feedback invariance, complementary—enrich the general arsenal of imaginative tools of thought. All philosophies share with science the need to work with concepts such as space, time, quantity, matter, order, law, causality, verification, reality.

A sound image of science must embrace each of these three functions. However, usually only one of the three is recognized. For example, folklore generally depicts the life of the scientist as isolated and divorced from life and beneficent action in the larger sense.[6]

ICONOCLASM. A second image of long standing is that of the scientist as iconoclast. Indeed, almost every major scientific advance has been interpreted as a blow against religion. To some extent science was pushed into this position by the ancient tendency to prove the existence of God by pointing to problems which science could not solve at the time. Newton thought that the regularities and stability of the solar system proved it "could only proceed from the counsel and dominion of an intelligent and powerful Being," and the same attitude governed thought concerning the earth's formation before the theory of geological evolution, the descent of man before the theory of biological evolution, and the origin of our galaxy before modern cosmology. This aspect of the conflict between science and religion results largely from a misunderstanding of both science and religion. To base religious beliefs on an estimate of what science can not do is as foolhardy as it is blasphemous.

The iconoclastic image of science has, however, other components not ascribable to an elementary misunderstanding of its functions. For example, Arnold Toynbee charges science and technology with usurping the place of Christianity as the main source of our new symbols. Neo-orthodox theologians call science the "self-estrangement" of man because it leads him into realms where no ultimate—that is, religious—concerns prevail. It is evident that these views fail to recognize the multitude of influences that shape a culture—or a person. Neither to Christianity nor to science can one properly assign more than a limited part in the interplay between man's psychological and biological factors on one hand, and the opportunities and accidents of his history on the other.

ETHICAL PERVERSION. The third image of science sees it as a force which can invade, possess, pervert and destroy man. The current stereotype of the soulless, evil scientist is the mad researcher of science fiction, or the nuclear destroyer—immoral if he develops the weapons he is asked to produce, traitorous if he refuses. According to this view, scientific morality is inherently negative. It causes the arts to languish, it blights culture and, when applied to human affairs, leads to regimentation and to the impoverishment of life. Science is the serpent seducing us into eating the fruits of the tree of knowledge—thereby dooming us.

The fear behind this attitude is genuine, but not confined to science. It is directed against all thinkers and innovators. Society has always found it hard to deal with creativity, innovation, and new knowledge. And since

6. See, for example, the disturbing findings of Margaret Mead and Rhoda Metraux, *Science, 126,* 384-390 (1957).

science assures a particularly rapid, and therefore particularly disturbing, turnover of ideas, it remains a prime target of suspicion.

Factors peculiar to our time intensify this suspicion. The discoveries of "pure" science often lend themselves readily to widespread exploitation through technology. Thus we are in an inescapable dilemma—irresistibly tempted to reach for the fruits of science, yet deep inside aware that our metabolism may not be able to cope with this ever-increasing appetite.

Probably the dilemma can no longer be resolved, and this increases the anxiety and confusion concerning science. A current symptom is the popular identification of science with the technology of superweapons. The bomb is taking the place of the microscope, Wernher von Braun the place of Einstein as symbols for modern science and scientists. All efforts to convince people that science itself can only give man knowledge about himself and his environment, and occasionally a choice of action, have been unavailing. The scientist *as scientist* can take little credit or responsibility either for facts he discovers—for he did not create them—or for the uses others make of his discoveries, for he generally is neither permitted nor specially fitted to make these decisions. They are controlled by considerations of ethics, economics or politics, and therefore are shaped by the values, fears and historical circumstances of the whole society.

There are other evidences of the widespread notion that science cannot contribute positively to culture. Toynbee, for example, gives a list of "creative individuals", from Xenophon to Hindenburg, from Buddha to Machiavelli, from Dante to Lenin, but does not include a single scientist. For this there is a significant equivalent on the level of casual conversation. For when the man-in-the-street—and many an intellectual—hears that you are a physicist or mathematician, he will almost invariably remark with a smile, "Oh, I never could understand that subject"; while intending a curious compliment, he also betrays his intellectual dissociation from scientific fields. It is not fashionable to confess to a lack of acquaintance with the latest ephemera in literature or the arts, but one may even exhibit a touch of pride in professing ignorance of the structure of the universe or one's own bodies, of the behavior of matter or one's own mind.

THE SORCERER'S APPRENTICE. The last two views held that man is inherently good and science evil. The next image is based on the opposite assumption—that man cannot be trusted with scientific knowledge. He has survived only because he lacked sufficiently destructive weapons; now he can immolate his world. Science, indirectly responsible for this new power, is here considered ethically neutral. But man, like the sorcerer's apprentice, can neither understand this tool nor control it. Unavoidably he will bring upon himself catastrophe, partly through his natural sinfulness and partly through his lust for power, of which the pursuit of knowledge is a manifestation.

When science is viewed in this light—at best as a glamorous but dangerous temptation—it clearly becomes easy to suggest a moratorium on science, a period of abstinence during which humanity somehow will develop adequate spiritual or social resources for coping with the possibilities of inhuman uses of modern technical results. Here I need point out only the two main misunderstandings implied in this recurrent call for a moratorium.

First, science of course is not an occupation—such as working in a store or on an assembly line—which one may pursue or change at will. For a creative scientist, it is not a matter of free choice what he shall do. Indeed it is erroneous to think of him as advancing toward knowledge—it is rather knowledge which advances toward him, grasps him, and overwhelms him. Even the most superficial glance at the life and work of a Kepler, a Dalton or a Pasteur would clarify this point. It would be well if in his education each person were shown by example that the driving power of creativity is as strong and as sacred for the scientist as for the artist.

The second point can be put equally briefly. In order to survive and to progress, one surely cannot ever know *too much* about one's environment. Salvation can hardly be thought of as the reward for ignorance. Man has been given his mind in order that he may find out where he is, what he is, who he is, and how he may assume the responsibility for himself which is the only obligation incurred for gaining knowledge.

Indeed, it may well turn out that the technological advances in warfare have brought us to the point where society is at last compelled to curb the aggressions that in the past were condoned and even glorified. Organized warfare and genocide have been practiced as long as recorded history, but never until now have even the warlords openly expressed fear of war. In the search for the causes and prevention of aggression among nations, we shall, I am convinced, find scientific investigations to be our main sources of understanding.

ECOLOGICAL DISASTER. A change in the average temperature of a pond or in the salinity of an ocean may shift the ecological balance and cause the death of a large number of plants and animals. The fifth prevalent image of science similarly holds that while neither science nor man may be inherently evil, the rise of science happened, as if by accident, to initiate an ecological change that now corrodes the only conceivable basis for a stable society. In the words of Jacques Maritain, the "deadly disease" science set off in society is "the denial of eternal truth and absolute values."

The main events leading to this state are usually presented as follows. The abandonment of geocentric astronomy implied the abandonment of the conception of the earth as the center of creation and man as its ultimate purpose. Then purposive creation gave way to blind evolution. Space, time and certainty were shown to have no absolute meaning. All *a priori* axioms were discovered to be merely arbitrary conveniences. Modern psychology and anthropology led to cultural relativism. Truth itself has been dissolved into probabilistic and indeterministic statements. Drawing upon analogy with the sciences, liberal philosophers have become increasingly relativistic, denying either the necessity or the possibility of postulating immutable verities, and so have undermined the old foundations of moral and social authority on which a stable society must be built.

It should be noted in passing that most applications of scientific concepts outside science merely reveal ignorance about science. For example, relativism in nonscientific fields is generally based on farfetched analogies. Relativity theory, of course, does not find that truth depends on the point of view of the observer, but, on the contrary, reformulates the laws of physics so that they hold good for every observer, no matter how he moves or where he stands. Its central meaning is that the most valued truths in science are wholly independent of the point of view.

Ignorance of science is also the only excuse for adopting rapid changes within science as models for antitraditional attitudes outside science. In reality, no field of thought is more conservative than science: Each change necessarily encompasses previous knowledge. Science grows like a tree, ring by ring. Einstein did not prove the work of Newton wrong; he provided a larger setting within which some contradictions and asymmetries in the earlier physics disappeared.

But the image of science as an ecological disaster can be subjected to a more severe critique. Regardless of science's part in the corrosion of absolute values, have those values really given us a safe anchor? *A priori* absolutes abound all over the globe in completely contradictory varieties. Most of the horrors of history have been carried out under the banner of some absolutistic philosophy, from the Aztec mass sacrifices to the auto de fé of the Spanish Inquisition, from the massacre of the Huguenots to the Nazi gas chambers. It is far from settled that any society of the past did provide a meaningful and dignified life for more than a small fraction of its members.

In the search for a new and sounder basis on which to build a stable world, science will be indispensable. We can hope to match the resources and structure of society to the needs and potentialities of people only if we know more about the inner working of man. Already science has much to say that is valuable and important about human relationships and problems. From psychiatry to dietetics, from immunology to meteorology, from city planning to agricultural research, by far the largest part of our total scientific and technical effort today is concerned with man, his needs, relationships, health, and comforts.

SCIENTISM. While the last four images implied a revulsion from science, scientism may be described as an addiction to science. Among the signs of scientism is the habit to divide all thought into two categories (up to date scientific knowledge, and nonsense), the view that the mathematical sciences offer the only permissible models for successfully employing the mind or organizing effort, and the identification of science with technology.

One main source for this attitude is evidently the persuasive success of recent technical work. Another resides in the revolutionary change in the nature of science through which we are passing, made possible by the perfection and dissemination of the methods of basic research by teams of specialists with widely different training and interests. Twenty years ago the typical scientist worked alone or with a few students and colleagues. Today he usually belongs to a sizable group working under a contract with a substantial annual budget. In the research institute of one university more than 1500 scientists and technicians are grouped around a set of multimillion-dollar machines; the funds come from Government agencies whose ultimate aim is national defense.

Everywhere the overlapping interests of basic research, industry and the military establishment have been merged in a way satisfactory to all three. Science has thereby become a large-scale operation with a potential for immediate and worldwide effects. The result is a splendid increase in scientific knowledge; but the side effects are analogous to those of sudden and rapid urbanization—a strain on communication facilities, the rise of an administrative bureaucracy, the depersonalization of some human relationships.

To a large degree, all this is unavoidable. The new scientific revolution will justify itself by the flow of results and the material benefits that will no doubt follow. The danger, the point where scientism enters, is that the fascination with the *mechanism* of this successful enterprise may change society and the scientist himself. For example, the unorthodox, often withdrawn individual, on whom most great scientific advances have depended in the past, does not fit well into the new system. And society will be increasingly faced with the seductive urging of scientism to adopt generally the pattern of organization of the new science.

MAGIC. Few nonscientists would suspect a hoax if it were suddenly announced that a stable chemical element lighter than hydrogen had been synthesized, or that a manned observation platform had been established at the surface of the sun. To most people it appears that science knows no inherent limitations. Thus, the seventh image depicts science as magic, and the scientist as wizard, *deus ex machina,* or oracle. The attitude to the scientist on this plane ranges from terror to sentimentality, depending on what motives one ascribes to him.

THE IMPOTENCE OF THE MODERN INTELLECTUAL. I hold that the prevalence of these false images is a main source of the alienation between the scientific and nonscientific elements in our culture, and that therefore few efforts can claim more urgent attention than the correction of this failure. Now it is quite correct—although not very novel—to pin much of the blame on the insufficient education in science which the general student receives at all levels. I have implied the great need, and most people are likely to agree now with this conclusion. But this is not enough. We must draw the full consequences of the discovery that not only the man in the street but almost all of our intellectual leaders today misunderstand or neglect science. And here we come to the central point, the crucial and chilling realization that *our intellectuals, for the first time in history, are losing their hold of understanding upon the world.*

The wrong images would be impossible were they not anchored in two kinds of ignorance. One kind is ignorance on the basic level, that of *facts*— what biology says about life, what chemistry and physics say about matter, what astronomy says about the development and structure of our galaxy, and so forth. The nonscientist realizes that the old common-sense foundations of thought about the world of nature have become obsolete during the last two generations. The ground is trembling under his feet; the simple interpretations of solidity, permanence, reality have been washed away, and he is plunged into the nightmarish ocean of four-dimensional continua, probability amplitudes, undecidable identities, indeterminacies, and so forth. He knows only two things about the basic conceptions of modern science: that he does not understand them, and that he is now so far separated from them that he will never find out what they mean.

On the second level of ignorance, the contemporary intellectual knows just as little how the main facts from the different sciences fit together in a picture of the world taken as a whole. He has had to leave behind him, one by one, those great syntheses which used to represent our intellectual and moral home—the world view of the book of Genesis, of Homer, of Dante, of Milton, of Goethe. In the mid-twentieth century, he finds himself abandoned in a universe which is to him an unsolvable puzzle either on the factual or the philosophical level. Of all the bad effects of the separation of culture and scientific knowledge, this feeling of bewilderment and basic homelessness is the most terrifying. Here is the reason, it seems to me, for the ineffectiveness and self-denigration of our contemporary intellectuals. Nor are the scientists themselves protected from this fate, for it has always been, and must always be, the job of the humanist to construct and disseminate the meaningful total picture of the world.

To illustrate this point we may examine a widely and properly respected work by a scholar who knows and warmly understands both the science and the philosophy of the sixteenth and seventeenth centuries. The reader is carried along by his authority and enthusiasm. And then, suddenly, one encounters a passage unlike any other in the book, an anguished cry from the heart:

It was of the greatest consequence for suceeding thought that now the great Newton's authority was squarely behind that view of the cosmos which saw in man a puny, irrelevant spectator (so far as a being, wholly imprisoned in a dark room, can be called such) of the vast mathematical system whose regular motions according to mechanical principles constituted the world of nature. The gloriously romantic universe of Dante and Milton, that set no bounds to the imagination of man as it played over space and time, had now been swept away. Space was identified with the realm of geometry, time with the continuity of number. The world that people had thought themselves living in—a world rich with colour and sound, redolent with fragrance, filled with gladness, love and beauty, speaking everywhere of purposive harmony and creative ideals—was crowded now into minute corners in the brains of scattered organic beings. The really important world outside was a world hard, cold, colorless, silent, and dead; a world of quantity, a world of mathematically computable motions in mechanical regularity. The world of qualities as immediately perceived by man became just a curious and quite minor effect of that infinite machine beyond. In Newton, the Cartesian metaphysics, ambiguously interpreted and stripped of its distinctive claim for serious philosophical consideration, finally overthrew Aristotelianism and became the predominant world-view of modern times.[7]

For once the curtain usually covering the dark fears modern science engenders is pulled away. How far is this view of modern man as a puny, irrelevant spectator lost in a vast mathematical system from the exultation of man that Kepler found through scientific discovery: "Now man will at last measure the power of his mind on a true scale, and will realize that God, who founded everything in the world on the norm of quantity, also has endowed man with a mind which can comprehend these norms!" Was not the universe of Dante and Milton so powerful and "gloriously romantic" precisely because it incorporated, and thereby rendered meaningful, the contemporary scientific cosmology alongside the current moral and aesthetic conceptions? Leaving aside whether Dante's and Milton's contemporaries, by and large, were really living in a rich and fragrant world of gladness, love and beauty, it is fair to speculate that if the new cosmos is felt to be cold, inglorious, and unromantic, it is not the new cosmology which is at fault, but the absence of the new Dantes and Miltons.

And yet, the author correctly reflects the present situation. What his outburst tells us, in starkest and simplest form, is this: By letting the intellectual remain in terrified ignorance about modern science, we have forced him into a position of tragic impotence; he is blindfold in a maze which he cannot decipher.

---

7. E. Burtt, *The Metaphysical Foundations of Modern Science.* (Doubleday Anchor Books issue of second edition, 1932), 238-239.

Once this is clearly seen, the consequence is also plain. I find it amazing that the intellectual today does not have even more distorted images and hostile responses with regard to science, that he has so far not turned much more fiercely against the source of apparent threats to his personal position and common-sense sanity,—in short, that the dissociation has not resulted in an even more severe psychosis.[8]

But this, I am convinced, is likely to happen, for there is at present no countercyclical mechanism at work. Some other emergencies of a related nature have been recognized and are being dealt with: We need more good scientists, and they are now sure to be produced in greater numbers; we need more support for studies in humanities and social science, and the pattern of Foundation sponsorship is growing gratifyingly. We sorely need to give our young scientists a larger and more thoughtful portion of humanistic studies in their education—and this can be done in principle with existing programs and facilities, for unlike the sciences the tools of study there are still in touch with our common sensibilities. But nothing that is being done or planned now is adequate to deal with the far more serious problem, the cultural psychosis engendered by the separation of science and culture.

One may of course, speculate how one could make science again a part of every intelligent man's literacy. A plausible program would include sound and thorough work at every level of education—imaginative new programs and curricula, strengthened standards of achievement, more recognition for excellence, strengthened adult education, including the presentation of factual and cultural aspects of science through the mass media. But while some efforts are being made here and there, the sum total is pitifully small and inadequate. No one has faced the real magnitude of the problem in view of the large range and amount of scientific knowledge needed before one can "know science" in any sense at all: moreover, while some time-lag between new discoveries and their wider dissemination has always existed, the increasing degree of abstraction and tempo of present science, coming at precisely a time of inadequate educational effort even by old standards, has begun to change the lag into a discontinuity.

This lapse, it must be repeated, is not the fault of the ordinary citizen; necessarily he can only take his cue from the intellectuals—the scholars, writers, and teachers who deal professionally in ideas. It is among the latter that the crucial need lies. Every great age has been shaped by intellectuals of the stamp of Hobbes, Locke, Berkeley, Leibniz, Voltaire, Montesquieu, Rousseau, Kant, Jefferson and Franklin—all of whom would have been horrified by the proposition that cultivated men and women could dispense with a good grasp of the scientific aspect of the contemporary world picture.

---

8. For a striking recent example see the virulent attack on modern science in the final chapter of Arthur Koestler's *The Sleepwalkers* (New York: 1959).

This tradition is broken; very few intellectuals are now able to act as informed mediators. Meanwhile, as science moves every day faster and further from the bases of ordinary understanding, the gulf grows, and any remedial action becomes more difficult and more unlikely.

To restore them to some kind of reciprocal contact within the concerns of most men—to bring science into an orbit about us instead of letting it escape from our intellectual tradition—that is the great challenge before intellectuals today.

INTELLECTUALS, EXPERTS, AND THE CLASSLESS SOCIETY

Thomas Molnar

THE CLASS-LESS SOCIETY. Society, Engels and Lenin promised their followers, some day will be "class-less." Collective ownership of the means of production, they insisted, will cause classes to disappear; and it will cause the state, always an instrument of class-rule, to "wither away."

A glance at the society Engels' and Lenin's followers have created will show them to have been completely wrong. A new social structure has indeed emerged there, but in it classes are at least as much in evidence as elsewhere, and the state flourishes—seeing to it, among other things, that the professionals of the intellect and red tape, the new privileged class, have a clear advantage over their compatriots. Even among Communists, the classless society has become an empty slogan. Only a few credulous Western intellectuals still take it seriously.

In the liberal-democratic West, things have gone otherwise—and Engels and Lenin look a little better as prophets. The state has not, of course, withered away. But the West's prosperity has been achieved less by compulsion than by social compromise, and less by imposition on the part of one group than by social discipline and self-restraint on the part of all groups: parliaments, parties, labor unions and consumers. Social mobility, based on free choice and laissez-faire economic doctrine, has worn down class distinction inherited from the past, and renders improbable rigid stratification in the future. And tax and wage policies have influenced matters in the same direction: everywhere in the Western world the tendency has been for some time to tax heavily people in high income brackets; while, in the United States for example, the workers have tripled and the professionals doubled their incomes. Everything tends to press the classes closer together, and to level standards of living. . . .

All this envisages, off at the end, a society without conflicting groups or organized opposition. Conflicting groups will not do because they put forward their particular "truths" as absolutes; those truths, according to Rousseau and Hegel, are—because particular—lies, and deserve no place

Reprinted from *Modern Age* (Winter, 1957-58), pp. 33, 34, 35, 36-37, 38-39, by permission of the author and the periodical.

under the sun. Society, then, must eliminate the damage they might produce —by elaborating a collective philosophy based on social cohesion. Renan, more tolerant and easy-going than the others, generously adds: if "other beliefs and thoughts are needed," they can be "personal and private to each individual." They must, in other words, be socially meaningless and inefficient, which means keeping them outside the realm of those forces that shape the public philosophy.

THE INTELLECTUALS. Such are the ideological foundations of the predictions of a class-less society for the western world. But they leave open the question: How will rapport between groups actually develop—even given a powerful public philosophy, based on the scientific concept of man, that establishes widespread confidence in the social body as a whole?

Political conflicts in the western world, writes Raymond Aron, are becoming less and less ideological, less and less political; what people care about, he thinks, is a system that increases the "volume of collective resources" —and "reduces the disparity of status between groups"—with a minimum of delay. Naturally enough, he adds, countries like the United States and France are governed by "governments of the working population." Samuel Lubell thinks so too: American voters, he believes, are turning their backs on extremists and ideologists in both parties; votes are determined by mercantile interests rather than by party philosophies and slogans. He speaks, therefore, of a "revolt of the moderates," leading to the "triumph of the middle class"; but his middle class, be it noted, includes almost the whole population. And Miss Barbara Ward, with England in mind, writes as follows: ". . . the ideological barriers between Left and Right are beginning to come down. . . . The disputes of the Fifties seem like shadow-boxing compared with the bitter struggles of the Twenties and Thirties."

Is there a causal connection between the declining vehemence of ideological commitments on the one hand, and material prosperity on the other? Some writers think so. When people are "experiencing . . . increasing and uninterrupted material contentment," writes C. Wright Mills, they are "not likely to develop economic resentments that would turn their political institutions into means of ideological conflict." Karl Mannheim put the point even more strongly; class struggles, he insisted, have their origin in economic scarcity; one class seizes the limited wealth that exists within a nation, and the depossessed strata make repeated attempts to wrest it away.

Well, the central issue may be economic to begin with; but it does not remain purely economic. Material dissatisfaction is inseparably connected with other grievances, resentments, and aspirations; and the longer conflict lasts, the greater the necessity for the contending sides to elaborate ideologies to justify their respective positions. Ideological debate subsequently turns these positions into all-embracing systems and philosophies; and as whole classes become involved with ideals, preferences, tastes, and ways of life, an intellectual leadership crystallizes within each class. Now the intellectual possesses the weapons needed in ideological conflict—in inexhaustible quantities and infinite variety. His, therefore, is the ultimate task of vindicating the class philosophy, of criticizing, denouncing, and ridiculing those of competing classes, and of expressing the aspirations of his class in propositions, in color and stone, and in verse and music. . . .

THE EXPERTS. The situation of the intellectuals is always difficult when, as Mannheim puts it, "the group with which they identify themselves arrives at a position of power." For at that moment, what we may call the second-zone intellectuals—the bureaucrats, experts, and social engineers—take over to organize the victory.

In our new, smoothly-operating societies, therefore, the intellectuals disappear from sight—or at least no longer serve as champions of classes in conflict and articulators of their ideologies. Their vacated positions are occupied by the trained engineers of cooperation, who invariably emerge in societies that are becoming level, classless, because such societies, organized as they are on the widest possible basis, feel the need to maintain and increase the level of production as the condition of prosperity, and to strengthen the social cohesion between producers, distributors, and consumers. These fundamental *groups,* be it noted, perform in contemporary western society functions that correspond less and less to those of the *classes* of medieval Europe (artisans, peasants, merchants, and nobility); and the relationship that obtains among them is not the traditional class-relationship. They no longer constitute, in Tawney's phrase, "the hands, the feet, and the head of a corporate body." Rather, each shares in, and performs, the others' functions, and has a stake equal to that of the others in the order and welfare resulting from this interplay. The social engineers are not to be confused, therefore, with Mr. Burnham's "managers," since their functions are not purely economic. Their task, again, is not that of exerting ideological influence, or assuming leadership of a class, but that of channeling the activities of their fellow-citizens who, as social equals, have analogous—therefore conflicting —interests and ambitions. Concretely, they preserve equilibrium by making use of, and further developing, existing mechanisms of adjustment, but without disturbing basic social relations or antagonizing any particular group. Social and economic transformations, which used to be accompanied by seemingly inevitable upheavals, now mostly take place, therefore, almost automatically—with the precision of laboratory operation. This, of course, does not mean that difficulties do not exist in classless societies, or that beneath the harmony there are no hidden antagonisms. But the intensive drive for power of divided societies is absent, and the political climate carries no charges of electricity.

Is the distinction I draw between the intellectual and the expert or social engineer valid? Let us think about it a moment. The "intellectual" was unknown as a social type before the sixteenth century, and will probably return to oblivion after the twentieth. During the Middle Ages and in ancient times, it was taken for granted that the intellectually prominent man would accept the *status quo* imposed from above (as, according to every indication, his post-twentieth-century descendant will accept the *status quo* imposed by his social peers). Our question must be asked, then, against the background of three or four centuries, when the intellectuals served first the middle class and then the proletariat, elaborating their respective ideologies and calling into question the symbols and taboos of their reigning opponents. These tasks were essentially *destructive,* and I give it as my opinion, in passing, that our philosophical confusion today is due partly to the onesidedness of their efforts. The contemporary social engineer, by contrast, is essentially a conservative organizer: far from questioning or criticizing the values his society holds, he endeavors to preserve them or adjust to them—or, if modifications seem necessary, to set into motion orderly mechanism of change. The social engineers are both a new aristocracy and a new elite: an aristocracy, because they are equipped with titles, diplomas, and other symbols of knowledge, and because their authority to dictate standards of taste, behavior, and success is more persuasive with every passing day. An elite, because they hold together, give shape to, and articulate the ideals of society that has produced them, and provides the background that makes their own lives intelligible.

There is, however, this great difference between the social engineers and the aristocracies of the past: the latter deemed their rights and privileges as God-given and sacred, thus not open to criticism on pragmatic grounds. The social engineers, on the contrary, well know that these rights ultimately depend upon the number of their satisfied clients, and on the latter's orderly circulation within the "open society." Planning and manipulation are, therefore, essential to them; they cannot afford to be fancy-free. They must work out a serious and precise technique all complete with code, jargon, trade-secrets and scientific support. There is, to be sure, still an air of romantic adventure attaching to their activities. But that is because classless societies have nowhere been completely established, and power-relationships within them are not yet settled. Yet power and controlling devices continue to accumulate in their hands, making it increasingly necessary for them to study and understand the nature and exigencies of their position with an eye to developing adequate techniques of manipulation. They clearly intend that the *milieu* shall ultimately conform to the *mechanism of control,* instead of the other way around. And their chances of realizing that intention are excellent, because the classless society, unlike previous societies, has no serious inner opposition to fear. . . .

The question now is whether the loss of ideology—and the consequent loss of a "heroic" role—will demoralize the intellectuals (after having scattered them over the social landscape). It will, certainly, discredit their free efforts in search of higher values. Society, to apply Tocqueville's phrase, finds itself in a state of "virtuous materialism which does not corrupt but enervates the soul." The cycle of social struggles, in other words, is practically closed, since (as Gunnar Myrdal puts it), "the dreamers, planners, and fighters of earlier generations are finally getting almost all they asked for."

In one sense, this turn of events is beneficial to the intellectuals: the loosening of ideological ties liberates them from a commitment which indeed gave them a title to glory, but also kept them in servitude. As means of interpreting the world, ideologies are original and fertile; as means of shaping it, they are risky and treacherous. Speaking generally, the intellectual is free for the first time since the wars of religion to use his conscience independently, without submitting it to the dictates and censorship of ideologies and partisan interests. He may now explore the human condition and the future without donning the distorting lenses of a class, and without "ulterior motives." His political and social views will profit by this change of optics. For he now has the possibility of a personal choice; instead of asserting himself by denying others, as Marxist dialectics obliged him to do, he may appraise the value of openness and charity toward his fellow man.

Secondly, he has gained in mobility what he has lost in status: he may fight his battles unselfishly, wherever he is needed. There will always be some to denounce him for not confining himself behind the bars of an intellectual zoo. But he need not mind. Enriched as he is by his experience of past loyalties, commitments, and alliances, and placed at last beyond their limitations, the intellectual may study and evaluate man's destiny as a whole, and the structure of the forces that compose and oppose it. His objective, I need hardly say, should not be to elaborate a positive science that he would put at the disposal of the social apparatus; rather it should be to open, in the teeth of the apparatus, avenues of transcendence, and deepen them in proportion as the apparatus becomes more extended and more nearly perfected.

There is an evident danger in such an enterprise; that of prescribing the necessary course of transcendence while insisting on its freedom from inertia. There are authors who would help build a utopia simply by subtracting, from the present world and its institutions and functions and creeds, those contents that irritate their own sensibilities and convictions. Thus Mr. Lewis Mumford speaks of de-nationalized governments, detheologized religions, and of world-citizens turned policemen to extirpate what he calls "outbreaks of private and collective criminality." Governments, religions, and citizens may become, at some future date, what Mr. Mumford expects and wishes them to be; but at present they are, respectively, national, theological, and non-custodial, and to speak of them otherwise is to build a utopia: that is, a counter-apparatus.

The tension between ideology—that is, partial truth—and the ideal of the whole truth is, I think, an extraordinarily fertile component of the human condition. This is not to say that similar tensions cannot be found in non-ideological conflicts. One of the central issues, perhaps the most vital issue, in our contemporary world is that of how to restore the tensions that seem to be an essential ingredient in any civilization. Karl Mannheim has called attention "to the increasing regression of the ideological and utopian elements from the mentality of the strata which are coming to dominate the present situation." He even goes so far as to ask whether the resulting diminution of all tension may not also mean the "diminution of political activity, scientific zeal—in fact of the very content of life itself?"

Mannheim's alarm would be justified if man's vital energies and mental and spiritual orientation were governed by the laws of physics. As this is not true, the future may not be so gloomy. Mannheim's views, after all, are prompted by his socialist convictions, according to which social classes are the real protagonists of history and individuals only pawns on its chessboard. This is ideological blindness: the truth is that the individual, the intellectual, only appears to be voiceless because in this period of transition he is in search of listeners. He may find them, it is true, only among scattered individuals and small groups, and in institutions that are committed to ideas which have passed the test of time. Such alliances, to be sure, would be meaningless, save that human existence is inseparably bound up with the life of symbols. But ideas, attitudes, and philosophies are not ghosts: they are, in first place, historical realities and, as such, possess an influence that far outlives the generation that sees their first flowering. They are, in the second place, rooted in human nature, and when translated into current language and behavior may regain much of their primitive significance. This explains why the intellectuals are today committed to history, tradition, and the organic life of societies. It also explains why, alongside with the concept of progress, the intellectuals propose the concept of heritage and conservation, point to the eternal ideal of justice, and confer upon old religions new life and new intellectual respectability. This preoccupation with history —and through history with the permanence of values and the value of permanence—explains the revival of political conservatism, flirtation with "elitism", and the demand for cultural non-conformism as a condition of diversity.

THE THREE ENEMIES OF INTELLECT

Jacques Barzun

... ARTISTS are today the most persistent denouncers of Western civilization; and their lay following zealously presses the indictment. Beside theirs, the political animus against society seems tame. This is something new, in form as well as spirit. For the artistic outcry tends to be vague, abstract, and often absurd. It affects to despise materialism and the world of trade, but the ground of attack is that trade gives artists too little material reward. Being intellectually feeble, these complaints cannot lead to action; they merely poison the air and the lives of those that breathe it.

This autointoxication, which contributes to the modern intellectual's sense of martyrdom, is linked with another social change that has stolen upon us unregarded—the recent education of the artist to the ways of Intellect. In itself, art can exist without learning and, in a sense, without reason. Painters, sculptors, musicians, actors, dancers, even poets and playwrights, resemble engineers and physical scientists in that they can follow modes of thought quite other than those of discursive intellect; some scarcely need literacy, as history proves; and they certainly have no obligation to traffic in established ideas. Some of the greatest have in fact been virtually inarticulate—to cite examples at random: Schubert, Daumier, George Stephenson, Ghiberti.

During the last century, the current has been reversed; artists of every kind have become men of words and ideas, bent on joining the Great Conversation. In youth, they no longer resist a liberal arts training; later, they accept academic posts, they set up as critics and social philosophers, they are caught—sometimes ridden—by political and other systems. This was notable in the Marxist decade and it still is so in the so-called religious revival of today. And now the artists have been joined by an increasing group of natural scientists, late-awakened by the noise of an explosion. In both groups, talent, education, and a fresh appetite for ideas produce an effervescence which has the coloring, though not always the substance, of Intellect.

Nor has the rapprochement been from one side only. The artist turning toward ideas has been met halfway by a public turning aside from words and greedy for speechless art. The new pastimes of the educated amateur are the arts of nonarticulate expression: music and painting. While fiction languishes and the theater is in the doldrums, ballet has risen to popularity, Sunday painting is fashionable, and chamber music thrives. Everywhere picture and sound crowd out text. The Word is in disfavor, not to say in disrepute—which is indeed one way of abolishing the problem of communication.

Nor should we be surprised: This shift in taste has been gathering momentum for three generations. From the Symbolist period on, Western art has been based on the repudiation of what is common—common speech, common life, common knowledge—and its replacement by the singular and indefinable. Excellent reasons can be shown for the choice, and the right of artists to do as they see fit is not here in question. But neither is the effect in doubt, for art has never been so quick and potent in its influence: the revulsion from words, syntax, and coherence accounts for the widespread anarchy in the handling of the mother tongue, as well as the now normal preference for the abnormal in our conceptions of the real. Whereas the 'experimental' in art used to take a generation to be recognized, now we encounter the latest modernisms overnight in the work of the commercial artist and the writer of advertising copy. The public approves and encourages, having learned to swallow and even to enjoy what shocks feeling and defies reason.[1]

Subtler, but equally strong, has been the result of what we pedantically call 'aesthetic experience.' For many people art, displacing religion, has become the justification of life, whether as the saving grace of an ugly civilization or as the pattern of the only noble career. In sustaining this role, art has put a premium on qualities of perception which are indeed of the mind, but which ultimately war against Intellect. The cant words of modern criticism suggest what these qualities are: *ambiguity, sensibility, insight, imagination, sensitive, creative, irony.* All these, in art, declare the undesirability, perhaps the impossibility, of articulate precision and thus defy, counteract, or degrade the chief virtue of Intellect.

The bearing of this observation must itself be understood precisely: there is a difference between the artist and the refugees from life who hide their nakedness in artistic toggery; there is a parallel difference between criticism which is the gateway of understanding and that which is a substitute for artistic work. I do not depart here from my lifelong conviction that art is miraculously precise and communicative in its own domain of fused spirit and

---

1. A trade magazine advises professional writers to make use of:

1. *Clever wackiness;* 2. *Exotic, quaint, or off-beat characters;* and 3. *Fresh and unusual props for showing characters.* Follows an example showing the hero's just resentment of his fiancée's mother by the 'symbolic' act of drowning a monkey. *The Writer,* 71:7, 1958, 14.

sensation. It awakens knowledge of a kind no other means can reach. But that kind is not the only kind, and the means that art uses are always less than explicit. This is the root of the distinction between poetry and prose, between painting and illustration; between narrative or dialogue that 'shows' and the kind that merely 'tells'; in short between Meaning and Information. And the point here is that explicitness in the mode of prose is also desirable: thanks to it, Intellect can steadily pursue one of its great tasks, which is to refine and enlarge the common language for ideas.

Now a devotion to art does not preclude being articulate in this mode, but an *exclusive* devotion, except in a professional, is almost surely hostile to Intellect. For cultivating art out of fear or spite means preferring always what is ambiguous, what touches only the sensibility, what titillates through irony, what plunges the imagination into a sea of symbols, echoes, and myths, from which insights may be brought up to the surface but no arguable views. And this preference is at bottom love of confusion—confusion sought as a release from responsibility. The purest emotions of the aethetic quest, it is said, are private; one partakes only after illumination, as formerly after mystical conversion. And it is true that the unique messages of poetry, music, painting, and serious fiction refuse to be decanted into common prose. When this is said in contempt of all other uses of the mind, it amounts to a denial of Intellect's declarative powers and social obligations.

That contempt and denial modern artists have not troubled to conceal. 'Every day,' said Proust in the opening sentence of his manifesto *Contre Sainte-Beuve,* 'I set less store by the intellect.' Today, after eighty years or more of this open war, most educated men and women have been persuaded that all the works of man's mind except art are vulgar frauds: law, the state, machinery, the edifice of trade, are worthless. More, men and women feel that they themselves are worthless, they despise their own existence, because it fails in loveliness when compared with the meanest *objet d'art.* The abandonment of Intellect in favor of communion through quartet playing and amateur ceramics has bred a race of masochist-idolaters, broken up into many sects, but at one in their worship of the torturing indefinite.

I dwell at this length on the influence of art upon the intellectual life of today because it is all-pervasive. A member of the educated class nowadays need not have any direct or vivid contact with art to fall under the sway of the aesthetical creed and its emotions. He feels about life, business, society, the Western world, what the art-inspired critics of the last eighty years have felt, and he speaks the phrases appropriate to his borrowed disgust. He may be a minor foundation official living rather comfortably on the earnings of some dead tycoon, but he talks like Baudelaire. Indeed, the attitudes I describe are no longer confined to those engaged in intellectual or semi-intellectual occupations. They have touched the wider public whose exposure to ideas is through the press, where readers find reflected not only the worship of art but also its attendant contempt of the world, both alike taken for granted as the natural response of any intelligent and 'sensitive' modern. A deep unconscious anti-intellectualism thus comes to be the natural adjunct of any degree of literacy and culture; and this at the very time when new social groups, fresh from the educational mills and thoroughly aestheticized, think of themselves as intellectuals and mean to live as artists.

But, it may be asked, is there not a great intellectual force, still more powerful than art and working against it, namely, the force of science? Science is exact, science is strict, science is influential—especially in the press where art must compete with it for attention. Why should Intellect be at the mercy of art?

The question is pertinent, and the answer not encouraging. For despite their differences, science and art have reenforced each other's effect. Through the increasing fantasy of its concepts and symbols, through its diverging technical tongues, science has also receded from the common world. Science too has helped to break up the unity of knowledge. In the name of untrammeled inquiry, scientists have planted citadels throughout the realm of mind, but have taken no thought of the means of intellectual exchange among them. The House of Intellect is lost somewhere in this no man's land. When scientists talk, as they sometimes do, about their supposedly common enterprise, they take one of two contrary views and sometimes both together. One is that science is radically unlike any other intellectual pursuit—in method, language, and type of mind. Science is numerical, objective, certain; nothing else is—as we imply in the common use of 'unscientific.' The second or 'enlightened' view is that the scientist's work is essentially akin to that of the poet. It relies on inspiration and a god-given power to handle symbols 'creatively.'

In spite of this second interpretation—a further tribute to aesthetic propaganda—and in spite of the influence of scientific jargon on common thought, the natural sciences and their practitioners continue to form a world apart. When their representatives meet with those of other branches of learning, the verbal deference does not signify much sympathy. The clans soon re-form and on each side the sense of apprehensive loneliness returns. What will 'they' be doing next? The question is charged with the promise of money and power. Is the public on 'our' side or theirs? I have myself heard scientists speak of a 'conspiracy of the humanities' to blacken science in general opinion, restrict research, and 'reverse the trend of modern progress.' What literary men say of the scientists, chaste ears ought to be spared.

When science won its place in academic and general opinion a century ago, the mutual hostility was perhaps justified, because the claims on each side were extravagant. But there has been ample opportunity since then to codify and make known the ways in which the knowledge of nature is like and unlike the knowledge of spirit. The visitor from Mars would surely suppose that these truths formed part of our elementary curriculum, a *pons asinorum* for all who make the least pretense to the life of the intellect. As things stand, the best that common knowledge can show is a pair of dull clichés about music being somehow related to mathematics, and poetry being 'in its way' as exact as science; but the how and the way are left prudently in the dark.

And this aloofness of the scientists has been seconded by their opponents' ambition. . . . The remnants of common intelligibility in their work disturb a good many nonscientists and spur them to achieve a scientific separateness. Why can *their* subjects not be rendered esoteric by special terminology and the use of numbers? Scholars . . . have improved the art of recognizing fewer and fewer peers, and many think they can do still better by imitating science. Indeed, some artists have also been seduced by science even while blaming it for their ills. In both groups, the imitation begins with externals—a pompous jargon, an affectation of method and rigor, and often also the pose of Truth's martyr crucified.

The motives here are obviously mixed, but among them is a desire for authority, which is not in itself unworthy: the mind should respect what the mind has brought forth and the truth is known by signs: let us multiply the signs of genuine knowledge and increase the respect owed to truth. But in so arguing, the imitators of physical science overlook the fact that every shrinking of the common ground of Intellect lessens the authority of each fragment. I am not speaking here of authority over the unlettered, but of authority among the educated, to whom it matters or should matter that intellectual authority is now dispersed and tenuous. They revere Einstein or Niels Bohr by rote, but hardly with the informed emotion which comes of even partial understanding. Their faith in a thinker's scope is so vacuous that when Einstein's misguided friends publish his nonscientific essays, thereby exposing his intellectual inadequacy, naïve astonishment is soon succeeded by excessive contempt, and another idol is overthrown that never was properly—that is, profitably—idolized.

The prestige of science remains of course pre-eminent, despite the superficial hold that science itself has on the minds of the intellectual class. And it is that prestige, acting as a perpetual goad to imitation, which makes science's share in the decay of Intellect equal to that of art. Each in its way undermines the sense of unity, defeats communication, and throws the individual back on his own resources in a world whose worth, and even whose reality, is challenged by these two imposing enterprises. We may conclude, then, that for a century more or less, Art and Science have been the chief

enemies of Intellect among intellectuals. But there is a third and closely related enemy, which is Philanthropy.

I use philanthropy to mean the liberal doctrine of free and equal opportunity as applied to things of the mind. This application has two results. The
first . . . is the corruption of judgment; the second . . . is the corruption of
the products of intellect themselves. In their corrupted use, 'opportunity' is
no longer wholly free and often not at all opportune. Rather, opportunity
turns into social pressure, and the desire for intellect becomes part of the urge
to share the wealth—a double imperative ceaselessly dinned into our ears:
'Patronize your local library, enjoy a museum seminar in your home, see
"what the Zoo can do for you"[2] You owe it to yourself to have an intellectual
life—learn Russian in your spare time, read the 101 classics during the next
1,001 nights, or at least take up the recorder and paint on Sundays. Remember
that education should never end: join a class after 5 P.M. Creativity is within
you; learning releases it. Education is the best recreation; square dancing
is recreation; square dancing is education. Have no fears: in our love is your
understanding.'

True to its origins, this philanthropy carries out the behests of pity; its
watchword is 'help.' The slightest response to the proffer of opportunity
creates a claim to special treatment. Help is abundant, overflowing, and
thanks to it willingness in the learner is enough: why distinguish intention
and performance? Philanthropically speaking—'in terms of eagerness'—the
aspirant is often superior to the passed master. Nor can there be a finer object
of philanthropy than struggling incompetence, since evangelical charity says:
give to those that want. The opposite, the worldly rule, would give to those
that have talents and would take away at least the opportunity from those
that have not. But this, proceeding from intellectual judgment, would be
cruel; it is indeed a flaw in the reign of love and welfare that Intellect seeks
to concentrate its resources rather than spread them as consolations for help-
lessness.

The connections of this philanthropy with modern art and science are
easy to trace. The evils that art discerns in the very nature of politics and
business, philanthropy also condemns and tries to make up for. It bars
competition, is suspicious of power, and ignores failure. For the usual prizes
of Philistine greed it substitutes the guerdons of higher lusts—a certificate
of proficiency in French or a scrapbook of two-by-four gummed reproduc-
tions of the old masters. Now none of this would be possible without the
surpluses that technology has created. The freehanded ways of intellectual
philanthropy reflect the abundance of paper, ink, books, schools, photographs,
recordings, and freelance lecturers, but also the more general sense of copi-

2. Leaflet from the New York Zoological Society, 1957.

ousness arising from the pride of science and the litany of numbers, numbers, numbers.

It hardly needs saying that though the whole world is now the playground of philanthropy, its headquarters everywhere are the schools. That their replacement of Intellect by philanthropy is not an exclusively American occurrence can be shown by a British example: 'Mr. G. H. Bantock expresses the concern that all thinking educationists are troubled with when they consider the present chaotic state of education in our society. Rightly, he considers it will fail to produce "the educated man"—though he carefully does not define this phenomenon. It concerns me more that the present system will lead to failure, not to produce the educated man, but to produce human beings with a capacity for life.'[3]

These last words tell us much. The talk of 'education' where none is wanted or needed, or where something else is meant, is characteristic of our time. But even more illuminating is the identity suggested between education and psychology or psychiatry, two demisciences ridden by philanthropic moralism. The doctrine of pity and help, originating in the church, the settlement house, and the clinic, has found in the modern psychologies a convenient means of carrying abroad the war against Intellect. Though the genius of Freud was unswervingly intellectual, it has given birth to a large progeny of adapters who, from generous as well as selfish motives, put philanthropy first. They mean to cure, or at least to 'help' at any cost. They respect, certainly, no intellectual limits or principles, and one by one the chief elements of our culture have fallen within the area of their devastation. Thus the school is not to teach but to cure; body and mind are not to use for self-forgetful ends but to dwell on with Narcissus' adoring anxiety; the arts, not to give joy and light but to be scanned for a 'diagnosis' of some trouble, a solution of some 'problem,' or else exploited for the common good in occupational therapy; and all other social or political institutions are not to serve man's material needs but to be brought to the bar of cultural justification.

The final twist in this transformation is that the clinician-publicists who carry on the war breathe love in hostile phrases while finding in Intellect untold aggressions to condemn. Their love hates Intellect because they feel and disapprove its impersonal calm, and also because its triumphs look like conquests not so much by, as over, common humanity. *Avant-garde* psychology, *avant-garde* art, and the philanthropy that is coeval with them, alike cherish the warm confusions of animal existence.

These foes of Intellect nevertheless make stern demands. Art, like professionalism, claims of its devotees exclusive allegiance. Science reserves the right to apply its method where it chooses and hopes for world empire.

---

3. Eric Baines, *The Listener*, May 16, 1957.

Philanthropy leaves no one alone, and its educational and psychological allies, taking universal welcome for granted, turn vindictive when challenged. For Intellect to say that its duty is clear and limited, that it cares little for happiness, that it puts other virtues ahead of good will and does not seek world peace, convicts it out of its own mouth. So much sobriety is not in fashion, it looks like provincialism, a refusal of enlightenment—complacency.

THE WRITER

Anton Tchekov

TRIGORIN. [*Making notes in his book*] Takes snuff and drinks vodka; always wears black dresses; is loved by a schoolteacher——

NINA. How do you do?

TRIGORIN. How are you, Miss Nina? Owing to an unforeseen development of circumstances, it seems that we are leaving here to-day. You and I shall probably never see each other again, and I am sorry for it. I seldom meet a young and pretty girl now; I can hardly remember how it feels to be nineteen, and the young girls in my books are seldom living characters. I should like to change places with you, if but for an hour, to look out at the world through your eyes, and so find out what sort of a little person you are.

NINA. And I should like to change places with you.

TRIGORIN. Why?

NINA. To find out how a famous genius feels. What is it like to be famous? What sensations does it give you?

TRIGORIN. What sensations? I don't believe it gives any. [*Thoughtfully*] Either you exaggerate my fame, or else, if it exists, all I can say is that one simply doesn't feel fame in any way.

NINA. But when you read about yourself in the papers?

TRIGORIN. If the critics praise me, I am happy; if they condemn me, I am out of sorts for the next two days.

NINA. This is a wonderful world. If you only knew how I envy you! Men are born to different destinies. Some dully drag a weary, useless life behind them, lost in the crowd, unhappy, while to one out of a million, as to you, for instance, comes a bright destiny full of interest and meaning. You are lucky.

TRIGORIN. I, lucky? [*He shrugs his shoulders*] H-m—I hear you talking about fame, and happiness, and bright destinies, and those fine words of yours mean as much to me—forgive my saying so—as sweetmeats do, which I never eat. You are very young, and very kind.

NINA. Your life is beautiful.

TRIGORIN. I see nothing especially lovely about it. [*He looks at his watch*] Excuse me, I must go at once, and begin writing again. I am in a hurry.

The passages selected are reprinted from Act Two of "The Seagull," in *Plays by Anton Tchekoff*, by permission of the publisher, Charles Scribner's Sons. Translated by Marian Fell. Title supplied by the Editor.

[*He laughs*] You have stepped on my pet corn, as they say, and I am getting excited, and a little cross. Let us discuss this bright and beautiful life of mine, though. [*After a few moments' thought*] Violent obsessions sometimes lay hold of a man: he may, for instance, think day and night of nothing but the moon. I have such a moon. Day and night I am held in the grip of one besetting thought, to write, write, write! Hardly have I finished one book than something urges me to write another, and then a third, and then a fourth—I write ceaselessly. I am, as it were, on a treadmill. I hurry for ever from one story to another, and can't help myself. Do you see anything bright and beautiful in that? Oh, it is a wild life! Even now, thrilled as I am by talking to you, I do not forget for an instant that an unfinished story is awaiting me. My eye falls on that cloud there, which has the shape of a grand piano; I instantly make a mental note that I must remember to mention in my story a cloud floating by that looked like a grand piano. I smell heliotrope; I mutter to myself: a sickly smell, the colour worn by widows; I must remember that in writing my next description of a summer evening. I catch an idea in every sentence of yours or of my own, and hasten to lock all these treasures in my literary store-room, thinking that some day they may be useful to me. As soon as I stop working I rush off to the theatre or go fishing, in the hope that I may find oblivion there, but no! Some new subject for a story is sure to come rolling through my brain like an iron cannonball. I hear my desk calling, and have to go back to it and begin to write, write, write, once more. And so it goes for everlasting. I cannot escape myself, though I feel that I am consuming my life. To prepare the honey I feed to unknown crowds, I am doomed to brush the bloom from my dearest flowers, to tear them from their stems, and trample the roots that bore them under foot. Am I not a madman? Should I not be treated by those who know me as one mentally diseased? Yet it is always the same, same old story, till I begin to think that all this praise and admiration must be a deception, that I am being hoodwinked because they know I am crazy, and I sometimes tremble lest I should be grabbed from behind and whisked off to a lunatic asylum. The best years of my youth were made one continual agony for me by my writing. A young author, especially if at first he does not make a success, feels clumsy, ill-at-ease, and superfluous in the world. His nerves are all on edge and stretched to the point of breaking; he is irresistibly attracted to literary and artistic people, and hovers about them unknown and unnoticed, fearing to look them bravely in the eye, like a man with a passion for gambling, whose money is all gone. I did not know my readers, but for some reason I imagined they were distrustful and unfriendly; I was mortally afraid of the public, and when my first play appeared, it seemed to me as if all the dark eyes in the audience were looking at it with enmity, and all the blue ones with cold indifference. Oh, how terrible it was! What agony!

NINA. But don't your inspiration and the act of creation give you moments of lofty happiness?

TRIGORIN. Yes. Writing is a pleasure to me, and so is reading the proofs, but no sooner does a book leave the press than it becomes odious to me; it is not what I meant it to be; I made a mistake to write it at all; I am provoked and discouraged. Then the public reads it and says: "Yes, it is clever and pretty, but not nearly as good as Tolstoi," or "It is a lovely thing, but not as good as Turgenieff's 'Fathers and Sons,'" and so it will always be. To my dying day I shall hear people say: "Clever and pretty; clever and pretty," and nothing more; and when I am gone, those that knew me will say as they pass my grave: "Here lies Trigorin, a clever writer, but he was not as good as Turgenieff."

THE POET

Stéphane Mallarmé

MY WORK was created only by *elimination,* and each newly acquired truth was born only at the expense of an impression which flamed up and then burned itself out, so that its particular darkness could be isolated and I could venture ever more deeply into the sensation of Darkness Absolute. Destruction was my Beatrice. I can speak of this now because yesterday I completed the first sketch of my work. It is perfectly outlined; it will be imperishable if *I* don't perish. I looked upon it without ecstasy or fear; I closed my eyes and *saw that it existed.*

But I am not proud of this, my dear fellow; in fact, I am rather sad. For I have not made these discoveries through the normal development of my faculties, but through the sinful, hasty, satanic, *easy* way of self-destruction which, in turn, produced not strength but the sensitiveness that was destined to lead me to this extreme. I can claim no personal merit in this; on the contrary, it is the fear of remorse (because, impatiently, I disobeyed the natural law) that makes me take refuge in the impersonal, as though indulging in a kind of self-vindication.

The most important thing for me is to live with the utmost care so as to prevent the sickness which, if it comes, will inevitably start in my chest. Up to now, school and lack of sunlight have been very bad for me; I need continual heat. Sometimes I feel like going to Africa and begging! When my work is completed, death won't matter; on the contrary, I shall *need* that rest! Now I must stop, because when my soul is exhausted, I begin to complain about my body or about society, and that is sickening.

I think the healthy thing for man—for reflective nature—is to think with his whole body; then you get a full harmonious thought, like violin strings vibrating in unison with the hollow wooden box. But I think that when thoughts come from the brain alone (the brain I abused so much last summer and part of last winter), they are like tunes played on the squeaky part of the first string—which isn't much comfort for the box; they come and go without ever being *created,* without leaving any trace. For example, I can't

Reprinted from *Mallarmé: Selected Prose Poems, Essays & Letters* (1956), pp. 95-96, by permission of the publisher, The Johns Hopkins Press. Translated by Bradford Cook. Title supplied by the Editor.

recall a single one of those sudden *ideas* I had last year. On Easter day I got a terrible headache from thinking only with my brain, after I had gotten it going with coffee; because it can't get going by itself, and my nerves were probably too tired to respond to any outside impression; I tried to stop thinking that way, and with a tremendous effort I braced the nerves in my chest so as to produce a vibration—still holding on to the thought I was then working on, which became the subject of the vibration, that is, an impression; and so that is the way I am beginning a poem I have been dreaming about for a long time. Ever since then, whenever the crucial hour of synthesis approaches, I say to myself: "I am going to work with my heart"; and then I feel my heart (at those times my whole life is undoubtedly centered in it), and the rest of my body is forgotten, except for the hand that is writing and the living heart, and my poem is begun—*begins itself*. Really, I am shattered. To think I have to go through all that to have a unified vision of the Universe. But if you don't do that, then the only unity you feel is your own existence.

THE PAINTER

Edgar Degas

THERE is courage indeed in launching a frontal attack upon the main structure and the main lines of nature, and cowardice in approaching by facets and details: art is really a battle.

It seems to me that today, if the artist wishes to be serious—to cut out a little original niche for himself, or at least preserve his own innocence of personality—he must once more sink himself in solitude. There is too much talk and gossip; pictures are apparently made, like stock-market prices, by the competition of people eager for profit; in order to do anything at all we need (so to speak) the wit and ideas of our neighbors as much as the businessmen need the funds of others in order to win on the market. All this traffic sharpens our intelligence and falsifies our judgment.

A picture is something which requires as much knavery, trickery, and deceit as the perpetration of a crime. Paint falsely, and then add the accent of nature.

The artist does not draw what he sees, but what he must make others see. Only when he no longer knows what he is doing does the painter do good things.

A picture is first of all a product of the imagination of the artist; it must never be a copy. If then two or three natural accents can be added, obviously no harm is done. The air we see in the paintings of the old masters is never the air we breathe.

Reprinted from *Artists on Art* (1958), compiled and edited by Robert Goldwater and Marco Treves, p. 308, by permission of the publisher, Pantheon Books. Translated by Robert Goldwater. Title supplied by the Editor.

Part IV

ROLE OF
INTELLECTUALS

OVERVIEW

THE BIBLE states: "But I say unto you, that every idle word that men shall speak, they shall give account thereof in the day of judgement. For by thy words thou shalt be justified, and by thy words thou shalt be condemned." Thus the responsibility of those who deal with words is great. It can be formulated in terms of the question whether intellectuals should take the responsibility of participating in political and social movements or whether they should refrain from doing so and be responsible only for what they write. This Part presents a variety of viewpoints on the question.

By "classic" position reference is made to the book by Benda which appeared in 1927. Benda popularizes the thesis of non-participation in political and social struggles. A year earlier Ortega also published an essay in which he wrote that intellectuals should withdraw from social questions. Benda defines the "clerks" as those whose activity essentially is not the pursuit of practical aims. In the past they were either indifferent to political passions or preached principles superior to such passions. But at the end of the nineteenth century the "clerks" adopted political passions and brought political passions into their activities as "clerks." Specifically they have betrayed their vocation as "clerks" by praising attachment to the particular and denouncing the feeling for the universal, and by praising attachment to the practical and denouncing the love of the spiritual.

In 1933 Gorky formulated the communist position on the responsibility of intellectuals. It is their duty to take a direct part in the practical work of changing the world. He castigates literary men for their individualism and lack of social responsibility. Art for art's sake and refined literature are attacked, because literature is viewed as a cause involving active collaboration with the proletariat. Creative writers must acquire the point of view from which "all the filthy crimes of capitalism" are exposed and "all the grandeur of the heroic work of the proletarian dictatorship" are highlighted. He castigates Soviet writers for not paying sufficient attention to such rich literary material as presented by hydroelectric canals and other themes involving the masses and "real life." The Marxist Georgi Plekhanov laid the philosophical background for the outlook of Gorky when he made one of the most philistine observations of all times. Plekhanov argued that Théophile Gautier's preoccupation with form was conditioned by his indifference to social-economic phenomena:

"The following quotation illustrates how completely Gautier failed to understand the relation of his 'idea of the beautiful' to social and political ideas:
'I would most joyfully renounce my rights as a Frenchman and a citizen to see an authentic picture by Raphael, or a beautiful woman naked—Princess Borghese, for instance, when she posed for Canova, or Julia Grisi entering her bath.'
Further than this one could not go. Yet all the Parnassians would probably have agreed with Gautier, though some of them might have made some reservations regarding the extremely paradoxical manner in which Gautier, particularly in his youth, expressed his demand for the 'absolute autonomy of art.' "

To consider further the question of whether intellectuals should participate in political and social struggles some recent positions are presented. MacLeish's essay evoked considerable controversy at the time it appeared in 1940. He criticizes the divisions according to which practical and political matters are the concern of practical and political men, and the concern of the intellectual is with purer and more enduring things. From this comes the mistaken point of view that intellectuals should not be concerned with political and social crises. This is partly due to the fact that the man of intellectual calling, the man who professes letters and an obligation to defend the labors of the mind and the structures it produces, no longer exists. The functions of such a man of intellectual calling have been divided into specialized roles. Thus the scholar, the scientist, the artist, and the writer, admit responsibility for the defense of civilization but at the same time pride themselves on acquiring detachment and objectivity.

Tate challenges MacLeish's thesis regarding the responsibility of the poet on several grounds. According to him it would be better to suppress poetry than to misuse it, to expect of it an order of action it cannot provide. Soviet Russia seems to do both; it suppresses poetry and supports party verse. Literary men themselves blame poets first when society goes wrong. Other intellectuals might be just as, if not more, responsible; and the dangers created by the accomplishments of the scientists are especially relevant in this connection. The great responsibility of the poet is to write poems. It is an irresponsible demand to ask poets to cease to be poets and to become the propagandists of a political ideal.

The essays which follow are presented in chronological order according to the date of their appearance. Like Tate, Eliot also states that the first responsibility of poets and writers of prose fiction should be toward their art. But as citizens, men of letters have the same responsibility as other citizens. Yet there are certain cultural matters of public concern on which the men of letters should express their opinion and exert their influence, not merely as citizens, but as men of letters. They should judge the conduct of politicians and economists when their activities are likely to have cultural consequences.

Silone believes that artists and other intellectuals in general have no right whatever to boast of any farsighted, disinterested or courageous part played by them in the preceding sad decades. Events have shown again that the calling of men of letters or of the arts is not, in itself, a guarantee of moral integrity or strength of character. The intellectual élite of a country does not coincide with a moral élite. Silone concludes by expressing concern with the reality of suffering, perhaps the only universal reality of human history.

Orwell says that the invasion of literature by politics was bound to happen, for a variety of forces have made a purely aesthetic attitude toward life impossible. But unfortunately, to accept political responsibility in recent times meant that the writer yield to leftist orthodoxies and "party lines," with all the timidity and dishonesty that that implies. The acceptance of *any* political discipline seems to be incompatible with the integrity of the writer. But this does not mean that the writer should keep out of politics. He should be active but as a citizen and not as a writer. He should even write about politics but only as an individual, an outsider. Thus in a time of conflict the creative writer must split his life into two compartments.

Like Silone, Camus is also concerned with suffering and says that the artist must simultaneously serve suffering and beauty. Because of what he refers to as "almost organic intolerance" toward having people humiliated and debased it is not possible for the artist to be unconcerned with life. This, however, does not mean that artists must sacrifice their nature to one social preaching or another. Considered as artists, they perhaps have no need to interfere in the affairs of the world, but considered as men, they do need to; which is similar to Orwell's position. In the past artists could at least keep silent in the face of tyranny but today tyrannies are improved and they no longer admit of silence or neutrality. Marxists and their followers reject the man of today in the name of the man of the future. That claim is religious in nature and Camus asks why it should be more justified than the one which announces the kingodm of heaven to come. These thoughts should be compared with those of Salomon in Part I and Hook in Part V.

THE TREASON OF THE INTELLECTUALS

Julien Benda

'I created him to be spiritual in his flesh; and now he has become carnal even in the spirit.'—(Bossuet, *Élévations*, VII, 3.)

IN ALL that I have said hitherto I have been considering only masses, whether bourgeois or proletarian, kings, ministers, political leaders, all that portion of the human species which I shall call 'the laymen', whose whole function consists essentially in the pursuit of material interests, and who, by becoming more and more solely and systematically realist, have in fact only done what might be expected of them.

Side by side with this humanity whom the poet has described in a phrase —'O curvae in terram animae et celestium inanes'—there existed until the last half century another, essentially distinct humanity, which to a certain extent acted as a check upon the former. I mean that class of men whom I shall designate *'the clerks'*, by which term I mean all those whose activity essentially is *not* the pursuit of practical aims, all those who seek their joy in the practice of an art or a science or metaphysical speculation, in short in the possession of non-material advantages, and hence in a certain manner say: 'My kingdom is not of this world.' Indeed, throughout history, for more than two thousand years until modern times, I see an uninterrupted series of philosophers, men of religion, men of literature, artists, men of learning (one might say almost all during this period), whose influence, whose life, were in direct opposition to the realism of the multitudes. To come down specifically to the political passions—the 'clerks' were in opposition to them in two ways. They were either entirely indifferent to these passions, and like Leonardo da Vinci, Malebranche, Goethe, set an example of attachment to the purely disinterested activity of the mind and created a belief in the supreme value of this form of existence; or, gazing as moralists upon the conflict of human egotisms, like Erasmus, Kant, Renan, they preached, in the name of humanity or justice, the adoption of an abstract principle

Reprinted from *The Treason of the Intellectuals* (1928), pp. 29-37, 50-65, 71-72, 81-86, by permission of the publisher, William Morrow & Company. Translated by Richard Aldington. References to Notes at the end of the book and the Notes themselves have been deleted by the Editor.

superior to and directly opposed to these passions. Although these 'clerks' founded the modern State to the extent that it dominates individual egotisms, their activity undoubtedly was chiefly theoretical, and they were unable to prevent the laymen from filling all history with the noise of their hatreds and their slaughters; *but the 'clerks' did prevent the laymen from setting up their actions as a religion, they did prevent them from thinking themselves great men as they carried out these activities.* It may be said that, thanks to the 'clerks', humanity did evil for two thousand years, but honoured good. This contradiction was an honour to the human species, and formed the rift whereby civilization slipped into the world.

Now, at the end of the nineteenth century a fundamental change occurred: *the 'clerks' began to play the game of political passions.* The men who had acted as a check on the realism of the people began to act as its stimulators. This upheaval in the moral behaviour of humanity operated in several ways.

FIRST: THE 'CLERKS' HAVE ADOPTED POLITICAL PASSIONS. First of all the 'clerks' have adopted political passions. No one will deny that throughout Europe to-day the immense majority of men of letters and artists, a considerable number of scholars, philosophers, and 'ministers' of the divine, share in the chorus of hatreds among races and political factions. Still less will it be denied that they adopt national passions. Doubtless, the names of Dante, Petrarch, d'Aubigné, certain apologists of Caboche or preachers of the Ligue will suffice to show that certain 'clerks' did not wait for our era to indulge in these passions with all the strength of their souls. But, upon the whole, these 'clerks' of the forum were exceptions, at least among the great ones. If, in addition to the great masters named above, I evoke the phalanx of Thomas Aquinas, Roger Bacon, Galilei, Rabelais, Montaigne, Descartes, Racine, Pascal, Leibniz, Kepler, Huyghens, Newton, and even Voltaire, Buffon and Montesquieu (to mention only a few) I think I may repeat that until our own days the men of thought or the honest men remained strangers to political passions, and said with Goethe: 'Let us leave politics to the diplomats and the soldiers.' Or if, like Voltaire, they took these passions into account, they adopted a critical attitude towards them, did not espouse them as passions. Or if, like Rousseau, Maistre, Chateaubriand, Lamartine, even Michelet, they did take these passions to heart, they did so with a generalizing of feeling, a disdain for immediate results, which in fact make the word 'passions' incorrect. To-day, if we mention Mommsen, Treitschke, Ostwald, Brunetière, Barrès, Lemaître, Péguy, Maurras, d'Annunzio, Kipling, we have to admit that the 'clerks' now exercise political passions with all the characteristics of passion—the tendency to action, the thirst for immediate results, the exclusive preoccupation with the desired end, the scorn for argument, the excess, the hatred, the fixed ideas. The modern 'clerk' has entirely ceased to let the layman alone descend to the market place. The modern clerk is determined to have the soul of a citizen and to make vigorous use of it; he is proud of that soul; his literature is filled with his contempt for the man who shuts himself up with art or science and takes no interest in the passions of the State. He is violently on the side of Michaelangelo crying shame upon Leonardo da Vinci for his indifference to the misfortunes of Florence, and against the master of the Last Supper when he replied that indeed the study of beauty occupied his whole heart. The time has long passed by since Plato demanded that the philosopher should be bound in chains in order to compel him to take an interest in the State. To have as his function the pursuit of eternal things and yet to believe that he becomes greater by concerning himself with the State—that is the view of the modern 'clerk'. It is as natural as it is evident that this adhesion of the 'clerks' to the passions of the laymen fortifies these passions in the hearts of the latter. In the first place, it abolishes the suggestive spectacle (which I mentioned above) of a race of men whose interests are set outside the practical world. And then especially, the 'clerk' by adopting political passions, brings them the tremendous influence of his sensibility if he is an artist, of his persuasive power if he is a thinker, and in either case his moral prestige.

Before proceeding any further, I feel I ought to make myself clear on certain points:—

(*a*) I have been talking of the *whole* of the men of thought anterior to our own age. When I say that the 'clerks' in the past opposed the realism of the laymen and that the 'clerks' of to-day are in its service, I am considering each of these groups as a whole; I am contrasting one general characteristic with another. This means that I shall not feel myself contradicted by a reader who takes pains to point out to me that so-and-so in the former group was a realist, and that so-and-so in the second is not, so long as this reader is obliged to admit that as a whole each of these groups does manifest the characteristic I have indicated. And also, when I speak of a single 'clerk', I am thinking of his work in its chief characteristic, i.e. in that part of his teaching which dominates all the rest, even if the remainder sometimes contradicts this dominant teaching. This means that I do not consider that I ought to refrain from looking upon Malebranche as a master of liberal thought because a few lines of his 'Morale' seem to be a justification of slavery, or upon Nietzsche as a moralist of war because the end of 'Zarathustra' is a manifesto of fraternity which outdoes the Gospels. And I see the less reason for doing so, since Malebranche as a defender of slavery and Nietzsche as a humanitarian have had no influence at all, and my subject is the influence which the 'clerks' have had in the world, and not what they were in themselves.

(*b*) Some will object to me: 'How can you treat men like Barrès and

Péguy as 'clerks' and blame them for lacking the true spirit of 'clerks' when they are so openly men of action, with whom political thought is obviously occupied solely with the needs of the present hour, solely spurred on by the events of the day, while the former scarcely ever gave expression to his political thought except in newspaper articles?' I reply, that this thought, which in truth is practically nothing but a form of immediate action, is given out by its authors as the fruits of the highest speculative intellectual activity, the result of the most truly philosophical meditation. Barrès and Péguy would never have consented to be looked upon as mere polemical writers, even in their polemical works. These men, who indeed are not 'clerks', gave themselves out to be 'clerks' and were considered as such, (Barrès gave himself out to be a thinker who condescended to the arena), and it is precisely as such that they enjoy a particular prestige among men of action. In this study my subject is not the 'clerk' as he is, but the 'clerk' such as he is considered to be and as he acts upon the world in that capacity.

I shall make the same answer with regard to M. Maurras and the other instructors of the *Action Française,* of whom it will be said even more truly that they are men of action and that it is indefensible to cite them as 'clerks'. These men claim to carry out their action by virtue of a doctrine derived from a wholly objective study of history, from the exercise of the most purely scientific spirit. And they owe the special attention with which they are listened to by men of action entirely to this claim that they are *men of learning,* men who are fighting for a truth discovered in the austerity of the laboratory. They owe it to their pose as combative 'clerks', but essentially *as 'clerks'.*

(c) Finally I should like to define my views on another point and to say that when the 'clerk' descends to the market place I only consider that he is failing to perform his functions when he does so, like those I have mentioned, for the purpose of securing the triumph of a realist passion, whether of class, race or nation. When Gerson entered the pulpit of Notre Dame to denounce the murderers of Louis d'Orléans; when Spinoza, at the peril of his life, went and wrote the words 'Ultimi barbarorum' on the gate of those who had murdered the de Witts; when Voltaire fought for the Calas family; when Zola and Duclaux came forward to take part in a celebrated lawsuit (Dreyfus affair); all these 'clerks' were carrying out their functions as 'clerks' in the fullest and noblest manner. They were the officiants of abstract justice and were sullied with no passion for a worldly object.[1] More-

---

1. I shall be told of 'clerks' who, apparently without degradation, have at some time or other taken the part of a race or a nation, even of their own race or nation. That is because they believed that the cause of that race or nation coincided at that time with the cause of abstract justice.

over, there exists a certain criterion by which we may know whether the 'clerk' who takes public action does so in conformity with his true functions; and that is, that he is immediately reviled by the laymen, whose interests he thwarts (Socrates, Jesus). We may say beforehand that the 'clerk' who is praised by the laymen is a traitor to his office. . . .

SECOND: THEY BRING THEIR POLITICAL PASSIONS INTO THEIR ACTIVITIES AS 'CLERKS'. The 'clerks' have not been content simply to adopt political passions, if by this one means that they have made a place for these passions side by side with the activities they are bound to carry on as 'clerks'. They have introduced these passions into those activities. They permit, they desire them to be mingled with their work as artists, as men of learning, as philosophers, to colour the essence of their work and to mark all its productions. And indeed never were there so many political works among those which ought to be the mirror of the disinterested intelligence.

You may refuse to be surprised by this in the case of poetry. We must not ask the poets to separate their works from their passions. The latter are the substance of the former, and the only question to ask is whether they write poems to express their passions or whether they hunt for passions in order to write poems. In either case one does not see why they should exclude national passion or the spirit of party from their vibrant material. Our political poets, who are not numerous however, have only followed the example of Virgil, Claudian, Lucan, Dante, d'Aubigné, Ronsard, and Hugo. Yet we cannot deny that political passion, as it is expressed by Claudel or d'Annunizo, a conscious and organized passion *lacking all simplicity,* coldly scornful of its adversary, a passion which in the second of these poets displays itself as so precisely political, so cunningly adapted to the profound cupidity of his compatriots and the exact point of weakness in the foreigner—we cannot deny, I say, that this political passion is something different from the eloquent generalities of the 'Tragiques of the Année Terrible.' A work like *La Nave,* with its national plan as exact and practical as that of a Bismarck, wherein the lyric gift is used to extol this practical character, seems to me something new in the history of poetry, even of political poetry. The result of this new departure on the minds of laymen may be judged by the present state of mind of the Italian people. But in our day the most remarkable example of the poets' applying their art to the service of political passions is that literary form which may be called 'lyrical philosophy', the most brilliant symbol of which is the work of Barrès. It begins by taking as its centres of vibration certain truly philosophical states of mind (such as pantheism, a loftily skeptical intellectualism) and then entirely devotes itself to serving racial passion and national feeling. Here the action of the lyric spirit is doubled by the prestige of the spirit of abstract thought (Barrès admirably caught the appearance of that spirit—he stole the tool, a philosopher has said of him), and in France as elsewhere the 'clerks' have thereby stimulated political passions among the laymen, at least in that very important section of them who read and believe they think. Moreover, in regard to poets and especially the poet I have just named, it is difficult to know whether the lyrical impulse lends its aid to a genuine and pre-existing political passion, or whether on the contrary this passion puts itself at the service of a lyrical impulse which is seeking inspiration. Alius judex erit.

But there are other 'clerks' who introduce political passion into their works with a remarkable consciousness of what they are doing, in whom this derogation seems more worthy of notice than in the poets. I mean the novelists and dramatists, i.e. 'clerks' whose function is to portray in as objective a manner as possible the emotions of the human soul and their conflicts —a function which, as Shakespeare, Molière, and Balzac have proved, may be carried out with all the purity I have here assigned to it. One may show how this function has been more than ever perverted by its subjection to political ends by the example of many contemporary novelists, not because they scatter 'tendencious' reflections throughout their narratives (Balzac constantly does so), but because instead of making their heroes feel and act in conformity with a true observation of human nature, they make them do so as the passion of the authors requires. Shall I cite those novels where the traditionalist, whatever his errors, always finally displays a noble soul, wheras the character without religion inevitably, and in spite of all his efforts, is capable of none but vile actions? Or the other novels where the man of the people possesses every virtue and vileness is the exclusive portion of the bourgeois? Or the novels where the author displays his compatriots in contact with foreigners and, more or less frankly, gives all moral superiority to his own people? There is a two-fold evil in this proceeding; not only does it considerably inflame political passion in the breast of the reader, but it deprives him of one of the most eminently civilizing effects of all works of art, i.e. that self-examination to which every spectator is impelled by a representation of human beings which he feels to be true and solely pre-occupied with truth. From the point of view of the artist and of the value of his activity alone, this partiality indicates a great degradation. The value of the artist, the thing which makes him the world's high ornament, is that he *plays* human passions instead of living them, and that he discovers in this 'play' emotion the same source of desires, joys and sufferings as ordinary men find in the pursuit of real things. Now, if this accomplished type of exuberant activity places itself at the service of the nation or of a class, if this fine flower of disinterestedness becomes utilitarian, then I say with the poet of the 'Vierge aux Rochers' when the author of *Siegfried* exhales his last sigh: 'The world has lost its import.'

I have pointed out that certain 'clerks' have put their activities as 'clerks' at the service of political passions. These are the poets, the novelists, the dramatists, the artists, i.e. they are men who may be permitted to give passion, even wilful passion, a predominant place in their works. But there are other 'clerks' in whom this derogation from the disinterested activity of the mind is far more shocking, 'clerks' whose influence on the laymen is much more profound by reason of the prestige attached to their functions. I mean the historians. Here, as with the poets, the phenomenon is a new one on account of the point of perfection it has reached. Assuredly, humanity did not await our age to see History putting itself at the service of the spirit of party or of national passion. But I think I may assert that it has never seen this done with the same methodical spirit, the same intensity of consciousness which may be observed in German historians of the past half century and in the French Monarchists of the past twenty years. The case of the latter is the more remarkable since they belong to a nation which has acquired eternal honour in the history of human intelligence by explicitly condemning pragmatic history and formulating, as it were, the character of disinterested history, through the works of Beaufort, Freret, Voltaire, Thierry, Renan, Fustel de Coulanges.[2] Yet the true novelty here is the admission of this spirit of partiality, the expressed intention to employ it as a legitimate method. 'A true German historian,' declares a German master, 'should especially tell those facts which conduce to the grandeur of Germany.' The same scholar praises Mommsen (who himself boasted of it) for having written a Roman history 'which becomes a history of Germany with Roman names'. Another (Treitschke) prided himself on his lack of 'that anemic objectivity which is contrary to the historical sense'. Another (Guisebrecht) teaches that 'Science must not soar beyond the frontiers, but be national, be German'. Our Monarchists do not lag behind. Recently one of them, the author of a *History of France,* which tried to show that the French Kings since Clovis were occupied in trying to prevent the war of 1914, defended the historian who presents the past from the point of view of the passions of his own time. By his determination in bringing this partiality to historical narrative the modern 'clerk' most seriously derogates from his true function, if I am right in saying that his function is to restrain the passions of the laymen. Not only does he inflame the laymen's passions more cunningly than ever, not only does he deprive them of the suggestive spectacle of a

---

2. See, for instance, Fustel de Coulanges's study *De la manière d'écrire l'histoire en France et en Allemagne*. It will be observed that this author's denunciation of the German historians exactly applies to certain French historians of recent years, with this difference: That the German alters history to exalt his nation and the Frenchman to exalt a political system. In general it may be said that the 'tendencious' philosophies of the Germans lead to national war, and those of the French to civil war. Is it necessary to repeat, after so many others, how much this proves the moral superiority of the latter?

man solely occupied by the thirst for truth, but he prevents the laymen from hearing speech different from that of the market place, speech (Renan's is perhaps the finest example) which, coming from the heights, shows that the most opposite passions are equally justified, equally necessary to the earthly State, and thereby incites every reader who has any capacity for getting outside himself to relax the severity of his passions, at least for a moment.

Let me say, however, that indeed men like Treitschke and his French equivalents are not historians; they are men of politics who make use of history to support a cause whose triumph they desire. Hence, it is natural that the master of their method should not be Lenain de Tillemont but Louis XIV, who threatened to withdraw Mezeray's pension if the historian persisted in pointing out the abuses of the old monarchy; or Napoleon, who ordered the chief of police to take measures for the history of France to be written in a manner favourable to his own throne. Nevertheless, the really cunning ones assume the mask of disinterestedness.

I believe that many of those whom I am here accusing of betraying their spiritual ministry, that disinterested activity which should be theirs by the mere fact of their being historians, psychologists, moralists, would reply to me as follows, if such a confession did not destroy their influence: 'We are not in the least the servants of spiritual things; we are the servants of material things, of a political party, of a nation. Only, instead of serving it with the sword, we serve it with the pen. We are *the spiritual militia of the material*.'

Among those who ought to show the world an example of disinterested intellectual activity and who nevertheless turn their function to practical ends, I shall also mention the critics. Everyone knows that innumerable critics to-day consider that a book is only good insofar as it serves the party which is dear to them, or as it manifests 'the genius of the nation', or as it illustrates a political doctrine in harmony with their own political system, or for other reasons of the like purity. The modern 'clerks', I said before, insist that the just shall be determined by the useful. They also want the useful to determine the beautiful, which is not one of their least originalities in history. Nevertheless, here again those who adopt such a form of criticism are not truly critics, but men of politics, who make criticism serve their practical designs. Here is a perfecting of political passion, the whole honour of which must be given to the moderns. Neither Pius XIV nor Napoleon apparently thought of using literary criticism in support of the social system in which they believed.[3] This new departure has brought forth its fruits. For instance, if you assert with the French Monarchists that the democratic

---

3. Yet the Jesuits thought of doing so to combat the Jansenists. (See Racine, *Port-Royal*, pt. i.)

ideal is inevitably bound up with bad literature, you are dealing that ideal a real blow in a country like France, which has a real devotion to literature, at least among those who will consent to believe that Victor Hugo and Lamartine were mere scribblers.

But the most remarkable thing about the modern 'clerk' in his desire to bring political passion into his work, is that he has done so in philosophy, more precisely, in metaphysics. It may be said that until the nineteenth century metaphysics remained the inviolate citadel of disinterested speculation. Among all forms of spiritual labour metaphysics best deserved the admirable tribute which a mathematician rendered the theory of numbers above all branches of mathematics, when he said: 'This is the really pure branch of our science, by which I mean that it is unsullied by any contact with practical application.' In fact thinkers free from any sort of earthly preference, like Plotinus, Thomas Aquinas, Descartes, Kant, and even thinkers strongly imbued with the superiority of their class or nation (like Plato and Aristotle), never thought of directing their transcendental speculations towards a demonstration of this superiority or the necessity of this adoption by the whole world. It has been said that the morality of the Greeks was national, but their metaphysics were universal. The Church itself, so often favourable to class or national interests in its morality, thinks only of God and Man in its metaphysics. It was reserved for our own age to see metaphysicians of the greatest eminence turning their speculations to the exaltation of their own countries and to the depreciation of other countries, fortifying the will to power of their compatriots with all the power of abstractive genius. Fichte and Hegel made the triumph of the German world the supreme and necessary end of the development of Being, and history has showed whether the action of these 'clerks' had an effect on the hearts of their laymen. Let me hasten to add that this spectacle of patriotic metaphysics is provided by Germany alone. In France, even in this age of nationalist 'clerks', we have not yet seen any philosopher (at least one who is taken seriously) build up a metaphysical system to the glory of France. Neither Auguste Comte nor Renouvier nor Bergson ever thought of making a French hegemony the necessary result of the world's development. Need I add what a degradation this has been for metaphysics, as it has been for art? It will be the eternal shame of the German philosophers to have transformed the patrician virgin who honoured the Gods into a harpy engaged in shrieking the glory of her children.

THIRD: THE 'CLERKS' HAVE PLAYED THE GAME OF POLITICAL PASSIONS BY THEIR DOCTRINES. But where the 'clerks' have most violently broken with their tradition and resolutely played the game of the laymen in their eagerness to place themselves in the real, is by their doctrines, by the scale of values they have set up for the world. Those whose preaching for twenty centuries had been to humiliate the realist passions in favour of something transcendental, have set themselves (with a science and a consciousness which will stupify history) to the task of making these passions, and the impulses which ensure them, the highest of virtues, while they cannot show too much scorn for the existence which in any respect raises itself beyond the material. I shall now describe the principle aspects of this phenomenon.

A. THE 'CLERKS' PRAISE ATTACHMENT TO THE PARTICULAR AND DENOUNCE THE FEELING OF THE UNIVERSAL. In the first place, the 'clerks' have set out to exalt the will of men to feel conscious of themselves as distinct from others, and to proclaim as contemptible every tendency to establish oneself in a universal. With the exception of certain authors like Tolstoi and Anatole France, whose teaching moreover is now looked on with contempt by most of their colleagues, all the influential moralists of Europe during the past fifty years, Bourget, Barrès, Maurras, Péguy, d'Annunzio, Kipling, the immense majority of German thinkers, have praised the efforts of men to feel conscious of themselves in their nation and race, to the extent that this distinguishes them from others and opposes them to others, and have made them ashamed of every aspiration to feel conscious of themselves as men in the general sense and in the sense of rising above ethnical aims. Those whose activity since the time of the Stoics had been devoted to preaching the extinction of national egotism in the interest of an abstract and eternal entity, set out to denounce every feeling of this kind and to proclaim the lofty morality of that egotism. In our age the descendants of Erasmus, Montaigne, Voltaire, have denounced humanitarianism as a moral degeneration, nay, as an intellectual degeneration, in that it implies 'a total absence of practical common sense'; for practical common sense has become the measure of intellectual values with these strange 'clerks'.

I should like to draw a distinction between humanitarianism as I mean it here—a sensitiveness to the abstract quality of what is human, to Montaigne's 'whole form of human condition'—and the feeling which is usually called humanitarianism, by which is meant the love for human beings existing in the concrete. The former impulse (which would more accurately be called humanism) is the attachment to a concept. It is a pure passion of the intelligence, implying no terrestrial love. It is quite easy to conceive of a person plunging into the concept of what is human without having the least desire even to see a man. This is the form assumed by love of humanity in the great patricians of the mind like Erasmus, Malebranche, Spinoza, Goethe, who all were men, it appears, not very anxious to throw themselves into the arms of their neighbours. The second humanitarianism is a state of the heart and therefore the portion of plebeian souls. It occurs among moralists in periods when lofty intellectual discipline disappears among them and gives way to sentimental exaltation, I mean in the eighteenth century (chiefly with Diderot) and above all in the nineteenth century, with Michelet, Quinet, Proudhon, Romain Rolland, Georges Duhamel. This sentimental form of humanitarianism and forgetfulness of its conceptual form explain the unpopularity of this doctrine with so many distinguished minds, who discover two equally repulsive commonplaces in the arsenal of political ideology. One of them is 'the patriotic bore' and the other 'the universal embrace'.[4]

The humanitarianism which holds in honour the abstract quality of what is human, is the only one which allows us to love *all* men. Obviously, as soon as we look at men in the concrete, we inevitably find that this quality is distributed in different quantities, and we have to say with Renan: 'In reality one is *more or less* a man, *more or less* the son of God ... I see no reason why a Papuan should be immortal.' Modern equalitarians, by failing to understand that there can be no equality except in the abstract and that inequality is the essence of the concrete, have merely displayed the extraordinary vulgarity of their minds as well as their amazing political clumsiness.[5]

Humanism, as I have defined it, has nothing to do with internationalism. Internationalism is a protest against national egotism, not on behalf of a spiritual passion, but on behalf of another egotism, another earthly passion. It is the impulse of a certain category of men—labourers, bankers, industrialists—who unite across frontiers in the name of private and practical interests, and who only oppose the national spirit because it thwarts them in satisfying those interests.[6]

In comparison with such impulses, national passion appears an idealistic and disinterested impulse. In short, humanism is also something entirely different from cosmopolitanism, which is the simple desire to enjoy the advantages of all nations and all their cultures, and is generally exempt from

---

4. The distinction between these two humanitarianisms is well expressed by Goethe when he relates (Dichtung und Wahrheit) the indifference of himself and his friends to the events of 1789. 'In our little circle, we took no notice of news and newspapers; our object was to know Man; as for men, we left them to do as they chose.' Need I recall that the 'humanities', as instituted by the Jesuits in the seventeenth century, the 'studia humanitatis', are 'the study of what is most essentially human', in no sense altruistic exercises.

5. This the Church has understood so well, and the corollary to this truth: That love between men can only be created by developing in them the sensibility for abstract man, and by combatting in them the interest for concrete man; by turning them towards metaphysical meditation and away from the study of history (see Malebranche). This is exactly the contrary direction to that of the modern 'clerks', but, once again, these 'clerks' have not the slightest desire to create love among men.

6. Thus they adopt the national spirit if it seems to serve their interests; for instance, the party of 'nationalist-socialists'.

all moral dogmatism.[7] But let us come back to this movement of the 'clerks' exhorting the peoples to feel conscious of themselves in what makes them distinct from others.

What will especially amaze history in this movement of the 'clerks' is the perfection with which they have carried it out. They have exhorted the peoples to feel conscious of themselves in what makes them *the most distinct* from others, in their poets rather than in their scientists, in their legends rather than in their philosophies, since poetry (as they perfectly well perceived) is infinitely more national, more separating than the products of pure intelligence.[8] They have exhorted the peoples to honour their poets' characteristics insofar as they are peculiar to them and are not universal. Recently a young Italian writer praised his language because it is only used in Italy, and poured scorn on French because it is employed universally. They have exhorted the peoples to feel conscious of themselves in *everything* which makes them distinct from others, not only in their language, art, and literature, but in their dress, houses, furniture, and food. During the past half century it has been a common experience to see serious writers (to go no further than France) exhorting their compatriots to remain faithful to French fashions, French hair-dressing, French dining rooms, French cooking, French cars. They have exhorted the peoples to feel themselves distinct even in their vices. The German historians, says Fustel de Coulanges, urge their nation to be intoxicated with its personality, even to its barbarity. The French moralist does not lag behind and desires his compatriots to accept their 'national determinism' in its 'indivisible totality', with its injustices as well as its wisdom, with its fanaticism as well as its enlightenment, its pettiness as well as its grandeur. Another, (Maurras) declares: 'Good or bad, our tastes are ours and it is always permissible to take ourselves as the sole judges and models of our lives'. Once again, the remarkable thing here is not that such things should be said, but that they should be said by the 'clerks', by a class of men whose purpose hitherto has been to urge their fellow-citizens

7. Certain nationalists, desirous of honouring cosmopolitanism, whose full value their intelligence perceives, and yet not wishing to sacrifice nationalism, declare that cosmopolitanism represents 'enlightened nationalism'. M. Paul Bourget, who gives this definition (*Paris-Times,* June, 1924), quotes Goethe and Stendhal as examples, 'the former of whom remained so profoundly German while striving to understand the whole movement of French thought, and the latter remained so profoundly French while he devoted himself to understanding Italy.' One wonders how these two masters showed the least, even enlightened, 'nationalism' by remaining profoundly German and profoundly French. Obviously M. Bourget confuses national and nationalist.

8. Almost all works of national propaganda among the small nations of Eastern Europe are anthologies of poetry. Very few are works of thought. See the words uttered by E. Boutroux in August, 1915, to the Committee of the Entente Cordiale, against the peoples who attach too much importance to the intelligence, which 'of itself tends to be one and common to all beings capable of knowledge'.

to feel conscious of themselves in what is common to all men, that they should be said in France by the descendants of Montaigne, Pascal, Voltaire, and Renan. . . .

The modern 'clerk' denounces the feeling of universalism, not only for the profit of the nation, but for that of a class. Our age has beheld moralists who have declared to the bourgeois world (or to the working classes) that, far from trying to check the feeling of their differences from others and to feel conscious of their common human nature, they should on the contrary try to feel conscious of this difference in all its profundity and irreducibleness, and that this effort is fine and noble, whereas every desire for union is here a sign of baseness and cowardice, and also of weakness of mind. This, as everyone knows, is the thesis of the 'Reflections on Violence', which has been praised by a whole galaxy of apostles of the modern soul. There is certainly something more novel in this attitude of the 'clerks' to class differences than in their attitude towards national differences. To discover the results of this teaching and the additional hatred (hitherto unknown) which it has given to either class in doing violence to its adversary, you have only to look at Italian Fascism for the bourgeois class, and at Russian Bolshevism for the working class.[9]. . .

B. The 'clerks' praise attachment to the practical, and denounce love of the spiritual. But the 'clerks' with their doctrines have inflamed the realism of the laymen in other ways besides praising the particular and denouncing the universal. At the very top of the scale of moral values they place the possession of concrete advantages, of material power and the means by which they are procured; and they hold up to scorn the pursuit of truly spiritual advantages, of non-practical or disinterested values.

This they have done, first of all, as regards the State. For twenty centuries the 'clerks' preached to the world that the State should be just; now they proclaim that the State should be strong and should care nothing about being just. (Remember the attitude of the chief French teachers during the Dreyfus affair.) Convinced that the strength of the State depends upon authority, they defend autocratic systems, arbitrary government, the reason of State, the religions which teach blind submission to authority, and they cannot sufficiently denounce all institutions based on liberty and discussion. This denunciation of liberalism, notably by the vast majority of contemporary men of letters, will be one of the things in this age most astonishing to History, especially on the part of the French. With their eyes fixed on the powerful

---

9. It is current knowledge that Italian Fascism and Russian Bolshevism both derive from the author of *Reflections on Violence*. He did, indeed, preach class egotism to some extent in a universal manner, but without any explicit preference for the interest of one class rather than that of another. In his preaching of egotism there is a kind of impartiality which does not lack grandeur, a quality not inherited by his disciples.

State, they have praised the State disciplined in the Prussian manner, where everyone has his post, and under orders from above, labours for the greatness of the nation, without there being any place left for particular wills. Owing to their cult of the powerful State (and also for other reasons I shall mention later), they want the military element to preponderate in the State, they want it to have a right to privileges and they want the civil element to agree to this right. (See *L'Appel au Soldat,* and the declarations of numerous writers during the Dreyfus affair.) It is certainly something new to see men of thought preaching the abasement of the toga before the sword, especially in the country of Montesquieu and Renan. And then they preach that the State should be strong and contemptuous of justice, above all in its relations with other States. To this end they praise in the head of the State the will to aggrandisement, the desire for 'strong frontiers', the effort to keep his neighbours under his domination. And they glorify those means which to them seem likely to attain these ends, i.e. sudden aggression, trickery, bad faith, contempt for treaties. This apology for Machiavellianism has inspired all the German historians for the past fifty years, and in France it is professed by very influential teachers, who exhort France to venerate her Kings because they are supposed to have been models of the purely practical spirit, exempt from all respect for any silly justice in their relations with their neighbours.

The novelty of this attitude among the 'clerks' can best be displayed by quoting the famous answer of Socrates to the realist in the *Georgias*:

'In the persons of Themistocles, Cimon and Pericles, you praise men who made their fellow citizens good cheer, by serving them with everything they desired without caring to teach them what is good and right in food. They have enlarged the State, cry the Athenians, but they do not see that this enlargement is nothing but a swelling, a tumour filled with corruption. This is all that has been achieved by these former politicians by filling the city with ports, arsenals, walls, tributes, and the like follies, and by not adding Temperance and Justice.'

Up to our own times, in theory at least (but it is with theories I am dealing here) the supremacy of the spiritual proclaimed in those words has been adopted by all those who, explicitly or otherwise, have proposed a scale of values to the world, whether through the Church, or the Renaissance, or the eighteenth century. One can guess the derisive laughter of a Barrès or any Italian moralist (to speak only of the Latin races) at this disdain of power for the benefit of justice, and their severity for the manner in which this son of Athens judges those who made his city materially powerful. For Socrates, in this respect the perfect model of the 'clerk' who is faithful to his essential function, ports, arsenals, walls are 'follies', and the serious things are justice and temperance. Those who to-day should perform the duties of a Socrates consider that it is justice which is a folly—'a cloud'—and the serious things are the arsenals, the walls. To-day the 'clerk' has made himself Minister of War. Moreover, one of the most revered modern moralists definitely approves of the judges who condemned Socrates, as good guardians of worldly interests.[10] And that is something which has not been seen among the educators of the human soul since the evening when Crito closed his master's eyelids.

I say that the modern 'clerks' have *preached* that the State should be strong and care nothing about being just; and in fact the 'clerks' do give this assertion the characteristic of preaching, of moral teaching. I cannot insist too often that in this lies their great originality. When Machiavelli advises the Prince to carry out the Machiavellian scheme of action, he invests those actions with no sort of morality or beauty. For him morality remains what it is for everyone else, and does not cease to remain so because he observes (not without melancholy) that it is incompatible with politics. 'The Prince,' says Machiavelli, 'must have an understanding always ready to do good, but he must be able to enter into evil when he is forced to do so'; thereby showing that for him evil, even if it aids politics, still remains evil. The modern realists are the *moralists* of realism. For them, the act which makes the State strong is invested with a moral character by the fact that it does so, and this whatever the act may be. The evil which serves politics ceases to be evil and becomes good. This position is evident in Hegel, in the Pangermanists and in Barrès; it is no less evident among realists like M. Maurras and his disciples, in spite of their insistence in declaring that they profess no morality. Perhaps these teachers do not profess any morality, at least expressly, in what concerns private life, but they very clearly profess a morality in the political order of things, if by morality is meant everything which puts forward a scale of good and evil. For them as for Hegel, the practical in politics *is the moral,* and if what the rest of the world calls moral is in opposition to the practical, then *it is the immoral.* Such precisely is the perfectly moralist meaning of the famous campaign of 'false patriotism'. It seems as if we might say that for M. Maurras the practical is the divine, and that his 'atheism' consists less in denying God than in shifting Him to man and his political work. I think I can describe the work of this writer accurately by saying that it is the *divinizing of politics.*[11] This displacement of morality

---

10. Sorel, *Le procès de Socrate.*

11. This has been perfectly obvious to all those guardians of the spiritual who have condemned it, whatever their motives may have been. More precisely, Maurras's work makes the passion of man to found the State (or to strengthen it) an object of religious adoration; it is really the worldly made transcendental. This displacing of the transcendental is the secret of the great influence exerted by Maurras on his contemporaries. These persons, especially in irreligious France, were plainly eager for such a doctrine, if one may judge by the outburst of gratitude with which they greeted it, and which seems to say: 'At last we are deliverd from God; at last we are allowed to adore ourselves in our will to be great, not in our will to be good; we are shown the ideal

is undoubtedly the most important achievement of the modern 'clerks', and the most deserving of the historian's attention. It is a great turning-point in the history of man when those who speak in the name of pondered thought come and tell him that his political egotisms are divine, and that everything which labours to relax them is degrading. The results of this teaching were shown by the example of Germany a decade ago.[12]

---

in the real, on earth and not in heaven.' In this sense, Maurras's work is the same as Nietzsche's ('be faithful to the earth'), with this difference, that the German thinker deifies man in his anarchic passions, and the Frenchman in his organizing passions. It is also the same as the work of Bergson and James, inasmuch as it says like them: the real is the only ideal. This *secularizing of the divine* may be compared with the work of Luther.

12. Machiavellian morality is plainly proclaimed in the following lines, where every open-minded person will recognize, except for the tone, the teaching of *all* the present teachers of realism, whatever their nationality: 'In his relations with other States, the Prince should know neither law nor right, except the right of the strongest. These relations place in his hands, under his responsibility, the divine rights of the Destiny and government of the world, and raise him above the precepts of individual morality into a higher moral order, whose content is enshrined in the words: Salus populi suprema lex esto.' (Fichte, quoted by Andler, op. cit., p. 33.) The advance on Machiavelli is obvious.

THE RESPONSIBILITY OF SOVIET INTELLECTUALS

Maxim Gorky

   ... THERE is nothing in modern times so edifying as the picture of the intellectual growth of masses and individuals in the Soviet Union. This picture compels me to look upon our scientific and technical workers as genuine heroes of our day. I am not only referring to the profound cultural-revolutionary value of their work in its various forms—this is not the place to speak of that. But I would like to say a few words about our scientist and our engineer as a social type.

He is a man of a new type. He is new, not only because he has resolutely rejected the precept "science for science's sake" professed by the scientific experts of the bourgeoisie, the precept of the searchers after "lasting truth"— our young scientist knows that there are no eternal truths and that every truth is nothing but an implement of knowledge, a step forward and upward. He is a new type of man because he differs from all other masters of culture in the fact that he is taking a direct part in the practical work of changing the world, that he is an indicator of the latent, "potential" talent of the working people. And one of his most valuable features is a feeling of responsibility—a truly socialist feeling, in my opinion. He feels his responsibility to the material with which he works, to the technical process in which he participates, to the collective body in whose midst he displays his capacity, to the party and class of which he is not a hireling, but one of the creative units. He is part of a working collective body, a necessary, and sometimes the chief part; he unites and concentrates the energy of the collective body in the process of labour. He cannot help feeling the deep meaning of his responsibility.

One involuntarily and not without a certain sadness compares the engineer and scientific worker with some of our other masters and conveyors of culture to the masses, as, for example, the actor and writer. The actor and writer are better known to society; they enjoy the attention, sympathy, and solicitude of society and the government far more than scientific and technical workers do. The labour of the masters of technology and science—not

Reprinted from *Culture and the People* (1939), pp. 189-198, by permission of the publisher, International Publishers Co., Inc. Title supplied by the Editor.

to mention the labour of the doctor, the sentinel and champion of the health of the people, or the labour of the teacher, who opens the eyes of children to the world surrounding them—is not yet as well paid as the labour of famous writers.

There are very serious grounds for asserting that the sense of social responsibility is far less developed among literary men than among other masters of culture. One might even ask: Does the writer recognise his responsibility to the reader, to the epoch, and to society, or does he feel responsible only to the critics? One very often observes a poor sense of responsibility in our literary men, or even no sense of responsibility at all, to the material they handle. The degree of individualism is much higher among literary men than among other masters of culture. It is said that this is due to the nature of their work. I do not undertake to judge. The individualism of the engineer and the scientist is determined by their speciality; the astronomer or astro-physicist need not necessarily be acquainted with geology or medicine, and a builder of locomotives or bridges probably need not be acquainted with ethnography and zoology.

But the writer should know, if not everything, at least as much as possible about the astronomer and the mechanic, the biologist and the tailor, the engineer and the shepherd, and so on. It is not enough to say of the bug that it is red or brown, which is what our writers usually say of the enemies of the proletariat. Our writers have a good knowledge and understanding of certain ancient aphorisms, such as: "Thou art a tsar; live thine own life." This wretched little aphorism is a false one. The tsars used to surround themselves with a vast host of servitors. And, in imitation of the tsars, literary barons also try to surround themselves with a retinue. The writers have not deleted another old aphorism from their lexicon: "Art for art's sake"—and some of the smart ones are trying to fabricate a refined literature, in imitation, for example, of Dos Passos. They are still disputing over the alleged contradiction between form and content, as though form is possible without content. For instance, a gun made of air—although air is also a material—is not a gun that can fire real shells. The more important the social significance of the material, the stricter, more precise, and clearer a form it demands. It seems to me high time this were understood.

There are quite a number of writers who are unconcerned about making the productions of their minds and pens at least relatively comprehensible to their readers. I have repeatedly raised this point before, but in vain. If you say even to a not very competent writer,—"Comrade, what you have written is not very good!", he gets annoyed, runs off to complain—and soon an article appears claiming that the writer mentioned is a genius. There are some who believe that since "it was so," then "it will be so"; they very assiduously delve into the filth of the past and, finding some survivals of it in the present, claim not without satisfaction that the past resembles the present. Mutually sympathetic groups are formed which vilify groups antipathetic to them; the *Literary Gazette* answers in the same coin—and this unseemly mix-up is called "literary life." As a knowledge of truth is obtained from a comparison of "contradictions," I, of course, am not opposed to groups, provided each of them is formed under the influence of a similar experience and does not try to hector and domineer, but to compare its experience with the experiences of others, and provided it does so honestly, with the object of attaining some higher ideological unity necessary for an alliance of writers.

It will be said: "He began with a toast, and has ended with a funeral oration." It looks very much like it, but not quite. For literature is a cause— and in our country and under our conditions—a very important cause. Moreover, the force of life is such that I am ready to believe that the dead may be resurrected.

Dear comrades, you are living in an atmosphere in which the collective labour of the masses is altering the physical geography of the earth; an atmosphere in which an unprecedented and amazingly audacious and successful struggle with nature has begun; an atmosphere which is re-educating wreckers, enemies of the proletariat, ingrained property-lovers, "socially dangerous" people, and making them useful and active citizens. Is it not time perhaps, comrades, for you, too, to re-educate yourselves and becomes genuine masters of your craft and active collaborators of the proletariat, which is working for the freedom and the happiness of the proletariat of all countries?

There is such a thing as a hummock view and a point of view. The distinction should be observed. We know that hummocks are a peculiarity of swamps, and that they are left after the swamp has been drained. Not much can be seen from a hummock. A point of view is different; it is formed as a result of a writer's observation, comparison, and study of the diverse phenomena of life. The broader the social experience of the writer, the more elevated is his point of view, the broader is his intellectual horizon, and the clearer can he see what is concerned with what and the reciprocal action of approaches and contacts on earth. Scientific socialism has created for us an elevated intellectual plateau, from which the past can be clearly observed and from which the only path into the future is visible, the path leading from "the realm of necessity to the realm of freedom." The successful progress of the work of the Party created by the political genius of Vladimir Lenin is convincing the proletariat of all countries, and even men of sense who are hostile to the proletariat as a class, that the path from "the realm of necessity to the realm of freedom" is not a fantasy. The death agony of the bourgeoisie known as fascism, and especially the frightful agony of the German bourgeoisie, shows even more convincingly that the path of the proletariat is the right one. The iron will of Joseph Stalin, the helmsman of the Party, is splendidly coping with deviations from the proper course and curing the crew of the Party vessel of all attacks of "dizziness." To this it should be added that history is ever more resolutely and effectively working for us.

This is optimism, you say? No. We must clearly perceive all the vileness and despicableness that is threatening us from abroad, that is threatening the first state in the history of mankind to be built by a proletarian dictatorship on the principles of scientific socialism. We must ruthlessly and mercilessly combat everything that is hostile to the fundamental aim of the proletariat and capable of retarding its cultural-revolutionary, socialist growth. And we must firmly realise that although in certain countries the movement of the proletariat towards power is being retarded, nevertheless there is no force that can halt it. Our system of political education of the masses teaches the truth, to which capitalism can retaliate only by force of arms; but the arms are in the hands of the proletariat. The shameful civic death of the "leaders" of the German Social-Democracy was the suicide of cowards terrified by the spread of revolutionary truth.

It is vitally essential for the creative work of our writers that they acquire the point of view from which—and from which alone—can be clearly seen all the filthy crimes of capitalism, all the vileness of its bloody intentions, and all the grandeur of the heroic work of the proletarian dictatorship. One can rise to this point of view only by ridding oneself of the professional, craft mesh, the mesh of commonplace in which we are slowly being entangled, perhaps without ourselves observing it. We must understand that by succumbing to the life of the commonplace, we run the risk of becoming parasites on the working class, public clowns, as the majority of the writers of the bourgeoisie have always been.

The anxiety which induces me to speak in this way is not peculiar to me; it is felt by Nikolai Tikhonov, one of our most talented writers, the author of the article "The Indifferent," and one senses it in friendly conversations with the more responsive of our young writers, those who are sincerely and eagerly concerned about the fate of literature and who understand its cultural and educational value. Anxiety is also caused by the indifference shown by writers to the organisation of their own all-Union congress. One asks: What will the literary men of the centre have to offer the hundreds of young writers from the regions and republics? What will they say to these young people? It is to be expected that the former members of the RAPP (Russian Association of Proletarian Writers.—*Trans.*), will once again repent their errors in public, and that, despite their repentance, their former enemies, friends, and colleagues will once again subject them to severe criticism, the sort of criticism that can teach nothing but is quite capable of increasing the irresponsibility of certain writers.

The other day the members of the Organising Committee were asked what they had done by way of preparation for the all-Union congress. They could not give a coherent answer, although the enquiry concerned a matter of "vital" interest to them.

The ability with which they pronounced lengthy and vague speeches revealed the anemia of their minds. Some of them demonstratively strolled past the groups engaged in conversation, seemingly admiring the wretched weather, and apparently convinced that geniuses they were and geniuses they would remain under all conditions. Not one of them regretted that he had not found time to visit the work on the White Sea and Baltic Canal; not one of them was acquainted with the results of the two years' work done by Angelo Omedo, one of the greatest hydrographers and hydro-electric engineers living, in Transcaucasia, the Caucasus, Central Asia, and Siberia; not one of them was interested in the state of the huge project for an Institute of Experimental Medicine; and, in general, the progress of the new culture is something that apparently lies beyond their field of vision, and that whatever knowledge they may have of it is derived solely from newspapers—not very nourishing pabulum for literary artists. For example, just now huts are being built outside Moscow for thousands of workers engaged in the construction of the Volga-Moscow Canal. These thousands of people of various types constitute splendid study material. I am not certain that any of my "colleagues of the pen" will devote the slightest attention to this rich material.

I have not forgotten that during these fifteen years our young literature has produced scores of very valuable books. But I have also not forgotten that the number of themes dealt with in these books is by no means very large, and that many of the themes, treated hastily and superficially, have been compromised, that is, spoilt.

One cannot help noting the fact that, with the exception of M. Ognyev and a few others, our writers have not produced a single valuable book on children—for fathers and mothers—not to speak of books for children, which are evidently considered to be unworthy of "high art." Nobody has dealt with the theme of the regeneration of the peasant in the factory, or of the intellectual and emotional transformation of members of the national minorities into Communist internationalists, we have not had a clear portrait of the woman-administrator, nobody has given us portraits of the scientific worker, the inventor, the artist—portraits of people many of whom were born in remote villages or in the filthy back-streets of the cities, or brought up in chimneyless huts together with the calves, or on city outskirts together with beggars and thieves. Yet many of them are already known to Europe as people of the highest talent. But in our own country they are unknown—or else have been forgotten.

Very narrow indeed is the outlook of our literary comrades; and the cause of this narrowness is—the hummock view. Millions and tens of millions of proletarians in all parts of the world are expecting ardent and vivid productions from us; they are expecting clear and simple descriptions of the great achievements of masses and individuals in which the miraculous energy of the masses is concentrated. However much the world bourgeois press may slander us, however assiduously it may invent abominable falsehoods about us, however diehard parliamentarians may lie and try to discredit our work, even this press is obliged to admit the success of our diplomacy. And the European proletariat, territorially situated closest to us, is hearing more and more frequently from the mouth of his enemy, the bourgeoisie, acknowledgements of the great achievements of "socialism in one country."

The writers of the Union of Soviet Socialist Republics must broaden their outlook in order to broaden and deepen their activities. This is demanded of them by the epoch, by the new history which the proletariat of the Soviet Union is creating; it is demanded by the children who will soon become adolescents and may put some rather disconcerting questions to their fathers; and, lastly, it is demanded by art.

The foreign and internal enemies will no doubt rejoice and say: "Here is Gorky, too, giving us some enjoyable spiritual food!" But their rejoicing will be misguided. I have no intention of feeding pigs. This article has been called forth by the great demands of real life in the Soviet Union. The enemies are constitutionally incapable of realising the greatness and value of these demands. The literature of the Soviet Union is developing well, but real life is splendid and magnificent. Literature must attain to the level of real life. That is the point.

THE IRRESPONSIBLES

Archibald MacLeish

HISTORY, if honest history continues to be written, will have one question to ask of our generation—people like ourselves. It will be asked of the books we have written, the carbon copies of our correspondence, the photographs of our faces, the minutes of our meetings in the famous rooms before the portraits of our spiritual begetters. The question will be this: Why did the scholars and the writers of our generation in this country, witnesses as they were to the destruction of writing and of scholarship in great areas of Europe and to the exile and the imprisonment and murder of men whose crime was scholarship and writing—witnesses also to the rise in their own country of the same destructive forces with the same impulses, the same motives, the same means—why did the scholars and the writers of our generation in America fail to oppose those forces while they could— while there was still time and still place to oppose them with the arms of scholarship and writing?

It is a question the historians will ask with interest—the gentle, detached, not altogether loving interest with which historians have always questioned the impotent spirits of the dead. Young men working in the paper rubbish of our lives, the old journals, the marginal notations, the printed works, will discover—or so they will think—that the scholars and the writers of our generation in this country had been warned of danger as men were rarely warned before. They will discover—or so they will think—that the common inherited culture of the West, by which alone our scholars and our writers lived, had been attacked in other countries with a stated and explicit purpose to destroy. They will discover that the purpose had been realized. They will discover that a similar purpose, backed by similar forces, created by similar conditions, was forming here. And it will seem to them strange—ironical and strange—that the great mass of American scholars and American writers made no effort to defend either themselves or the world by which they lived.

They will make of course the necessary reservations. They will note that societies of scholars and associations of writers adopted resolutions de-

Reprinted from *The Nation* (May 18, 1940), pp. 618-619, 620-623, by permission of the periodical and Duell, Sloan & Pearce, Inc. Copyright 1940, by Archibald MacLeish.

claring their devotion to civilization. They will note that certain young novelists and poets, the most generous and gallant of their time, unable to endure the outrage and injustice, gave up their lives as writers and enlisted in the hopeless armies to fight brutality with force. But of those who truly faced this danger not with their bodies but with their minds, of those who fought the enemies of the intellect with the weapons of the intellect, of those who fought this danger with the weapons by which this danger could be overcome, they will record the names of very few. And they will ask their question: Why did we, scholars and writers in America in this time, we who had been warned of our danger not only by explicit threats but by explicit action, why did we not fight this danger while the weapons we used best—the weapons of ideas and words—could still be used against it?

It is not a question for which we are altogether unprepared. We have been writing out our answer for many years now in action and inaction, in words and in silence—in learned articles in the scientific journals and in controversial articles in the general magazines, in books, in blank faces after the passionate words, in bored eyes refusing to believe. The answer we have prepared, the answer we have written out for history to find, is the answer Leonardo is said to have given Michelangelo when Michelangelo blamed him for his indifference to the misfortunes of the Florentines. It is the answer of our kind at many other times and places. "Indeed," said Leonardo, "indeed, the study of beauty has occupied my whole heart." The study of beauty, of history, of science, has occupied our whole hearts, and the misfortunes of our generation are none of our concern. They are the practical and political concern of practical and political men, but the concern of the scholar, the concern of the artist, is with other, purer, more enduring things.

This is the answer we have written down for history to find. I doubt whether it will satisfy the ironic men who come to plague us on that waterfront where Teresias was made to drink the blood and answer. I think, indeed, it will not satisfy them. For it has not satisfied ourselves. We say with great firmness and authority, speaking by our words and by our silence, that the misfortunes of our generation are economic and political misfortunes from which the scholar can safely hold himself apart. We say this with all the authority of the political scientists of the past, to whom the misfortunes of the people were always political and economic and of no concern to the poet, the pure scholar, the artist intent upon his art. We say it also with the authority of the political scientists of the present, to whom all phenomena of whatever kind are, by hypothesis, economic and political. But though we say it we do not believe it. For we have observed these misfortunes. They have been acted out for us to see. And what we have seen is this: that the misfortunes of our time are not the misfortunes the philosophers, the theorists, the political scientists have described to us. They are not the practical concern of the practical man and therefore matters of indifference to the scholar. On the contrary, it is the practical man and the practical man alone—the man whose only care is for his belly and his roof—who can safely be indifferent to these troubles. The things he lives by are not menaced. And it is precisely the scholar, the poet—the man whose care is for the structures of the intellect, the houses of the mind—whose heart is caught. For it is the scholar's goods which are in danger.

It is perhaps because we have seen this and yet refuse to see it that our minds are so confused and our counsels so bewildered. Nothing is more characteristic of the intellectuals of our generation than their failure to understand what it is that is happening to their world. And nothing explains that failure so precisely as their unwillingness to see what they have seen and to know what they do truly know. They continue to speak of the crisis of their time as though the war in Europe were that crisis—and the war, they say, is no concern of theirs. They continue to speak of the crisis as though the imperialistic maneuvers, the struggles for markets, the propaganda in the newspapers and the radio were the crisis—and the maneuvers of imperialism, the propaganda of the press, and the struggles for trade, they say, are no concern of theirs. And yet they know—they know very well because they have seen—that these things are not the crisis but merely its reflections in the mirrors of action. They know that behind the war, behind the diplomatic gestures, behind the black print on the page and the hysterical voices on the air there is something deeper and more dangerous—more dangerous to *them*. They know that it is a condition of men's minds which has produced these things—a condition which existed and exists not only in Europe but in other parts of the world as well and not least in our own country. And they know that this condition of men's minds is not a practical, a political, phenomenon of no concern to the scholar and the man of thought, but something very different. . . .

It is to this disorder and not to some political and partisan dissension, not to some accidental economic breakdown—it is to this direct, explicit, and intentional attack upon the scholar's world and the scholar's life and the scholar's work that American scholarship has been indifferent. Or if not indifferent, then inactive; merely watchful—fearful, watchful, and inactive. And it is there that history will place its question: How could we sit back as spectators of a war against ourselves?

I think, speaking only of what I have seen myself and heard, I think it is neither lack of courage nor lack of wisdom but a different reason which has prevented our generation of intellectuals in this country from acting in its own defense. I think it is the organization of the intellectual life of our time. Specifically, I think it is this: that intellectual responsibility has been divided in our time and by division destroyed. The men of intellectual duty, those who should have been responsible for action, have divided themselves into two castes, two cults—the scholars and the writers. Neither of these accepts responsibility for the common culture or for its defense.

There was a time a century ago, two centuries ago, when men who practiced these professions would have accepted such responsibility without an instant's hesitation. A century ago the professions of the writer and the scholar were united in the single profession of the man of letters, and the man of letters was responsible in everything that touched the mind. He was a man of wholeness of purpose, of singleness of intention, a single intellectual champion, admittedly responsible for the defense of the inherited tradition, avowedly partisan of its practice. Where those who practice these several professions today divide the learned world and the creative world between them in irresponsible and neutral states, the man of letters inhabited both learning and the world of letters like an empire.

He was a man of learning whose learning was employed not for its own sake in a kind of academic narcissism but for the sake of decent living in his time. He was a writer whose writing was used not to mirror an abstract and unrelated present but to illuminate that present by placing it in just relation to its past. He was therefore and necessarily a man who admitted a responsibility for the survival and vitality of the common and accumulated experience of the mind, for this experience was to him the air he breathed, the perspective of his thinking. Learning to him was no plump pigeon carcass to be picked at for his private pleasure and his private fame but a profession practiced for the common good. Writing was not an ornament, a jewel, but a means to ends, a weapon, the most powerful of weapons, a weapon to be used. Whatever threatened learning or the ends of learning challenged the man of letters. Whatever struck at truth or closed off question or defiled an art or violated decency of thinking struck at him. And he struck back with every weapon masters of the word could find to strike with. Milton defending freedom of the mind in sentences which outlive every name of those who struck at freedom, Voltaire displaying naked to the grin of history the tyrants who were great until he made them small, Bartholomew de las Casas gentling cruel priests and brutal captains with the dreadful strokes of truth —las Casas, Milton, and Voltaire were men of letters, men who confessed an obligation to defend the disciplines of thought not in their own but in the general interest.

Had men like these been living in our time, had the intellectuals of our time been whole and loyal, it would, I think, have been impossible for the revolution of the gangs to have succeeded where success has been most dangerous—in the perversion of the judgments of the mind. Murder is not absolved of immorality by committing murder. Murder is absolved of immorality by bringing men to think that murder is not evil. This only the perversion of the mind can bring about. And the perversion of the mind is only possible when those who should be heard in its defense are silent.

They are silent in our time because there are no voices which accept responsibility for speaking. Even the unimaginable indecencies of propaganda, even the corruption of the word itself in Germany and Russia and Spain and elsewhere, even the open triumph of the lie produced no answer such as Voltaire in his generation would have given. And for this reason—that the man who could have been Voltaire, who could have been las Casas, does not live: the man of intellectual *office,* the man of intellectual *calling,* the man who *professes* letters—professes an obligation as a servant of the mind to defend the mind's integrity against every physical power—professes an obligation to defend the labors of the mind and the structures it has created and the means by which it lives, not only privately and safely in his study, not only strictly and securely in the controversies of the learned press, but publicly and at the public risk and danger of his life. He does not exist because the man of letters no longer exists. And the man of letters no longer exists because he has been driven from our world and from our time by the division of his kingdom. The single responsibility, the wholeness of function of the man of letters, has been replaced by the divided function, the mutual antagonism, the isolated irresponsibility of two figures—the scholar and the writer.

Why this substitution has come about—whether because the methods of scientific inquiry, carried over into the humanities, destroyed the loyalties and habits of the mind or for some other reason—I leave to wiser men to say. The point is that there has been a substitution. The country of the man of letters has been divided between his heirs. The country that was once the past and present brought together in the mind is now divided into past on one side, present on the other.

Past is the scholar's country; present is the writer's. The writer sees the present on the faces of the world and leaves the past to rot in its own rubbish. The scholar digs his ivory cellar in the ruins of the past and lets the present sicken as it will. A few exceptions noted here and there—men like Thomas Mann—the gulf between these countries is complete. And the historical novels fashionable at the moment, the vulgarizations of science, the digests of philosophy, only define its depth as a plank across a chasm makes the chasm deeper. That it should be necessary to throw such flimsy flights from one side to the other of the learned world shows how deeply and disastrously the split was made.

That scholarship suffers or that writing suffers by the change is not asserted. Scholarship may be more scientific: writing may be purer. Indeed, there are many who believe, and I among them, that the time we live in has produced more first-rate writers than any but the very greatest ages, and there are scholars of a scholarship as hard, as honest, as devoted as any we have known. But excellence of scholarship and writing are not now in question. What matters now is the defense of culture—the defense truly, and in the most literal terms, of civilization as men have known it for the last two thousand years. And there the substitution of the modern scholar-writer, however pure his scholarship, however excellent his writing, is a tragic and immeasurable loss. For neither the modern scholar nor the modern writer admits responsibility for this defense. They assert on the contrary, each in his particular way, an irresponsibility as complete as it is singular.

The irresponsibility of the scholar is the irresponsibility of the scientist upon whose laboratory insulation he has patterned all his work. The scholar in letters has made himself as indifferent to values, as careless of significance, as bored with meanings as the chemist. He is a refugee from consequences, an exile from the responsibilities of moral choice. His words of praise are the laboratory words—objectivity, detachment, dispassion. His pride is to be scientific, neuter, skeptical, detached—superior to final judgment or absolute belief. In his capacity as scholar the modern scholar does not occupy the present. In his capacity as scholar he loves the word—but only the word which entails no judgments, involves no decisions, accomplishes no actions. Where the man of letters of other centuries domesticated the past within the rustling of the present, making it stand among us like the meaning of a statue among trees, the modern scholar in his capacity as scholar leaves the present and returns across the past, where all the men are marble.

It is not for nothing that the modern scholar invented the Ph.D. thesis as his principal contribution to literary form. The Ph.D. thesis is the perfect image of his world. It is work done for the sake of doing work—perfectly conscientious, perfectly laborious, perfectly irresponsible. The modern scholar at his best and worst is both these things—perfectly conscientious, laborious, and competent: perfectly irresponsible for the saving of his world. He remembers how in the Civil Wars in England the scholars, devoted only to their proper tasks, founded the Royal Society. He remembers how through other wars and other dangers the scholars kept the lamp of learning lighted. He does not consider that the scholars then did other things as well as trim the lamp wicks. He does not consider either that the dangers change and can be greater. He has his work to do. He has his book to finish. He hopes the war will not destroy the manuscripts he works with. He is the pure, the perfect type of irresponsibility—the man who acts as though the fire could not burn him because he has no business with the fire. He knows, because he cannot help but know, reading his papers, talking to his friends—he knows this fire has consumed the books, the spirit, everything he lives by, flesh itself, in other countries. He knows this but he will not know. It's not his business. Whose business is it then? He will not answer even that. He has his work to do. He has his book to finish. . . .

The writer's irresponsibility is no less. Where the modern scholar escapes from the adult judgments of the mind by taking the disinterested man of science as his model, the modern writer escapes by imitation of the artist. He practices his writing as a painter does his painting. He thinks as artist, which is to say he thinks without responsibility to anything but truth of feeling. He observes as artist, which is to say that he observes with honesty and truthfulness and without comment. His devotion, as with every honest painter, is devotion to the thing observed, the actual thing, the thing without its consequences or its antecedents, naked of judgment, stripped of causes and effects. The invisible world, the intellectual world, the world of the relation of ideas, the world of judgments, of values, the world in which truth is good and lies are evil—this world has no existence for the honest artist or for the honest writer who takes the artist for his model.

He sees the world as a god sees it—without morality, without care, without judgment. People look like this. People act like that. He shows them looking, acting. It is not his business why they look so, why they act so. It is enough that he should "make them happen." If he concerns himself with motive at all he concerns himself with the "real" motive, meaning the discreditable motive which the actor conceals from himself. His most searching purpose is to find, not the truth of human action, but the low-down, the discreditable explanation which excuses him from care. The suggestion that there are things in the world—ideas, conceptions, ways of thinking—which the writer-artist should defend from attack—the suggestion above all that he was under an obligation to defend the inherited culture—would strike him as ridiculous.

Artists do not save the world. They practice art. They practice it as Goya practiced it among the cannon in Madrid. And if this war is not Napoleon in Spain but something even worse than that? They practice art. Or they put the art aside and take a rifle and go out and fight. But not *as artists*. The artist does not fight. The artist's obligations are obligations to his art. He has no others. Not even when his art itself, his chance to practice it, his need to live where it is practiced may be in danger. The writer-artist will write a bloody story about the expense of blood. He will present the face of agony as it has rarely been presented. But not even then will he take the weapon of his words and carry it to the barricades of intellectual warfare, to the storming of belief, the fortifying of conviction where alone this fighting can be won.

There are examples in history of civilizations made impotent by excess of culture. No one, I think, will say of us that we lost our intellectual liberties on this account. But it may well be said, and said with equally ironic emphasis, that the men of thought, the men of learning, in this country were deceived and rendered impotent by the best they knew. To the scholar impartiality, objectivity, detachment were ideal qualities he taught himself laboriously and painfully to acquire. To the writer objectivity and detachment were his writer's pride. Both subjected themselves to inconceivable restraints, endless disciplines to reach these ends. And both succeeded. Both writers and scholars freed themselves of the subjective passions, the emotional preconceptions which color conviction and judgment. Both writers and scholars freed themselves of the personal responsibility associated with personal choice. They emerged free, pure, and single into the antiseptic air of objectivity. And by that sublimation of the mind they prepared the mind's disaster.

If it is a consolation to the philosophers of earlier civilizations to know that they lost the things they loved because of the purity of their devotion, then perhaps this consolation will be ours as well. I doubt that we will profit by it or receive much praise.

TO WHOM IS THE POET RESPONSIBLE?

Allen Tate

AND FOR WHAT? The part of the question that I have used as the title has been widely asked in our generation. I have seldom heard anybody ask the second part: *For what?* I shall have to assume, without elucidating it, a certain moral attitude towards the idea of responsibility which is perhaps as little popular in our time as the accused poetry that has given rise to the controversy. Thus I take it for granted that nobody can be held generally responsible, for if our duties are not specific they do not exist. It was, I think, the failure to say what the modern poet was responsible *for* that made it easy to conclude, from the attacks ten years ago by Mr. MacLeish and Mr. Van Wyck Brooks, that in some grandiose sense the poet should be held responsible to society for everything that nobody else was paying any attention to. The poet was saddled with a total responsibility for the moral, political, and social well-being; it was pretty clearly indicated that had he behaved differently at some indefinite time in the near or remote past the international political order itself would not have been in jeopardy, and we should not perhaps be at international loggerheads today. We should not have had the Second World War, perhaps not even the First.

The historical political suspicion of poetry is one thing; but the attacks that I have alluded to were by men of letters, one of them a poet—and this is another thing altogether. I do not know to what extent the Marxist atmosphere of the thirties influenced the attacks. In trying to get to the bottom of them one may dismiss too quickly the Communist party-line as a perversion of the original Platonic rejection of poetry which holds that the arts of sensible imitation are a menace to the political order. One must dismiss it respectfully, because it contains a fundamental if one-eyed truth: that is to say, from Plato on there is in this tradition of thought the recognition that, however useful poetry may be as a civilizing virtue, it should not be allowed to govern the sensibility of persons who run the state. One may scarcely believe that Sophocles *as poet* was appointed *strategos* in the Samian war, even though that honorific office followed upon the great success of the *Antigone* in the

Reprinted from *The Man of Letters in the Modern World* (1955), pp. 23-33 of the Meridian Books edition, by permission of the author. Copyright 1951 by *The Hudson Review*, 1953 by Henry Regnery Company, 1955 by Meridian Books.

Dionysia of 440 B.C. What I am getting at here is that, were we confronted with an unreal choice, it would be better to suppress poetry than to misuse it, to expect of it an order of action that it cannot provide. (Stalinist Russia seems to do both· it suppresses poetry and supports party verse.) In any literary history that I have read there is no record of a poet receiving and exercising competently high political authority. Milton wrote Cromwell's Latin correspondence, and tracts of his own; but he was never given power; and likewise his successor, Andrew Marvell. We have read some of Shelley's more heroic assertions, in "The Defense of Poetry," into the past, where we substitute what Shelley said ought to have been for what was. The claim that poets are "unacknowledged legislators" is beyond dispute, if we understand that as legislators they should remain unacknowledged and not given the direction of the state. This limit being set, we are ready to understand what Shelley really had to say—which is the true perception that there is always a reciprocal relation between life and art, at that point at which life imitates art.

If poetry makes us more conscious of the complexity and meaning of our experience, it may have an eventual effect upon action, even political action. The recognition of this truth is not an achievement of our own age; it is very old. Our contribution to it I take to be a deviation from its full meaning, an exaggeration and a loss of insight. Because poetry may influence politics we conclude that poetry is merely politics, or a kind of addlepated politics, and thus not good for anything. Why this has come about there is not time to say here, even if I knew. One may point out some of the ways in which it has affected our general views, and hence see how it works in us.

How does it happen that literary men themselves blame the poets first when society goes wrong? The argument we heard ten years ago runs somewhat as follows: The rise of Hitlerism (we were not then looking too narrowly at Stalinism) reflects the failure of our age to defend the principles of social and political democracy, a failure resulting from the apathy of responsible classes of society, those persons who have charge of the means of public influence that was formerly called language (but is now called "communications"). These persons are the writers, more particularly the poets or "makers," whose special charge is the purity of language and who represent the class of writers presumably at its highest. The makers, early in the nineteenth century, retired to a private world of their own invention, where they cultivated certain delusions—for example, their superiority to practical life, the belief in the autonomy of poetry, and the worship of the past. Some of them, like Baudelaire, actively disliked democracy. Their legacy to our tortured age turned out to be at once the wide diffusion and the intensification of these beliefs, with the result that we became politically impotent, and totalitarianism went unchecked.

This argument is impressive and we cannot wholly dismiss it; for directed somewhat differently it points to a true state of affairs: there was a moral and political apathy in the western countries, and there was no decisive stand against Nazism until it was too late to prevent war. Did the men of letters, the "clerks," have a monopoly upon this apathy? We may answer this question from two points of view. First, is there anything in the nature of poetry, as it has been sung or written in many different kinds of societies, which would justify putting so great a burden of *general* responsibility upon the man of imagination? Secondly, was there no other class of "intellectuals" in the modern world—scientists, philosophers, or statesmen—who might also be called into account?

If we address ourselves to the second question first, we shall have to observe that philosophers, scientists, and politicians have by and large assumed that they had no special responsibility for the chaos of the modern world. Mr. Einstein not long ago warned us that we now have the power to destroy ourselves. There was in his statement no reference to his own great and perhaps crucial share in the scientific progress which had made the holocaust possible. If it occurs, will Mr. Einstein be partly to blame, provided there is anybody left to blame him? Will God hold him responsible? I shall not try to answer that question. And I for one should not be willing to take the responsibility, if I had the capacity, of settling the ancient question of how much natural knowledge should be placed in the hands of men whose moral and spiritual education has not been impressive: by such men I mean the majority at all times and places, and more particularly the organized adolescents of all societies known as the military class.

Here we could meditate upon (or if we like better to do it, pray over) the spectacle, not military, widely reported in the newspapers, of the President of Harvard University congratulating his colleagues with evident delight when the first atom bomb was exploded in the desert. Among those present at Los Alamos on July 14, 1945, at five-thirty in the morning, were Mr. Conant and Mr. Bush. "On the instant that all was over," reported the *New York Times,* "these men leaped to their feet, the terrible tension ended, they shook hands, embraced each other and shouted in delight." We have no right to explore another man's feelings, or to say what should please him. Nobody then or since has said that Mr. Conant's emotions, whatever they may have been on that occasion, were irresponsible. Nor do I wish to use Mr. Conant or any other scientist, or administrator of the sciences, as a whipping-boy for his colleagues. Yet it is a fact that we cannot blink, that the Renaissance doctrine of the freedom of unlimited enquiry has had consequences for good and evil in the modern world. This doctrine has created our world; in so far as we are able to enjoy it we must credit unlimited enquiry with its material benefits. But its dangers are too notorious to need pointing out. An elusive *mystique* supports the general doctrine, which may be stated as follows: We must keep up the enquiry, come hell and high water.

One way to deal with this modern demi-religion is to say that a part of its "truth" must be suppressed. I am not ready to say that: I am only ready to point out that it is not suppression of *truth* to decline to commit wholesale slaughter even if we have the means of committing it beyond the reach of any known technique of the past. Is it suppression of truth to withhold from general use the means of exploiting a technique of slaughter? How might it be withheld, should we agree that it is both desirable and possible to do so? If we let government suppress it, government will in the long run suppress everything and everybody else—even democratic government. There is no just way of holding individuals and classes responsible for the moral temper of an entire civilization.

At this point the theologians and humanists, the men of God and the men of man, appear—or at any rate formerly appeared. The Christian religion, in its various sects, has been blamed for its historic conservatism in refusing to sanction the advances of science as they were made. It is my impression that this supposedly Christian skepticism is Arabic in origin. It was the followers of Averroës in Europe who upheld the secret cult of natural knowledge against the Thomists and the Scotists, who more than the disciples of Roger Bacon stood for the diffusion of scientific enquiry. It is significant that the one science of the ancient world that impinged directly upon the daily lives of men—medicine—was held to be esoteric; the school of Hippocrates hid the secrets of the "art" lest the uninitiate abuse them and pervert them to the uses of witchcraft. This is not the place, and I am not competent enough, to follow up this line of speculation. I have wished only to observe that before the Christian dispensation, and well into it, the professors of special knowledge tried to be responsible for the public use of their techniques. We have not, so far as I know, a record of any of their reasons for what we should consider an illiberal suppression of truth. But if we think of the Greek world of thought as having lasted about nine hundred years, down to the great pupils of Plotinus—Iamblichus and Porphyrius—we may see in it a sense of the whole of life which must not be too quickly disturbed for the prosecution of special scientific interests. Nature was investigated, but it was a nature whose destiny in relation to a transcendental order was already understood. The classical insight into this relation was, as usual, recorded very early in a myth—that of the brothers Prometheus and Epimetheus—which now gives signs of recovering the authority which in the modern world it had yielded to myths that science had created about itself.

The responsibility of the scientist has not, I am sure, been defined by this digression: I have merely suggested that if anybody have a specific responsibility it may be the scientist himself. His myth of omnipotent rationality has worked certain wonders; but perhaps a little too rapidly. In Shelley's "Defense of Poetry" there is a sentence that persons who press the poet to legislate for us seldom quote: "Our calculations have outrun conception; we have eaten more than we can digest." Shall we hold the scientists responsible for this? Have they made the child sick on green apples? I do not say that they have. But the child is sick. If the scientist is not responsible, are philosophers, statesmen, and poets, particularly poets, responsible?

Before I return to the poet's responsibility, I shall consider briefly the possible responsibility of other persons, excluding this time the scientists, about whom it has become evident that I know little; and I can scarcely do more than allude to the other intellectual classes whose special disciplines might conceivably implicate them in care for the public good. Of the philosophers I likewise speak with neither information nor knowledge. Like Mr. Santayana, I might somewhat presumptuously describe myself as "an ignorant man, almost a poet." But one gets strongly the impression that the classical metaphysical question—What is the nature of Being?—is semantically meaningless in our age, a mere historicism reserved for the frivolous occasions of lecture-room philosophy. Our going philosophy is reported to me as a curious, apostolic activity known as the "philosophy of science," an attempt to devise a language for all the sciences which through it would arrive at "unity." This is no doubt a laudable program, unity being usually better than disunity, unless the things to be joined do not like each other, or, again, unless the union take place at a level of abstraction at which certain things become excluded, such as human nature, of which the Nazi and the Stalinist unities for some reason took little account. But these are unities of the political order. What have the philosophers of unified science to do with them? They glanced at them, I believe, in resolutions passed at philosophical congresses, or in interviews for the press, where we were told that things will continue to go badly until men behave more rationally. Rationality usually turned out to be liberalism, or the doctrine that reason, conceived in instrumental terms, will eventually perfect us, even though our situation may be getting worse every day. This, it seems to me, was the contribution of certain philosophers to the recent war. Was the contribution responsible or irresponsible? Common sense ought to tell us that it was neither; and common sense tells us that not all philosophers talked this way. Everybody knows that modern philosophers, like their brother scientists, and not unlike their distant cousins the poets, are pursuing specialisms of various kinds; and from the point of view of these interests, the investigation of the nature of being, with the attendant pursuit of the love of wisdom, is no more within their purview than it is within mine. In his extra-laboratory pronouncements the merged philosopher-scientist sounds uncomfortably like his famous creation in allegorical fiction, the "man in the street"—the man without specialisms who used to sit on the cracker barrel, and who, in all ages since hats were invented, has talked through his hat. Perhaps it was neither responsible nor irresponsible: it was merely dull to use the prestige of the philosophy of science as the stump from which to deliver commonplaces that were already at your and my command and that were doing us so little good that they might be suspected of having caused a part of our trouble. Reason—in the sense of moderate unbelief in difficult truths about human nature—and belief in the perfectibility of man-in-the-gross, were the great liberal dogmas which underlay much of our present trouble. The men in charge of nature never told me that I ought to try to perfect myself; that would be done for me by my not believing that I could do anything about it, by relying upon history to do it, by the invocation of ideals that many of us thought were democratic, by the resolutions of committees, conventions, and associations; and not least by condescending affirmations of faith in the Common Man, a fictitous person with whom neither the philosopher-scientist nor I had even a speaking acquaintance. Will it not be borne in upon us in the next few years that Hitler and Stalin *are* the Common Man, and that one of the tasks of democracy is to allow as many men as possible to make themselves uncommon?

Thus it is my impression that belief in a false liberal democracy was not lacking among certain classes of "intellectuals" in the period between the wars: the period, in fact, in which Mr. MacLeish and Mr. Brooks said that we had staggered into a war that might have been prevented had the men of letters not given us such a grim view of modern man from their ivory towers, or simply refused to be concerned about him. If the more respectable "intellectuals" were not heeded in the call to democratic action, would the mere literary men have been heeded? Was the poet's prestige so great that his loss of democratic faith (assuming he had lost it) set so bad an example that it offset the testimony to the faith of even the statesman?

By the statesman one means, of course, the politician, though one would like to mean more, whether he carry the umbrella or the infectious smile, the swastika or the hammer-and-sickle. It would seem to have been the specific duty of the politician to have kept the faith and forestalled the rise of Nazism, though it was not generally supposed that it was up to him to do anything about Soviet Russia, which was tacitly assumed, if not by you and me, then by the leaves in Vallombrosa, to be on our side. My own disappointment in the politican is somewhat mitigated by the excuse which his failure provides for the poet: if he could not baulk the enemy, whom he directly confronted, what chance had the poet?—the poet, whose best weapon in history seems to have been Shelley's fleet of toy boats, each bearing a cargo of tracts, which he committed to the waters of Hyde Park.

I am sorry to sound frivolous; I confess that the politicial responsibility of poets bores me; I am discussing it because it irritates me more than it bores me. It irritates me because the poet has a great responsibility of his own: it is the responsibility to be a poet, to write poems, and not to gad about using the rumor of his verse, as I am now doing, as the excuse to appear on platforms and to view with alarm. I have a deep, unbecoming suspicion of such talking poets: whatever other desirable things they may believe in, they do not believe in poetry. They believe that poets should write tracts, or perhaps autobiographies, encourage the public, further this cause or that, good or bad, depending upon whose political ox is being gored.

My own political ox was at least driven into a fence-corner when Mr. Pound thumped his tub for the Axis; but what I cannot easily forgive him was thumping any tub at all—unless, as a private citizen, dissociated from the poet, he had decided to take political action at some modest level, such as giving his life for his country, where whatever he did would be as inconspicuous as his ejaculatory political philosophy demanded that it be. But on Radio Rome he appeared as Professor Ezra Pound, the great American Poet. Much the same can be said of Mr. MacLeish himself. It is irrelevant that I find his political principles (I distinguish his *principles* from his *views*), in so far as I understand them, more congenial than Mr. Pound's. The immediate *views* of these poets seem to me equally hortatory, quasi-lyrical, and ill-grounded. We might imagine for them a pleasant voyage in one of Percy Shelley's boats. If society indicted and condemned poets for the mixture and the misuse of two great modes of action, poetry and politics, we might have to indict Mr. Pound a second time, as it could conceivably be done in some Swiftian social order; and we should have in fairness to provide an adjoining cell for Mr. MacLeish.

The relation of poetry and of other high imaginative literature to social action was not sufficiently considered in the attacks and counter-attacks of the past ten years. No one knows precisely what the relation is; so I shall not try here to define it; though what I am about to say will imply certain assumptions. There is no doubt that poetry, even that of Mallarmé, has some effect upon conduct, in so far as it affects our emotions. To what extent is the poetry itself, even that of Mallarmé, an effect? The total complex of sensibility and thought, of belief and experience, in the society from which the poetry emerges, is the prime limiting factor that the poet must first of all be aware of; otherwise his language will lack primary reality, the nexus of thing and word. The failure to consider this primary reality produces willed poetry which usually ignores the human condition. The human condition must be faced and embodied in language before men in any age can envisage the possibility of action. To suggest that poets tell men in crisis what to do, to insist that *as poets* they acknowledge themselves as legislators of the social order, is to ask them to shirk their specific responsibility, which is quite simply the reality of man's experience, not what his experience ought to be, in any age. *To whom* is the poet responsible? He is responsible to his *con-science,* in the French sense of the word: the joint action of knowledge and judgment. This conscience has long known a severe tradition of propriety in discerning the poet's particular kind of actuality. No crisis, however dire, should be allowed to convince us that the relation of the poet to his perma-nent reality can ever change. And thus the poet is not responsible to society for a version of what it thinks it is or what it wants. *For what* is the poet responsible? He is responsible for the virtue proper to him as poet, for his special *arête*: for the mastery of a disciplined language which will not shun the full report of the reality conveyed to him by his awareness: he must hold, in Yeats' great phrase, "reality and justice in a single thought."

We have virtually turned the argument of the attack around upon itself. For it was an irresponsible demand to ask the poet to cease to be a poet and become the propagandist of a political ideal, even if he himself thought it a worthy ideal. If the report of the imagination on the realities of western culture in the past century was as depressing as the liberal mind said it was, would not the scientist, the philosopher, and the statesman have done well to study it? They might have got a clue to what was wrong. They were, I believe, studying graphs, charts, and "trends"—the indexes of power—but not human nature. The decay of modern society is nowhere more conspicuous than in the loss of the arts of reading on the part of men of action. It was said at the beginning of the war that the traditions of modern literature repre-sented by Proust had powerfully contributed to the collapse of Europe. It was not supposed that the collapse of Europe might have affected those traditions. If the politicians had been able to read Proust, or Joyce, or even Kafka, might they not have discerned more sharply what the trouble was, and done some-thing to avert the collapse? I doubt it; but it makes as much sense as the argument that literature can be a cause of social decay. If, for example, Mr. Churchill had been able to quote the passage about Ciacco from the *Inferno,* or the second part of *The Waste Land,* instead of Arthur Hugh Clough, might we have hoped that men would now be closer to the reality out of which sound political aspiration must arise?

I leave this subject with the observation that poetry had to be attacked for not having done all that men had expected of it at the end of the nine-teenth century. "The future of poetry is immense," said Matthew Arnold. It had to be immense because, for men like Arnold, everything else had failed. It was the new religion that was destined to be lost more quickly than the old. Poetry was to have saved us; it not only hadn't saved us by the end of the fourth decade of this century; it had only continued to be poetry which was little read. It had to be rejected. The primitive Athenians, at the Tharg-elian festival of Apollo, killed two human beings, burnt them, and cast their ashes into the sea. The men sacrificed were called *pharmakoi*: medicines. We have seen in our time a powerful attempt to purify ourselves of the knowledge of evil in man. Poetry is one of the sources of that knowledge. It is believed by some classical scholars that the savage ritual of the *pharmakoi* was brought to Athens by Barbarians. In historical times effigies made of dough were substituted for human beings.

THE MAN OF LETTERS AND THE FUTURE OF EUROPE

T. S. Eliot

I WISH first to define the sense in which I shall use the term "man of letters." I shall mean the writer for whom his writing is primarily an *art,* who is as much concerned with style as with content; the understanding of whose writings, therefore, depends as much upon appreciation of style as upon comprehension of content. This is primarily the poet (including the dramatic poet), and the writer of prose fiction. To give emphasis to these two kinds of writer is not to deny the title "man of letters" to writers in many other fields: it is simply a way of isolating the problem of responsibility of the man of letters *qua* man of letters; and if what I have to say is true for the poet and the novelist, it will also be true for other writers in so far as they are "artists."

The first responsibility of the man of letters is, of course, his responsibility towards his art, the same, which neither time nor circumstance can abate or modify, that other artists have: that is, he must do his best with the medium in which he works. He differs from other artists, in that his medium is his language: we do not all paint pictures, and we are not all musicians, but we all talk. This fact gives the man of letters a special responsibility towards everybody who speaks the same language, a responsibility which workers in other arts do not share. But, in general, special responsibilities which fall upon the man of letters at any time must take second place to his permanent responsibility as a literary artist. However, the man of letters is not, as a rule, exclusively engaged upon the production of works of art. He has other interests, like anybody else; interests which will, in all probability, exercise some influence upon the content and meaning of the works of art which he does produce. He has the same responsibility, and should have the same concern with the fate of his country, and with political and social affairs within it, as any other citizen; and in matters of controversy, there is no more reason why two men of letters should hold identical opinions, and support the same party and programme, than why any other two citizens should. Yet there are matters of public concern, in which the man of letters should

Reprinted from *The Sewanee Review* (Summer, 1945), pp. 333-337, 338, 339-342, by permission of the author. This essay originally appeared in *The Norseman* (1944).

express his opinion, and exert his influence, not merely as a citizen but as a man of letters: and upon such matters I think that it is desirable that men of letters should agree. In proceeding to suggest some of these, I have no expectation that all men of letters *will* agree with me: but if I confined myself to statements to which all men of letters, as men of letters, could give immediate assent, I should only be uttering platitudes.

The man of letters as such, is not concerned with the political or economic map of Europe; but he should be very much concerned with its cultural map. This problem, involving the relations of different cultures and languages in Europe, must have presented itself first, to the man of letters, as a domestic problem: in this context, foreign affairs are merely an extension of domestic affairs. Nearly every country, that has been long settled, is a composite of different local cultures; and even when it is completely homogeneous in race, it will, between east and west, or more often between north and south, exhibit differences of speech, of customs, and of ways of thinking and feeling. A small country of course, is usually assumed by foreigners to be much more unified than it really is: and although the educated foreigner is aware that Britain contains within its small area several races and several languages, he may underestimate the importance of both the friction, and the often happy combination toward a common end, of the different types. It is a commonplace that industrialism (of which totalitarianism is a political expression) tends to obliterate these differences, to uproot men from their ancestral habitat, to mingle them in large manufacturing and business centres, or to send them hither and thither as the needs of manufacture and distribution may dictate. In its political aspect, industrialism tends to centralize the direction of affairs in one large metropolis, and to diminish that interest in, and control over, local affairs by which men gain political experience and sense of responsibility. Against this tendency, "regionalism"—as in the demand, from time to time, for greater local autonomy in Scotland or in Wales —is a protest.

It has often been the weakness of "regionalist" movements, to assume that a cultural malady can be cured by political means; to ascribe, to individuals belonging to the dominant culture, malignant intentions of which they may be innocent; and, by not probing deep enough into the causes, to prescribe a superficial remedy. By the materalist, these regional stirrings are often regarded with derision. The man of letters, who should be peculiarly qualified to respect and to criticize them, should be able to take a longer view than either the politician or the local patriot. He should know that neither in a complete and universal uniformity, nor in an isolated self-sufficiency, can culture flourish; that a local and a general culture are so far from being in conflict, that they are truly necessary to each other. To the engineering mind, the idea of a universal uniformity on the one hand or the idea of complete autarchy on the other, is more easily apprehensible. The union of local cultures in a general culture is more difficult to conceive, and more difficult to realize. But the man of letters should know that uniformity means the obliteration of culture, and that self-sufficiency means its death by starvation.

The man of letters should see also, that within any cultural unit, a proper balance of rural and urban life is essential. Without great cities—great, not necessarily in the modern material sense, but great by being the meeting-place of a society of superior mind and more polished manners—the culture of a nation will never rise above a rustic level; without the life of the soil from which to draw its strength, the urban culture must lose its source of strength and rejuvenescence. *Fortunatus et ille qui deos novit agrestes.*

What we learn from a study of conditions within our own countries, we can apply to the cultural economy of Europe. The primary aim of politics, at the end of a great war, must be, of course, the establishment of a peace, and of a peace which will endure. But at different times, different notions of what conditions are necessary for peace may prevail. At the end of the war of 1914-18, the idea of peace was associated with the idea of independence and freedom: It was thought that if each nation managed all its own affairs at home, and transacted its foreign political affairs through a League of Nations, peace would be perpetually assured. It was an idea which disregarded the *unity* of European culture. At the end of this war, the idea of peace is more likely to be associated with the idea of *efficiency*—that is, with whatever can be *planned*. This would be to disregard the *diversity* of European culture. It is not that "culture" is in danger of being ignored: on the contrary, I think that culture might be safer if it were less talked about. But in this talk of "culture," the notion of a European culture—a culture with several sub-divisions, other than national boundaries, within it, and with various crossing threads of relationship between countries, but still a recognizable universal European culture—is not very prominent: and there is a danger that the importance of the various cultures may be assumed to be in proportion to the size, population, wealth and power of the nations. . . .

I have suggested that the cultural health of Europe, including the cultural health of its component parts, is incompatible with extreme forms of both nationalism and internationalism. But the cause of that disease, which destroys the very soil in which culture has its roots, is not so much extreme ideas, and the fanaticism which they stimulate, as the relentless presssure of modern industrialism, setting the problems which the extreme ideas attempt to solve. Not least of the effects of industrialism is that we become mechanized in mind, and consequently attempt to provide solutions in terms of *engineering,* for problems which are essentially problems of *life*. . . .

The responsibility of the man of letters at the present time, according to this point of view, is neither to ignore politics and economics, nor, certainly, to desert literature in order to precipitate himself into controversy on matters which he does not understand. But he should be vigilantly watching the conduct of politicians and economists, for the purpose of criticizing and warning, when the decisions and actions of politicians and economists are likely to have cultural consequences. Of these consequences the man of letters should prepare himself to judge. Of the possible cultural consequences of their activities, politicians and economists are usually oblivious; the man of letters is better qualified to foresee them, and to perceive their seriousness.

I should not like to give the impression that I assume there to be a definite frontier, between the matters of direct and those of indirect concern to the man of letters. In matters of Education, for instance, he is less directly concerned with the problems of organization and administration of popular instruction, than he is with the *content* of education. He should certainly be aware, of what many persons seem to be ignorant, that it is possible to have a high state of culture with very little education, and a great deal of education without any consequent improvement of culture: from some points of view he will not take education quite so seriously as other people seem to do. But he is very much concerned with the maintenance of *quality,* and with the constant reminder of what is easily overlooked: that, if we had to choose, it would be better that a few people should be educated well, than that everyone should be educated moderately well. He should also be particularly concerned with the maintenance of those elements in education which the several European nations have in the past had in common. We are not only in danger of, we are actually suffering from, excessive nationalism in education. The common higher elements of European secular education are, I presume, the cultivation of Latin and Greek language and literature, and the cultivation of pure science. At a time when science is chiefly advertised for the sake of the practical benefits, from invention and discovery, which the application of science may confer, the reminder is perhaps not inappropriate, that applied science is always liable to be contaminated by political and economic motives, and that inventions and discoveries appeal to people as often for their usefulness in getting the better of other people, in peace and in war, as for their common benefits to mankind. And also, that it is not the use of the same machines and the enjoyment of the same comforts and therapeutic aids, that can establish and develop a common mind, a common culture. I speak of science with some hesitation: but I am wholly convinced that for the preservation of any European culture, as well as for the health of its national components, a perpetual cultivation of the sources of that culture, in Greece and Rome, and a continual refreshment from them, are necessary. I should say Israel also, but that I wish to confine myself, so far as that is possible, to the cultural, rather than the religious aspect.

There are other matters over which the man of letters should exercise constant surveillance: matters which may, from time to time, and here and there, present themselves with immediate urgency. Such are the questions which arise in particular contexts, when the freedom of the man of letters is menaced. I have in mind, not merely questions of censorship, whether political, religious or moral: my experience tells me that these issues must be faced as they arise. I have in mind also the dangers which may come from official encouragement and patronage of the arts; the dangers to which men of letters would be exposed, if they became, in their professional capacity, servants of the state. Modern governments are very much aware of the new invention "cultural propaganda," even when the governors are not remarkably sensitive to culture: and, however necessary cultural propaganda may be under modern conditions, we must be alert to the fact that all propaganda can be perverted.

As I said earlier, I do not expect that all men of letters, in every country of Europe, will concur with my *views;* but I venture to hope that some of them will agree, that there is a range of public problems in which we all have, irrespective of nationality, language or political bias, a common interest, and about which we might hope to have a common mind; and I hope that some will agree that I have stated some of these problems. Such agreement would give more content to the phrase "the republic of letters." The "republic" or (to use a stronger term) the "fraternity" of letters does not, fortunately, demand that all men of letters should love one another—there always have been, and always will be, jealousy and intrigue amongst authors: but it does imply that we have a mutual bond, and a mutual obligation to a common ideal; and that on some questions we should speak for Europe, even when we speak only to our fellow-countrymen.

ON THE PLACE OF THE INTELLECT AND THE PRETENSIONS OF THE INTELLECTUAL

Ignazio Silone

THE SPEECH I am going to make was not composed for delivery before a large audience; it consists rather of ideas that I should have preferred to have exchanged individually, with each one of you, or, to be more exact, with some of those whom I see among you; for it is common knowledge that conversation is much more in a writer's line than speechmaking. It is this characteristic of writers that gives books their special quality, with which other techniques of communication cannot compete. This special quality will always remain their justification in the face of the cinema and the theatre; for the reading of a book, even in the most collectivized society, will always be a personal and solitary act, a quiet conversation between two men. That is one of the reasons why, when a writer makes a speech to a large assembly, his most sincere words have a note of confession.

Well, I have come before you, writers from all the countries of the world, simply to reaffirm in the great and brilliant republic of letters a certain humble presence that is also a survival. (I use the word 'humble' in its ancient sense of *prope humo*.) And it is my duty to explain clearly to you the significance of that presence in the contemporary situation.

What presence? I certainly do not refer to any definite territory or country, or to the reappearance of an Italian representative at your deliberations, even though the latter is a notable event; I am thinking rather of a different region and another country—that invisible, underground country without frontiers which we created, together with some who are with us here today and others who are no longer alive, during the long years of persecution; that country of which we wish to remain free and loyal citizens.

Mention of this survival brings me to the first reflection that I propose to bring to your notice today. Nowadays, whenever a meeting of writers, or artists, or 'intellectuals' in general yields to the temptation of pronouncing

Reprinted from *Horizon* (December, 1947), pp. 319-325 by permission of the author. Translated by Eric Mosbacher. (A speech made at the International PEN Club Conference at Basle, 1947.)

judgment on men's conduct during the tragic events of recent years, it is essential that somebody should undertake the task of putting them on guard against any hypocritical self-satisfaction. What, in short, I intend to say, is that it will be agreed on mature reflection that writers, artists and intellectuals in general have no right whatever to boast of any disinterested, far-sighted or courageous part played by them in the sad decades through which we have passed. And despite the fact that this statement is entirely inconsistent with any feeling of self-satisfaction of the kind to which I have alluded, I notice that it is sufficient to make it to secure general assent. No special effort of memory is required on the part of those who might desire to check its accuracy, for the painful experiences through which we have passed are only those of yesterday. Events have once more demonstrated that the professional exercise of letters or of the arts does not, in itself, provide any guarantee of moral integrity or strength of character. Events have shown that wherever a crisis has overtaken a ruling class the majority of writers and artists have not remained immune from the aberrations and perplexities inseparable from that state of crisis. If we widen our perspective to include the whole of the educated section of society, we can say that these same events have demonstrated the complete ineffectiveness of the so-called humanities, that is to say, of those very studies that should by definition have a formative effect on character. But I hasten to add that it should not be thought that this is a feature characteristic of, or peculiar to, our time.

Why? To me the explanation seems plain. The choice between liberty and slavery presents itself to the writer in the form of a choice between his sincerity and his willingness to conform. That choice has to be made at a level of the mind at which literary or artistic notions or aesthetic sensibility count for very little. It is clear that, with all the difficulties, vexations and limitations imposed by external circumstances, what really matters is something very different indeed.

It is for this reason that intellectuals have always shared the virtues and failings of their people, their social environment and their time; and it is naive to attempt to postulate an 'intellectual' platform for the crisis of our time, a unanimous position based on any general principles. I should like, with your permission, to remind you that artists, in addition to the ordinary external limitations imposed on them by society—difficulties which they share with other men and which are superable even if they involve sacrifice—are faced with difficulties of professional psychology which constitute a far more intimate threat to their capacity for choice, which in extreme cases may atrophy all normal sense of responsibility.

It seems almost as though the exclusive exercise of the profession of letters or of the arts, with prolonged absorption of all the faculties in the creative effort, can produce a monstrous displacement or deformation of the personality which may cause the artist to run a grave risk of losing the ordinary sense of the relations between himself and others, the ordinary sense of rights and duties, the ordinary standards of moral judgment and of ending by feeling himself a world unto himself and the actual centre of the universe. The intellect, diverted from its proper function, which is the humble and courageous service of truth, is degraded to the task of perpetually chasing after ephemeral success and perpetually providing justification for the inevitable self-betrayals that results from that pursuit. Every important social event, every political or social change, dictatorship, war, revolution, pestilence or famine, comes to be judged by the changes that it may involve for the artist's own reputation. Unpopularity comes to be regarded as the worst of all evils. Modern psychology has given a name that you all know to this illness of the mind, but, fortunately for the reputation of our profession, the psychologists will never be able to provide even approximate statistics of those who are afflicted by it.

Besides, morality can never be measurable by statistics, nor can there be any statistical register of those thinkers and artists who, fully aware of historical development as a whole, or clearly perceiving the sublime dignity of humanity, careless of unpopularity or of any other changes, are willing, in case of need, to oppose their own country, their own class or their own party. But we are dealing, as experience shows, with a phenomenon not confined to the educated classes. Intellectuals as a class can neither claim to have shown exemplary conduct during the past decades, nor does there seem to me to be any justification for claiming for them now any particular function in the guidance of public opinion. It is certainly dangerous and difficult to talk of a moral *élite* in any country; but in any case it would be extremely hazardous to suggest that it coincided with that country's intellectual *élite*. I hasten to add that this disagreeable conclusion is intended to be a plain statement of historical fact; it is not intended to establish any standard of relative values, which would be absurd. It might, in fact, be the starting-point for a longer speech on the place of the intellect and the pretensions of the intellectual.

This latter is so widespread that to seek to condemn any particular national group of writers, as was done at this conference a few days ago, appears to me to be an unworthy piece of scapegoat hunting. To be perfectly frank, I do not know if, in recent years, there has been a single country or a single party in which the intellect has not been degraded to the humiliating function of an instrument of war. I assure you that I do not intend to hurt anyone's feelings or to cast the least doubt on the good faith of those writers who actively and at their own risk and peril took part in the ideological war. What I mean to say is that now that the war is over, nobody can deny that the use made by the military leaders of the work of those writers and of the eloquent slogans invented by them was identical with the use made of this or that war weapon. In fact, as soon as there was no more use for them, the principles of liberty, human dignity and universal security were put back into store, just as if they were tanks. That is why we now have this peace, which is not peace but at best an uncertain armistice.

I feel I can ignore the risk of being misunderstood. A man of the resistance, of a resistance that lasted for twenty years and was ready to last for centuries if necessary, of a resistance that by any calculation began and developed when many of the future wartime opponents of Fascism admired and supported it, I can assure you that my words are inspired by no unforeseen sense of disillusionment. At no moment or phase of the war did I doubt that the solidarity in fact established between the cause of democratic liberties and that of a definite *bloc* of powers, though it might be a highly important historical coincidence and a useful, opportune and necessary alliance, was not, and could not be, complete or permanent. It was an uncomfortably critical position towards the Allies, but it made it possible to forecast with relative ease what is actually happening now. The key to that forecast, and it is still valid today, is in the following warning: never identify the cause of moral values with that of a state. The spirit bloweth where it listeth. It is clerical presumption to wish to prescribe for it any definite domicile.

But why continue with such pessimistic thoughts in such a festive assembly as this and in such circumstances as today's? I should not recall these things merely for the purposes of recrimination. But, actually, these questions are always topical. At every congress of writers is there not some significant allusion to new and inevitable ideological crusades? But these zealots must be told firmly that there can be no graver threat to moral values in any period than to regard them as historically bound to the old political and social forms. Only by the sacrifice of intellectual honesty is it possible to identify the cause of truth with that of an army. But if siding with one antagonistic power against another is intellectually dishonest now, on the political plane it is a dangerous error, because it means capitulating in advance to the threat of another world catastrophe, admitting its inevitability, providing its justification, and hastening its occurrence. This is certainly the most dangerous aberration to which an intellectual can succumb. But we must not conceal from ourselves the deep causes that make such aberrations possible.

The military victory of the so-called democratic powers has left unsolved the problems from which Fascism and National-Socialism arose. A certain cynical clear-sightedness has deprived the men of this post-war period of the naive illusions of the last. Those among the young who fail to satisfy the whole of their intellectual appetite in biting their finger-nails find no better nourishment than the meagre left-overs of the formerly despised nine-teenth century. And in these conditions it is obvious that that desperate aridity of mind that Nietzsche called 'European nihilism', which some considered peculiar to Nazism, was by no means merely the result of military defeat, but is to be found in a more or less acute form in all countries. The denunci-ation and punishment of a few scapegoats is certainly not sufficient to save ourselves from it.

I know of no party, no church, no institution that can at present be con-sidered uncontaminated by this terrible scourge. Nihilism is making a pretence of a creed in which one does not believe; it is the smoke of incense before an empty shrine; it is the exaltation of self-sacrifice and heroism as ends in themselves; it is liberty that is not in the service of life; liberty that has to have recourse to suicide or crime in order to prove itself. It is the subordination of truth and justice to selfish utility; it is the primacy of tactics and cunning in every form of collective relationship. Every one of you will have shared with me the experience of having been appealed to by this or that political party to protest against some injustice to which its adherents were said to have been subjected in some part of the world. But you will have noticed, as I did, that these same parties remain mute and indifferent when the same or even greater injustices are committed in countries gov-erned by their friends. Similarly, we hear vehement protests by the highest religious authorities from time to time because the men or the interests of the Church are molested in some country. But so far not one of us has had the pleasure of hearing the Pope protesting against the persecution by Catholic governments of their political enemies or the adherents of other faiths. Thus we now observe (and there have not been lacking some small instances of it during this conference) how those very men, who, during recent years, suffered most from, and rightly protested against, the in-human madness of the Nazi racial doctrines, have no objection now to im-posing bans and restrictions on their conquered adversaries of yesterday that reproduce very faithfully the essential *motifs* of the theories that they condemn. But justice invoked only when it is convenient is nihilist justice, a mask for crude and naked utilitarianism.

Now it must be evident to every serious person that no judgement of the crisis of our time can be formulated except on the basis of its universal char-acter. It is not by finding scapegoats that we can obliterate from our con-sciousness the awareness of this general decadence, of this universal guilt. This is not the occasion to recall the ways and means by which the human race has overcome its periods of nihilist aridity in the past. But you will permit me to observe that it would be a mistake for writers to expect their salvation from others. What is at stake is not a way of writing or speaking or behaving, but a way of feeling. Salvation lies not in the profession of any ideas or theories, or in joining this or that political party or this or that Church, because the decay, as anyone can observe for himself, is common to believers in the most varied doctrines. Before any useful distinction can be made between the various groups or trends or parties, there is a question of fundamental honesty to solve, and that is to find the inalienable sense of one's own responsibility, to re-establish sincere, direct and lasting contact with the tragic reality that underlies the human state. For the Christian the symbol of that tragic reality is the Cross. The human anatomy reminds us of the Cross by its very shape. In our personal life it is the permanent unease of the human heart, not to be allayed by any progress of civilization. On the historical plane it is principally the sufferings of the poor, known by different names in different times and places. In China they are called coolies; in South America—*peones;* among the Arabs—fellahin: or they can be called simply proletarians or Jews. But always and everywhere we find the same reality of suffering, perhaps the only really universal reality of human history.

I ask you to believe that I am sorry if a note of vehemence, foreign to my intentions, has crept into my speech. My intention, I repeat, was simply to re-state in the vast and brilliant world of letters a certain presence that is also a survival; to re-state a determination of fidelity, a determination not to betray.

WRITERS AND LEVIATHAN

George Orwell

THE POSITION of the writer in an age of State control is a
subject that has already been fairly largely discussed, although most of the
evidence that might be relevant is not yet available. In this place I do not
want to express an opinion either for or against state patronage of the arts,
but merely to point out that *what kind* of state rules over us must depend
partly on the prevailing intellectual atmosphere: meaning, in this context,
partly on the attitude of writers and artists themselves, and on their willingness or otherwise to keep the spirit of liberalism alive. If we find ourselves
in ten years' time cringing before somebody like Zhdanov, it will probably
be because that is what we have deserved. Obviously there are strong tendencies towards totalitarianism at work within the English literary intelligentsia already. But here I am not concerned with any organised and conscious movement such as Communism, but merely with the effect, on people
of goodwill, of political thinking and the need to take sides politically.

This is a political age. War, Fascism, concentration camps, rubber trunch-
eons, atomic bombs, etc., are what we daily think about, and therefore to a
great extent what we write about, even when we do not name them openly.
We cannot help this. When you are on a sinking ship, your thoughts will be
about sinking ships. But not only is our subject matter narrowed, but our
whole attitude towards literature is coloured by loyalties which we at least
intermittently realise to be non-literary. I often have the feeling that even
at the best of the times literary criticism is fraudulent, since in the absence
of any accepted standards whatever—any *external* reference which can give
meaning to the statement that such and such a book is "good" or "bad"—
every literary judgement consists in trumping up a set of rules to justify
an instinctive preference. One's real reaction to a book, when one has a reaction at all, is usually "I like this book" or "I don't like it", and what follows is a rationalisation. But "I like this book" is not, I think, a non-literary
reaction: the non-literary reaction is: "This book is on my side, and therefore I must discover merits in it." Of course, when one praises a book for
political reasons one may be emotionally sincere, in the sense that one does

feel strong approval of it, but also it often happens that party solidarity demands a plain lie. Anyone used to reviewing books for political periodicals is well aware of this. In general, if you are writing for a paper that you are in agreement with, you sin by commission, and if for a paper of the opposite stamp, by omission. At any rate, innumerable controversial books—books for or against Soviet Russia, for or against Zionism, for or against the Catholic Church, etc.—are judged before they are read, and in effect before they are written. One knows in advance what reception they will get in what papers. And yet, with a dishonesty that sometimes is not even quarter-conscious, the pretence is kept up that genuinely literary standards are being applied.

Of course, the invasion of literature by politics was bound to happen. It must have happened, even if the special problem of totalitarianism had never arisen, because we have developed a sort of compunction which our grandparents did not have, an awareness of the enormous injustice and misery of the world, and guilt-stricken feeling that one ought to be doing something about it, which makes a purely æsthetic attitude towards life impossible. No one, now, could devote himself to literature as single-mindedly as Joyce or Henry James. But unfortunately, to accept political responsibility now means yielding oneself over to orthodoxies and "party lines", with all the timidity and dishonesty that that implies. As against the Victorian writers, we have the disadvantage of living among clear-cut political ideologies and of usually knowing at a glance what thoughts are heretical. A modern literary intellectual lives and writes in constant dread—not, indeed, of public opinion in the wider sense, but of public opinion within his own group. As a rule, luckily, there is more than one group, but also at any given moment there is a dominant orthodoxy, to offend against which needs a thick skin and sometimes means cutting one's income in half for years on end. Obviously, for about fifteen years past, the dominant orthodoxy, especially among the young, has been "left." The key words are "progressive", "democratic" and "revolutionary", while the labels which you must at all costs avoid having gummed upon you are "bourgeois", "reactionary" and "Fascist." Almost everyone nowadays, even the majority of Catholics and Conservatives, is "progressive", or at least wishes to be thought so. No one, so far as I know, ever describes himself as "bourgeois", just as no one literate enough to have heard the word ever admits to being guilty of anti-Semitism. We are all of us good democrats, anti-Fascists, anti-imperialists, contemptuous of class distinctions, impervious to colour prejudice, and so on and so forth. Nor is there much doubt that the present-day "left" orthodoxy is better than the rather snobbish, pietistic Conservative orthodoxy which prevailed twenty years ago, when the *Criterion* and (on a lower level) the *London Mercury* were the dominant literary magazines. For at the least its implied objective is a viable form of society which large numbers of people actually want. But it also has its own falsities which, because they cannot be admitted, make it impossible for certain questions to be seriously discussed.

The whole left-wing ideology, scientific and Utopian, was evolved by people who had no immediate prospect of attaining power. It was, therefore, an extremist ideology, utterly contemptuous of kings, governments, laws, prisons, police forces, armies, flags, frontiers, patriotism, religion, conventional morality, and, in fact, the whole existing scheme of things. Until well within living memory the forces of the left in all countries were fighting against a tyranny which appeared to be invincible, and it was easy to assume that if only *that* particular tyranny—capitalism—could be overthrown, socialism would follow. Moreover, the left had inherited from liberalism certain distinctly questionable beliefs, such as the belief that the truth will prevail and persecution defeat itself, or that man is naturally good and is only corrupted by his environment. This perfectionist ideology has persisted in nearly all of us, and it is in the name of it that we protest when (for instance) a Labour government votes huge incomes to the King's daughters or shows hesitation about nationalising steel. But we have also accumulated in our minds a whole series of unadmitted contradictions, as a result of successive bumps against reality.

The first big bump was the Russian Revolution. For somewhat complex reasons, nearly the whole of the English left has been driven to accept the Russian régime as "socialist", while silently recognising that its spirit and practice are quite alien to anything that is meant by "socialism" in this country. Hence there has arisen a sort of schizophrenic manner of thinking, in which words like "democracy" can bear two irreconcilable meanings, and such things as concentration camps and mass deportations can be right and wrong simultaneously. The next blow to the left-wing ideology was the rise of Fascism, which shook the pacifism and internationalism of the left without bringing about a definite restatement of doctrine. The experience of German occupation taught the European peoples something that the colonial peoples knew already, namely, that class antagonisms are not all-important and that there is such a thing as national interest. After Hitler it was difficult to maintain seriously that "the enemy is in your own country" and that national independence is of no value. But though we all know this and act upon it when necessary, we still feel that to say it aloud would be a kind of treachery. And finally, the greatest difficulty of all, there is the fact that the left is now in power and is obliged to take responsibility and make genuine decisions. . . .

To accept an orthodoxy is always to inherit unresolved contradictions. Take for instance the fact that all sensitive people are revolted by industrialism and its products, and yet are aware that the conquest of poverty and the emancipation of the working class demand not less industrialisation, but more and more. Or take the fact that certain jobs are absolutely necessary and yet are never done except under some kind of coercion. Or take the fact that it is impossible to have a positive foreign policy without having powerful armed forces. One could multiply examples. In every such case there is a conclusion which is perfectly plain but which can only be drawn if one is privately disloyal to the official ideology. The normal response is to push the question, unanswered, into a corner of one's mind, and then continue repeating contradictory catchwords. One does not have to search far through the reviews and magazines to discover the effects of this kind of thinking.

I am not, of course, suggesting that mental dishonesty is peculiar to socialists and left-wingers generally, or is commonest among them. It is merely that acceptance of *any* political discipline seems to be incompatible with literary integrity. This applies equally to movements like pacifism and personalism, which claim to be outside the ordinary political struggle. Indeed, the mere sound of words ending in -ism seems to bring with it the smell of propaganda. Group loyalties are necessary, and yet they are poisonous to literature, so long as literature is the product of individuals. As soon as they are allowed to have any influence, even a negative one, on creative writing, the result is not only falsification, but often the actual drying-up of the inventive faculties.

Well, then, what? Do we have to conclude that it is the duty of every writer to "keep out of politics"? Certainly not! In any case, as I have said already, no thinking person can or does genuinely keep out of politics, in an age like the present one. I only suggest that we should draw a sharper distinction than we do at present between our political and our literary loyalties, and should recognise that a willingness to *do* certain distasteful but necessary things does not carry with it any obligation to swallow the beliefs that usually go with them. When a writer engages in politics he should do so as a citizen, as a human being, but not *as a writer*. I do not think that he has the right, merely on the score of his sensibilities, to shirk the ordinary dirty work of politics. Just as much as anyone else, he should be prepared to deliver lectures in draughty halls, to chalk pavements, to canvass voters, to distribute leaflets, even to fight in civil wars if it seems necessary. But whatever else he does in the service of his party, he should never write for it. He should make it clear that his writing is a thing apart. And he should be able to act co-operatively while, if he chooses, completely rejecting the official ideology. He should never turn back from a train of thought because it may lead to a heresy, and he should not mind very much if his unorthodoxy is smelt out, as it probably will be. Perhaps it is even a bad sign in a writer if he is not suspected of reactionary tendencies to-day, just as it was a bad sign if he was not suspected of Communist sympathies twenty years ago.

But does all this mean that a writer should not only refuse to be dictated to by political bosses, but also that he should refrain from writing *about* politics? Once again, certainly not! There is no reason why he should not write in the most crudely political way, if he wishes to. Only he should do so as an individual, an outsider, at the most an unwelcome guerrilla on the flank of a regular army. This attitude is quite compatible with ordinary political usefulness. It is reasonable, for example, to be willing to fight in a war because one thinks the war ought to be won, and at the same time to refuse to write war propaganda. Sometimes, if a writer is honest, his writings and his political activities may actually contradict one another. There are occasions when that is plainly undesirable: but then the remedy is not to falsify one's impulses, but to remain silent.

To suggest that a creative writer, in a time of conflict, must split his life into two compartments, may seem defeatist or frivolous: yet in practice I do not see what else he can do. To lock yourself up in the ivory tower is impossible and undesirable. To yield subjectively, not merely to a party machine, but even to a group ideology, is to destroy yourself as a writer. We feel this dilemma to be a painful one, because we see the need of engaging in politics while also seeing what a dirty, degrading business it is. And most of us still have a lingering belief that every choice, even every political choice, is between good and evil, and that if a thing is necessary it is also right. We should, I think, get rid of this belief, which belongs to the nursery. In politics one can never do more than decide which of two evils is the less, and there are some situations from which one can only escape by acting like a devil or a lunatic. War, for example, may be necessary, but it is certainly not right or sane. Even a general election is not exactly a pleasant or edifying spectacle. If you have to take part in such things—and I think you do have to, unless you are armoured by old age or stupidity or hypocrisy—then you also have to keep part of yourself inviolate. For most people the problem does not arise in the same form, because their lives are split already. They are truly alive only in their leisure hours, and there is no emotional connection between their work and their political activities. Nor are they generally asked, in the name of political loyalty, to debase themselves as workers. The artist, and especially the writer, is asked just that —in fact, it is the only thing that politicians ever ask of him. If he refuses, that does not mean that he is condemned to inactivity. One half of him, which in a sense is the whole of him, can act as resolutely, even as violently if need be, as anyone else. But his writings, in so far as they have any value, will always be the product of the saner self that stands aside, records the things that are done and admits their necessity, but refuses to be deceived as to their true nature.

THE ARTIST AND HIS TIME

Albert Camus

I. *As an artist, have you chosen the role of witness?*
This would take considerable presumption or a vocation I lack. Personally I don't ask for any role and I have but one real vocation. As a man, I have a preference for happiness; as an artist, it seems to me that I still have characters to bring to life without the help of wars or of law-courts. But I have been sought out, as each individual has been sought out. Artists of the past could at least keep silent in the face of tyranny. The tyrannies of today are improved; they no longer admit of silence or neutrality. One has to take a stand, be either for or against. Well, in that case, I am against.

But this does not amount to choosing the comfortable role of witness. It is merely accepting the time as it is, minding one's own business, in short. Moreover, you are forgetting that today judges, accused, and witnesses exchange positions with exemplary rapidity. My choice, if you think I am making one, would at least be never to sit on a judge's bench, or beneath it, like so many of our philosophers. Aside from that, there is no dearth of opportunities for action, in the relative. Trade-unionism is today the first, and the most fruitful among them.

II. *Is not the quixotism that has been criticized in your recent works an idealistic and romantic definition of the artist's role?*
However words are perverted, they provisionally keep their meaning. And it is clear to me that the romantic is the one who chooses the perpetual motion of history, the grandiose epic, and the announcement of a miraculous event at the end of time. If I have tried to define something, it is, on the contrary, simply the common existence of history and of man, everyday life with the most possible light thrown upon it, the dogged struggle against one's own degradation and that of others.

It is likewise idealism, and of the worse kind, to end up by hanging all action and all truth on a meaning of history that is not implicit in events and that, in any case, implies a mythical aim. Would it therefore be realism

Reprinted from *The Myth of Sisyphus and Other Essays* (1959), pp. 147-151, by permission of the publisher, Vintage Books, Alfred A. Knopf, Inc. Translated by Justin O'Brien.

to take as the laws of history the future—in other words, just what is not yet history, something of whose nature we know nothing?

It seems to me, on the contrary, that I am arguing in favor of a true realism against a mythology that is both illogical and deadly, and against romantic nihilism whether it be bourgeois or allegedly revolutionary. To tell the truth, far from being romantic, I believe in the necessity of a rule and an order. I merely say that there can be no question of just any rule whatsoever. And that it would be surprising if the rule we need were given us by this disordered society, or, on the other hand, by those doctrinaires who declare themselves liberated from all rules and all scruples.

III. *The Marxists and their followers likewise think they are humanists. But for them human nature will be formed in the classless society of the future.*

To begin with, this proves that they reject at the present moment what we all are: those humanists are accusers of man. How can we be surprised that such a claim should have developed in the world of court trials? They reject the man of today in the name of the man of the future. That claim is religious in nature. Why should it be more justified than the one which announces the kingdom of heaven to come? In reality the end of history cannot have, within the limits of our condition, any definable significance. It can only be the object of a faith and of a new mystification. A mystification that today is no less great than the one that of old based colonial oppression on the necessity of saving the souls of infidels.

IV. *Is not that what in reality separates you from the intellectuals of the left?*

You mean that is what separates those intellectuals from the left? Traditionally the left has always been at war against injustice, obscurantism, and oppression. It always thought that those phenomena were interdependent. The idea that obscurantism can lead to justice, the national interest to liberty, is quite recent. The truth is that certain intellectuals of the left (not all, fortunately) are today hypnotized by force and efficacy as our intellectuals of the right were before and during the war. Their attitudes are different, but the act of resignation is the same. The first wanted to be realistic nationalists; the second want to be realistic socialists. In the end they betray nationalism and socialism alike in the name of a realism henceforth without content and adored as a pure, and illusory, technique of efficacy.

This is a temptation that can, after all, be understood. But still, however the question is looked at, the new position of the people who call themselves, or think themselves, leftists consists in saying: certain oppressions are justifiable because they follow the direction, which cannot be justified, of history.

Hence there are presumably privileged executioners, and privileged by nothing. This is about what was said in another context by Joseph de Maistre, who has never been taken for an incendiary. But this is a thesis which, personally, I shall always reject. Allow me to set up against it the traditional point of view of what has been hitherto called the left: all executioners are of the same family.

V. *What can the artist do in the world of today?*

He is not asked either to write about co-operatives or, conversely, to lull to sleep in himself the sufferings endured by others throughout history. And since you have asked me to speak personally, I am going to do so as simply as I can. Considered as artists, we perhaps have no need to interfere in the affairs of the world. But considered as men, yes. The miner who is exploited or shot down, the slaves in the camps, those in the colonies, the legions of persecuted throughout the world—they need all those who can speak to communicate their silence and to keep in touch with them. I have not written, day after day, fighting articles and texts, I have not taken part in the common struggles because I desire the world to be covered with Greek statues and masterpieces. The man who has such a desire does exist in me. Except that he has something better to do in trying to instill life into the creatures of his imagination. But from my first articles to my latest book I have written so much, and perhaps too much, only because I cannot keep from being drawn toward everyday life, toward those, whoever they may be, who are humiliated and debased. They need to hope, and if all keep silent or if they are given a choice between two kinds of humiliation, they will be forever deprived of hope and we with them. It seems to me impossible to endure that idea, nor can he who cannot endure it lie down to sleep in his tower. Not through virtue, as you see, but through a sort of almost organic intolerance, which you feel or do not feel. Indeed, I see many who fail to feel it, but I cannot envy their sleep.

This does not mean, however, that we must sacrifice our artist's nature to some social preaching or other. I have said elsewhere why the artist was more than ever necessary. But if we intervene as men, that experience will have an effect upon our language. And if we are not artists in our language first of all, what sort of artists are we? Even if, militants in our lives, we speak in our works of deserts and of selfish love, the mere fact that our lives are militant causes a special tone of voice to people with men that desert and that love. I shall certainly not choose the moment when we are beginning to leave nihilism behind to stupidly deny the values of creation in favor of the values of humanity, or vice versa. In my mind neither one is ever separated from the other and I measure the greatness of an artist (Molière, Tolstoy, Melville) by the balance he managed to maintain between the two. Today, under the pressure of events, we are obliged to transport that tension into our lives likewise. This is why so many artists, bending under the burden, take refuge in the ivory tower or, conversely, in the social church. But as for me, I see in both choices a like act of resignation. We must simultaneously serve suffering and beauty. The long patience, the strength, the secret cunning such service calls for are the virtues that establish the very renascence we need.

One word more. This undertaking, I know, cannot be accomplished without dangers and bitterness. We must accept the dangers: the era of chair-bound artists is over. But we must reject the bitterness. One of the temptations of the artist is to believe himself solitary, and in truth he hears this shouted at him with a certain base delight. But this is not true. He stands in the midst of all, in the same rank, neither higher nor lower, with all those who are working and struggling. His very vocation, in the face of oppression, is to open the prisons and to give a voice to the sorrows and joys of all. This is where art, against its enemies, justifies itself by proving precisely that it is no one's enemy. By itself art could probably not produce the renascence which implies justice and liberty. But without it, that renascence would be without forms and, consequently, would be nothing. Without culture, and the relative freedom it implies, society, even when perfect, is but a jungle. This is why any authentic creation is a gift to the future.

Part V

INTELLECTUALS AND MODERN IDEOLOGIES

OVERVIEW

ACCORDING to a chronicle published in 1515: "I tried to find out whether Erasmus of Rotterdam was an adherent of that party, but a certain merchant said to me: 'Erasmus est pro se'" (Erasmus stands alone). But the great passion of many modern intellectuals has been to find ideologies to which they can commit themselves. Particular care has been taken to present a diversity of viewpoints and interpretations on the controversial subjects involved in the relation of intellectuals to modern ideologies. Several views are given on democracy, the relation of the intellectuals to liberalism and conservatism is respectively discussed by proponents of these positions and socialism, communism, and capitalism are illuminated from diverse sides.

According to James democracy is on trial; its critics affirm that in a democracy the inferior and the vulgar is preferred. The major democratic problem is to have the majority take their cue from better leaders; therefore the mission of intellectuals is to raise the tone of democracy. Higher education must create appreciation of excellence and loss of appetite for mediocrities. In a democracy where everything else is so shifting, the alumni of the colleges are the only permanent presence that corresponds to the aristocracy in older countries. No prouder name could be adopted by the college-bred than "intellectuals."

Wilson presents a different point of view: he maintains that democracy is not based on radical empiricism, the kind of philosophy James propounds, but on the acceptance of a transcendental order that is above all men. The denial of the existence of the spiritual and the transcendent by many intellectuals has caused much of the conflict between them and the democratic citizen. The path of reconciliation between the learned and the people is the common acceptance of a transcendent order. The intellectuals who reject the higher order of human experience are seekers of power. Such intellectuals believe in science through which, with the help of the state, a new and planned society can be realized. In such an order there is no room for the values and traditions of the ordinary man who will be told what to think. This analysis might be compared with the point of view of Laski in Part III.

According to Ascoli the main function of intellectuals is to act as an impersonal instrument; to reproduce and interpret social reality which is not of their making. In a democracy the final decisions for what happens in

(278)

society does not lie with intellectuals. They do not have any custodian or master who passes on their work, no protector but the elusive master, society. It is by society that they are held responsible for their work.

Niebuhr argues that not all forms of liberal dissent can be identified with communism. The common Marxist dogma does not create an affinity between communism and socialism; many leaders and intellectuals of socialist or liberal faith have fought communism. However, many liberals have been complacent about the danger of communist conspiracy. Marxists have had a remarkable influence over liberals. The Marxist pretension that man can become master of history appealed particularly to one part of liberal secularism, exemplified by August Comte. But this Marxist pretension has inevitably led to tyranny. Just as men can neither be masters of their historical fate nor mere prisoners of destiny, an economy can neither be totally regulated nor totally unregulated.

According to Kirk the plight of the intellectual is partly due to his commitment to presumptuous human reason unassisted by religious humility, imagination and traditional wisdom. Such intellectuals want to mold society nearer to their heart's desire, rather than to adhere to traditional humanism by improving private mind and character. American tradition is opposed to persons claiming to speak for the intellect and the intellect alone. The domination of higher education in America by church-founded colleges tended to prevent any opposition between tradition and intellectuality, while popular government made it difficult for the intellectually alienated to maintain that they were kept under by some iron political domination. The thinking American did not speak of himself as a member of a distinct order for there existed no nobility or church or central bureaucracy in the European sense to exclude him. Only under the growing influence of Marxism and other ideologies in the 1920's and the discontent of the Depression did a number of educated Americans start to call themselves intellectuals. Today there is urgent need for a genuine clerisy; scholars with religious aims and aspirations.

The relation of intellectuals to various forms of socialism has been particularly important to the modern world, and an extensive literature has grown up about this. Essays by persons of diversified background and views are presented: Kautsky, Lafargue, and Hook are hostile to capitalism and favor one form of socialism or another; Nomad is also anti-capitalist. These essays are balanced by Mises, Hayek, and Jouvenel who are critical of socialism. It should be noted that the terms "socialism" and "communism" are not defined precisely in order to accomodate a number of variations on the theme of socialism. Also the term "liberalism" has not been defined for the same reason; in some instances the term is used in entirely different senses by different authors.

According to Michels, Marxism was largely the work of bourgeois intellectuals and it is a historical law that class movements are led by members of the classes against which they are aimed. He distinguishes among the following kinds of intellectual socialists: those with a social conscience; scientists convinced of the necessity for or the practicability of socialism; demagogues or quacks; men who desire revenge for personal misfortune or for being declassed; and satiated rich men and philanthropists. Intellectuals at first are inclined to have utopian illusions concerning the character of the proletariat and then tend to get disillusioned. To the workers the intellectual at first appears as the savior; when the movement matures intellectuals are still indispensable because of the increasing complexity of problems; but they are felt to be not wholly faithful to the cause. But it would be false to assume that leaders drawn from the proletariat manifest greater political dependability than those coming from the educated bourgeoisie. There are two main groups of intellectuals; those who are one way or another supported by the state and will defend it and those who are not, who when their position seems hopeless furnish the yeast for social revolutions.

Lafargue believes that intellectuals should overthrow capitalism and appeals to their self-interest to accomplish this. He maintains that capitalism has degraded the intellectuals below the economic level of manual laborers. But the degradation attendant on the transformation of intellectual faculties into merchandise has not made intellectuals indignant. The triumph of socialism cannot wait upon hesitant intellectuals. Although they have been degraded by centuries of capitalistic oppression, intellectuals do not manifest examples of civic courage and moral dignity. They are far below the moral plane of the working class and the socialist party. The capitalists hire as supervisors and managers of their business enterprises, and political system, intellectuals who think they are a part of the capitalist class but in reality are only its servants. These intellectuals can never detach themselves from the capitalist class but those below them, whose number is steadily increasing and whose lot is becoming worse, belong to socialism. Here Lafargue appears to make the distinctions between two groups of intellectuals also made by Michels. If intellectuals would recognize their real interests they would flock to socialism not because of philanthropy, the misery of the workers, and not through affectation or snobbery, but to save themselves. Thus science and art would be liberated from the slavery of commercialism.

Kautsky not only indicates reasons why intellectuals should be socialists but also describes in some detail what the position of the intelligentsia will be under the new order. According to him the intelligentsia does not have class consciousness but its members unite with various classes and parties and furnish their intellectual leaders, which point was also made by Mannheim in Part II. Kautsky advances two major reasons why he thinks intellectuals adhere to socialism: the theoretical superiority of socialism and the increasing realization on the part of the intellectuals that it is among the broad popular section of the proletariat that there is the greatest interest in and highest regard for art and science. Culture and science under socialism will differ from conditions that obtain under capitalism in three respects. Under capitalism education and science are monopolized by the state; in some fields of science the apparatus for investigation has become so expensive that with a very few exceptions only the state can afford it. In the proletarian regime everyone will have within his reach all knowledge, and science will become free with the abolition of class antagonisms. Secondly, the means of individual intellectual production, such as the ink and the pen or the palette, will not be socialized and at the same time the number of persons engaged in such production will increase under socialism, which must aim at making culture a universal good. Finally, under socialism the danger that the state, replacing such capitalists as the publishers and theater owners, would dominate intellectual life by its central power is excluded by the fact that municipalities and free unions will indulge in the promotion of intellectual production. In the field of material production central direction is necessary but in the intellectual field free production will prevail.

Nomad takes an anti-communist, anti-fascist and anti-capitalist point of view. He asserts that sandwiched between the capitalist and the manual workers is a heterogeneous and growing stratum of intellectuals, a point of view which was also expressed by some previous writers. The "ins" are satisfied with the existing system, enjoy a bourgeois standard of living, and are in fact minor partners of capitalism as a whole. The "outs" are underpaid or unemployed, are opposed to the system, want to abolish capitalism, and are active in radical or fascist movements. This distinction between two types of intellectuals is, of course, also made by Michels and Lafargue. The first time the "outs" came into their own was in the Soviet regime which after the Revolution evolved an enormous hierarchy of intellectuals who enjoy bourgeois comforts and work in terms of the formula: "From the workers according to their abilities, to the bureaucrats according to their needs." This new form of exploitation where inequalities are merely less than under capitalism nevertheless shows that exploitation under socialism is just as possible as under capitalism. Intellectuals are flocking to radical parties for they see in the Soviet Russian example the possibility of putting an end to their insecurities and the prospect of making themselves masters of a country. The desire for a short cut to power was also largely responsible for many intellectuals joining fascist ranks. Thus the dissatisfaction of the manual workers offers an opportunity for intellectuals to take the place of the old masters. But intellectual leadership of whatever ideology is amoral in its policies and deceives the masses. There is an ever recurring competition for power between various groups of educated malcontents, which includes also some disinterested idealists, leading or aspiring to lead the dissatisfied masses. In connection with Nomad's view one is reminded of Bakunin's advice, which Michels calls the "heroic postulate," that in order to prevent the rise of a new ruling group in the persons of the leaders of a successful revolution, the leaders should immediately disappear or commit suicide.

Attention has to be paid to another form of socialism, the National Socialism of Germany. According to Röpke many German professors, especially in the social sciences, prepared the people's mind for National Socialism. There were also grave lapses among the natural scientists and those on the faculties of medical science. Despite honorable exceptions German professors incurred a great load of responsibility for the success of National Socialism and this responsibility grows when the behavior of intellectuals after 1933 is examined. The number of professors who lost their posts for being true to their convictions after Hitler came into power was very small. The presence of some intellectual resistance does not obliterate the fact that German universities not only failed to stand firm but actually were the worst centers of infection.

Hook says that many intellectuals created a literature of affirmation regarding communism and the Soviet Union which was exploited politically to the utmost. While National Socialism attracted intellectuals not because of a principle but because of national enthusiasm and mysticism centered on the person of Hitler, intellectuals were attracted to communism for a variety of reasons among which idealistic motives were important. It might be noted in passing that communism attracted for a while even really first rate artists and thinkers, as for example Gide and Berdyaev. According to Hook, unlike other great myths, the communist myth of a good society was presumably to take place in a definite locus in space and time, which promise is prone to increase disillusionment. This Marxist myth is comparable to the French positivist expectation of establishing the Kingdom of God on earth which Salomon analyzes in Part I. It took time for some intellectuals to become disenchanted with the Soviet myth and the intellectuals' responsibility for their own illusions is heavy. Their self-deception was due to the fact that they looked to politics for absolute security and for salvation; they substituted faith for intelligence; abandoned too soon their own heritage of political democracy; and they did not understand the genuine sense in which the social problem is a moral problem.

The hostility of many intellectuals to capitalism has been indicated. For a variety of reasons artists have been especially contemptuous. However, before three essays are presented which are favorable to capitalism, it is interesting to note that one of the most important of modern poets, Valéry, argues that historically as well as logically the commerce in ideas and freedom of the mind are related to the commerce in things, to business and that "Finally, all the dreams of mankind, which figure in our various kinds of fables—flight, submersion, the apparition of absent things, the word fixed, transported, and detached from its period and its source—and many strange things which had not even been dreamed of—have now issued from the impossible and from the mind. The fabulous is bought and sold. The manufacture of wonder-machines provides a living for thousands of people. But the artist has played no part in this creation of prodigies. It springs from science and wealth. The bourgeois has invested his capital in phantasms and is speculating in the ruin of common sense."

Mises also bases his analysis of the anti-capitalism of intellectuals on the factor of resentment but he explains more fully how this arises than Schumpeter in Part II, and Michels, Nomad, and Hayek in this Part. In a society based on caste and status, the individual can ascribe adverse faith to conditions beyond his control. But under capitalism, where the principle of to each according to his accomplishments prevails, everybody's station in life depends on his own doing. Those who fail to attain the position they think they deserve develop resentment, and the more sophisticated ones elaborate the philosophy of anti-capitalism. Intellectuals often come into contact with those who are more successful and this causes special feelings of frustration and resentment.

Hayek views intellectuals as "professional secondhand dealers in ideas" who play the decisive role in determining the view the masses will get of the work of experts and of original thinkers. The climate of opinion in any period is essentially a set of general preconceptions by which intellectuals judge the importance of new facts and opinions. New ideas are not judged on their merits but the readiness with which they fit into the ideology of intellectuals. Among the impulses that predispose intellectuals toward socialism is their assumption that engineering techniques can be applied to society and that the direction of all forms of human activity according to a single coherent plan will bring great improvements. The utopian character of socialist thought particularly appeals to intellectuals who are uninterested in practical matters. Moreover, to exceptionally able men there are many avenues to power, but to the dissatisfied intellectual socialism is the chief means to attain power; a similar point of view is also expressed by Nomad. The old-fashioned liberals must learn from the success of socialists that it was their courage to be utopian which gained them the support of intellectuals; they must elaborate a program that will appeal to imagination and courage.

Jouvenel approaches the problem of the anti-capitalism of intellectuals from a different point of view. He says that to the intellectual the social device of capitalism offers a displeasing picture because in his terms self-seeking men provide consumers with things they want or can be induced to want—not what they should have. The historian's bias reflects the attitude of a large sector of the intelligentsia who adopted an unfavorable view of capitalism. The hostility to the money-maker is a recent attitude on the part of the secular intelligentsia. In succession intellectuals turned against the church; the sword and its highest political manifestation, the political sovereign; and then the purse. Intellectuals and businessmen function by wholly different standards. The businessman offers to the public "goods" defined as anything the public will buy; the intellectual seeks to teach what is "good." The world of business is to the intellectual one in which the values are wrong, the motivations low, the rewards misaddressed. Yet capitalism today is more praiseworthy than previously when it was less bitterly denounced by intellectuals, which suggests that a change must have occurred in the intellectuals themselves.

DEMOCRACY AND THE COLLEGE-BRED

William James

. . . WHAT THE COLLEGES—teaching humanities by examples which may be special, but which must be typical and pregnant—
should at least try to give us, is a general sense of what, under various dis-
guises, *superiority* has always signified and may still signify. The feeling
for a good human job anywhere, the admiration of the really admirable,
the disesteem of what is cheap and trashy and impermanent—this is what
we call the critical sense, the sense for ideal values. It is the better part of
what men know as wisdom. Some of us are wise in this way naturally and
by genius; some of us never become so. But to have spent one's youth at
college, in contact with the choice and rare and precious, and yet still to
be a blind prig or vulgarian, unable to scent out human excellence or to
divine it amid its accidents, to know it only when ticketed and labeled and
forced on us by others, this indeed should be accounted the very calamity
and shipwreck of a higher education.

The sense for human superiority ought, then, to be considered our line,
as boring subways is the engineer's line and the surgeon's is appendicitis.
Our colleges ought to have lit up in us a lasting relish for the better kind
of man, a loss of appetite for mediocrities, and a disgust for cheapjacks. We
ought to smell, as it were, the difference of quality in men and their proposals when we enter the world of affairs about us. Expertness in this might
well atone for some of our awkwardness at accounts, for some of our ignorance of dynamos. The best claim we can make for the higher education,
the best single phrase in which we can tell what it ought to do for us, is, then,
exactly what I said: it should enable us to *know a good man when we see
him*.

That the phrase is anything but an empty epigram follows from the fact
that if you ask in what line it is most important that a democracy like ours
should have its sons and daughters skillful, you see that it is this line more
than any other. "The people in their wisdom"—this is the kind of wisdom

Reprinted from *McClure's Magazine* (February, 1908), pp. 420-422, by permission of
Paul R. Reynolds & Sons. Copyright 1911 by Henry James. Delivered originally as an
address at a meeting of the Association of American Alumnae at Radcliffe College, on
November 7, 1907. Title supplied by the Editor.

(285)

most needed by the people. Democracy is on its trial, and no one knows how it will stand the ordeal. Abounding about us are pessimistic prophets. Fickleness and violence used to be, but are no longer, the vices which they charge to democracy. What its critics now affirm is that its preferences are inveterately for the inferior. So it was in the beginning, they say, and so it will be world without end. Vulgarity enthroned and institutionalized, elbowing everything superior from the highway, this, they tell us, is our irremediable destiny; and the picture-papers of the European continent are already drawing Uncle Sam with the hog instead of the eagle for his heraldic emblem. The privileged aristocracies of the foretime, with all their iniquities, did at least preserve some taste for higher human quality and honor certain forms of refinement by their enduring traditions. But when democracy is sovereign, its doubters say, nobility will form a sort of invisible church, and sincerity and refinement, stripped of honor, precedence, and favor, will have to vegetate on sufferance in private corners. They will have no general influence. They will be harmless eccentricities.

Now, who can be absolutely certain that this may not be the career of democracy? Nothing future is quite secure; states enough have inwardly rotted; and democracy as a whole may undergo self-poisoning. But, on the other hand, democracy is a kind of religion, and we are bound not to admit its failure. Faiths and utopias are the noblest exercise of human reason, and no one with a spark of reason in him will sit down fatalistically before the croaker's picture. The best of us are filled with the contrary vision of a democracy stumbling through every error till its institutions glow with justice and its customs shine with beauty. Our better men *shall* show the way and we *shall* follow them; so we are brought round again to the mission of the higher education in helping us to know the better kind of man whenever we see him.

The notion that a people can run itself and its affairs anonymously is now well known to be the silliest of absurdities. Mankind does nothing save through initiatives on the part of inventors, great or small, and imitation by the rest of us—these are the sole factors active in human progress. Individuals of genius show the way, and set the patterns, which common people then adopt and follow. *The rivalry of the patterns is the history of the world.* Our democratic problem thus is statable in ultra-simple terms: Who are the kind of men from whom our majorities shall take their cue? Whom shall they treat as rightful leaders? We and our leaders are the x and the y of the equation here; all other historic circumstances, be they economical, political, or intellectual, are only the background of occasion on which the living drama works itself out between us.

In this very simple way does the value of our educated class define itself: we more than others should be able to divine the worthier and better leaders.

The terms here are monstrously simplified, of course, but such a bird's-eye view lets us immediately take our bearings. In our democracy, where everything else is so shifting, we alumni and alumnae of the colleges are the only permanent presence that corresponds to the aristocracy in older countries. We have continuous traditions, as they have; our motto, too, is *noblesse oblige;* and, unlike them, we stand for ideal interests solely, for we have no corporate selfishness and wield no powers of corruption. We ought to have our own class-consciousness. "Les intellectuals"! What prouder club-name could there be than this one, used ironically by the party of "red blood," the party of every stupid prejudice and passion, during the anti-Dreyfus craze, to satirize the men in France who still retained some critical sense and judgment! Critical sense, it has to be confessed, is not an exciting term, hardly a banner to carry in processions. Affections for old habit, currents of self-interest, and gales of passion are the forces that keep the human ship moving; and the pressure of the judicious pilot's hand upon the tiller is a relatively insignificant energy. But the affections, passions, and interests are shifting, successive, and distraught; they blow in alternation while the pilot's hand is steadfast. He knows the compass, and, with all the leeways he is obliged to tack toward, he always makes some headway. A small force, if it never lets up, will accumulate effects more considerable than those of much greater forces if these work inconsistently. The ceaseless whisper of the more permanent ideals, the steady tug of truth and justice, give them but time, *must* warp the world in their direction.

This bird's-eye view of the general steering function of the college-bred amid the driftings of democracy ought to help us to a wider vision of what our colleges themselves should aim at. If we are to be the yeast-cake for democracy's dough, if we are to make it rise with culture's preferences, we must see to it that culture spreads broad sails. We must shake the old double reefs out of the canvas into the wind and sunshine, and let in every modern subject, sure that any subject will prove humanistic, if its setting be kept only wide enough.

Stevenson says somewhere to his reader: "You think you are just making this bargain, but you are really laying down a link in the policy of mankind." Well, your technical school should enable you to make your bargain splendidly; but your college should show you just the place of that kind of bargain —a pretty poor place, possibly—in the whole policy of mankind. That is the kind of liberal outlook, of perspective, of atmosphere, which should surround every subject as a college deals with it.

We of the colleges must eradicate a curious notion which numbers of good people have about such ancient seats of learning as Harvard. To many ignorant outsiders, that name suggests little more than a kind of sterilized conceit and incapacity for being pleased. In Edith Wyatt's exquisite book of

Chicago sketches called "Every One his Own Way" there is a couple who stand for culture in the sense of exclusiveness, Richard Elliot and his feminine counterpart—feeble caricatures of mankind, unable to know any good thing when they see it, incapable of enjoyment unless a printed label gives them leave. Possibly this type of culture may exist near Cambridge and Boston, there may be specimens there, for priggishness is just like painter's colic or any other trade-disease. But every good college makes its students immune against this malady, of which the microbe haunts the neighborhood-printed pages. It does so by its general tone being too hearty for the microbe's life. Real culture lives by sympathies and admirations, not by dislikes and disdains—under all misleading wrappings it pounces unerringly upon the human core. If a college, through the inferior human influences that have grown regnant there, fails to catch the robuster tone, its failure is colossal, for its social function stops: democracy gives it a wide berth, turns toward it a deaf ear.

"Tone," to be sure, is a terribly vague word to use, but there is no other, and this whole meditation is over questions of tone. By their tone are all things human either lost or saved. If democracy is to be saved it must catch the higher, healthier tone. If we are to impress it with our preferences, we ourselves must use the proper tone, which we, in turn, must have caught from our own teachers. It all reverts in the end to the action of innumerable imitative individuals upon each other and to the question of whose tone has the highest spreading power. As a class, we college graduates should look to it that *ours* has spreading power. It ought to have the highest spreading power.

In our essential function of indicating the better men, we now have formidable competitors outside. McClure's Magazine, the American Magazine, Collier's Weekly, and, in its fashion, the World's Work, constitute together a real popular university along this very line. It would be a pity if any future historian were to have to write words like these: "By the middle of the twentieth century the higher institutions of learning had lost all influence over public opinion in the United States. But the mission of raising the tone of democracy, which they had proved themselves so lamentably unfitted to exert, was assumed with rare enthusiasm and prosecuted with extraordinary skill and success by a new educational power; and for the clarification of their human sympathies and elevation of their human preferences, the people at large acquired the habit of resorting exclusively to the guidance of certain private literary adventures, commonly designated in the market by the affectionate name of ten-cent magazines."

Must not we of the colleges see to it that no historian shall ever say anything like this? Vague as the phrase of knowing a good man when you see him may be, diffuse and indefinite as one must leave its application, is there any other formula that describes so well the result at which our institutions *ought* to aim? If they do that, they do the best thing conceivable. If they fail to do it, they fail in very deed. It surely is a fine synthetic formula. If our faculties and graduates could once collectively come to realize it as the great underlying purpose toward which they have always been more or less obscurely groping, a great clearness would be shed over many of their problems; and, as for their influence in the midst of our social system, it would embark upon a new career of strength.

PUBLIC OPINION AND THE INTELLECTUALS

Francis G. Wilson

IF ONE SEEKS the fundamental cleavage between different types of intellectuals, it is no easy quest. It has been stated in various ways by many who have sought the fundamental issues of philosophy. But if one keeps in mind the relation of men to a human order, the issue may be stated like this: Is there such a thing as a transcendent order, or is all reality, including social and private experience, immanent? Is reality only the here and now? Is this the only divinity that men can know, and can it be discovered only by some application of what may be called positivism in social science? The predominant Greek philosophy that has survived as the core of many centuries of liberal education asserted the existence of a transcendent order, and so did Christian thought, whether based on Plato or Aristotle, or on a more direct examination of the implications of the Bible and Church tradition. The soul of man was open to something more than empirical data. Thus, Greek and Christian thought were looking for a spiritual reality transcendent to all men, whether they were among the learned or the vulgar. In more recent times, it is precisely the denial of such an order that has made up much of modern epistemology and metaphysics. Indeed, it has been the effort of many intellectuals to deny metaphysics by denying the existence of the spiritual and the transcendent. And it has been precisely this denial that has caused much of the conflict between the intellectuals and the democratic citizen.

It is said that Plato's God was always busy with geometry; and that, according to some scholars, is a peculiarly aristocratic and snobbish idea of science. It was a science beyond the comprehension of ordinary men; it was beyond the possibility of their participation in it. One may say, naturally, that Plato failed as a statesman or as advisor to kings and tyrants, but that in his *Laws* he seems to be trying to construct a society that would raise men to the highest level of which they are capable, and that in truth it was to a level very far from any modern idea of democracy. The dialectic that the rulers were to study in the *Republic* was only for a few, who in turn could direct the rest of society with wisdom. Here was a transcendental order clearly

Reprinted from *The American Political Science Review* (June, 1954), pp. 331-339, by permission of the author and the journal.

anti-democratic in implication. However, in Aristotle, both in the *Ethics* and in the *Politics,* the conservative mind comes closer to ordinary human habit, and there is a much more generous attitude toward what common people may think. They may still be directed by philosophers who have in mind a transcendent order, but the ordinary man participates in virtue. Moreover, the collective judgment of men is praised in Aristotle as a good standard for political behavior. One feels that the criticism of the city state in its time of decay was much milder in Aristotle than in Plato, even though Aristotle held that some men were slaves in their nature. On the other hand, Aristotle's praise of the common judgment was stated in the light of higher rational standards that were drawn from a knowledge of the purposes of nature. And some have gone so far as to assert that Aristotle had a profound influence even on the Stoic ideas of the natural equality of men. These points are emphasized because it seems that the path of reconciliation between the learned and the vulgar is the common acceptance of a transcendent order. This order may be known more intimately by those who are philosophers, but it is shared in and known to some extent by the education of all men in the habits of virtuous living. In this situation reason and faith have a common and supplemental function, and faith does not become the object of derision by those who have stressed the unlimited creativeness and autonomy of the educated reason. But it is also clear that there is a great dualism in human existence, for all men are existentially in both an immanent and a transcendent order, and the higher objectives of the transcendental are never to be realized in their fullness in that which is immanent and directly social.

It may seem paradoxical, but the intellectual who accepts a transcendental order that is above all men can be more easily reconciled to democracy and the forces of public opinion than one who does not. Such a view stands in criticism of much of the current theory of democracy. For in the intellectually predominant view of the present, democracy is almost incompatible with any standards that philosophy and religion may propose. It is asserted by some that only a philosophy of pragmatism is compatible with democracy. In other words, democracy must be based on something like William James' radical empiricism, or the instrumentalism of John Dewey. Or, one might say that because no standard of human justice can be proved, the only standard is that which is approved by some majoritarian procedure.

If this proposition states the current situation, it must arise from some qualities within the intellectual himself; it must be a kind of existential statement of the tensions of his life. In a direct sense, the answer may be found in the attitude of the intellectual toward political power. Those who deny a transcendental realization must attain whatever objectives they have in mind in the organization of society, and this primarily through the force of the state. Thus, they are driven to seek power, or sometimes in futility to deride it. On the other hand, those who, like Boethius, seek the consolation of philosophy, may speak of the vanity of the world. The order of wisdom is both here and beyond, and knowledge can be its own reward and spiritual consolation. Such an intellectual's primary activities are teaching and writing, so that the *artes liberales* will become the proud possession of the coming generation. He is happiest when he is directing a school, the Lyceum of the Academy in Athens, or perhaps the cathedral schools that preceded the foundation of the Western universities. What he asks is freedom from the ruler, not freedom to direct the government.

One is driven, therefore, to the conclusion that the intellectual who rejects the higher order of human experience is existentially a seeker of power. The free commitment of his will may be to him a painful experience, but in the end he has tried to remake the world; that is, historically, he has sought to be the servant and the advisor of kings. His writings, like those of Pierre DuBois or Marsilius of Padua in the fourteenth century, become the manifestos of the new and planned society. From the time of the rise of science and the troubles of the Reformation and Counter-Reformation, the idea of a utopia has been congenial to such intellectuals. From the eighteenth century to our time there has always been an intellectually-led political revolution in the making. The Tudor humanist, for example, might stress obedience to the king, but he was also a dreamer of the kind of society that autonomous human knowledge might make. Humanism was far more committed to the historic belief in a divine order than was the intellectualism of the eighteenth century, but the humanist was trying to be a philosopher and a bureaucrat. Consider, for example, the controversy over the objectives of Thomas More in his *Utopia*. Some have said that he was merely justifying English imperialism, but most students have said either that he was trying to reform society or that he was deriding the possibility of any reform. More was a great servant of the king, and he finally died as a martyr for his religious faith. But in the *Utopia* he seems to be struggling with the problem of personal power. Should he seek power in order to reform the world, or should he say that the injustice of the world could not be cured, owing to the corruption of men and government? Latterly, some have said that More was really arguing with himself as to whether he should be a lover of wisdom and the liberal arts or seek to reshape society nearer to the heart's desire. There is no question here of what the people may want, for the philosopher is able to say what justice is and what is proper for the people. But as a bureaucrat he would surely be at war with common opinion.

If we consider the seventeenth century, the picture is more clear. The ideal of science has dawned, and the literary humanism of a previous time is being pushed aside or into a darkened background where it has been ever since. Men seek now to wrest away the secrets of nature through mathematics, and through new methods that are scientific. They would, like Francis Bacon, another servant of the throne and author of the first scientific utopia, the *New Atlantis,* develop a new technology and create a kingdom governed by scientists who are continually engaged in scientific experimentation. But it is the government of a society that is at stake; it is science and politics hand in hand, and there is no room for the traditions and values of ordinary men who might turn away from the chilly efficiency of the new technology. When you do not believe in the traditional religious and humanistic values, as a modern you believe in science. And when you believe that the methods of natural and physical science can be applied to the social relations of people, you must turn to the state, for the state is the means whereby the new objectives can be attained. Likewise, one does not bother with ideas of natural rights and limitations on power when the state becomes the chief agency for the attainment of scientific results, whether those results are simple technology or the creation of a new social theory, as Robert Owen proposed.

At this point a digression into the history of political ideas is appropriate. With the beginning of the seventeenth century, certain major and traditional views in politics had emerged. There were the Calvinists, the Lutherans, the Anglicans, the Catholics, the minor and dissenting religious sects, and there were those who against all other traditions sustained the authority of the state and who were the proponents of various doctrines of sovereignty. It is clear, of course, that all of these views were internally divided, but each one took a position on the central issue of time: the relation of religion and politics. One can generalize as follows: those who supported a religious tradition, especially when it was on the defensive, were likely to be exponents of the consent of the governed, tyrannicide, and the power of the traditional estates or parliaments of the realm. They were more inclined than the defenders of sovereignty to seek the support of the general population. On the other hand, it was a time of the emergence of the modern conception of the authority of the state, modelled not a little on the authority of the Roman Empire and the Civil Law which had been used as a support for imperial power. Those who asserted the sovereignty of the monarch were not interested in what the people thought, but only in their obedience to the law. The doctrine of sovereignty was a kind of civil theology that was to take the place of the various Christian theologies which struggled against each other in Western Europe. Under the Tudors and the Stuarts, English official doctrine might be moving toward the assertion of the divine right of kings as the civil theology of Anglicanism, and Lutheranism had similar though not so well stated doctrines. But the divine right of kings was simply a passing phase of the argument. It is not the argument upon which the power of the modern state was built.

The question involved here is the function of intellectuals in relation to what might be called the general currents of popular opinion. It is clear that the religious traditions appealed with success to the citizen body, otherwise the religious wars would not have been fought, kings would not have been assassinated, and general and violent repression of religious dissent would not have been possible. To be brief, the secular, empirical, and scientific intellectuals were on the side of political authority, and to them a strong monarchy became all too often a symbol of the denial of the power of the people. The intellectuals framed the new theory of power. Though the lawyers had long used the model of the Roman Emperor in the analysis of kingly power, the secular mind used the new mathematical and scientific theories to justify the supremacy of the state over all dissent. In other words, much of the political theory of the time that now finds itself ensconced in the standard treatises is a defense of political power. The lawyers, the humanists, the poets, the philosophers, and the writers of systematic works in political analysis were generally on the side of sovereignty. One should not underestimate the force of protest, the defense of consent, and the emergent theory of constitutional liberty. But down to the eve of the French Revolution the *philosophes* were often supporters of the monarchy and they were contemptuous of the ideas of the ordinary citizen. Ignorance, faction, and sedition comprised the treadmill of the common man. The idea of the centralized and powerful state was rationalized by the intellectuals; it is a lasting, but perhaps unhappy, contribution to the history of modern times.

In no small degree Machiavelli became the symbol of the organized power of the state, though he was denounced often by those who used him most. Sir Thomas Browne said of him: "I confess that every county hath its Machiavel, every age its Lucian, whereof common Heads must not hear, nor more advanced Judgments too rashly venture on: it is the Rhetorik of Satan and may pervert a loose or prejudicate belief." In contrast, Francis Bacon, one of the great apostles of scientific method, and who was slightly senior to Browne, read avidly the Italian historians such as Paolo Sarpi, and he said: "We are much beholden to Machiavel and others that wrote what men do, and not what they ought to do." Here is an essential credo of the new science of national power; here is the principle that description and not values forms the core of the effort of the student of politics. The people must be managed and prevented from organizing so that discontent can never be a force on government. Thomas Hobbes, on the other hand, had few reservations as to the action of a totalitarian state. Not only must the common people be told what to think; the preacher and the professor must be dealt with in the firmest way. But Hobbes tried his hand at theology, and he rather fancied himself as a theologian. He reduced obedience to God to obedience to the theology that was incorporated into the civil statutes of the realm. Anyone who resisted the prince or the government was not only violating a civil law and worthy of condign punishment, but was also a rebel against his God. Moreover, the sovereign could command whatever he could get away with. Religion was thus reduced to a necessary annoyance; at best it was a department of government, as under the peculiar English system. Behind Hobbes' religious ideas, moreover, was a materialistic and utilitarian philosophy that in effect left no room for natural or divine law, for under Hobbe's covenant of death each individual had conceded all to the sovereign power of the state.

Fortunately for England, the long decades of disturbances and revolution ended, and a man like Locke could take many of the same philosophical ideas and create a moderate political philosophy that even led in the direction of religious toleration. And that great skeptic Hume, like William James, insisted that we must believe, but always under a powerful government that did not allow for the religious assertiveness of other days. In both Locke and Hume, the ideas of the common man get a hearing, and the stabilized custom, tradition, and public opinion of a nation may be considered in the calculations of public policy. But one of the great sources of modern liberty is the insistence on a genuine religious liberty, and though Locke moved far in that direction—farther than Milton—religious freedom was not a fact of political life. For example, Spinoza is cited for his defense of intellectual freedom, but it was the freedom of the philosopher that he defended. Spinoza's comments on religious liberty are often omitted from the books giving selections from his works. In his *Tratactus Theologico-Politicus* he argues in Chapter XIX that the right over matters spiritual lies wholly with the sovereign, and that the outward form of religion should be in accordance with public peace, if we would obey God aright. This is Hobbes all over again—the sharp Erastianism, or state supremacy over religion, that was characteristic of the critical and intellectual mind of the time. Some, like Giambattista Vico in his *New Science,* might argue that in the custom of nations the right of the common man to share in society is an embodiment of the natural law, but Vico was a forgotten figure in his Neapolitan isolation until almost the beginning of the nineteenth century.

With these ideas in mind, some comment must be made on the modern age of revolutions that began with the French Revolution. The philosophers of France in the eighteenth century played a large role in bringing about the revolution, for the intellectual origins of the French Revolution are among the most important, as Daniel Mornet has argued in his study of the subject. The intellectuals, such as Rousseau, provided the ideas that a Robespierre might use, even to the establishment of the worship of reason. Ever since the eighteenth century the battle over political ideology has centered on the philosophy of the French Revolution. A liberal must believe in it, and a conservative cannot. Burke and Wellington stand against Sieyès and Napoleon, and their successors adopt similar intellectual and ideological postures. The revolutionist would destroy the things the people love in the name of the people; the conservative would preserve the things the people love in the name of duty. But the participants in ideological battle may be consoled by Alexis de Tocqueville, who believed that the French Revolution had already occurred before 1789, and that the institutions of France had long since undergone a deep-seated remodelling.

The philosophical battle over the French Revolution and its successor revolutions is different in at least one respect from the present struggle over the Russian Revolution. Those who accepted the French Revolution and those who rejected it believed that values in social life could be demonstrated or proved. Values such as justice, liberty, natural rights, were accepted by both sides; Burke and Thomas Paine were trying to prove the same thing, but with widely variant theories of how to prove them. But since then values have tended to become myths and power has tended to become technique in the atheistic humanism of the nineteenth century, as in the thought of Feuerbach, Comte, and Nietzsche. Against the relativist and pragmatic democratic intellectual, the Marxian, the supporter of the Russian regime and its expansion, insists he has a scientific answer to everything. And in the cold light of the all-encompassing ideal of science, it is hard for the intellectual to say why the values of democracy can stand against dialectical materialism. To say, as some of the followers of John Dewey have done, that group experience, the dominance of the group, will give us answers, is surely futile, when the processes of group interaction produce the irreconcilable conflicts of modern times. C. Wright Mills in his recent book *White Collar* has suggested that to many intellectuals the revolution has become vulgar and the system of democratic society is accepted in a purely mechanical manner. To resist the new revolution, there must be an alternative faith. While we have many enthusiasts for revolution like Richard Price among us, there are few of the insight of Edmund Burke.

But common men still believe in many things. They are largely theistic and opposed to the secular intellectual whenever they understand what the clamor of wordy battle is all about. If the common herd, as Browne said, follows the intellectual you may have a revolution to remake society; but if the functioning citizen distrusts the intellectual leaders of important segments of society, the progress of society may be retarded, and retarded sharply in battle concerning values that are as old as the struggles between Plato and the Sophists. In a democratic society where there is a free communication of ideas and free elections, the people can at least make some sort of effective choice of what is offered them by those who edit the pharmacopoeia of the better world.

What then do the intellectuals promise? They promise a secular democracy, in which somehow spiritual values must take care of themselves. It is said that with psychology, the frustrations of the common man can be removed; with engineering and science, we can produce more worldly goods than he can consume; with economics, we can give assurance of a stable economy and high wages; with proper government policies, there can be liberty and security, and the lasting peace that poet and saint have so long prophesied. Art can be made popular and it can be appreciated; there will be plenty of novels to read, and entertainment will not lack. The great revolution, it is sometimes said, has already come and is behind us. The new frontiers of welfare beckon. But in all this there is another note: public opinion must be obedient; it must follow, and not be recalcitrant. Men must select the proper leaders and then not criticize them. It is surely uncertain whether the democratic citizen of our time is going to accept this prescription and such a leadership. It is not certain that he has accepted the secular democracy.

INTELLECTUALS AND DEMOCRACY

Max Ascoli

IN ACCORDANCE with democratic trends, in America as well as in the countries where traditional democracy has not been rejected, intelligence is scarcely fettered with exacting duties and responsibilities. Its functions being mainly preventive and negative, its duties are mainly technical: to give a certain coloration to events so as to facilitate their assimilation, to keep the stage clean for the new stream of happenings. But the final responsibility for what happens in society does not lie with the intellectuals; they voice, they clarify, they reproduce what is and what has been in the enormous scale required for information and education. Artists, and especially writers, unremittingly do their work of human reclamation, bringing to the light of expression situations buried under the marshes of silence or of conventionalism. But in any case the intellectuals cannot be responsible for the situations which they reproduce or for the facts which they analyze or even for the ideas which they voice. They have organized and adjusted their craft after the hidden rules and requirements of democracy but they cannot bear the responsibility for the material which is the object of their work, any more than the physical scientist can be responsible for the materials that he samples from nature. According to various viewpoints, this irresponsibility that the intellectual enjoys once he has passed the test of technical skill is called either objectivity or intellectual freedom. But in a democracy no more than in any other form of political or social organization can they bear the final responsibility. They follow every stream, register every tendency, enter into every land where organized efforts of men go. They are experts, not promoters. They have to reproduce and assimilate reality, not shape it. They have been crippled and equipped with orthopedic instruments precisely in order to reproduce a chaotic nature with man-made tools. The democratic system has laid more stress upon this independence, done more to enlarge the gap between intelligence and its subject matter, than any other. Once the intellectuals have accepted the rules laid down by society, and adjusted themselves to them, they cannot bear the final responsibility for society. This responsibility must lie somewhere else, with somebody else.

Reprinted from *Intelligence in Politics* (1936), pp. 246-254, by permission of the publisher, W. W. Norton & Company, Inc. Title supplied by the Editor.

But in a democracy the final responsibility lies nowhere and with nobody. Or it lies perhaps in society, but society is huge. It is everybody and nobody. Between these two terms, so opposite and so close, groups of more determined men may stand, working through propaganda and pressure, and assuming the representation of society through default of other pretenders. These groups badly need the help of intellectual technicians, but they as well as their technicians have always to direct their actions to goals and with methods acceptable to the elusive master, society. A democracy offers no barriers, no protections, only a few frames of law which may be helpful so long as men have imagination enough to see power in them. A democracy permeates every stratum of society, softens the corrosion of thought, smooths the outbursts of passion; it is certainly the shrewdest form of social organization because it seems to make no dent on time and decadence, having arranged a preventive deal with time and decadence. It has no permanent ruling class that may be disintegrated, it has no visible principles that may be deprived of content. The intellectuals are at the advanced and unprotected posts; they are bound by economic ties, by the danger of ridicule that comes from their persistence in sublimity, by the actual pettiness of their work, by their sheer numbers. But, on the other hand, they have not in front of them any organized group or class or caste bearing the final responsibility for society. They have only society.

Technicians at the service of nobody, protected by nobody, the intellectuals are in tune with democracy so long as their work is negative and preventive. Both external and internal pressure conspire to keep them loyal to this task. In some fields they have succeeded splendidly. The conflict of political ideals dramatically exploded in the middle of the last century had been stabilized in the same terms for decades and decades, until and after the World War. Liberalism had reached its highest expression in Tocqueville and in John Stuart Mill, socialism in Marx; political compromises, pedantic scholarship and journalistic vulgarization have prevented sustained thinking and avoided sharp clashes; theories cushioned by scholarly doctrines and by spurious popular offspring have been sheltered in a scientific quarantine, surrounded by a cloud of blissful misinterpretation. Certainly, if political changes which loomed possible after the middle of the last century materialized only in the first quarter of this century, it was to a great extent thanks to the softening of intellectual vigor brought about by scholastic pedantry and by journalism. And it makes little difference whether the intellectuals were conservative or revolutionary.

But society can drift toward situations unforeseen in history; unloosed economic and social forces can produce depressions or turmoils that defy the chastening work of intellectuals. No matter how devastating these forces may be, intellectuals are dragged along by them, and have to give them some expression and order. They are tamed by democracy, and at the same time they do not have any custodian or master who may pass on their work, no protector but this elusive master, society. Their expression of these forces may be in the form of demands for radical changes, and such changes may occur. But the forces which urge the changes are, in democratic times, moving and impersonal; the intellectual who has voiced them is caught in his individual personality as if he were responsible. The force may be revolutionary or reactionary, the intellectual who voices it may be worshiped or crucified; the chances are that when the tide has turned he will be left alone to bear the brunt of events. The more dominant the impersonal forces, the greater becomes the responsibility of the intellectual for his perhaps casual, perhaps coerced expression.

The political philosopher of our days cannot address his advice to a prince, or draw a draft that a king, a dynasty, or an oligarchic class will pay. Yet intellectuals have been accustomed since immemorial times to work in the interest and through the medium of a king or a dynasty, or an oligarchic class; sometimes the intellectual and his class have even been obliged to share in the payment. In normal times, when the circulation of ideas and expressions is buttressed by confidence, this is scarcely realized; but times of panic and of reckoning do come. It seems cruelty to have responsibility without power, precisely when the intellectual is most fettered by his need of adjustment to democratic society. But no matter how low he is reduced in a democracy, no matter how elusive his expression may be, he offers the target of an individual personality. The worst misfortune for a Machiavelli in former times was to be an unheard adviser or a bad guesser; the Machiavelli of our time is primarily reproached for being a poor doer. Everyone is permitted to be a Machiavelli in our time, provided that he is able to carry on with his ideas, shaping the insidious material that democracy offers. The practical man who does not achieve his goal is simply unsuccessful; the intellectual in the same condition is called wrong, and not only his whole personality but the whole influence of intelligence upon practical things is challenged. So the entire class sometimes has to pay when some of its members fail.

A democratic society drifts through political events, dark and self-contained, at the same time conservative and loose. Its tentacular organs for the apprehension of ideas, for the assimilation of experience, are like alarm signals softened to gentle buzzes in an enveloping cloudy fog. Its slow, retarded movement may drift anywhere; the organs of consciousness may be driven along with the rest without making too great a disturbance. Exposed and insecure, hampered in their individuality and swollen in number, the intellectuals are kept irresponsible toward the subject matter of their work—and that is called freedom; and entirely responsible for the effect of their work upon society at large—and that is called power. In the delicate equilibrium of a democracy this precarious situation of the intellectuals seems to be a guarantee of stability. If the system of hidden prohibitions, of dominant impersonal entities were revealed to itself in the light of clear consciousness, then the equilibrium would be broken, and in gaining consciousness of itself every democracy would slide into intolerance. When a democracy turns intolerant and totalitarian the intellectuals are definitely crushed. A certain intellectual atony may prevent the intellectuals from rushing to their doom. This seems to be a rather meager security, especially when in times of distress intellectuals may be awakened. Democracy seems to be protected by being forbidding and confused, a protection that fades away when it is invested with intelligence or love. Even in countries where democracy has overcome the test of endurance, and intelligence is more admirably adjusted to it, even in America, the casual, home-grown democracy can tolerate with difficulty the unrest brought about by the need of planning and reasoning.

Only in its own despair and fear and final self-mutilation does intelligence seem to have some temporary guarantee against being destroyed, and some hope of becoming adjusted to democratic politics. Its last recourse seems to be a moderate, learned or journalistic dullness. Intellectuals in our days are massed and packed on the thin edge between traditional and totalitarian democracy. In whatever direction they move they may precipitate an avalanche, and in the avalanche they know they will be the first to be destroyed. Intelligence in modern politics can plunge politics into unfathomable disastrous new forms. It is a position where the responsibility is even more merciless than the danger, yet it inclines more to inaction than to strenuous and sustained work. Of the new dimension created by democracy one thing is certain and measurable: that the intellectuals are located in its most vital section. The democratic world does not revolve on the axis of intelligence, yet the intellectuals are packed on the pivotal parts of its structure; too pivotal for what they can bear or decide by themselves. Where the edge between the two slopes of democracy offers some appearance of greater compactness and of resistance to sudden avalanches, there the measurement of the function and responsibility of intelligence in politics is still possible.

LIBERALS AND THE MARXIST HERESY

Reinhold Niebuhr

THE SPATE of Congressional investigations, ostensibly intended to ferret out remnants of disloyalty in the schools and colleges, in the churches, and in the entertainment industries, are manifestations of an old tension between the business community of America and the so-called "intellectuals." The former has achieved formal political power for the first time in two decades and it seems intent on evening the score and venting its resentments against its critics of the past decades. The more unscrupulous and demagogic representatives of the Republican Party seek to do this by proving the critics to be involved, directly or indirectly, with the hated conspiracy all good men abhor. The temptation to embarrass the critics of a business civilization was strong, even for those who are not given to the arts of demagogy, for it is a fact that the critics were informed by various shades and versions of a dogma which, in its most consistent form, led to the sorry realities of a Communist tyranny.

It is, of course, necessary in the interest of democratic justice and for the sake of our unity with the remainder of the free world, to resist unscrupulous efforts to obscure all shades and distinctions on the Left, and to prove every critic to be in either explicit or implicit connivance with a hated enemy. But it is also necessary for those of us who account ourselves among the critics to confess to the remarkable influence of the Marxist dogma on our viewpoints, even while we resist the efforts of the demagogues to identify every form of dissent with Communism.

The term "intellectuals" is somewhat vague, particularly in America; but it designates, however inexactly, the more articulate members of the community, more particularly those who are professionally or vocationally articulate, in church and school, in journalism and the arts. It is altogether healthy that these articulate members of the community should assume the task of criticism or should have had that task imposed upon them by the criteria of their several disciplines, whether religious, academic or esthetic. It is as natural as it is inevitable that the so-called men of affairs, whether in business or government, should be inclined to be more complacent, whether

---

Reprinted from *The New Republic* (October 12, 1953), pp. 13-15, by permission of the author and the periodical.

because preoccupation with practical affairs prevents critical thinking or because their interest creates an ideological stake in the *status quo,* or because practical experience endows men with a wisdom proving the tenets of the critics abstract and illusory. Since the latter factor is present in the attitudes of the business community, though in a minor role, it behooves those of us who were and are the critics of our civilization to confess to the power of an abstract dogma over our minds, even while we resist the unscrupulous efforts to relate every form of dissent with the extreme form of the dogma, or even with disloyalty.

The most obvious distinction in the interest of fairness is to note the rigorous resistance to Communism by Democratic Socialists in all nations. The attitudes of Norman Thomas in this country, of the late Ernst Reuter in Berlin, and Henri Spaak in Belgium and many others is sufficient refutation of the outrageous charge that a common Marxist dogma creates an affinity between Communism and Socialism. Socialism and Communism may be brothers; if so, they are, as the late socialist leader Kurt Schummacher observed, like Cain and Abel. The common Marxist dogma not only failed to guarantee affinity with Communism, but it has not prevented Socialism from being a creative force, when it expressed itself in loyalty to and in the context of a democratic community. A large part of the free world is indebted to the Socialist movement for the establishment of justice. The efforts of our vigilantes to brand the movement with the mark of Cain therefore alienates our friends and seems to substantiate prejudices of their own about our life.

It must be admitted that the intellectuals, committed or uncommitted to Socialist parties, do not have as good a record of discernment as do the party leaders. Some of them, like the late Harold Laski, could not make up their minds whether to condemn Russia as a tyranny or to exalt her as the harbinger of a new culture. Mr. Laski was equally uncertain whether to extol our own nation as an open society or to condemn us as a capitalistic one. In a similar fashion, the Swedish social scientist, Gunnar Myrdal, despite his intimate relation with our culture, was prompted by the Marxist dogma to adopt a defeatist attitude toward our future. He was so sure our economy would collapse after the war that he persuaded Sweden to engage in a very unadvantageous trade agreement with Russia. The examples of Laski and Myrdal will remind us that intellectuals are more easily swayed by Marxist dogma than the workingmen who constitute the bulk of the Socialist movement and who, as Lenin confessed, would not rise unaided, above a "trade-union psychology." That is, they would reject utopian illusions and be content with proximate goals of justice.

In America the Marxist ideology had a surprisingly strong hold on the intellectualist critics of capitalism, despite the absence of a Socialist movement giving their ideas relevance. The "New Deal," a characteristically pragmatic effort to resolve the debate between classical economics and Marxism, was consciously or unconsciously dependent upon the thought of the late Lord Keynes. It fell under the criticism of intellectuals prompted by obvious Marxist prejudices. But their Marxism was not consistent; it included every shade of opinion from open hospitality to Communism, to secret or open sympathy for the Communist cause.

Many of the intellectuals who were at first attracted by Communism were subsequently repelled by the realities of Communist politics, particularly as these revealed themselves in the purge trials of the early 30s, the Nazi-Soviet pact and the chicane of the Communist Party in the Spanish Civil War. A group of very distinguished intellectuals have left a record of their initial illusions and subsequent disillusion in the symposium *The God That Failed:* a moving revelation both of the spiritual and political confusions of our day and a proof that moral sensitivity and utopian longings were responsible for their attraction to Communism. The realities of Communist politics are in such vivid contrast to the moral motives for original allegiance that those converts who have not broken with Communism have become more and more pathetic in seeking to cover their mistaken loyalty with ever more implausible interpretations of present realities. Some have assumed an attitude of neutrality and "objectivity," pretending to be able to criticize both Soviet and American policies with equal severity and with equal justification.

Of those who have renounced their Communist faith, some have, in the violence of their reaction, embraced the dogmas of the extreme Right, thus exchanging creeds but not varying the spirit and temper of their approach to life's problems. A few have found profit or prestige as professional anti-Communists. Others—for example, the redoubtable young editor, James Wechsler, and the famous Mayor Reuter of Berlin—have expiated an earlier Communist loyalty by a rigorous anti-Communist, but thoroughly liberal, democratic faith. It is ironic that men who extricated themselves with least hurt to their spirit are now declared suspect by our vigilantes because they have not proved their repentance by adhesion to some dogma of the Right or by imitating its hysteria.

Among the intellectuals who have not explicitly disavowed earlier Communist sympathy, many have gradually taken a more and more critical attitude toward Communist politics. Some of these would probably be surprised if confronted with early writings in which they made ridiculous estimates of Russia as the holy land of a new culture. The number actually involved in the Communist conspiracy was very small. Professor Hook is probably right, however, in charging liberal sentiment on the Left with the error of complacency toward the danger of conspiracy. Many thought of Communism chiefly as a heresy with which they might not agree but which must be granted that tolerance the traditional liberal extends to all dissent. They were thus as undiscriminating as the Right, which was eager to identify every form of dissent with disloyalty or even with treason. The Hiss trial had particular significance. It was a traumatic experience on the Right, for it seemed to confirm all of its worst fears and established prejudices. The Left, however, assumed Hiss' innocence and regarded the proceedings against him as no more than an effort to attack the Roosevelt Administration. In Europe Hiss' innocence is still widely taken for granted.

While fairness demands that distinctions among the opinions on the Left be established, the intellectuals must with corresponding honesty admit the universality of the Marxist dogma over their minds. In one sense the breadth and extent of that is not a mystery. The critics of a business civilization wished to challenge the moral and intellectual assumptions guarding the complacency of the culture. Those assumptions had been stated by Adam Smith, who based his thought upon an earlier physiocratic dogma. According to that dogma, freedom in economic life would automatically bring justice, if only men would rigorously refrain from interfering with the operation of "nature's laws." This view assumed an analogy between historical and natural events which was not true; and it guaranteed social harmonies which the social tensions of a growing technical society violently contradicted. If the injustices of a business society were to be challenged what would seem more relevant than the Marxist dogma? The social realities seemed to validate its presuppositions rather than the optimism of the liberal dogma. Furthermore, it lacked the rigorous and enervating determinism of the liberal dogma and appealed to the human impulse to master historical destiny.

Pious criticisms of Marxist determinism are somewhat ironic, considering that the business community follows a more deterministic creed. The danger in the Marxist creed derives, not from its determinism, but from its pretension that men can, at a particular climax in human affairs, triumph not only over injustice but over man's ambiguous role in history and become masters of history. This ambition to achieve mastery of historical destiny conformed to one part of liberal secularism, exemplified by August Comte. There is, therefore, good reason for the power of the Marxist dogma over the minds of the intellectuals and critics of a business civilization. Unfortunately for them, and for our civilization, the Marxist dogma was as mistaken as the dogma upon which capitalistic culture rests. It was doubly unfortunate that the Marxist errors led to worse injustices than those which prevailed in our free society. The dogma of the Right sought to reduce the power of the state; but it preserved the multiplicity of power centers in society. The dogma of Marxism assumed that the socialization of property would eliminate economic power from human affairs. This was a great mistake, for it led to the concentration of both economic and political power in a single oligarchy. The resulting tyranny must therefore be regarded not as the fortuitous corruption of an original Marxist ideal but as the inevitable fruit of its illusions.

All the errors in the rightist dogma could not efface its one virtue: preserving a multiplicity of power centers in society. And all the virtues of the Marxist dogma could not efface the evil effects of its single great error: creating a monopoly of power. The moral embarrassment of the intellectuals derives from accepting Marxist dogma too uncritically, failing to perceive its error. In the democratic world, Marxism did not lead to the noxious consequences of the totalitarian state chiefly because the dogma was not consistently expressed or applied.

The fact is that an economy can neither be totally regulated nor totally unregulated; just as men can be neither masters of their historical fate nor mere prisoners of destiny. Neither dogma is totally true. Modern communities do not live in the harmony assumed by the one dogma, nor do they move inevitably to a climax of social tension as the other dogma assumes. So the healthiest modern nations have distilled truth from the tension between both equally untenable dogmas and have preserved their health by practices which followed neither too consistently. That is probably why Britain is spiritually the healthiest of modern nations, however precarious her economic health may be. There the creed of the business community was qualified by an older aristocratic tradition, and the creed of a quasi-Marxist party was leavened by an older and more pragmatic Christian radicalism. Thus the struggle between contradictory creeds was mitigated, and the comparative equality of strength between the social forces, holding allegiance to each creed, has prevented the unequivocal triumph of either. America, by comparison, is less favorably endowed. The absence of a strong Marxist movement has led to the triumph of the opposite creed without serious challenge; and the present effort of our vigilantes to wipe out or discredit every form of critical dissent not only makes our political thinking inflexible but deepens the rift between ourselves and the free nations of Europe and Asia.

Oddly enough our business community is more pragmatic in the management of its affairs than in its political creed. Whether because of its practical wisdom or because of the policies of a political movement which it opposed and abhorred, our history has not been as catastrophic as it seemed that it might be in the 1930s. Then, general defeatism among the critics, and among some of the defenders of our economy was one of the primary reasons for Marxism's attraction. Recently a friend wrote to congratulate me on my accuracy in predicting the inevitable corruptions of power in the Soviet state in a book I wrote in 1934. Upon rereading the book to enjoy the experience of justified prophecy, I discovered that my wisdom was not as perfect as the friend suggested. *Reflections on the End of an Era* was a perfect revelation of the pessimistic assumptions, prompted by Marxist thought, which had informed one who was challenging at least some of the Marxist illusions. History is fortunately not as predictable as those who invent a logic to contain it imagine. Our civilization is not as free of problems as the conservative dogmatists pretend. But we were able to survive the stresses of the war with rather more residual health than was anticipated. The Nazi peril was moreover something quite different from the final desperate defensive action of capitalism Marxist analysis made it. In reality it was a lower middle-class revolt against a weakened civilization.

It is an ironic fact that the actual "class struggle" between owners and workers has been less severe, and characterized by more accommodations of interest, in America than in Europe. We therefore enjoy a measure of political and moral health. But the ideological struggle between the defenders and the intellectual critics of our economy has been more severe than in Europe. It threatens at the present time to sow confusion both within our boundaries and between ourselves and our allies. Thus adherence to inflexible dogmas, and dishonesty in taking advantage of an ideological foe, threatens to undo whatever a wisdom in practical affairs has established in this nation.

THE AMERICAN INTELLECTUAL:
A CONSERVATIVE VIEW

Russell Kirk

W E HEAR a great deal nowadays about the lamentable plight of the American intellectual. I think that the American educated man, or at least the American who has submitted to a certain amount of formal instruction, is indeed in an unhappy situation; and part of his unhappiness is the consequence of his calling himself an "intellectual." That term implies defecated rationality, the exaltation of pure logic, presumptuous human reason unassisted by religious humility and traditional wisdom, above veneration and conscience. I do not think that we are going to effect much improvement in education until we confess to ourselves that there is something greater than pure individual reason. That higher wisdom is religious truth.

Until a very few generations ago, men took it for granted that the essence of true education was religious knowledge. Theology was queen of the sciences; professors and teachers, Catholic or Protestant, were men in holy orders, or at least men thoroughly schooled in theology, apologetics, Biblical studies, and the wealth of Christian thought. A learned man was a clerk, a cleric. Nor was this true simply of the Christian nations: Judaism, Mohammedanism, Buddhism, Brahmanism, and all the higher religions had in their charge the education of the people. As philosophy, art, law, and all the more important elements of civilization developed out of religious principle and faith, so formal schooling was the creation of the church, and instruction in religious truth remained until very late the primary aim of schools and universities. Here in America, the whole tone and temper of learning and society was immeasurably influenced by our church-founded universities and colleges.

Yet in America, as in most of the rest of the world, a divorce between religion and education began to take effect about the middle of the nineteenth century, with the rise of scientific materialism, aggressive secularism, state educational institutions, and the triumph of technology. Knowledge, simple

Reprinted from *Beyond the Dreams of Avarice* (1956), pp. 3-10, 12-15, by permission of the author and publisher, Henry Regnery Company. This essay originally appeared in a shorter version in *The Pacific Spectator* (Autumn, 1955) under the title "The American Intellectual: A Conservative View" which title has been employed here.

secular instruction, might teach a man all that he needs to know in this life, the zealots of the new order insisted. Religion, these reformers maintained, was unscientific, irrational: at best, it was a personal, private, mystical experience, not fit to be discussed in schools. The clerisy—the body of preachers and teachers imbued with a sense of religious consecration—gave way to the intellectuals. And from the consequences of this neglect of religious wisdom, we have suffered terribly, and we are destined to suffer for a great while yet. Newman, more than a century ago, prophesied these consequences:

In morals, as in physics, the stream cannot rise higher than its source. Christianity raises men from earth, for it comes from heaven; but human morality creeps, struts, or frets upon the earth's level, without wings to rise. The Knowledge School does not contemplate raising man above himself; it merely aims at disposing of his existing powers and tastes, as is most convenient, or is practicable under circumstances. It finds him, like the victims of the French Tyrant, doubled up in a cage in which he can neither lie, stand, sit, nor kneel, and its highest desire is to find an attitude in which his unrest may be least.

Now the unrest and the ill repute of the American intellectual, I think, are caused primarily by this divorce of knowledge from religious truth; and I propose to say a little about defecated intellectuality.

Not long ago someone wrote to Bertrand Russell inquiring after his definition of an "intellectual." Lord Russell replied most forthrightly:

"I have never called myself an intellectual, and nobody has ever dared to call me one in my presence.

"I think an intellectual may be defined as a person who pretends to have more intellect than he has, and I hope that this definition does not fit me."

Earl Russell, being well acquainted with the signification of words, spoke with some authority on the modern usage of "intellectual." The word has had rather an interesting history. In the seventeenth century, it was indeed employed as a noun, chiefly to describe a person who holds that all knowledge is derived from pure reason. It had even then, and earlier, a denigratory implication. The more common term for this concept was "intellectualist." Bacon writes critically, in the *Advancement of Learning,* of the intellectualist as an abstract metaphysician: "Upon these intellectualists, which are, notwithstanding, commonly taken for the most sublime and divine philosophers, Heraclitus gave a just censure." Bishop Parker remarks how "These pure and seraphic intellectualists forsooth despise all sensible knowledge as too grosse and materiall for their nice and curious faculties." Hume demolished the eighteenth-century intellectuals, or intellectualists, who took Reason for their guide to the whole nature of man; they were the *a priori* reasoners, upon the model of Locke; Hume does not employ the word "intellectual," however. Coleridge—again, however, not using the word—attacked them as the devotees of the mere Understanding, "the mere reflective faculty," as distinguished from the Reason, or organ of the supersensuous.

As a noun descriptive of persons, "intellectual" scarcely appeared at all in nineteenth-century dictionaries. So far as the term was employed, it meant the "sophisters and calculators" whom Burke had denounced, the abstract *philosophes;* it was a category despised equally, though for different reasons, by Romantics and Utilitarians. It is scarcely surprising, then, that the word retains a disparaging signification. It was closely linked with an unimaginative secularism: Newman attacked Sir Robert Peel for embracing it. All in all, "intellectual" meant just what Bacon meant by it, a person who overrates the understanding. By implication, an intellectual neglected the imagination, the power of wonder and awe, and the whole great realm of being which is beyond mere rational perception.

Fairly early in the twentieth century, however, a group of persons began to describe themselves as intellectuals. Throughout the nineteenth century, a man no more would have thought of calling himself an intellectual than a woman would have thought of calling herself a bluestocking. The words used to describe persons possessed of what Burke called "a liberal understanding" were varied, and none of them wholly satisfactory: scholar, bookman, philosopher, university man. Coleridge coined a new word to describe the teachers and preceptors of society, including the clergy and the lay scholars: the clerisy. A principal reason why no one word adequately described such a class of persons was that, in most of Europe and America, and especially in Britain and the United States, intellectuality was not the particular property of any class or order. A banker, like Grote, might possess the liberal understanding; or a politician, like Disraeli or Franklin Pierce; or a judge, like Tocqueville or Chancellor Kent; or a wine-merchant's son, like Ruskin; or an engraver and printer, like Blake. Thus it was reserved to the twentieth century to try to make "intellectual" a distinct term of commendation.

The current employment of "intellectual" appears to be derived from the jargon of Marxism. It is directly linked with the notion of a body of schooled and highly rational persons bitterly opposed to established social institutions —outcasts in a sense, men who go out to the Cave of Adullam, uprooted, rootless, radical folk, what Gissing called "the unclassed." *Les intellectuels* was the term of contempt employed by the factions of the Right, during the Dreyfus controversy, to describe the café-revolutionaries, the men who had broken with tradition, the enemies of patriotism, order, and the wisdom of the ages. It implied an opposition between the life of the mind and the life of society—or, at least, an inimicality between "advanced social thinkers" and the possessors of property and power. It also implied, commonly, a contempt for religious ideas and establishments. In the definition of the twentieth-century dictionaries, an intellectual is "a person of a class or group professing or supposed to possess enlightened judgment with respect to public or political questions." The link with social and political action is significant of the aims and limitations of the twentieth-century intellectuals. A "liberal understanding" in Burke's sense, Newman's "liberal education," the world of contemplation and silence, was not what they were after: they wanted to mould society nearer to their hearts' desire, not to adhere to traditional humanism by improving private mind and character.

The Marxists seem to have been the first body of "intellectuals" to call themselves just that. In their sense, "intellectuals" was the Anglicized form of the Russian *intelligentia,* more awkwardly if more literally translated as "intelligentsia." In nineteenth- and twentieth-century Russia, the *intelligentia* were the emancipated and revolutionary body of educated or half-educated people, university students and graduates, who felt that the old Russia was hopelessly reactionary and mindless—and that, indeed, it held no place for them. They considered themselves enemies of established society and the church, opposed both to convention and to the state, self-liberated from prejudice and prescription. In all charity, it must be said that though they thought of themselves as emancipated, in fact often they merely were unbuttoned. Out of this *intelligentia* came the Nihilists—and, in the fullness of time, the Narodniks and the Mensheviks and the Bolsheviks. This curious class, a kind of intellectual proletariat, is described by Dostoievski, in its earlier stages; Conrad's *Under Western Eyes* examines these people, too, particularly through the character of Razumov—who, though unsuccessfully reacting against the emancipated *intelligentia,* cannot free himself from their temper and society. The *intelligentia* were displaced persons, schooled beyond their proper expectations in life, severed from tradition but unable to find comfortable niches in the world of modernity.

An intelligentsia of this description increased rapidly in numbers throughout much of Europe in the latter half of the nineteenth century, and began to be a force in all sorts of odd corners of the world; its lineaments may be discerned now in nearly every Latin-American state, and in India, Indonesia, and even the modern towns of Africa. It never has attained to corresponding influence in the English-speaking states, however, in part because of the traditional liberal learning there (closely joined to the old religious and humanistic disciplines and the concept of free and dignified personality in all walks of life), in part because representative government and social mobility have provided safety-valves.

What Dr. Albert Salomon, in *The Tyranny of Progress,* calls the "coffee-house intellectual," then, so subversive in the Continent, represented no real threat to things established in the English-speaking states. Pitt and Liverpool might find it prudent to keep an eye upon the radical journalist and pamphleteer; but as the mob was Tory, so was the great majority of scholars and writers. Burke, when he exposed the designs of Dr. Price and the "constitutional societies," found the clergy—dissenting or Anglican—actually more radical than Grub Street was. Oxford and Cambridge, Harvard and Yale, throughout the eighteenth and nineteenth centuries, scarcely were seedbeds of revolt; while the newspaper-office and the publishers' string of writers did not turn out Trotskys. Café-society (in the French or German sense, not the gossip-column signification) did not dominate the realm of scholarship and authorship and political speculation in Britain and America. "Mr. Trotsky of the Central Cafe," in Vienna, could walk into the street and make a revolution; but he had no Anglo-Saxon counterpart.

Until recent years, London and New York knew little of this atmosphere. The scholar and the writer were not alienated men. Not until the 1920's, in Britain and America, was there much talk of the treason of the intellectuals; and that was because the word "intellectual" was seldom employed, for lack of any distinct class to which it might be attached. Only as Britain and America lost their comparative isolation from European ideology, and only as there began to grow up in these nations a body of persons educated beyond their expectations in life, opposed to established social institutions, did the word "intellectual" obtain currency and the place of the intellectual in English and American society begin to be argued about. And it remains true, as Lord Russell's sardonic remark suggests, that not many people in these nations want to be called intellectuals—and that some of the more intelligent and best-educated Englishmen and Americans are most hostile to what I have called "defecated intellectuality." Burke could imagine nothing more wicked than the heart of a thoroughbred metaphysician—that is, presumptuous rationality, the cult of Reason, divorced from religion, tradition, honor, and duties. This remained almost the universal Anglo-American attitude until recent years.

Emerson did not write about the "American intellectual"; he wrote of the American Scholar; indeed, he disliked the concept of "a sort of Third Estate with the world and the soul," a body of persons claiming to speak exclusively for the intellect, and for the intellect only. The aversion to defecated intellectuality may be observed not only among our statesmen—Washington, John Adams, Webster, Lincoln, Theodore Roosevelt—but among our men of letters and speculation: take Hawthorne, Melville, Lowell, Henry Adams, and George Santayana, to speak almost at random. Some of our writers and critics might remark sadly the deficiency of contemplation and the higher imagination in America, but they did not aspire to set up the "intellectuals" as a distinct caste. Had not the New England farmer who read good books as much a right to be considered an intellectual being as any coffee-house Bohemian? Was Calhoun, reading in his solitary way at Fort Hill, any less a thinking man than an Amherst professor? Who was the "intellectual"—

Clarence King or William Graham Sumner? Schooling was easily enough available to almost anyone that wanted it; the domination of higher education in America by church-founded colleges tended to prevent any opposition between tradition and intellectuality; while popular government made it difficult for the intellectually alienated to maintain that he was kept under by some iron political domination. Thus we hear next to nothing about "the role of the intellectual," as a distinct breed, until the alteration of American character and the triumph of urbanization, within this century, bring to the United States conditions in some degree analogous to those of Europe.

I have suggested that the concept of the "intellectual" is closely joined to class-antagonism and radical political alteration. The thinking man in America generally has not spoken of himself as a member of a distinct order, precisely because class has been so amorphous in this country. He was not excluded by the nobility or the church or the central bureaucracy: there existed no nobility, and no church establishment, and no bureaucracy in the European sense, to exclude him. He might be lonely, but he was not oppressed; if he felt himself neglected or almost friendless, still he attributed his condition to the ancient preoccupation of the mass of men with material ends, not to organized obscurantism in high places. Only when a doctrinaire hostility toward traditional religion, "capitalism," and established political forms began to make itself felt in America, particularly with the growing influence of Marxism and other European ideologies in the 1920's and the vague discontents of the Depression, did a number of educated Americans commence to call themselves intellectuals.

So the American Intellectuals were identified from the first with a political and social movement loosely called "Liberalism"—very different in some respects from the English liberalism it thought it emulated, and ranging all the way from a mild secularism to outspoken sympathy with Communist Russia. Often it was linked, philosophically, with Pragmatism, and with various experimental undertakings in education and practical morality. It tended rapidly to become an ideology, as Mr. David Riesman and others have suggested recently, with its secular-dogmas and its slogans. Mr. Lionel Trilling and Mr. William J. Newman have stated that they use the terms "liberal" and "intellectual" almost synonymously. The "progressive" assumption in America (with some justification, during the 'twenties and 'thirties) has been that if a man thinks, he must vote for "liberal" candidates. . . .

I confess, in short, to being one of those scholars whom John Dewey detested, endeavoring as I do (in Dewey's words) "to justify rationally the religious-tribal beliefs, moral preoccupations and privileges of their noble masters." (What Dewey meant by this disagreeable description was any educated man who might be inclined to believe that there was light in the world before John Dewey lit his torch.) It is precisely because I respect the scholar, the professor, the scientist, and the lonely thinker that I am hostile toward the clique of "We Happy Few," the closed corporation of the half-educated who call themselves intellectuals—and who then proceed to discard the wisdom of our ancestors and to try to remould human nature and society after an image contrived from their own petty stock of private rationality. I think that a man who believes we wandered in darkness, until Marx and Freud and Dewey took us by the hand, is doing everything in his puny power to injure the mind of our civilization—however humanitarian his intention may be. My model for the scholar is that described by Orestes Brownson in his address "The Scholar's Mission," at Dartmouth College, in 1843:

I understand by the scholar no mere pedant, dilettante, literary epicure or dandy; but a serious, robust, full-grown man; who feels that life is a serious affair, and that he has a serious part to act in its eventful drama; and must therefore do his best to act well his part, so as to leave behind him, in the good he has done, a grateful remembrance of his having been. He may be a theologian, a politician, a naturalist, a poet, a moralist, or a metaphysician; but whichever or whatever he is, he is it with all his heart and soul, with high, noble,—in one word, *religious* aims and aspirations.

The scholar of religious aims and aspirations is a man of true freedom of mind. Much of what is said and written nowadays about academic freedom is so much cant. Too often the defenders of the liberties of the Academy take for their motto that of Rabelais' Abbey of Thélème. "Do as you will." This anarchic freedom never really existed in any university, and never can. The Christian knows that true freedom is not simply to "do as you will." For the Christian, freedom is submission to the will of God; and this is no paradox. We are free in proportion as we recognize our real duties and our real limitations. Then we may act within the just confines of our nature, and act with courage. But if we claim an anarchic freedom, we all become so many Cains. The scholar who claims an anarchic freedom may become a sour, conspiratorial, envious creature, like Professor Mulcahey, in Miss Mary McCarthy's novel *The Groves of Academe*.

And a second description of freedom runs through Christian thought, as it ran through the Stoic philosophy and through Indian tradition: freedom is the absence of desire. Exalt the Self, the solitary human atom, above authority, tradition, and conscience, and you make yourself, in the name of freedom, the victim of *hybris*.

Real intellectual freedom must be in accord with submission to the will of God and with subjection of desires. And every right is married to some duty. Academic freedom is married to the duty to seek and to teach the truth. The scholar is protected in his right to think and to say things which might not be tolerated in the market-place because of the assumption that he is a man devoted to the conservation and the advancement of Truth. If, deserting Truth, he lusts after Power, then he loses his claim to the special freedom of the Academy. And as a friend of mine says who has had much experience of American universities, when some professors nowadays talk about academic freedom, language has lost its meaning for them. They really are not talking about academic freedom, but only about academic power. They are very little interested in conserving or advancing Truth, and are still less interested in securing intellectual or academic freedom for others. What they mean, when they say "academic freedom," is power to dominate the wills of their colleagues and to force the minds of their students into an ideology that they happen to fancy. It is because of these persons that academic freedom is endangered today. No order falls except from its own weakness; and if academic freedom is lost, it will be because the scholar has forgotten that he is a Bearer of the Word. He will have become an intellectual in the root-meaning of that term.

In this time of equalitarian conformity, boredom, and mechanization, when Things are in the saddle and the triumph of technology threatens to suppress the truly human person, we require intellectual power and virtue more than ever before—and courage to resist popular infatuations. "The scholar is not one who stands above the people," Brownson says, "and looks down on the people with contempt. He has no contempt for the people; but a deep and all-enduring love for them, which commands him to live and labor, and, if need be, to suffer and die, for their redemption; but he never forgets that he is their instructor, their guide, their chief, not their echo, their slave, their tool." We now need a genuine clerisy as never before we needed such in America. But I do not believe we are going to obtain anything of the sort if we endeavor to create an intelligentsia, a rootless class of half-educated persons after the European model. The reflective and conscientious American needs to do his duty as an intellectual leader; but he needs to remember that in such a society as ours, the restriction of intellectuality to a presumptuous caste may be disastrous. We may turn out some millions of intellectuals, but we may simultaneously do our worst to stifle the wise man and the truly liberal understanding.

INTELLECTUAL SOCIALISTS

Roberto Michels

THE GREATEST contribution of intellectualism to a practical movement is Marxism. By transferring socialism from the utopian to the scientific level of thought and by demonstrating the existence of an objective, economically inevitable trend toward socialism it intellectualized the modern labor movement, endowing proletarian interests with the ethical aspects of a universal cultural movement, and made it conscious of a "scientific function"—bearing the germ of a new society.

This achievement, which has had such boundless political consequences, was largely the work of bourgeois intellectuals; indeed it may be stated as a historical law that class movements are led by members of the classes against which they are aimed. Marx correctly said in the *Communist Manifesto* that it was the tragic fate of the bourgeoisie to be the teacher of its economic and social archenemy, because it is compelled in its constant battles ("at first with the aristocracy; later on, with those portions of the bourgeoisie itself, whose interests have become antagonistic to the progress of industry: at all times, with the bourgeoisie of foreign countries") "to appeal to the proletariat, to ask for its help, and thus, to drag it into the political arena," supplying it with a weapon, in the form of education, which is destined to be turned against the teacher. In addition the bourgeoisie becomes the fencing master of the proletariat when as a result of constant interclass contact members of the bourgeoisie, especially many intellectuals, are detached and use their knowledge and spirit to inspire the working masses to struggle against existing conditions.

Intellectual socialists are of the following main types: ethicists, armed with social conscience; scientists, convinced of the necessity for or the practicability of socialism; demagogues; quacks, selling confused ideological merchandise; men of the Coriolanus type, who desire revenge for personal misfortune, including in a depersonalized, class sense the so-called intellectual proletariat, the declassed; and satiated rich men, philanthropists or *grands seigneurs*. These types fall into two principal categories: "missionaries" and "interested

Reprinted from "The Intellectuals," in *Encyclopedia of the Social Sciences,* Vol. VIII (1932), pp. 120-123, by permission of the publisher, The Macmillan Company. Title supplied by the Editor.

parties." There are of course innumerable mixed types. Sometimes special groups of intellectuals tend by virtue of their particular experiences to drift toward socialism more rapidly or more generally than the whole body of their fellows. For example, the percentage of intellectual Jews in socialist ranks is relatively large. This fact may be explained by the analytical and critical qualities which the social experience of the Diaspora has bred in the Jewish mind. In pre-war central and eastern Europe furthermore social oppression, especially as expressed in the *numerus clausus* in the universities, when it did not divert the ablest Jews into business caused them to suffer keenly at the hands of prejudiced authority. In addition many were forced to study abroad, an experience which accentuated the comparative looseness of the Jew's connection with the traditions of the peoples among whom he dwelt and laid an emotional basis for internationalist ideology. Other groups of intellectuals who have suffered from similar discriminations have shown comparable trends to radicalism of varying degrees; such are aliens, religious dissidents and, latterly in the United States, Negroes. In the case of the Jewish intelligentsia their international relations and relationships and frequently an element of Hebraic Messianism contribute to their radicalization.

Ethically the alliance of bourgeois and talented intellectuals with socialist parties signifies a capacity for entering into the alien fate of the masses and adapting their personal, individual fates to it. While the worker may be driven to socialism merely as an instinctive reaction to his class position, the intellectual reacts in terms of distress involving his intellectual life. He acts under ethical or intellectual constraint, except in those cases where he is instinctively or consciously seeking to use the proletariat as the raw material for a personal political adventure.

As a matter of fact intellectuals are in some ways untrustworthy as leaders of political parties of any character. By their very nature they are often led, especially in parliamentary struggles, to an attitude which tends to blur natural social antagonisms and to hamper the play of class forces. For example, there has developed among parliamentarians in England an atmosphere of sport, "fair play" and friendly agreements among opposing politicians, all of whom are "members of this club"; and in France despite the severity of election and parliamentary struggles an attitude called camaraderie, which combines esprit de corps with an attitude of mutual responsibility, binding deputies of the most diverse parties closer to each other than a deputy is bound to a rank and file member of his own party.

Disgusted by the behavior of their own class and its individual members, intellectuals first tend to have utopian illusions concerning the character of the proletariat; and their subsequent discovery that workers are also human beings sometimes makes them cynical. The purer their intentions and the higher their ideals, the sooner they lose courage in the face of mass cowardice, brutality or egoism. Especially those seeking revenge are led to open or veiled desertion of their ideals by each outstanding success of their policies. They endeavor to lead the masses along paths which lie close to their personal interests and, when the masses are unwilling to follow, sever connections to seek a career upon the basis of the notoriety achieved through them. Again, radical intellectuals tend toward impossibilism; through favorable circumstances they may lead a movement to a victory which they ruin through excesses and undue severity. More often, becoming dogmatic and pedantic, they ride a movement to death for the sake of "immortal" principles. This tendency toward extremism arises also from the nature of mental work, which can be easily dissociated from hard reality, from the intellectual's experience in the transvaluation of all values and from the vehemence of emotions and convictions, newly released in fighting his former class. Regarded as apostates, deserters and fanatics intellectuals are most hated in the milieu of their birth and hence tend to set up rigid principles which justify their conduct. Moreover the intellectual who engages in social conflict frequently serves a movement poorly or even deserts it because of his dislike of so-called detailed work.

The attitude of the working masses toward the intellectuals who serve them as leaders has its own mode of change. When a movement is still naïve and inchoate, the intellectual who offers his services appears as a savior and as such worthy of confidence and admiration. Even when the supply of intellectual leaders has increased and new, "really proletarian" leaders have begun to develop from the workers' ranks, the intellectual is indispensable because of the increasing complexity of the problems of the party and auxiliary organizations, the broadening of political aims and the invasion of new arenas of struggle, such as parliament. Now, however, the moral position of intellectuals becomes less unassailable; they are accused of job hunting and careerism and are felt to be a foreign body. Furthermore their struggles and intrigues among themselves compromise them in the eyes of the masses. It would, however, be false to assume that leaders drawn from the ranks of the proletariat manifest greater political dependability than those coming from the educated bourgeoisie, the process of becoming middle class is rapid among both labor leaders and the upper strata of the workers, and these too may desert the cause. Nevertheless, labor leaders of proletarian origin tend to discipline severely, to displace and even to mistreat colleagues of upper class origin from a sort of feeling of class struggle. Some intellectuals have tried to win greater confidence from the masses by sacrificing their forms of life to their principles on the theory that words are less effective as propaganda than the silent example of daily life. The ideal of self-denial incidentally involves a heroic postulate laid down by Bakunin: immediate disappearance or suicide of the leaders after the success of the revolution in order to prevent the rise of a new ruling class in their persons.

While educational categories can be defined only in terms of examinations and diplomas and have no economic significance, Karl Renner's characterization of intellectuals as "those beyond economics" is misleading. Neither those in the liberal professions nor those drawing state salaries are free from the effects of the business cycle in respect to real or money income. Nor are clear divisions along social and economic lines absent among intellectuals. For example, in England students of the old, aristocratic universities of Oxford and Cambridge rank socially above those of the new and more plebian universities of Manchester and London, and university graduates tend to fall into the middle of the upper middle class according to the amount and type of their training and economic success attained in their professions. Such facts as well as the geographical dispersion of intellectuals make it hard to organize them.

The social status of student bodies is conditioned among other things by the fact that for several years, during which their contemporaries as laborers, merchants and managers of industry produce and earn, they as students only consume and that they enjoy a far reaching qualitative as well as a quantitative autonomy of work known as academic freedom. Thus the university period is a sort of capital investment of time and money, and the very fact of this investment proves that students—aside from scholarship holders or stipendiaries—come from a possessing class. The few exceptions are candidates for entrance to the bourgeoisie, the university acting as a bridge from a lower to a higher stratum of society.

While there is thus a definite logical and empirical connection between property and education, it cannot be said that each class has a fixed amount of education as an immanent peculiarity or necessary cultural attribute. With the exception of the old English universities the student body does not belong ipso facto to the bourgeoisie, and intellectuals must not be confused with the bourgeoisie. In eighteenth century France intellectualism was a transition to the *noblesse de robe;* there was then a sharp distinction between manufacturers or merchants and bourgeois intellectuals as subclasses.

Intellectuals in the lower income groups are termed the intellectual proletariat, a phenomenon which arises as a consequence of an overabundance of persons offering their knowledge in the market. Always a pathological condition, it is caused by an intellectual overestimation of formal education in general; by sudden stoppage in the consumption of intellectual commodities due to general impoverishment; by industrial backwardness which forces youth into the civil service or a liberal profession, both of which are unprofitable because overrun; and to a small extent by personal negligence and foolishness resulting in ruined careers. Intellectuals who do not find a satisfactory place in the social order are retrospectively déclassés: they have been lost to their class of origin (birth); and prospectively *spostati* (dislodged): they have not proved their ability to win good jobs. While it is obvious that the size of the intellectual proletariat is related to the rapidity of social change, the intellectual proletariat does not consist merely of unsuccessful members of the upper classes. It also includes the sons of small manufacturers and artisans, who seriously menaced by large scale industry turn to an intellectual profession and endeavor to obtain a place at the government trough. From the standpoint of the political state there are two main groups of intellectuals: those who have obtained such places and those who have unsuccessfully tried to do so. The first, considered the most loyal of citizens, are always ready because of class egotism and personal selfishness to defend the state which feeds them, no matter what questions are at stake. The others are sworn enemies of government policies, eternally restless spirits which lead the bourgeois opposition and even revolutionary proletarian parties. The number of intellectual proletarians fluctuates widely; but although the state from time to time is compelled to transform thousands of dangerous opponents into active protectors and clients by making them officials, in general the tendency of government officialdom is to grow more slowly than would satisfy middle class elements. Having, however, some expectation of socio-economic advance the intellectual proletariat constitutes a transition class and reflects its characteristics. When this element is impatient or loses hope of improvement it may be absorbed by the lower classes. Poor persons of education become consciously antagonistic to the educated well to do. They furnish the yeast for social revolutions and champion the masses in the class struggle, which in part becomes a struggle for power of two economically differentiated educated classes.

Estimates of the social value of intellectuals differ widely. Plato, for example, characterized the ideal republic as one in which philosophers would be kings and kings philosophers. Most intellectuals continued to cherish such a view of their kind: after the Napoleonic era the intelligentsia proposed a prominent role for itself, Saint-Simon's doctrine of the producer, for example, calling for a supreme council of scientists to direct economic life: and today intellectuals in many countries insist on their peculiar ability to govern reasonably, fairly and efficiently. The nineteenth century was profoundly influenced by the bourgeois intelligentsia and valued it highly. Early in the twentieth century some intellectuals began an intense spiritual self-criticism, a trend which is still going on and which has found in France its richest expression. Today some writers try to base upon the well known fact that both workers and employers entrust the political advocacy of their interests to intellectuals a theory that the intellectual fulfils a special function of social initiative, creativeness and leadership.

Some Marxists hold that the intelligentsia can maintain its intellectual power and freedom and properly fulfil its creative function only by affiliation with the working class. This view has some support in the fact that while the possession of education, as of riches, the power to command services and exclusiveness, is a hallmark of the bourgeoisie, intellectuals are bourgeois of slight social rank if they are bourgeois merely through the possession of education, and that while mental work is considered by the bourgeoisie to be more honorable than manual labor—when it is more profitable—to do no work at all and to live on one's income is considered most honorable of all.

In the syndicalism of the Sorel school the function of the intelligentsia shrinks from that of teacher to that of pupil. At the French socialist convention of Toulouse in 1908 Lagardelle defined the intellectual's task not as teaching the proletariat but only as interpreting the proletariat's experiences, using its data and employing its new principles for general cultural work. In any case this function of interpreting the experience which has been accumulated by the proletariat would presuppose the highest degree of intellectualism.

On the other hand, some thinkers have branded the political function of intellectuals as uncreative and sterile and, in so far as it serves the masses, pernicious and intrinsically false. Edouard Berth, Sorel's disciple, complains bitterly that producers entrust the championing of their interests to intellectuals who enthralled by demagogy and without economic interests sell themselves like harlots to all parties for money and kind words, while at bottom they are unable to serve any.

SOCIALISM AND THE INTELLECTUALS

Paul Lafargue

THE CAPITALISTS have degraded the intellectuals below the economic level of the manual laborers. This is their reward for having so magnificently prepared the way for the bourgeois revolution of the eighteenth century.

Jaures in his preface to the "Socialist History of France" says that "the intellectual Bourgeoisie, offended by a brutal and commercial society and disenchanted with the bourgeois power, is rallying to the support of socialism." Unfortunately nothing could be less exact. This transformation of the intellectual faculties into merchandise, which ought to have filled the intellectuals with wrath and indignation, leaves them indifferent. Never would the free citizen of the ancient republics of Athens and Rome have submitted to such degradation. The free man who sells his work, says Cicero, lowers himself to the rank of the slaves. Socrates and Plato were indignant against the Sophists who required pay for their philosophic teaching, for to Socrates and Plato thought was too noble a thing to be bought and sold like carrots and shoes. Even the French clergy of 1789 resented as a mortal insult the proposition to pay a salary for worship. But our intellectuals are accustoming themselves to such degradation.

Spurred on by the mercantile passion, they are never better satisfied with themselves or with society than when they succeed in selling their intellectual merchandise at a good price; they have even come to the point of making its selling price the measure of its value. Zola, who is one of the most distinguished representatives of literary intellectualism, estimates the artistic value of a novel by the number of editions sold. To sell their intellectual merchandise has become in them such an all-absorbing principle that if one speaks to them of socialism, before they inquire into its theories, they ask whether in the socialistic society intellectual labor will be paid for and whether it will be rewarded equally with manual labor.

Imbeciles! they have eyes but they see not that it is the capitalist bourgeoisie which establishes that degrading equality; and to increase its wealth degrades intellectual labor to the point of paying it at a lower rate than manual labor.

Reprinted from *Socialism and the Intellectuals* (1900), pp. 10-13, 16-17, 20-22, Charles H. Kerr & Company.

We should have to put off the triumph of socialism not to the year 2000 but to the end of the world if we had to wait upon the delicate, shrinking and impressionable hesitancy of the intellectuals. The history of the century is at hand to teach us just how much we have a right to expect from these gentlemen.

Since 1789 governments of the most diverse and opposed character have succeeded each other in France; and always, without hesitation the intellectuals have hastened to offer their devoted services. I am not merely speaking of those two-for-a-cent intellectuals who litter up the newspapers, the parliaments and the economic associations; but I mean the scientists, the university professors, the members of the Institute; the higher they raise their heads, the lower they bow the knee.

Princes of science, who ought to have conversed on equal terms with kings and emperors, have marketed their glory to buy offices and favors from ephemeral ministers. Cuvier, one of the mightiest geniuses of the modern era, whom the revolution took from the household of a nobleman to make of him at 25 years one of the museum professors, Cuvier took the oath of allegiance and served with fidelity the Republic, Napoleon, Louis XVIII, Charles X and Louis Philippe, the last of whom created him a peer of France to reward him for his career of servility.

To devote one's self to all governments without distinction is not enough. Pasteur placed his glorious name at the service of the financiers, who placed him in the administrative council of the Credit Foncier, side by side with Jules Simon, with dukes and counts, with senators, deputies and ex-ministers, in order to entrap the "lambs." When De Lesseps was equipping his colossal swindle of the Panama canal, he enrolled the intellectuals of the Institute, of the French Academy, of literature, of the clergy, of all the circles of higher life. . . .

It is not in the circle of the intellectuals, degraded by centuries of capitalist oppression, that we must seek examples of civic courage and moral dignity. They have not even the sense of professional class-consciousness. At the time of the Dreyfus affair, a certain minister discharged, as if he had been a mere prison guard, one of the professors of chemistry in the Polytechnic school who had had the rare courage to give public expression to his opinion. When in a factory the employer dismisses a workman in too arbitrary a fashion, his comrades grumble, and sometimes quit work, even though misery and hunger await them in the street.

All his colleagues in the Polytechnic school bowed their heads in silence; each one crouched in self-regarding fear, and what is still more characteristic, not a single partisan of Dreyfus in the Society of the Rights of Man or in the ranks of the press raised a voice to remind them of the idea of professional solidarity. The intellectuals who on all occasions display their transcendental ethics, have still a long road to travel before they reach the moral plane of the working class and of the socialist party.

The scientists have not only sold themselves to the governments and the financiers; they have also sold science itself to the capitalist-bourgeoisie. When in the eighteenth century there was need to prepare the minds of men for the Revolution, by sapping the ideologic foundations of aristocratic society, then science fulfilled its sublime mission of freedom; it was revolutionary; it furiously attacked Christianity and the intuitional philosophy. But when the victorious bourgeoisie decided to base its new power on religion, it commanded its scientists, its philosophers and its men of letters to raise up what they had overthrown; they responded to the need with enthusiasm. They reconstructed what they had demolished; they proved by scientific, sentimental and romantic argument the existence of God the father, of Jesus the son and of Mary the virgin mother. I do not believe history offers a spectacle equal to that presented in the first years of the nineteenth century by the philosophers, the scientists and the literary men, who from revolutionaries and materialists suddenly transformed themselves into reactionaries, intuitionalists and Catholics. . . .

The great capitalist bourgeoisie does not choose to work, either with its hands or its brain; it chooses merely to drink, to eat, to practice lewdness and to look dignified in its beastly and cumbersome luxury; it does not even deign to occupy itself with politics; men like Rothschild, De Lesseps, Vanderbilt, Carnegie, Rockefeller, do not run for office; they find it more economical to buy the officers than the voters, and more convenient to put their clerks into the ministries than to take part in parliamentary struggles. The big capitalists interest themselves only in the operations of the stock exchange, which afford the delights of gambling; they dignify these by the pompous name of "speculations,"—a word formerly reserved for the highest processes of philosophical or mathematical thought. The capitalists are replacing themselves in the supervision and management of the great industrial and commercial enterprises by intellectuals, who carry them on, and usually are well paid for doing so. These intellectuals of industry and politics, the privileged portion of the wage class, imagine that they are an integral part of the capitalist class, while they are only its servants; on every occasion they take up its defense against the working class, which finds in them its worst enemies.

Intellectuals of this description can never be led into socialism; their interests are too closely bound to the capitalist class for them to detach themselves and turn against it. But below these favored few there is a swarming and famishing throng of intellectuals whose lot grows worse in proportion to the increase of their numbers. These intellectuals belong to socialism. They ought to be already in our ranks. It ought to be true that their education would have given them intelligence to deal with social problems, but it is this very education which obstructs their hearing and keeps them away from socialism. They think their education confers on them a social privilege, that it will permit them to get through the world by themselves, each making his own way in life by crowding his neighbor or standing on the shoulders of everyone else. They imagine that their poverty is transitory and that they only need a stroke of good luck to transform them into capitalists. Education, they think, is the lucky number in the social lottery, and it will bring them the grand prize. They do not perceive that this ticket given them by the capitalist class is fixed, that labor, whether manual or intellectual, has no chance to do more than earn its daily pittance, that it has nothing to hope for but to be exploited, and that the more capitalism goes on developing, the more do the chances of an individual raising himself out of his class go on diminishing.

And while they build castles in Spain, capital crushes them, as it has crushed the little merchants and the little manufacturers, who thought they, too, with free credit and a little luck, might become first-class capitalists, whose names should be written in the Great Book of the Public Debt.

The intellectuals, in all that has to do with the understanding of the social movement, do not rise above the intellectual level of those little bourgeois who scoffed so fiercely at the bunglers of 1830, who, after being ruined and merged in the proletariat, none the less continue to detest socialism; to such a degree were their heads perverted by the religion of property. The intellectuals, whose brains are stuffed with all the prejudices of the bourgeois class, are inferior to those little bourgeois of 1830 and 1848 who at least knew the smell of gunpowder; they have not their spirit of combativeness, they are true imbeciles,—if we restore to this word its original Latin meaning of unsuited for war. Without resistance they endure rebuffs and wrongs and they do not think of uniting, of organizing themselves to defend their interests and give battle to capital on the economic field. . . .

The intellectuals ought to have been the first of all the various groups to revolt against capitalist society, in which they occupy a subordinate position so little in keeping with their hopes and their talents, but they do not even understand it; they have such a confused idea of it that Auguste Comte, Renan, and others more or less distinguished have cherished the dream of reviving for their benefit an aristocracy copied after the model of the Chinese mandarin system. Such an idea is a reflection of past ages in their heads, for nothing is in more absolute opposition with the modern social movement than such pretensions. The intellectuals in previous states of society formed a world outside and above that of production, having charge only of education, of the direction of religious worship, and of the political administration.

The mechanic industry of these societies combine in the same producer, manual labor and intellectual labor; it was for example the same cabinet-maker who designed and worked out the piece of furniture, who bought its first material and who even undertook its sale. Capitalist production has divorced two functions which once were indissolubly united; on the one side it puts the manual workers, who become more and more servants of the machine, and on the other the intellectual workers, engineers, chemists, managers, etc. But these two categories of workers, however different and contrary they may be in their education and habits, are welded together, to the point that a capitalist industry can not be carried on without manual laborers any more than without intellectual wage-workers.

United in production, united under the yoke of capitalist exploitation, united they should be also in revolt against the common enemy. The intellectuals, if they understood their own real interests, would come in crowds to socialism, not through philanthropy, not through pity for the miseries of the workers, not through affectation and snobbery, but to save themselves, to assure the future welfare of their wives and children, to fulfill their duty to their class. They ought to be ashamed at being left behind in the social battle by their comrades in the manual category. They have many things to teach them, but they have still much to learn from them; the working men have a practical sense superior to theirs, and have given proof of an instinctive intuition of the communist tendencies of modern capitalism which is lacking to the intellectuals, who have only been able by a conscious mental effort to arrive at this conception. If only they had understood their own interests, they would long since have turned against the the capitalist class the education which it has generously distributed in order better to exploit them; they would have utilized their intellectual capacities, which are enriching their masters, as so many improved weapons to fight capitalism and to conquer the freedom of their class, the wage-working class.

Capitalist production, which has overthrown the old conditions of life and of work, has elaborated new forms, which already can be discerned without supernatural vision, but which to the intellectuals remain sealed under seven seals. One of the leading lights of intellectualism, M. Durkheim, in his book, "The Division of Labor," which made some noise in university circles, can not conceive of society except on the social pattern of ancient Egypt, each laborer remaining, his life through, penned up in one single trade. However, unless one is so unfortunate as to be affected by the hopeless near-sightedness of the normal school, one can not help seeing that the machine is suppressing trades, one after the other, in a way to let only one survive, that of the machinist, and that when it has finished its revolutionary work which the socialists will complete by revolutionizing capitalist society, the producer of the communist society will plow and sow with the machine today, will spin, will turn wood or polish steel tomorrow, and will exercise in turn all the trades to the greater profit of his health and his intelligence.

The industrial applications of mechanics, chemistry and physics, which, monopolized by capital, oppress the worker, will, when they shall be common property, emancipate man from toil and give him leisure and liberty.

Mechanical production, which under capitalist direction can only buffet the worker back and forth from periods of over-work to periods of enforced idleness, will when developed and regulated by a communist administration, require from the producer to provide for the normal needs of society, only a maximum day of two or three hours in the workshop, and when this time of necessary social labor is fulfilled he will be able to enjoy freely the physical and intellectual pleasures of life.

The artist then will paint, will sing, will dance, the writer will write, the musician will compose operas, the philosopher will build systems, the chemist will analyze substances not to gain money, to receive a salary, but to deserve applause, to win laurel wreaths, like the conquerors at the Olympic games, but to satisfy their artistic and scientific passion; for one does not drink a glass of champagne or kiss the woman he loves for the benefit of the gallery. The artist and the scientist may then repeat the enthusiastic words of Kepler, that hero of science: "The elector of Saxony with all his wealth can not equal the pleasure I have felt in composing the Mysterium Cosmographicum."

Will not the intellectuals end by hearing the voice of the socialist calling them to the rescue, to emancipate science and art from the capitalist yoke, to liberate thought from the slavery of commercialism?

INTELLECTUALS UNDER SOCIALISM

Karl Kautsky

. . . PERHAPS the most striking phenomenon of the last fifty years is the rapid and unbroken rise of the proletariat in moral and intellectual relations.

Not many decades ago the proletariat was so low that there were even socialists that expected the worst results for culture from the conquest of the proletariat. In 1850 Rodbertus wrote: "The most threatening danger at present is that we shall have a new barbarian invasion, this time coming from the interior of society itself to lay waste custom, civilization and wealth."

At the same time Heinrich Heine declared that the future belonged to the communist. "This confession, that the future belongs to the communist, I make in sorrow and greatest anxiety. This is in no way a delusion. In fact, it is only with fear and shuddering that I think of the epoch when these dark iconoclasts come to power; with their callous hands they will destroy all the marble statues of beauty, etc."

Undeniably it has now become wholly different. It is not by the proletariat that modern civilization is threatened. It is those very communists who to-day constitute the safe refuge of art and science, for which they stand in the most decisive manner.

So it is that the fear is rapidly disappearing, which after the Paris Commune dominated the whole capitalist class; the fear that the conquering proletariat would come into our culture like the Vandals in their race migrations and on its ruins found a government of barbaric ascetics.

It is partially owing to the disappearance of this fear that sympathy with the proletariat and with socialism is on the increase among the bourgeois intellectuals.

Like the proletariat, class intelligence is a peculiarity of the capitalist system of production. I have already shown that this system makes such demands upon the ruling class that they have neither the interest nor the leisure to care for the business of government, or to cultivate art and science, as did the aristocracy of Athens or the clergy of the best days of the Catholic Church. The whole sphere of the higher intellectual activity, that was for-

Reprinted from *The Social Revolution* (1903), pp. 44-49, 167-183. Charles H. Kerr & Company. Title supplied by the Editor.

merly a privilege of the ruling classes, is now left by these to paid laborers, and the number of these professional scholars, artists, engineers and functionaries is increasing rapidly.

Taken as a whole these constitute the so-called "intellectuals," the "new middle class," but they are distinguished from the old middle class above all by the lack of any especial class consciousness. Certain divisions of them have a peculiar caste consciousness, very often a blindness of caste, but the interests of each one of these divisions is too peculiar for any common class consciousness to develop. Its members unite with various classes and parties and furnish the intellectual fighters for each. One portion defends the interests of the ruling class for whom many of the intellectuals serve professionally. Others have championed the cause of the proletariat. The majority, however, have up to the present time remained entangled in the little bourgeois circles of thought. This is not alone because many of them sprung from this class, but also because their social position as "middle class" is like that of the small bourgeois, a midway position between the proletariat and the ruling class.

It is in these divisions of the intellectuals, as remarked above, that a continually increasing sympathy for the proletariat is evident. Because they have no especial class interest, and are most accessible through their professional, scientific point of view, they are easiest won for our party through scientific considerations. The theoretical bankruptcy of bourgeois economics, and the theoretical superiority of Socialism must become clear to them. Through this they must continually discover that the other social classes continuously strive to still further debase art and science. Many others are finally impressed by the fact of the irresistible advance of the Social Democracy, especially when they compare this with the continuous deterioration of Liberalism. So it is that friendship for labor becomes popular among the cultured classes, until there is scarcely a parlor in which one does not stumble over one or more "Socialists."

If these circles of the cultured class were synonomous with the bourgeoisie, then to be sure we would have won the game, and a social revolution would be superfluous. With this class it is easy to discuss things, and from them a quiet gradual development will meet no forcible hindrance.

Unfortunately, however, they are only a portion of the bourgeoisie, though, to be sure, just those who speak and write in the name of the bourgeoisie, but not those who determine their acts. And men as well as classes must be judged, not by their words, but by their deeds.

It must also be remembered that it is the least effective fighters and least combative portion of the bourgeoisie in which sympathy for the proletariat is developing.

Heretofore, while socialism was branded among all cultured classes as criminal or insane, capitalist elements could only be brought into the Socialist movement by a complete break with the whole capitalist world. Whoever came into the Socialist movement at that time from the capitalist elements had need of great energy, revolutionary passion, and strong proletarian convictions. It was just this element which ordinarily constituted the most radical and revolutionary wing of the Socialist movement.

It is wholly different to-day, when Socialism has become a fad. It no longer demands any especial energy, and no break with capitalist society to assume the name of Socialist. It is no wonder then that more and more these new Socialists remain entangled in their previous manner of thought and feeling.

The fighting tactics of the intellectuals are at any rate wholly different from those of the proletariat. To wealth and power of arms the latter opposes its overwhelming numbers and its thorough organization. The intellectuals are an ever diminishing minority with no class organization whatever. Their only weapon is persuasion through speaking and writing, the battle with "intellectual weapons" and "moral superiority," and these "parlor Socialists" would settle the proletarian class struggle also with these weapons. They declare themselves ready to grant the proletariat their moral support, but only on condition that it renounces the idea of the application of force, and this not simply where force is hopeless—there the proletariat has already renounced it—but also in those places where it is still full of possibilities. Accordingly they seek to throw discredit on the idea of revolution, and to represent it as a useless means. They seek to separate off a social reform wing from the revolutionary proletariat, and they thereby divide and weaken the proletariat.

Up to the present time this is practically the only result of the beginnings of the conversion of the "Intellectuals" to Socialism. . . .

We have here hitherto only investigated the problem of material production which is most fundamental. But upon this basis there arises a production of artistic works, scientific investigation and literary activities of various forms. The continuation of this production is no less necessary for modern civilization than the undisturbed continuance of the production of bread and meat, coal and iron. A proletarian revolution, however, renders its continuance in the former manner impossible. What has it to substitute therefor? That no reasonable man to-day fears that the victorious proletariat will cause a return to the old condition of barbarism or that it will fling art and science and superfluous rubbish into the lumber room, but that on the contrary it is just among those broad popular sections of the proletariat that the most interest and the highest regard for art and science is to be found, I have already shown in my essay concerning "Reform and Revolution." But my whole inquiry is not so much in the nature of an investigation into what the victorious proletariat might do as to what by virtue of the power of logic and facts it can and must do.

There will be no lack of the necessary material objects for art and science. We have already seen that it is one of the strong points of the proletarian regime that through the abolition of private property in the means of production the possibility will be created of wiping out in the quickest possible manner the ruins of the outgrown means and methods of production which to-day prevent the unfolding of the modern productive powers and which beneath the present dominion of private property can only be slowly and incompletely swept out of the road by competition. The wealth of society must thereby at once attain a level far above that inherited from capitalist society.

But material objects alone are not sufficient to secure this elevation. Wealth alone does not give rise to a great ideal life. The question is whether the conditions of production of material goods in socialist society are consistent with the necessary conditions of a highly developed intellectual production. This is strongly denied by our opponents.

Let us next examine some forms of existing intellectual production. It takes on three forms: production through organs of society for direct satisfaction of social needs; then, the production of goods in individual industries, and finally the production of goods under capitalist industry.

To the first form of intellectual production belongs the whole system of education from kindergartens to universities. If we disregard the insignificant private schools, this is to-day almost wholly in the hands of society and is conducted by the State not for the purpose of making profits or on account of gain. This holds above all of the modern national and municipal schools, but also of those which are mainly ruins descended from the Middle Ages, but which still exist under clerical organization and community support, and which are especially prominent in the land of Anglo-Saxon culture.

This social educational system is of the highest significance for the intellectual life, especially for the scientific, and this is not simply through its influence upon the growing youth. It controls ever more and more scientific investigation in that its teachers, especially in the high schools, have more and more a monopoly of scientific apparatus without which scientific investigation is to-day almost impossible. This is especially true in the field of the natural sciences whose technique has become so highly developed that, aside from a few millionaires, the State alone is able to supply the means demanded for the establishment and maintenance of the necessary scientific apparatus. But in many branches of social science, ethnology and archaeology and others, the scientific apparatus of investigation has become ever more comprehensive and expensive. Because of this, science becomes ever more and more an unremunerative occupation, by which a man cannot live and to which only those people can devote themselves who are paid by the State unless they have been very fortunate in the choice of their parents—or of their wives. Attainment of the necessary preliminary knowledge for productive scientific activity demands again a great and ever increasing amount of money. So it is that science is more and more monopolized by the governmental powers and the possessing classes.

At the very least a proletarian regime can abolish the conditions which hamper scientific activity at present. It must formulate its educational system, as was previously pointed out, so that each genius will have within his reach all the knowledge that the social educational system has at its disposal. It will increase enormously the demand for educated people, and therewith also for the power of scientific investigation. Finally it will operate through the abolition of class antagonisms to make the investigators in the sphere of social science, where employed by the State, internally and externally free. So long as there are class antagonisms there will be very different standpoints from which society will be observed. There is no greater hypocrisy or self-deception than the talk about an existing science which is above class antagonisms. Science exists only in the heads of investigators and these are the products of society and cannot get out of it or reach above it. Even in a socialist society science will be dependent upon social conditions, but these will then at least be uniform and not antagonistic.

Even worse than the internal dependence upon social conditions, from which no investigator can free himself, is the external dependence of many of those from governmental or other dominating institutions, for example, clerical. These compel the intellectual workers to direct their views according to those of the governing classes and will not permit them to investigate freely and independently, and it compels them to seek in a scientific manner for arguments that will justify the existing order and repel the aspiring classes. So the class dominion operates directly to demoralize science. The intellectual workers will have every reason to breathe freer when the proletarian regime sweeps away the direct and indirect dominion of the class of capitalists and land owners. The intellectual life so far as it is connected with education has nothing to fear and everything to hope from the victory of the proletariat.

How is it, then, with the production of intellectual commodities? In this connection we will first study individual production. Here painting and sculpture come most prominently into consideration, together with a portion of literary writing.

A proletarian regime will no more make this form of commodity production impossible, than it will abolish the little private industry in material production. Just as little as the needle and thimble, will brush and palette, or ink and pen belong to those means of production which must under all conditions be socialized. But one thing is well possible and that is that with the cessation of capitalist exploitation the number of purchasers that heretofore constituted the market for the commodities produced by the little artistic industry will be reduced. This will certainly not be without influence on the articles of artistic production. It will not abolish such production but only alter its character. The easel painting and statuettes which can most easily change their places and possessors, that can be placed wherever we wish, are the special form of commodity production in art. They include those forms of artistic work that can easiest take the form of commodities, which, like jewelry, can be accumulated and stored either for the purpose of re-selling at a profit or to hoard as treasures. It is possible that their production for the purposes of sale will find many obstacles in a socialist society. But in place of these, other forms of artistic production will appear.

A proletarian regime will immensely increase the number of public buildings. It will endeavor to make attractive every place occupied by the people, whether for labor, for consultation, or for pleasure. Instead of accumulating statuettes and pictures that will be thrown into a great impersonal market from whence they finally find a place utterly unknown to the artist and are used for wholly unthought of purposes, the artist will work together with the architect as was the case in the Golden Age of art in Athens under Pericles and in the Italian Renaissance. One art will support and raise the other and artistic labor will have a definite social aim so that its products, its surroundings and its public will not be dependent on chance.

On the other side the necessity to produce artistic works for sale as commodities will cease. Above all there will no longer be need to offer individual labor for profit or as wage labor, or for the production of commodities.

I have already pointed out that a proletarian regime would endeavor, as is perfectly evident from the standpoint of the wageworker, to shorten the labor time and raise the wages. I have also shown to how high a degree this can be done, particularly in the line of highly developed capitalist production, simply through the concentration of industry in the most perfect centers of production and through the most perfect utilization of these most perfect industries. It is by no means fantastic to conclude that a doubling of the wages and a reduction of labor time to half of the present one is possible at once, and technical science is already sufficiently advanced to expect rapid progress in this field. The further one goes in this direction the more the possibility increases for those who are engaged in material production to give themselves up also to intellectual activity and especially to those forms that bring no material gain, but rather find their reward in themselves and which are the highest forms of intellectual activity. The greater increased leisure may in part, indeed in overwhelming part, lead to pure intellectual *enjoyment*. With the talented the creative genius will be free and the union of material with artistic, literary and scientific production will be made possible.

This union, however, will not be simply possible. It will be an *economic necessity*. We have seen that a proletarian regime must aim to make culture a universal good. If we should seek to extend culture in the present sense of the word it would end in making the growing generation useless for material production and hence would undermine the foundations of society. To-day the social division of labor is developed in such a manner that material and intellectual labor are well-nigh mutually exclusive. Material production exists under such conditions that only the few who have been favored by nature or by special conditions are able to engage in the higher intellectual labor. On the other side intellectual labor as it is carried on to-day makes those who follow it incapable of and disinclined toward physical labor. To give culture to all mankind under such conditions would simply make all material production impossible because then no one would be found who could or would carry it on. If we are to make the higher intellectual culture a common good without endangering the existence of society, then not simply pedagogical but economic necessity demands that this be done in such a manner that the growing generation will be made familiar in schools not simply with intellectual but also with physical labor and the habit of uniting intellectual and material production will be firmly rooted.

The proletarian regime must proceed from two directions to secure the union of material and intellectual production and to free the latter in the mass of the population from its present material fetters. On the one side this must be done through the continuous shortening of the labor time of the so-called hand laborers. This will come as a result of the increasing productivity of labor whereby more time will be continuously granted for intellectual labor to those engaged in material production. On the other side this will be accomplished by an increase of the physical labor of the cultured, an unavoidable result of the continual increase in numbers of the latter.

It is, however, plain that with this union, physical labor for gain and for the necessary labor in the interest of society, and intellectual labor for the free exercise of personality would be freed from every social compulsion. For intellectual labor is much more incompatible with such compulsion than physical. This liberation of intellectual labor by the proletariat is not the pious wish of the Utopian but the economically necessary consequence of its victory.

Finally we must observe the third form of intellectual production—that which is capitalistically exploited. Since the first of these three forms of intellectual production includes mainly science and the second the fine arts, so what we have to say now applies to the utilization of all spheres of intellectual activity, but particularly, however, to the heroes of the pen and the stage, to whom now stand opposed as capitalist directors of industry, the publishers, periodical owners and theater directors.

Capitalist exploitation in such a form is impossible of continuance under a proletarian regime. It rests, however, upon the fact that to get even a questionable intellectual production to the public requires an expensive technical apparatus and extensive co-operative powers. The individual cannot here act for himself. Does that, however, not mean that here again the alternative to capitalist industry is national industry? If this is so, must not the centering of so great and important a part of the intellectual life in the State threaten in the highest degree that intellectual life with uniformity and stagnation? It is true that the governmental power will cease to be a class organ, but will it not still be the organ of a majority? Can the intellectual life be made dependent upon the decisions of the majority? Would not every new truth, every new conception and discovery be comprehended and thought out by the insignificant minority? Does not this new order threaten to bring at once the best and keenest of the intellectual thinkers in the various spheres into continuous conflict with the proletarian regime? And even if this creates increased freedom for the artistic and scientific development would not this be more than offset by the fetters that it will lay upon the intellectual activity when this can only be pursued by social means? Here is certainly an important but not an insoluble problem.

We must first notice that as for all production so also for the social necessities of intellectual production the *State* will from the beginning not be the only leading and means-granting organ which will come into consideration, but there will also be *municipalities*. Through these alone all uniformity and every domination of the intellectual life by central power is excluded. As another substitute for the capitalist industry in individual production, still other organizations must be considered; those of *free unions* which will serve art and science and the public life and advance production in these spheres in the most diverse ways, or undertake them directly as even today we have countless unions which bring out plays, publish newspapers, purchase artistic works, publish writings, fit out scientific expeditions, etc. The shorter the hours of labor in material production and the higher the wages the more will these free unions be favored. They must increase in numbers, in enthusiasm and in the intelligence of their members as well as in the resources which the intellectuals can contribute to support the common cause. I expect that these free unions will play an even more important role in the intellectual life. It is their destiny to enter into the place now occupied by capital and individual production and to organize and to lead the social nature.

Here also the proletarian regime leads not to greater bondage but to greater freedom.

Freedom of education and of scientific investigation from the fetters of capitalist dominion; freedom of the individual from the oppression of exclu-

---

MASTERS—OLD AND NEW

Max Nomad

A S A SAYING credited to Machiavelli has it, "nobody has yet killed his own successor." That dictum has often been applied to the coming "final struggle" between the beneficiaries of decaying capitalism and their proletarian successors. Its soothing value to the still waiting inheritors is certainly incontestable.

When feudalism lay in its death throes its enemies predicted the succession of the rule of the people. That "people" turned out to be the modern bourgeoisie. With capitalism in a similar predicament, history seems to be repeating itself and playing the same trick upon the "proletariat."

The beneficiary of that momentous piece of sleight-of-hand is no longer in hiding. Sandwiched between the capitalists and the manual workers there has emerged an ever growing stratum of neo-bourgeois or not-yet-quite-bourgeois engaged in mental or near-mental occupations. "Intellectual workers," "privileged employees of capital," "new middle class"—these are the various terms used interchangeably for this amazing variety of people: office-holders, teachers, professional men, technicians, clergymen, commercial and financial experts, journalists, writers, artists, politicians, professional revolutionists and agitators, trade union organizers and so on. In short, a vast crowd of educated and semi-educated people, all of them "propertyless," who may or may not have a college degree, but can make a livelihood without resorting to manual or lower clerical labor.

Sometimes scions of the prosperous capitalists, of the "privileged employees" or of the lower middle classes, and sometimes self-educated upstart workers, the intellectuals are divided into various income groups, just as the property holders are. Some of them, the "ins," are satisfied with the existing system; others, the "outs," the underpaid or unemployed, are just as strenuously opposed to it. The "ins" devour an enormous part of the national wealth: they enjoy a bourgeois standard of living, and in their large mass are always ready to side with the existing system against the manual workers.

In short, formally "employees," the "ins" are, in fact, due to their higher educational qualifications, *minor partners* of the capitalists as a whole: the

Reprinted from *The Making of Society* (1937), edited by V. F. Calverton, pp. 882-93, The Modern Library, Random House, Inc.

sive, exhaustive physical labor; displacement of the capitalist industry in the intellectual production of society by the free unions,—along this road proceeds the tendency of the proletarian regime in the sphere of intellectual production.

We see that the problems in the field of production are of a contradictory nature. The capitalist system of production has created the task of formulating the social process of production in a simple and systematic manner. This task consists in placing the individual in a fixed order to whose rules he must conform. On the other side this same manner of production has more than ever brought the individual to a self-consciousness, placed him on his own feet and freed him from society. More than ever mankind demands to-day the possibility of developing a personality and its relation to other men in order to determine in the freest manner the more sensitive and individual of these relations, especially the marriage relation, but also their relation as artists and thinkers to the external world.

Regulation of social chaos and liberation of the individual—these are the two historical tasks that capitalism has placed before society. They appear to be contradictory, but they are simultaneously soluble because each of them belongs to a different sphere of social life. Undoubtedly whoever should seek to rule both spheres in the same manner would find himself involved in insoluble contradictions. It is on this point that anarchism is wrecked. Anarchism arises out of the reaction of the little bourgeois against the repressive and oppressive capitalism. The little handworker who was accustomed to direct his labor according to his own pleasure rebels against the discipline and the monotony of the factory. His ideal remains the free labor of the individual and when this is no longer possible he seeks to replace it by common working together in free unions wholly independent of each other.

The "new middle class," the intellectuals, is, as we have already seen many times, in its social position only a refined and more sensitive expression of the earlier little bourgeois. Its manner of working develops in them the same need for free labor, the same repugnance to discipline and uniformity. So it is that their social ideal becomes the same as that of the small bourgeois, that is the anarchist. But that which is a progressive ideal in their sphere of production shows itself to be reactionary in the field of material production where it corresponds to the conditions of production of the now extinct hand work.

In the present stage of production there are only two possible forms of *material production* so far as production in quantities is concerned, aside from a few remnants which are mainly curiosities: on the one side *communistic* with social property in the means of production, and the systematic direction of production from a central point, or the *capitalistic*. The anarchistic system of production can, under the best conditions, be only a transi-

tory episode. Material production leads to chaos unless the communistic basis of the law of value determined by free competition above what the consequence is for individual industry under free tion. It determines the correct proportionality of individual means of production to one another and prevents any one from swamping society with commodities or leaving it without bread. Production of commodities under the present conditions of social production must continuously take on some form of capitalist production, as countless productive co-operatives have shown. To strive for an anarchist ideal in material production is at best a Sisyphus task.

It is wholly different with intellectual production. This is built upon material production, on the surplus of products and labor powers which proceed from material production. It is possible only when material life is secured. If the latter falls into confusion then our whole existence is threatened. Consequently it is absolutely unimportant for society in what relations the existing surplus of products and labor powers are applied to the individual fields of free intellectual creation. The exception to this is the educational system which has its special laws, and has not yet been turned over to free competition in any society, but has been socially regulated. Society would fall into bad condition if all the world should set to work at the manufacture of one kind of commodities such, for example, as buttons, and thereby direct too much labor power to this, so that not enough was left for the production of others, such, for example, as bread. On the other hand the relation between lyric poems and tragedies, works on Assyriology and botany which are to be produced is no essential one; it has neither maximum nor minimum point. If to-day there should be twice as many dramas as yesterday, and at the same time one-half as many lyrics, or if to-day twenty works on Assyriology should appear and only ten Botanical, while yesterday the relations were reversed, still the existence of society would not be touched in the slightest thereby. These facts find their economic expression in that the law of value, in spite of all psychological theories of value, only holds good for material production and not for intellectual. In this field a central direction of production is not only unnecessary, but absolutely foolish. Here free production can rule without the necessity of production of commodities of value or of capitalist production.

Communism in material production, anarchism in the intellectual. This is the type of socialist production system which will arise from the dominion of the proletariat or, in other words, out of the social revolution by the logic of economic facts whatever may be the wishes, ideas and theories of the proletariat.

lesser nobility, as it were, within the great bourgeois aristocracy of the modern age. And in proportion as the *major partner,* the capitalist, becomes a mere consuming parasite, leaving most of the functions of technical and commercial management to his "paid employees"—in the same proportion these "employees" become the potential successors of their employers. But, being satisfied with their social position, they are naturally a conservative element; they are not in a hurry to dispossess their masters (or major partners); for any serious interference with the property relations may disturb the social peace and endanger their own privileged incomes.

Against these defenders of the status quo are arrayed the "outs," the unemployed or underpaid journalists, lecturers, college graduates and undergraduates, "lawyers without clients and doctors without patients" (Marx), educated ex-workers in search of a white-collar position—in short all that motley army of impecunious or starving intellectuals, near-intellectuals and would-be intellectuals, who are dissatisfied with the existing system and are very often militantly active in the various radical or fascist movements. It is the members of this group who have the ambition of eliminating the capitalist class of parasitic consumers and of establishing their own rule in a system based on government control or ownership of industries, and an unequal distribution of incomes.

The first case in history when this group came into its own was the Bolshevik revolution and the establishment of the so-called Soviet system. That system has evolved an enormous hierarchy of intellectuals who are bureaucrats at the same time: administrative office-holders, technical managers and engineers, judges, savants, journalists, writers, professors, higher transport and postal employees, Marx-theologians, army officers, actors, singers, scientific spies, bank accountants, trade union and sports organizers —all of them government employees who owe their bourgeois comfort to the labor of the uneducated workers and peasants. Having eliminated the old parasitic strata of feudal lords and capitalist proprietors, these officeholders have become the only consumers of privileged incomes. The badge of admission to this new privileged class is a certain amount of education or training exceeding the average level of the manual workers. That amount of higher education or training guarantees its owner a soft job and a salary which is above the average wage of the manual worker.

It is this class which, being identical with the government, has become the collective owner of the country's socialized economy—its industries and its land. The workers and peasants are merely the nationalized laborers, menials and serfs of the new ruling class which has combined the fiction of the "proletarian dictatorship" with that of "the factories and fields belonging to the workers and peasants."

The bolshevik form of class rule and inequality of incomes is not a distortion of the original equalitarian character of socialism, as some sentimental souls may believe. Stripped of its emotional content and reduced to the simplest economic terms, socialism has always meant merely *government ownership of the means of production.* In other words, socialism means primarily a change in the *form of production,* or in the *ownership of the means of production.* The rest is poetry and propaganda. The question of *distribution* has always been considered a secondary matter by the various socialist schools after the first and most important task of socialization had been carried out. Practically all socialist theorists take it for granted that immediately after the socialist revolution, during "the first phase of communism," to use an expression of Marx, there would be no equality of incomes. It is only under "the higher phase of communism," after God knows how many generations or centuries, that the principle of "from each according to his abilities, to each according to his needs," would be applied. A formula which is as hazy as it is deceitful. For who is to determine a man's needs? None other apparently than the bureaucrats, the same men who in present-day Russia determine that a high class manager "needs," or, let us say, "deserves," several thousand rubles a month, while for an ordinary laborer or other plain worker one hundred or one hundred fifty a month is sufficient. In other words, for the future as for the present the real meaning of that formula is to be conceived as "from the workers according to their abilities, to the bureaucrats according to their needs".

Only the beneficiaries of such glaring inequalities of income can assert that the means of production under the new dispensation are "owned by the workers." They are owned, collectively of course, by those who hire and fire; by those who constitute the government machine, the bureaucrats, the sum total of all educated people who have good apartments in city and countryside, who have the best food, the use of the available automobiles, domestic servants, and all the other comforts from which the enormous majority of manually working "owners" are excluded. Only paid propagandists, or would-be "ins" of such a new system of exploitation, can speak of a "proletarian state" because the maximum proportion of inequality is "merely" one to one hundred, instead of being one to one thousand as in the typically capitalist countries.

The Soviet example has proven that *exploitation is just as much possible under socialism as under any other previous social system.* (Granting of course, that any system of planned, socialized economy, historically speaking, represents a great step forward as compared with the productive process under private capitalism with its calamities resulting from the business cycles). If one were to indulge in prophecy one could make a guess that *the coming universal form of exploitation of man by man, as foreshadowed by Russia's system of government ownership and inequality of incomes, will simply be called socialism,* and that in the ears of the underdog this word will, in time, assume the same connotation of master-and-slave-relationship as feudalism and capitalism. Like the previous social systems that relationship will be self-perpetuating. For while the *entire offspring of the new masters is given all the facilities of higher education, only the most gifted children of the lower orders get those opportunities of the higher schooling that will enable them to rise above the level of manual labor.* Whether it is inaugurated by communists or socialists, whether it maintains the strictest political one-party absolutism, Bolshevik style, or is ready to permit democratic competition of various political currents—the *distribution* within the new system is to be based upon the immemorial aristocratic principle of giving the greater share to the "more deserving." "Socialism is not equalization" Otto Bauer, greatest theorist of the socialist wing of Marxism, wrote in his magazine "Kampf" in May 1936. "It levels society by *abolishing the classes,* thus removing the privileges deriving from descent or property. But it differentiates society by rewarding those whose achievements for society are particularly outstanding, and by raising them above the masses in matters of *income* [my emphasis—M.N.] and social prestige."[1] (The "abolition of classes" under socialism with the higher incomes going to the more deserving, i.e. to the bureaucracy and occasional "shock workers," is on a par with the bourgeois theory of the "non-existence of classes" under a system of capitalist democracy where every one has the vote and an "equal opportunity" of acquiring property. Under socialism "every one" owns an "equal share" in the nation's means of production, and has an "equal opportunity" of becoming an office-holder, provided he had selected the right parents or was endowed with those special gifts which in America enable "every" office-boy to become a high-class executive.)

No wonder then that ever increasing sections of the more enlightened part of the intelligentsia in non-fascist Europe and America are flocking now to the various radical parties. They see in the Russian example the possibility of putting an end to their economic insecurity, the hope of throwing off the financial magnates, and the prospect of themselves becoming masters of the country. They are the pioneers of their class—opposed not only by the well-paid "ins" who are satisfied with their present condition, but by a large number of other educated "outs" and déclassés as well.

If a large part of the intellectuals in various countries, instead of turning socialist or communist, join the fascist ranks, they do so largely for the same reason for which many workers likewise don the black or brown shirt. No

---

1. In a lecture delivered in Vienna (*Arbeiter-Zeitung* of September 25, 1932) Paul Goebbels, Hitler's chief propaganda expert, expressed the following opinion: "We say 'to every one his due.' Hence we take the *aristocratic* point of view: not according to property or rank, but according to ability and achievement." Cynic though he may be, the Fascist Goebbels, by frankly admitting the aristocratic nature of this principle, is more honest than Socialist or Communist Marxists who defend inequality of rewards as a "proletarian" theory.

doubt, the influence of reactionary ideology plays a certain part in the process. But it is largely their impatience, their desire for a short cut to power, that is responsible for the success of the new gospel. Many of the fascist intellectuals would join the communist movement, if they saw that it had any chances, or at least intentions of winning *immediately*. For by now it has become obvious to most observers that the leading communists of the non-fascist countries have altogether ceased to be revolutionaries: that ever since 1923 they have been ordinary Russian patriots abroad, *actually* opposed to any revolutionary steps that might disturb the international status quo in which the U.S.S.R. has been interested for many years. Like the socialists of pre-war times the communists—meaning of course the official leadership—have become a party of "gradualist" anti-capitalist *protest* and *reform,* and *not* of anti-capitalist *revolt.* (It is only the extreme-left fringe of radicalism, as represented by the followers of Trotsky and of various anarchist or syndicalist groups, that now advocates going beyond the mere defense of the bourgeois-democratic status quo.)

The fascists in power, in spite of the reverence they show towards all the taboos of the past, are not just flunkeys of the capitalist class, as most of the socialists and communists believe or pretend to believe. They are their *major partners;* they swallow an ever growing share of the nation's wealth; and while in some countries they are now greatly favoring the munition magnates, their taxes and assessments are impoverishing the bourgeoisie as a whole in order to feed an enormous bureaucratic machine. That machine is both a "protector" of the rich, and their blackmailing parasite at the same time; largely comparable to the Praetorians of the Roman Empire, who, while permitting the property-owners to exist, actually were the masters of the country and lived at the expense of all the other classes of the population.

The fascists' present close association with capitalism does not imply that this association will have to be permanent. History is replete with cases where mercenaries of various sorts, Mamertines, Praetorians, Mamelukes, Condottieri, became the masters of those who hired them. There is an openly anti-capitalist wing within the Italian fascist party which recommends the "road to Moscow," i.e. the expropriation of the capitalists. Mussolini himself, if driven to a corner, will not hesitate to turn Bolshevik if by doing so he can save the rule of his party—the rule of the most determined section of the Italian intelligentsia. His widely publicized threats to do away with capitalism, and the serious character of these threats, contributed their share in preventing capitalist Europe from interfering with his Ethiopian expedition. Similar anti-capitalist tendencies are becoming more and more discernible among certain unorthodox German Nazis, as well as within Japan's officers' caste and its bureaucratic and would-be bureaucratic hangers-on.

There is no reason why the rank and file as well as the leaders of the job-hungry fascist intellectuals should be opposed to the elimination of the capitalists—*provided they themselves can get the best positions to the exclusion of their leftist competitors.* Socialism, as a new form of class rule, is possible under all forms of philosophical "superstructures." A system embodying the mastery of the office-holders' class is just as compatible with a Paretist-Mussolinian aristocratic nationalism and its glorification of the "élite," as it is with a Marxist-Leninist "proletarian internationalism" with its no less aristocratic "proletarian vanguard," or with Bauer's democratic socialism which takes for granted the higher incomes enjoyed by men of "achievement" and "prestige." Just as private capitalism can gather its profits both under the Voltairian iconoclasm of the French Republic and under its crassest opposite—the medieval Emperor-God worship of a militarist semi-absolutism, Japanese style.

Thus the abolition of capitalism, the result of the "final revolution" championed by the various political parties of the underdog, eventually leads to the establishment of a new class rule, of a new exploitation of man by man. That new form of class rule must naturally call forth a violent dissatisfaction both among the down-trodden manual workers and among the step-brothers or poorer relations of the new bureaucratic masters. There arises the urge towards a new "final revolution" in which the old process is repeated under the guise of a changed vocabulary. For whether they call themselves left communists, syndicalists or anarchists, the victorious rebels against the bureaucracy of a socialized form of exploitation cannot help establishing a new bureaucracy, a new ruling aristocracy—in other words, follow the example of the Russian communists. For the process of revolution is always the same: Seizure of power; organization of a revolutionary government; its defense against the reactionaries at first; and then its consolidation against the masses as well in the interest of a better paid aristocracy of office-holders, technicians, and other members of the educated layers of society.

Does this all, in its final analysis, amount to the old philosophy of "thus it had been, thus it is, thus it will be?" In other words, does this conclusion consign the poor to statistics and to eternal slavery?

No, this "skepticism," if skepticism there be, is the very opposite of submission to fate. On the contrary, it implies permanent revolt against any status quo: capitalist exploitation of today, as well as socialist inequality of tomorrow. It is directed both against the property-owning oppressors of today and the job-holding "liberators" of tomorrow; against the middle class of yesterday which used the workers in its struggle against feudal tyranny; and against the *new middle class* of today which uses them against the capitalist bourgeoisie; against the college-trained apologists of the coming form of slavery, and against their competitors from the ranks of the self-educated ex-workers.

However, that "skepticism" likewise implies the realization of certain phenomena which hitherto have been consistently overlooked or glossed over: The acknowledgment of the non-proletarian neo-bourgeois character of the educated non-capitalist strata of society roughly comprised under the designation of "intellectual workers" to whom the dissatisfaction and the struggles of the manual workers offer an opportunity for taking the place of the old masters; and the admission of the tragic dualism involved in the composition of the labor movement with its inevitable partnership between mass and leadership. A partnership which, though to a certain extent beneficial to the masses, invariably results in a conflict between the interests of the leading élite and those of the masses constituting the following.

Those leading élites, even if they rise from the working masses themselves, being more educated and consequently better endowed than their following, are essentially aristocratic in character, no matter whether they profess to be democratic, anarchist, socialist-communist, syndicalist or fascist. Like all aristocratic groups they are inevitably Machiavellian or amoral in their policies, keeping up their "morale" with all sorts of philosophical justifications ("rationalizations") and resorting constantly to a conscious or unconscious deception of the masses. For all their activities and endeavors converge in the single purpose of obtaining and maintaining all power and its resulting benefits for their specific revolutionary or counter-revolutionary group. And to strengthen their hold upon the masses they evolve certain religious features within their respective movements—the analogy with the material growth and the spiritual decay of many of the great religions being particularly striking. The intolerance and ruthless suppression of any unorthodox opinion, as well as the divine veneration bestowed upon the Leader are the common characteristics of most of these groups, whether they place themselves at the extreme right or at the extreme left.

The desire to concentrate all the power and the privileges deriving from it within a restricted circle results in an ever recurring competition for power between various groups of educated malcontents leading, or aspiring to leadership of, the dissatisfied masses. Some of these groups may be more crude than the others in their efforts to win the masses; some of them may be in the pay of domestic capitalists or of foreign bureaucrats; but at bottom even the most "honest" and "consistent" group cannot claim to be "really proletarian" in its aims. For every *organization* wants only one thing: power, that is privilege, for itself and for its more active members. That competition for power between the various groups is a guaranty against stagnation and against the perpetuation of the status quo. Under the present conditions of a decaying private capitalism it is bound to hasten the inauguration of some system or other of a socialized economy.

After the elimination or a considerable restriction of the capitalist owners, that competition for power leads to an internecine struggle between various groups of intellectuals and educated ex-workers for predominance within the government machine, that is, the office-holding class, now ruling supreme.

It is the ever recurring struggle between the Trotzkys and the Stalins, or the Roehms and the Goerings, caused by the oligarchical tendencies prevailing within each ruling class. *The urge to win forces the rebellious rivals to appeal to the dissatisfaction of the manual workers and of the lower clerical force and to assist them in obtaining a larger share of the national income.* This process is accompanied by the rise of the most educated and most intelligent elements among the manual workers themselves, joining either of the contending groups or making their own bid for power.

Each of the contending parties or groups constituting the opposition is bound to include disinterested idealists or "romanticists" whose sentiments are with the horny-handed underdog and who, consciously at least, care neither for power nor for personal advantage. These quite naturally will push forward any mass struggle for better conditions, as expressed in higher wages, shorter hours and jobs for the unemployed. And they will denounce the leaders who for one reason or another may be suspected of restraining the masses or of selling them out. Yet the very success of his revolutionary opposition may force the disinterested rebel, in a given situation, to accept the responsibilities of leadership and power—and to imitate the example of those whom he had just denounced; when he will in turn be opposed by a new set of fighters who, again, may go through the same cycle. Until that blessed time, when the miracle of all miracles, the "good master" will have made his appearance.

The permanent change of masters and the accompanying striving of the masses in the direction of an ever greater *approach* towards equality in the enjoyment of the good things of life forms the basic content of the historical process. That process knows of no millennium when full harmony has been achieved once for all eternity. There is no "happy ending" just as there is no "final revolution" that will eliminate all further class struggles. For the working masses every "final victory" proclaimed by their victorious leaders, even if it is a real step forward, can be only another starting point in their endless struggle *for more and always more.*

The chasm separating the great toiling majority from the men of "outstanding achievement," from those wielding the most efficient combination of knowledge, intelligence and ruthlessness, from the socialist and communist aristocracy of superior brains and incomes—may never be bridged completely. But the "evil passions" (Bakunin) of the underdog, his legitimate envy of, and hatred for, his luckier "betters," will drive him forward—under ever changing leaders. Those leaders may fall by the side, martyrs in defeat or masters in victory, but the struggle will go on.

That struggle is the *permanent revolution.* Permanent—not as conceived by those who would cut short their "dialectical process" the moment they themselves are enthroned over a socialized world; but in the real meaning of the word.

NATIONAL SOCIALISM AND INTELLECTUALS

Wilhelm Röpke

> Once a movement breaks out, may God protect
> us from the journalists and the professors.
> ADALBERT STIFTER *in a letter
> to Gustav Heckenast* (1849)

THERE IS SCARCELY another class in Germany that failed so fatally as that of the intellectuals in general, with the exception of a large part of the clergy of both confessions and some notorious university professors. This failure was so fatal because it resulted in a crippling of the conscience of the German nation. At a later stage we shall go thoroughly into the deeper historical roots of the betrayal of their mission by the German intellectual leaders. It was, in point of fact, a long process of degeneration and perversion of which we have here to describe the final steps. . . .

. . . Such were the forces that tirelessly sapped the foundations of German civilization and prepared the chaos that followed. These were the men whom we had to denounce as guilty of spiritual arson. But before the foreigner bursts out in all too righteous indignation, let us remind him that abroad there were the same groups as in Germany ready to lap up the same sort of propaganda. One of the best-known works of the *Tat* group—Ferdinand Fried's muddled book *Das Ende des Kapitalismus*—found eager and sympathizing readers in a French translation, and many were the writers in the Western countries who played the same tune. What is still more serious is that in Great Britain and elsewhere today such a book as Carr's *Conditions of Peace* should have had a remarkable reception, although it corresponds in many respects to the German pattern of the *Tat* group. Indeed, it even seems as if this book is only a particularly striking symptom of a much broader current that has been noted today in Britain by attentive observers.

Professor Carr belongs to an English university. In Germany also, and, indeed, in Switzerland, where the university professor has always had excep-

Reprinted from *The Solution of the German Problem* (1946), pp. 51, 53-55, 60-61, 62-63, 65-67, by permission of the author and the publisher, George Allen and Unwin, Ltd. Translated by E. W. Dickes. Title supplied by the Editor.

tional standing, even more than elsewhere, it was from the universities that most of the other intellectuals drew the disintegrating poison that they then distributed, duly packed and processed, to the mass of the people. This is not the place for drawing the portrait of the German professor who became generations ago in so many faculties the caricature of any intellectual leader of integrity—a specialist with no political sense but any amount of self-confidence and usually a bad temper. As a rule the professor of this type was a splendid worker and often a master in his special field, but he became a pretentious idiot the moment he blundered into vital questions of the state and society. That type of professor was always ready to hold a stirrup for the government, whether by expounding the economic basis of Bismarck's protectionism, or by supporting a saber-rattling policy in foreign affairs, or by furthering the propaganda of the German Navy League, or by defending the unrestricted U-boat warfare, or finally by burning incense at the altar of Nazism. Here again we are concerned only with indicating the last stages of this betrayal of the mind and placing our finger on the almost inexpiable guilt of many German university professors in preparing people's minds for the Nazi hordes, and later, when Nazism put their courage as intellectual leaders to the test, proving ready, in good faith or bad, to palliate its assaults on culture and law and morality and to swallow its absurdest theories and even sing their praises. This is a harsh accusation, but it comes in this book from one of those very professors, who in his long years in German universities had the best of opportunities of studying the work of this type of professional politicaster and noting its appalling influence on academic youth. The writer knows, too, from his own experience, the difficulty the others, the honorable type, had in holding their own in this stuffy atmosphere. The academic freedom that progressive governments were at pains to respect had indeed become here more and more a charter for irresponsibles.

It is particularly disgraceful for the German universities that it was there that the method of the base appeal to the mob first made its way in the form of anti-Semitism, and with ever growing success. At the end of the nineteenth century, Theodor Mommsen, in his public controversy with the anti-Semitic Treitschke, had made a strong effort, to his great credit, to stave off the beginning of the movement, speaking for an earlier and nobler Germany; but later there was no opposition of equal weight. No observer with any but a myopic vision could deny the existence of a very grave Jewish question, and in Germany it had become more and more critical in the last generation in particular; but this is no excuse for the coarse anti-Semitism that became more and more dominant in the German universities. I had experience myself of the length to which anti-Semitism had been carried, when I tried once to point out to my colleagues, at a general meeting of professors, the great services done by Jewry for the German language and culture in eastern and southern Europe—with the result that I found my position as professor at Marburg University most seriously affected. Now that this anti-Semitism has worked immeasurable harm to Germany, it is to be hoped that most of the German professors will have realized where that course has landed them. . . .

It was here, too, at the German universities, that in the lecture rooms, among the associations, and at every opportunity that offered, there were cultivated *a brutal nationalism, a stupid national pride, an unreasoning hatred of the victor powers, and an inhuman contempt for international law.* It was here that a war of revenge was most energetically preached, and the way thus prepared for the triumph of Nazism. Here the young students were systematically fed on lies and trained in unreason. It was the University of Berlin that at that time placed on its war memorial the inscription *"Invictis victi victuri"*—"To the unconquered the conquered who will conquer"—and it was a professor of theology (Seeberg) that invented this.

Naturally the faculties of social science provided a special opportunity for practicing intellectual treachery and preparing the way for Nazism. Thus it is mainly the names of jurists and philosophers that could here be given. In Germany there were, indeed, few faculties of law that were not filled with the spirit of obdurate antiliberalism, antidemocratism, nationalism, and anti-Semitism, and it was this spirit that was thus carried into the life of the country by those who later became judges, administrative officials, and lawyers. It was in these faculties that the saps were pushed forward that undermined the edifice of the Weimar Republic, weak as it was in any case. In these faculties was forged in every possible variant the theory of the anti-liberal total state—by a Berlin professor named Smend, who invented for it the name of "sociological state," by the Bonn professor Carl Schmitt, who later played so sinister a part, by the Viennese professor Othmar Spann, and by many of less note. All these teachings fell on a soil that had been most efficiently prepared by such "muck spreaders" as Spengler's brilliant but perverse *Decline of the West.*

It can be said to the honor of the German economists that the part they played up to the start of the Third Reich was far less pernicious than that of the jurists. It may even be claimed that the great majority of them remained loyal to the spirit of social understanding and of comprehensive assessment in which that science, when it is pursued with a genuine regard for economic and social facts, gives special training. In addition to this the younger generation of German economists was seeking at that time with energy and understanding and impartiality a return to the tradition of the strict economic doctrine that had suffered eclipse under the dominance of the historical school. If there was any faculty in which a breath of the liberal spirit was to be found, it was the faculty of economics, and this accounted for the emphasis with which this group of professors fought against the economic doctrines of Nazism, and especially against the insane system of autarchy. There were exceptions, some of them of the worst sort, such as Othmar Spann, already mentioned, and Werner Sombart, who had much in common with him in character and mentality. Sombart had already given evidence of his quality during the First World War in his unspeakable pamphlet *Händler und Helden* ("Traders and Heroes"); and later, in his book *Deutscher Sozialismus* (1934), he supplied a model collection of pet theories of Nazism. These writers were seconded by a bevy of lesser spirits, whose names may be permitted to fall into oblivion.

There were many grave lapses among the representatives of medicine and of the natural sciences (with the creditable exception of a few individuals and branches), and the general atmosphere of the medical faculties often exceeded that of the legal faculties in unintelligence. The philologists and the historians maintained the good tradition for the longest time, though here, too, there was no lack of professors whose honest work in their own field did not prevent them from making most unfortunate excursions into politics. It is true that the average historians did not renounce their devotion to the neo-Prussian tradition, and certainly in this field there were plenty of preachers of the baldest nationalism who felt themselves to be epigoni of Treitschke. German historical science was no less indisputably influenced by the tendency to a certain naturalism that began with Ranke; we shall have more to say about this tendency, which contributed immensely to creating the general mental atmosphere in which Nazism first became possible. Finally, there was scarcely a single German historian who was able to judge with the impartiality of the universal historical outlook the development of Greater Prussia since 1866, still less the origin and course of the First World War. But it is difficult to discover any prominent historian who so directly prepared the way for Nazism as did professors of constitutional law or of political science. As for the philologists, many of them, particularly the specialists in the Romance and Anglo-Saxon languages, can be referred to only in terms of deep respect. To mention only one example, it must not be forgotten that Ernst Robert Curtius, in his book *Deutscher Geist in Gefahr* ("German Spirit in Danger"), published in 1932, courageously and energetically set himself against the fatal process already far advanced; while no one familiar with the subject need be reminded of the importance of Karl Vossler's work. Even in Germanic philology the strict scientific discipline that philology especially inculcates kept most of its students clear of nationalist cultural charlatanry. Here again a single name may stand for many, that of the Berlin Germanic scholar Konrad Burdach, who had the courage to tell the Germans plainly that in the Middle Ages they had had no truly national culture, and that Middle High German epic poetry was mainly an art of translation from the French. Neither must it be forgotten that the eminent philosopher Karl Jaspers (Heidelberg University) had challenged in 1932 the evil spirit of the times in his book on *Die geistige Situation der Zeit* ("The Spiritual Situation of the Times") with a courage that never failed him afterward throughout the tribulations of the Third Reich.

In spite of all bright spots, the general picture we have had to draw of the influence of the German professors down to the Third Reich remains dark enough, and we hope their best representatives will agree with us when we conclude that a great load of responsibility has here been incurred. But the responsibility grows to infinite dimensions when we examine the behavior of the German professors after 1933.

The Nazis knew only too well that the German universities were among the strongholds it was most important for them to capture if they were to gain the indispensable dominance over the German soul—a stronghold scarcely less important than the churches. Accordingly they left no stone unturned to gain this end, and where they had no success with intimidation or brutality they tried persuasion or transparent indulgence. . . .

In Italy many university professors refused to take the oath to fascism and bravely held their ground. In Germany the number of professors who lost their posts after 1933 through being true to their convictions was exceedingly small. Most of the professors then dismissed under a so-called "Law for the Restoration of the Professional Civil Service" (which, of course, in reality undermined it) were victims of the racial legislation. It is impossible to say what they would otherwise have done; but to judge from the attitude of those Jewish professors who at first imagined themselves to be safe on account of their special standing, and who often looked down contemptuously on their dismissed colleagues, Jew or Gentile, there seems ground for a good deal of skepticism.

In view of all this it is not to be wondered at that after the Nazis had tricked their way into power the representatives of learning in general behaved with what can be described only as either cowardice or cynical opportunism or mental and moral perversion. Even in those branches of knowledge that had shown themselves capable of resistance so far, there now came a collapse that for years made an end of any usefulness of the universities as a mental and moral counterweight to the official barbarism, and it seemed as if, now that there was no longer any need for self-restraint, they were going over to the lowbrow camp with flags flying. It was a scene of prostitution that has stained the honorable history of German learning, and represents one of the worst and most fateful examples of group responsibility.

Here again justice certainly demands that we should set certain limits to our condemnation; once more we must be careful not to be too summary in our verdict. On the one hand there were cases of brave resistance, standing out all the more brightly from the poor record of the majority, cases that ended—if nothing worse happened—with the silent disappearance of not a few scholars of high repute, while those who now set the tone were brought so much the more into the foreground. On the other hand, the general picture was falsified, by no means to the benefit of traditional learning, by the fact that everywhere worthless fanatics, careerists, incapable young lecturers, or purely partisan "intellectuals," men who had never caught a breath of the true spirit of science, occupied the professorial chairs so ardently aspired to, gained control of the journals, wrote new approved textbooks, carried on the learned societies, and represented the German universities in relation to the outer world. In a sense there was repeated on a small scale in the universities what had happened to the German nation as a whole: they were driven into active or passive complicity, but they must not be judged on the same basis as those who had done the driving.

The general picture, however, was most depressing. This applies especially to the cases, unfortunately by no means few, in which former socialists, democrats, or liberals not only capitulated miserably, but even gave active service in the former enemy ranks, trying to bury their past in oblivion by means of an undignified display of zeal. We cannot refrain here from mentioning these unfortunate lapses; on the other hand, the utmost respect is due to the courage of many former democrats. . . .

In accordance with the totalitarian character of the new regime, there was scarcely a single branch of learning on which Nazism did not try to set its stamp—there were even a "German" mathematics and a "German" physics —but, naturally, certain fields were especially imperiled. These included, above all, jurisprudence, economics, history, and certain branches of medicine. They were made instruments of the state and its ideology to such an extent that very few professors had the courage, the strength of character, and the high intellectual capacity not merely for keeping silent but actually for assuring the undeviating progress of their honest scientific labor. Among these mention should be made of the economists Walter Eucken (Freiburg), Constantin von Dietze (Freiburg), Wilhelm Gehlhoff (Brunswick), and Wilhelm Gerloff (Frankfurt). As for history, it provided striking confirmation of the dictum of Edgar Quinet: *"Dans la servitude rien ne se corrompt si vite que l'histoire"*—"Nothing, if it loses its independence, is so quickly corrupted as history." It was only through a spiritual corruption of this sort that it was largely historians, archeologists, and art critics who everywhere in the occupied countries of Europe, to the utter disgrace of learning, became mental myrmidons of the Nazis and looted archives and museums.

We have described at this length the pernicious part played by the German universities because it shows us the process of mental and moral degeneration in the quarter from which, after the churches, the strongest resistance ought to have come. *Corruptio optimi pessima*—the German universities not only failed to stand firm but actually were among the worst centers of infection. . . .

All these reproaches affect the leaders of intellectual life in Germany in two ways. Against the very worst they are a charge of having paved the way for barbarism, long before its eruption in 1933, and a different charge against those who showed cowardice and stupidity after the trick that set barbarism in the saddle. We have already stated the extenuating circumstances that in justice have to be admitted. It would also be thoroughly pharisaical if the world were no longer willing to bear in mind that lack of character, the conforming spirit, and opportunism seem unfortunately to be a general characteristic of our epoch, and it was precisely the class of university professors that failed, and not only in Germany, when the need came for courageous defense of the ultimate values and convictions of our civilization. It should also not be forgotten how quickly the intellectuals outside Germany showed themselves ready to take the keenest interest in Nazism, and how many of them were easily won over by the Nazis as paid or unpaid helpers. We have not even been spared the repulsive spectacle of some of these members of the "intellectual Foreign Legion" of Nazism turning later into thoroughly unfair denouncers of Germany.

These same demands of justice compel us further to insist on the fact that after those first fateful years of the Third Reich there came an undoubted change among the German intellectuals, which indicated a continuing process of courageous reflection and self-assertion after the catastrophe had come for which generations of decadent and irresponsible writers had prepared the way. Just as the epidemic was preceded by a long period of intellectual incubation, it may very well have been precisely the German intellectuals who first came to their senses, who were the first to be filled with acute horror of the reality that some of them had foreseen in desolate dreams, and who realized the path that of necessity, when a certain philosophy was carried to the last extreme, led to Oradour-sur-Glane, to Maidanek, and to the devastation of the cities of Europe. True as it is that these intellectuals were infected for a period, shorter or longer, with Nazism, or may have sailed with the wind through lack of character, it would be wrong to suppose that they were permanently converted to Nazism and had sunk to the level of party functionaries. It may, indeed, fairly be said that, if the great majority of them ever really succumbed to the poisonous influence of Nazism, they had since for a considerable time been actively trying to get rid of it.

This was the more noteworthy since the war into which Nazism had driven Germany had naturally, as everywhere else, and as at all times, a strong integrating effect, of which we have already spoken, and placed every intellectual under the temptation to identify himself, at least "for the duration," with the regime. This was all the more to be expected since, in a tragically vicious circle, the Allied powers in their exasperation seemed to envisage for the Germans a fate that would make them suffer for the deeds of the regime. Thus the German intellectuals must have traveled very far when many of them, in spite of their divided feelings, preferred to see their country's fall rather than the continuance of the regime. I know a German professor who, when he learned of Rudolf Hess's flight to Scotland, brought one of his last bottles of Rhine wine from his cellar, to celebrate an event that seemed to him to portend the end of the war. If anyone does not see at once what that implies, let him try to imagine a German professor doing the same thing if the German Crown Prince had flown to England in 1917. Everybody will agree that the idea is unthinkable, and this throws a strong light on the fundamental contrast between then and now. It makes, of course, no difference that my professor had mistaken the true character of Hess's escapade. And what are we to think of another good conservative intellectual, who had the courage to write to me during the war that there was nothing to be seen in the streets any longer but the "horrible uniforms"? Would he have written that in 1918?

All this does not in the least alter the fact that many German intellectuals have loaded themselves with an enormous responsibility. The thing that matters, however, is that probably some of them would actually contradict us if we had any idea of trying to find excuses for them. It is this that shows the moral revolution of which we shall have later to speak particularly. . . .

COMMUNISM AND THE INTELLECTUAL

Sidney Hook

THE contemporary struggle of political ideals has a long history. But it became focal and dramatic with the Russian Revolution of October, 1917, and the formation of the Soviet state. W. H. Auden, the English poet, in comparing the times of Wordsworth with our own, writes:

> Like his, our lives have been coeval
> With a political upheaval,
> Like him, we had the luck to see
> A rare discontinuity
> Old Russia suddenly mutate
> Into a proletarian state.

There are tremendous differences, of course, between the French and Russian Revolutions and their respective developments; and Auden would no longer refer to Russia as a proletarian state. It is undeniable, however, that the Russian Revolution has been the only historical event that has inspired in so many different fields, from philosophy to poetry, reactions of comparable magnitude to those which followed the Fall of the Bastille.

One important difference, relevant to our analysis, in the cultural responses to the French and Russian Revolutions, is the extent to which they took on a *narrow* political character. The responses that greeted the French Revolution were episodic, spontaneous, in varying degrees sympathetically *critical,* and above all *autonomous* in their subsequent development. But those evoked by the October Revolution, after the first few years, were organized, and then in divers ways moulded until their expression took the form of total acceptance.

Neither the French Assembly nor the Convention nor the Directorate nor even the Empire, which some historians view as consolidating the gains of the French Revolution, had an international organization which established political parties in other countries and channelled sympathetic cultural movements along definite lines. The Soviet regime, however, through the Communist International, organized and controlled political parties whose

Reprinted from "The Literature of Political Dissillusionment," in *American Association of University Professors Bulletin* (Autumn, 1949), pp. 451-458, 460-461, 462-463, 465-467, by permission of the author and the *Bulletin*. Title supplied by the Editor.

following provided, so to speak, the acoustic medium in which intellectuals influenced by the October Revolution could hear over and over again the echo of their own sentiments. The existence of this audience and special public was put to good use by the agencies established to effect cultural liaison between sympathetic intellectuals and the political movements inspired by the Soviet regime. Leagues of writers, associations of artists, councils of scientists, proliferated in every large country of the world. The upshot was a mobilization and concentration of intellectual talent on behalf of a political ideal unequalled in the annals of any period.

The enthusiasm generated by the October Revolution was not synthetic even though it was exploited politically to the utmost. In many cases it had the sincerity of a religious conversion. It encountered opposition, sometimes strong opposition. But it throve on it. It produced an impressive body of literature in affirmation of the philosophy, program, and practices of the Soviet regime. This literature of affirmation was in no way unique except in volume, for the American and French Revolution, as well as the national upheavals in Italy and Germany during the 19th century, had also given rise to libraries of passionate and interpretive sympathetic studies. What seems to me to be historically distinctive about the cultural and literary phenomena associated with the Russian Revolution is the literature of disillusionment with which the spiritual Odyssey of so many converts to the Bolshevik faith has terminated, and who now recognize with Auden:

> O Freedom still is far from home
> For Moscow is as far as Rome
> Or Paris.

Indeed, most of them would say that Moscow is farther.

This literature of disillusion constitutes a distinct genre of writing in contemporary letters if only because of its international character and the common pattern of rediscovery and rededication to certain values of the Western tradition that had not been so much denied as ignored. Russell, Auden, Spender, and Orwell in England; André Gide, Souvarine and Serge in France and Belgium; Ignazio Silone in Italy; Panait Istrati in Greece; Arthur Koestler in Central Europe; Anton Ciliga in the Balkans; Eastman, Dos Passos, Wilson, Hicks, Farrell in the United States are among the more noteworthy figures who have contributed to this literature.

As literature it must be sharply distinguished from the revelations of former members of the Communist Party who were revolted, or felt themselves threatened, by the pattern of conspiracy, espionage, and subversive infiltration in which all members of the Communist Party are personally involved. I am not discussing the "professional revolutionists," but intellectuals who are concerned more with ideology than organization, and who in some ways are more influential than exclusively political personalities.

The evolution of attitudes in most of these men differs from the apostacies of Wordsworth and Dostoyevsky, whose early revolutionary enthusiasm and doctrines became transformed into their polar opposites. We do not find in their works sentiments comparable to those expressed in Wordsworth's *Ecclesiastical Sketches* or *Devotional Incitements;* and if their writings do not reach the great artistic heights of Dostoyevsky's bitter legend of the *Grand Inquisitor,* neither do they celebrate the central role which Dostoyevsky assigned to miracle, mystery, and authority in human life.

If we ask what led so many sensitive and generous spirits to ardent and sometimes sacrificial support of Soviet communism, we find a mixture of motives inexplicable in terms of the hedonistic determinism of Bentham or the economic determinism of Marxian orthodoxy. Neither self-interest nor fear nor vanity moved them to break with the conventional pieties and allegiances of the world in which they had been nurtured. In almost equal measure, they were impelled by a revulsion against the dismal spectacle of the postwar West which tottered without faith and with little hope from one crisis to another, and by an enthusiasm for the ideals of equality and human liberation broadcast in the official decrees and laws of the early Soviet regime. Both the revulsion and enthusiasm were rooted in a moral sensibility whose fibres had been fed from sources deeply imbedded in the traditions of the West. Not one of the neophytes to the Communist faith was conscious of accepting an alien creed no matter how foreign the idiom in which it was clothed. The words in which one English convert to the Soviet idea describes her road to the Kremlin holds true with minor variations for the entire band of fellow-pilgrims:

> I came to communism via Greek history, the French revolutionary literature I had read in childhood, and the English 19th century poets of freedom. . . . In my mind Pericles' funeral oration, Shelley's and Swinburne's poems, Marx's and Lenin's writings, were all part and parcel of the same striving for the emancipation of mankind from oppression.[1]

Stephen Spender, another English poet, in an effort to show that there is a continuity between the liberal idealists and philosophical radicals of the past century, on the one hand, and the Communists of the present century, on the other, between Blake, Godwin, and J. S. Mill and Lenin, Trotsky, and Stalin, wrote:

> I am a communist because I am a liberal. Liberalism seems to me to be the creed of those who, as far as it is possible in human affairs, are disinterested, if by disinterestedness one understands not mere passivity but a regard for objective truth, an active will towards political justice. During an era of peace and progress,

---

1. Freda Utley, *Lost Illusion* (Philadelphia: Fireside Press, rev. ed., 1948), pp. 2, 43.

the liberal spirit is identical not only with political discussion, but also with scientific inquiry, speculative thought and the disinterested creation of works of art.[2]

What Spender is saying is that he is a communist because he believes in disinterestedness, objective truth and justice, free political discussion and inquiry, and creative integrity—a cluster of values every one of which, oddly enough, has been vehemently denounced as bourgeois prejudices by the pundits of dialectical materialism ever since the early days of the Soviet regime. Spender has long since repudiated communism without foreswearing his liberalism.

Compare these strains of rationalism and humanism with the *motifs* in the apologies of those adherents to German National Socialism like Rauschning, Strasser, and Thyssen, who renounced the Nazi regime. What elements in the Nazi practice and doctrine magnetized *their* minds, emotions, and will? "A national awakening," "a surface discipline and order," "a vast display of energy and achievement" whose new tempos and accelerated rhythms lift men out of "the humdrum of daily life"—these are some of the things of which they speak. No ideals continuous with the heritage of either secular or Christian humanism moved these men and their fellows but only the pull of the dynamism of power. Here was no attempt to achieve either a revolution from within or a transformation of basic institutions, but in Rauschning's phrase "a revolution of nihilism." Not principle—not even mistaken principle—drew them on, but a frenetic national enthusiasm, and a mysticism centered on the person of Hitler. "I looked into his eyes and he into mine; and at that I had only one desire, to be at home and alone with that great, overwhelming experience." This extravagant outburst, Rauschning tells us, came not from an hysterical woman "but from a judge in a high position, talking to his colleagues."

A candid appraisal of the literature of Nazi disillusion shows that it is qualitatively of an entirely different order from that of the erstwhile partisans of the Soviet idea. Those who broke with Hitler did so because their stomachs were not strong enough to assimilate, as a constant diet, the atrocities to which they had originally resigned themselves as incidental and temporary —like Rauschning; or because their private interests were jeopardized by someone who they expected would be their creature because he had been bought—like Thyssen; or because their personal ambitions were frustrated— like Strasser.

I have contrasted these two types of literature of disillusion to underscore how misleading is the simple equation often drawn between Bolshevism and Nazism. In respect to their repudiation of many features of the democratic

2. *Forward from Liberalism* (London: Victor Gollancz, 1937), p. 202.

process they are, of course, identical, but in respect to the power of the Soviet and Nazi myths to attract the liberal spirits of the West they are vastly different. One need not agree with Toynbee that Russian Bolshevism is a species of Christian heresy to recognize the seductive effect of its use of categories drawn from the Western culture it would destroy. Just as the early Christians used the temples of pagan worship to make the new religion more palatable to peoples whose rulers had been converted, so the ideology of Bolshevism parades with a vocabulary of freedoms and rights freighted with connotations precious to all genuine humanists. That is why it is a more formidable opponent of free cultures than movements openly dedicated to their destruction. It is especially formidable in drawing to itself politically innocent men and women of good will and strong emotions whose minds are unfortified with relevant information, and who have not yet learned that only an intelligence hardened by skepticism is a safeguard against the credulities born of hope.

It is worthy of note that most of those who succumbed to the Soviet myth were devoid of political experience. They were led to their first political affair by emotional compulsion rather than by sober computation of the consequences of adopting a given proposal and its alternatives, which constitutes the every day life of rational politics. Just as the necessity for loving creates its own object, so the necessity for believing selects the myth that appears best fitted to one's need and hopes. And, given the cultural climate—the naiveté, the vague longing for "higher things," and the vast ignorance of political fact—what seemed more congenial than the Soviet idea, the apparent offspring of moral idealism and scientific law? It not only held out guarantees of fulfillment of their highest hopes but provided a metaphysics to give them cosmic support.

All the great myths of history, from Augustine's *City of God* to Sorel's *General Strike,* have been able to sustain themselves because nowhere could they be exemplified, lived with, tested in terms of their fruits in experience. The Soviet myth of a humane, rationally ordered, classless, democratic society, however, was glorified not as an otherworldly ideal but as an historical fact with a definite locus in space and time. In staking out a claim in history, it subjected not only its power but its intent to the logic of events. We have no way of knowing the actual extent to which those who are native to the Soviet Union believe in the Soviet myth, carefully inculcated as it is in every textbook from the kindergarten to the university and reinforced by an omnipresent secret police whose forced labor camps girdle the country. But we do know, judging by the literature under review, that the first doubts in the minds of the pilgrims from other countries arose when they actually lived in the land of their dreams or pondered on the critical reports of those who had.

Some day a psychologist or poet will do justice to the drama of doubt in the mind of these political believers. Few individuals ever surrendered their belief in God with more agony, soul-searching, and inner resistance than these latter-day apostles of revolutionary brotherhood surrendered their belief in the monolithic validity of the monolithic state system.

It is an elementary truth of the psychology of perception that what a man sees depends often upon his beliefs and expectations. The stronger the beliefs the more they function like *a priori* notions whose validity is beyond the tests of experience. Hopes can be so all-consuming that they affect even the range and quality of feeling. The consequence is that the shocks of reality, in terms of which the natural pragmatism of the human mind experiences actuality, lose their educational office. To say that a man is seized and transformed by an abstraction is a metaphor but it expresses the empirical fact that an idea-system, instead of functioning as a guide to conduct, can operate in such a way as to transform habits, feelings, and perceptions of the individual to a point where marked changes of personality are noticeable.

It was to be expected that the Western intellectuals who saw the Soviet Union firsthand would screen their impressions through the closely knit frame of doctrinal abstractions. It took some time before the cumulative shock of events tore a hole in this frame through which the facts of experience could pour. Only then did the agony of self-doubt begin. With varying details each one tells the same story. Once the evils of the system were recognized as evils, it was hoped they would disappear in time. When they grew worse with time, they were justified as necessary elements of the future good. When this necessity was challenged, the mind dwelt upon worse evils that could be found in other countries. But this provoked two gnawing questions. Were the evils in other countries really worse? And in any case, in the countries they came from, evils could be publicly criticized: why not here?

The process of disenchantment was all the harder because in the course of their original conversion so much tortured dialectic had been expended in defense of what now seemed to be indefensible. As a rule it requires more intellectual courage to renounce an illusion than to espouse one. For others are usually involved in such renunciations. These men and women felt a moral responsibility for those, and to those, who had been influenced by their enthusiasms. They knew that they would be showered with abuse, defamed as turncoats, that their former friends would construe the avowal of any doubt as evidence of personal fear or self-seeking despite the overwhelming evidence that neither popular favor nor material goods ranked high in their scale of values. They knew they faced loneliness and isolation. Bertrand Russell, the first of this group, and, as one would expect, the quickest to see through the myth, once confessed that he lost more friends by his criticism of Soviet terror than by his absolute pacifism during a war in which his country was locked in a battle for life and death with Germany. . . .

What, then, were the specific experiences which led to disenchantment with the Soviet myth? And at the outset it must be declared that it was *not* the discovery of the miserable living conditions of the Russian masses. Although they had been sadly unprepared for what they found by the extravagant claims made by Soviet partisans abroad, they found reassurance in the promises of future five-year plans. What struck them most forcibly was the *cruelty,* the unnecessary cruelty, which pervaded almost every aspect of Soviet administrative practice.

This cruelty was not sadistic or demonic as in some Fascist countries; it was systematic, a matter of state policy, carried out to teach object lessons to those who could not possibly profit by it because they were destroyed in the process. The use of bread as a political weapon was not unknown in the past, but its calculated withdrawal for purposes of insuring absolute conformity was something new. The same was true for the use of correctional labor camps for political prisoners. Ciliga, Serge, and others bitterly contrast the conditions in which political prisoners, including Lenin and his lieutenants, lived under the Czar with the conditions under which those charged with political offenses lived under Stalin. And in a nationalized economy under dictatorial controls almost any offense can be regarded as political. Even theft of a handful of grain from a collective farm, moving from one town to another, not to speak of crossing a border without proper papers, are crimes against the state and punishable as such.

This cruelty was manifest not only in bureaucratic indifference but by official reminders that mercy, charity, or pity were evidence of bourgeois decadence. According to our informants, there was a total absence of concern for the individual person, an attitude in high official quarters and low, which regarded the lives of *human* beings as if they were so much raw material like iron, coal, and scrap to be consumed in the fires of production in order to swell the figures of output. . . .

Most of the excesses against which the disillusioned intellectuals of the West protested did not at first concern their own professional fields. They protested as *human beings* against the degradation imposed on other human beings; or as *socialists* against mounting inequalities of power and position which, in fact, produced new class distinctions; or as *Marxists* against the wilful disregard of objective historical conditions, and the blindness to the limits of endurance of human flesh. To all such protests came the reply, "reasons of state." Those who received this reply confess that although they could not *see* these "reasons of state," they were puzzled and confused by the retort. After all, there are so many variables in history, the future is so indeterminate, who knows with certainty what is necessary for what?

But there was one kind of persecution for which the excuse "reasons of state" could not be offered with the slightest plausibility. This was the cultural terror which raged in every field of the arts and sciences. All of these Western intellectuals lived in countries in which the slightest attempt to suppress a book or painting or a piece of music was sure to meet with fierce public opposition even when the censorship was tangential. And at the worst, restrictions affected sales, not one's freedom and not one's life. To undergo the experience of a *total* censorship and control shocked and stunned them. For it was a control not only over what was written but also over what was painted and sung, not only over political thought but over thought in philosophy and science, not only over *what* was created but also over *how* it was created—the style and manner as well as theme and content. Nothing like it has ever existed in the modern world. In making art and philosophy a matter for the police, it violated the sense of dignity and authenticity among these writers and artist and thinkers of the West. It also affronted their sense of integrity as craftsmen.

It had been hard enough for them to accept Stalin's description of the intellectual as "an engineer of the human soul." When the engineer was required, however, to build not only to another's specifications but according to technical rules and laws laid down by those who had never undergone the discipline and training of the craftsmen, they felt that some kind of atavistic cultural barbarism was being forced upon them. When, on top of this, the penalties and sanctions of refusing to knuckle under entailed, because of the state monopoly of all means of publication and communication, the withdrawal of the means of life for the dependent thinker and writer and his family, and in stubborn cases deportation and death, mystification gave way to passionate revulsion.

They were mystified because of the demonstrable uselessness of these cultural purges to the declared objectives of the Soviet regime. What bearings, for example, on any declared social policy were involved in the purge of Soviet physicists and astronomers for expressing disbelief in absolute space and time, a corollary of the theory of relativity? Or the condemnation of abstraction in modern art, romanticism in the novel, formalism in poetry, and atonality in music? The decrees laid down with the awful authority of the Central Committee of the Communist Party and specifying the correct line in these fields must be read in order to realize how minutely this control extended to the very details of the arts and sciences. Or one could cite the dogmas of "Soviet biology"—a phrase reminiscent of late unlamented "Nazi biology"—which renders taboo the Mendelian-Morgan theory of gene transmission in favor of Engel's Lamarckian notion, already disproved in his day, concerning the inheritance of acquired characters.

Not even this theory has any logical consequences of a political nature.

Professor H. J. Muller, the famous American geneticist and Nobel Prize winner, who witnessed at firsthand the tragic purge of Russian biologists, has observed that one can just as well argue from the theory of inherited acquired characters that the children of the ruling classes, because of the advantages of their environment, become superior types of human beings in comparison with the children of the masses, as that any human being can be transformed by environmental changes into a genius. Needless to say both inferences are false. In insisting that the truth of a scientific theory had to be judged by its alleged social or political consequences, the Soviet regime, to the amazement of the Western intellectuals, was challenging what had become axiomatic since the time of Galileo. . . .

It would be inappropriate to conclude this survey of political disillusionment without some evaluation of the weaknesses in the outlook of these Western intellectuals which contributed to their tragic self-deception. Even granting the partial truth of their plea that it was not so much *they* who changed as the Soviet system, it still remains undeniable that they were at fault in not conceiving the possibilities of change. But much more than this can be said in criticism. Even when all allowances are made for human fallibility their responsibility for their own illusions remains heavy.

First, they looked to politics for something politics alone can never bring to the life of men—that absolute certainty, that emotional "sumptuosity of security," to use James' phrase, which, if attainable at all, can be most easily reached through a revealed religion they had already, and properly, rejected. In identifying themselves with those in the seats of power, they abdicated their true functions as intellectuals—to be the critical conscience of the smug and contented; and to fulfill their mission as the creatively possessed, the eternal questers after truth under all conditions. There is no loyalty to any community or state or party or church which absolves the individual from loyalty to himself. Whatever good the "saving remnant" can bring to the world, it must at least save the purity of the enkindling flame which by accident of natural grace burns within them.

Secondly, in their zeal for salvation by total political faith, they forgot that politics is always made by men, and that no doctrine or institution is a safeguard against its own abuses. They were doomed to be disillusioned because they forgot that no social change can make gods or even angels out of men, that to be human is to be tempted, and that no one can be forever tempted without erring either out of weakness or ignorance. This is another way of saying that they were naïve and immature about human psychology.

Third, they made the mistake of all the typically *religieux* of forgetting that in the affairs of *this* world, at least, faith can never be a substitute for intelligence. The transformation of the economic order is not a single problem that can be settled by fiat, poetic or philosophical. It is a series of problems, all very difficult, requiring prolonged study, in the absence of which a talent with paint or words or tones is not a sufficient qualification. They were immature in imagining that the field of economic behavior, from which as a youth the great physicist, Planck, had withdrawn because of its difficulty, could be stormed with the weapons of moral indignation.

Fourth, they had abandoned too soon their own heritage of political democracy. They grossly underestimated the power of the self-corrective procedures of democracy to remedy, and in time to abolish, the major economic disabilities and injustices of our age. Intent upon viewing everything *else* in historical perspective, they refused to take an historical perspective to Western democracy, and to observe the substantial progress that had been made since the time Marx described the pitiful conditions of the English proletariat in *Capital,* a book so sacred to most of them that they never read it. They failed to see that, so long as the processes of political democracy remained intact, it was possible to carry the moral imperatives of the democratic way of life just as far as our courage, effort and powers of persuasion reached.

Fifth, they did not understand the genuine sense in which the social problem is a moral problem, i.e., that no social institution or system is an end in itself but a means for realizing the primary values of security, freedom, justice, knowledge, and kindness. Since the world is just as much a consequence of the means we use as of the end we profess, the end that actually comes to be depends upon the moral qualities of the means used. They had often heard that the end justifies the means but they never stopped to examine the evidence in order to see whether the means used were actually bringing the end-in-view closer or pushing it farther away. Even if they had, it is doubtful whether they would have recognized negative evidence. For the strange fact is that despite their assurance of the scientific character of their convictions, none of them could indicate, even theoretically, what possible evidence would lead them to abandon or modify their political beliefs. Everything that happened counted as positive evidence. Until their basic attitude changed, experience could never refute what they held to be empirical truths.

Whatever the responsibility of these writers for their own illusions, the record of their disillusionment is a record of growing intellectual and emotional maturity. No one has a right to be censorious of them, and least of all those who complacently accept all social changes, whose emotions of sympathy for their fellowman are never engaged, and who leave all the risks of thought and action to others. What was possible to believe in 1919 or 1929 was no longer possible in 1939 except to the morally obtuse or corrupt. The very existence of this literature is a challenge to subsequent generations of writers who feel called to enlist themselves as foot-soldiers in a political crusade. We should be grateful to them for providing texts not only in the costs of human folly but in the grandeur of human faith and humility.

As long as there are human beings there will always be ideals and illusions. They cannot be foresworn. But perhaps the greatest lesson to which this literature points is that good sense in the quest for the good life in the good society depends not so much on *what* ideals are held as on *how* they are held; not so much on the nature of our beliefs as on the methods by which they are reached.

Underlying all other differences among human beings is the difference between the absolutist and the experimental temper of mind. The first converts its unreflective prejudices into first principles, and its shifting certitudes into a fanaticism of virtue which closes the gates of mercy against all who disagree. The second, although resolute in action, knows that finality of judgment is not possible to men, and is therefore prepared to review the evidence on which it stakes its ultimate commitments. It is this willingness to reconsider first principles in the light of relevant evidence and other alternatives which is the sign of both the liberal and the mature mind.

THE RESENTMENT AND THE ANTI-CAPI-TALISTIC BIAS OF AMERICAN INTEL-LECTUALS

Ludwig von Mises

In A SOCIETY based on caste and status, the individual can ascribe adverse fate to conditions beyond his own control. He is a slave because the superhuman powers that determine all becoming had assigned him this rank. It is not his doing, and there is no reason for him to be ashamed of his humbleness. His wife cannot find fault with his station. If she were to tell him: "Why are you not a duke? If you were a duke, I would be a duchess," he would reply: "If I had been born the son of a duke, I would not have married you, a slave girl, but the daughter of another duke; that you are not a duchess is exclusively your own fault; why were you not more clever in the choice of your parents?"

It is quite another thing under capitalism. Here everybody's station in life depends on his own doing. Everybody whose ambitions have not been fully gratified knows very well that he has missed chances, that he has been tried and found wanting by his fellow man. If his wife upbraids him: "Why do you make only eighty dollars a week? If you were as smart as your former pal, Paul, you would be a foreman and I would enjoy a better life," he becomes conscious of his own inferiority and feels humiliated.

The much talked about sternness of capitalism consists in the fact that it handles everybody according to his contribution to the well-being of his fellow men. The sway of the principle, *to each according to his accomplishments,* does not allow of any excuse for personal shortcomings. Everybody knows very well that there are people like himself who succeeded where he himself failed. Everybody knows that many of those whom he envies are self-made men who started from the same point from which he himself started. And, much worse, he knows that all other people know it too. He reads in the eyes of his wife and his children the silent reproach: "Why have you not been smarter?" He sees how people admire those who have been more successful than he and look with contempt or with pity on his failure.

What makes many feel unhappy under capitalism is the fact that capitalism grants to each the opportunity to attain the most desirable positions which, of course, can only be attained by a few. Whatever a man may have gained for himself, it is mostly a mere fraction of what his ambition has impelled him to win. There are always before his eyes people who have succeeded where he failed. There are fellows who have outstripped him and against whom he nurtures, in his subconsciousness, inferiority complexes. Such is the attitude of the tramp against the man with a regular job, the factory hand against the foreman, the executive against the vice-president, the vice-president against the company's president, the man who is worth three hundred thousand dollars against the millionaire and so on. Everybody's self-reliance and moral equilibrium are undermined by the spectacle of those who have given proof of greater abilities and capacities. Everybody is aware of his own defeat and insufficiency.

The long line of German authors who radically rejected the "Western" ideas of the Enlightenment and the social philosophy of rationalism, utilitarianism and laissez faire as well as the policies advanced by these schools of thought was opened by Justus Möser. One of the novel principles which aroused Möser's anger was the demand that the promotion of army officers and civil servants should depend on personal merit and ability and not on the incumbent's ancestry and noble lineage, his age and length of service. Life in a society in which success would exclusively depend on personal merit would, says Möser, simply be unbearable. As human nature is, everybody is prone to overrate his own worth and deserts. If a man's station in life is conditioned by factors other than his inherent excellence, those who remain at the bottom of the ladder can acquiesce in this outcome and, knowing their own worth, still preserve their dignity and self-respect. But it is different if merit alone decides. Then the unsuccessful feel themselves insulted and humiliated. Hate and enmity against all those who superseded them must result.

The price and market system of capitalism is such a society in which merit and achievements determine a man's success or failure. Whatever one may think of Möser's bias against the merit principle, one must admit that he was right in describing one of its psychological consequences. He had an insight into the feelings of those who had been tried and found wanting.

In order to console himself and to restore his self-assertion, such a man is in search of a scapegoat. He tries to persuade himself that he failed through no fault of his own. He is at least as brilliant, efficient and industrious as those who outshine him. Unfortunately this nefarious social order of ours does not accord the prizes to the most meritorious men; it crowns the dishonest unscrupulous scoundrel, the swindler, the exploiter, the "rugged individualist." What made himself fail was his honesty. He was too decent to resort to the base tricks to which his successful rivals owe their ascendancy. As conditions are under capitalism, a man is forced to choose between virtue and poverty on the one hand, and vice and riches on the other. He, himself, thank God, chose the former alternative and rejected the latter.

This search for a scapegoat is an attitude of people living under the social order which treats everybody according to his contribution to the well-being of his fellow men and where thus everybody is the founder of his own fortune. In such a society each member whose ambitions have not been fully satisfied resents the fortune of all those who succeeded better. The fool releases these feelings in slander and defamation. The more sophisticated do not indulge in personal calumny. They sublimate their hatred into a philosophy, the philosophy of anti-capitalism, in order to render inaudible the inner voice that tells them that their failure is entirely their own fault. Their fanaticism in defending their critique of capitalism is precisely due to the fact that they are fighting their own awareness of its falsity.

The suffering from frustrated ambition is peculiar to people living in a society of equality under the law. It is not caused by equality under the law, but by the fact that in a society of equality under the law the inequality of men with regard to intellectual abilities, will power and application becomes visible. The gulf between what a man is and achieves and what he thinks of his own abilities and achievements is pitilessly revealed. Daydreams of a "fair" world which would treat him according to his "real worth" are the refuge of all those plagued by a lack of self-knowledge.

The common man as a rule does not have the opportunity of consorting with people who have succeeded better than he has. He moves in the circle of other common men. He never meets his boss socially. He never learns from personal experience how different an entrepreneur or an executive is with regard to all those abilities and faculties which are required for successfully serving the consumers. His envy and the resentment it engenders are not directed against a living being of flesh and blood, but against pale abstractions like "management," "capital" and "Wall Street." It is impossible to abominate such a faint shadow with the same bitterness of feeling that one may bear against a fellow creature whom one encounters daily.

It is different with people whom special conditions of their occupation or their family affiliation bring into personal contact with the winners of the prizes which—as they believe—by rights should have been given to themselves. With them the feelings of frustrated ambition become especially poignant because they engender hatred of concrete living beings. They loathe capitalism because it has assigned to this other man the position they themselves would like to have.

Such is the case with those people who are commonly called the intellectuals. Take for instance the physicians. Daily routine and experience make every doctor cognizant of the fact that there exists a hierarchy in which all medical men are graded according to their merits and achievements. Those more eminent than he himself is, those whose methods and innovations he must learn and practice in order to be up to date were his classmates in the medical school, they served with him as internes, they attend with him the meetings of medical associations. He meets them at the bedside of patients as well as in social gatherings. Some of them are his personal friends or related to him, and they all behave toward him with the utmost civility and address him as their dear colleague. But they tower far above him in the appreciation of the public and often also in height of income. They have outstripped him and now belong to another class of men. When he compares himself with them, he feels humiliated. But he must watch himself carefully lest anybody notice his resentment and envy. Even the slightest indication of such feelings would be looked upon as very bad manners and would depreciate him in the eyes of everybody. He must swallow down his mortification and divert his wrath toward a vicarious target. He indicts society's economic organization, the nefarious system of capitalism. But for this unfair regime his abilities and talents, his zeal and his achievements would have brought him the rich reward they deserve.

It is the same with many lawyers and teachers, artists and actors, writers and journalists, architects and scientific research workers, engineers and chemists. They, too, feel frustrated because they are vexed by the ascendancy of their more successful colleagues, their former schoolfellows and cronies. Their resentment is deepened by precisely those codes of professional conduct and ethics that throw a veil of comradeship and colleagueship over the reality of competition.

To understand the intellectual's abhorrence of capitalism one must realize that in his mind this system is incarnated in a definite number of compeers whose success he resents and whom he makes responsible for the frustration of his own farflung ambitions. His passionate dislike of capitalism is a mere blind for his hatred of some successful "colleagues."

The anti-capitalistic bias of the intellectuals is a phenomenon not limited to one or a few countries only. But it is more general and more bitter in the United States than it is in the European countries. To explain this rather surprising fact one must deal with what one calls "society" or, in French, also *le monde.*

In Europe "society" includes all those eminent in any sphere of activity. Statesmen and parliamentary leaders, the heads of the various departments of the civil service, publishers and editors of the main newspapers and magazines, prominent writers, scientists, artists, actors, musicians, engineers, lawyers and physicians form together with outstanding businessmen and scions of aristocratic and patrician families what is considered the good society. They come into contact with one another at dinner and tea parties, charity balls and bazaars, at first-nights, and varnishing-days; they frequent the same restaurants, hotels and resorts. When they meet, they take their pleasure in conversation about intellectual matters, a mode of social intercourse first developed in Italy of the Renaissance, perfected in the Parisian salons and later imitated by the "society" of all important cities of Western and Central Europe. New ideas and ideologies find their response in these social gatherings before they begin to influence broader circles. One cannot deal with the history of the fine arts and literature in the nineteenth century without analyzing the role "society" played in encouraging or discouraging their protagonists.

Access to European society is open to everybody who has distinguished himself in any field. It may be easier to people of noble ancestry and great wealth than to commoners with modest incomes. But neither riches nor titles can give to a member of this set the rank and prestige that is the reward of great personal distinction. The stars of the Parisian salons are not the millionaires, but the members of the Académie Française. The intellectuals prevail and the others feign at least a lively interest in intellectual concerns.

Society in this sense is foreign to the American scene. What is called "society" in the United States almost exclusively consists of the richest families. There is little social intercourse between the successful businessmen and the nation's eminent authors, artists and scientists. Those listed in the Social Register do not meet socially the molders of public opinion and the harbingers of the ideas that will determine the future of the nation. Most of the "socialites" are not interested in books and ideas. When they meet and do not play cards, they gossip about persons and talk more about sports than about cultural matters. But even those who are not averse to reading, consider writers, scientists and artists as people with whom they do not want to consort. An almost unsurmountable gulf separates "society" from the intellectuals.

It is possible to explain the emergence of this situation historically. But such an explanation does not alter the facts. Neither can it remove or alleviate the resentment with which the intellectuals react to the contempt in which they are held by the members of "society." American authors or scientists are prone to consider the wealthy businessman as a barbarian, as a man exclusively intent upon making money. The professor despises the alumni who are more interested in the university's football team than in its scholastic achievements. He feels insulted if he learns that the coach gets a higher salary than an eminent professor of philosophy. The men whose research has given rise to new methods of production hate the businessmen who are merely interested in the cash value of their research work. It is very significant that such a large number of American research physicists sympathize with socialism or communism. As they are ignorant of economics and realize that the university teachers of economics are also opposed to what they disparagingly call the profit system, no other attitude can be expected from them.

If a group of people secludes itself from the rest of the nation, especially also from its intellectual leaders, in the way American "socialites" do, they unavoidably become the target of rather hostile criticisms on the part of those whom they keep out of their own circles. The exclusivism practiced by the American rich has made them in a certain sense outcasts. They may take a vain pride in their own distinction. What they fail to see is that their self-chosen segregation isolates them and kindles animosities which make the intellectuals inclined to favor anti-capitalistic policies.

THE INTELLECTUALS AND SOCIALISM

F. A. Hayek

IN ALL democratic countries, in the United States even more than elsewhere, a strong belief prevails that the influence of the intellectuals on politics is negligible. This is no doubt true of the power of intellectuals to make their peculiar opinions of the moment influence decisions, of the extent to which they can sway the popular vote on questions on which they differ from the current views of the masses. Yet over somewhat longer periods they have probably never exercised so great an influence as they do today in those countries. This power they wield by shaping public opinion.

In the light of recent history it is somewhat curious that this decisive power of the professional secondhand dealers in ideas should not yet be more generally recognized. The political development of the Western World during the last hundred years furnishes the clearest demonstration. Socialism has never and nowhere been at first a working class movement. It is by no means an obvious remedy for an obvious evil which the interests of that class will necessarily demand. It is a construction of theorists, deriving from certain tendencies of abstract thought with which for a long time only the intellectuals were familiar; and it required long efforts by the intellectuals before the working classes could be persuaded to adopt it as their program.

In every country that has moved toward socialism the phase of the development in which socialism becomes a determining influence on politics has been preceded for many years by a period during which socialist ideals governed the thinking of the more active intellectuals. In Germany this stage had been reached toward the end of the last century; in England and France, about the time of the first World War. To the casual observer it would seem as if the United States had reached this phase after World War II and that the attraction of a planned and directed economic system is now as strong among the American intellectuals as it ever was among their German or English fellows. Experience suggests that once this phase has been reached it is merely a question of time until the views now held by the intellectuals become the governing force of politics.

Reprinted from *The University of Chicago Law Review* (Spring, 1949), pp. 417-420, 421-423, 425-433, by permission of the author and the publisher, The University of Chicago Press.

The character of the process by which the views of the intellectuals influence the politics of tomorrow is therefore of much more than academic interest. Whether we merely wish to foresee or attempt to influence the course of events, it is a factor of much greater importance than is generally understood. What to the contemporary observer appears as the battle of conflicting interests has indeed often been decided long before in a clash of ideas confined to narrow circles. Paradoxically enough, however, in general only the parties of the Left have done most to spread the belief that it was the numerical strength of the opposing material interests which decided political issues, whereas in practice these same parties have regularly and successfully acted as if they understood the key position of the intellectuals. Whether by design or driven by the force of circumstances, they have always directed their main effort toward gaining the support of this "elite," while the more conservative groups have acted, as regularly but unsuccessfully, on a more naive view of mass democracy and have usually vainly tried directly to reach and to persuade the individual voter.

The term intellectuals, however, does not at once convey a true picture of the large class to which we refer and the fact that we have no better name by which to describe what we have called the secondhand dealers in ideas is not the least of the reasons why their power is not better understood. Even persons who use the word intellectual mainly as a term of abuse are still inclined to withhold it from many who undoubtedly perform that characteristic function. This is neither that of the original thinker nor that of the scholar or expert in a particular field of thought. The typical intellectual need be neither: he need not possess special knowledge of anything in particular, nor need he even be particularly intelligent, to perform his role as intermediary in the spreading of ideas. What qualifies him for his job is the wide range of subjects on which he can readily talk and write, and a position or habits through which he becomes acquainted with new ideas sooner than those to whom he addresses himself.

Until one begins to list all the professions and activities which belong to this class, it is difficult to realize how numerous it is, how the scope for its activities constantly increases in modern society, and how dependent on it we all have become. The class does not consist only of journalists, teachers, ministers, lecturers, publicists, radio commentators, writers of fiction, cartoonists, and artists—all of whom may be masters of the technique of conveying ideas but are usually amateurs so far as the substance of what they convey is concerned. The class also includes many professional men and technicians, such as scientists and doctors, who through their habitual intercourse with the printed word become carriers of new ideas outside their own fields and who, because of their expert knowledge on their own subjects, are listened to with respect on most others. There is little that the ordinary man of today learns about events or ideas except through the medium of this class; and outside our special fields of work we are in this respect almost all ordinary men, dependent for our information and instruction on those who make it their job to keep abreast of opinion. It is the intellectuals in this sense who decide what views and opinions are to reach us, which facts are important enough to be told to us and in what form and from what angle they are to be presented. Whether we shall ever learn of the results of the work of the expert and the original thinker depends mainly on their decision.

The layman, perhaps, is not fully aware to what extent even the popular reputations of scientists and scholars are made by that class and are inevitably affected by its views on subjects which have little to do with the merits of the real achievements. And it is specially significant for our problem that every scholar can probably name several instances from his field of men who have undeservedly achieved a popular reputation as great scientists solely because they hold what the intellectuals regard as "progressive" political views; but I have yet to come across a single instance where such a scientific pseudo-reputation has been bestowed for political reasons on a scholar of more conservative leanings. This creation of reputations by the intellectuals is particularly important in the fields where the results of expert studies are not used by other specialists but depend on the political decision of the public at large. There is indeed scarcely a better illustration of this than the attitude which professional economists have taken to the growth of such doctrines as socialism or protectionism. There was probably at no time a majority of economists, who were recognized as such by their peers, favorable to socialism (or, for that matter, to protection). In all probability it is even true to say that no other similar group of students contains so high a proportion of its members decidedly opposed to socialism (or protection). This is the more significant as in recent times it is as likely as not that it was an early interest in socialist schemes for reform which led a man to choose economics for his profession. Yet it is not the predominant views of the experts but the views of a minority, mostly of rather doubtful standing in their profession, which are taken up and spread by the intellectuals.

The all-pervasive influence of the intellectuals in contemporary society is still further strengthened by the growing importance of "organization." It is a common but probably mistaken belief that the increase of organization increases the influence of the expert or specialist. This may be true of the expert administrator and organizer, if there are such people, but hardly of the expert in any particular field of knowledge. It is rather the person whose general knowledge is supposed to qualify him to appreciate expert testimony, and to judge between the experts from different fields, whose power is enhanced. The point which is important for us, however, is that the scholar who becomes a university president, the scientist who takes charge of an institute or foundation, the scholar who becomes an editor or the active promoter of an organization serving a particular cause, all rapidly cease to be scholars or experts and become intellectuals in our sense, people who judge all issues not by their specific merits but, in the characteristic manner of intellectuals, solely in the light of certain fashionable general ideas. The number of such institutions which breed intellectuals and increase their number and powers grows every day. Almost all the "experts" in the mere technique of getting knowledge over are, with respect to the subject matter which they handle, intellectuals and not experts. . . .

It is not surprising that the real scholar or expert and the practical man of affairs often feel contemptuous about the intellectual, are disinclined to recognize his power, and are resentful when they discover it. Individually they find the intellectuals mostly to be people who understand nothing in particular especially well, and whose judgment on matters they themselves understand shows little sign of special wisdom. But it would be a fatal mistake to underestimate their power for this reason. Even though their knowledge may be often superficial and their intelligence limited, this does not alter the fact that it is their judgment which mainly determines the views on which society will act in the not too distant future. It is no exaggeration to say that once the more active part of the intellectuals have been converted to a set of beliefs, the process by which these become generally accepted is almost automatic and irresistible. They are the organs which modern society has developed for spreading knowledge and ideas and it is their convictions and opinions which operate as the sieve through which all new conceptions must pass before they can reach the masses.

It is of the nature of the intellectual's job that he must use his own knowledge and convictions in performing his daily task. He occupies his position because he possesses, or has had to deal from day to day with, knowledge which his employer in general does not possess, and his activities can therefore be directed by others only to a limited extent. And just because the intellectuals are mostly intellectually honest it is inevitable that they should follow their own convictions whenever they have discretion and that they should give a corresponding slant to everything that passes through their hands. Even where the direction of policy is in the hand of men of affairs of different views, the execution of policy will in general be in the hand of intellectuals, and it is frequently the decision on the detail which determines the net effect. We find this illustrated in almost all fields of contemporary society. Newspapers in "capitalist" ownership, universities presided over by "reactionary" governing bodies, broadcasting systems owned by conservative governments have all been known to influence public opinion in the direction of socialism, because this was the conviction of the personnel. This has often happened not only in spite of but perhaps even because of the attempts of those at the top to control opinion and to impose principles of orthodoxy.

The effect of this filtering of ideas through the convictions of a class which is constitutionally disposed to certain views is by no means confined to the masses. Outside his special field the expert is generally no less dependent on this class and scarcely less influenced by their selection. The result of this is that today in most parts of the Western World even the most determined opponents of socialism derive from socialist sources their knowledge on most subjects on which they have no firsthand information. With many of the more general preconceptions of socialist thought the connection of their more practical proposals is by no means at once obvious, and in consequence many men who believe themselves to be determined opponents of that system of thought become in fact effective spreaders of its ideas. Who does not know the practical man who in his own field denounces socialism as "pernicious rot" but when he steps outside his subject spouts socialism like any left journalist?

In no other field has the predominant influence of the socialist intellectuals been felt more strongly during the last hundred years than in the contacts between different national civilizations. It would go far beyond the limits of this article to trace the causes and significance of the highly important fact that in the modern world the intellectuals provide almost the only approach to an international community. It is this which mainly accounts for the extraordinary spectacle that for generations the supposedly "capitalist" West has been lending its moral and material support almost exclusively to those ideological movements in the countries farther east which aimed at undermining Western civilization; and that at the same time the information which the Western public has obtained about events in Central and Eastern Europe has almost inevitably been colored by a socialist bias. Many of the "educational" activities of the American forces of occupation in Germany have furnished clear and recent examples of this tendency.

A proper understanding of the reasons which tend to incline so many of the intellectuals toward socialism is thus most important. The first point here which those who do not share this bias ought to face frankly is that it is neither selfish interests nor evil intentions but mostly honest convictions and good intentions which determine the intellectuals' views. In fact it is necessary to recognize that on the whole the typical intellectual is today more likely to be a socialist the more he is guided by good will and intelligence and that on the plane of purely intellectual argument he will generally be able to make out a better case than the majority of his opponents within his class. If we still think him wrong we must recognize that it may be genuine error which leads the well-meaning and intelligent people who occupy those key positions in our society to spread views which to us appear a threat to our civilization.[1] Nothing could be more important than to try and understand the sources of this error in order that we should be able to counter it. Yet those who are generally regarded as the representatives of the existing order and who believe that they comprehend the dangers of socialism are usually very far from such understanding. They tend to regard the socialist intellectuals as nothing more than a pernicious bunch of highbrow radicals without appreciating their influence, and, by their whole attitude to them, tend to drive them even further into opposition to the existing order.

If we are to understand this peculiar bias of a large section of the intellectuals we must be clear about two points. The first is that they generally judge all particular issues exclusively in the light of certain general ideas; the second that the characteristic errors of any age are frequently derived from some genuine new truths it has discovered, and they are erroneous applications of new generalizations which have proved their value in other fields. The conclusion to which we shall be led by a full consideration of these facts will be that the effective refutation of such errors will frequently require further intellectual advance, and often advance on points which are very abstract and may seem very remote from the practical issues.

It is perhaps the most characteristic feature of the intellectual that he judges new ideas not by their specific merits but by the readiness with which they fit into his general conceptions, into the picture of the world which he regards as modern or advanced. It is through their influence on him and on his choice of opinions on particular issues that the power of ideas for good and evil grows in proportion with their generality, abstractness, and even vagueness. As he knows little about the particular issues, his criterion must be consistency with his other views, suitability to combine them into a coherent picture of the world. Yet this selection from the multitude of new ideas presenting themselves at every moment creates the characteristic climate of opinion, the dominant *Weltanschauung* of a period which will be favorable to the reception of some opinions and unfavorable to others, and which will make the intellectual readily accept one conclusion and reject another without a real understanding of the issues.

In some respects the intellectual is indeed closer to the philosopher than to any specialist, and the philosopher is in more than one sense a sort of prince among the intellectuals. Although his influence is farther removed from practical affairs and correspondingly slower and more difficult to trace than that of the ordinary intellectual, it is of the same kind and in the long run even more powerful than that of the latter. It is the same endeavor

1. It was therefore not (as has been suggested by one reviewer of *The Road to Serfdom*, Professor J. Schumpeter), "politeness to a fault" but profound conviction of the importance of this which made me, in Professor Schumpeter's words, "hardly ever attribute to opponents anything beyond intellectual error."

toward a synthesis, pursued more methodically, the same judgment of particular views in so far as they fit into a general system of thought rather than by their specific merits, the same striving after a consistent world view, which for both forms the main basis for accepting or rejecting ideas. For this reason the philosopher has probably a greater influence over the intellectuals than any other scholar or scientist, and more than anyone else determines the manner in which the intellectuals exercise their censorship function. The popular influence of the scientific specialist begins to rival that of the philosopher only when he ceases to be a specialist and commences to philosophize about the progress of his subject—and usually only after he has been taken up by the intellectuals for reasons which have little to do with his scientific eminence.

The "climate of opinion" of any period is thus essentially a set of very general preconceptions by which the intellectual judges the importance of new facts and opinions. These preconceptions are mainly applications to what seem to him the most significant aspects of scientific achievements, a transfer to other fields of what has particularly impressed him in the work of the specialists. One could give a long list of such intellectual fashions and catchwords which in the course of two or three generations have in turn dominated the thinking of the intellectuals. Whether it was the "historical approach" or the theory of evolution, nineteenth century determinism and the belief in the predominant influence of environment as against heredity, the theory of relativity or the belief in the power of the unconscious—every one of these general conceptions has been made the touchstone by which innovations in different fields have been tested. It seems as if the less specific or precise (or the less understood) these ideas are, the wider may be their influence. Sometimes it is no more than a vague impression rarely put into words which thus wields a profound influence. Such beliefs as that deliberate control or conscious organization is also in social affairs always superior to the results of spontaneous processes which are not directed by a human mind, or that any order based on a plan laid down beforehand must be better than one formed by the balancing of opposing forces, have in this way profoundly affected political development. . . .

In particular, there can be little doubt that the manner in which during the last hundred years man has learned to organize the forces of nature has contributed a great deal toward the creation of the belief that a similar control of the forces of society would bring comparable improvements in human conditions. That, with the application of engineering techniques, the direction of all forms of human activity according to a single coherent plan, should prove to be as successful in society as it has been in innumerable engineering tasks is too plausible a conclusion not to seduce most of those who are elated by the achievement of the natural sciences. It must indeed be admitted both that it would require powerful arguments to counter the strong presumption in favor of such a conclusion and that these arguments have not yet been adequately stated. It is not sufficient to point out the defects of particular proposals based on this kind of reasoning. The argument will not lose its force until it has been conclusively shown why what has proved so eminently successful in producing advances in so many fields should have limits to its usefulness and become positively harmful if extended beyond these limits. This is a task which has not yet been satisfactorily performed and which will have to be achieved before this particular impulse toward socialism can be removed.

This, of course, is only one of many instances where further intellectual advance is needed if the harmful ideas at present current are to be refuted, and where the course which we shall travel will ultimately be decided by the discussion of very abstract issues. It is not enough for the man of affairs to be sure, from his intimate knowledge of a particular field, that the theories of socialism which are derived from more general ideas will prove impracticable. He may be perfectly right, and yet his resistance will be overwhelmed and all the sorry consequences which he foresees will follow if he is not supported by an effective refutation of the *idées mères*. So long as the intellectual gets the better of the general argument, the most valid objections of the specific issue will be brushed aside.

This is not the whole story, however. The forces which influence recruitment to the ranks of the intellectuals operate in the same direction and help to explain why so many of the most able among them lean toward socialism. There are of course as many differences of opinion among intellectuals as among other groups of people; but it seems to be true that it is on the whole the more active, intelligent, and original men among the intellectuals who most frequently incline toward socialism, while its opponents are often of an inferior caliber. This is true particularly during the early stages of the infiltration of socialist ideas; later, although outside intellectual circles it may still be an act of courage to profess socialist convictions, the pressure of opinion among intellectuals will often be so strongly in favor of socialism that it requires more strength and independence for a man to resist it than to join in what his fellows regard as modern views. Nobody, for instance, who is familiar with large numbers of university faculties (and from this point of view the majority of university teachers probably have to be classed as intellectuals rather than as experts) can remain oblivious to the fact that the most brilliant and successful teachers are today more likely than not to be socialists, while those who hold more conservative political views are as frequently mediocrities. This is of course by itself an important factor leading the younger generation into the socialist camp.

The socialist will, of course, see in this merely a proof that the more intelligent person is today bound to become a socialist. But this is far from being the necessary or even the most likely explanation. The main reason for this state of affairs is probably that, for the exceptionally able man who accepts the present order of society, a multitude of other avenues to influence and power are open, while to the disaffected and dissatisfied an intellectual career is the most promising path to both influence and the power to contribute to the achievement of his ideals. Even more than that: the more conservatively inclined man of first class ability will in general choose intellectual work (and the sacrifice in material reward which this choice usually entails) only if he enjoys it for its own sake. He is in consequence more likely to become an expert scholar rather than an intellectual in the specific sense of the word; while to the more radically minded the intellectual pursuit is more often than not a means rather than an end, a path to exactly that kind of wide influence which the professional intellectual exercises. It is therefore probably the fact, not that the more intelligent people are generally socialists, but that a much higher proportion of socialists among the best minds devote themselves to those intellectual pursuits which in modern society give them a decisive influence on public opinion.[2]

The selection of the personnel of the intellectuals is also closely connected with the predominant interest which they show in general and abstract ideas. Speculations about the possible entire reconstruction of society give the intellectual a fare much more to his taste than the more practical and short-run considerations of those who aim at a piecemeal improvement of the existing order. In particular, socialist thought owes its appeal to the young largely to its visionary character; the very courage to indulge in Utopian thought is in this respect a source of strength to the socialists which traditional liberalism sadly lacks. This difference operates in favor of socialism, not only because speculation about general principles provides an opportunity for the play of the imagination of those who are unencumbered by much knowledge of the facts of present-day life, but also because it satisfies a legitimate desire for the understanding of the rational basis of any social order and gives scope for the exercise of that constructive urge for which liberalism, after it had won its great victories, left few outlets. The intellectual, by his whole disposition, is uninterested in technical details or practical difficulties.

---

2. Related to this is another familiar phenomenon: there is little reason to believe that really first class intellectual ability for original work is any rarer among Gentiles than among Jews. Yet there can be little doubt that men of Jewish stock almost everywhere constitute a disproportionately large number of the intellectuals in our sense, that is of the ranks of the professional interpreters of ideas. This may be their special gift and certainly is their main opportunity in countries where prejudice puts obstacles in their way in other fields. It is probably more because they constitute so large a proportion of the intellectuals than for any other reason that they seem to be so much more receptive of socialist ideas than people of different stocks.

What appeal to him are the broad visions, the specious comprehension of the social order as a whole which a planned system promises.

This fact that the tastes of the intellectual were better satisfied by the speculations of the socialists proved fatal to the influence of the liberal tradition. Once the basic demands of the liberal programs seemed satisfied, the liberal thinkers turned to problems of detail and tended to neglect the development of the general philosophy of liberalism, which in consequence ceased to be a live issue offering scope for general speculation. Thus for something over half a century it has been only the socialists who have offered anything like an explicit program of social development, a picture of the future society at which they were aiming, and a set of general principles to guide decisions on particular issues. Even though, if I am right, their ideals suffer from inherent contradictions, and any attempt to put them into practice must produce something utterly different from what they expect, this does not alter the fact that their program for change is the only one which has actually influenced the development of social institutions. It is because theirs has become the only explicit general philosophy of social policy held by a large group, the only system or theory which raises new problems and opens new horizons, that they have succeeded in inspiring the imagination of the intellectuals.

The actual developments of society during this period were determined, not by a battle of conflicting ideals, but by the contrast between an existing state of affairs and that one ideal of a possible future society which the socialists alone held up before the public. Very few of the other programs which offered themselves provided genuine alternatives. Most of them were mere compromises or half-way houses between the more extreme types of socialism and the existing order. All that was needed to make almost any socialist proposal appear reasonable to these "judicious" minds which were constitutionally convinced that the truth must always lie in the middle between the extremes, was for some one to advocate a sufficiently more extreme proposal. There seemed to exist only one direction in which we could move and the only question seemed to be how fast and how far the movement should proceed.

The significance of the special appeal to the intellectuals which socialism derives from its speculative character will become clearer if we further contrast the position of the socialist theorist with that of his counterpart who is a liberal in the old sense of the word. This comparison will also lead us to whatever lesson we can draw from an adequate appreciation of the intellectual forces which are undermining the foundations of a free society.

Paradoxically enough, one of the main handicaps which deprives the liberal thinker of popular influence is closely connected with the fact that until socialism has actually arrived he has more opportunity of directly influencing decisions on current policy and that in consequence he is not only not tempted into that long run speculation which is the strength of the socialists, but actually discouraged from it, because any effort of this kind is likely to reduce the immediate good he can do. Whatever power he has to influence practical decisions he owes to his standing with the representatives of the existing order, and this standing he would endanger if he devoted himself to the kind of speculation which would appeal to the intellectuals and which through them could influence developments over longer periods. In order to carry weight with the powers that be he has to be "practical," "sensible," and "realistic." So long as he concerns himself with immediate issues he is rewarded with influence, material success, and popularity with those who up to a point share his general outlook. But these men have little respect for those speculations on general principles which shape the intellectual climate. Indeed, if he seriously indulges in such long run speculation he is apt to acquire the reputation of being "unsound" or even half a socialist, because he is unwilling to identify the existing order with the free system at which he aims.[3]

If, in spite of this, his efforts continue in the direction of general speculation, he soon discovers that it is unsafe to associate too closely with those who seem to share most of his convictions and he is soon driven into isolation. Indeed there can be few more thankless tasks at present than the essential one of developing the philosophical foundation on which the further development of a free society must be based. Since the man who undertakes it must accept much of the framework of the existing order, he will appear to many of the more speculatively minded intellectuals merely as a timid apologist of things as they are; at the same time he will be dismissed by the men of affairs as an impractical theorist. He is not radical enough for those who know only the world where "with ease together dwell the thoughts" and much too radical for those who see only how "hard in space together clash the things." If he takes advantage of such support as he can get from the men of affairs, he will almost certainly discredit himself with those on whom he depends for the spreading of his ideas. At the same time he will need most carefully to avoid anything resembling extravagance or over-statement. While no socialist theorist has ever been known to discredit him-

---

3. The most glaring recent example of such condemnation of a somewhat unorthodox liberal work as "socialist" has been provided by some comments on the late Henry Simons' *Economic Policy for a Free Society* (1948). One need not agree with the whole of this work and one may even regard some of the suggestions made in it as incompatible with a free society, and yet recognize it as one of the most important contributions made in recent times to our problem and as just the kind of work which is required to get discussion started on the fundamental issues. Even those who violently disagree with some of its suggestions should welcome it as a contribution which clearly and courageously raises the central problems of our time.

self with his fellows even by the silliest of proposals, the old-fashioned liberal will damn himself by an impracticable suggestion. Yet for the intellectuals he will still not be speculative or adventurous enough and the changes and improvements in the social structure he will have to offer will seem limited in comparison with what their less restrained imagination conceives.

At least in a society in which the main requisites of freedom have already been won and further improvements must concern points of comparative detail, the liberal program can have none of the glamour of a new invention. The appreciation of the improvements it has to offer requires more knowledge of the working of the existing society than the average intellectual possesses. The discussion of these improvements must proceed on a more practical level than that of the more revolutionary programs, thus giving a complexion which has little appeal for the intellectual and tending to bring in elements to whom he feels directly antagonistic. Those who are most familiar with the working of the present society are also usually interested in the preservation of particular features of that society which may not be defensible on general principles. Unlike the person who looks for an entirely new future order and who naturally turns for guidance to the theorist, the men who believe in the existing order also usually think that they understand it much better than any theorist and in consequence are likely to reject whatever is unfamiliar and theoretical.

The difficulty of finding genuine and disinterested support for a systematic policy for freedom is not new. In a passage of which the reception of a recent book of mine has often reminded me, Lord Acton long ago described how "[at] all times sincere friends of freedom have been rare, and its triumphs have been due to minorities, that have prevailed by associating themselves with auxiliaries whose objects differed from their own; and this association, which is always dangerous, has been sometimes disastrous, by giving to opponents just grounds of opposition. . . ."[4] More recently, one of the most distinguished living American economists has complained in a similar vein that the main task of those who believe in the basic principles of the capitalist system must frequently be to defend this system against the capitalists—indeed the great liberal economists, from Adam Smith to the present, have always known this.

The most serious obstacle which separates the practical men who have the cause of freedom genuinely at heart from those forces which in the realm of ideas decide the course of development is their deep distrust of theoretical speculation and their tendency to orthodoxy; this more than anything else, creates an almost impassable barrier between them and those

---

4. Acton, *The History of Freedom*, 1 (1922).

intellectuals who are devoted to the same cause and whose assistance is indispensable if the cause is to prevail. Although this tendency is perhaps natural among men who defend a system because it has justified itself in practice, and to whom its intellectual justification seems immaterial, it is fatal to its survival because it deprives it of the support it most needs. Orthodoxy of any kind, any pretense that a system of ideas is final and must be unquestioningly accepted as a whole, is the one view which of necessity antagonizes all intellectuals, whatever their views on particular issues. Any system which judges men by the completeness of their conformity to a fixed set of opinions, by their "soundness" or the extent to which they can be relied upon to hold approved views on all points, deprives itself of a support without which no set of ideas can maintain its influence in modern society. The ability to criticize accepted views, to explore new vistas and to experiment with new conceptions, provides the atmosphere without which the intellectual cannot breathe. A cause which offers no scope for these traits can have no support from him and is thereby doomed in any society which like ours, rests on his services.

It may be that a free society as we have known it carries in itself the forces of its own destruction, that once freedom has been achieved it is taken for granted and ceases to be valued, and that the free growth of ideas which is the essence of a free society will bring about the destruction of the foundations on which it depends. There can be little doubt that in countries like the United States the ideal of freedom has today less real appeal for the young man than it has in countries where they have learnt what its loss means. On the other hand, there is every sign that in Germany and elsewhere, to the young men who have never known a free society, the task of constructing one can become as exciting and fascinating as any socialist scheme which has appeared during the last hundred years. It is an extraordinary fact, though one which many visitors have experienced, that in speaking to German students about the principles of a liberal society one finds a more responsive and even enthusiastic audience than one can hope to find in any of the Western democracies. In Britain also there is already appearing among the young a new interest in the principles of true liberalism which certainly did not exist a few years ago.

Does this mean that freedom is valued only when it is lost, that the world must everywhere go through a dark phase of socialist totalitarianism before the forces of freedom can gather strength anew? It may be so, but I hope it need not be. Yet so long as the people who over longer periods determine public opinion continue to be attracted by the ideals of socialism, the trend will continue. If we are to avoid such a development we must be able to offer a new liberal program which appeals to the imagination. We must make the building of a free society once more an intellectual adventure, a deed of courage. What we lack is a liberal Utopia, a program which seems neither a mere defense of things as they are nor a diluted kind of socialism, but truly liberal radicalism which does not spare the susceptibilities of the mighty (including the trade unions), which is not too severely practical and which does not confine itself to what appears today as politically possible. We need intellectual leaders who are prepared to resist the blandishments of power and influence and who are willing to work for an ideal, however small may be the prospects of its early realization. They must be men who are willing to stick to principles and to fight for their full realization, however remote. The practical compromises they must leave to the politicians. Free trade or the freedom of opportunity are ideals which still may arouse the imaginations of large numbers, but a mere "reasonable freedom of trade" or a mere "relaxation of controls" are neither intellectually respectable nor likely to inspire any enthusiasm.

The main lesson which the true liberal must learn from the success of the socialists is that it was their courage to be Utopian which gained them the support of the intellectuals and therefore an influence on public opinion which is daily making possible what only recently seemed utterly remote. Those who have concerned themselves exclusively with what seemed practicable in the existing state of opinion have constantly found that even this has rapidly become politically impossible as the result of changes in a public opinion which they have done nothing to guide. Unless we can make the philosophic foundations of a free society once more a living intellectual issue, and its implementation a task which challenges the ingenuity and imagination of our liveliest minds, the prospects of freedom are indeed dark. But if we can regain that belief in the power of ideas which was the mark of liberalism at its greatest, the battle is not lost. The intellectual revival of liberalism is already under way in many parts of the world. Will it be in time?

THE TREATMENT OF CAPITALISM BY CONTINENTAL INTELLECTUALS

Bertrand de Jouvenel

To THE INTELLECTUAL the social device of capitalism offers a displeasing picture. Why? In his own terms, here are self-seeking men in quest of personal aggrandizement. How? By providing consumers with things they want or can be induced to want. The same intellectual, puzzlingly, is not shocked by the workings of hedonist democracy; here also self-seeking men accomplish their aggrandizement by promising to other men things they want or are induced to demand. The difference seems to lie mainly in that the capitalist delivers the goods. And all through the West the fulfilling of political promises seems to be a function of capitalist achievement. Another aspect of the capitalist device which makes it unpleasant to the intellectual is the "degradation of workers to the condition of mere instruments." In Kant's words, it is always immoral to treat other men as means and not as ends. Experience teaches us that this is not an uncommon behavior, nor is it peculiar to capitalism. It is Rousseau's view that such treatment is inherent in civilized society, which multiplies random contacts based on utility rather than on affection, and that it becomes more and more widespread as contacts increase and interests overlap. Marx's view is less philosophical, more dependent on history. The nascent capitalist, he says, found already at hand a population which had been treated as tools by previous exploiters before being seized by the enterprising bourgeois, and the existence of a proletariat which could be treated in such a way originated in the expropriation of the farmers. This is what obliged the workers, bereft of their own means of production, to work for others who disposed of such means. If this theory (obviously inspired by the enclosures) were true, capitalism would have found it most difficult to obtain "wage slaves" in the countries where land was most readily available (i.e., in the United States).

It is not impossible that the mental picture of capitalism has suffered from a dichotomy which classical economists found necessary for logical purposes —the dichotomy of the consumer and the worker. The entrepreneur was

Reprinted from *Capitalism and the Historians* (1954), edited by F. A. Hayek, pp. 97-123, by permission of the author, editor, and the publisher, The University of Chicago Press.

(385)

represented as serving the consumer and using the worker. Such a dichotomy can be introduced even in the case of Robinson Crusoe, whose physical resources (considered as "the worker") can be represented as exploited in the service of his needs (considered as "the consumer"). This reification of two aspects of the public was intellectually tenable at the outset of what is known as the capitalist era. Heretofore, indeed, the buying public of manufacturers had been sharply distinguished from the working public of artisans, engaged chiefly in producing luxuries consumed by the rich, who lived on unearned takings from the produce of the land. But precisely in the capitalist era the wage-earning producer of industrial consumer goods and the market buyer of such goods have become increasingly identified. It would be a striking illustration of social evolution to find out what fraction of manufactured consumer goods has gone to the wage-earners employed in manufacturing. This fraction has constantly increased under capitalism, so that the dichotomy has become ever a more theoretical concept. It is almost unnecessary to point out that the dichotomy is intellectually useful in any economy where division of labor obtains; in the same manner the Soviet worker is used in the service of the Soviet consumer. The difference lies in the fact that he is used more mercilessly as a worker and gets less as a consumer.

A large part of the Western intelligentsia of today forms and conveys a warped picture of our economic institutions. This is dangerous, since it tends to divert a salutary urge to reform from feasible constructive tasks to the unfeasible and the destructive. The historian's contribution to the distortion of the picture has been under discussion, especially his interpretation of the "Industrial Revolution." I have little to add. Historians have done their obvious duty in describing the miserable social conditions of which they found ample evidence. They have, however, proved exceptionally incautious in their interpretation of the facts. First, they seem to have taken for granted that a sharp increase in the extent of social awareness of and indignation about misery is a true index of increased misery; they seem to have given little thought to the possibility that such an increase might also be a function of new facilities of expression (due partly to a concentration of workers, partly to greater freedom of speech), of a growing philanthropic sensitivity (as evidenced by the fight for penal reforms), and of a new sense of the human power to change things, mooted by the Industrial Revolution itself. Second, they do not seem to have distinguished sufficiently between the sufferings attendant upon any great migration (and there was a migration to the towns) and those inflicted by the factory system. Third, they do not seem to have attached enough importance to the Demographic Revolution. Had they used the comparative method, they might have found that a massive influx into the towns, with the resultant squalor and pauperism, occurred as well in countries untouched by the Industrial Revolution, where they produced waves of beggars instead of underpaid workers. Given population pressure, would conditions have been better without capitalist development? The condition of underdeveloped and overcrowded countries may provide an answer.[1] Methodological oversights of this type, however, dwindle into insignificance in comparison with conceptual errors.

The vast improvement achieved in workers' conditions over the last hundred years is widely attributed to union pressure and good laws correcting an evil system. One may ask, on the other hand, whether this improvement would have occurred but for the achievements of this evil system, and whether political action has not merely shaken from the tree the fruit it had borne. The search for the true cause is not an irrelevant pursuit, since an erroneous attribution of merit may lead to the belief that fruit is produced by shaking trees. Lastly, one may ask whether the "hard times" so bitterly evoked, and for which capitalism is arraigned, were a specific feature of capitalist development or are an aspect of a rapid industrial development (without outside help) to be found as well under another social system. Does the Magnitogorsk of the 1930's compare so favorably with the Manchester of the 1830's?

It is remarkable that the historian should fail to "forgive" the horrors of a process which has played an obvious part in what he calls "progress," precisely in an age addicted to "historicism," where excuses are currently found for horrors going on today on the plea that they will lead to some good, an assertion as yet incapable of proof. Surely indignation is best expended on what is happening today, events which we may hope to influence, rather than on what is beyond recall. Nonetheless, instances readily come to mind of authors who have stressed the hardships of the British working classes in the nineteenth century while finding nothing to say about the violent impressing of Russian peasants into kolkhozes. Here bias is blatant.

Can we find specific reasons for the historian's bias? I think not. The attitude of the historian would present a special problem only if it could be shown that it was he who originally brought to light the evils of capitalism previously unnoticed by the remainder of the intelligentsia, thereby altering

---

1. Do we not see such countries in dire need of capital for the employment of surplus labor crowded off the land? Be it noted that such labor can be employed on terms which seem to us humane only on condition that its produce serves foreign and richer markets. But, in so far as it destines its wares for the home market, hours have to be long and pay short to make merchandise salable to a poor population. Indeed, the initial factories seeking to serve an ample fraction of the local population cannot fail to employ their workers on terms much lower than those which were previously commanded by artisans serving only a narrow market of wealthy landowners. Therefore the Industrial Revolution is logically accompanied at the outset by a fall in real wages, if one compares, somewhat unduly, the previous reward of the artisan with the present reward of the factory worker.

the point of view of his fellow-intellectuals. But this is not in accordance with the facts. Unfavorable views of capitalism, whole systems of thought directed against it, were prevalent in large sectors of the intelligentsia before historians exposed the past wrongs of capitalism or indeed before they paid any attention at all to social history. It is probably the main achievement of Marx to have fathered this pursuit, which originated and developed in an anticapitalist climate. The historian is no aimless fact-finder. His attention is drawn to certain problems under the influence of his own or other current preoccupations related to the present day. These induce him to seek certain data, which may have been rejected as negligible by former generations of historians; these he reads, using patterns of thought and value judgments which he shares with at least some contemporary thinkers. The study of the past thus always bears the imprint of present views. History, the science, moves with the times and is subject to the historical process. Furthermore, there is no philosophy of history but by the application of philosophy to history. To sum up, the historian's attitude reflects an attitude obtaining in the intelligentsia. If he manifests a bias, it is one pertaining to the intelligentsia in general. Therefore it is the intellectual's attitude which must claim our attention.

Sociology and social history are disciplines much favored nowadays. We would turn to them for help. Unfortunately, their scholars have given little or no attention to the problems centering on the intellectual. What is and what has been his place in society? To what tensions does it give rise? What are the specific traits of the intellectual's activity, and what complexes does it tend to create? How have the attitudes of the intellectual to society evolved, and what are the factors in this evolution? All these problems, and many more, should be tempting to social scientists. Their importance has been indicated by major thinkers (such as Pareto, Sorel, Michels, Schumpeter, and, first and foremost, Jean Jacques Rousseau). The infantry of science, so to speak, has not followed; it has left this vast and rewarding field of study uncharted. We must therefore make shift with the scanty data in our possession, and we may perhaps be excused for the clumsiness and blundering of an ill-equipped attempt.

The history of the Western intelligentsia during the last ten centuries falls easily into three parts. During the first period the intelligentsia is levitic; there are no intellectuals but those called and ordained to the service of God. They are the custodians and interpreters of the Word of God. In the second period we witness the rise of a secular intelligentsia, kings' lawyers being the first to appear; the development of the legal profession is for a long time the main source of secular intellectuals; amusers of noblemen, progressively raising their sights, provide another, very minor, source. This secular intelligentsia grows slowly in numbers but rapidly in influence and conducts a great fight against the clerical intelligentsia, which it gradually supersedes in the main functions of the intelligentsia. Then, in a third period coinciding with the Industrial Revolution, we find a fantastic proliferation of the secular intellectual, favored by the generalization of secular education and the rise of publishing (and eventually broadcasting) to the status of a major industry (an effect of the Industrial Revolution). This secular intelligentsia is by now far and away the most influential, and it is the subject of our study.

An enormous majority of Western intellectuals display and affirm hostility to the economic and social institutions of their society, institutions to which they give the blanket name of capitalism. Questioned as to the grounds of their hostility, they will give *affective* reasons: concern for "the worker" and antipathy for "the capitalist"; and *ethical* reasons: "the ruthlessness and injustice of the system." This attitude offers a remarkable superficial resemblance to that of the clerical intelligentsia of the Middle Ages (and a striking contrast, as we shall see, to that of the secular intelligentsia up to the eighteenth century). The medieval church centered its attention and its work on the unfortunate. It was the protector of the poor, and it performed all the functions which have now devolved on the welfare state: feeding the destitute, healing the sick, educating the people. All these services were free, provided out of the wealth shunted to them by church taxes and huge gifts, vigorously pressed for. While the church was forever thrusting the condition of the poor before the eyes of the rich, it was forever scolding the latter. Nor is its attitude to be viewed merely in the light of a mellowing of the heart of the wealthy for their own moral improvement and the material advantage of the poor. The rich were not only urged to give but also urged to desist from their search after wealth. This followed most logically from the ideal of the Imitation of Christ. The seeking of worldly goods beyond bare necessity was positively bad: "Having food and raiment, let us therewith be content. But they that will be rich fall into temptation and a snare and into many foolish and hurtful lusts which drown men in destruction and perdition. For the love of money is the root of all evil" (I Tim. 6:7-10). Obviously a faith which warned men against worldly goods ("Love not the world, nor the things that are in the world" [I John 2:15]) could not but regard the most eager and successful seekers after such goods as a vanguard leading the followers to spiritual destruction. The moderns, on the other hand, take a far more favorable view of worldly goods. The increase of wealth seems to them a most excellent thing, and the same logic should therefore lead them to regard the same men as a vanguard leading the followers to material increase.

This latter view would have been most unrealistic in the material conditions of the Middle Ages. In so far as wealth was drawn from land which received no improvements, and in so far as the well endowed did not make productive investments, there was nothing but disadvantage to the many in the existence of the wealthy (though this existence did give rise to the artisan industries from which there long after evolved the industries serving the people; further, it was instrumental in the development of culture). It is perhaps a fact worthy of notice that the modern use of profit, expansion from retained earnings, arose and was systematized in the monasteries; the saintly men who ran them saw nothing wrong in extending their holdings and putting new lands under cultivation, in erecting better buildings, and in employing an ever increasing number of people. They are the true original of the nonconsuming, ascetic type of capitalist. And Berdyaev has truly observed that Christian asceticism played a capital part in the development of capitalism; it is a condition of reinvestment. It is tempting to mention that modern intellectuals look favorably on the accumulation of wealth by bodies bearing a public seal (nationalized enterprises), which are not without some similarity to monasterial businesses. They do not, however, recognize the same phenomenon when the seal is missing.

The intellectual thinks of himself as the natural ally of the worker. The partnership is conceived, in Europe at least, as a fighting one. The image is imprinted in the intellectual's mind of the long-haired and the blue-bloused standing side by side on the barricades. It appears that this image originated in the French Revolution of 1830 and became generally popular during the Revolution of 1848. The picture was then projected backward into history. A permanent alliance between the thinking few and the toiling many was assumed, a view to which romantic poetry gave expression and currency. The historian, however, can find no evidence of such an alliance in the case of the secular intelligentsia. No doubt the clergy was committed to the solace and care of the poor and unfortunate, and indeed its ranks were continuously replenished from the lowest orders of the people; the clerical intelligentsia was thus the channel whereby the talented poor rose to command princes and kings. But the lay intelligentsia, growing away from its clerical root, seemed to turn its back on the preoccupations of the church. Evidence of its interest in what came in the nineteenth century to be called the "social question" is up to that time remarkably scant. There is, however, abundant evidence of a sustained fight by the lay intellectuals against the welfare institutions of their day, administered by the church. During the Middle Ages the church had amassed immense wealth from pious gifts and foundations for charitable purposes. From the Renaissance to the eighteenth century these accumulations were returned to private possession through far-reaching confiscation. In this process the intellectuals played a major role. Servants of the temporal power, they started from the simple fact that the wealth of the church was least amenable to tax; they moved by degrees to the idea that property was more productive in private hands and hence that private enterprise was the best servant of the prince's treasure. Finally, it became a truism that the prince lost his due and the subject his chance by the piling-up of wealth in undying hands (cf. D'Aguesseau's report on perpetual foundations).[2] The lay intellectuals took little account of the social needs fulfilled by the institutions which they sought to destroy. Beggars should be rounded up and led to forced labor; this was the great remedy, in sharp contrast to the medieval attitude. It is not an undue comparison to liken the attitude of the secular intelligentsia to that of the most rabid opponents of the social services in our day, except that they went so much further, taking an attitude which we may find recurring in our times a few generations hence, if the social services should happen to claim a large part of the national wealth in a poor economy.

In direct contradiction to the friars who were to live in poverty with the poor, the secular intellectuals started out as companions and servants of the mighty. They can be called friends of the common man in the sense that they fought against distinctions between the high- and the lowborn and that they favored the rising plebeian—in point of fact, the merchant.[3] There was a natural bond of sympathy between the merchant and the civil servant, both waxing important but both still treated as social inferiors. There was a natural resemblance in that both were calculators, weighers, "rational" beings. There was, finally, a natural alliance between the interests of the princes and those of the merchants. The strength of the prince bound up with the wealth of the nation and the wealth of the nation bound up with individual enterprise; these relationships were perceived and expressed as early as the beginning of the fourteenth century by the secular councilors of Philip the Fair of France. The legal servants of the princes tended to free property from its medieval shackles in order to encourage an expansive economy benefiting the public treasury. (All the terms here are anachronistic, but they do not misrepresent the policies of those times.)

Hostility to the money-maker—*l'homme d'argent*—is a recent attitude of the secular intelligentsia. Any history of European literature must cite the names of the numerous money-makers who patronized intellectuals and apparently earned the affection and respect of their protégés; thus the courage shown by the men of letters who defended Fouquet (after the imprisonment

---

2. This report, which prefaced the French Royal Edict of August, 1749, lays down the principle that the accumulation of land in collective hands which never release their holdings impedes the availability of capital to the individual, who should find it possible to obtain and control a "fund of wealth" to which he may apply his energy. Readers of this and other state papers will perhaps subscribe to the equation: "The ideas of the French Revolution, I mean those which inspired the ministers of Louis XV."

3. The merchant, of course, was also an industrial promotor, since he ordered from artisans the goods which he offered for sale.

of this financier and finance minister by Louis XIV) testifies to the depth of the feelings which he had inspired. The names of Helvetius and D'Holbach must of necessity figure in any history of the ideas before the French Revolution. These two *hommes d'argent* were much admired by their circle, while the person most popular with French intellectuals at the time of the Revolution was the banker Necker. Again, in the Revolution of 1830, a banker—Laffitte—occupies the front of the stage. But this is the parting of the ways. Later, intellectuals cease to admit the friendship of capitalists, who, in turn, cease to be possible figureheads, as Necker had been.[4]

Strangely enough, the fall from favor of the money-maker coincides with an increase in his social usefulness. The moneyed men whom the French intellectual of the seventeenth and eighteenth centuries had liked so well had been chiefly tax farmers (publicans). The economics of tax farming are simple. The farming companies rented the privilege of collecting a given tax by paying a certain sum to the exchequer. They saw to it that much more than the official levy flowed in to their coffers; the margin constituted their gross income. When the costs of collection had been subtracted, the remainder was clear profit. This procedure is certainly more deserving of the name "exploitation" than any modern form of profit-making. Moreover, these profits were only rarely used for investments enriching the country. The tax farmers were renowned for their ostentatious consumption. As their privilege was valuable, they conciliated influential people at court by "helping them out" very freely. Thus the tax farmer combined all the features commonly attributed to the "bad capitalist" without any of the latter's redeeming features. He produced nothing, he profited in proportion to the harshness of his agents, and he retained his privilege by corruption. What a paradox it is that this type of money-maker should have been popular with the intellectual of his day and that unpopularity should have become the lot of the money-maker at the time when his chief form of money-making became the manufacture of goods for popular use!

Until the late eighteenth century the secular intelligentsia was not numerous; its average intellectual level was therefore high. Moreover, its members were educated in ecclesiastical schools, where they received a strong training in logic, which the "scientific education" of our day seems unable to replace. Therefore these minds were prone to consistency; it is remarkable how common a quality consistent reasoning was in their works, as compared to those of our contemporaries. For minds thus equipped, as soon and in so far as they insulated earthly concerns from spiritual truths, the criterion of earthly good was bound to be what we call efficiency. If, with Descartes, we insulate what occurs in space and comes directly to our notice, we can validly state that

---

4. One of the later instances being, of course, that of Engels.

one movement is greater or less than another and validly call the "force" which causes it greater or less. If social events are regarded as movements, some of which are considered desirable, then it is "good" that these should be produced, the forces which tend to produce them are "good," and devices tending to call them forth and apply them to the object are better or worse in proportion to their efficiency. It is a naïve belief of many European intellectuals that "efficiency" is an American idol, recently installed. But it is not so. In anything which is regarded *instrumentaliter,* as an agent for the production of another thing, the greater or lesser capacity of the agent is to be taken into account, and Descartes repeatedly spoke in this sense of the greater or lesser *virtus* of the agent. It seems clear that, the more one tends to a monist conception of the universe which sets up the wealth of society as the result to be attained, the more one must be inclined to equate efficiency in the service of wants and desires with social good. Strangely enough, however, such an evolution of intellectual judgment did not occur in the last hundred and fifty years coincidentally with the evolution toward materialist monism. Ethical judgments disastrously detached from their metaphysical basis sprang up in disorderly growth to plague temporal action.

It seems at least plausible to seek some relation between this change of attitude and the wave of romanticism which swept over the Western intelligentsia. Factory builders trampled over the beauties of nature precisely when these were being discovered; the exodus from the country coincided with a new-found admiration for country life. A sharp change of surroundings divorced men from ancient ways precisely when folkways were coming into fashion. Finally, town life became life with strangers precisely at the moment when civil society was proclaimed insufficient for man's comfort, and the necessity of communal feeling and affection was stressed. All these themes are to be found in Rousseau. This major philosopher was well aware that the values which he cherished were in opposition to the progress of Western society; therefore, he wanted none of this progress: no successive quickening of new wants, no monstrous bellying of towns, no vulgarization of knowledge, etc. He was consistent. Western intellectuals, however, were not to be diverted from their enthusiasm for progress. Therefore, at one and the same time, they thought of industrial development as a great spreading of man's wings and of all its features which were in sharp contrast with the "shepherd" values as deplorable blemishes. Avidity was responsible for these blemishes, no doubt—and also for the whole process! There is a natural homogeneity of the attitudes relative to a certain general process.

The intellectual is really of two minds about the general economic process. On the one side, he takes pride in the achievement of technique and rejoices that men get more of the things which they want. On the other hand, he feels that the conquering army of industry destroys values and that the discipline reigning there is a harsh one. These two views are conveniently reconciled by attributing to the "force" of "progress" everything one likes about the process and to the "force" of "capitalism" everything one dislikes.

It is perhaps worthy of note that precisely the same errors are made in respect to economic creation as are made on the metaphysical level in respect to Creation, since the human mind has but limited capacities and lacks variety even in its mistakes. The attribution to essentially different forces of what is considered good and what is considered bad in the tightly knit process of economic growth of course recalls Manichaeism. Error of this type is not dispelled but tends to be aggravated by retorts taking Pope's line that all is well and that every unpleasant feature is the condition of some good.

It is not surprising that the discussion of the problem of evil in society should tend to follow the pattern of the more ancient and far-reaching discussion of the problem of evil in the universe, a matter upon which far more intellectual concentration has been brought to bear than upon the more limited modern version. We find the secular intelligentsia passing judgment on temporal organization, not from the point of view of adequacy to the end pursued, but from the point of view of ethics (though the ethical principles invoked are never clearly stated or perhaps even conceived). One hears Western students stating that the welfare of the workers must be the aim of economic leaders; that, although this aim is achieved in the United States and not achieved in the U.S.S.R., it does inspire the Soviet leaders and not the Western leaders (or so the students say); and that therefore the former are to be admired and the latter condemned. Here one finds one's self very clearly in a case of jurisdiction *in temporalia, ratione peccati.* The secular intellectual in this instance does not judge social devices as devices (and the device which achieves the workers' good out of the leaders' indifference *ex hypothesi* is surely an excellent device as compared to that which produces no workers' good out of the leaders' solicitude!), but he steps into the shoes of a spiritual guide, with perhaps insufficient preparation.

Taking a sweeping view of the attitudes successively adopted by the lay intelligentsia of the West, we shall say that it started out in reaction to the spiritual jurisdiction of the clerical intelligentsia, in the services of the temporal powers, and concerned itself with bringing rationality into the organization of earthly pursuits, taken as given. Over the centuries it battered down the power of the church and the authority of revelation; thereby it gave free rein to the temporal powers. Temporal power takes the two basic forms of the sword and the purse. The intelligentsia favored the purse. After liquidating the social power of the church, it turned upon the sword-bearing classes, especially upon the greatest sword-bearer, the political sovereign. The weakening of the ecclesiastical power and of the military power obviously gave full freedom to the moneyed power. But then the intelligentsia turns again, proclaiming a spiritual crusade against the economic leaders of modern society. Is this because the intelligentsia must be at odds with any ruling group? Or are there special causes of antagonism toward business executives?

The intellectual wields authority of a kind, called persuasion. And this seems to him the only good form of authority. It is the only one admitted by intellectuals in their utopias, where the incentives and deterrents of material reward and of punishment are dispensed with. In real societies, however, persuasion alone is inadequate to bring about the orderly co-operation of many agents. It is too much to hope that every participant in an extensive process will play his part because he shares exactly the vision of the promoter or organizer. This is the hypothesis of the "General Will" applied to every part and parcel of the economic body; it goes to the extremes of unlikeliness. It is necessary that some power less fluctuating than that gained from persuasion should lie in the hands of social leaders; the intellectual, however, dislikes these cruder forms of authority and those who wield them. He sniffs at the mild form of authority given by the massing of capital in the hands of "business czars" and recoils from the rough sort of authority given by the massing of police powers in the hands of totalitarian rulers. Those in command of such means seem to him coarsened by their use, and he suspects them of regarding men as wholly amenable to their use. The intellectual's effort to whittle down the use of alternatives to persuasion is obviously a factor of progress, while it may also, carried too far, lead society into the alternatives of anarchy and tyranny. Indeed, the intellectual has been known to call upon tyranny for the propping-up of his schemes.

The intellectual's hostility to the businessman presents no mystery, as the two have, by function, wholly different standards, so that the businessman's normal conduct appears blameworthy if judged by the criteria valid for the intellectual's conduct. Such judgment might be avoided in a partitioned society, avowedly divided in classes playing different parts and bound to different forms of honor. This, however, is not the case of our society, of which current ideas and the law postulate that it forms a single homogeneous field. Upon this field the businessman and the intellectual move side by side. The businessman offers to the public "goods" defined as anything the public will buy; the intellectual seeks to teach what is "good," and to him some of the goods offered are things of no value which the public should be discouraged from wanting. The world of business is to the intellectual one in which the values are wrong, the motivations low, the rewards misaddressed. A convenient gateway into the intellectual's inner courtyard where his judgments are rendered is afforded by his deficit preference. It has been observed that his sympathy goes to institutions which run at a loss, nationalized industries supported by the treasury, colleges dependent on grants and subsidies, newspapers which never get out of the red. Why is this? Because he knows from personal experience that, whenever he acts as he feels he should, there is unbalance between his effort and its reception: to put it in economic jargon, the market value of the intellectual's output is far below factor input. That is because a really good thing in the intellectual realm is a thing which can be recognized as good by only a few. As the intellectual's role is to make people know for true and good what they did not previously recognize as such, he encounters a formidable sales resistance, and he works at a loss. When his success is easy and instantaneous, he knows it for an almost certain criterion that he has not truly performed his function. Reasoning from his experience, the intellectual suspects whatever yields a margin of profit of having been done, not from belief in and devotion to the thing, but because enough people could be found to desire it to make the venture profitable. You may plead with the intellectual and convince him that most things must be done this way. Still he will feel that those ways are not his. His profit-and-loss philosophy can be summed up in these terms: to him a loss is the natural outcome of devotion to a-thing-to-be-done, while a profit, on the other hand, is the natural outcome of deferring to the public.

The fundamental difference of attitude between the businessman and the intellectual can be pinned down by resort to a hackneyed formula. The businessman must say: "The customer is always right." The intellectual cannot entertain this notion. A bad writer is made by the very maxim which makes him a good businessman: "Give the public what it wants." The businessman operates within a framework of tastes, of value judgments, which the intellectual must ever seek to alter. The supreme activity of the intellectual is that of the missionary offering the Gospel to heathen nations. Selling spirits to them is a less dangerous and more profitable activity. Here the contrast is stark between offering "consumers" what they should have but do not want and offering them what they avidly accept but should not have. The trader who fails to turn to the more salable product is adjudged a fool, but the missionary who would so turn would be adjudged a knave.

Because we intellectuals are functionally teachers of truth, we are prone to take toward the businessman the very same attitude of moral superiority which was that of the Pharisee toward the Publican, and which Jesus condemned. It should be a lesson to us that the poor man lying by the wayside was raised by a merchant (the Samaritan) and not by the intellectual (the Levite). Dare we deny that the immense improvement which has occurred in the condition of the toiling many is chiefly the work of the businessmen?

We may rejoice that we minister to the highest wants of mankind; but let us be honestly fearful of this responsibility. Of the "goods" offered for profit, how many can we call positively harmful? Is it not the case of many more of the ideas we expound? Are there not ideas nefarious to the workings of the mechanisms and institutions which insure the progress and happiness of commonwealths? It is telling that all intellectuals agree to there being such ideas, though not all agree as to which are obnoxious. Far worse, are there not ideas which raise anger in the bosoms of men? Our responsibility is heightened by the fact that the diffusion of possibly mischievous ideas cannot and should not be stopped by the exertion of the temporal authority, while the merchandising of harmful goods can be so stopped.

It is something of a mystery—and a promising field of investigation for historians and sociologists—that the intellectual community has waxed harsher in its judgments of the business community precisely while the business community was strikingly bettering the condition of the masses, improving its own working ethics, and growing in civic consciousness. Judged by its social fruits, by its mores, by its spirit, capitalism of today is immeasurably more praiseworthy than in previous days when it was far less bitterly denounced. If the change in the attitude of the intelligentsia is not to be explained by a turn for the worse in what they assess, is it not then to be explained by a change which has occurred in the intelligentsia itself?

This question opens a great realm of inquiry. It has for long been assumed that the great problem of the twentieth century is that of the industrial wage-earner's place in society; insufficient notice has been taken of the rise of a vast intellectual class, whose place in society may prove the greater problem. The intellectuals have been the major agents in the destruction of the ancient structure of Western society, which provides three distinct sets of institutions for the intellectuals, the warriors, and the producers. They have striven to render the social field homogeneous and uniform; the winds of subjective desires blow over it more freely; subjective appreciations are the criterion of all efforts. Quite naturally, this constitution of society puts a premium upon the "goods" which are most desired and brings to the forefront of society those who lead in the production of "goods." The intelligentsia has then lost to this "executive" class the primacy which it enjoyed when it stood as "the First Estate." Its present attitude may be to some degree explained by the inferiority complex it has acquired. Not only has the intelligentsia as a whole fallen to a less exalted status, but, moreover, individual recognition tends to be determined by criteria of subjective appreciation by the public, which the intelligentsia rejects on principle; hence the countervailing tendency to exalt those intellectuals who are for intellectuals only.

We do not presume to explain, and the foregoing remarks are the merest suggestions. Our ambition is merely to stress that there is something to be explained and that it seems timely to undertake a study of the tensions arising between the intelligentsia and society.

Part VI

INTELLECTUALS
IN VARIOUS
COUNTRIES

OVERVIEW

THE FIRST four paragraphs from Stalin are particularly important for they are from his report to the Extraordinary Eighth Congress of Soviets of November 25, 1936 "On the Draft Constitution of the U.S.S.R." Stalin argues that the working intellectuals are not a class but a stratum which recruits members from the two classes—workers and peasants. These toiling intellectuals are entirely new because of their recruitment and because they serve the people. Intellectuals are equal members of Soviet society, side by side with workers and peasants. The other selection is from his report to the Central Committee of the Eighteenth Congress of the Communist Party delivered in 1939. He criticizes those who regard the Soviet intellectuals as an alien force, even as a force hostile to the workers and peasants. The theme that Soviet intellectuals are really new in contrast to the old is repeated. There were among the old intellectuals some who were revolutionary and threw in their lot with the working class. Since the establishment of the Soviet regime, those intellectuals who sided against it in the October Revolution have been smashed; another section of the old intellectuals, the greater part of which is well along in years, eventually decided to serve the Soviet government; the rank and file of the old intellectuals joined forces with the people and supported the Soviet government. Parallel with this break up of the old intellectuals, a new Socialist intellectual class has come into being which requires a theory teaching the necessity of cordial attitudes and respect. The old theory which was directed against the bourgeois intellectuals is not applicable to the new socialist intellectuals.

The situation of the intellectuals in the communist world is presented by Milosz in terms of a character in a Polish novel, Murti-Bing, who succeeded in producing pills containing a "philosophy of life." The men who took these pills changed completely, became serene, and the problems that worried them disappeared. Today in the communist world one must die physically or spiritually or one must be reborn by taking Murti-Bing pills. These pills are especially tempting to the intellectual who yearns for a new faith, for with the decline of religion he feels alienated. Murti-Bing contains a dialectical philosophy which will provide a pattern of life and through it the intellectual feels that he belongs to society and has a useful role in it. Such intellectuals have a fear of thinking for themselves. The culture of the communist world and the picture they have of the outside world prove to the intellectuals that things cannot be different, that they belong to a new and conquering world. At the end of the Polish novel those who took the Murti-Bing pills become schizophrenics, which is what is happening to many intellectuals in the communist world.

The intellectuals in Latin America are an important, and frequently the most important, part of the ruling group. Almost unanimously these intellectuals value Hispanic culture and consider the United States culture inferior. They do not think that technology represents something valuable. However, since the 1920's many Latin American intellectuals have given grudging recognition to technology and industrialization but they deal with these matters in a theoretical manner. They value a non-utilitarian education highly, and have developed the cult of the academic title, especially the "doctore." Intellectuals also believe that leisure enobles, while labor, especially technical labor, degrades. In contrast, as the next essay shows, in Asia the vision of an industrialized society, as represented by the U.S.S.R., appeals to many intellectuals. Bell's essay makes a similar analysis regarding Asia as well as Africa.

Padhye argues that intellectuals and the middle class from which they sprang have been responsible for the defeat of colonialism in Asia, and they are now called upon also to lead in the task of reconstruction. Intellectuals were ideally suited to the negative task of driving out the colonial rulers but they seem to be spiritually ill-equipped in the face of the fact of independence and the tasks of reconstruction. In this connection it can be noted that a somewhat similar situation occurred regarding the role of intellectuals in the French and Russian Revolutions, as shown by Tocqueville and Seton-Watson in Part I. In Asia the social fabric was sustained by religious ritual and by social conventions. Modern rational education undermined ritual and convention and this had two closely interrelated consequences: it deepened the split between intellectuals and the people and created a terrible void in the minds of intellectuals. The growth of revivalism testifies to this hunger of the spirit. Those who have not been able to reconcile their rational beliefs with religious cults, are looking for a substitute which not only satisfies their inner void but also provides ready answers. Communism provides such answers and has also the essentials of a satisfying religion and therefore has great appeal, as is also emphasized by Milosz. Asian intellectuals are frustrated because their youthful dreams have been disappointed by Asian reality and because there is not much scope for their training. They are also unhappy about their isolation from the people. The picture of a high-powered industrialized society appeals to the desperate desire of intellectuals for integration, for they also believe that in such a society they will have a secure and legitimate place. They forget that this sort of integration involves total conformity and assures them only a subordinate role. Reconstruction on the basis of democratic decentralization would give intellectuals a more dynamic relationship with the people than mechanical integration by a vast centralized plan on the Soviet pattern.

Bell's piece contrasts the situation of the intellectuals in Asia and Africa with that of the West. The rising states of Asia and Africa are fashioning new ideologies which are parochial, instrumental, and are created by political leaders. This appears to be a different view than that taken by Padhye. The impetus for these ideologies are economic development and national power, and in this appeal the Soviet Union and Communist China have become models. In contrast in the West, nineteenth century ideologies which had the title "intellectual" for themselves. The writer is the peak of intelligence in appears to be similar to the one expressed by Molnar in Part III. These ideologies, in contrast to those of present-day Asia and Africa, were universalistic and humanistic.

According to Lüthy, despite the existence in France of numerous and outstanding non-leftist intellectuals, only men of the Left have claimed the title "intellectuals" for themselves. The writer is the peak of intelligence in France, while in Germany it is the professor and in America the expert. In France the political republic is subject to the moral guardianship of the republic of letters. In the postwar period for several years the Left intelligentsia in the face of communism was stricken with impotence in both its traditional functions—as critics of society and as prophets of utopia. In 1952 unpolitical writers and also those who compromised themselves with Vichy, triumphantly celebrated the debacle of the "intellectuals." France is the only country in which cultural propaganda is rooted in a great tradition. French culture is profoundly intellectual and it is being challenged in such places as Latin America and the Near East not only by its old rivals but by the industrial civilization of America. All French intellectuals are concerned with the materialist vulgarity of mass culture, without necessarily being anti-American, neutralist, and pro-communist.

Mann shows that in Germany the writer does not have prestige because he is without an office and is on his own. Nothing is considered more respectable than the university professor who has an office, rank, and a title. As shown in Part III it is against this domination of the university professor that Schopenhauer, Kierkegaard and Nietzsche protested. The man of letters, the publicist, made a belated appearance in Germany and the German intellectual *par excellence* is Heine; a whole branch of German intellectuals derives from him. The nineteenth century also witnessed the emergence of another type of intellectual, the sociologist of the Left. In this century there developed a divorce between the political and intellectual life of the nation, a condition which is comparable to Russia as was shown by Seton-Watson and to France a century earlier as was shown by Tocqueville. This divorce came to an end in 1914 when intellectuals generally supported the war; in its aftermath intellectuals took various sides. After World War II a prosperous and busy country came into being which was hardly expected by anyone, least of all the intellectuals. In such a country there is little market for the products of either the left-wing or the right-wing intellectuals.

According to Spender intellectuals in England in the last two decades have been concerned with their effectiveness as a social force. Some English intellectuals believed that they could be socially effective through political programs while others thought that they could be so without them. Until 1939, English intellectuals felt themselves to belong to a continuing tradition. With the outbreak of the war the pre-war illusion that the individual intellectual could be the exponent in his work of a philosophy which could change society, disappeared. With this development a great deal of conviction went out of contemporary English literature. The last lingering illusion of the British intellectuals were the fantasies that the immsense cooperative effort of the war would be used to rebuild Britain. But the young writers did not in their writing take planning seriously and were concerned with their own experiences, and with their personal relationships. Nineteen-fifty created a new situation for intellectuals—a crisis of conscience arising out of American policies, particularly out of the Korean situation.

Nine essays are presented on the intellectual in the United States. In addition to presenting a variety of outlook, the essays also vary in their subject matter; some are theoretical discussions, while others treat more concrete aspects of the situation of intellectuals in the United States.

According to Phillips, new and genuinely creative impulses in our time tend to take the form of bohemianism, in a kind of permanent mutiny against utility and conformity. Although the intelligentsia which came to the fore with the rise of bourgeois society was not bound by any common creed, still they managed through the years to build a tradition. One might almost put down as an aesthetic law that continuity is the condition of creative invention. Characteristic of the American intelligentsia is its inability to achieve a detached and self-sufficient group existence that would permit it to sustain its traditions through succeeding epochs, and to keep abreast of European intellectual production. The history of American letters comprises efforts by solitary writers or by intellectual groups to differentiate themselves and set a new current in motion, with inevitable wearing out, and the necessity for a fresh start over again. Not until the last two or three decades did any literary "schools," promoted by an active literary intelligentsia, make their appearance in the United States. But their inspiration was European. The intelligentsia in America, for all its efforts to preserve its intellectual identity, seems to have a deep-seated need to accept as its own—if only periodically—the official voice of society.

Barrett makes the following distinctions among writers: Poets belong to the little magazines which among a vast quantity of rubble once in a while unearth a genuine talent. Ladywriters contributed during 1945-55 a few good writers of feminine sensibility. The snotty young men of the thirties were Marxists and social militants; they had the role of rebels but they have been superseded by institutionalized writers. Many have become institutionalized by working for large magazines and others by accepting university appointments. These developments have superseded Bohemia and its adjunct, the little magazines. Under these conditions according to Barrett the professional writer as an independent person no longer seems to exist.

Buckley's comments on American intellectuals concern their public rather than cultural position. The principal responsibility of intellectuals is to make distinctions and this is not being done in the United States; therefore the nation's problems are not getting solved. The failure of intellectual leaders to make distinctions, thus leading to confusion in which progress is not possible, is illustrated in a couple of examples. Intellectuals have developed the capacity to suspend virtually *en masse* their critical judgment on those occasions where a rigorous application of standards, the careful drawing of distinctions, leads to inconvenient conclusions. On account of this breakdown Americans have failed to take proper measure of their enemy. The commitment of intellectuals to democracy, which is a method and not a policy, and to academic freedom, has proved inordinate and obsessive. The only defense against the shortcomings and abuses of the collective action of the state is concerted resistance by individuals and this resistance can only issue from an undamaged critical faculty and from moral sense.

Viereck concentrates on the more specific issue of the relation of intellectuals to communism. According to him American workingmen have an innate impulse toward anti-communism and toward capitalist democracy. On the other hand many bourgeois intellectuals have an innate soft spot for some kind of almost unconscious fellow-traveling with communism; but their guilt should not be exaggerated. In America fellow-traveling arose among upper middle class intellectuals who were psychologically—not economically—discontented; a psychological emphasis made by many other previous essays. Polls have shown that the obstacle to understanding the real nature of communism and Soviet Russia was the possession of intellect, education, and wealth. The delusions of many American intellectuals in this respect influenced American policy toward Soviet Russia. While today American intellectuals are rejecting these misconceptions they still have not rejected sufficiently the confusion of criminal deeds with free thought.

The previously given two essays are critical of American intellectuals. The two essays that follow are friendly toward them and express pleasure that the status of intellectuals is rising. Riesman analyzes the situation today with reference to recruitment of professors and students. He points out that intellectuals have risen in power in a society that more and more requires intellectuals, or at least educated specialists. There has been a general rapprochement between the values of universities and business values. The life of the businessman and the life of the professor have become less and less distinct. He also believes that along with the general rise in the standards of education, professors have become brighter and better.

Lipset provides some of the data to support Riesman's contention that the status of American intellectuals is rather high. Lipset's analysis makes a clear distinction between the real and the presumed status of American intellectuals. He points out that their actual status is much better than they believe it to be. He shows the pitfalls of comparing the status of American and European intellectuals. Then he cites considerable evidence to demonstrate that in terms of American conditions, American intellectuals do have a rather high status. He further shows that in relation to such comparable careers as government service, American intellectuals are well off in terms of income.

Lukacs approaches the predicament of American intellectuals from a different point of view although he agrees with Lispet and Riesman on the status of American intellectuals. According to Lukacs democracy favors intellectual classes but not necessarily intellectual professions. The difference between intellectual class and intellectual profession, between the recognition of a category of persons designated as intellectuals and the recognition of intellectual virtues and vices is fundamental. The emergence of intellectual classes is due to the passing of aristocratic society and in our times of inherited property; the general intellectualization of life; and the fact that in our times administration consumes even more time and energy than production. What is needed is not an intellectual class, not even an intellectual élite, but a sincere dedication of men to the intellectual profession.

The concluding two pieces deal primarily with the theme of alienation. Rosenberg defines alienation as the loss by the individual of personal integrity through the operation of social processes. The intellectual has attained in the past fifteen years prosperity and social prestige but he is the most dependent of wage earners. He cannot escape the conviction of guilt for his part in also depriving others of their individuality. He cannot help but feel himself to be a betrayer of humanity in his own mind. What is new in America is a self-conscious intellectual caste whose disillusionment has induced its members to volunteer to serve as tools. Having accepted self-alienation in trade for social status, the post-radical intellectual can see nothing in the future but other-direction and a corporately styled personality.

Hook says that the lamentations about the alienation of the creative artist in American culture are difficult to understand since American intellectuals face less obstacles to doing significant work or finding a significant audience than they did fifty or one hundred years ago. The notion that American university life is a Golgotha of the intellectual spirit is absurd. Creative life in America suffers more from mediocrity than from frustration. Marx's notion of self-alienation applies primarily to the worker who is compelled to labor at something which neither expresses nor sustains his own needs and interests as a person. The unalienated man according to Marx is the one that does significant work. The artist for Marx is the unalienated man *par excellence* to the extent that he does not produce *merely* a commodity. As some previous essays indicated, the Marxist view involves the myth that all artists, once the market economy disappears, will be able to do creative work. Another conception of alienation popular with some sociologists and bohemians applies to artists who break with the conventions or norms of their family, society, or class. This is the most popular conception of the alienated artist in America and is the shallowest. Non-conformist artists have created their own audience and feel unalienated in the Marxist sense despite hostile critics. Many intellectuals mistake the indifference of the world or their private agonies—which may be very well due to lack of creative capacity or to an ambition incommensurate to their talents—for unerring signs of election to an alienated élite. There are no specific virtues in the attitudes of conformity and non-conformity for they are relational terms. What is important is to know to what and with what intellectuals are conforming or not conforming and how—and to some of the greatest intellectuals the question is not at all relevant. The social function of the American intellectual is to continue the tradition of critical integrity. Too many American intellectuals are the creatures of fashion; it is sufficient for the majority to believe anything, for them to oppose it.

THE OLD AND THE NEW INTELLIGENTSIA

Joseph Stalin

... LET US pass on to the question of the intelligentsia, to the question of engineers and technicians, of workers on the cultural front, of employees in general, and so on. The intelligentsia, too, has undergone great changes during this period. It is no longer the old hidebound intelligentsia which tried to place itself above classes, but which actually, for the most part, served the landlords and the capitalists. Our Soviet intelligentsia is an entirely new intelligentsia, bound up by its very roots with the working class and the peasantry. In the first place, the composition of the intelligentsia has changed. People who come from the aristocracy and the bourgeoisie constitute but a small percentage of our Soviet intelligentsia; 80 to 90 per cent of the Soviet intelligentsia are people who have come from the working class, from the peasantry, or from other strata of the working population. Finally, the very nature of the activities of the intelligentsia has changed. Formerly it had to serve the wealthy classes, for it had no alternative. Today it must serve the people, for there are no longer any exploiting classes. And that is precisely why it is now an equal member of Soviet society, in which, side by side with the workers and peasants, pulling together with them, it is engaged in building the new, classless, Socialist society.

As you see, this is an entirely new, working intelligentsia, the like of which you will not find in any other country on earth. . . .

. . . As we know, Soviet society consists of two classes, workers and peasants. And it is of this that Article 1 of the Draft Constitution speaks. Consequently, Article 1 of the Draft Constitution properly reflects the class composition of our society. It may be asked: What about the working intelligentsia? The intelligentsia has never been a class, and never can be a class— it was and remains a stratum, which recruits its members from among all classes of society. In the old days the intelligentsia recruited its members from the ranks of the nobility, of the bourgeoisie, partly from the ranks of the peasantry, and only to a very inconsiderable extent from the ranks of the workers. In our day, under the Soviets, the intelligentsia recruits its members mainly from the ranks of the workers and peasants. But no matter where

Reprinted from *Problems of Leninism* (1945), pp. 545, 559-560, 638-640. Foreign Languages Publishing House. Title supplied by the Editor.

it may recruit its members, and what character it may bear, the intelligentsia is nevertheless a stratum and not a class.

Does this circumstance infringe upon the rights of the working intelligentsia? Not in the least! Article 1 of the Draft Constitution deals not with the rights of the various strata of Soviet society, but with the class composition of that society. The rights of the various strata of Soviet society, including the rights of the working intelligentsia, are dealt with mainly in Chapters X and XI of the Draft Constitution. It is evident from these chapters that the workers, the peasants, and the working intelligentsia enjoy entirely equal rights in all spheres of the economic, political, social, and cultural life of the country. Consequently, there can be no question of an infringement upon the rights of the working intelligentsia. . . .

In spite of the fact that the position of the Party on the question of the Soviet intelligentsia is perfectly clear, there are still current in our Party views hostile to the Soviet intelligentsia and incompatible with the Party position. As you know, those who hold these false views practise a disdainful and contemptuous attitude to the Soviet intelligentsia and regard it as an alien force, even as a force hostile to the working class and the peasantry. True, during the period of Soviet development the intelligentsia has undergone a radical change both in its composition and status. It has come closer to the people and is honestly collaborating with the people, in which respect it differs fundamentally from the old, bourgeois intelligentsia. But this apparently means nothing to these comrades. They go on harping on the old tunes and wrongly apply to the Soviet intelligentsia views and attitudes which were justified in the old days when the intelligentsia was in the service of the landlords and capitalists.

In the old days, under capitalism, before the revolution, the intelligentsia consisted primarily of members of the propertied classes—noblemen, manufacturers, merchants, kulaks and so on. Some members of the intelligentsia were sons of small tradesmen, petty officials, and even of peasants and workingmen, but they did not and could not play a decisive part. The intelligentsia as a whole depended for their livelihood on the propertied classes and ministered to the propertied classes. Hence it is easy to understand the mistrust, often bordering on hatred, with which the revolutionary elements of our country and above all the workers regarded the intellectuals. True, the old intelligentsia produced some courageous individuals, handfuls of revolutionary people who adopted the standpoint of the working class and completely threw in their lot with the working class. But such people were all too few among the intelligentsia, and they could not change the complexion of the intelligentsia as a whole.

Matters with regard to the intelligentsia have undergone a fundamental change, however, since the October Revolution, since the defeat of the foreign armed intervention, and especially since the victory of industrialization and collectivization, when the abolition of exploitation and the firm establishment of the Socialist economic system made it really possible to give the country a new constitution and to put it into effect. The most influential and qualified section of the old intelligentsia broke away from the main body in the very first days of the October Revolution, proclaimed war on the Soviet government, and joined the ranks of the saboteurs. They met with well-deserved punishment for this; they were smashed and dispersed by the organs of Soviet power. Subsequently the majority of those that survived were recruited by the enemies of our country as wreckers and spies, and thus were expunged by their own deeds from the ranks of the intellectuals. Another section of the old intelligentsia, less qualified but more numerous, long continued to mark time, waiting for "better days"; but then, apparently giving up hope, decided to go and serve and to live in harmony with the Soviet government. The greater part of this group of the old intelligentsia are well on in years and are beginning to go out of commission. A third section of the old intelligentsia, mainly comprising its rank-and-file, and still less qualified than the section just mentioned, joined forces with the people and supported the Soviet government. It needed to perfect its education, and it set about doing so in our universities. But parallel with this painful process of differentiation and break-up of the old intelligentsia there went on a rapid process of formation, mobilization and mustering of forces of a new intelligentsia. Hundreds of thousands of young people coming from the ranks of the working class, the peasantry and the working intelligentsia entered the universities and technical colleges, from which they emerged to reinforce the attenuated ranks of the intelligentsia. They infused fresh blood into it and reanimated it in a new, Soviet spirit. They radically changed the whole aspect of the intelligentsia, moulding it in their own form and image. The remnants of the old intelligentsia were dissolved in the new, Soviet intelligentsia, the intelligentsia of the people. There thus arose a new, Soviet intelligentsia, intimately bound up with the people and, for the most part, ready to serve them faithfully and loyally.

As a result, we now have a numerous, new, popular, Socialist intelligentsia, fundamentally different from the old, bourgeois intelligentsia both in composition and in social and political character.

The old theory about the intelligentsia, which taught that it should be treated with distrust and combated, fully applied to the old, pre-revolutionary intelligentsia, which served the landlords and capitalists. This theory is now out-of-date and does not fit our new, Soviet intelligentsia. Our new intelligentsia demands a new theory, a theory teaching the necessity for a cordial attitude towards it, solicitude and respect for it, and cooperation with it in the interests of the working class and the peasantry.

That is clear, I should think.

It is therefore all the more astonishing and strange that after all these fundamental changes in the status of the intelligentsia people should be found within our Party who attempt to apply the old theory, which was directed against the bourgeois intelligentsia, to our new, Soviet intelligentsia, which is basically a Socialist intelligentsia. These people, it appears, assert that workers and peasants who until recently were working in Stakhanov fashion in the factories and collective farms and who were then sent to the universities to be educated, thereby ceased to be real people and became second-rate people. So we are to conclude that education is a pernicious and dangerous thing. [*Laughter*.] We want all our workers and peasants to be cultured and educated, and we shall achieve this in time. But in the opinion of these queer comrades, this purpose harbours a grave danger; for after the workers and peasants become cultured and educated they may face the danger of being classified as second-rate people. [*Loud laughter*.] The possibility is not precluded that these queer comrades may in time sink to the position of extolling backwardness, ignorance, benightedness and obscurantism. It would be quite in the nature of things. Theoretical vagaries have never led, and never can lead, to any good.

Such is the position with regard to our new, Socialist intelligentsia.

MURTI-BING

Czeslaw Milosz

IT WAS ONLY toward the middle of the twentieth century
that the inhabitants of many European countries came, in general unpleas-
antly, to the realization that their fate could be influenced directly by intricate
and abstruse books on philosophy. Their bread, their work, their private
lives began to depend on this or that decision in disputes on principles to
which, until then, they had never paid any attention. In their eyes, the
philosopher had always been a sort of dreamer whose divagations had no
effect on reality. The average human being, even if he had once been exposed
to it, wrote philosophy off as utterly impractical and useless. Therefore the
great intellectual work of the Marxists could easily pass as just one more
variation on a sterile pastime. Only a few individuals understood the meaning, causes and probable results of this general indifference.

A curious book appeared in Warsaw in 1932. It was a novel, in two
volumes, entitled *Insatiability*. Its author was Stefan Ignacy Witkiewicz, a
painter, writer and philosopher, who had constructed an ontological system
akin to the monadology of Leibniz. His book, like his earlier novel, *Farewell
to Autumn,* could not hope for a large number of readers. The language used
by the author was difficult, full of his own neologisms. Brutal descriptions of
erotic scenes alternated with whole pages of discussions on Husserl, Carnap
and other contemporary ontologists. Besides, one could not always tell
whether the author was serious or joking; and the subject matter seemed to
be pure fantasy.

The action of the book took place in Europe, more precisely in Poland,
at some time in the near future or even in the present, that is, in the 'thirties,
'forties or 'fifties. The social group it portrayed was that of musicians, painters, philosophers, aristocrats and higher-ranking military officers. The whole
book was nothing but a study of decay: mad, dissonant music; erotic perversion; widespread use of narcotics; dispossessed thinking; false conversion to
Catholicism; and complex psychopathic personalities. This decadence reigned
at a time when Western civilization was said to be threatened by an army
from the East, a Sino-Mongolian army that dominated all the territory stretching from the Pacific to the Baltic.

Reprinted from *Partisan Review* (September-October, 1951), pp. 540-551, 554-556,
by permission of the author and the periodical. Translated by Jane Zielonko.

Witkiewicz's heroes are unhappy in that they have no faith and no sense of meaning in their work. This atmosphere of decay and senselessness extends throughout the entire country. And at that moment, a great number of hawkers appear in the cities peddling Murti-Bing pills. Murti-Bing was a Mongolian philosopher who had succeeded in producing an organic means of transporting a "philosophy of life." This Murti-Bing "philosophy of life," which constituted the strength of the Sino-Mongolian army, was contained in pills in an extremely condensed form. A man who used these pills changed completely. He became serene and happy. The problems he had struggled with until then suddenly appeared to be superficial and worthless. He smiled indulgently at those who continued to concern themselves with such problems. Most affected, were all questions pertaining to unsolvable ontological difficulties. A man who swallowed Murti-Bing pills became impervious to any metaphysical concerns. He treated wild excesses of art, arising out of an "insatiety of form," as outmoded stupidities. He no longer considered the approach of the Sino-Mongolian army as a tragedy for his own civilization. He lived in the midst of his countrymen like a healthy individual surrounded by madmen. More and more people took the Murti-Bing cure, and their resultant calm contrasted sharply with the nervousness of their environment.

The epilogue, in a few words: the outbreak of the war led to a meeting of the armies of the West with those of the East. In the decisive moment, just before the great battle, the leader of the Western army surrendered to the enemy; and in exchange, though with the greatest honors, he was beheaded. The Eastern army occupied the country and the new life, that of Murti-Bing realized, began. The heroes of the novel, once tormented by philosophical "insatiety," now came to the service of the new society. Instead of writing the dissonant music of former days, they composed marches and odes. Instead of painting abstractions, as before, they turned out socially useful pictures. But since they could not rid themselves completely of their former personalities, they became outstanding cases of schizophrenia.

So much for the novel. Its author often expressed his belief that religion, philosophy and art are living out their last days. Yet he found life without them worthless. On September 17, 1939, learning that the Red Army had crossed the eastern border of Poland, he committed suicide by taking veronal and cutting his wrists.

Today, Witkiewicz's vision is being fulfilled in the minutest detail throughout a large part of the European continent. Perhaps sunlight, the smell of the earth, little everyday pleasures, and the forgetfulness that work brings can ease somewhat the tensions created by this process of fulfillment. But beneath the activity and bustle of daily life is the constant awareness of an irrevocable choice to be made. One must either die (physically or spiritually), or else one must be reborn according to a prescribed method, namely, the taking of Murti-Bing pills. People in the West are often inclined to consider the lot of converted countries in terms of might and coercion. That is wrong. There is an internal longing for harmony and happiness that lies deeper than ordinary fear or the desire to shield one's self against misery or physical destruction. The fate of completely logical, non-dialectical people like Witkiewicz is a warning for many an intellectual. All about him, he sees the frightening example of internal exiles, irreconcilable, non-participating, eroded by hatred. In order to understand the situation of a writer in a "popular democracy," one must seek the reasons for his activity and ask how he maintains his equilibrium. Whatever one may say, the New Faith affords great possibilities for an active and positive life. And Murti-Bing is more tempting to an intellectual than to a peasant or laborer. For the intellectual, the New Faith is a candle that he circles like a moth, eventually to be consumed by its flame. Blood flowed freely in Europe during the religious wars; and he who joins the New Faith today is paying off the debt of that European tradition. We are concerned here with more significant questions than mere force.

I shall try to speak of the profound longings in a man as if one really could analyze the essence of his blood and flesh. If I should try to describe the reasons why a man becomes a revolutionary I would be neither eloquent enough nor restrained enough. I admit that I have too much admiration for those who fight evil, whether their choice of ends and means be right or wrong. I draw the line, however, at those intellectuals who *adapt* themselves, although the fact that they are adapted and not genuine revolutionaries in no way diminishes their newly acquired zeal and enthusiasm.

There are, I believe, a few key concepts which may lead us to understand why men accept Murti-Bing.

The society portrayed by Witkiewicz is distinguished by the fact that religion has ceased to exist as a force. Religion long ago lost its hold on men's minds not only in the popular democracies, but elsewhere as well. As long as a society's best minds were occupied by theological questions, it was possible to speak of a given religion as the way of thinking of the whole social organism. All the matters which most actively concerned the people were referred to it and discussed in its terms. But that belongs to a dying era. We have come by easy stages to a lack of a uniform system of thought that could unite the peasant ploughing his field, the student poring over his books, and the mechanic working on an assembly line. Out of this lack arises the painful sense of detachment or abstraction that oppresses those who are the "creators of culture." Religion has been replaced by philosophy, which, however, has strayed into spheres increasingly less accessible to the layman. The discussions of Witkiewicz's heroes about Husserl can scarcely interest a reader of even better than average education; whereas the peasants remained bound to the Church, but only emotionally and traditionally. Music, painting and poetry have become something completely foreign to the great majority of people. To bridge the gap between art and the masses a theory developed that art should become a substitute for religion. "Metaphysical feelings" were to be expressed in the "compression of pure form"; and so form soon came to dominate content.

The great longing of the "alienated" intellectual is to belong to the masses. It is such a powerful longing that, in trying to appease it, a great many of them who once looked to Germany or Italy for inspiration have now become converted to the New Faith. Actually, the rightist totalitarian program was exceptionally poor. The only gratification it offered came from collective *warmth*: crowds, red faces, shouting, marches, arms outstretched in salute. It was difficult, however, to find rational satisfactions. Neither racist doctrines nor hatred of other nations, nor the glorification of one's own national traditions could efface the feeling that the entire program was improvised to deal with problems of the moment. But Murti-Bing is different. It lays scientific foundations. At the same time, it scraps all vestiges of the past: post-Kantian philosophy, fallen into disrepute because of its remoteness from reality; art designed for those who, having no religion, dare not admit that to seek the "absolute" through a juxtaposition of colors and sounds is cowardly and inconclusive thinking; and the semi-magic, semi-religious mentality of the peasants. All these are replaced by a *single* system, a single language of ideas. The truck driver and elevator operator employed by a publishing firm read the same Marxist classics as its director or staff writers. A day laborer and an historian can reach an understanding on this basis of common reading. Obviously, the difference that may exist between them in mental level is no smaller than that which separated a theologian from a village blacksmith in the Middle Ages. But fundamental principles are universal; the great spiritual schism has been obliterated. Dialectical materialism has united everyone; and philosophy (that is, dialectics) once more determines the patterns of life. It is beginning to be regarded with a respect that one has only for a force on which one's food, happiness and safety depend. The intellectual has once more become *useful*. He, who once devoted himself to his thinking and writing in his free moments away from a paying job in a bank or post office, has now found his rightful place on earth. He has been restored to society. Whereas, the businessmen, aristocrats and tradespeople who once considered him a harmless blunderer have now been dispossessed. They are indeed delighted to find work as cloak-room attendants and to hold the coat of a former employee of whom they said, in pre-war days, "It seems he writes." We must not oversimplify, however, the gratifications of personal ambition;

they are merely the outward and visible signs of social necessity, symbols of a recognition that strengthens the intellectual's feeling of *belonging*.

Even though one seldom speaks about metaphysical motives that can lead to a complete change of one's political opinions, such motives do exist and can be observed in some of the most eminent, most intelligent, and most neurotic people. Let us imagine a spring day in a city situated in some country similar to that described in Witkiewicz's novel. One of his heroes is taking a walk. He is tormented by what we may call the *suction of the absurd*. What is the significance of the lives of the people he passes, of the senseless bustle, the laughter, the pursuit of money, the stupid animal diversions? By using a little intelligence he can easily classify the passers-by according to type; he can guess their social status, their habits and their preoccupations. A fleeting moment reveals their childhood, manhood and old age; and then they vanish. A purely physiological study of one particular passer-by in preference to another is meaningless. Yet if one penetrates into the minds of these people, one discovers utter nonsense. They are totally unaware of the fact that nothing is their own, that everything is part of their historical formation; their occupations, their clothes, their gestures and expressions, their beliefs and ideas. They are the force of inertia personified, victims of the delusion that each individual exists as a self. If at least these were souls, as the Church taught, or the monads of Leibniz! But these beliefs have perished. What remains is an aversion to the domination of the detail, to the mentality that *isolates* every phenomenon, such as eating, drinking, dressing, earning money, fornicating. And what is there beyond these things? Should such a state of affairs continue? Why should it continue? Such questions are almost synonymous with what is known as hatred of the bourgeoisie.

Let a new man arise, one who, instead of submitting to the world, will transform it. Let him create his own historical formation, instead of yielding to its bondage. Only thus can he redeem the absurdity of his physiological existence. Man must be made to understand this, by force and by suffering. Why shouldn't he suffer? He ought to suffer. Why can't he be used as manure, as long as he remains evil and stupid? If the intellectual must know the agony of thought, why should he spare others this pain? Why should he shield those who until now drank, guffawed, gorged themselves, cracked inane jokes and found life beautiful?

The intellectual's eyes twinkle with delight at the persecution of the bourgeois, and of the bourgeois mentality. It is a rich reward for the degradation he felt when he had to be part of the middle class, and when there seemed to be no way out of its cycle of birth and death. Now he has moments of sheer intoxication when he sees the intelligentsia, unaccustomed to rigorously tough thinking, caught in the snare of the revolution. The peasants, burying hoarded gold and listening to foreign broadcasts in the hope that a war will save them from collectivization, certainly have no ally in him. Yet he is warm-hearted and good; he is a friend of mankind. Not mankind as it is, but as it *should* be. He is not unlike the inquisitor of the Middle Ages; but whereas the latter tortured the flesh in the belief that he was saving the individual soul, the intellectual of the New Faith is working for the salvation of the human species in general.

His chief characteristic is his fear of thinking for himself. It is not merely that he is afraid to arrive at dangerous conclusions. His is a fear of sterility, of what Marx called the misery of philosophy. I myself am not entirely free of a like fear as I write these words. Let us admit that a man is no more than an instrument in an orchestra directed by the muse of History. It is only in this context that the notes he produces have any significance. Otherwise even his most brilliant solos become simply a highbrow's diversions. We are not concerned with the question of how one finds the courage to oppose one's self to the majority. It is a much more poignant question that one poses to one's self: can one write well outside that one real stream whose vitality springs from its harmony with historical laws and the dynamics of reality? Rilke's poems may be very good; but if they are good, that means there must have been some reason for them in his day. Contemplative poems, such as his, could never appear in a popular democracy; not only because it would be difficult to publish them, but because the writer's impulse to write them would be destroyed at its very root. The objective conditions for such poetry have disappeared; and the intellectual of whom I speak is not one who believes in writing for the bureau drawer. He curses and despairs over the censorship and demands of the publishing commissions. Yet at the same time, he distrusts profoundly the values of unlicensed literature. The publishing license he himself receives does not mean that the editor appreciates the artistic merits of his book, nor that he expects it to be popular with the public. That license is simply a sign that the author reflects the transformation of reality with scientific exactness. Dialectical materialism in the Stalinist version both reflects and directs this transformation. It creates social and political conditions in which a man ceases to think and write otherwise than as is necessary. He accepts this "must" because nothing worthwhile can exist outside its limits. Herein lie the claws of dialectics. The writer does not surrender to this "must" merely because he fears for his own skin. He fears for something much more precious—the significance of his work. He believes that the by-ways of "philosophizing" lead to a greater or lesser degree of graphomania. Anyone gripped in the claws of dialectics is forced to admit that the thinking of private philosophers, unsupported by citations from authorities, is sheer nonsense. If this is so, then one's total effort must be directed toward following the line, and there is no point at which one can stop. A, which inevitably leads to B, is the first and unnoticed Murti-Bing pill. It is easily swallowed because it comes concealed in the various dishes that constitute the diet of the contemporary intellectual. No untrained mind or barren spirit could ever notice this first, disguised pill. Since I am no philosopher, it is my ambition not to analyze its ingredients, but merely to study its distribution.

The pressure of the state machine is nothing compared with the pressure of a convincing argument. I attended the artists' congresses in Poland in which the theories of Socialist realism were first discussed. The attitude of the audience toward the speakers delivering the required reports was decidedly hostile. Everyone considered Socialist realism to be an officially imposed theory that would have, as Russian art demonstrates, deplorable results. Attempts to provoke discussion failed. The hall remained silent. Usually, however, one daring artist would launch an attack, full of restrained sarcasm, with the silent but obvious support of the entire audience. He would invariably be crushed by superior reasoning plus practicable threats against the future career of an undisciplined individual. Given the conditions of convincing argument plus threats, the necessary conversion will take place. That is mathematically certain.

The faces of the listeners at these congresses were not too legible, for the art of masking one's feelings had already been perfected to a considerable degree. Still one was aware of successive waves of emotion: anger, fear, amazement, distrust, and finally thoughtfulness. I had the impression of participating in a demonstration of mass hypnosis. These people could laugh and joke afterwards in the corridors. But the harpoon had hit its mark; and henceforth wherever they may go, they will always carry it with them. Do I believe that the dialectic of the speakers was unanswerable? Yes, as long as there was no fundamental discussion of methodology. No one among those present was prepared for such a discussion. It would probably have been a debate on Hegel, whose reading public was not made up of painters and writers. Moreover, even if someone had wanted to start such a debate, he would have been silenced. Such discussions are permitted—and even then, fearfully—only in the upper circles of the Party.

These artists' congresses reveal the inequality between the weapons of the dialectician and those of his adversary. A match between the two is like a duel between a foot soldier and a tank. Not that every dialectician is so very intelligent or so very well educated: but all his statements are enriched by the cumulated thought of the masters and their commentators. If every sentence he speaks is compact and precise, that is not due to his own merits, but to those of the classics he has studied. His listeners are defenseless. They could, it is true, resort to arguments derived from their observations of life; but such arguments are just as badly countenanced as any questioning of fundamental methodology. The dialectician rubs up against his public at innumerable meetings of professional organizations and youth groups in clubs, factories, office buildings, and village huts throughout the entire converted area of Europe. And there is no doubt that he emerges the victor in these encounters.

It is no wonder that a writer or painter doubts the wisdom of resistance. If he were sure that art opposed to the official line can have a lasting value, he would not hesitate. He would earn his living through some more menial job within his profession; write or paint in his spare time; and never worry about publishing or exhibiting his work. He believes, however, that in most cases such work would be artistically poor; and he is not too far wrong. As we have already said, the objective conditions he once knew have disappeared. The objective conditions necessary to the realization of a work of art are, as we know, a highly complex phenomenon, involving one's public, the possibility of contact with it, the general atmosphere, and above all freedom from involuntary subjective control.

I can't write as I would like to [a young Polish poet admitted to me]. My own stream of thought has so many tributaries, that I barely succeed in damming off one, when a second, third or fourth overflows. I get halfway through a phrase, and already I submit it to Marxist criticism. I imagine what X or Y will say about it, and I change the ending.

Paradoxical as it may seem, it is this subjective impotence that convinces the intellectual that the one method is right. Everything proves it is right. Dialectics: I predict the house will burn; then I pour gasoline over the stove. The house burns; my prediction is fulfilled. Dialectics: I predict that a work of art incompatible with Socialist realism will be worthless. Then I place the artist in conditions in which such a work *is* worthless. My prediction is fulfilled.

Let us take poetry as an example. Obviously there is poetry of political significance. Lyric poetry is permitted to exist on certain conditions. It must be: (1) serene; (2) free of any elements of thought that might trespass against the universally accepted principles (in practice, this comes down to descriptions of nature and of one's own feelings for friends and family); (3) understandable. Since a poet who is not allowed to *think* automatically tends to perfect his form, he is accused of formalism.

It is not only the literature and painting of the popular democracies that prove to the intellectual that *things cannot be different*. He is strengthened in this belief by the news that seeps through from the West. The Western world is the world of Witkiewicz's novel. The number of its aesthetic and philosophical aberrations is myriad. Disciples imitate disciples; the past imitates the past. This world lives as if there had never been a second World War. Eastern Europe knows this life; but knows it as a stage of the past that isn't worth looking back on. Even if the new problems are so oppressive that they can break a great many people, at least they are contemporary. And mental discipline and the obligation to be clear are undoubtedly precious. The work of really fine Western scholars and artists escapes notice. The only new names that are known are those of "democrats"—a delicate circumlocution that means one is not dealing with a pagan. In short, the recompense for all pain is the certainty that one belongs to the new and conquering world as its propaganda would have one think.

Mystery shrouds the political moves determined on high, in the distant Center. People speak about prominent figures in hushed voices. In the vast expanses of Euro-Asia, whole nations can vanish without leaving a trace. Armies number into millions. Terror becomes socially useful and effective. Philosophers rule the state—obviously not philosophers in the traditional sense of the word, but dialecticians. The conviction grows that the whole world will be conquered. Great hordes of followers appear on all the continents. Lies are born from seeds of truth. The philosophically uneducated, bourgeois enemy is despised for his inherited inability to think. (Classes condemned by the laws of history perish because their minds are paralyzed.) The boundaries of the Empire move steadily and systematically westward. Unparalleled sums of money are spent on scientific research. One prepares to rule all the people of the earth. Is all this too little? Surely this is enough to fascinate the intellectual. As he beholds these things, historical fatalism takes root in him. In a rare moment of sincerity he may confess cynically, "I bet on this horse. He's good. He'll carry me far."

A delinquent has a hard time, however, when the moment comes for him to swallow Murti-Bing in its *entirety*. He becomes such a nervous wreck, that he may actually fall ill. He knows it means a definite parting with his former self, his former ties and habits. If he is a writer, he cannot hold a pencil in his hand. The whole world seems dark and hopeless. Until now, he paid a minimal tribute: in his articles and novels, he described the evils of capitalist society. But after all, it isn't difficult to criticize capitalism; and it can be done absolutely honestly. The charlatans of the stock exchange, feudal barons, self-deluding artists, and the instigators of nationalistic wars are figures who lend themselves readily to his pen. But now he must begin to *approve*. (In official terminology this is known as a transition from the stage of critical realism to that of Socialist realism. It occurred in the newly established popular democracies about the year 1950.) The operation he must perform on himself is one that some of his friends have already undergone, more or less painfully. They shake their heads sympathetically, knowing the process and its outcome. "I have passed the crisis," they say serenely. "But how he is suffering. He sits at home all day with his head in his hands." . . .

In the epilogue of Witkiewicz's novel, his heroes, who have gone over to the service of Murti-Bing, become schizophrenics. The events of today bear out his vision, even in this detail. One can survive the "crisis" and function perfectly, writing or painting as one must; but the old moral and aesthetic standards continue to exist on some deep inner plane. Out of this arises a split within the individual that makes for many difficulties in the daily life of popular democracies. It facilitates the task of ferreting out heretical thoughts and inclinations; for, thanks to it, the Murti-Bingist can feel himself into his opponent with great acuteness. *The new phase and the old phase* are co-existent in him; and together they render him an experienced psychologist, a keeper of his brother's conscience.

One can expect that the new generation, raised from the start in the new society, will be free of this split. But that cannot be brought about quickly. One would have to rid one's self completely of the Church, which is a difficult matter, and one that demands patience and tact. And even if one could eliminate this reverenced mainstay of irrational impulses, national literatures would remain to exert their malignant influence. For example, the works of the greatest Polish poets are marked by a dislike of Russia; and the dose of Catholic philosophy one finds in them is alarming. Yet the state must publish certain of these poets and must teach them in its schools for they are the classics, the creators of the literary language, and are considered to be the forerunners of the Revolution. To place them on the index would be to think non-dialectically and to fall into the sin of "leftism." It is a difficult dilemma, more difficult in the converted countries than in the Center, where the identification of national culture with the interests of humanity has been achieved to a much greater degree. (But trouble exists even there, for its youth, despite sensible persuasion, insists upon reading Dostoevsky.) Probably, therefore, the schizophrenic as a type will not disappear in the near future.

Someone might contend that Murti-Bing is a medicine that is incompatible with human nature. That is not a very strong argument. The Aztecs' custom of offering human sacrifices to their gods or the mortification of their own flesh practiced by the hermits in the early centuries of Christianity scarcely seem praiseworthy. Yet they were practiced successfully. The worship of gold has become a motive power second to none in its brutality. Seen from this perspective, Murti-Bing does not violate the nature of human kind.

Whether a man who has taken the Murti-Bing cure attains internal peace and harmony is another question. He attains a relative degree of harmony, just enough to render him active. It is preferable to the torment of pointless rebellion and groundless hope. The peasants, who are incorrigible in their petty-bourgeois attachments, assert that "a change must come, because *this can't go on.*" This is an amusing belief in the natural order of things. A tourist, as an anecdote tells us, wanted to go up into the mountains; but it had been raining for a week. He met a mountaineer walking by a stream, and asked him if it would continue to pour. The mountaineer looked at the swelling stream and voiced the opinion that it would not. When asked on what basis he had made his prediction, he said "Because it would overflow." Murti-Bing holds such magic judgments to be fossil remains of a past era. The "new" is striving to overcome the "old," but the "old" cannot be eliminated all at once.

The one thing that seems to deny the flawlessness of Murti-Bing is the apathy that is born in people, and that continues to live in spite of their feverish activity. It is hard to define; and at times one might suppose it to be a mere optical illusion. In the last analysis, people bestir themselves, work, go to the theater, applaud speakers, take excursions, fall in love, and have children. Yet there is something impalpable and unpleasant in the human climate of such cities as Warsaw or Prague. The collective atmosphere, resulting from an exchange and a re-combination of individual elements, is bad. It is an aura of strength and unhappiness, of internal paralysis and external mobility. Whatever we may call it, this much is certain: if Hell should guarantee its lodgers magnificent quarters, beautiful clothes, the tastiest food and all possible amusements, but condemn them to breathe in this aura forever, that would be punishment enough. No propaganda, either pro or con, can capture so elusive and little-known a phenomenon. It escapes all calculations. It cannot exist on paper. Admitting, in a whispered conversation, that something of the sort does exist, one must seek a rational explanation for it. Undoubtedly the "old," fearful and oppressed, is taking its vengeance by spilling forth its inky fluid like a wounded octopus. But surely the Socialist organism, in its growth toward a future of guaranteed prosperity, is already strong enough to counteract this poison; or perhaps it is too early for that. When the younger generation, free from the malevolent influence of the "old," arises, everything will change. Only, whoever has observed the younger generation in the Center is reluctant to cast such a horoscope. Then we must postpone our hopes to the remote future, to a time when the Center and every dependent state will supply its citizens with refrigerators and automobiles, with white bread and a handsome ration of butter. Maybe then, at last, they will be satisfied.

Why won't the equation work out as it should, when every step is logical? Do we have to use non-Euclidean geometry on material as adaptable and plastic as a human being? Won't the ordinary variety satisfy them? What in the hell does a man need?

THE "PENSADORES" OF LATIN AMERICA

William S. Stokes

THE PENSADORES AND TECHNOLOGY. Among those with status, dignity, and influence in the community, few rank higher in the continuum than the *pensadores* or intellectuals—the poets, novelists, essayists, artists, and professional people. They are an important element, frequently the most important, in the upper-middle classes which govern everywhere in Latin America. The *pensadores* have almost unanimously expressed the conviction that the values of Hispanic and Anglo-American culture are in conflict. More than that, the central theme in the thinking of the great majority of the intellectuals is the belief in the superiority of the values of Hispanic culture and the inferiority of the values of United States culture. Hispanic values must be defended and protected at all costs from the encroachment of the United States culture. I have elsewhere explored the evidence of cultural anti-Americanism of the nineteenth and twentieth centuries in Latin America.[1]

There is no school of literature in Latin America which argues that technology represents values which should be adopted, cherished, and used as a means to a more meaningful life. Indeed, Professor Eduardo Neale-Silva, distinguished professor of romance languages at the University of Wisconsin and authority on José E. Rivera, has informed me that he does not know of a single novel of any recognized author which treats technology as a legitimate, valuable part of Hispanic culture. Although I have not made a quantitative analysis of the content of the novels of Latin America of the nineteenth and twentieth centuries, I have made sample studies from time to time which would lead me to believe that almost without doubt a majority of the novelists of Latin America are largely indifferent to technology.

The Mexican Revolution, which began in 1910-11 and is still continuing, at least in the sense of controlling government, is generally regarded as the most important social, political, and economic movement in Latin America

Condensed and adapted by the author from "The Drag of the 'Pensadores'," in *Foreign Aid Re-examined* (1958), edited by James W. Wiggins and Helmut Schoeck; printed by permission of the author, the editors, and the publisher, Public Affairs Press. Title supplied by the author.

1. Stokes, William S. "Cultural Anti-Americanism in Latin America," in Anderson, George L. (Ed.). Issues and Conflicts (Lawrence, Kansas: University of Kansas Press, 1959), pp. 315-338.

since independence. The object of the Revolution was to effect a fundamental break with the past. More specifically, the Revolution sought to solve the problems of poverty, disease, and hunger which caused widespread distress among the masses. The Revolution therefore offered the *pensadores* an unexcelled opportunity to recommend that science and technology be made central values in the new social order. The evidence demonstrates that the revolutionary novelists did nothing of the kind. Indeed, there is not a single novel by any recognized revolutionary novelist in which technology or the desirability of technological change is the central theme. The subject is simply ignored.

However, there are many illustrations of novels and essays which criticize passionately all aspects of technology when it is introduced into a Latin American country by United States private interests. For example, Miguel Angel Asturias and Joaquín Gutiérrez dramatize alleged "exploitations" of the United Fruit Company in Central America. Baltazar Castro blames United States mining interests in Chile for the frustrations of Chilean workers, and Rómulo Gallegos never deals kindly with the men in his novels who represent the values of United States culture—Mr. Builder in *La trepadora* (the Climber), Mr. Danger in *Doña Bárbara,* Mr. Davenport in *Canaíma,* and Mr. Hardman in *Sobre la misma tierra* (Upon the Same Earth).

Of course, novelists, essayists, historians, and other *pensadores* have not been able to ignore technology in recent decades. The masses everywhere in Latin America have been demanding higher material standards of living. All political movements which have gained power have succeeded in part because their leaders have promised the masses to increase standards of living. "Industrialization" is one of the most-repeated words in the Spanish and Portuguese languages at the present time. Since about the 1920's, therefore, many *pensadores* have given grudging recognition to technology and some have expressed a kind of doleful acceptance of the necessity for changes. However, when the *pensadores* write about industrialization or technological change they almost always do so in theoretical or abstract or doctrinal terms —"las cuestiones primeras" (the primary or fundamental questions), as they put it. They are infinitely more interested in speculation as to the theoretical rôle of technology within the broad context of culture than they are in empirical investigation into the meaning and practical operation of technology in any of the fields in which they desperately need improvements. They have appropriated terms to describe mechanism (such as *maquinismo* and *cosificación*) in life which have overtones of distaste and disapproval.

There is, of course, a voluminous literature critical of United States investments and the operation of United States companies in Latin America. I have hundreds of such references in my files, and I have described and documented economic anti-Americanism elsewhere.[2] Some of the flavor of present-day hostility to United States private economic operations is seen in the argument of Vicente Saenz, perhaps the most prolific of the anti-American writers in Latin America today. He uses the word "suctioning" (*succionadoras*) to describe the activities of United States companies in Latin America. He likens such companies to the pirates and slavers of the sixteenth and seventeenth centuries and asserts that they have contributed to Latin America none of the benefits of their civilization, no culture, not even hygiene. The "economic imperialism" of the "great North American plutocracy"— the "monopolies" of "foreign capital"—have left Latin American mines empty of their riches and soils exhausted of their fertility. The resources of Latin America are going down the "financial gullet" of the "insatiable monopolistic octopus," more fearful than the alligator or the crocodile. Those governments in Latin America which permit United States companies to operate are guilty, according to Saenz, of *entreguismo* (giveaways).

The Value of Non-Utilitarian Education—The Cult of the Doctor. Every work on higher education in the colonial period I have seen has emphasized the excessively literary, abstract, and dogmatic nature of the courses and instruction. Students studied grammar, rhetoric, Latin, and religious dogma (apologetics, theology, ethics) to the virtual exclusion of natural science, modern languages, or literature. The discoveries of Newton, Bacon, Descartes, Copernicus, and others led to some changes toward the end of the colonial period. There was at least some recognition of experimental science and the inductive method. The methodology and content of the instruction created cultural values which still persist, according to Fernando de Azevedo:

> This tendency to put quantity above quality, erudition above culture, the value of eloquence above the passion of ideas, the 'more or less' instead of exactitude, if it did not have its origins in it, certainly was strengthened by the traditional type of teaching . . . in which it was not so much a question of appreciation as of sheer accumulation, and in which the spirit of exactitude, profundity, penetration, critical and aesthetic maturity was (as it still is today) sacrificed to the acquisition of an encyclopedic learning.[3]

The university was one of the institutions in the colonial period with maximum status. Professors were willing to offer their services practically without compensation in order to enjoy the prestige which their position brought to them. The courses which they taught were largely non-utilitarian, certainly non-mechanical or technical, but this enhanced the prestige of

2. Stokes, William S. "Economic Anti-Americanism in Latin America," *Inter-American Economic Affairs* (Winter, 1957), pp. 3-22.

3. de Azevedo, Fernando. *Brazilian Culture* (New York: Macmillan Company, 1950), p. 388.

education. Learning was valued for its own sake. The sons of the elite coveted higher education for the titles and prestige it brought to them rather than for the training it might provide.

Of course, higher education in Latin America has changed since the colonial period. However, it is also true that the colonial institutions have directly influenced the Latin American universities of today: (1) higher education still has maximum status in the community; (2) learning is still regarded as a value in itself, and therefore the courses offered still tend to be theoretical, non-empirical, and non-utilitarian; (3) the symbols of education are still passionately sought and service to the community which titles should guarantee is largely avoided. Almost everyone wants to be a medical doctor who does not practice, a doctor of pharmacy who does not mix prescriptions, a doctor of engineering who does not build, even a doctor of veterinary science who does not personally inject the diseased animal with the medicine it needs. The high status of titles such as *doctor* (*doutor* in Portuguese), *Lic.* (licentiate, lawyer), *Ing.* (engineer), and *Arq.* (architect) is seen in the excessive use of the symbols. Everyone has his calling card with whatever symbol of status he can claim ostentatiously displayed. Letters are signed with the title added. Name plates for homes and apartments display the information. Men are careful to address each other in the ceremonial fashion. In politics the *doctor* and *general* (words are the same in English) compete with each other for control of government. The only exception to the cult of the doctor is Chile, which has prohibited the use of titles except for medical doctors.

The figures on enrollment in institutions of higher learning in Latin America show that relatively few students study to be scientists, technicians, inventors, businessmen, administrators, agronomists, or research specialists. Practically none of the graduate students conduct scientific research in the human and physical resources of their own countries with a view to discovering ways in which the general interest and welfare might specifically be advanced. The evidence in support of these generalizations is readily available in standard sources for the period up to World War II.

In order to bring enrollment figures down to date, I wrote (in 1957 and 1958) to what I considered to be the 80 most important institutions of higher learning in Latin America. I asked for total enrollment by fields for the most recent year for which such figures were available. The figures I collected show that a large percentage of students enter the traditional fields of law, medicine, and engineering. Medicine and engineering are frequently taught more at theoretical than practical levels in Latin American countries, and many men with degrees in these fields do not practice their profession. They are more likely to become government bureaucrats, if they find it necessary to work at all. The figures indicate that training to become farmers, veterinaries, specialists in animal husbandry, miners, or businessmen is almost always far down on the list of preferences. This is significant, because the most obvious methods of increasing standards of living involve modernizing agriculture, exploiting mineral resources, and developing manufacturing enterprises of various sorts.

I devised a sample which included 13 universities from 8 countries plus the figures for all the colleges and universities of Brazil for the years 1950-52. The total number of students in all of these universities was 82,135, out of which 54,540 or almost 66½ percent were in law, medicine, and engineering. Law, medicine, and engineering were the top three choices in Brazil (composite figures for 115 colleges and universities) and in 9 out of the other 13 universities in the sample. There were 30 schools of law in Brazil with 11,455 students and only 12 schools of agriculture with 1,188 students, a ratio of almost 10 law students to each student in agriculture. There were only 539 students studying veterinary science in all of Brazil. Argentina depends on agriculture and stock raising for a large part of its national income, yet at the Universidad Nacional de la Plata, there were in 1956 2,169 students in Juridical and Social Science and only 62 students in agronomy and 42 students in Veterinary Science, etc.

Latin American governments and United States agencies aid graduates of Latin American universities to come to the United States for additional instruction. It is to be expected that most of such students will select courses of study in the scientific and technical fields, because the terms of their scholarships or grants frequently make such selection necessary. However, exact information has not been available. I therefore wrote to the graduate schools of all universities in the United States with about 2,000 graduate students or more enrolled in 1956.

Cursory examination of the statistical data in this sample suggests that Latin Americans enrolled in graduate schools in the United States are more inclined to select utilitarian, practical, and technical courses of study than is the case with Latin American students in their own universities. However, closer examination of the figures reveals that even in the United States large numbers of Latin Americans prefer to work in fields that are more theoretical and cultural than scientific and practical. At least this can be said: Latin America has produced more doctors of law than their culture has required for hundreds of years. Specialization in law surely should not have high priority among Latin American graduate students in the United States if their desire is to contribute to rapid technological change and the raising of standards of living in their respective countries. At the other extreme, one of the things Latin America most desperately needs to alleviate widespread poverty is modern, efficient, scientific agriculture. If we add together all the figures for agriculture, agricultural economics, soils, soils science, poultry husbandry, agronomy, agricultural extension, plant pathology, dairy husbandry, dairy industry, horticulture, and veterinary science, we get 49 graduate students in all out of a total of 466. At the same time, there were 45 Latin American graduate students enrolled in law. There were only 28 students enrolled in business and public administration. And out of the total of 466 graduate students (in the sample for 1956-57), only 2 were in commerce.

THE VALUE OF LEISURE AND NOBLE EMPLOYMENT. The *pensadores* have long expressed the belief that leisure ennobles and labor, especially technical labor, degrades. Indeed, this psychological attitude toward production probably explains better than any other single factor why the Latin American countries are, in varying degrees, backward in the material sense.

The value of leisure and the hostility to technical pursuits can be traced back hundreds of years in Hispanic culture. All scholarly evidence indicates that the *peninsulares* (Spanish born in Spain) dominated the social, economic, and political life of the Spanish-speaking colonies in the New World. A similar situation prevailed in Brazil. The *Peninsulares* were the religious and military officers, the viceroys, captain-generals, governors, intendants, judges, heads of the universities, and great landowners. They demonstrated their social superiority through "conspicuous consumption." They tried to outdo each other in acquiring land; they took pride in their patriarchal "big house;" they wore expensive clothing and personal adornments, had many servants, and ostentatiously proclaimed their lack of association with manual, productive labor or any kind of vile employment. The manual, productive labor and all kinds and types of vile employment were performed first by the Indians through systems of forced labor and later by Negroes who were brought in as slaves and finally by the mixed races produced by *mestizaje* (miscegenation).

The Industrial Revolution could have effected profound changes in the value system of the Hispanic countries. However, the Industrial Revolution did not impress the *pensadores* in the Iberian countries or in Latin America.

The generalization is largely accurate for almost all of Latin America since independence that manual labor and technical activity have low social status. Ostentatious use of leisure (travel, patronage of the arts, conspicuous consumption) has maximum social status. Everyone has contempt for the kind of labor described in the following terms: "manual, productive labor;" "menial labor;" "physical labor;" "labor with the hands;" "mechanical labor;" and "vile employment." These are terms used in works by Carlos Octavio Bunge, José Ingenieros, Manuel González Prada, Juan Agustín García, and many others who have written about Latin American psychology. These noted Latin American writers all agree that in Hispanic culture work degrades; leisure ennobles. In 1955 in an important essay, Sérgio Buarque de Holanda attempts in part to explain why Spain and Portugal never accept work and production as values in themselves. He says: "Action on things, on the material universe, implies submission to an external object, acceptance of a law extraneous to the individual. Not being required by God, it does not add anything to His glory, nor does it increase our own dignity. On the contrary, one may say it impairs and vilifies it. Menial and mechanical labor searches a goal external to man, and intends to attain perfection of a work different from him."[4]

The most important implications of the value of leisure and noble employment are obvious. There is little incentive among the best educated and most cultured people in society to use their brains and hands in production and distribution. They do enough to acquire the leisure which they seek and no more. The lower classes of people, of course, have to work to live. However, they are affected by the value system of the *pensadores*. They do not work up to their potentialities. Quite the contrary. They do everything possible to obtain shorter hours, more vacations, more security from discipline or loss of employment.

Both the theory and practice of capitalism suffer in Latin America from the value system of the *pensadores*. Indeed, capitalism has low status as an economic system. However, almost everywhere in Latin America the ruling classes are alarmed by the increasing demands of the lower classes for higher material standards of living. Almost everywhere they seek an easy way out. Whereas capitalism has low status, collectivism has high status. Even when a country has been able to achieve socialism, the basic values with respect to work nevertheless persist. For example, one has only to study the case of Uruguay, the country which has achieved the maximum development toward socialism. The public servants are many, obviously many more than are needed to operate the government's enterprises. They have acquired the 29-hour work week for themselves, and most of them do not work the full 29 hours. Indeed, I have found in visiting one government ministry or building after another groups of serenely idle government workers in every one of them.

CONCLUDING REMARKS. In most of Latin America there are good people, good land, and good resources. Why are they not used to produce higher material standards of living for all classes of people than is the case at the present time? The evidence indicates that the *pensadores* have not in the past and do not in the present see in technology a value which should be grasped eagerly and made a central part of Hispanic culture. The evidence indicates that when people have a choice as to what kind of education they

---

4. Buarque de Holanda, Sérgio. *Raíces del Brasil* (Mexico: Fondo de Cultura Económica, 1955), p. 17.

want, they choose courses of study which are more in the humanistic tradition than in the industrial, scientific tradition. Finally, the evidence indicates that mechanical work and production have low status and leisure high status generally throughout Latin America.

Therefore, I would conclude that if Latin America desires a revolution, a fundamental breaking with the past, in at least the economic aspects of life, what Latin America needs more than anything else is ideas and values. There have been few such revolutions in the last 2,000 years of Western Civilization. One of the few began in the United States a relatively short time ago. This was in large part a revolution that was made possible by ideas and values. In making this statement, I am aware of the school of thought which argues that the United States is rich because the riches and resources were here for the taking. I have to reject this point of view if for no other reason than the fact that I have observed riches and resources in Latin America which seemed available for the taking. In my opinion, the greatest contribution the United States could make to Latin America would be to share with the *pensadores* our knowledge of the ideas and values which provided the motivation and incentive to all men to develop and express their talents. From what I could see in South America in the summer of 1955, the activities of the United States Information Agency are ineffective in the realm of ideas. The program is oriented to a kind of low-level advertising campaign involving the use of slogans and pamphlets condemning Communism and boasting about the United States rather than the serious, scholarly approach which would have more effect with the *pensadores* who have status and influence in Latin America.

THE INTELLECTUAL IN MODERN ASIA

Prabhakar Padhye

THE INTELLECTUAL in any age is like a seismograph that registers even the most incipient changes in the world around it. Education and training cultivate his faculties, and his developed imagination adds to his sensitivity. He not only reflects the changes around him but, by his imaginative advocacy, even intensifies them.

The intellectual in contemporary Asia has, therefore, become tremendously important. Asia today is surcharged with an atmosphere of revolution. The continent is undergoing fundamental changes. These changes are of a complex nature, at once political, economic, and cultural. Most of all they are emotional. They are vibrating the innermost life of the people.

The dominant factor in the Asian—particularly the Southeast Asian—scene today is the defeat of colonialism. Foreign colonialism is on the defensive, and the disappearance of its uneasy remnants is only a matter of time. Most of the people of the area have become free and are facing the problems of political, economic, and even psychological, reconstruction.

The intellectuals and the middle class from which they sprang were responsible for this profound transformation, and they are now called upon to lead in the task of reconstruction also. But unfortunately they seem to be spiritually ill-equipped to bear the responsibility.

Here is a remarkable paradox. The independence movements were led mainly by the intellectuals, but they now find themselves curiously unable to handle the new post-independence problems.

The explanation of this paradox can be found in the Western education and training that they have received. It must be admitted that the education that the colonial powers provided to the people created the motive-pattern of the educated middle class, which was fired by the ideals of freedom and which provided the leadership for these movements. These patriotic intellectuals were perhaps ideally suited for the negative task of driving out the colonial ruler. But the moment they were faced with the fact of independence

Reprinted from *Cultural Freedom in Asia* (1956), edited by Herbert Passin, pp. 68-71, 73-81, by permission of the author and publisher, Charles E. Tuttle Company. Another version of this essay appeared in *Quest* (October-November, 1955), under the title "The Intellectual in Modern Asia," which title the Editor has employed.

and all the problems that came in its wake they found their Western education not the sure blessing that they had supposed it to be.

It should be remembered that the old colonial rulers were not exactly actuated by high motives in imparting this education. (There were of course noble exceptions like Lord Macaulay, Lord Elphinstone, and Sir Charles Metcalfe in India.) They educated the "natives" mainly to staff their services. And the education they imparted was often artificial and unsuited to the cultural patterns and temperament of the people.

To begin with, the philosophy that inspired their systems of education was totally at variance with the traditional philosophy and outlook on life of the peoples of the region. The Eastern philosophies of life are based on a peculiar relation to nature. "Progress" to the Asian people does not mean the "conquest of nature," but rather the realization of a harmonious relationship of interdependence between man and nature. Their attitude towards nature is not one of mastery, but of gratitude and reverence. They do not look upon nature as something to be conquered and put to the material use of man, but as something to be tended, cultivated, and befriended. The people of Asia look upon themselves as a part of nature; their aim is to realize a harmony between the human order and the natural order. The Asian art of life consists in living in harmony and understanding with one's fellow beings and with nature. Nature here as elsewhere creates wonder and awe, but these feelings lead to reverence rather than to fear, to love rather than to opposition.

The reason for this difference (which is one of the fundamental differences between ancient religion and modern science) is not hard to find. The Asian philosophies of life were developed and fashioned in an environment where nature is bountiful and has been very generous to man. Perhaps the opposite is true in the West. Western man has to face the rigours of nature and to master her in order to eke out a living. The cold climate of Europe and America has made their peoples vigorous and hard working, whereas the warm climate of Asia tends to make the people indolent and carefree.

Asian intellectuals today have been naturally influenced by the philosophies and attitudes that inspire the modern systems of education. One would, of course, expect them to resist this influence because of the long tradition of Asian culture of which they are the heirs. This culture should give them the necessary power of resistance because it is informed by philosophies of great profundity, and it is embellished by an art of life of rich and sensitive texture. But these philosophies have been languishing for hundreds of years, and the traditional art of life has been losing its living touch. What sustained the social fabric in spite of this deterioration was religious ritual and the hold of social conventions. But modern rational education made nonsense of these conventions and rendered the ritual ridiculous.

It should be remembered that the very basis of traditional ritual and convention was being knocked out by the introduction of Western modes of production. These changes had already shaken the foundations of the Asian social structure and severely disturbed the life of the people. But modern rational education carried the changes from the physical to the mental plane. This has deepened the contradiction between the intellectuals and the people. This complication of Western education has turned the educated minority, who live mostly in towns and cities, and the masses of people, who live mostly in the villages, into entities that not merely think different thoughts and speak different languages, but regard each other with a strange incomprehension.

This is especially true of those who have had the opportunity to go to Western universities and be educated there in Western ideas and ways of life. They return home so thoroughly steeped in Western habits, Western practices, and Western views on life that they find the land of their birth more alien and the ways of life here more strange than the West. They are utterly unable to adjust themselves to the realities here. They return with dreams of personal and national advancement, but these dreams are soon cruelly shattered, leaving them sullen and frustrated. . . .

The Asian intellectual is frustrated because his youthful dreams have cruelly foundered on the rocks of Asian reality. He is woefully disappointed because he realizes that his knowledge and training, of which he is legitimately proud, are useless since the Asian situation does not offer much scope for them. He burns with a sense of failure because in spite of his technical training he does not find a suitable vocation; he may even have to engage in "trade." And finally his alienation from the people completely disenchants him. His inability to function creatively in society drives him to frustration and anger. This frustration assumes tortuous forms, and some intellectuals even become professional detractors of their country's efforts and achievements. What happens to them mainly, however, is that they lose their sense of relation to the task of reconstruction that their country has to undertake.

Psychologically there is a terrible void inside them. There is no faith and no conviction to sustain them. They suffer from a terrible feeling of alienation and disenchantment, which threatens to make permanent misanthropes of them. The hunger of the spirit threatens to make them permanently sick, sick in mind and sick in heart.

It should be recognized that this spiritual vacuity was perhaps inevitable. The intellectuals seem to have been victims of the conspiracy of history. The spiritual sustenance that a people draws from the philosophies of its culture was not available to them because these philosophies had been moribund for centuries. The masses of people could at least draw sustenance from ritual and conventions which, though badly shaken by the physical and economic changes of the colonial period, could still have some meaning for them. But for the intellectuals this possibility was largely destroyed by the modern rational education they had received. It is true that this education was inspired by sincere philosophies and it is also true that these philosophies profoundly influenced some of the finest minds in Asia who, in fact, became the pioneers of the new awakening. But it should be remembered that these philosophies were fundamentally alien and that in any event, alien rulers could hardly impart a total philosophy of life to a conquered people. Furthermore, the philosophies of the alien conquerors were badly mixed up with the religious propaganda of the missionaries who appeared on the horizon determined to match the physical conquest of the people with their spiritual conquest; and this created inner antagonisms. Again, these philosophies started crumbling at home (that is, in the metro- politan countries) even before they took root here.

In India (including the present Pakistan), philosophers and poets like Ramkrishna Paramhansa, Vivekanand, Aurobindo Ghosh, Rabindranath Tagore, and Mohamad Iqbal, started revitalizing and reinterpreting the old cultures, but their efforts were not immediately linked up with the pressing material problems of the people. This was done, in magnificent fashion, by Mahatma Gandhi. He gave the people a philosophy that had the power of a new faith. For a generation or so this philosophy inspired some of the finest minds and made life meaningful to thousands of young intellectuals. But most of the Mahatma's efforts had to be confined to the independence campaign, and before he had any time to apply the dynamic of his philosophy to wider spheres of life he was snatched away. Deprived of this dynamic, a vacuum has developed in the spirit of the Indian intellectual. This may be true in other parts of Southeast Asia also. It is a dangerous situation, for nature "abhors a vacuum," and the vacant minds of the Asian intellectuals are being rapidly filled by a comprehensive ideology which has been all prepared to march in.

I do not mean to say that all intellectuals have been suffering from this spiritual hunger, that all are frustrated, and that all are suffering from the gnawings of alienation. Again, alienation may not necessarily be a sign of sickness. The imagination of the artist or the writer may derive great strength from the sense of alienation. It may mean liberation, and it may lend freshness to his outlook; it may, in fact, whet his imagination and activate his creative spirit. But in most cases this alienation is an artificial thing, for man is essentially a social being, and he always pines to "belong." He desires to live under a common roof with his fellow beings, to join them in cooperative activity. He desires to be integrated into the scheme of things. The crowded life and busy tempo of the cities (where the intellectual generally lives) may create the defense-mechanism of aloofness, but that really is superficial; at heart he wants to be part of society.

Some of the striking intellectual phenomena in Asia can be traced to this hunger of the spirit. The growth of revivalism in India and Pakistan, for instance. A mind defeated by contemporary problems tends to take refuge in the glories of the past, and that is what is visibly happening in the Indo-Pakistan subcontinent. The Islamic revival in Indonesia can also be traced to this. A recrudescence of several religious cults (with surprisingly primitive beliefs and practices) and their growing prestige even among the educated classes is another instance. Big gatherings and congresses of the devotees of such cults based on magic and spiritism have been held in recent times and have been attended and blessed by well-known scholars and leaders. Booksellers have reported a marked spurt in the sale of religious literature not primarily of the higher philosophical order.

For those who are unable to reconcile their rational beliefs with these cults there has come in a ready substitute which not only satisfies their inner cravings but also promises ready answers to all the practical problems that have baffled their minds. The substitute is communism.

Communism, in the last analysis, is a religion that believes in reason and the world of here and now. For communists, "reason" means dialectical materialism, and "this world" is the place on which to build heaven. Dialectical materialism assures the triumph of the Cause, whatever the obstacles. The doctrine proclaims communism as the end-product of the historical process. Communists act as the agents of Historical Necessity. Communism is therefore not only a faith, but a Triumphant Faith, and an Armed Faith. It has all the essentials of a satisfying religion. It enables its followers not only to understand the historical process, but to participate in it. Everyone has a definite place within it. This participation not only bestows on him the glory of self-sacrifice but also the opportunity to affect human destiny.

Communism is a philosophy of human development and a technique of political action that satisfies many of the dominant urges of the intellectuals. Western-educated intellectuals have been influenced by the triune ideals of the French Revolution—Liberty, Equality, and Fraternity. To these, the moderns have added the fourth ideal of Planned Economic Development. The modern intellectuals, starved of emotion and imagination, have had a profound need to believe that the triumph of communism is the triumph of these ideals, even though in actual fact these ideals have been thoroughly violated. They have been able, therefore, to accept the so-called "economic liberation" as a proper substitute for political liberty, which according to them is in any case illusory. They are not disturbed by Stalin's dismissal of "equality" as a "petty-bourgeois ideal" because hatred of the rich has provided an adequate psychological substitute. The nature of communist "fraternity" has been exposed to the full horror of democrats by the treatment meted out to one-time comrades, but they are not worried because the bond of party loyalty has the force of the mediaeval Islamic brotherhoods. And even if the communist betrayal of these ideals has sometimes been too blatant to bear, they have been willing to accept them as unavoidable sacrifices in the interest of rapid economic development. The speed of economic construction is so important to them that they are willing to forget many things. That this economic development is lopsided, that it leans on heavy industry designed for a quick switch over to war production, that it is based on the immoral practice of forced labour, and that it has its own crises of over-bureaucratization, does not bother them. It is the fact that economic life is planned and organized that has an irresistible fascination for them. For education has led them to an acceptance of the concept of mastering nature, which is what communism preaches. It has to be admitted that this attitude has great relevance for the countries of Asia, where a long era of exploitation has largely undone the benefits of bountiful nature. But it is not for this that the intellectuals care nothing for the beauties of the Oriental philosophies of the integration of man with nature and of love between man and man.

The picture of a high-powered industrialized society appeals to their desperate desire for integration. They feel that they can find their secure and legitimate place in the structure of the planned society that the communists will build. Of course, there is integration in democratic societies also; but it is a spiritual kind of integration based on the integrity of every individual. In an economically precarious society this spirtual integration is continuously threatened. Naturally, our modern intellectuals tend to attach more importance to the integration of the Soviet type. But they forget that what they call integration in Soviet society is ultimately pure conformity, against which the heart of every genuine intellectual must legitimately rebel. Intellectual growth is impossible in an atmosphere of total conformity, and a mind that is not allowed the delights of independent thinking cannot flower to its full bloom. Asian intellectuals, who tend to ignore the difference between integration and conformity, easily fall for the blandishments of communist doctrine and propaganda.

Our alienated intellectual has been pining for this feeling of integration. He is intensely unhappy about his isolation from the people. Though outwardly he might like to flaunt his "cultural" superiority, inwardly he is disturbed by a feeling of guilt. Communism gives him a good opportunity to get rid of this feeling. The communist emphasis on modernization and planning places a special value on the talents of the intellectuals, who can thus retain their sense of superiority and yet have the feeling of being integrated with the interests and destiny of the people. More than this, they can retain their white collars and still go around as revolutionaries, as privileged servants of the "supreme revolution of the times."

This feeling of integration so completely and satisfactorily fills the spiritual void in our intellectuals that they have a hard time giving up their beliefs even when some of its vital planks have been knocked out by experience. An Asian intellectual can overnight give his allegiance to communism but generally takes years before he can finally shed it; and then, like the American Negro writer, Richard Wright, he feels a terrible emptiness, only this time it is filled with a strange sense of meaninglessness. Professor Paul Linebarger of the School of Advanced International Studies (Johns Hopkins University) has recorded his experience of the captured communists in Korea and Malaya thus: "men who defected from communism had a very real sense of being spiritually forlorn." This is even more true of the intellectuals.

The dominant problem in Asia today is, of course, the economic problem. The Asian people are passionately yearning for economic development and material well-being. You cannot convince the intellectuals here by denying the achievements of Soviet Russia or by singing the praises of nonmaterial values (although one must emphasize their importance and must also point out that excessive preoccupation with material development will distort the vision of our people and dehumanize our culture). But it should be possible to demonstrate that the ruthless Soviet methods of centralized, high-powered industrialization will not bring about the economic development of Asian countries (as they did in Russia) because the man-resources ratio is extremely adverse here whereas it was supremely favourable in Russia. It should be possible to convince the reasonable intellectuals that the ruthless Soviet methods of high-powered industrialization might give us the steel frame of dictatorship but certainly cannot give us the necessary steelmills.

It is true that extreme poverty and material degradation tend to make the people indifferent to freedom; but it is not true that they cannot be roused to the dangers of dictatorship. People aspire to economic betterment, but they also aspire to a share in decisions affecting their own fate. This is as real as the urge for material comfort. It may not be possible, in the undeveloped conditions of Asia, to bestow sizeable material comforts on the people in the immediate future; but there is no reason why this growing urge for participation should not be satisfied. Conventional centralized democracy may not be able to do this; but surely it should be possible to think of a variety of democracy that would decentralize power and bring its magnetic touch to large masses of people on various levels. Communist dictatorship, in the first place, does not respect this desire of the people to share in power; and, secondly, by its very nature it cannot decentralize power. If the Asian intellectuals are persuaded that it is possible to give more power to the people, their natural idealism would welcome it, and this itself would mean the beginning of a revolution in their outlook.

It can be easily demonstrated to the intellectuals that the satisfaction of the power urge of the people can be a means of economic development even as the satisfaction of their property instinct. But the communists too go to the peasants and workers with the slogans of "land to the peasants" and "factories to the workers." The peasants and workers may not immediately understand that once the communists take power, first the factories and then the land would be handed over to a new bureaucracy which would manage them in the name of the people and grow fat and rich in the process. But the intellectuals can see the point and realize that *control* over the means of production can yield as much power and special privilege as formal ownership does.

The intellectuals, with their heightened imagination and broadened vision, should be able to see that the touch of power can galvanize the broad masses of the people, rouse their energies, and fill them with the conviction that they are the masters of their own destiny, that they are participating in a revolution to shape the destiny of themselves and of their fellow men: the intellectuals should be able to realize the importance of enfranchising the people (as Bevan has said) not only at the ballot box but also in the fields and factories. A decentralization of this kind would release the forces of a unique democratic dynamic and put the instruments of social, political, and economic action into the hands of those who would be affected by it. This requires, of course, tremendous confidence in the ability of the people and their direct participation in civic and economic activities. This would give our intellectuals a relationship with them that would be more honest and organic an integration than the mechanical integration that is possible in a bureaucratic role in the vast centralized plan of the Soviet pattern. This would make the intellectuals really comrades and not masters of the people. Such a relationship would be emotionally more satisfying and more profound.

This dynamic relationship between the intellectual and the people would galvanize the life of the community. It would mean a full-blooded cultural efflorescence which would inspire the life of the people with the magic of creative delight. It would revive the culture of the masses and provide them the elements of joy that they have been woefully lacking for many years. The culture of a nation always springs from the people. It can never be imposed from above. It is a living example of decentralization in the most delicate and vibrant aspects of human life. Any attempt to encage it in a centralized plan is bound to make it lifeless and mechanical. A system of organization that evokes the participation of the people at all levels of life would naturally lead to the advancement of folk culture, which is a vital element in the national culture of all countries, particularly those of Southeast Asia. Such an awakening is bound to lead to the resurrection of the philosophies of the East, which visualize a grand harmony based, to quote Dr. Supomo, President of the University of Indonesia, on "the unity between God and man, unity between man and other creatures, and unity between the material world and the spiritual world"—in short, harmony between man and nature. Such a consummation will provide the elements of faith (in the most scientific sense of the term), starved of which our intellectuals have become walking skeletons of frustration and faithlessness!

Only a philosophy that embraces this conception of decentralization and popular participation in power has the capacity to defeat the appeal of doctrines like communism and to release our intellectuals from their deadly lure. Wherever philosophies of this type have arisen, communism has been put on the defensive—intellectually at least. I do not mean to say that any particular doctrine like Revolutionary Gandhism, or Radical Humanism, or Decentralized Socialism, or Buddhist Socialism, has all the answers; but they have all shown remarkable attractive power. Nor do I mean that they have been put into practice in whole societies or that they have defeated totalitarianism once and for all. But they will. However, before they achieve this success, they will have to be revitalized (as Gandhism is being revitalized by *Bhoodan* and *Jeevandan*) in actual practice. They will have to be integrated. They will have to be strengthened. Here is a sublime quest for thinkers and philosophers.

THE END OF IDEOLOGY IN THE WEST

Daniel Bell

THE DIFFERENCES between the intellectual and the scholar, without being invidious, are important to understand. The scholar has a bounded field of knowledge, a tradition, and seeks to find his place in it, adding, in mosaic fashion, to the accumulated, tested knowledge of the past. The intellectual begins with *his* experience, *his* individual perceptions of the world, *his* privileges and deprivations, and judges the world by these sensibilities. Since his own status is of high value (because of the tradition of learning), his judgments of the value of the society reflect the treatment accorded him. Any man might say, "The world owes me a living," but society could easily reject the claim if the man has no talent or contribution to make. But the status of the intellectual, because of the presumed intrinsic value of the position, is a different one; and no society can reject the intellectual's claim out of hand. In a business civilization, the intellectual felt that the wrong values were being honored, and rejected the society. Thus there was a "built-in" compulsion for the free-floating intellectual to become political. The ideologies, therefore, which emerged from the nineteenth century had the force of the intellectuals behind them.

Today, these ideologies are exhausted. (This is not to say that such ideologies as Communism in France and Italy still do not have political weight or a driving momentum gained from other sources.) The reasons for this important sociological fact are complex and varied. (The Moscow Trials, the Nazi-Soviet pact, the concentration camps, the suppression of the Hungarian workers, form one chain; the modifications of capitalism, the rise of the Welfare State, another. On a philosophic level one can trace the decline of simplistic rationalistic beliefs and the emergence of new stoic-theological images of man, e.g., Freud, Tillich, Jaspers, etc.) They have been traced, in probing ways, by Raymond Aron and Edward Shils.[1] But out of

Reprinted from *The End of Ideology* (1960), pp. 372-375, by permission of the author and the publisher, The Free Press of Glencoe, Illinois.

1. Raymond Aron, *The Opium of the Intellectuals* (New York, 1958); Edward Shils, "Ideology and Civility," *Sewanee Review*, Vol. LXVI, No. 3, Summer, 1958, and "The Intellectuals and the Powers," in *Comparative Studies in Society and History*, Vol. I, No. 1, October, 1958.

all these explanations, one simple consequence emerges: these old ideologies have now lost their "truth" and their power to move the old radical intelligentsia. Few serious intellectuals any longer have the passion and belief in them that can be communicated to others. Few serious minds believe any longer that one can set down "blueprints" and through "social engineering" bring about a new utopia of social harmony.

At the same time, the older "counter-beliefs" have lost their intellectual force as well. Few "classic" liberals insist that the state should play no role at all, and few serious conservatives, at least on the Continent, believe that the Welfare State is the road to "serfdom." In the Western world, therefore, there is today a rough consensus on intellectual issues: the acceptance of a Welfare State; the desirability of decentralized power; a system of a mixed economy and of political pluralism.

And yet, the extraordinary fact is that while the old nineteenth-century ideologies and intellectual debates have become exhausted, the rising states of Asia and Africa are fashioning new ideologies with a different appeal for their own people. These are the ideologies of industrialization, modernization, Pan-Arabism, color, and nationalism. In the distinctive difference between the two kinds of ideologies lies the great political and social problems of the second half of the twentieth century. The ideologies of the nineteenth century were universalistic, humanistic, and fashioned by intellectuals. The mass ideologies of Asia and Africa are parochial, instrumental, and created by political leaders. The driving forces of the old ideologies were social equality and, in the largest sense, freedom. The impulsions of the new ideologies are economic development and national power.

And in this appeal, Russia and China have become models. The appeal of these countries is no longer the old idea of the free society, but the new one of economic growth. And if this involves the wholesale coercion of the population and the rise of new elites to drive the people, the new repressions are justified on the ground that without such coercions economic advance cannot take place rapidly enough. And even for some of the liberals of the West, "economic development" has become a new ideology that washes away the memory of old disillusionments.

It is hard to quarrel with an appeal for rapid economic growth and modernization, and few can dispute the goal, as few could ever dispute an appeal for equality and freedom. But in this powerful surge—and its swiftness is amazing—any movement that instates such goals risks the sacrifice of the present generation for a future that may see only a new exploitation by a new elite. For these new countries, the question is not one of Communism, for the content of that doctrine has long been forgotten by friends and foes alike. The question is an older one: whether new societies can grow by building democratic institutions and allowing people to make choices—and sacrifices—voluntarily, or whether the new elites, heady with power, will impose totalitarian means to transform their countries. Certainly in these traditional and old colonial societies where the masses are apathetic and easily manipulated, the answer lies with the intellectual classes and their conceptions of the future.

Thus one finds, at the end of the fifties, a disconcerting caesura. In the West, among the intellectuals, the old passions are spent. The new generation, with no meaningful memory of these old debates, and no secure tradition to build upon, finds itself seeking new purposes within a framework of political society that has rejected, intellectually speaking, the old apocalyptic and chiliastic visions. In the search for a "cause," there is a deep, desperate, almost pathetic anger. The theme runs through a remarkable book, *Convictions,* by a dozen of the best young Left Wing intellectuals in Britain. They cannot define the content of the "cause" they seek, but the yearning is clear. There is the search for what William James called "the faith ladder," which in its vision of the future cannot distinguish possibilities from probabilities, and converts the latter into certainties. Richard Chase, the American critic, in a thoughtful assessment of American society, *Democratic Vistas,* insists that the greatness of nineteenth-century America for the rest of the world was its radical vision of man (e.g., Whitman), and calls for a new radical criticism today. But the problem is that the old politico-economic radicalism (e.g., socialization of industry) has lost its meaning, while the stultifying aspects of contemporary culture (e.g., television) cannot be redressed in political terms; at the same time, the avant-garde, particularly in art, is completely accepted and has driven out the older, academic styles. The irony, further, for those who seek "causes" is that the workers, whose grievances were once the driving energy for social change, are more satisfied with the society than the intellectuals. They have not achieved utopia, but their expectations were less than those of the intellectuals, and the gains correspondingly larger. The young intellectual is unhappy because the "middle way" is for the middle-aged, not for him; it is without passion and is deadening. Ideology, which by its nature is an all-or-none affair, and temperamentally the thing he wants, is intellectually devitalized, and few issues can be formulated any more, intellectually, in ideological terms.

But the emotional energies—and needs—exist, and the question of how one mobilizes these energies is a difficult one. Politics offers little excitement. Some of the younger intellectuals have found an outlet in science or university pursuits, but often at the expense of narrowing their talent into mere technique; others have sought self-expression in the arts, but in the wasteland they lack the necessary tension that creates new forms and styles.

Whether the intellectuals in the West can find passions outside of politics is moot; unfortunately, social reform does not have any unifying appeal, nor does it give a younger generation the outlet for "self-expression" and "self-definition" that it wants. The trajectory of enthusiasm has curved East, where, in the new ecstasies for economic utopia, the "future" is all that counts.

And yet, if the intellectual history of the past hundred years has any meaning—and lesson—it is to reassert Jefferson's wisdom (aimed at removing the dead hand of the past, but which can serve as a warning against the heavy hand of the future as well), that "the present belongs to the living." This is the wisdom that revolutionists, old and new, who are sensitive to the fate of their fellow men, rediscover in every generation. "I will never believe," says a protagonist in a poignant dialogue written by the gallant Polish philosopher Leszek Kolakowski, "that the moral and intellectual life of mankind follows the law of economics, that is by saving today we can have more tomorrow; that we should use lives now so that truth will triumph or that we should profit by crime to pave the way for nobility."

And these words, written during the Polish "thaw," when the intellectuals had asserted, from their experience with the "future," the claims of humanism, echo the protest of the Russian writer Alexander Herzen, who, in a dialogue a hundred years ago, reproached an earlier revolutionist who would sacrifice the present mankind for a promised tomorrow: "Do you truly wish to condemn all human beings alive today to the sad role of caryatids . . . supporting a floor for others some day to dance on? . . . This alone should serve as a warning to people: an end that is infinitely remote is not an end, but, if you like, a trap; an end must be nearer—it ought to be, at the very least, the labourer's wage or pleasure in the work done. Each age, each generation, each life has its own fullness. . . ."[2]

---

2. To see history as changes in sensibilities and style or, more, how different classes or people mobilized their emotional energies and adopted different moral postures is relatively novel, though the history of moral temper is, I feel, one of the most important ways of understanding social change, and particularly the irrational forces at work in men. The great model for a cultural period is J. H. Huizinga's *The Waning of the Middle Ages,* with its discussion of changing attitudes toward death, cruelty, and love. Lucien Febvre, the great French historian, long ago urged the writing of history in terms of different sensibilities, and his study of Rabelais and the problem of covert belief (*Le problème de l'incroyance du XVIème siècle*) is one of the great landmarks of this approach. Most historians of social movements have been excessively "intellectualistic" in that the emphasis has been on doctrine or on organizational technique, and less on emotional styles. Nathan Leites' *A Study of Bolshevism* may be more important, ultimately, for its treatment of the changing moral temper of the Russian intelligentsia than for the formal study of Bolshevik behavior. Arthur Koestler's novels and autobiography are a brilliant mirror of the changes in belief of the European intellectual. Herbert Lüthy's study of the playwright Bert Brecht (*Encounter,* July, 1956) is a jewel in its subtle analysis of the changes in moral judgment created by the acceptance of the image of "the Bolshevik." The career of Georg Lukacs, the

Hungarian Marxist, is instructive regarding an intellectual who has accepted the soldierly discipline of the Communist ethic; other than some penetrating but brief remarks by Franz Borkenau (see his *World Communism* [New York, 1939], pp. 172-75), and the articles by Morris Watnick (*Soviet Survey* [London, 1958], Nos. 23-25), very little has been written about this extraordinary man. Ignazio Silone's "The Choice of Comrades" (reprinted in *Voices of Dissent* [New York, 1959]) is a sensitive reflection of the positive experiences of radicalism. An interesting history of the millennarian and chiliastic movements is Norman Cohn's *The Pursuit of the Millennium* and, from a Catholic viewpoint, Father Ronald Knox's study *Enthusiasm*.

THE FRENCH INTELLECTUALS

Herbert Lüthy

FRANCE is emphatically not one of the countries in which the word "intellectual" has an ironic or derisive connotation. In the course of French history it has, however, acquired a very definite ideological coloration. The "intellectual" is quite naturally linked to the Left—with all the infinite vagueness that belongs to the idea of Left in France: Reason and the Encyclopædia, Progress and the Republic. . . . Nowhere else do the intellectuals still form a kind of closed society, a *corps constitué*—a mandarinate—as they do here. The famous "Manifesto of the Intellectuals" of 1898, with which at the height of the Dreyfus Affair the representatives of the critical intellect declared war on the supporters of tradition and authority, and which for decades fixed the meaning of the word "intellectual," was essentially a manifesto of the École Normale Supérieure, that official nursery of the enlightened, republican French spirit. In that great moment, the whole French Left rallied round the venerable institute on the Rue d'Ulm, and the loyalties that were then forged remained alive right down to the years of the Second World War.

Of course, any such claim to a monopoly of intellect has an element of usurpation. Even the most traditional of the anti-Dreyfusards had their intellectual standard-bearers, not only the great names of the academic nobility, the de Broglies, de Vogüés, and d'Haussonvilles, but also the brilliant writers and journalists around Barrès, among whom Charles Maurras soon emerged as the unsurpassable embodiment of all those "deformations" which are usually attributed to "rootless intellectuals"—doctrinaire rationalism, abstract logomachy, and excessive systematisation. Every public polemic is necessarily conducted by intellectuals on both sides, and every ideology ever developed—even the most "anti-intellectual" doctrine of blood and soil—has been formulated and represented by intellectuals. But in France only the men of the Left—those jurors who sat on the Supreme Court of Reason and who were united in nothing but their antipathy to Authority and the Church —claimed the title of "intellectuals" for themselves, and it was a claim they were successful in establishing.

Reprinted from *Encounter* (August, 1955), pp. 5-15, by permission of the author and the periodical.

The hierarchy of intelligence and culture is organised differently in every country. In Germany the peak of Olympus is—or was—occupied by the professors; in America by the experts; in France—as befits a country in which literature is the public conscience, the public consciousness, and, in a famous phrase of Victor Hugo's, "civilisation itself"—by the writer. Not politicians or specialists but writers are, in France, the supreme oracles on public affairs. The phrase, *"littérature engagée,"* was created by the writers and journalists of the Resistance who for a few years dominated the literary and political scene; and it was finally degraded into the catchword of a clique. But the thing itself is old; since the 18th century, every major French writer has been an *"écrivain engagé."* Diderot, Voltaire, Chateaubriand, Hugo, Renan, Zola, Péguy, and Gide were no less "engaged" than Sartre and his disciples, and no one finds it extraordinary that a Nobel Prize winner for literature, François Mauriac, should appear every week as a political journalist who polemicises against Deputies and Ministers. Here the human- istic hierarchy of values has remained unshaken; like the princes of the Renaissance, though far more humbly, every French statesman, general, or diplomat strives after the laurels of literary success as the supreme justification of his public life. It is not yet certain that history will say of General de Gaulle, "What a great commander!" or "What a great statesman!"—but how much more important it seems to him that history should say, "What a great stylist!"

In France it is the *homme de lettres* who issues authoritative dicta on the political and social questions of the day—not as an expert, but as a moralist. The political republic is still subject to the moral guardianship of the republic of letters. It is a state of affairs that astounds and fascinates literary men from countries less given to ideocracy. But if the representatives of the French republic of letters intervene in day-to-day politics, one should not forget that it is never merely the particular political issue that is under dis- cussion. What is being enacted, rather, is an almost ritual confrontation between different conceptions—whose roots go deep into the past—of what "the real France" consists of. It is a struggle over ultimate symbols far more than a struggle over proximate realities.

THE LOST UTOPIA. In so far as the clash between Vichy and the Resistance was a matter of internal politics—and it was this to so great an extent that defeat, occupation, and liberation often seemed only the occasion and pretext for the settling of old scores—it reproduced in a striking manner the opposing line-up of the Dreyfus Affair. For the republic of letters, the liberation of France was a seizure of power by the "intellectuals," in the exact sense of the 1898 manifesto; and here the "revolution" was more radical and more ruthless than in the political republic. Publishing houses, presses, newspapers, and magazines were confiscated by the intellectual

Resistance groups, the "collaborationist" writers were condemned to professional death (i.e. denied the right to publish), and a book or a bit of film
criticism had less chance of escaping the vengeance of the victors than
fortunes made on the Atlantic Wall or the exercise of police and policy-
making functions in the Vichy government. In the measurement of crime
and punishment, too, literature stood at the top of the hierarchy, far above
politics and economics.

In the following years, this dominance of the intellectuals shared the
fortunes of the ruling political Left; its inner convulsions and divisions
were the same, and its ideology faltered before the same decisive issue: the
"this-worldly religion" of Communism, in the face of which the Left intelligence was stricken with impotence in both its traditional functions—as
critic of society and as prophet of utopia. Within its ideological frame of
reference, the "positive values" it represented had been pre-empted by the
Communist world-power, the myth of the Great Revolution had been incarnated (and perverted) by the Soviet Union; and as if overcome by dizziness, the intellectuals teetered on the rim of the extinct volcano of yesterday's
utopia, while the public watched spellbound to see if they would fall in. In
their polemic against the "anti-Communist intellectuals," Sartre and his
friends were basically right when they insisted on the impossibility of a
fundamental rejection of Communism that was not also, at the same time,
a renunciation of the traditional ideas and conception of the French intelligentsia. ("We have the same values as a Communist. . . . We may think
he compromises them. . . . But they are still ours.")

The whole spiritual atmosphere of the first post-war years was bewitched
by this "dialogue of the intellectuals with Communism," a dialogue which
was as fruitful as a conversation with a prison wall. The Communist contribution was, of course, limited to the monotonous repetition of a few
slogans; but even the genuine, rational arguments which passed between
the not-yet Communists and the no-longer Communists—the "sympathisers"
who stood hesitant, fascinated, and shuddering, before the gates of the
Party, and the "renegades" who had the fall from innocence behind them—
took the form of two endless monologues in different languages about completely different things. For one side, what was involved was the defence of
an ideological frame of reference without which its spiritual world seemed
to come apart; for the other what mattered was the analysis and exposure of
the Communist reality—by which they at once ceased to be "intellectuals" in
the received sense.

For ten years, the French intellectuals discussed the great questions of the
age before a mirror, so to speak, and what they were looking for was not
objective knowledge but the striking of a proper attitude—the right traditional posture. The "testament," the "personal document" which, almost

without literary transposition, reproduced the author's more or less profound reflections as he read his daily newspaper, the diary published day by day, and journalism *tout court* became the dominant forms of this literature of men who were so busy keeping up appearances that they barely had time to formulate their thoughts, far less to organise them. Through all the events of the post-war era, the aim was to preserve one's good conscience and intellectual balance by carefully measured protests against tyranny in Spain and tyranny in Czechoslovakia, race dicrimination in America and forced labour in Russia, executions in Persia and executions in Budapest. In the end, everything that happened in some part of the world came to be viewed in terms of an Incarnate Reason busy with the supreme problem of its own consistency. The one theme of *"littérature engagée"* finally became—itself; and *"engagement"* ended in solipsism. Jean-Paul Sartre especially, even in his polemics and his plays, never had any other subject or any other conversation-partner but himself; and there sprang up in his wake a whole literature, written by intellectuals for intellectuals about intellectuals, in which every ripple in the local pond became a stage in the development of the Human Spirit.

This post-war period, which in literature ran its course under the sign of the twin constellation Sartre-Camus, came to its end in the fall of 1952 with a bitter and rancorous polemic between the two men, of which Sartre remarked with foresight that it would look to a detached observer like a wrangle between Vadius and Trissotin, the two vain poets in Molière's *Femmes Savantes*. The whole choir of "unpolitical" writers, devoted merely to entertainment or to belles lettres—but also all those writers who had once compromised themselves with Vichy—triumphantly celebrated the débâcle of the "intellectuals," under whose moral authority they had chafed for so long. The purged of yesterday returned in triumph to the spotlight; it was the time of the rebirth of the non-ideological reviews, from the *Nouvelle Revue Française* to *La Parisienne,* and of the decline of the political-literary *revues engagées* of the type of *Les Temps Modernes* and *Esprit*. This literary counter-revolution corresponded exactly with the course of French post-war history in general; the "Antoine Pinay era" meant the collapse of the Resistance mythology in politics and literature; the death-agony of Gaullism; the beginning of disenchantment with Communism; the end of the inflation and of the great working-class strikes; and the evaporation of that apocalyptic mood in which the intellectuals had lived since the end of the war. Since then, Sartre has busied himself for more than two years—significant in itself of the ideological cul-de-sac in which he finds himself—in an interminable, fragmentary, and tangled exegetical effort to elucidate the significance of the last Communist essay in rowdyism: the miserably unsuccessful protest-demonstration of May 28th, 1952, against

"Ridgway la Peste," which the Party itself condemned shortly afterwards as a "sectarian error," and which was long ago forgotten by everyone—everyone except Jean-Paul Sartre, who is still calling on world history, the Church Fathers, and Hegel's World-Spirit to prove that it was at that very moment, when the Proletariat refused to follow it, that the Communist Party embodied the Proletariat most completely, because most tragically.

More interesting, as well as more meaningful, is Albert Camus' tireless search for a more genuine utopia to replace the Communist-confiscated myth of the Great Revolution. His is an almost religious endeavour to snatch the "original truth" of the human rebellion against fate and injustice out of the hands of the false priests who have seized it. But the temple of a new Mediterranean sun-cult which Camus has raised on the rim of the burned-out crater of the Revolution is not yet a convincing piece of architecture.

To be sure, neither Sartre nor Camus has said his last word yet. As long as a writer is alive and working, his account remains open. But a literary decade in which these two names seemed the official representatives of the Zeitgeist has come to an end.

SELF-PORTRAIT OF THE MANDARINS. It marks a kind of period after one of the most confused chapters of French literary history that Sartre's companion, Simone de Beauvoir, should have felt the time was ripe to write a history of this period in the form of a *roman à clef.* The title, *Les Mandarins,* exhibits a good deal more ironic detachment than the book itself. The documentary value of the novel, and its artistic failure, lies precisely in the fact that its author lacks all detachment from the group of intellectuals it portrays—all detachment, that is, but the instinctive detachment of a woman toward this species of men who spend all their time in general discussions, when they are not busy writing. The crapulous aspect of the book which made it a best-seller in France—a kind of Kinsey report on the sexual behaviour of the homo sapiens of Saint Germain des Prés—need not occupy us here. But the remaining two-thirds of this astonishing book consists chiefly of endless discussion between those writers who for a few years represented for the world the "new" spirit of France, and these conversations are so genuine—they are, indeed, genuine to the point of absolute dullness—that they read like stenographic reports. This is accompanied by a convenient and arbitrary distortion of the facts about her protagonists. The "poetic liberties" which Mme de Beauvoir allows herself with personages who were taken directly and very recognisably from life derive from that subtle art of polemical insinuation and misquotation which Sartre himself manipulates so brilliantly. Almost every one of the central figures of the novel can be immediately and unmistakably identified behind their transparent pseudonyms, and almost every situation corresponds to an actual occurrence; but everything is displaced, transposed, misdrawn, and adorned with invented or distorted episodes. (Not to speak of the painful tastelessness of the contrived happy ending, in which the narrator is left established as the wife of one of the two spiritual leaders of *"littérature engagée"*—who are now politically and personally reconciled—and the mother-in-law of the other.) This "historical document" must therefore be approached with caution.

But all the book's unreliability is made up for by the priceless naïveté with which, for hundreds of pages, the author earnestly and conscientiously reports the dullest and most threadbare of the clichés with which her intellectuals carry on their political-philosophic arguments, never doubting for an instant either their importance or their profundity. Here she has really added nothing and subtracted nothing: this is exactly the way the Cold War, the Future of Mankind, Communism, Capitalism, and The Revolution were discussed and morally judged in these editorial offices—just so abstractly, just so foolishly, and with just such an absence of all knowledge and all serious analysis.

This unending monologue in an intellectual hothouse has an almost eerie unreality; there is a complete lack of contact with the present time or place. These revolutionary intellectuals seem to have no thoughts for the needs and problems of their own country, just emerging from war and disorganisation. All the discussions revolve endlessly about the single, decisive, fascinating, and insoluble question of whether entrance—or non-entrance—into the Communist Party is compatible with intellectual integrity. But about what goals are to be sought thereby, what changes striven for, what a Communist seizure of power would really mean for their country or even for their own lives—of this not a word. It is a purely symbolic action whose propriety or impropriety for intellectuals has been made into a theme for dialectical disputation. Not one of the contemporary problems of the political and economic organisation of France is mentioned even in passing; nothing moves these spirits but the Manichean duel of eternal principles, which is not even a conflict but a motionless, dramatic confrontation of light and darkness, good and evil, justice and injustice—and even this not as a confrontation within their own country, but as a distant gigantomachy whose protagonists are "Capitalism," personified in the United States, and "Communism," personified in the Soviet Union. For these intellectuals, who had set themselves the goal of overturning the world, the real France and the real Europe simply did not exist. What makes this all the more touching is their conviction that they are hardened political realists, for whom there is no worse insult than to be called "idealists," and who are ready to sacrifice all their ideas and values for the sake of "action"—an abstract action-in-itself about whose goals the reader remains completely in the dark.

Ideological casuistry is not a fertile soil for literature. Simone de Beauvoir's novel of ideas is at the same time a novel of idea-lessness that takes refuge in ideology. Its heroes are writers to whom nothing occurs but pamphlets and newspaper articles, because "politics" leaves them no time to think. In one of his weekly columns, François Mauriac recently raised the question—only immediately to answer it in the negative so far as he himself is concerned—of whether the entrance of the French writer into journalism did not have other grounds than the sheer impulse toward political activity.

In the mixture of motives that drives us to act, let us not yield to the temptation to choose only those which flatter us. . . . Are we, in reality, fleeing from the work we have to do, or from an exhausted soil from which we no longer expect anything worth the effort? In that case, if we have become journalists it is not because our thirst for injustice has increased but our powers of creation have diminished.

This insidious question has never struck the heroes of "The Mandarins." They know exactly why nothing occurs to them any more: it is the result of their revolutionary sense of duty, their clear insight into the historical situation. "First we must win the struggle in the political field. . . . What must be avoided is the creation in the world of a war situation. . . . We must also avoid allowing this victory to be exploited by capitalism. . . . There are many things that must be prevented before we can amuse ourselves by writing books that no one, perhaps, will read," Dubreuilh, the philosopher and leader of the group, explains; and he refuses to publish the reminiscences he wrote during the war in order not to "furnish arms to Reaction." And the novelist-playwright-moralist Perron, in his turn, spends sleepless nights oppressed by the responsibility of his newspaper editorship.

There had been no need for special competence to work in the Resistance and to found an illegal newspaper; he had thought things would go on like that. . . . But if he wanted to get to the bottom of things it would take him years: economics, history, philosophy, he would never be finished! Just to come more or less to terms with Marxism—what a task! There would be no question of writing any more.

And finally this central paragraph from a long conversation between the supreme mandarin and his wife, in which the doctrine of the *sacrificium intellectus* is formulated with an almost classic purity:

Today the revolution is in the hands of the Communists, and in their hands alone; they will be found again perhaps, let us hope so; but if we persist in maintaining them, at this moment, we serve the counter-revolution. . . . I know very well that many things that were important to me are out of place now; I have come to wish for a future very different from the one I imagined; only I cannot change myself; and so I see no place for myself in that future.—In other words you hope for the victory of Communism, although you know that you could not live in a Communist world?—That's about it. I will write about that. That will be the conclusion of my book.

Thus, given his ideological frame of reference, within which the opposition "Russia-Communism-Revolution" and "America-Capitalism–Counter-revolution" marked the polarity of Left and Right, good and evil, the high mandarin of the French intelligentsia knew—or thought he knew—on which side his sympathies lay; but he could find no place there for himself or for "his values." And the Mandarin's France has shared his fate: it has become a no-man's-land which had no place in this post-war world. For if, as we have seen, the real France—its people, it institutions, and its problems —never appears in the political deliberations of its mandarins, there does flicker through this revealing book a strange, abstract France, an "Idea of France" with which the mandarins completely identify themselves, even with a considerable amount of intellectual chauvinism. And perhaps the key to the riddle lies here. For it would be easy to find a similar dissociation of the "Idea of France" from the prosaically real France in other writings of a very different tendency—perhaps most completely of all in the memoirs of General de Gaulle. How is it possible, one asks oneself, to venerate one's own country so completely as an Idea and yet despise its material reality so profoundly?

PRESTIGE AND THE INTELLECTUALS. In the endless monologue of the mandarins there sounds from time to time the discordant, sardonic voice of an uninvited guest, whose Mephistophelian features Mme de Beauvoir has painted with a loving hatred: Scriassine, the incarnation of the ex-Communist. In the opening pages he is already present, insinuating himself into the first New Year's celebration after the liberation of Paris to disturb the optimistic gathering with his message of doom. "The French intellectuals are in an impasse. . . . Their art, their thought, will only retain meaning if a certain civilisation succeeds in maintaining itself; and if they wish to save this civilisation, they will have nothing left to contribute either to art or to thought." The hostess sees through him immediately: an American agent! ("You don't mean that if there is a conflict you would wish for an American victory!") and there is no doubt about his evil intentions: "All Scriassine wanted was to silence the French writers." Nevertheless, this Cassandra evokes the fundamental theme of the whole book, which is nothing but a depiction of that impasse.

Intertwined with this episode there is a second one, whose real meaning is submerged in a waste of sentimental and erotic complications. In the last winter of the war, Henri Perron makes a much-envied lecture and vacation trip to Portugal—on behalf of the French Foreign Ministry, we learn quite incidentally. He brings back to the Ministry a memorandum from the Portuguese opposition which, betrayed to Salazar by the British and American capitalist, "places its one hope in France." A hundred pages later, a high official of the Quai d'Orsay, a former Resistance comrade, explains to him that this hope is completely unrealistic. "How can France do anything for Portugal, or for anyone else, when it can do nothing for itself?" And here an inner monologue follows which would be one of the best things in the book if Mme de Beauvoir did not have a mania for motivating every spiritual shock (including her own discovery that the Americans are fascists and warmongers) by a tedious erotic misadventure. The scene is Henri Perron's discouraged return from the Quai d'Orsay through the outwardly-untouched streets of Paris, which suddenly seems to him a ruined city:

He crossed the street and leaned on the parapet of the quay. Seen from Portugal, France still kept the stubborn radiance of a dead star, and Henri had let himself be taken in by it. Suddenly he saw that he lived in the dying capital of a very small country. The Seine flowed in its bed, the Madeleine, the Chamber of Deputies were in their place, and the Obelisk too; one might have thought the war had miraculously spared Paris. . . . But in truth the proud city erected on the heart of the world had been annihilated. Henri was no longer anything but the unimportant citizen of a fifth-rate power, and *L'Espoir* nothing but a local gazette. . . . He opened the door of the restaurant and heard his name being whispered. Yesterday he would still have been flattered; now while he made his way through the crowd of habitués he was angered to think how he had let himself be duped by this shabby mirage; what a derisory triumph, to be a great writer of Guatemala or Honduras! Yesterday he had thought himself the inhabitant of a privileged part of the world, from which every sound reverberated through the entire globe; but now he knew that all his words died at his feet.

There is more in this inner monologue than patriotic grief or offended national pride. "France is our only hope"—that was the exhilarating message brought back by the travelling lecturers sent swarming into the world by the propaganda services of the French Government after the Liberation. The travelling salesmen of French prestige reaped a rich harvest, and feasted—in a kind of despairing self-intoxication—on the restored glory of the nation. In 1945, France no longer possessed anything but her historical and cultural prestige, and on that basis she undertook to build a world position. Measured by the diplomatic honours and privileges that were granted France in the councils of the victors, the attempt was successful; but the gap between the promise and the reality was too great, and the awakening was unavoidable—especially among the intellectuals themselves, who carried the "light of the dead star" into the world. For the prestige of that France which they served was their own personal prestige, that of the French spirit and of French literature. That, beyond this, the international weight of a nation should also be measured by its political, economic, and military strength came to them as a painful surprise, almost a barbaric insult.

The practice of sending intellectuals, writers, and artists abroad to add to one's national prestige has become common since the First, and even more so since the Second World War. But no other country—except perhaps for Spain within the limited orbit of *Hispanidad*—so invests its cultural missions with pathos as does France: the pathos of its claim to universality as "human civilisation" itself, its urge to the redemption and unification of mankind through the French spirit. The many-faceted and deeply-rooted conception of "the mission of France" manifests its continuity in a succession of avatars; from the Christian crusading idea of the *"Gesta Dei per Francos,"* through the absolute monarchy's policy of cultural as well as military hegemony, up to and beyond the revolutionary imperialism of the Jacobins and the Empire. The power of this "French Idea" is precisely that it can take many forms and expressions—from the revolutionary "world-nation" to the policy of colonial assimilation; from the formation of an aristocratic élite to the message of liberty and equality proclaimed in the "principles of 1789"; from the enlightened rationalism of that France which proclaimed itself the "torch-bearer of Reason and Knowledge" to the world-spanning network of mission schools, officially fostered and protected even in the most anti-clerical days of the Third Republic—and even down to the prophetic anger of George Bernanos's last works, which summoned France to a crusade against the materialistic herd-philosophy of the machine age. Behind this *"rayonnement de la France"* stands not only a national personality which is culturally the most finished in the West, but also a mighty, centralised cultural apparatus, inherited from the age of absolute monarchy and extended afterwards with ever-increasing consistency, that has drawn the whole spiritual and artistic life of the country to Paris and placed it, directly or indirectly, at the disposal of the state.

France is the only country in which modern "cultural propaganda" is genuinely rooted in a great tradition which goes directly and unbrokenly back to the prestige politics of the Renaissance and the absolute monarchs. Francis I's "court of muses" and the *"magnificence"* of Louis XIV were nothing else, though they were directed at a more tightly-knit and selected society than modern propaganda can aim at. The conspicuous lavishness at official functions, the systematic cultivation of Europe's courtly society, the wooing of the élite with titles, honours, pensions, and sinecures—all this took up no small proportion of the hard-pressed budgets of the *ancien régime* than do the *"action artistique,"* the *"expansion universitaire,"* and the *"relations culturelles"* of the Fourth Republic. Napoleon I, who brought the Paris opera with him to his peace congresses, and Napoleon III, who built Paris into the cultural capital of the world, found faithful heirs in republican France; and the post-war period has brought this centralisation and state control to such perfection that it remains endurable only because of the political anarchy at the apex. All the strands of the nation's cultural life, the academies, art schools, libraries, research institutes and museums, the national and subsidised theatres, the orchestras, film studios, and publishing houses, converge like a spider's web at the Ministry of Education, which in turn has its subsidiary lines of communication to the authors' and composers' associations, the semi-official overseas organisations, and the Quai d'Orsay.

It would be astonishing if this century-old concern for self-advertisement and external splendour had not had some effect on the inner self-awareness of French civilisation. It has created a natural solidarity between the intelligence of the country and its national prestige which comes aggressively to the surface in times of crisis, and which even the most individualistic and nonconformist of intellectuals cannot escape, because it is not a question of solidarity with a régime or a form of government but with the "Idea of France," and with the primacy of French—and thus of his own—civilisation. Here there is no question of exclusion, just as in the French schools abroad there is never any conflict between Catholic and *laïque* tendencies. When Jean Cocteau, the nonconformist *par excellence,* becomes one of the official immortals of the Académie, when André Breton and his household demons, Lautréaumont and de Sade, are lectured on at the Sorbonne as classics of French literature, one thinks of an old phrase of Sartre's about the "nationalisation of the writer." And even the little *chansonnier* who appears in Brussels, the mannequin who travels to New York with the latest styles, the cook who works in London, or the governess who teaches manners to an Argentine millionaire's son—all feel themselves to be ambassadors of *"la chanson française," "le goût français"* and *"la civilisation française."*

At the core of the whole complex stands the French language itself. "Its credit will share the fortunes of our state," Montaigne remarked in one of his essays. It would be hard to find a similar remark in any other country of the 16th century. Fifty years later the French language had actually become a public institution, with its government council, the Académie Française, which codified and purified its vocabulary, and its legislators who laid down the rules of its grammar and syntax with the same pedantic thoroughness that the lawyers applied to the public life of the country. Perhaps the iridescent French *"esprit"* was always closely connected with this incomparable stability of its syntax—like the fixed, unalterable choreography of the ideological game to which it devoted itself—and even the hermetic, Expressionist, Dadaist, and Surrealist poets lived on the fixedness of the linguistic structure they undertook to shatter. This pre-eminence of the French language has survived French politico-military hegemony in Europe by a full century— the most fragile of all linguistic empires, because it rested neither on numbers nor extension, nor on commercial and technical superiority, but only on the prestige of the language itself and its intrinsic qualities. Even today, every position is still fought for in stubborn rearguard actions: in every new international organisation the struggle for pre-eminence is renewed; the growing use of English and of multilingual arrangements in international conferences is mourned as the decay of all diplomatic tradition and the source of Baby-

Ionian confusion; and in the day-to-day activities of French foreign policy, the conclusion of cultural accords which will assure the French language of first place, or at least most-favoured status, in the educational systems of other countries take precedence over such things as economic agreements and trade treaties.

It would be ridiculous to see in this a mere satisfaction of national vanity. The French linguistic *imperium* has for a long time now—for example, in a purely technical way, in the choice of diplomatic personnel—set a premium on a French education, an understanding of the French mentality, and it has created everywhere a fundamentally Francophile ambiance which is not without its political effect. Beyond this, the international supremacy of French taste, French fashion, and the French way of life were an economic factor of the first rank in their influence on tourism and on the luxury and fashion industries—all exports with an especially high margin of "increment-value."

THE "SALVATION OF MAN". It is only with this background in mind that it becomes quite clear to what an extent France has been driven in the past fifty years to an almost desperate defence against all the fundamental tendencies of our times. Hers is an aristocratic, courtly, individualistic, and profoundly intellectual culture, in an age of industrial mass-civilisation in which the old cultured classes on whose influence French cultural hegemony rested have been, in part expropriated, in part destroyed, and everywhere dethroned. In Central and Eastern Europe, one of the oldest and best-organised of France's cultural spheres of influence, the landslide of the last two decades has taken with it not only the entire network of French institutes, schools, and cultural agreements, but the whole French-educated aristocracy. Even before the Second World War, the 18th-century-style cultural diplomacy of the French, which sought to counter the commercial and industrial superiority of Germany with literary *conférenciers,* had in the end reaped nothing but disappointments. In the remaining zones of influence that still exist outside the teetering colonial empire, in Latin America and the Near East, French prestige is engaged in a hard fight, not only with its old rivals, but above all with the industrial civilisation of America, which has a greater appeal to all "undeveloped countries" than French literature and French Egyptology. And here, too, that social reshifting has come into play which sweeps aside, together with the old leisured classes, all sympathy with the French model of civilisation. The age of social levelling, of the "common man," the demand for well-being and a share in the goods of civilisation for all, do not favour the world-hegemony of the French ideal of civilisation.

These are distant and underground processes, which seldom reach the consciousness of the average Frenchman, or even the average intellectual. But the calamities of this 20th century, which have swept the ground from under France's spiritual *imperium,* are also clearly visible in the daily life of

the motherland; in a multitude of small occurrences on the most visible—
and most sensitive—surfaces of existence. The most obvious—and also, for
the artists and literati of Paris, the most irritating—symbol of this change is
the transformation in the social and cultural structure of tourism. Even in the
between-war period, which was itself only a dull reflection of the *"belle
époque,"* the foreign visitors to France came predominantly from the propertied and more or less aristocratic classes of Central and Eastern Europe,
Latin America, and even a "good old England" then still in existence. They
all had at least some tincture of French culture, and they made it a point of
pride to speak French and to show that they were connoisseurs of wine and
literature, gourmets and *hommes d'esprit* in the French style. This clientèle
has mostly disappeared. It is true that the worst crisis of the first post-war
years has been overcome, but the new tourism of the "common man"—
whose tone is set by the average American, the average Englishman, and
lately by those tourists from what remains of Central Europe who are pro-
pelled through the country in busloads—possesses fewer of these distinctions.
The new tourist does not step piously on to the holy soil of civilisation, but
visits France as he would any other foreign country, finds ruined houses not
historic but wretched, the sanitary facilities of the middling hotel inadequate,
and the horde of tip-seeking lavatory-guardians oriental. He submits less and
less often to the tyranny of the wine list and the menu, and it is the hotels
and resturants that now must suit *his* barbarous taste.

The little innkeeper, the dance-hall artist, the necktie-seller, and even
the ladies of the Place Pigalle can see this "decline of the cultural level" in
their own lives, and are only too quick to adjust to it. And the intellectual
sees in it visible confirmation of what his "philosophy" tells him: in the day
and night-life of Montmartre, as well as in the world-wide rearguard action
of aristocratic taste, "Americanism" appears as the great enemy of the "French
Ideal." A good many really hysterical outbursts, like the crusade against
"Coca-colonisation," or the anger at an American-sponsored cultural festival
in Paris—*"Messieurs, sur le plan de la culture, de la civilisation, de l'esprit,
la France ne reçoit les conseils de personne; elle en donne!"*—can be explained
by this irritation. Out of this deeply-wounded sense of national pride there
has sometimes developed an intellectual chauvinism which can go to the
wildest lengths of persecution mania; in the last few years, for example,
writers and critics of repute have repeatedly developed the thesis that Shakespeare or Goethe were never really significant figures, and that their great
names are the product of an "organised bluff" promoted by the Germans or
the English in order to contest the legitimate pre-eminence of the French
language and literature.

From this perspective, the impasse of Simone de Beauvoir's mandarins,
and the tragicomedy of their search for something to replace their former

certainties, are perhaps more understandable. For them the prestige of France —which was their own prestige—remained bound to the Jacobin myth of the Great Revolution; although France had long ago become a conservative country, forced to defend an old way of life and an old cultural heritage against the industrial revolution of modern times. The "Idea of France," whose once-revolutionary message they wished to go on proclaiming, had lost all relation to the real France. They could do nothing, ideologically, with the reality of France; and, at bottom, they wished to know nothing about it; it had nothing to do with their "French Idea." It was only in the rejection of "Americanism" that they found a—purely negative—contact with the real problems of France, and this negation became the one fixed point of their position. None of them was ever really excited or even genuinely interested by Russian Communism, and even the fate of the working class did not occupy too large a share of their thoughts. But frankly to oppose American civilisation with the aristocratic and individualistic values of traditional France would have meant acknowledging themselves to be conservatives, which was intolerable. And so they clothed their deeply conservative rejection of modern mass-civilisation in the form of an ideological decision to take sides against "American Capitalism" in the cold war—only, indeed, to stumble then against the insight that "our values have no place in Communism." Nothing would do them more good than to decide just once to apply the Marxist analysis of "the ideological superstructure" to their own ideological constructions—for the revolutionary pose of the mandarins is the very prototype of what the Marxist would call "false consciousness."

But the Jacobin message is not the only message France has, and its old civilisation is by no means on its deathbed. Rather, it is passing through a crisis of adjustment to a radically altered world, in which it has all the more difficulty in finding its bearings because it spent the decisive years of the transition under the narcosis of Vichy—and the years afterwards under the self-intoxicating myth of victory. It is by no means inconceivable that a conservative idea of culture, a reasoned defence of aristocratic values against the technical frenzy of the modern world, will find an echo in those very countries where technical and organisational development has reached its highest point; and the rejection of a certain materialist vulgarity, which is all too easily caricatured as "Americanism," does constitute a kind of natural common denominator of all French intellectuals, from Sartre to André Siegfried, without necessarily implying anti-Americanism, neutralism, or pro-Communism. Those who most easily found their bearings in this situation were the writers of the Catholic tradition, who had never believed in technical progress and the blessings of a materialist civilisation. It is just this opposition to the "modern world"—as the late, almost posthumous fame of Claudel bears witness—that has won for them in this post-war period a prominence in

French intellectual life which they have not had for a hundred years. The radical rejection of modern mass-civilisation was Bernanos's last message, as it was the utopia of Antoine de Saint-Exupéry's posthumous *Citadelle*. Here lay the original inspiration for Mounier's philosophy of Personalism, and it is to this group, at bottom, that Albert Camus has, after many detours, attached himself with his appeal to the archaic "Mediterranean spirit"—his personal "revolt" is the exact negation of the ideology of Revolution. And far beyond this group, the "salvation of man," i.e., preventing the sovereign individual from being transformed into a mere cog of organised society, has become the very *leit-motif* of French literature, attaining its greatest expressiveness in André Malraux's post-war work on the philosophy of art.

Today, with the end of the "mandarinate," both the peak of the crisis and the period of pure negation seem to be past. That France should once more take, and earn, her place in the world, instead of drawing back resentfully into her memories of *"la belle époque"*—this, beyond all its ideological confusions and political ambiguities, was the core of the "Mendès-France myth" and of that still formless "New Left," under the banner of which Malraux, Mauriac, and Camus have found themselves united. There is no irreconcilable contradiction between the will to defend and reinvigorate one's own traditional cultural values and the equally determined will to free France from the suffocating burden of its "stagnation by consent." There is no contradiction between the great experiment of Jean Vilar's "Théâtre National Populaire," which has presented Corneille's aristocratic, stilted, and heroic tragedies before enthusiastic audiences in the working-class suburbs of Paris, and the endeavour to give the same workers better tools, more rational methods of production, and a higher standard of living. If a synthesis on these lines is achieved, France will not have to fear for her prestige in the world.

THE GERMAN INTELLECTUALS

Golo Mann

IN A SHORT STORY by the German romantic poet, Clemens Bretano, the narrator (who is Bretano himself) is asked about his profession. For some reason, unclear even to himself, he cannot bring himself to say that he is a writer. And so, after some hesitation, he answers: Scribe. . . . That was around 1800. Some one hundred and thirty years later a German professor was challenged in his seminar to say what he thought of Ludwig Klages, a then well-known philosopher. "Klages," he answered, "I consider a genuine thinker, especially in his early writings. But why not be frank about it? Klages is on his own, a free-lance, without office, without secure income. So, in order to win his bread, he must create all kinds of sensations and write books which are sheer nonsense. If he were protected by a university, he would not have to write such stuff; besides, his colleagues would make life hard for him if he did. . . ."

How often have I heard similar views expressed—and frequently with less sympathy! There was nothing more respectable than the university professor; nothing more dubious, economically and morally, than the "intellectual," the "writer," the "man of letters." In Germany, to be taken seriously, one had to have an office, a rank, a title. That may be due, in part, to the Lutheran notion of a "calling"; in part to the fact that the country had a capital city only at rare moments of its history, so that a metropolitan public was lacking and the writer had to seek princely patronage, together with the office of librarian, preacher, tutor, theatre-manager, and the like. A free-lance publicist could hardly exist until late in the 19th century. When he finally emerged, the public looked at him as something foreign, bohemian, and probably subversive. Every *Studienrat* (teacher in a secondary school) felt superior to a Maximilian Harden or indeed, in retrospect, to a Heinrich Heine.

In contrast, the university professor was very near the top of the social pyramid even when he dealt with subjects—historical or literary criticism, social theory and general philosophy—which were not so far from the "intellectual's" fields of endeavour. He was a high servant of the State or, until

Reprinted from *Encounter* (June, 1955), pp. 42-49, by permission of the author and the periodical.

the early 20th century, of his Prince; in old Austria he held the honorary rank of, I believe, colonel in the imperial army. Apart from his social rank, he has held a central place in the history of his country—which cannot be said of the free-lance writer. When, towards the end of the 18th century, there happened that expansion of intellectual forces on which the German mind has lived ever since, it was largely—not entirely—guided into academic channels. Kant in East Prussia, then Schelling in Bavaria, Fichte in Berlin, Hegel in Heidelberg and Berlin, all became immeasurable influences. Ever since, great professors have been intellectual leaders. They were the conservatives of the late Metternich period (Niebuhr, Ranke), the liberals of the eighteen-forties (Uhland, Dahlmann, Droysen), the Bismarckians (Treitschke, Sybel), the Wilhelminians (Harnack, Willamowitz, Sombart), the anti-Wilhelminians (Max Weber, Friedrich Meinecke). There were prose-writers of great power among them as well as men of almost self-caricaturing pompousness. I do not wish to imply that they were as a whole superior to their Western colleagues, that Mommsen was a greater writer than Boissier, or Treitschke than Seeley. But in Britain and France the university had competition; the great novelist, the successful man of letters far outshone the scholar. In Germany, the university enjoyed something like a monopoly of respectable intellectual existence. Schopenhauer, who was not a professor, was very proud but at the same time very bitter about it. Actually, he had tried to become one. So had Ludwig Feuerbach; so, even, had Karl Marx.

The position of the German professor has been slightly declining of late; partly because during the Hitler period he did not cut a very impressive figure; more generally because of that deep and broad process which, for the lack of a better term, we may call the Americanisation of German society. But even in 1954, a public opinion poll concerning the hierarchy of the various callings brought this unequivocal result: there is nothing higher than the university professor. He still ranks above the industrialist, the trade union leader, the parliamentarian. The same poll gave the writer a standing far below that of the teacher in an elementary school.

Hired by the State to do a certain job, the professor recognised authority, Luther's *Obrigkeit*. He had nothing to do with politics, a well-known professor of philosophy once remarked in my presence.—But would you not try to help, when the house was afire?—No, he calmly answered, when the house was afire, he would call the firemen. To fight fire, to master a political or economic crisis, was a skill which had to be learned. He had not learned it, but had learned to philosophise. . . . If, however, the professor dealt with politics, it was the natural thing to do so in the interest of the State, to back up with historical arguments, say, the German mission of Prussia if he were teaching at a Prussian university.

There are great and numerous exceptions to this academic conformism. Rather, there was a period when it did not exist.

The Revolution of 1848 has been called (by Namier) the "Revolution of the Intellectuals," an appropriate term even for Germany. At that time, liberalism was chiefly represented by professors of whom, including the legists, some three hundred were sitting in the Frankfurt national assembly. The movement failed miserably. This settled the fate of the professors, in the eyes of the nation and even in their own. They no longer asked how society should be ordered but, rather, how things had come to pass as they had, and why they were quite as good as they were. Hegel triumphed over Kant, Bismarck over Hegel.

Meanwhile, the publicist, the man of letters who writes as he pleases, on any topic of his choosing but largely on politics, had made his belated appearance. It started with a bang during the Napoleonic time of trouble and immediately reached a very high point; more powerful editorials than those by Gentz, on the right, or by Goerres, on the left, Germany has never had a chance to read. In the early eighteen-thirties, the writers of the "Young-German" school were winning fame: less solemn than their predecessors, more "Western," urbane, frivolous. Their star is the immortal Heinrich Heine.

Heine—the German intellectual, if there ever was one. An emigré who preferred Paris to any city of his native country. A journalist who made his living mainly by reporting on France for German papers. A bohemian spend-thrift, always in debt, taking money where it could be found, even from King Louis Phillipe. A philosopher of genius, but unsystematic, throwing out and wasting ideas as they came to him, in articles, essays, poems; unpredictable in philosophy and politics; playing with ideas but never entering a permanent alliance with any; prophetic as a commentator but not a mover of things historical; a socialist afraid of the "masses"; an aristocrat hating aristocracy; a rebel by birth and, there is no denying it, thoroughly subversive despite all his charm, his sadness, his personal conservatism; vulgar, at times truly infamous in his polemics; at the same time a poet, and a fine poet. It was exactly this last point which never ceased to puzzle the "true German" critic: how a fatherlandless scoundrel could write such beautiful poetry; how a German poet could lead such a worthless existence.

In truth, the influence of Heine was not entirely to the good. He was the inventor of a new style in political poetry, criticism, satire, aphoristic philosophy, travel reporting. He was an inventor of dazzling genius; but it proved easy to imitate him—including his various poses, his irresponsibility, egotism, frivolity, his hatreds, all his obvious tricks. After the great Heine there came many smaller ones, in the 19th and, even more, the early 20th century. A whole branch of the race of German intellectuals derives from Heine and its members have not helped us much. To them, the world was almost always wrong, especially the German world. Right was what they were pleased to choose; the "proletariat" (with which, in fact, they had dismally little to do),

France, later the Soviet Union, above all the clique to which they belonged (as long as the main battle did not take place within the clique).

The early 1840's also saw the appearance of another type of German intellectual, the "Young-Hegelian," the sociologist of the left. He (Bruno Bauer, Arnold Ruge, Ludwig Feuerbach, etc.) was less happy than the Heine type, for he was neither poet nor brilliant journalist. He was the professor *raté,* the sharp-witted, aggressive, and bitter social scientist whom the reactionary State would not employ and the public would not read. Free and independent these men were—independent, that is, from the State; but not independent of dreary worries, always forced to outbid one another and bitterly quarrelling among themselves. The greatest of them was Marx; who, having contributed his fair share of quarrelling and hating, could turn to his lasting achievements as an economist, thanks to the generosity of that prosperous industrialist, Engels. The sociologist of the far left, Marxian or semi-Marxian, had his heyday under the Weimar republic. At that time, the State did employ him. How much good it did to the democratic State, I shall not judge.

Of Bismarck it is known that he made an amazing offer to Marx: to write for him, with complete freedom to propagate Communism at the same time. That weird episode is characteristic of Bismarck's attitude towards the intellectual life of his time and his nation. He clearly did not belong to the race of the intellectuals. His memoirs, beautifully written as they are, have next to nothing to say about general problems, ideas, constitutional issues. Where he does say something about them, he makes sense; but it happens in barely one out of a hundred pages. The rest is all diplomacy, court-gossip, intrigues, administrative stuff, and malignant personal portraits. All the same, the arch-conservative Baron kept in touch with the intellectuals of the left. He won some of the bankrupt radicals of the 1848 period over to his service; he deeply enjoyed his secret conferences with Lassalle; he made the offer to Marx which has just been mentioned. In his old age he saw Harden at his table—that talented but profoundly dubious publicist of the Wilhelminian era. Bismarck felt lonely among the stiff bores of his own class. A brilliant conversationalist himself, he liked to converse with quick-witted men. Communist utopias he feared far less than the intrigues of his Emperor's wife. At ideas he laughed. But they could be used for propaganda purposes; tools to be picked up, tried out, and thrown away.

Bismarck's government gave work to some intellectuals, but did not elevate their status as a class—very far from it. Nor could they find a real chance of self-realisation in the political parties which now, at last, came into their own. These were not intellectuals' parties. They were interest-lobbies, decked out with some ideological claptrap. There were two exceptions: the Catholic Centre and the Social Democrats. The German Catholic intellectual has always had a spiritual home, a public to talk to, superiors to watch and to protect him; his fate has been enviable in this respect. The Social Democratic party was dedicated to a highly sophisticated theory, Marxism. It took professional intellectuals to create Marxism as well as to keep it alive, to interpret and revise it; while it took factory hands to create a workers' party. Hence the dualism within the party. Lassalle lamented the simplicity of his followers, "the many hard and hot hands" he had to shake; and one of his orders of the day, much to the hilarity of his enemies, began with the words: "Workingmen! Before I leave for the spas of Switzerland. . . ." His successor, Bebel, the true founder, an old worker himself, disliked brainy people. ("If a bourgeois wants to join you, look him over closely; if he is an intellectual, twice as closely.")

There had been a time in Germany when philosophers were near the government (Hegel), even when they were the government (Humboldt). There had been a time, the 1840's, when liberal intellectuals, while being excluded from the government, could reasonably hope to conquer it one day and when, therefore, they took Affairs of State seriously. So long as the State was authoritarian, anachronistic, obnoxious, there was hope that there would one day be a great, blessed change. But the State of the ageing Bismarck and of William II was in many ways no longer anachronistic. It was still authoritarian and military but also bourgeois; even the organised workers mustered considerable political influence. It was an efficient, powerful State, a prosperous, modern society. All the same, the State was stupid, the emperor ridiculous, the parties, including the socialist opposition, bureaucratic, ossified, uninspiring. Consequently, there developed something like a divorce between the political and the intellectual life of the nation, on various levels. Imperial Germany, with her princes, diplomats, court-preachers, generals, judges, industrialists, official poets, did not take notice of what was happening in the sphere of free thought. Nor was she taken notice of by the better writers; she was nothing to be worked for or fought against; at best, she could be ridiculed. On the other hand, political writers, critics, polemists, did not win much respect from their non-political colleagues, or from the nation as a whole, which considered them outlandish and completely negative. One must confess that the most famous publicists of the Wilhelminian era could not entirely refute this charge.

That intellectuals, like artists, are egotistical is a trivial fact. They want to succeed, to impress; and as what they are doing seems important to them, so do they who are doing it, and the more so when the world remains unmoved. It is a matter of degree. In a man like Ferdinand Lassalle, histrionic vanity had already reached striking proportions. In Maximilian Harden, in Alfred Kerr, in the Viennese Karl Kraus, it became maniacal and repulsive. Harden in his way understood diplomacy, Kraus the German language,

Kerr the drama (he greatly helped the rise of Gerhart Hauptmann). But they were not fortunate influences, all three of them. Unbearably mannered in their style, sensationalist, apocalyptically hating and castigating each other as well as most people, they were negative representatives of the Wilhelminian period and did not really outlive it. For Kraus it can at least be said that he remained adamant in his pacifism during the First World War. Harden, like Kerr, turned to a hectic worship of war and power. It is a strange experience today to go through the pages of Harden's review, *Die Zukunft*. Brilliant they are at times, and not entirely without prophetic sense. But what an inflated lurid style! What lack of taste, of mere decency! And how stale the whole work!

In August 1914, the divorce between the intellectuals and the State came suddenly to an end, much to the satisfaction of the weaker, if not of the stronger partner. Those who had so far led the chilly intellectual life, away from the main stream, now jumped into the crowded waters of enthusiasm. Everybody, or almost everybody, wanted to share the wonderful experience— if not as a soldier, then with his pen. Psychological warfare-bureaux—the name did not yet exist—swallowed a good number of writers and lecturers. There were the notorious "war manifesto of the intellectuals," the battle cries of professors and poets, the songs of hatred; on the more serious side, the brilliant paradoxes of Thomas Mann's *Reflections of a Non-political Man,* the geopolitical phantasies of Friedrich Maumann, the warlike metaphysics of Max Scheler. It has been argued that by giving some meaning to a catastrophe which had none, but which was there in any case, the intellectuals did a service to the community. It depends how one looks at it. A Voltaire would find more folly than helpfulness in that *trahison des clercs.*

The so-called revolution of 1918-19 was more of a collapse than of a rising. At least, it created a power-vacuum and where this exists various people will try to step in and fill it with the embodiments of their ideas. Within the Social Democratic party the tough practical men triumphed over the radicals and restored law and order with the help of General Hindenburg. But there were regional upheavals of a more extreme character. If ever unpractical men played at revolution, it was the men who set up a soviet republic in Munich in March 1919: young intellectuals, fresh from Heidelberg University, who, with a little more luck, might have become disciples of Stefan George the poet, or of the sociologist Max Weber, the sterner, better man—in which case they might now be respected, grey-haired teachers somewhere in America. As it was, they became the victims, first of Marxism, then of Lenin's intoxicating example, and now the hour had come when they had to prove the solidity of their science of revolution. They perished in the attempt, some of them; one hates to imagine the writer Gustav Landauer, a fine Shakespeare scholar and an idealist, being beaten to death with rifle-butts by Prussian soldiers. In justice, one must add that these idealists tried to do what was none of their business, that many of them were foreigners in Bavaria and even in Germany, that their attempt was utterly rootless, hopeless, senseless from the start, and that they should not have done it. The notion, popular in Germany ever since 1848, of the crazy, obnoxious *Literat* who should be kept out of politics by any means, if necessary with rifle-butts, has been greatly strengthened by this tragic adventure.

From that time on, there was no escape from politics. To have one's say about the world situation, the crisis, the future of civilisation, the past war and the next one, became the intellectual's normal endeavour—even the anti-political intellectual's. The philosophy which came to be called the "Conservative Revolution," was itself political; highly contradictory, to be sure, vague, dynamic, but anti-constitutional and political nevertheless. Their representatives, much as they despised *littérateurs* and the craft of writing books, expressed their contempt in books which they wrote and they clearly lived the life of *littérateurs;* the terrible Oswald Spengler not being an exception.

The middle-of-the-roaders continued Germany's humanist, liberal, and European tradition. They were republicans, democrats, protagonists of a lasting Franco-German understanding, the League of Nations, Count Coudenhove's Pan-Europe, progress without revolution, and so on. Not that the republic, as a whole, had much use for them. The political parties which now ruled directly, no longer through bargaining with an imperial government, had changed their names rather than their character after the Kaiser's abdication. They were as uninspiring as before and so were Weimar's heads of government: elderly administrators, former city managers, financiers, industrialists, bureaucrats, at best trade-unionists. They were as foreign to the German literature of their age as Bismarck had been and with less justification; German literature had been stale and mediocre in Bismarck's time, while it was very much alive in the nineteen-twenties. The man of experience who gets things done, as against the scribbler who moves whole worlds in his mind while in reality he does not know a marriage certificate from a wage contract—that, essentially, was their attitude, as it had been Bismarck's before them.

Exceptions are worth mentioning, although they do not disprove the rule. Rathenau, foreign minister in 1922, was a rare combination of industrialist and philosopher, an intellectual with tremendous practical achievements to his credit. He was also an outsider in the government, suspected and blindly hated by a large sector of the nation exactly because he was an intellectual, and a Jew to boot; I remember what joyful noise we schoolboys made when we learned about his assassination. Stresemann made at least one brave effort to show his interest in the world of books. A Prussian minister of education,

C. H. Becker, went so far as to found the institution which came to be called the "Prussian Writers' Academy." (Its exact name was "Prussian Academy of the Arts, Section for Literature.") It was an attempt to make writing something official, like in France, to give the man of letters a dignified place in the state. Alas, few people took the Prussian Writers' Academy seriously. It was considered as republican, as purposeless, and, not entirely without reason, as a flat imitation of the French Academy.

On the far Left we find, apart from the Communists, the non-committed leftist intellectual, Heine's heir. He had ridiculed the Kaiser, now he ridiculed the republic which evidently was not lacking in pathetic aspects—though, being better in her potentialities than anything that might succeed her, she would nevertheless have deserved help, rather than hilarious contempt. Heine's heir lived from saying No; from accusing, unmasking, and putting the world in the wrong, a function which gave a secure superiority to the accuser. Indeed, one could hardly see how things could ever improve unless he himself were given command—the slimmest chance of which would have made him run for cover.

What an intellectual Babylon of voices, that Weimar Republic! Talking of decline, of crisis, of doom—but joyful talking. Philosophers demonstrating that there was no longer time for any philosophy, sociologists unmasking all creeds, values, moral standards as "ideological," economists calmly proving that five or six million unemployed had come to stay and would not be gotten rid of in any future, legists affirming that the very notion of natural justice was a hoax and that any positive law, duly codified, was as good as any other—far too many people assiduously sawing off the branch on which other people or they themselves were sitting. There was then, I should say, too much intellectual freedom in Germany; and all of a sudden there was none.

Most modes of life have their characteristic temptations, and so has that of the intellectuals, academic or other. The German intellectuals have given in to them as much as have the intellectuals of other countries, to say the least.

There is the pretention to know what cannot and must not be known, the secret law of the ages:—We understand the past, the present, the future, we have the key to it, we or someone we choose to follow. We understand Necessity. We also know that Necessity is good, was good, shall be good. Or again, that the notions of good and bad make no sense when applied to the Inevitable. Hence we are far above the many who ignore where they are going and think they are free to choose, poor fellows. . . .

If this presumption of looking behind the stage of history and discovering the strings which are pulling the actors is characteristic of certain writers everywhere, it is especially characteristic of a large sector of the German mind: the Hegelians, the Marxians, the Spenglerians, and a host of lesser schools and men. There is a profound lack of charity connected with it, as the French critic, Edgar Quinet, noticed already in the eighteen-thirties.

These are the yes-men. There are also the no-men—those who, confronted by history, past or in the making, put on a permanently hurt look. With a little reason, everything could have been straightened out; but it was not and there is little hope that it ever will. Because the rulers are so stupid. . . . This feeling of a considerable superiority is something that yes-men and no-men have in common. Similar also are the practical consequences of both attitudes. The yes-men see no need for, the no-men no hope in, strenuous limited efforts of their own. On a more restricted level, the contrast between the yes-men and the no-men appears in the attitude towards one's own nation. German intellectuals were either of an aggressive patriotism or of a cosmopolitanism marked by a super-critical, if not hostile and contemptuous, view of their own nation. The golden mean did exist, of course, but not as naturally as in Britain and France. (America is a different story.)

Related to this is the polarity between the "Western" and the "Pure German" intellectual, which goes back to the beginnings of modern Germany. To be a free publicist—say, the editor of a politico-philosophical review in Berlin in 1795—meant to imitate French and English styles; for there was no German model to work on. Ever since, the free intellectual has had a somewhat outlandish, Western air around him. Frequently he did imitate Anglo-Saxon and French examples, both in what he had to say and in the way he said it. For this the great progressive papers of the Wilhelminian and Weimar period, the *Frankfurter Zeitung* and the *Berliner Tageblatt,* are striking instances. The reaction is equally old. When a Prussian baron, Achim von Arnim, founded his "Christian Round-Table" in Berlin around 1810, it was, I think, the first attempt to organise an intellectual milieu which would be purely Germanic. Jews, Frenchmen, and friends of France were rigorously excluded from von Arnim's club; and its members, like Heinrich von Kleist, may be said to represent a new type of German writer: highly poetical, at the same time savagely political and nationalist, the producer of ideas about State and Nation which could not be identified with any Western tradition. The conflict between the two German intellectual schools, the Western and the Germanic, has been going on ever since, among various groups, around various issues.

The Westerner easily passed for subversive, merely negative, socially useless if not dangerous, a dubious product of metropolitan swamps. So did the Jewish intellectual; and both were identified for all practical purposes. Already, around 1800, literary critics who were not Jewish were jokingly referred to as "indirect Jews." Nobody but the Jews had made Bonaparte an emperor, a German patriot complained; as they were supposed one hundred and twenty years later to have caused Germany's defeat in the First World War through their diabolic machinations.

There is a grain of substance behind such nonsense. Among German intellectuals of the Western type, the Jewish percentage has been high, for good historical reasons. The Western intellectual, following his French prototype, did throw in his lot with the causes of progress, democracy, free science, positivism, socialism, and so on. That great movement, having its negative as well as its constructive aspects, its intellectual backers can be rightly charged with both, and sometimes, according to their character, more with the one than with the other. It was, I believe, de Maistre—also Burke—who predicted that the progressive intellectual was making a mistake from the point of view of his own interest; that his natural place was with the aristocracy and the church; and that, having helped to destroy the old order, he would not find in the new that worthy position of which he was dreaming. There have been moments in recent history when de Maistre's prediction seemed sagacious enough—exceptional moments, we hope.

Somehow, most of us expected that the history of the nineteen-twenties would repeat itself after 1945. The humanists made ready to fight the nationalists once again; the apocalyptics pulled their manuscripts out of the drawer where they had been hiding since 1933, to renew their prophecies about the decline of the West, the destruction of man by the machine, and so on. Nobody was prepared for the West-Germany we have today, that incredibly busy, prosperous, crowded, pleasure-seeking place; least of all the intellectuals. It happened that way. And as it happened, intellectual positions changed, as well as functions.

One can still hear the complaint that the writer has no respected place. The President of the Federal Republic himself is making regretful allusions to this fact. On the other hand—there are always other hands—the intellectual can keep himself busy enough, what with all those congresses, public discussions, summer-schools, publicity and self-publicity campaigns, Unesco, Franco-German reconciliation, Pan-Europe, cultural attachéships, trips to America, exchange services and, above all, the radio, that inexhaustible market for words. As a man above or outside society, prophet or bohemian, he will find life unrewarding. As a member of a consumers' society he can win a market for his goods and services; and then he can do what any German likes to do nowadays: marry young, rent an apartment, perhaps own a car, live a regular life. If he is talented and clever, he will write novels on topical subjects which have a chance to appear in an *Illustrierte* and to become best-sellers—the only way for a novel to pay its way. He will work for the radio, the press, if he is very lucky for the movies. In any case, his work is a job like another, nothing particularly solemn; not the writing of "doomsday accounts of our souls," as Ibsen defined the art of the writer.

There are still those who write for the sake of truth rather than with their eyes on the market. But they are few and their readers are few; a fine highbrow review like *Merqur* barely sells 3,000 copies. The broad cultured and leisured public which existed in Wilhelminian and pre-Hitler days is gone— in that public, too, the Jews had a very high percentage.

One should add that both spheres, that of the intellectual entertainment industry and that of the absolute creative effort, are still connected at various points. Some find energy enough to participate in both, and the radio gives generous support to higher literature through its "night-studios" and other special offerings comparable to the BBC's Third Programme. As a whole, however, the situation of the German intellectual tends to become similar to that of his American colleague—minus the colleges, those great if none too comfortable refuges of the American highbrow. The German secondary schools (Gymnasiums) are still almost completely isolated from intellectual life, traditionalist, narrow, bureaucratic. Universities are few, tightly organised, and very much afraid of overstaffing their faculties.

Where there is no market for a Spengler, no Spengler will appear. Today, the prophets of doom are silent; those of a "Conservative Revolution," a purified spartan German community, hardly audible. Silent is their counterpart, the "leftist intellectual," Heine's heir, who has practically vanished from the German scene. (He leads a ghostly and distrusted existence in the Eastern Zone, filling the pages of the same red-covered weekly, *Die Weltbuehne,* with the same giggling vituperations as in 1925.) A left there is, but not a very literary one; trade unions which, through well-trained economists and well-paid lawyers, are studying the theoretical basis for their action. The age-old conflict between the Western and the "pure German" intellectual has died down, for everybody is somehow pro-Western now and everybody a good German to boot. Gone are the passionate polemics of the Weimar period, the sensational propositions, the mutual accusations. A cool but general agreement on the essentials prevails, as between parties in parliament so between intellectuals. Politics itself is no longer in the centre of interest, not even for those who are unhappy over Adenauer's Germany, who think her materialistic, business-dominated, unimaginative, reactionary, and what not. Theirs is an esoteric community and the values they serve are not to be realised by any political action. It is nothing but the old *l'art pour l'art*—an unmistakable symptom of normalcy, of a stable society.

These symptoms may delude us. Normalcy, after all, is itself something abnormal when balanced against the crazy Berlin situation, the Eastern Zone, the Oder-Neisse frontier, and all the monstrosities of a still recent past. When one remembers the Germany of nine or eleven years ago—some do— the present appears as if created by witchcraft. That country has surprised us before; it may do it again. But the present is what it is, and looking at the way the Germans are building, they seem to trust the future.

THE ENGLISH INTELLECTUALS AND THE WORLD OF TO-DAY

Stephen Spender

THE TERM 'intellectual', used frequently in discussions about the role of the intellectual in society, the attitude of intellectuals to problems of war and peace, and so on, has come to mean: 'a thinking person, often a writer, who has a sense of social responsibility to which he wants to give voice.' This definition, if vague, is also rather narrowly limited: for an intellectual might be a mathematical genius, a chess champion, or a specialist in some technical field. However, here I am going to use the word in the special sense in which it is often taken for granted.

Amongst the intellectuals it has been possible to discern a growing preoccupation, over the last twenty years, with their own effectiveness as a social force. They wish to be able to influence contemporary history, if only so as to prove to themselves that they live in a society where they can continue their work. This desire to influence society in order to create a suitable background for his own writing is as characteristic of a writer like D. H. Lawrence, who seemed utterly to abhor professional politicians, as of those writers who joined the International Brigade during the Spanish Civil War. Lawrence wished to influence the direction of civilization as much as any social revolutionary has ever done. He thought, though, that political action was not the way to do it. Society could be changed, he believed, by changing the relationship between men and women, and men and men, making it more instinctual. So that when certain intellectuals claim to be political whilst others, like Mr Herbert Read, renounce politics, all this means is that some believe that society can be altered by political programmes, and others by measures which are included in no existing political programme. Those who call themselves anarchists, or existentialists, have no representation for their views in parliaments. There is in our time a kind of secret parliament of the intellectuals, containing, like the parliament of the Weimar Republic, about thirty different parties. Yet the anarchism of Mr Read, or the Christianity of Mr Eliot, like the revolution in human relations propagated by D. H. Lawrence, would, if pushed to their extremes, ultimately change the face of

Reprinted from *The Twentieth Century* (June, 1951), pp. 482-488, by permission of the author and the periodical.

society. An intellectual is political if he has the slightest hidden feeling in his heart that (even though he may hate Shelley for having stated such a claim), he is potentially an 'unacknowledged legislator of mankind'. The potential legislators include, among others, W. H. Auden, T. S. Eliot and Aldous Huxley, however remote these may be from the actual political scene. For all these hold views which, if applied, would affect the political structure and behaviour of our society. The question of 'non-political' or 'political' is largely an argument amongst intellectuals about means whereby they hope they may save civilization from the destructive aspects of contemporary professional politics.

Until 1939, the English intellectuals felt themselves to belong to a continuing tradition, which would be extended into the future. The remark of one of them (was it Lytton Strachey?) during the first World War: 'I am the civilization for which you are fighting', expressed the attitude of Bloomsbury. To exist and shine and write well, and, above all, to be sensitive, justified one's existence as a writer, and, indeed, imposed on society the duty of continuing as a kind of material background of a civilization of perceptive people. It was the duty of the intellectual not to take side in the struggles around him; and there was a feeling that if he did so he was betraying a civilization which was detached from political and perhaps even religious faith.

In the 1930's it became evident to a good many intellectuals that sensibility was not enough. The fabric of civilization upon which post-impressionism and the novels of Virginia Woolf rested was threatened. In this decade, English politics showed themselves to be bankrupt of means to prevent war. The intellectuals, with their gifts of intuition and sensibility, were put into the position of perceiving very clearly approaching disasters the existence of which the governing class simply denied.

In this situation, the intellectuals reacted in different ways. Some of them became actively political, others, like D. H. Lawrence, looked to a revolution in human relations which although outside politics, would transform society, some, like T. S. Eliot, tried to bolster up the Church. It is significant that Eliot's first full-length play, *The Rock,* was performed in order to obtain funds for building more churches in London.

Yet all these attitudes had something in common: the belief that the individualist position, however unreal and remote from actuality in appearance, was socially effective. It sustained or transformed or, in some way which was supposed to be beneficial, influenced society. And the intellectual who was a writer, was a responsible person, a civilizing force, a defender of the 'cultural heritage', whether as traditionalist, or revolutionary. The surrealists claimed to represent a revolution which was 'deeper' (in a psychological sense) and therefore more radical, than communism.

With 1939, with the outbreak of war, the stubborn pre-war illusions that the individual intellectual could be the exponent in his work of a philosophy which would change society, disappeared. In a world of universal conscription, all attitudes were simplified into those of assent or dissent. If you approved of the war you were absorbed into it; if you didn't you made your ineffective pacifist protest which may have satisfied your own conscience but which could have little effect on a community where the protesting pacifists were protected from Fascism and concentration camps, and fed, by the fighting assenters. In addition to this, all the protests and affirmations of the anti-Fascists of the Spanish war, were now systemized and swallowed up in official governmental anti-Nazi propaganda, while the anti-Fascists themselves were often rejected from the services, being regarded as ideologically suspect, and despised as amateurs, now that anti-Fascism had become a professional game.

Of course, many intellectuals played distinguished parts in the services or the bureaucracy; but as critics of society, critics of life, they had shrunk to passive spectators, pinning their despair or their hopes to external events which they could hardly influence. The difference between the surrealists before the war and the apocalyptics during it, is that the surrealists regarded themselves as the centre of a volcano pouring lava out of the individualist subconscious, whereas the apocalyptics regarded themselves as witnesses of disasters which were taking place within society itself and overwhelming *them*.

Shortly before he died, George Orwell remarked to me that social prophets like D. H. Lawrence died when their intellectual position had become untenable. 'It is impossible to think of any coherent attitude which Lawrence could have taken up after 1939,' Orwell said. 'He might even have found himself in the position of having to support the Nazis.' Lawrence's belief that society could be changed within individual relationships could only demonstrate the weakness of Lawrence; and Lawrence died of an ailment which was as much the sickness of his philosophy as of himself. Or, conversely, the sickness of society was too much for Lawrence and destroyed him.

This view, which may seem fanciful, nevertheless illustrates the point that the epoch of individualist literary prophets, offering their experience of living as a kind of secret formula for saving society, was ended. And with its end, a great deal of conviction went out of contemporary English literature.

The last lingering illusion which kept some intellectuals going was fantasies about the 'post-war world.' These were based on the idea that when the war was over, the immense co-operative, collectivized effort which had gone into making armaments and conscripting industry, would be switched to rebuilding Britain. It was possible, looking at things from this point of view, to regard catastrophes like the destruction of large parts of the East End of the City of London, and of Coventry, as only the negative aspects of a huge slum-clearance project. After the war we would be able to build magnificent parks, containing tall tenement buildings, to replace the slums. Yet although the intellectuals of the Left comforted themselves by advertizing these dreams, they were really dreams of the same apocalyptic nature as the ones of a destructive social volcano, which I have described. Reconstruction came from the outside, as the result of an external catastrophe, and the planners were potential spectators of an effort which was expected from society, not from themselves.

It is to the credit of the young writers who emerged during the time that they did not, in their writing at all events, take planning seriously. They were concerned with their own experiences, and with their personal relationships. They were trying to stake out a claim to a little area of personal experience, but they rejected, often with disgust, all idea that this would either change society or prove a sheet anchor—like Eliot's traditionalism—in a storm. It was simply a personal attitude, and that was the only truthful one, they seemed to say. At most it was a medium of communication between persons who felt equally lost and who were equally in search for some beauty, some love, some conversation in a hut while the bullets were rattling across the plain. If they could admire attitudes like those of Eliot and Edith Sitwell, which seemed rooted in the past and offered no hope for the future, they rejected utterly the writers of the thirties who had tried to make the life of the imagination intervene in the world of social events, and who felt in some way personally responsible for apocalyptic events. Their gods were writers with forceful and publicly irresponsible private personalities, like Dylan Thomas and George Barker.

The test of such an attitude, which by implication demanded that the young writers should produce an enormous force of personality out of a vacuum, was whether it produced such personalities. If it had done so, the vacuum would have been filled because these personalities would, as they developed in their work, have taken up attitudes which were philosophical and social, wider than merely personal ones. However, the 1940's remained dominated by Dylan Thomas, who had begun publishing in the mid-1930's, and whose personality alone had the vitality and richness to produce a rhetorical poetry which had genuine force. The apocalyptic and personalist movements of the 1940's dissolved into the vapidness of empty passionate gestures. Poets like Vernon Watkins and John Heath Stubbs who were bigger than the movements with which they were at first identified, proved to be purists or scholars. It is characteristic that *Nine,* the only literary review devoted almost entirely to the works of new writers (apart from its publishing the works of Roy Campbell) is devoted largely to scholarship of a rather esoteric kind, translations, and literary oddities.

At the end of the 1940's, what seemed most 1940ish had died of sheer boredom with itself and of others with it. The complete lack of sales for poetry in England, the almost total disappearance of all the literary reviews is not just the fault of the 'public'. It is a symptom of the bankruptcy of a decade. The older writers like Eliot and the Sitwells have actually increased in popularity, and the writers of the 1930's, supposedly out of fashion, have nevertheless held their own. What has happened is simply that the 1940's were an almost total failure; and that the 1950's must either see a continuation of the decline, or a new start.

This picture would seem very depressing, if literary productivity were our only intellectual activity. But of course it is not. What has happened recently has been a splitting off of literature from serious contemporary thinking. It is the same kind of split as has occurred in America, where, at the most serious turning point in recent American history, the writers who are publicized as representing youth are Truman Capote, Tennessee Williams and Carson McCullers. These writers surely represent a reaction *from* rather than towards events. Of course, if this reaction away from the historic into the exclusively personal is sufficently strong, it acquires significance in the way that Keat's poetry is significant. But it has to be extremely powerful to hold its own against the pressure of the events it rejects, or it is liable to be snuffed out, or to die of narcissistic self-love.

One strange but greatly respected figure is perhaps even more a link between the 1930's and the 1950's than Dylan Thomas. This is David Gascoyne. Gascoyne, like Thomas and Barker, began writing in the mid-'thirties. At this time he was a surrealist. During the Spanish war he went to Spain and broadcast from Barcelona. Then he lived for a time in France where he became a follower of the poet Jouve, some of whose work he translated. Gascoyne has also translated poems of Hoelderlin, and there is a mystic-philosophic side to his writing. He has in fact written long philosophic essays which baffle publishers, and have not been printed.

The significance of Gascoyne is that although he rejected the crude political simplifications of the 1930's, he never rejected the aim of seeking in his poetry for a solution of the problem of contemporary history. He never renounced what was surely best in the 1930's: the expression of the individual's sense of personal guilt for political and social disasters. That the younger writers should attack the older ones not for their politics and their ill-digested thinking, but for their having a sense of social responsibility, shocked him. The centre of Gascoyne's philosophy is that each person is involved in, and responsible for all, sharing an awareness of a particular modern situation which is potentially sharable by all. The business of the poet, in Gascoyne's view, is to make people more fully aware of what they already dimly feel: that an immense change has taken place in people's minds of recent years, for they have become conscious of being involved in a common fate which is a world-fate; and they are also conscious of the fact that it is necessary for humanity now to take a great step forward—to develop a new kind of world consciousness. Unless such a stage of wholeness is attained, men will fall back into a disunity greater even than we have now. In conversation, Gascoyne has spoken to me of the atom bomb as an event which broke down the barriers between people's minds—as a mental event, that is to say, which made people realize that they were living in a new situation of wholeness, where world unity was the only solution of their problems.

Here I have summarized very roughly—and perhaps not altogether accurately—the thinking of a writer who may be at times difficult and vague. But Gascoyne is not tarred with the brush of having been a 'political' writer, and yet his writing and thinking call upon his contemporaries to face a contemporary situation which is much larger than themselves. He is important because he transforms what was essentially the problem of the 1930's—the problem of responsibility—into new terms, which are not overtly political or social.

When I think of my own life and work, I realize that the war was simply a gap of more than ten years—from 1938 until 1950—in my development. I amused myself with diversions and speculations which seemed serious to me at the time, because the depressing circumstances in which we lived made me take them seriously. But really, I have only rediscovered the thread which I had lost in 1938 during recent months. I mention this, because I think that my own experience is also true of other people. The war created a gap in all our lives, and at the end of it we discovered that our own fates were no longer within our control. Hence the post-war wave of discouragement in which writers became officials, editors abandoned reviews which, in fact, were doing rather well, and the public ceased to be interested in 'young writers' who were Dead End Kids in the Waste Land.

Quite suddenly, however, since the outbreak of the Korean War, we seem to have entered an entirely new phase in which the role of the intellectuals may again become extremely important.

As I have pointed out, in the 'thirties the intellectuals felt that they could and should intervene in a political situation in which they brought to bear powers of analysis and intuition beyond those of the English and French Governments of that decade. The outcome of this was that their intervention proved ineffective, and what to them had been a cause experienced differently by many individuals, became mechanical slogans of official anti-Nazi propaganda. There followed the intellectual vacuum of the 1940's. But now a new situation not at all like the 1930's, except in having a political background, has quite suddenly arisen in 1950.

This new situation is a crisis of conscience quite different, but perhaps more significant than that of the 1930's. As in the 1930's, it is a crisis primarily of the Left, but it extends much further than this. Moreover, unlike the 1930's, it is more likely to divide than unite the Left. This crisis has been precipitated by the action of the United Nations in Korea, and by American policies throughout the world, which have suddenly confronted all thinking people with the question of what they really stand for, and what values are being asserted by the West in the present conflict. The same kind of people who in the 1930's felt called upon to act, to-day feel called upon to analyse the situation into which they have found themselves thrown: a situation in which progressives who have been striving for years to improve the conditions of the masses, suddenly find themselves forced into opposition to these masses, in the name of democratic freedom. To-day it is war against the Chinese, but it is evident that to-morrow it might be against the Indians or the Africans. If we are involved in conflicts with the very people for whose freedom we have so long been struggling, what are the values of our own freedom which we defend against Chinese coolies? This is stating the question in its crudest form, but beyond it there lie other challenges which go to the very root of all the values of our civilization. The problem is to define our own freedom: and, since freedom is not empty activity but the freedom to believe certain things and to live according to certain values, these values themselves and this way of life are also challenged. In the next decade it seems likely that thinkers of the West will have not only to analyse the increasingly complex and bewildering situation in which they find themselves, but also to define the values of democracy.

THE INTELLECTUALS' TRADITION

William Phillips

... ALL new and genuinely creative impulses in our time, as Trotsky once observed in a study of the Russian symbolists, tend to take the form of bohemianism, as the *avant-garde* in a kind of permanent mutiny against the regime of utility and conformity, proclaims its faith in the freedom, the irresponsibility, and the higher integrity of art.

Now, the complexion of the intelligentsia has undergone many changes —their extremities of belief being a fairly late development—but throughout their history, and despite their growing tendencies toward atomization, they have maintained the kind of institutional stability vital to the production of art. Obviously, it was through such a unified and self-perpetuating group that our cultural continuity has been preserved, and the individual artist has been provided with a sustaining tradition of convention and experiment, without which he could never hope to be more than a gifted eccentric. In addition, however, as society lost its earlier unity of belief, which the artist shared and took as his starting point, the very plight of the intelligentsia and the more or less homogeneous outlook it had acquired served as a philosophical mooring for the modern artist. Thus, even today, while their bent is entirely against any kind of social authority or discipline, nevertheless the intelligentsia, in their role of intellectual conservation and in their tightly knit traditions, perform for modern times a function that an institution like the church, for instance, had in the medieval period. And, in an historical sense, the church was actually the organized body of intellectuals in the middle ages, for at the height of its dominion it was the conveyor of all secular, as well as spiritual, culture, and it was set apart from the laity as much by its intellectual as by its hieratical distinction. The church, like its modern successors, tried jealously to maintain its cultivated and inbred esthetic traditions by absorbing, sometimes through actual physical possession, the more-popular forms of folk-art at the time. In opposition to such spontaneous performances as the sword plays, for example, which arose in the primitive agricultural community much the same way as the early dramatic rites of the Greeks, the church used all its powers to keep art primarily a vehicle for its own myth.

Reprinted from *Partisan Review* (November-December, 1941), pp. 483-490, by permission of the periodical.

If the secular intellectuals who came to the fore with the rise of a bourgeois society in Europe were not bound by any common creed, still they managed through the years to build what might be called a tradition of approach or perspective. In the realm of literature this tradition amounted to a highly elaborate sense of its achievements and its tasks, thus providing the creative imagination with a fund of literary experiences—a kind of style of work—to draw on. For the old-world writer, from about the seventeenth century on, had to mediate between the great scramble of the new order and the authority of the past, between the boundless perspectives for the individual personality and the material forces tending more and more to confine it, between scepticism and faith, between the city and the country. . . . And he was able to do so to the extent that he shared the generalized vision of the intelligentsia as a whole; or where any great divergence of belief existed, he simply took his cue from the collective opinion of some dissident group. The fact is that European literature made little headway in the smaller, marginal countries—or appeared late in a backward region like Russia—that, on the contrary, it enjoyed the greatest success in those nations that set the social and intellectual pace for the rest of the continent. (It was, after all, in Italy, the original home of the new mercantilism, that the beginnings of humanist theory and renaissance art first appeared.) Not only did most of the problems and crises of European expansion come to a head in France and England (and in Germany somewhat later), but, in addition, these countries were sufficiently prosperous and were becoming sufficiently urbanized to support a scientific and literary intelligentsia. Hence they were able to rationalize the general European predicament and to provide a tentative equilibrium of opinion for all political and intellectual pursuits. While the lagging industrial nations had to be content with sporadic cultural expressions, which were largely an adaptation of the more advanced currents to the local ethos, the great tradition of French and English art maintained itself at the crest of the upheavals and large-scale movements that marked the growth of bourgeois society. One can hardly conceive of a Julien Sorel, balancing himself on the contradictions between ambition and personality, in, say, Warsaw or Madrid—or the domestic drama of the eighteenth century being born outside the boom of British trade at the time and the plebeian sentimentality that accompanied it.

It is plain that we have here more than a coincidence of geographical and social factors. Indeed, the major impulses of European art can be traced in practically every instance to the existence of an active intelligentsia, crucially involved in its contemporary history, and sufficiently self-conscious to be able to assimilate some new experience to the norms of its past. One might almost put down as an esthetic law that continuity is the condition for creative invention. Thus the dream of fulfillment released by the French

Revolution lingered on in the modern mind: disengaged from its social frame and turned inward, it served, at one pole, as a basis for the series of movements dedicated to the primacy of art; while at the other extreme, stripped of its critical and tendencious spirit, it lay behind the celebrations of progress that appeared toward the end of the last century. In fact, the increasing complexity of contemporary literature is at least partially to be accounted for by the variety of traditional memories and associations that fill the consciousness of the writer today. And in such works as *The Wasteland* and *Finnegans Wake,* where this natural tendency has been converted into a deliberate method, both Joyce and, to a less extent, Eliot have actually set out to dissolve their immediate perceptions in the timeless reality of the past.

Now, in the case of American literature, unlike that of the old world, we have a kind of negative illustration of the relation of the intelligentsia to art. For the outstanding features—not to speak of the failures—of our national culture can be largely explained by the inability of our native intelligentsia to achieve a detached and self-sufficient group existence that would permit it to sustain its traditions through succeeding epochs, and to keep abreast of European intellectual production. One need hardly stress such symptoms in American writing as shallowness, paucity of values, a statistical approach to reality, and the compensatory qualities of forthrightness, plebeianism, and a kind of matter-of-fact humanism: they have been noted in a number of historical studies; and, to be sure, our cultural innocence has been practically a standing complaint of American criticism. As Howells had Bromfield Corey remark in *The Rise of Silas Lapham:* "A Greek got his civilization by talking and looking, and in some measure a Parisian may still do it. But we, who live remote from history and monuments, we must read or we must barbarize."

Obviously, our history has been too rapid and too expansive for the American mind to settle down and take stock of itself. Moreover, the city, as the symbol of modern civilization, did not fully emerge until after the Civil War, with the result that our intellectual life, in its formative years, could not escape the atomizing influence of ruralism. And, what is perhaps more important, the lusty pioneer motif running through American letters, with its strong tinge of hinterland philosophy, exerted a constant regional pull on the intelligentsia and tended to sanction an individual rather than a group solution of the cultural problem.

Our early literary expressions were, of course, little more than British amenities feeling their way through strange, primitive surroundings. Nor could the Puritan outlook serve as the ground-work for a tradition. Essentially prohibitive and regional, it was a kind of frontier Calvinism, destined to be superseded by a more materialist creed—in keeping with the rough-and-tumble spirit of aggrandizement that was possessing the country as a whole. Hawthorne, of course, whose imagination was tortured by the Puritan demons of guilt and decay, was the prime literary beneficiary of the Puritan mind; but, on the whole, it entered into later writing mainly as a negative factor, a repressed strain, as in Melville, where it was in a sense a purged element; and through the nineteenth century it persisted largely as a characteristic moral wholesomeness.

The Concord school may be said to mark the first appearance, in full intellectual dress, of an American intelligentsia. Revolting against the all-absorbing commercialism of the day and against the bleakness of the Puritan heritage, they set out quite consciously to form, as Emerson put it, "a learned class," and to assimilate the culture of Europe into a native tradition. Yet, just as they had no established past to draw on, so they were unable to transmit a full-blown literary mentality to succeeding generations. Emerson was, of course, intoxicated with the pioneer spirit, with the hard-bitten realism of the plain people, and his bias was strongly agrarian in its emphasis on bare hands and the self-reliant mind. He was essentially a transcendental commoner, and for all his cultural yearning, his philosophy was at bottom an affirmation of individual fulfillment in a boundless American expansion. Thus, in later years he turned upon New England, the seat of his own cultural development, to cast a loving eye on the turbulent settlements of the West, where he found the dawn of our native genius. No wonder, then, that the entire tendency, of which Emerson was, perhaps, the most representative figure, was soon reabsorbed, in the main, by the life and philosophy of the general mass, whose premises it accepted, and to whom it made its prime appeal.

This, in essence, is the story of American letters: momentary efforts by solitary writers or by intellectual groups to differentiate themselves and to set a new current in motion, with the inevitable petering out, and the necessity for a fresh start over again. Hence our unusual number of literary sports. By the time Whitman, for example, was ready to affirm again the democratic ethos and the frontier excitements of the new cities, he had to start from scratch, with the result that his vision was largely a matter of itemized experience, devoid of those central symbols and values that are handed down by a creative tradition. The case of Poe is even more striking: he was the first truly bohemian writer in America (if we except the peculiar rustic bohemianism of Thoreau), and throughout his life practically the only one. Hence he lacked those professional resources of esthetic and social subversion that are normally provided by an organized bohemia. In only a negative, escapist sense, did his poetry have a characteristically bohemian content; although it gave the lead to Baudelaire, his poetry fell short of the programmatic experimentalism of his French contemporaries; even his essays, as Henry James once remarked, were excessively amateurish and provincial; and his verse constantly tended, in an over-felicitous fashion, toward a lovelorn provincialism. What saved Poe, I suppose, was a happy coincidence of talent, morbidity, and the capacity for absorbing those literary strains that served the needs of his sensibility.

Not until the last two or three decades did any literary "schools," promoted by an active literary intelligentsia, make their appearance here. But their inspiration was largely European, and, in a basic sense, they never really succeeded in lifting themselves above the conceptual plane of American writing as a whole. Consider the Marxist or proletarian school; perhaps the most confident, aggressive, and most thoroughly international of recent trends. One might have expected that a movement so completely regulated by an organized body of left-wing intellectuals, committed to an all-embracing philosophy and to the principle that literature must serve as a vehicle for revolutionary ideas—that such a movement would have been able to grasp the effects of our social experience on our national mythology in more significant terms than the simple rites of awakening and conversion. As it was, radical novelists in this country took the short cut to integration by substituting data for values and the specious unity of the narrative for the interplay of historical meanings. Sharing the general aversion and distrust of ideological fiction, they failed to create a single intellectual character —either revolutionary or conservative—thus depriving themselves of their very medium of understanding, for it is only through the consciousness of such a character that it is possible, it seems to me, to depict the modulations and tensions of belief that make up the political movement.

If any one figure can be said to be a symbol of our entire culture, it is Henry Adams, whose active life covered almost the entire phase of our modern development and whose work sounded its principal themes. In its spiritual bafflements, its peculiarly native mixture of materialism and religious feeling, its desperate search for some central tradition, his *Education* reads like a diary of our speculative conscience. A product of the New England mind, he was soon cast adrift by what he called the "multiplicity" of the world—his repeated use of the word suggests a morbid fondness for it—and he began his life-long probe into history for some principle of unity, some contemporary equivalent of the ideal unity he believed to have existed in the thirteenth century. In a measure, he thought he discovered this principle in a dynamic law of history, but it served only to confirm his dilemma, for the law merely proved all over again the increasing complexity and disintegration of society; and, besides, his experimental bent led him to distrust theoretical constructions because they tend to "falsify the facts." He turned to science. But he could not overcome his feeling that its authority was limited to purely secular matters; and even in this sphere the prevailing chaos all but defied the efforts to create order, or, as Adams put it, "the multiplicity baffling science." Finally, there was God, the supreme and infallible, synthesizing force; yet he could derive no conclusive satisfaction from his faith because his Calvinist leanings toward a personal creed precluded any belief in a single unifying system. What was left?—nothing but to return, after completing the cycle of his researches, to a kind of methodological groping for a common denominator of belief. "The old formulas had failed, and a new one had to be made. . . . One sought no absolute truth. One sought only a spool on which to wind the thread of history without breaking it."

In a sense, this has been our persistent tradition—this periodic striving for a unified outlook and the inevitable return to a clean slate all over again—though one hesitates to describe it as such because it is exactly this discontinuity that is the mark of our inability to form a complex, intellectual tradition. In this respect, the American intelligentsia exhibits a kind of ambivalent psyche, torn between the urge toward some degree of autonomy and an equally strong tendency to self-effacement, for it is largely its natural inclination to merge with the popular mind that has prevented any such lasting intellectual differentiation as has been achieved in European art and thought. Generally, these dual impulses have found expression in the repetitive cycle of our literary history, but on occasion they have also appeared side by side—in figures like Emerson and Whitman, and, to some extent, Dreiser,—as a combination of populist sensibility with some broad cultural vision. And, is not the predilection for the real, the fatal attraction for the overwhelming minutiae of every-day life, that characterizes so much of American writing, but the creative equivalent of the instability of the intelligentsia?

In the last few decades, we have run the gamut of three important trends, and we are at present in the midst of one more movement to stir the embers of the past, to discover once more the secrets of the national spirit. Yet, except for the natural persistence of certain states of mind, one cannot discern any organic linkage between these successive currents. The regional nostalgia that appeared in such writers as Masters or Frost, which, incidentally, can hardly be said to be a direct outgrowth of the earlier expansive naturalism, was literally brushed aside by the great rebellion of the twenties against provincialism, gentility, and the native bent for minute self-portraiture. At one pole, were the provocations of modernism, with their libertarian effects in the social sphere; at the other stood figures like Mencken and Lewis, attacking the moral and intellectual proprieties. As for the Marxist school, which held sway in the following decade, and whose demise was as sudden and mechanical as its birth, it could scarcely have been expected to establish a line of continuity, since, in addition to the strong resistance it naturally encountered, it believed one of its chief historical assignments to be the task of erasing the traces of the bourgeois past. But it is surely ironic that the current appeal to immerse ourselves in the splendors of the American tradition should ignore the critical acquisitions and revaluations of these last decades.

In a typically compulsive way, this effort to frame a new cultural myth has not only made a clean break with the Marxist outlook, but in its special concern with the indigenous, it is patently a negation of everything the twenties stood for. Thus we have the astonishing phenomenon of a writer like Van Wyck Brooks now forsaking his earlier studies in creative frustration for a gayer—and more successful—version of the literary life in America. One cannot find, it seems to me, a surer sign of the lack of a *felt* tradition—of one that can be assumed—than in such a wilful endeavor to invoke it into being. In a recent address Brooks, who is apparently intent on carrying the quest for a native heritage to the most comic and painful extremes, called for a purge of such figures as Joyce and Eliot—of the truly characteristic works of the modern tradition. As for a "usable past"—Brooks has finally discovered it in the humanitarian pieties of none other than Whittier.

Our concern at the moment, however, is not with the career or the latest views of Van Wyck Brooks, but with the current epidemic of literary nationalism in which Brooks is simply an advanced case. And what is this nationalist revival—this militant provincialism—if not a new phase of self-abnegation on the part of the intelligentsia? Once again they are renouncing the values of group-detachment as they permit themselves to be drawn into the tides of prevailing opinion. In a complete reversal of role, they have come to echo all the stock objections to the complex and ambiguous symbolization of modern writing: and the improvised tradition they now offer in its place—is it not the popular, Sunday version of our history? The immediate effect is bound to be some kind of creative disorientation. But even more important, from the viewpoint of our culture as a whole, it is evident that this constant fluctuation between dissidence and conformity, this endless game of hide-and-seek with the past, cannot but thwart the production of a mature and sustained literature. And the intelligentsia in America, for all its efforts to preserve its intellectual identity, seems to have a deep-seated need to accept as its own—if only periodically—the official voice of society.

WRITERS IN AMERICA

William Barrett

WHO, then, are the writers for the little magazines? I once attempted a classification of the main types, for which I can only say, first, that it is probably not much more nonsensical than most classifications of human beings and, second, that it provides a number of useful pigeonholes for my own experience of the decade. This classification runs:

(1) the poets;
(2) ladywriters;
(3) the snotty young men;
(4) the academics.

Let us take each group in turn:

Poets belong to the little magazine; they have no place else to go. An occasional poem and then only a poem of a certain kind, may find its way into the pages of *The New Yorker,* with a much more satisfying check in payment; but the poet knows *that* is no audience for poetry. If one considers the bulk of the poetry that appears issue by issue in the little magazines, not merely alighting on a few favored names here and there, then one is bound to draw some dismal conclusions about the general atmosphere for poetry now prevailing. The bulk of this poetry, to be perfectly blunt, is bad, and not merely indifferently bad but bad in a way that suggests perversion of some kind. The perversion in this case is that it is a caricature of modern poetry in its bleakness, intellectualization, and remoteness of feeling. Eliot's revolution in poetry brought about a revaluation of John Donne and the metaphysical poets, and irony and intellectual toughness became the great virtues of the day; unfortunately, these real and at the time (circa 1910–20) very necessary virtues hardened in this country into a critical orthodoxy, and the kind of criticism prevailing in the pages of the little magazines was not of a kind even faintly to suggest to our young and aspiring poets that behind the ingeniousness and intellectual wit of their images should be some evidence of a direct and personal involvement with their subject. Had not John Crowe Ransom once rebuked an elder scholar for having said that be-

Reprinted from "Declining Fortunes of the Literary Review: 1945-57," in *The Anchor Review,* Number Two, (1957), pp. 148-158, by permission of the author. Title supplied by the Editor.

hind all Donne's conceits there was *passion?* How critically naïve, how positively *square,* to demand of a poet what was once the primal element in all poetry! (Here the distinction between highbrow and lowbrow hardly cut at the root of the matter, which is the decline of feeling in a whole civilization, a fact as visible in the pages of the literary review as in the secondhand and ready-made images that flicker across the television screens.) Watching this poetry issue after issue, one had somewhat the feeling of taking part in a conspiracy of silence, and I used to dream from time to time of an issue which would have several blank pages with the notice that no poems worth printing had been found in the last months; this might have been a useful editorial act, at least a reminder to some of the readers that they were not necessarily to take seriously all the poetry that appeared in the magazine's pages.

Of course, these cavils are fortunately but half the story, and their service in the cause of poetry will probably be the brightest star in the record of the little magazine. The fact is that really first-rate poets and first-rate poems are very few and far between, and that a vast quantity of rubble is the price one pays for unearthing a single diamond. Considering the engulfing facts of the commercial literary market, we are lucky (and also indebted to the little magazine) that we have any poetry or poets left at all.

The ladywriter, the second of our categories, is a thorny and obscure subject, which I mention here as a separate group not primarily for any difference of literary quality (though this difference is there), but because their economic status is likely to be different, for several reasons, from the male's, and any general discussion of the status of writers always tends to come down to very stubborn bread-and-butter facts. Of course, this species ranges all the way from the literary bobby-soxer to the most intellectually formidable of women whose daggers of the mind were honed to ten times the sharpness of their male counterparts. The years 1945–55 were good ones for the literature of feminine sensibility, and even some of the younger and more sensational male talents capitalized on this style. Sometimes the little reviews inclined to be rather gallantly protective of their pet lady-writers, but of course every group has to be clubby somewhere. No collective can ever be totally pure—that is the nature of a collective; and even so loosely federated a one as the literary highbrows has at any time its own undeclared sense of focal points of pressure—in short, of that dread and necessary thing, literary politics. The highbrows happen only to be pure on different matters and different reputations from the middlebrow.

The third category, "the snotty young men," brings us, I think, to the more central issues in this decade's history, at least as it is reflected in the little magazine. The term is not meant in any derogation; indeed the snotty young men are very valuable for the literary review, and a certain number of them are indispensable to keep the bounce in its pages: they can be counted on to throw bricks when and where needed, and generally to remind readers how awful things really are. Of course, they do get tiresome and strident, and there is a certain monotony in their targets; but if they were not around to remind us, we might forget that things are often even worse than the snotty young men make them out to be. They are young men fresh out of college, or maybe doing some graduate work, but still relatively unattached and free. Their unattached status makes them the last contemporary survivors of that old free-floating intelligentsia which was once the backbone of the European literary reviews and of our own American ones during earlier periods. That is why the history of these young men is very much the history of the little magazine over the last few decades.

Their fathers in the twenties were "all those sad young men" of Scott Fitzgerald. Their themes were different then (personal emancipation, the escape from the provincialism of American life, and the discovery of Europe), the sad young men had considerably more naïveté but also more poetry, and they moved about in a more casual and spacious period. A dollar went a long way in Europe; you could move around freely for quite a while before tying yourself down; and various side-line jobs, needed now and then to keep body and soul together, didn't seem to take as much out of the person. In the thirties, their next metamorphosis, these young men were Marxists and social militants. Since everyone was poor in the decade of the Great Depression, again the young man could drift around with an easier conscience. The leisure of a Bohemia (though a much grubbier one) was still possible: there were gaps, open spaces, in the social life, and indeed one great big gap of national unemployment. With the forties and the War there ensued a gradual closing down of horizons. The snotty young men inherited from their forebears the social role of rebels, but the positive content of the two previous decades was gone: the revolution in letters of the twenties had been assimilated, and revolutionary politics was no longer possible. In Europe some new themes emerged in the forties, and a writer like Malraux was able to make his leap out of the thirties by recognizing that the social issues with which the intellectuals had occupied themselves led back to a much more total and ultimate problem, Man himself; even so inveterate a journalist as Arthur Koestler, with his eye perpetually glued to political events in the foreground, began to hear in their background the haunting music of the Absolute. But America is a country that has no taste for the metaphysical and the totally problematic, and no new idea took hold here to fill the vacuum left by the thirties. Thus the snotty young men, when I came to know them at first hand in 1945, retained out of all their grand youthful illusions of rebellion not much more than a dissent that had become purely cultural and critical, and this was the thin gruel that fed even our liveliest reviews during the period: the highest calling left seemed to be to denounce the fake, to keep a steady eye on the high and serious even if the period could not quite produce these itself—in short, the dreary war upon the middlebrow. Premises of an Age of Criticism. And now in the midst of the great smuggery of the Eisenhower boom even this dissenting shade, gaunt and emaciated as he is, seems on his way to final interment: the snotty young men vanish into the Academy.

The decade, so far as the literary intellectual is concerned, seems to me to be summed up precisely in this contracting, shrinking, closing down of horizons. This summation may sound rather abstract, but in my small corner of the world it was experienced at first hand as something very concrete. I remember very vividly an evening right after the War, about the time when I first became connected with *Partisan Review,* with a friend at a Greenwich Village bar: the place was packed with uniforms, for though demobilization was going on, it was hardly fast enough to please anybody. The air was alive with a kind of postwar excitement that, though we did not know it then, was to disappear from these spots almost as fast as the uniforms. (The sexes, too, in and out of uniform, were a little bit more open and mixed; the specialization had not yet quite set in which was to divide bars strictly into straight and pansy places.) Through the hubbub I remember my friend shouting to me, "Nineteen-nineteen! Nineteen-nineteen!" Granted that he was a poet and a little bit high at the time, he did not seem to be prophesying anything fantastic but simply stating what many of us felt to be in the air. We were at the end of a long tunnel, there was light showing ahead, and beyond that all sorts of horizons opened. Unfortunately, between that evening and the present was to be interposed a long line of disasters that neither of us dreamed of at the time: the paralyzing stalemate of the Cold War; peacetime conscription in the United States and a gigantic military budget, which absorbs in so many subtle ways the energies of the nation; the Korean War; and now a New Boom in which prosperity is so rife that everybody is straining body and soul to make more and more money that turns out to be just enough to keep one's head above water, an atmosphere where the young already seem to be sodden with middle age. In 1945, for example, it was still possible to get cheap and livable cold-water flats in Greenwich Village, where one could hole up for a while against the encroaching demands of being a respectable member of society; these disappeared in the postwar housing shortage, and in the span of ten years the Village has been transformed into an overpriced middle-class housing project, sprinkled with gift shops and tourist bars, but without any significant relation to the cultural life of the nation. Even the painters, at present the hardiest members of Bohemia, have moved out. That 1945 did not turn out to be another 1919 is now a matter of sad record; a period as creative as the twenties did not follow this War; instead the whole social life became somber, immense, massive—institutionalized.

The closing down of human horizons is always at once both material and spiritual. What has been going on here, to put it in the more abstract language of sociology, is the process of the institutionalizing of all forms of social life. The literary review has not escaped, for the process is at once so universal and subtle that it engulfs everyone and everything. The material achievements of modern society, as everybody knows, are due to the rational organization of production with its corresponding minute subdivision of human functions— in a word, the factory system. Unfortunately, the factory system does not stay in the factory. A few years ago *Fortune* magazine printed a couple of amazing articles on the corporation wife, which showed that the modern corporation had so far encroached upon ordinary human relations that in some cases a woman's fitness for marriage was to be assessed by the corporation's requirements. (One can imagine the day when Big Business with all those stacks of IBM cards will be able to determine whether a young woman might make a good wife for an executive of General Motors but not, say, of Du Pont.) Well, we have also the corporation writer: a writer isn't just a writer any more, he's a *Time* writer, a *New Yorker* writer, a Hollywood writer, or a television writer. Even in the field of the little review, it became disturbing during my editorial years to note how one began to recognize this or that kind of writing as a *Kenyon* or a *Partisan Review* piece. A glance over the early files of *The New Yorker* is extremely instructive on this process of the Americanization (specialization) of writing: over the past twenty-five years this magazine has polished its formula to the point of perfection and— *rigor mortis*. The employment policy there nowadays, I am informed, is to get them young, preferably before thirty, so that you can build them quicker and tighter into the institution. Sound corporation policy.

Now, a literary review demands for its existence a society which still has some gaps in it, open spaces, interstices; where the human spirit is still flexible enough so that when a man puts himself into print he is not automatically putting on the uniform of his specialization. In such a society *movements* (for or against something or somebody) can be launched and supported; and literary reviews are kept afloat only in the ebb or flow of a movement of some kind. The "movement" may be only a few young men with a couple of ideas about which they are enthusiastic. The enthusiasm is necessary, it gives the sense of things opening up. The great creative talents cannot be predicted in advance, but their arrival can be prepared a little, and in any case editors cannot sit around inertly waiting but have to have something to say in the meantime. Without its "movement" the literary review inevitably becomes a kind of academic miscellany. The history of the little magazines in the past twenty-five years confirms this. *The Dial* had some wonderful talents to draw upon, though it also printed in its pages things that had all the vanished and impossible naïveté of its period; what it did have which we do not have today was the literary atmosphere of the twenties, which was a movement in itself. T. S. Eliot's *Criterion,* particularly in its earliest years, participated in the excitement of a literary revolution that Eliot and Pound had launched during the previous decade. *Partisan Review* in its earlier years, when most people say it was better, may have printed a good many pieces that do not wear well now but had a liveliness and bounce then because they expressed something in the air to which people responded. With the tightening up all along the line in our national life during the decade past, the literary reviews have become invaded more and more by the spirit of the museum: instead of struggling to keep things open and alive, they are engaged in enshrining the dead.

Recently, a new institutionalizing force has gone to work on the literary reviews: the government, or certain agencies of the government, and some foundations interested in the national welfare have at last become interested in these magazines. The highbrow reviews, which once went unnoticed or, if they got any notice at all, were usually kicked around in the more popular press, now turn out to be in the national interest after all! For they may help to convince foreign intellectuals that America is not really (as foreigners sometimes think) a barbarously commercial country, and of course foreign intellectuals sway public opinion in their countries much more powerfully than American intellectuals do here. Thus the literary review is enlisted in the propaganda battle of the Cold War. Certainly, it is flattering for the literary reviews to be given at long last this mite of recognition, and with all the millions poured down the drains in securing good public relations for our country it is only just that the literary reviews should get their very tiny drop. Nevertheless, one would be naïve to expect that this is going to do very much for literature itself. The situation is one in which all kinds of cultural rackets multiply: fellowships for the most fanciful projects and junkets to foreign countries for a whole tribe of cultural ambassadors who in most cases can be counted on to rub the foreigners' fur the wrong way. If the Cold War persists and the fantastic bureaucracy which it has inevitably spawned continues to proliferate in all directions, we may expect that the Cultural Racketeer, sliding smoothly from one grant to another, will become a permanent fixture on our scene. Patronage was once indispensable to the arts; but when the patronage is institutional and the money is poured down bureaucratically from the top, we have to view all this new prosperity for the literati in very sober relation to other things now going on in the national life—particularly in relation to a peculiar kind of stilted and unspontaneous self-consciousness that we Americans have been developing toward the arts. When Samuel Beckett's *Waiting For Godot* was produced on Broadway this past season, it was felt necessary to organize a formal discussion group in the theater afterward in order to explain the "meaning" of the play. Nothing like this happened in the European capitals, where the play, incidentally, enjoyed very much longer runs. This American need to have things "explained" is, no doubt, part of our laudable desire for facts and information, but pushed too far it can only end by threatening art itself, because the demand for an "explanation" will not let the experience be what it is. The more bureaucratized life becomes, the more we expect everything to fit into its pigeonhole, carry its identifying rubric, and so brandish its own "explanation" before it. The explanation ends by taking the place of the experience. The habit of believing that everything can be managed from the top down inevitably begets a secondhand and cerebral attitude toward experience. Maybe a corporation can be managed that way, but hardly literature, and certainly not a good many other things in life more important than literature and on which literature in the end depends. Even where money is given with no bureaucratizing pressures (and for the most part this has been the case), we would be foolish to think this will suffice to produce the new movement or new thing we are all looking for. Nature is stubborn, and things still insist on growing from the bottom up, not the top down.

In the midst of all this our Snotty Young Man, naturally enough, has also surrendered to the institutionalizing process, and he too has found his institution: he has gone over into the Academy. (The third of our categories passes into the fourth—the literary evolution of a decade.) In some cases he has made his separate peace in commercial publishing or even government service, but the Academy has been the most frequent, as it may be the best, solution. Though somewhere along the line he may have written a formal study of Rimbaud, he has not—in any case I know—imitated his subject and gone off to run guns in Abyssinia. Instead, he has settled down in the company of those whom John O'Hara calls "critics and professional pipe smokers," and the soothing odor of tweed and pipe tobacco begins to be diffused more and more thickly through the pages of what, for lack now of any other adjective, have still to be called our *avant-garde* magazines. No doubt the appointment of literary men to university chairs has made some small breach in the dikes and set a fresh, if as yet small, current moving in the academic world; so that the picture is not altogether without its favorable side. In the meantime, however, our young man (and not so young any more) is left to wrestle with all the inertias of academic specialization, so that perhaps even yet he has not altogether escaped that lonely burden of being the dissident one. More often, however, he gives the impression that if Bohemia Lost comes back to his mind at all it is only with a very unreal romanticism (from which we have had a few bad stories in the little magazines) or else with irritation that the years spent there have cost him a couple of academic promotions. He, if anyone does, knows that Bohemia belongs to the past, that modern society has closed down on it, and that the literary review, which once drew its sustenance from that quarter, is no longer possible.

THE BREAKDOWN OF THE INTELLECTUALS
IN PUBLIC AFFAIRS

William F. Buckley, Jr.

I CONTEND that the principal responsibility of the thinking man is to make distinctions. Physics primers remind us that "all of the progress of mankind to date has resulted from the making of careful measurements." That is a way of saying that distinctions are necessary to purposive thought. Evidence that distinctions are not consistently being made is at least a prima facie indication that thinking men are not exercising their primary responsibility; and so long as they do not, civilization cannot profit from what man has to offer: and the nation's problems do not get solved.

That the nation's problems are not being solved is plain, and there is nothing to be gained by a lurid demonstration of the fact. We should bear in mind that the major problems that beset us are not the result of importunate demands on destiny; nor do our demands go against the grain of history and human nature. We want security for our country, and peace and freedom and security for our people. If ever the collective ambitions of a people were licit, ours surely are; and this fact, if one bears in mind that we are the most powerful people in the world, makes it all the more extraordinary that fortune does not indulge our moderate demands. Yet things are *not* going our way, as anyone knows who will reflect on the overarching reality of our day, the growth of the Soviet Empire. Communism—with its unnatural, primitive, total appetite, is on the march, and the West yields before it.

The question is why. There is, of course, no more complex question than that one, and I do not pretend to begin to answer it. I merely assert that one reason why we are losing is that the nation's intellectual leaders, because they have other commitments, are taking imprecise measurements, and in the confusion, progress is not possible.

Let me give a couple of examples, drawn mostly from contemporary and

Condensed and adapted from *Up from Liberalism* (1959) by the author; printed by permission of the author and the publisher, McDowell, Obolensky, Inc. Title supplied by the author.

recent history, of the failure to make distinctions, after which I shall put forward a hypothesis.

1. *Were Sacco and Vanzetti guilty?* It is a part of the American creed that they were not. Yet what happened is that for failure to distinguish, those who felt that Sacco and Vanzetti were unfairly tried (as I do) transmuted this conviction into an affirmation of Sacco and Vanzetti's innocence of the crime for which they were executed. And that is something else again.

Most students of law appear to agree that in the proceedings against Sacco and Vanzetti, there was reversible error; therefore, Sacco and Vanzetti should not have been executed—at least not as the result of that trial. Very well. But may we not explore the question whether they were actually guilty of the murder? Speculation on the point is not encouraged; for as I say, it has become a part of the American creed that they were *martyrs*. "The momentum of the established order required execution of Sacco and Vanzetti," reminesced the editor of the *Boston Herald*. And yet I *believe* the evidence points strongly to the guilt of Sacco and Vanzetti, and I *know* I could prove from an examination of the rhetoric used in the typical account of the case—for example, in Mr. Schlesinger's first volume on the *Age of Roosevelt*—that the relevant distinction is *not* kept in mind. But is this important? Yes, for two reasons. The commitment of the intellectual community to the innocence of Sacco and Vanzetti profoundly affects the current mood, particularly respecting the problem of internal security. And belief in the martyrdom of Sacco and Vanzetti is a part of the syndrome I am attempting to identify. Sacco-Vanzetti, like Dreyfuss, like Galileo, is the stuff of which long shadows are cast.

2. *Was Owen Lattimore a Communist?* Certainly not, one is told by the majority of the academicians. The charges against him were dropped by the court, were they not?

They were. And one repeats, Was Owen Lattimore a Communist? The decision of the Court of Appeals to set aside the indictment of Mr. Lattimore had nothing whatever to do with the question whether, during the period when he directed the policies of the Institute of Pacific Relations, he worked —as an investigating committee of the Senate put it—as a "conscious, articulate instrument of the Soviet conspiracy." The legal case against Lattimore was dropped on a technicality which shed no light on the central problem involved. Yet Johns Hopkins University—and the academic community in general—pounced on the technicality as constituting total exoneration of Lattimore. Academic communities are usually asking that they be allowed to police their own personnel, that it is their business, not that of congressional committees, or vigilante groups, or, worse, alumni, to decide whether a teacher has abused his profession—but here they joyfully consigned to a totally incompetent court of law the responsibility to decide in their behalf, not merely the *legal* merits of the Lattimore case, over which the Court did have competence, but other questions, over which only Johns Hopkins and Mr. Lattimore's professional peers had competence, as well. I believe that a study of the 13-volume investigation of the Institute of Pacific Relations not only affirms the conclusion of the Senate Committee but does it so conclusively as to render dissent from it (there was none in the Committee— eleven out of eleven Senators concurred) positively perverse.

I have a letter from the President's office at Massachusetts Institute of Technology addressed to an alumnus who had written in to question the reinstatement last year of Professor Dirk Struik. Answered Mr. James G. Kelso, Executive Assistant to Dr. Killian, "Upon the dropping of all charges against Professor Dirk Struik by the Commonwealth of Massachusetts, he was restored to teaching duties at the Institute. We are not a legal body with powers of trying or conducting a case. If the authorities cannot find suitable charges, it seems hardly our role to do so."

Now if Professor Struik were to begin teaching that far from the apple's falling down on Newton, Newton fell up on the apple; and that the shortest airplane route between Georgia and Washington is via Phoenix, Arizona, the Commonwealth of Massachusetts would not find, in its statute books, grounds for action against Mr. Struik. But would MIT? For the Commonwealth of Massachusetts there is no mechanism by which to judge whether Professor Struik is a competent teacher of physics and, let us hope, there never will be. But does this relieve MIT of the responsibility of setting up its own standards of professional behavior? The question for MIT is not whether being a concealed Communist is against the laws of Massachusetts, but whether, to qualify to teach at MIT, one must meet rather more fastidious requirements than merely staying out of Massachusetts jails.

But MIT and Johns Hopkins—and just about the entire academic fraternity—whom one might have expected to be startled by the evidence of Mr. Lattimore's and Mr. Struik's abuse of their calling, and resolved to settle for nothing less than an exhaustive examination, *conducted by themselves,* have allowed, respectively, a court and a legislature to bail them out. They have slurred over a distinction that one might have expected men of lesser critical faculties to observe.

What happened to the mission of the intellectuals, so perfectly defined 700 years ago by Albertus Magnus? That mission, he said, "is to tell whether an action is good or bad, not by passing sentence, as do the judges, but according to the truth, as do the sages; and to do this truly, whoever may be the author of the action, and whatever his position, be it above, or below, our own."

If I had merely singled out aberrational lapses of judgment, my contention could be rejected that there is here a syndrome of a national affliction; but I have not. I draw attention not to the sins of commission, but of omission. It is not the enormities of Schlesinger, or Owen Lattimore, or Struik that arrest me: what matters is that the MIT's, the Johns Hopkins, and many intellectuals, fail to so classify them. Whether they fail to do so because they fail to understand that that is what they are, or whether they have transcending commitments which keep them silent, is essentially a psychological question, one which I shall not go into any more than is necessary. The point is the effective critical apparatus of America has broken down in matters of urgent national concern. The intellectual class has developed the capacity to suspend virtually *en masse* the critical judgment on those occasions where a rigorous application of standards, the careful drawing of distinctions, leads to inconvenient conclusions. That is a major breakdown.

Our nation is primarily imperilled by the march of international Communism. The threat which costs us forty-five billion dollars a year, preempts the creative energies of some of our most talented scientific minds, and forces upon us the abhorrent institution of conscription, is a threat which, had it been properly assessed a generation ago, might have been disposed of by the strategic use of a few dozen manacles. Even ten years ago, the problem, though much more difficult, was, relative to today's easy to solve. Perhaps a better way to put it is that ten years ago it was a problem one could afford to postpone only at the price of seeing the enemy develop hydrogen bombs and intercontinental rockets. But consistently, a generation ago—ten years ago—now, down to and including the present moment, our policy has reflected our failure to think rigorously. There is always with us the desire—never entirely excreted—to think well of the Soviet experiment; there is the desire to believe that time and tide will draw Communism's teeth; there is the selective obsession with peace—I say selective, because today's pacifism contrasts sharply with the bellicosity shown by the intellectuals toward Hitler—all contribute to the intellectual breakdown. On account of that breakdown we fail to take the measure of the enemy, and it is from that failure—not, I like to think, from the fact the moral resources are simply not there—that our lack of will derives. What does this lead to? "I believe," said President Eisenhower at Geneva in 1955, in an effusion heard round the world, "that the Soviet Union wants peace every bit as much as we do."

Who is really to blame for so egregious a misestimate as this (and all it means coming from the man who writes American foreign policy)? What have the distinction-makers done, that the President should, by their counsel, avoid such an error? "You people"—Eisenhower might say in self-defense—"haven't yet spotted Owen Lattimore as a fellow-traveler—what are you getting after me for if I think Marshal Zhukov is a man of peaceful intentions?"

The question has not been asked—and as things are going will not be, until Apocalypse; and it is not easily answered. Meanwhile our governors, who are not for the most part men of independent critical resources, draw, as they must, on the thinking community for counsel; and, on account of the thinking community's failure, themselves fail in their job.

The commitment by the intellectuals to democracy has proved, I think, to be inordinate, obsessive, and fetishistic. It is part of their larger absorption with *method,* and *method* is the fleshpot of those who live in metaphysical deserts. Democracy, Erik von Kuehnelt-Leddihn rightly observes, is the lubricant of relativism. Democracy (like the United Nations) is a procedure, not a policy; yet in it all the hopes of an intellectual epoch were vested. Many intellectuals tend to look upon democracy as an extension of the scientific method, as the scientific method applied to social problems. In an age of relativism, one tends to look for flexible devices for measuring this morning's truth. Such a device is democracy; and indeed, democracy becomes epistemology. Democracy will render reliable political truths just as surely as the marketplace sets negotiable economic values. If democracy certifies Harry Truman, who are we to call him down?—And since we are prepared to believe, a priori, that democracy simply could not punish a God-fearing people as, some people suggest, they were indeed punished when Mr. Truman became President—then is not Truman really like Lincoln? "Truth will emerge victorious in the free contest of ideas"— there is the root superstition of today's intellectuals. Do they believe in it? Yes, in that they carry it to its theoretical extreme in establishing academic policy. No, in that they do not (could not), in their own behavior, practise what they preach. It is established doctrine, under academic freedom, that a school may not consciously (even via released time for religious instruction) further one point of view over against another. "A university does not take sides on the questions that are discussed in its halls," a committee of scholars and alumni of Yale reported in 1952. "In the ideal university all sides of any issue are presented as impartially as possible." To do otherwise is to violate the neutrality of a teaching institution, to give advantage to one idea over and against another, thus prejudicing the race which, if all the contestants were let strictly alone, truth is bound to win.

That is the distilled voodoo of academic freedom—and it could only be taken seriously in an age when people will move mountains rather than believe, when the nightmare of academic theorists is that someone will apprehend one of those truths the university is allegedly chasing after all the time. What a horrifying dilemma! For the university would then be face to face with those consequences of finding the truth that one is always told we are bravely prepared to accept—but *what* consequence is theoretically permissible? The rejection of its opposite as error? No: that is a presumption not permitted under academic freedom. What then? Nothing—except the repudiation of that truth—or else, on better thought, the reclassification of it as untruth or—*always* good—partial truth.

The notion that, in education, all ideas should start out, so to speak, even in the race (*who can say with absolute confidence that Communism is in error? It has not lost many races lately*) is, in my judgment, sheer caricature, it is relativism (*see what happens when you have orthodoxy? Before you know it, Sacco and Vanzetti are lying there dead*)—relativism gone mad, the final rout of reason (*Just what laws did Professor Struik break?*) at the hands of sophistry, the denial of the validity of three millenniums of purposive thought.

The modern intellectual has gone absolutist where he should be relativist, and relativist where he should be absolutist. It is an immutable fact that Communism, because its premises contradict the nature of man, is wrong: and it should be treated as wrong, absolutely. It is a fact that academic freedom and democracy must be judged by their works, hence one's enthusiasm for them must be tempered by time and place and circumstances; must, in a word, be relative. It is a *fact* that the exertions of the human mind and spirit have left us with an intellectual patrimony that were we to live one thousand years, we could not fully absorb, or adequately cherish: and yet the theory of higher education seeks primarily to sate the god *method*: with the emphasis on the search for new truths, rather than the apprehension of old ones. And so as regards truths, we are become like the girls of Randall Jarrell's novel, whose capacity for tolerance was so industriously stimulated by the faculty of Benton College that the girls "yearned for the discovery of life on the moon, so that they could prove that *they* weren't prejudiced against moon men."

So diverse are the problems that plague man that it is unwise to speculate as to their central cause. No cause more elaborated than original sin seems adequate—even so, let me venture this: the direct problems that face the world are the making of governments in action; for only government can exercise the leverage necessary to transform individual vices into universal affliction. It took government to translate *Das Kapital* into concentration camps; it takes positive action by government to preserve many of the imbalances in our economic system; only government, with its monopoly of force, can perpetuate injustices that individuals, given the freedom to do so, would redress. It was long ago understood, in the evolution of political theory, that just about the only *in*tolerable answer to big government is *no* government. Government there must be, this side of paradise, so that the challenge is, and always will be, how to restrain and direct that government without which we cannot get on. The facile answer of the 19th century, when the body of the world's progressive social theorists seized intoxicatingly upon literacy and self-rule as the solvents of the enlightened and domesticated state, has proved naive. The insufficiency of democracy as a guarantor of enlightened public action is now perceptible. The only defense against the shortcomings and abuses of collective action by the state is concerted resistance by individuals. That resistance can only issue from an undamaged critical faculty, and moral sense. If the entire thinking class indulges itself in the suppression of the intellect and the conscience, anything can happen: wars that should not be fought, are fought; and wars that should be fought are not fought; and human impulses that should be restrained are not restrained, and human impulses that should not be restrained, are restrained; and great nations are humbled.

"BLOODY-MINDED PROFESSORS": SHAME OF THE INTELLECTUALS

Peter Viereck

"The power of vested interests is usually exaggerated when compared with the gradual *encroachment of ideas*. . . . Indeed the world is ruled by little else. . . . Madmen in authority, who hear voices in the air, are distilling their frenzy from some *academic* scribbler of a few years back."

—JOHN MAYNARD KEYNES

"If we liberals were right on certain single aspects of the Russian Revolution, we were wrong, disgracefully wrong, on the question as a whole. We were wrong because, in our . . . vision of a new world springing from the womb of this Russian experiment, we permitted ourselves to condone wrongs that we knew must be wrongs."

—JOHN HAYNES HOLMES, *America's leading liberal clergyman, 1939 (after the Hitler-Stalin pact)*

IN ONE of his breathtakingly apt phrases, Winston Churchill called our communists and their sympathizers *not* a gang of ruthless and bloody-minded gangsters but "a gang of ruthless and bloody-minded professors." The phrase is apt because Churchill, by implication, has spotted a central problem of our century: the strike of the middle-class intellectuals, their reluctance to conserve the very heritage that protects from Russia their freedom and their security.

Just as American workingmen have an innate impulse toward Red-baiting and toward capitalist democracy, so many bourgeois intellectuals, artists, and writers (what Churchill means by "professors") still have an innate soft spot for some kind of almost unconscious fellow-traveling with communism. I wish more of my fellow "professors," to use Churchill's phrase a third time, would analyze the reasons for their (our) soft spot—in addition to spending so much of their leisure deploring loyalty oaths for professors. We will fight these potentially dangerous oaths more effectively, and protect more effectively our indispensable academic freedom, by analyzing objectively our own

Reprinted from *Shame and Glory of the Intellectuals* (1953), pp. 109-111, 120-126, by permission of the publisher, The Beacon Press.

soft spot. To replace our alienation from our own society with greater mutual trust, we must improve—rather than servilely accept—our imperfect society. But equally we must improve—rather than self-pity—our own imperfect selves.

Conversely, on the opposite side of this social split, I wish more business tycoons would spend more of their leisure analyzing the following question. Since America is not merely prosperous but a relatively free and decent place to live in, why are its patriotic and capitalist slogans so unattractive, psychlogically and esthetically, that they repel educated Americans and attract only the uneducated?

Totalitarianism has had an innate attraction for an able minority of literary intellectuals as far back as Plato. He in turn expelled his fellow poets from his totalitarian republic, thus anticipating the modern popular impulse to send "all long-hair radicals back where they came from." Bad tempers on all sides may abate if all sides remember that it is nothing new— has been true for centuries—that *some* intellectuals have an inherent soft spot for totalitarian revolution and that, therefore, *all* intellectuals are distrusted by their nonintellectual fellows. We have seen it all before: the sensitive artists saying (with Wordsworth) of a brutal, insensitive revolution, "Bliss was it in that dawn to be alive," and the victims of that revolution chanting:

> Je suis tombé à terre,
> Le nez dans le ruisseau;
> C'est la faute à Voltaire,
> C'est la faute à Rousseau![1]

Today American victims of a later world revolution, paying a price in Korea for the illusion that you can appease the Soviet terror, are chanting prose versions of this old anti-Jacobin ditty: "C'est la faute à. . . ." For Voltaire, they are substituting any number of more recent and less distinguished intellectuals and ideologues, including all the professors who reassured America that communists are not communists but agrarians, Chinese Jeffersons, fellow-progressives in a Popular Front, or (to quote one book title) "people on our side."

Then as now, the guilt of intellectuals and educators gets wildly exaggerated. Then as now, there has been some truth—amid the obvious exaggerations—in some of the accusations. Intellectuals are more susceptible to the leftist totalitarian lure than any other group in America: only a small minority of them, of course, but proportionately a higher minority than of such other groups as farmers, businessmen, and manual workers. . . .

---

1. "I crashed to the ground, my nose in the gutter;
   It's the fault of Voltaire, it's the fault of Rousseau!"

In America, fellow-traveling has never been a working-class movement or a spontaneous people's movement. American pro-communism, and even much of European communism, is a spontaneous movement only among the educated intellectuals of the upper middle class. It arises among that section of them which is psychologically—*not* economically—discontented and self-outlawed. (That these, in turn, with their educational leadership, may set a mass movement in motion under certain unusual economic conditions, is another and *later* matter.)

Marx, Engels, Lenin, Trotsky, Bukharin—most of the original communist leaders—were intellectuals of the upper middle class, not suffering economically but suffering intensely psychologically. This must be qualified by adding that Lenin's family belonged to the petty nobility (the Tsar's professional service-aristocracy) as well as to the rich upper middle class. Among top communists, Stalin was one of the few to spring (like Hitler and Mussolini) from humble—so-called democratic—origins. But this fact had far less to do in shaping Stalin than his being picked by the Greek Orthodox church as one of the favored semi-intellectuals trained for the priesthood. Thereby he, too, was able to find his way indirectly to the alienated upper classes, the first prerequisite to communism.

Evidence is available about the composition and origins of the small Bolshevik party that seized power in November, 1917. The overwhelming majority of its members were definitely not workers, but middle-class intellectuals. Is this fact sufficiently known and sufficiently analyzed in America? As late as 1921-22, even after the triumph of the revolution and the adherence of some of the propagandized masses to the Bolshevik party, a *majority* of its members were still not workers but intellectuals.

Even more, far more is this true of America. The American worker is the most anticommunist bulwark of freedom in the world today. He believes in democratic trade unionism, working *within* the capitalist system for increased living standards and increased civil liberties. Though intended as slander, there is reassuring truth in the definition of "Trade unions" in the 1951 edition of the *Soviet Dictionary of Foreign Words:* "primarily opportunists and adherents of class collaboration with the bourgeoisie."

It is only half the story to explain the anticommunism of American workers by their having the highest living standards of any workers in the world. Just as the pro-communism of rich middle-class intellectuals defies economic determinism, so does the anticommunism of American workers; it, too, is partly motivated also by noneconomic factors. For trade unionism has a rarely-discussed psychological appeal in addition to its much-discussed and obvious economic appeal. Communism appeals to those suffering from the frustration and loneliness of an impersonal, cash-nexus relationship with their neighbors. The middle class suffers most from that; in consequence, its intellectuals become the leaders of communism in all countries. Trade unions not only bring obvious economic gains to the Anglo-American worker. They also replace for him the cash-nexus with a sense of belonging. They give him a human, cultural, social, and recreational unity with his neighbors, not merely an economic one. They give him an organic sense of community, more medieval (guild-style) than modern—if modern means a separatist, atomistic liberalism.

Therefore, America's anticommunist trade-unions (in contrast with the reckless, revolution-provoking anarchism of the Republican Old Guard) are our most conservative, revolution-preventing force. Their *voluntary* sense of community is the best guaranty against communist or fascist collectivism, which appeals—with its *coercive* sense of community—to all who are starved for an organic human nexus. Part of the same pattern is the much-mocked bar (pub in England); it, too, gives the worker but never the middle-class clerk a belonging-ness that undercuts the psychological appeal of communism-fascism. Despite "Seven Nights on the Barroom Floor" and "The Drunkard's Progress," I would even put in a good word for the saloon, the old-fashioned pre-Prohibition saloon, which so horrified the "properly" educated (that is, half-educated) middle class, whose lace-curtain psychology barred them from participating in this great American folklore. In that same unifying folklore, the unmentionable burlesque show also occupies an honorable place, as the only spontaneous, non-fancied-up folk art of our day.

Since the problem is global, let the camera flash back for an instant to a very different continent:

The significant thing about all these [pro-communist] leaders . . . is that they almost without exception are middle-class, and most of them from the fairly well-to-do middle class with a tendency toward the intellectual side. Many of them are somewhat bookish men. . . . They feel that their talents are not appreciated, a common disease of the intellectual, particularly in the Orient.

These words by a reliable American foreign correspondent[2] were not written of the Russian Bolsheviks of 1917 nor of American fellow-travelers—though they might just as well have been—but of communist sympathizers in the Iran of 1952. Over three different continents, a single world-wide pattern of the pro-communist personality emerges.

In 1945, Elmo Roper took a poll on whether America should offer still greater concessions to communist Russia. Roper classified the responses according to the education and income of those who replied. A sharp split in American opinion was revealed. Workers and low-income groups distrusted Russia and opposed concessions. Rich Americans, what Marx would

---

2. Albion Ross, "Iran's 'Secret' Tudeh Party," despatch of August 16 from Teheran in New York *Times,* August 17, 1952, Sunday editorial section.

call the bourgeoisie, trusted Russia and wanted still further American concessions to Russia. Roper classified these answers not only by wealth but by intellectuality and by knowledge of Russian and world affairs. The uneducated and the nonintellectual, in Roper's words of 1945,

were much less aware of the necessity of co-operation with Russia and much more inclined to charge Russia with dark and sinister intentions. . . . Those who knew something about Russia gave broad, balanced, opinions—critical on some scores and laudatory on others, but with the balance leaning strongly toward friendly understanding.

In 1946, a Gallup poll asked: "Do you believe Russia is trying to build herself up to a ruling power, or is Russia just building up protection against being attacked in another war?" Again answers were classified by education and income. The most optimistic replies came from "the professional and business group." They split almost 50-50 on this question. The most pessimistic replies came from what Gallup called the uneducated "manual workers." Sixty per cent of these "oppressed proletarians" predicted—in contrast with experts and professors—that Russia aimed for world power and expansion.

In other words, the main obstacle to understanding that communists are communists (not good neighbors, not agrarian reformers) was the possession of education, intellect, or great wealth. No wonder one editor made the following comment on all this in 1952: "to predict accurately in 1945 that Russia would act as Russia has acted, you had to be as dumb and poorly informed as an ox."

The misinterpretation of Soviet world conquest by the best educated non-oxen of the West did not merely affect the realm of abstract theory. It affected the course of actual history. To what extent it did so, cannot be accurately assessed. Here we enter the imponderable realm of the indirect influence exerted by "intellectual atmosphere"—in this case, a trust-Russia atmosphere. One assessment of the historical results of this atmosphere has been formulated by Norman Angell, the winner of the Nobel peace prize. He can hardly be called an imperialist warmonger, or unliberal, or anti-intellectual. His assessment of the trust-Russia atmosphere, among our unproletarian, upper-middle-class liberals, probably exaggerates its concrete territorial or military influences and consequences. But he does offer a real insight into at least the spirit of what was happening:

We defeated Hitler in a second war for democracy and then (against all the counsels of the "imperialist" Churchill) insisted upon a strategy which left the military domination of those states to Stalin, largely *because liberals and leftists* in both Britain and the United States believed Stalin and what he stood for to be so much more democratic than Churchill and what that "Tory imperialist" stood for.[3]

3. Norman Angell, *The New Leader,* May 26, 1952, p. 11. Italics mine.

To Angell's insufficiently-qualified comment, you must add: Stalin could have and probably would have taken Eastern Europe militarily (though hardly Manchuria) even without Yalta. For this was a time when armed resistance to Soviet expansion would have been politically impossible in terms of the still deceived, still Popular Fronting public opinion of western Europe.

But the issue is not: what would he have taken anyway? The issue is: why did we give the seal of Western moral approval upon what would otherwise have been an open act of highway robbery? Confronted by such an open act, without the Yalta moral sugarcoating, our public opinion—which hampered resistance to Russian aggression till 1947—would at least have hardened earlier. This would have permitted rearmament and a Truman doctrine and an Atlantic pact many months earlier, instead of having to undergo that fatal delay of unilateral disarmament—until Churchill's noble Fulton speech and Stalin's own actions brought Stalin's Western dupes back to their senses. Back from the Popular Front illusion.

That illusion may be defined as the view that communists are merely misguided, overhasty liberals, moving in the same general "forward-looking" and "anti-fascist" direction as the rest of us. This illusion views communists as a problem of "civil liberties for nonconformists," instead of as a murderous Red army of invasion on behalf of a Russian fascist ruling class. This illusion made well-groomed and plausible-sounding maniacs of precisely the highest intellectual liberal circles, as shown not only by their above Roper-poll reactions but by their books, lecture courses, and liberal weeklies.

If you have forgotten the prevalence of this illusion—so I wrote in an *Atlantic Monthly* article of April 1940, and so I repeat again today—then simply read the list of 165 (allegedly 400) supposedly liberal intellectuals, not the worst nor the best elements of our culture, who in August 1939 signed a disgraceful pro-communist manifesto. This denounced "the fantastic falsehood that the fascist states and Soviet Russia equally menace the democratic way"; it called "Soviet and fascist policies diametrically opposed," and called Russia the great "bulwark" of peace. To repeat the list of signers now, in part the élite of the world of liberal weeklies, would embarrass some honest men who subsequently changed their minds for the better. Suffice it to recall again in 1952, as my article originally did in 1940, one tragi-comic coincidence: this manifesto was featured in *The Nation* the very week of the Hitler-Stalin pact!

Originating in the '30's, the Popular Front illusion provided during 1944-47 the moral sugar-coating to Russia's aggressions. It did so by blending into what might be called the optimistic "Yalta spirit," namely the spirit of thinking that Stalin would behave more peacefully and democratically than Hitler. Thereby the Popular Front illusion has dealt a blow to peace and liberty, and likewise to lucid reasoning, of still unassessed proportions. Just possibly it will turn out to be (if Russia annihilates the West) the most antisocial act ever committed in the history of mankind by any comparably decent and well-intentioned intelligentsia.

Today American intellectuals are rejecting these misconceptions, so far as foreign policy toward aggression in Korea goes. But they have still not rejected sufficiently the most successful communist hoax ever perpetrated: the confusion of criminal deeds with free thought, the confusion of communist military conspiracy with the sacred cause of civil liberties. One can only echo and underline the phrase, "so grave and urgent that a man breaks out in a cold sweat," in the following comment on this whole problem by John Dos Passos:

A living organism that fails to react to danger is sick or dying. The questions raised in the mind by the moral lynching of Whittaker Chambers by the right-thinking people of this country are so grave and urgent that a man breaks out in a cold sweat to think of them. Can it be that the "liberals" who control communications in the press and the radio and the schools and the colleges . . . refuse, in the light of all the evidence, to recognize the existence of a conspiracy of assassins bent on the destruction of the right-thinking liberals, as much as on the destruction of the rest of us? The day that this mystery becomes clear, the day when this strange delusion is swept out of the public mind, that day we will be able to go to bed secure in the thought that, if the United States is doomed by forces of history too great for us to overcome, at least we will go down fighting.[4]

---

4. *Saturday Review*, May 24, 1952; p. 11.

THE SPREAD OF "COLLEGIATE" VALUES[1]

David Riesman

THERE has been a great change both in recruitment into the academic life and in the distinctness of that life vis-à-vis our common life in the last generation. College faculties have been expanding too fast to permit the slow and careful grooming of a few hand-picked scholars. Indeed, in some fields men now may become professors at an age at which they would once still have been teaching assistants. A bright assistant professor today may be more sought out than a famous full professor even ten or fifteen years ago. The competition of the three state universities of Michigan is only an example of the raiding that goes on quite generally. A great many factors have cooperated to produce these changes. The country is richer, which means that it needs fewer people to tend its farms and factories and can locate more of them in the professions and in the other more or less intellectual careers such as communications, management, and teaching itself. It can also afford to keep people in school longer and to send many more of them to college. And people have more leisure in which to absorb some of the "cultural" values previously associated with attending college; the better large-circulation magazines and networks, paper books, and "art" movies spread intellectual values, at least sporadically. More people travel, visit Europe, read *Gourmet* magazine, and in general feel entitled to follow the style set by those who have attended college. In the process America has become not only more urbanized but also in many ways more urbane.

Correspondingly, I believe that the small liberal arts colleges of the Midwest may not show up as the great recruiting grounds for scholars twenty years from now. The sharpness of the conflict between science and religion is attenuated today; it seldom drives people into a creative tension that results in their becoming biologists or psychologists. Nor do the remaining Protestant colleges seem to me very ascetic. Moreover, there are fewer boys who

Reprinted from "The Academic Career: Notes on Recruitment and Colleague-ship," in *Daedalus* (*Winter*, 1959), pp. 152-157, by permission of the author, the journal, and Basic Books.

1. Based on a talk given in April 1958 at a symposium on "The College Teacher" at Wayne State University. Opportunity to work on problems of higher education discussed in this paper has been facilitated by a grant from the Carnegie Corporation.

want to get off the farm by becoming teachers; there are fewer farms, and those that remain are often large and complex businesses.

At the same time, I am inclined to think that the big cosmopolitan universities are no longer channeling their best students largely into such socially approved careers as law, medicine, business, and the diplomatic service, but are increasingly serving also to recruit scholars.[2] This is in part because their student bodies have become less "social," and include many relatively poor boys who once would have gone to local and often to denominational colleges. For example, the Minneapolis *Star & Tribune* now sends small-town newsboys on scholarships to Yale and Harvard, boys who in an earlier day, if they had attended college at all, would have gone to Carleton or St. Olaf's or Gustavus Adolphus or the University of Minnesota. One result may be that in the future institutions such as Carleton and St. Olaf's will not show up quite so well as they did in the Wesleyan studies, while Harvard and Yale may show up somewhat better.

For the small-town newsboy skimmed out of the Midwest by the increasing talent hunts of the national universities, the transition from high school to college may still be very sharp and dramatic, even traumatic. But as I have implied, college is not so sharp a break from home as it once was for the many youngsters whose high schools have already anticipated college (as some of the wealthy suburban high schools do) and whose parents are themselves collegiate. It follows that, while youngsters who are *entirely* given over to intellectual or artistic values may still feel quite alone, those who have a partial but not exclusive interest in those values no longer need feel, either at home or in high school, that they belong to a minority culture. While, as we all know, a great deal has been said about anti-intellectualism in America during the McCarthy years and later, it is at least arguable that these very attacks on the intellectuals are, *inter alia,* a response to their rising power in a society that more and more requires intellectuals, or at least educated specialists, to get its work done. Whereas once bankers were hated and

2. Social class factors, however, still tend to dictate choice of profession among graduates of the more exclusive prep schools. Cf. Charles McArthur and Lucia Beth Stevens, "The Validation of Expressed Interests as Compared with Inventoried Interests: A Fourteen-Year Follow-Up," *Journal of Applied Psychology,* Vol. 3, No. 3 (1955), pp. 184-189.

For an exploratory study concerning the attractions college teaching has for students, see Maurice L. Farber and W. A. Bousfield, "College Teaching as a Profession," *Journal of Higher Education,* Vol. 29 (1958), pp. 70-72. See Robert H. Knapp and H. B. Goodrich, *Origins of American Scientists* (Chicago: University of Chicago Press, 1952); and Robert H. Knapp and Joseph J. Greenbaum, *The Younger American Scholar: His Collegiate Origins* (Chicago: University of Chicago Press and Wesleyan University Press, 1953); compare John L. Holland, "Undergraduate Origins of American Scientists," *Science,* Vol. 126, No. 3271 (1957), pp. 433-437.

feared in part because they controlled the "mystery" of the gold standard, today scientists and intellectuals control the relevant mysteries, and, as Edward Shils points out in *The Torment of Secrecy,* give rise to analogous fears of domination and analogous opportunities for demagogic attack.

The increasing attention to intellectual values is especially striking among some businessmen. In recent years many large corporations have instituted executive training programs so that their middle-management people, who have often been trained as engineers or as business administration majors, can transcend narrow professional horizons and model themselves on the going version of the industrial statesman. And industrial statesmanship today takes a great interest in colleges, because increasingly businessmen do go to college (as the Warner and Abegglen studies show[3]), use colleges for executive training and development purposes, and meet professors as consultants, market researchers, and social equals. The hope Justice Brandeis expressed before the First World War—that business would become a profession—approaches reality as managers become increasingly aware of the need to handle complex data in making decisions rather than playing hunches or following tradition. Despite ritualistic speeches on ceremonial occasions, big business— little business, including farming, is an entirely different story—has become much less Philistine and much less hostile to intellectual values.

This, of course, is not to say that sheer distinterested intelligence brought to bear on matters of national concern is everywhere welcome. While at present a general liberalism permeates the country at large, there are definite limits, and few voices are raised anywhere to attack nationalism as such or our own militarism. In fact, many universities are as much bases for fighting the Cold War as any S.A.C. outpost: they do research on weapon systems, or military-sponsored social science research on presumptive enemies and allies.

Another limit on academic liberalism occurs in the sphere of religion. Just as most professors are good patriots, so also, if they have not joined the general "return to religion," they are (whatever Fundamentalist senators may think) hardly ever atheistic. For good reasons as well as bad ones, the academy is less of a threat to certain basic values of the American community, and the outlook of the big businessman and of many a professor is not so different as either may still hopefully or sadly think. In contrast with the situation Veblen satirized, the leading universities are not dominated by small-town business values. Rather, a process of mutual infiltration has occurred.

These developments render somewhat paradoxical the attitudes I find among many of my own students and those at other leading colleges: namely, a posture of contempt for business and a belief that, in contrast, teaching

3. See W. Lloyd Warner and James C. Abegglen, *Big Business Leaders in America* (New York: Harper & Brothers, 1955), and *Occupational Mobility in American Business and Industry, 1928-1952* (Minneapolis: University of Minnesota Press, 1955).

offers respectability and even integrity. (I should make clear that this is not a political contempt, for these students are very rarely directly political; it is rather a cultural, moral, or intellectual contempt.) Some students come to this outlook because they harbor aristocratic values and look down on businessmen as the English gentry traditionally looked down on people in trade. But others are themselves the children of small businessmen, and they have overgeneralized from their parental occupations, with their often rapacious ethics and lack of intellectual range, to the large managerial businesses I have been describing. That is, small business is still competitive, still what Veblen would have called a "pecuniary" occupation, in the sense that it deals with bargains and mere tricks of trade, not with large engineering and industrial conceptions. The result is that the younger generation, seeking not only social but also intellectual mobility away from the parental small business (and, in this group, increasingly coming from Jewish and Catholic families rather than Protestant ones), have their eye on the professions as the road to status and opportunity. Academic careers then become alternatives either as belated second choices—for instance, a student ending up as a biologist because he could not get into medical school—or as first choices,[4] decided with the blessing of parents and peers.

Many of the parents of these young people, whose values contrast with those of an older day, do not want them in the business but rather out of the business—although, of course, still self-supporting. And many of the occupations that once would have raised the parents' protest today may seem a golden opportunity. Van Cliburn may persuade them that the piano is not a road to ruin; Charles Van Doren may persuade them that one can make money as an English teacher. Less and less are professors regarded as members of a small, deviant but semi-elite group—although, as we shall see, those who teach the humanities often so consider themselves—but rather as people who have gone into a business that isn't business.

Certainly, as I have said, the life of the businessman and the life of the professor become less and less distinct. The professor is no longer to be regarded as a stuffy fellow. He has become a man of the world, perhaps traveling on an expense account, attending a conference in Washington one day and flying to a UNESCO meeting in Paris the next. In honor of his new status, the avant garde novelist may now portray him as having sex appeal and even a lurid sex life. As universities become bigger and bigger, it is hard for them not to judge their output by business standards or at least bureaucratic ones (as I am told the Michigan legislature has recently been judging the

---

4. I am concerned here with general social factors rather than idiosyncratic ones that influence career choices. For an illustration of the latter, compare the discussion of the medical "call" in the first chapters of Robert W. White, *Lives in Progress* (New York: Dryden Press, 1952).

educational institutions of that state). I have heard professors in the social sciences pass judgment on each other in terms that would not be different if they were engaged in production control. They speak of a man's "output" or his "productivity" as measurable and even quantifiable things, and yards of print take the place of foot-pounds or B.T.U. (Natural scientists, having the most money, are also exposed to these tendencies.[5])

Many professors in classics, in literature, in history, and in the humanities generally believe themselves to espouse the traditional academic values. But in the process of homogenization of values that I have been describing, this becomes more and more difficult, and we see the paradox that some of the embattled humanists engage in "selling" the humanities as good for whatever ails the U.S.A. with the same public-relations fervor that they deprecate in Madison Avenue. The social sciences stand somewhere between, trying to drag an uneasy foot out of the humanities while not quite managing to locate the other foot in the profitable camp of the natural sciences. But in fact, as I shall try to indicate, it is impossible to tell whether a man is a humanist or not by the label of his discipline; and I have seen a number of colleges where the anthropologists are more humanistic than the teachers of English, the physicists by far more humanistic than the economists or the sociologists.

As to these comparisons, however, I should add a word of caution against pushing them too far. One of the characteristics of any older generation, markedly of the present older generation in the universities, is to talk about the good old days. In general, it is safe to say that the old days were not so good and not so different as most of us believe. There were plenty of professors at the turn of the century who espoused business values, just as there were many ministers who did, and they did so with a vulgarity that one could hardly match today among businessmen. Correspondingly, there were other professors a generation ago who really were stuffy, pretentious without being literate, erudite without understanding, pedantic without being critical. Along with the general rise in standards of education, I believe college teachers have become brighter and better.[6]

5. Norbert Wiener, "The Megabuck Era," *New Republic,* Vol. 138, No. 1 (27 January 1958), p. 10.

6. This is probably a debatable point. I concede that there has been some dilution of the profession in terms of the qualities of the scholar as well as those of the gentleman, but I am convinced that the products of the leading graduate schools are better educated than many of their teachers.

THE REAL STATUS OF AMERICAN INTELLECTUALS

Seymour M. Lipset

IT IS a surprising fact, that the image of the American intellectual as held by his fellow citizens is quite different from what he himself thinks they hold. While there is considerable evidence showing that the average intellectual feels himself neglected and scorned, his work poorly valued by the community, the community itself places him fairly high when polled on the relative status of occupations. In one such study of the ranks of ninety-six occupations, conducted in 1947 by the National Opinion Research Center of the University of Chicago, college professors ranked above every nonpolitical position except that of physicians; artists, musicians in a symphony orchestra, and authors ranked almost as high.[1] Essentially, this study suggests that those in the intellectual occupations enjoy about the same prestige in America as do important businessmen, bankers, and corporation directors.[2] In 1950 a second national opinion survey reported similar results. This study asked people to place various jobs in the "upper, middle, working, or lower classes." Professors came out fourth among twenty-four categories, and 38 per cent of those polled placed them definitely in the "upper" class.[3]

Adapted by the author from "American Intellectuals: Their Politics and Status," in *Daedalus* (Summer, 1959), pp. 467-473; printed by permission of the author, the journal, and Doubleday & Company, Inc. This article is a part of the book *Political Man,* copyright 1959, 1960, by Seymour M. Lipset. Title for the adaptation has been supplied by the author.

1. National Opinion Research Center, "Jobs and Occupations," in R. Bendix and S. M. Lipset, eds. *Class, Status and Power* (Chicago: The Free Press of Glencoe, 1953), pp. 412-414.

2. It is interesting to note that studies made in different countries and at different times indicate that the relative prestige of occupations is everywhere similar. Essentially, all the studies indicate that occupations which require high levels of educational attainment (intellectuals and professionals) or which command considerable power (business elite and politics) are ranked high everywhere. For discussion and references see S. M. Lipset and R. Bendix, *Social Mobility in Industrial Society* (Berkeley: University of California Press, 1959), pp. 14, 111.

3. Richard Centers, "Social Class, Occupation, and Imputed Belief," *American Journal of Sociology,* 1953, 58: 546.

It may be argued that national surveys reporting the opinions of the total population are not significant, since what counts is the opinion of the elite. The social science professors interviewed for *The Academic Mind* considered that big businessmen and high government officials simply do not respect intellectuals. Yet studies that have compared the differential ratings made by people from different classes indicate that those in high social and economic positions actually think far better of intellectual pursuits than do those in the working and lower classes.[4]

Perhaps the best evidence that intellectual occupations, particularly college teaching, do enjoy a high status in America derives paradoxically from the same professors cited above, the majority of whom reported that they thought their occupation would be ranked relatively low by businessmen and politicians. These professors, who constitute a good sample of university social scientists, turn out to come from "relatively high status . . . family backgrounds," as the data in Table I indicate.

TABLE I

SOCIAL ORIGINS OF UNIVERSITY SOCIAL SCIENTISTS

Source: Paul F. Lazarsfeld and Wagner Thielens, Jr., *The Academic Mind* (Chicago: The Free Press of Glencoe, 1958), p. 7.

Father's Occupation	*Per Cent*
Teacher	8
Other professional	23
Managerial	25
White collar and small business	15
Farmer	13
Manual laborer	15
No information given	1
	100 (2451)

Though professors prefer to believe that they are undervalued by people outside the intellectual community, the fact that they are able to attract to their ranks men from relatively privileged origins suggests that their occupation is highly valued. Almost half the respondents have fathers who are in managerial posts or professions other than teaching. Only 15 per cent are the children of manual workers. A comparison of these data with those reported on different samples of the American business elite, the heads of the largest corporations, indicates that the origins of both groups are roughly similar.[5] Actually, the comparison may be unfair to the academic profession,

4. See John D. Campbell, *Subjective Aspects of Occupational Status* (unpublished Ph.D. thesis, Harvard University, 1952).

5. See Lipset and Bendix, *op. cit.*, pp. 128-137, for a summary of the various business-elite studies.

since the sample of college professors is drawn from all institutions of higher learning in the United States, whereas the professors at the better institutions (which are on the average the larger schools) come from higher socioeconomic backgrounds: 62 per cent of those at very large schools (above 9000 students) are from managerial or professional families, as contrasted with 49 per cent at very small schools (700 or below); two-thirds of the social scientists at private nondenominational schools are from high-status backgrounds, as compared with 44 per cent at institutions with religious affiliation or at teachers colleges.[6] Since the social sciences are not generally those disciplines with the highest prestige within a university, it is likely that the social origins of humanists and natural scientists are even higher. But the facts we already have as to the attitudes of the general population and the family backgrounds of social scientists constitute a powerful argument for the thesis that academic and other intellectual occupations in the United States are high in social prestige.

THE CONTRADICTIONS OF REAL AND PRESUMED STATUS. Since the American intellectual's self-image seems contradicted by the evidence cited above the question naturally follows: why then does the intellectual feel that he is looked down on?

I suspect that in large measure his feelings of inferiority derive from his glorified conception of the status of the European intellectual and from his using the European situation as a comparison.[7] Anyone who has ever been in a discussion about the life of an intellectual in this country knows that sooner or later someone will remark that in England, Germany, France, or Italy a writer, painter, composer, or professor really counts. There, such a man is recognized by the public and by the political and economic elites.

It is certainly true that there is a difference between the European and the American treatment of the intellectual. This difference is no more or less than the difference between a fairly rigid class society and a society that

6. Lazarsfeld and Thielens, *op. cit.,* pp. 23, 26.

7. "In Emerson's day professors and their fellow intellectuals had not come to be regarded as a special group; they were not then, nor have they ever come to be, looked up to, rewarded, and honored as in Europe" (Merle Curti, "Intellectuals and Other People," *The American Historical Review,* 1955, 60: 260). It may be that the grass always looked greener elsewhere, particularly to intellectuals who want to prove it is so, and who as important foreign travelers are often involved in exchanges with many sections of the native elite whom they rarely meet regularly at home. Thus, writing in the 1880's, James Bryce tells us that intellectual eminence in America "receives, I think, more respect than anywhere in Europe, except possibly in Italy, where the interest in learned men, or poets, or artists, seems to be greater than anywhere else in Europe. A famous writer or divine is known by name by a far greater number of persons in America than would know a similar person in any European country. He is one of the glories of the country" (James Bryce, *The American Commonwealth* [Toronto: The Copp Clark Pub. Co., Ltd., 1891], Vol. II, p. 621).

emphasizes equality. In Europe, open or apparent deference is given *all* those with higher status, whether engineers, factory owners, or professors, whereas in this country it is not given anyone in such categories to the degree it is abroad.[8] As A. G. Nicholas has pointed out in comparing the situation of the American and the British intellectual, the latter "has been in some degree sheltered by his very position in what Bagehot called a 'deferential society.' Not *very* deferential to him, perhaps; less deferential than to the landowner, the administrator, the soldier, the clergyman or the lawyer, over all of whom the protective gabardine of the appellation 'gentleman' has fallen more inclusively, with fewer loose ends sticking out. Nevertheless the [British] intellectual has shared in it too, whether he was behaving as a rebel or as a hired apologist."[9]

Obviously intellectuals receive a gratifying social deference in many parts of Europe—but so do all positions of high status. What the American intellectual who envies his European brother fails to see is that he is really objecting to the egalitarianism of the United States, rather than to a lower evaluation of his occupation by its citizens. Unconsciously, he thinks in European terms, adopting the criteria of conservative middle- and upper-class European travelers and *émigrés* in America who have found American egalitarianism distasteful.[10]

THE EFFECTS OF ISOLATION AND LOW INCOME. Two other sources of the low self-appraisal of American intellectuals that do not follow directly from American egalitarian values are the seeming isolation of intellectuals from other sections of the elite (particularly their lack of direct contact with political power) as compared with that of European intellectuals, and their income, as contrasted with that of business executives and professional men.

It is true that the average American intellectual has less direct contact with other sections of the elite, particularly with men who wield political power, than does the average European intellectual. Why is this true? The fact is that there are, in absolute as well as proportionate terms, more intel-

---

8. For an elaboration of these ideas on the subject to American egalitarianism, one which attempts to show how the elaborate efforts of upper-status Americans to establish distinctions of family rank result from the strength of the egalitarian ideology, see S. M. Lipset, "Social Trends in America," in Lyman Bryson, ed., *A Concise Guide to Knowledge* (New York: McGraw-Hill Book Co., Inc., in press).

9. A. G. Nicholas, "Intellectuals and Politics in U.S.A.," *Occidente,* 1954, *10:* 47.

10. "With his deep sense of class and status, integration in American society is not easy for the *émigré.* The skilled engineer or physician who, after long years of internship, flunking license exams, washing dishes or laboratory floors, finally establishes himself in his profession, discovers that he does not enjoy the same exalted status that he would have had in the old country. I met several Croatian doctors in the Los Angeles area who were earning $25,000 to $35,000 a year, but still felt declassed" (Bogdan Raditsa, "Clash of Two Immigrant Generations," *Commentary,* January 1958, *25:* 12).

lectuals in America, and they are more widely dispersed geographically than in any other country. This matter of numbers can be quite important. For example, in 1929 *all ten* professors of economics in Australia met and told the government they believed it would be disastrous for the country to go off the gold standard. The Labor government of the day was not happy about this, but it felt it should not move against the "experts." There are far too many such experts in America for them to have such a corporate influence. In this country there are more than fifteen hundred colleges and universities, while Great Britain has about fifteen, West Germany less than twenty, Norway one, Denmark two, Sweden four. In the United States, the Boston area has about 9000 teachers of college and university rank, and the northern California area of which San Francisco is the center has 14,000. In Greater New York City alone there are well over 20,000 persons teaching in about forty institutions of higher learning.

No city in the world approaches New York in the number of intellectuals employed in publishing houses, magazines, and other intellectual enterprises, in addition to those in universities. While New York may be said to be the intellectual capital of the United States, there are important groups of intellectuals scattered round the country whose combined number is far greater than those in or adjacent to New York. Important schools of painters and writers exist in various parts of the country, from Seattle and Los Angeles on the West Coast to New Mexico, New Orleans, Chicago, and Boston. The two leading universities in the country (as judged by faculty caliber ranked by authorities in the various academic disciplines) are located in metropolitan Boston and San Francisco.

The sheer numbers of intellectuals in the urban centers, as well as the enormous size of the country, necessarily limit the extent to which intellectuals in the same field are acquainted with one another, let alone with those in other fields such as politics or business. Academics in large cities often know well only those within their own disciplines; and I can testify from direct experience that social relations among people in the same specialization in different universities in the same large community are rare. There are over sixty historians employed full time on the faculty of Columbia University. The Berkeley faculty harbors more than thirty sociologists, more than are employed by all the British or Canadian universities. Groups of artists, *avant-garde* writers, and those employed in publishing houses exist in many cities, but their membership is often too large to permit much contact with other groups. The relative isolation of the American college professor from all groups, intellectual or other, is borne out by the Lazarsfeld-Thielens study of social scientists. Over three-fifths of the respondents (62 per cent) reported that "their main social contacts are confined to the university," a figure that rises to above 70 per cent among those at the more distinguished colleges and universities.[11] Conversely, in countries with a smaller elite, there is necessarily much intermingling. As Irving Kristol, who has edited *Encounter* in London and *Commentary* and *The Reporter* in New York, has put it, "What has astonished me, and what astonishes any American, is the extent to which almost all British intellectuals are cousins. . . . In America it is otherwise, to put it mildly. . . . It is by no means unimaginable that the senior editors of *The New Yorker* should never have met the senior editors of *Time*."[12] Dwight Macdonald, whose writing experience also includes both cities, has commented, "As an alumnus of both of these magazines, I can testify this is accurate; intellectual circles in New York are neither concentric, interlocking, nor tangential, and one knows 'personally' . . . only a small proportion of the authors whose books and articles one reads. The London intellectual community is much broader, including businessmen, lawyers, and even publishers, even Members of Parliament."[13]

The government of the United States, even when the Republicans are in office, does employ and consult professors and other intellectuals. According to John Fischer, "The Eisenhower administration employs more professors than the New Deal ever did."[14] (The Republican need for intellectuals may be seen in the fact that the two professors who have recently written sympathetic appraisals of the party, Arthur Larson and Malcolm Moos, have since been employed as Presidential aides in the White House.) The great majority, of course, are unlikely to be thus singled out, but I would guess that as many, if not more, professors and other intellectuals are employed or consulted at high levels by the state and federal governments as in most European nations. It is only when the comparison is made in terms of proportion between one class in one country and that in another that Americans rate lower—there are just so many more of them.[15]

Thus, while the size and decentralization of American intellectual life remove the individual intellectual from contact with other sections of the elite and give him a sense of deprivation when he compares his situation with what he conceives to be that of his British or French counterpart, an analysis

11. Lazarsfeld and Thielens, *op. cit.*, pp. 31-32.

12. Irving Kristol, "Table Talk," *Encounter*, October, 1955, 5, pp. 60-61.

13. Dwight Macdonald, "Amateur Journalism," *Encounter*, November 1956, 7: 19. For later comments by Macdonald on the same subject, see his letter, "Politics and Partisans," *Columbia University Forum*, Fall 1958, 2: 3.

14. John Fischer, "The Editor's Easy Chair," *Harper's*, March 1958, p. 18.

15. It has also been suggested that the separation of the political capital, Washington, from the intellectual capital, New York, likewise contributes to the feelings of isolation from political power on the part of many intellectuals. "The only type of intellectual who is likely to congregate in Washington is . . . one who has decided to make politics his full time business" (A. G. Nicholas, *op. cit.*, p. 44).

of the causes of this deprivation do not justify the conclusion drawn by many intellectuals that they are being ostracized or rejected by nonintellectuals.

Another point, and a very sore one, in the negative image the American intellectual has of himself is his income. Compared with businessmen and independent professional men, he is impecunious.[16] His argument goes like this: people are paid according to what they are worth, and consequently lower pay implies lower value. This syllogism omits the important fact that there are really two income structures in modern Western countries, the private one and the public one. The public position of high status is always more poorly paid than is a corresponding private one. A lawyer at the peak of his profession, as for example, a justice of the Supreme Court of the United States, earns a good deal less than does many a corporation lawyer in private practice. When Eisenhower's cabinet officers left private employment, they had to take considerable cuts in salary.

To consider a comparable group of intellectuals, the leading professors at major American universities earn salaries that compare favorably with those paid in all but the very summit of high-level posts in government or other nonprofit institutions. Thus the minimum salary for full professors at certain good universities is at present $12,000 for the academic year and many earn above this minimum. Many professors make considerably more money on the side, in consulting fees from corporations and governments, in fees for articles, lectures, and books. Data in the study of social-science professors cited previously show that 62 per cent of all in this field have outside sources of income, and that the more productive faculty members (earning presumably the highest regular salaries) are most likely to secure extra income. It is true, of course, that many professors could earn more in private industry, but this very fact disproves the contention of those who claim that their talents are undervalued. The truth is that professors, like the lawyers who become judges or elective officials rather than corporation counselors, really believe that the noneconomic rewards of the job are better than monetary gains.

16. But Raymond Aron tells us that in France, some intellectuals "cast their eyes longingly across the Atlantic, where certain specialists of the written word, whom one would hesitate to call intellectuals achieve considerable incomes." (Raymond Aron, *The Opium of the Intellectuals* [New York: Doubleday & Company, 1957], p. 219).

INTELLECTUAL CLASS OR INTELLECTUAL PROFESSION?

John Lukacs

THE universal tendency of our times toward social and political equality creates conditions that are unusually favorable for intellectual classes while they are not necessarily favorable for the intellectual profession. The age of modern democracy favors intellectuals while it does not necessarily promote a regimen of reason.

This may sound surprising: most people, including intellectuals, think and say the opposite. From their earlier optimism about democracy and the Common Man they have come around to believe that the modern masses are contemptuous of and hostile to intellectuals. At the same time they continue to believe that, were it not for reactionary managerial and political forces, the progress of mankind would continue away from Ages of Faith into Ages of broadening Reason. Both of these assumptions are, by and large, wrong; and their frequent coexistence within one mind is symptomatic of the general intellectual schizophrenia of our times. That condition in itself deserves attention; still, its description does not belong here. Let me only remark that the extraordinary confusion of the Western mind now is an historical consequence of great transformations, when old systems crumble and when new beliefs are not yet recognizably formed. It was about five hundred years ago that another great and confusing transformation had developed in the Western world: and in many ways its symptoms of intellectual confusion had been similar to ours.

But I am not dealing here with the great intellectual problem of what happens during transitions from Ages of Faith to Ages of Reason. I am concerned with the actual and, to some extent, unique emergence of intellectual classes. There are three developments that have been leading to this. First, it is obvious that with the passing of aristocratic societies, at a time when distinctions of birth have become less and less important, other distinctions were bound to emerge, since every society has distinctions of some kind. In our times these are no longer those of inherited property; they are, rather,

Adapted by the author from "Intellectuals, Catholics, and the Intellectual Life," in *Modern Age* (Winter, 1957-1958), pp. 49-53; printed by permission of the author and the periodical. Title supplied by the author.

those of recognized achievement; and there are reasons why recognized intellectual achievements have become more and more important. For, in the second place, we are now witnessing the general intellectualization of life: never in the history of mankind have there been so many schools, books, experts, written instructions, records, formulations and analyses of every kind of human endeavor, including sleeping, eating, love-making. In the third place, then, we live in times when administration consumes even more time and energy than does production; we are more and more governed by large administrative bureaucracies; and these, in turn, depend more and more on Intellectuals.

In the United States, in the home of Franklin's *homo faber,* of better and better mousetrap-makers, where the virtues of honest manual labor had been extolled more than perhaps anywhere else, by 1956 more people were employed in administration than in production. I know that not every file-clerk or, indeed, not every expert is an intellectual—according to the present usage of that noun. But my contention is that the present usage of the noun, and the concepts associated with it, may be rather senseless. I question whether we may speak of an intellectual class in the same way that we may speak of nobles, serfs, yeomen, bourgeoisie, scribes, mandarins in certain places and times.

For it is at least arguable that there is no such thing as *an* intellectual. It is at least significant that this noun has come into the English language relatively recently, around 1880; and that its original employment was Russian. Thus a word has come to the "West" from a semi-barbaric nation where it connoted a tiny minority of men and women capable of intellectual activity, a highly isolated and restricted caste. Curiously enough, the origins of the noun-like usage are Marxist as well as Russian; it has been a standard Marxist concept and later a Communist slogan to speak of "Workers, Peasants and Intellectuals" that is, brain-workers and body-workers. There is reason to believe that its introduction into common English and American was partly due to Russian Socialists; there is no doubt that the related word "intelligentsia" is of purely Russian mould, the "ts" in it being a simple transliteration of a Russian letter and sound. I think I need not describe in detail how the existence of intellectual *cadres* is a principal part of the structure of Communist states. But the rise of a meritocracy of intellectuals and experts develops elsewhere, too, even though the traditional Western and Christian concept of human nature does not permit this implied categorical separation of body from spirit, of physical from intellectual activity, of "non-intellectuals" from "intellectuals."

In the American Webster's *New Collegiate Dictionary* "intellectuals" and "intelligentsia" are virtually synonymous by now; this is not so in the Oxford, and not in the Larousse; it is relatively a new development. It was in the

1890's that the notion of an intellectual class first appeared in America. It was also in the 1890's that Germanic forms of philosophy, of social thought, and the German method of scholarship began to replace in prestige as well as in practice the domination of the earlier Anglo-Saxon and Celtic semi-classical and Biblical traditions of learning. Ever since that time the influence of American intellectuals has grown apace with their separation from the rest of the people. It is therefore that the intellectual as a prototype of a class is nowhere better observeable than in the United States, where we may find him in his occasional most human and best, but also in his most separated, anemic, worst form, in the form of a veritable caricature of his representative class category.

I submit that the standard complaint about "American anti-intellectualism" is nonsense in a population which invents and venerates brain trusts, I.Q.'s, quiz champions, educational science; which reads and writes more than ever before; which relies with a cramped trust on the opinions of experts, commentators, scientists, analysts, pundits, evaluators and all kinds of professors; whose political leaders constantly clamor for more brain-power; where there are scarcely any limits to the respectability of any kind of "education" or "research" and of public funds for it; which in its very sensual experiences—consider the prevalence of sex-manuals or the heavy scientific emphasis on the advertisement of food—has become thoroughly intellectualized. Thus we must dismiss the widely accepted cliché about the European "intellectual tradition" and about "traditional American anti-intellectualism." Together with it, we must reconsider that other shibboleth, the "practicality" of American minds when contrasted to the "aesthetic intellectualism of Europe": we must recognize how often, because of their thin-scientific and nominalist education, it is Americans who stubbornly stick to certain abstractions (in the name of *facts,* of course) at the expense of reality.

Nor is it arguable that American society mistreats its own intellectuals. I can say from my own experience that scholars, artists, writers or plain teachers are considerably respected by almost every stratum of the American people, provided that they are decent men and women with decent manners —and sometimes even without the latter provision. It is true of course that honest, decent, convinced men and women may be shunned because of their unorthodox ideas, unorthodox proposals, or unorthodox behavior: but this is *no longer* a specifically contemporary American phenomenon. Or consider how, after everything is said, Intellectuals in America are paid much better for their work than almost anywhere else in the Western world, which is more than a merely material index in a country where earning capacity and social status are rather intimately entangled. This does not necessarily mean that they are paid very well; but it means that they are neither mistreated or disrespected. I have thought for a long time that the epithet "egghead" and, indeed, all popular expressions of superficial anti-intellectualism are, in reality, backhanded compliments to Intellectuals, expressions in which sour grapes and a certain vague kind of envy are minor, and a lack of self-confidence major, components.

Around 1955 I read somewhere the self-pitying contention that the American public treats Communists and intellectuals with the same basic suspicion. This nonsense may be easily refuted when one keeps in mind that to be accused of *being* a Communist and to be accused of *not being* a real intellectual are both derogatory; conversely, that while pseudo-Communists are preferred over real ones, the reverse is true of pseudo-intellectuals.

By the end of the 1950's it is, more than ever, a profitable thing to be a recognized intellectual, to form part of the intellectual class in America. For about two centuries every American seeking popular approbation, every man running for office has strenuously tried to represent himself in farmer's overalls. But this is all over now. The shoe is on the other foot. Remember that recent reincarnation of populism, McCarthy, the *bête noire* of American intellectuals: how he shot across the country wearing horn-rimmed glasses, accompanied by a bevy of hand-picked anti-communist experts, always with briefcase in hand, pointing at its contents: "I Have Here The Facts!" . . .

In our days everyone would like to be recognized as an intellectual; but I am by no means sure that this is "a good thing." This is the story of all liberal intellectual illusions, the story of the Sorcerers and of their Apprentices all over again: there are millions who go to universities, intellectuals get a better deal than ever before; and yet the better kind among them are not very happy. But of course: like universal suffrage or social engineering or city planning or the marvels of liberating science, it turned out to be all very different from the way they had envisaged it. The intellectual class itself is becoming divided into producers and operators, while the levels of intellectual achievement of art, of writing and reading, of teaching and learning, deteriorate further. This is why it may be best if all of us would recognize that the noun intellectual makes little sense in this country now. For the now accepted sense of the noun excludes not only the overwhelming majority of a people who, after all, know how to read and write and who went through at least twelve years of schooling and the greater part of whom are no longer employed in manual occupations; it excludes, too, the great majority of college graduates, and the majority of engineers, doctors, lawyers.

What are these people, then? And what are their counterparts? Is every college professor or every buyer of paperback books automatically "an intellectual"? Is it still possible to separate the American population into intellectuals and non-intellectuals? I do not think so; but the answer is not that of new definitions. I do not think that we need worry unduly about the present confusion of intellectuals with non-intellectuals; we ought to worry, instead, about the recognized privileges and vanities of an intellectual class that obscure the true functions, the duties and burdens of the intellectual profession.

The present confusion flows from the misunderstanding of the difference between the aristocratic and the minority principles. The latter is general and "functional"; the former is particular and moral. The latter refers to the quantitative distribution of influence; the former to the quality of that influence. In every form of society and under every kind of government there is always a minority whose influence and leadership prove decisive. Yet the recognition of the principle that leadership, as every human privilege, should issue from a recognition of superior duties is a unique mark of the Western and Christian tradition. In this respect democracy and aristocracy are not antithetical, since the social ideals in the West were born out of a concern for the rights of the downtrodden and of the rights of minorities through a broadening application of the standards of chivalry. This respect for the small, the recognition that everybody is born equal, this generous willingness to give everyone the highest opportunities of self-betterment are not very evident in civilizations unrelated to ours. The spirit of true chivalry; the romantic temper within the recognized noble effort of fighting for good causes even when they are losing; the ideals of romantic love; a sense of humor; the reflective capacity for self-analysis; the courage to face oneself; a deep knowledge of human limitations complemented by an unlimited trust in Free Will; the preference of the straight and noble over the adorned and the pretentious; all in all, a respect for personal dignity forms the core of the heritage which is our own. I see even the best examples in Oriental civilizations, a Confucius or a Dostoevsky, falling on their faces with self-debasing humility before a corrupt Khan or a Tsar. The dignity of human achievement, thus, is not a problem of definitions or of proclamations or of technical or intellectual classification. At least the ideals of chivalry rose from the desire to imitate Christ; and they ought not to be relegated to the past, to the memories of elegant swordsmanship; it is chivalry and generosity that are so sadly missing from the virtues of our intellectual class. The fourteen requirements of the ideal knight described by Raoul de Houdenc in *Ailes de Prouesse* in 1230 are not requirements which we may pigeonhole under "liberal," "conservative," "reactionary," or "progressive." They are aristocratic, since they are marked by self-imposed duties and not by expected privileges; they are Christian; they reflect a distinction not of different *positions* but of different *aspirations*. And our trouble is not that the positions but that the aspirations of our recognized Intellectuals are insufficient.

The present crisis of the Western world is a spiritual crisis. To some extent it is due to grave Western intellectual errors that have gained prestige during the now gradually closing Age of Reason. A reaction against some of these errors has set in in many places, very much including the United States: but this is no cause for rejoicing or relief. A decline in personal liberties, in moral and intellectual standards, in the quality of independent opinion mark the dangerous character of this otherwise natural reaction.

During the excesses of an Age of Reason certain conservatives and Christians warned against an absolute and exclusive trust in the human intellect. During the present transition marked by the appearance of emotional mass movements, it may be the supreme and difficult duty of good men, of scholars, and of believing Christians to prevent the evolution of excessive dogmatic habits of mind to the detriment of charity and of reason. Nor are they allowed to dismiss smugly the Age of Reason as godless and dark. Here the generosity of Anselm and of Augustine but not the rabidities of Tertullian or of Joachim of Flora are worthy of emulation.

"The intellectual profession," "the intellectual life," "intellectual honesty," "intellectual courage," "intellectual sensitivity"—these are proper and recognizable things; they deal with vocations, they designate tendencies. But "the intellectual," "the class of intellectuals," "the intelligentsia" refers to an improper category: these nouns are not compatible with the Western Christian tradition. We must consider that the only civilization whose government was built partly on the minority principle of an intellectual élite was China with its mandarin system. The result was a degenerate and rotten government by eunuchs.

What *we* need is not an intellectual class, not even an intellectual élite, but a sincere dedication of men within the intellectual professions. That, in turn, must issue from the recognition that moral and intellectual performance, that mind and soul, spirit and body are not separable. It is therefore that the present American emphasis on the increase of "qualified" cadres of intellectuals is so questionable. It is part and parcel of the relatively recent devolution wherein learned men moved *down* toward the category of recognized intellectuals and experts rather than *up* toward the more self-sufficient and traditional concept of scholars and lovers of truth and of art; and this, in turn, is but part and parcel of the same broader devolution wherein ideas have superseded principles, methods have obscured purposes and means rose above ends during the present phase of a great transition.

When it comes, then, to the argument of "disrespect" it is, again, at least possible that this has reflected, at least in part, the inner, uneasy insecurity with which members of intellectual classes are prone to regard themselves. It is not possible to grant much respect to a man who, deep down, has little respect for himself and for his profession. Conversely, a man who has respect for himself and for his profession is bound, in the long run, to acquire the respect of others. That manifestations of this respect may appear in such ugly forms as envy, suspicion, shunning is, unfortunately, quite possible; but a man who has a true respect for his own profession will not—or, rather, he should not—be deterred therefrom.

The problems of our age seem to be marked much less by a disrespect for the mind than by a disrespect for the heart. We live in a world that is suspicious, nervous, and loveless, though it keeps reading, studying, and wishing to know. There exists, to say the least, little proof that intellectuals are different: that they are noble, generous, full of courage, and that suspicion, pettiness, opportunism and conformism are largely absent from their ranks. Thus a reforming not of the positions but of the aspirations of intellectuals may be very necessary: I have in my mind, first and far above all, the new forthcoming generation of young American teachers and scholars.

It is one thing to rephrase or to restate a new Christian hierarchy of values. It is another, and a much more difficult thing, to restore them. I fear that the creation of a professionally respected Christian intellectual élite will not do. Our teachers, scholars, and learned men now need such non-intellectual qualities of character as have always proved to have been not merely valuable supplements but essential components of personal integrity as well as to the proper exercise of their profession. They are courage (and not complacency); humility (and not self-pity); self-questioning (and not inner fear); generosity (and not pettiness); an unwillingness to make one's own moral convictions dependent on circumstances; and, above all, Love—that high kind of charity that reveals to us how the main purpose of knowledge is not so much certainty than it is understanding.

In the foreseeable future, these qualities will be needed more and more; the strain of their demand may prove, at times, alarming. These qualities have, in the past, marked the artistic or scholarly devotion of men, Christians and non-Christians, who tried to prevent and, indeed, at times halted the dreary degeneration of pragmatism into intellectual dogmatism. Mere restatements of a hierarchy of values without their profound sense and actual practice will not prevent a future degeneration of intellectual dogmatism into moral pragmatism. Without these non-intellectual qualities those shocking nadirs are reached where the intellectual cliques of the Jacobins and the intellectual timeservers around Torquemada, and more recently, Goebbels as well as Ehrenburg left their marks.

The difference between intellectual class and intellectual profession, between the recognition of a category of persons designated as intellectuals and the recognition of intellectual virtues and vices is generic and fundamental. I believe that many Americans dedicated to the intellectual life understand, deep down, this difference. For it is, too, the difference between what is organic and what is inorganic; between what is human and what is artificial; between what is romantic and what is merely sentimental; between what is manly and what is merely virile; between what is purposeful and what is methodical; between men and women with an inner dedication on one hand and the fretful pomposity of unsure pedants on the other.

AMERICA'S POST-RADICAL CRITICS

Harold Rosenberg

AMONG the grand metaphysical themes of this period, the most persistent and popular has been that of "alienation," the loss by the individual of personal identity through the operation of social processes. The tone of the post-War imagination was set by Orwell's *1984;* since the appearance of that work, the victim of "the dehumanized collective that so haunts our thoughts" (as William H. Whyte, Jr., described it in *The Organization Man*) has passed from the realm of fiction into the testimony of the sociologist and cultural anthropologist. Riesman's *The Lonely Crowd,* with its "other-directed" phantoms of automobile showrooms and PTA meetings, left no doubt among Americans that the familiar feeling of being someone else, or "nothing," was not a mere after-effect of seeing the wrong movie. With Whyte's *The Organization Man,* Spectorsky's *The Exurbanites,* Mills' *White Collar,* Packard's *Hidden Persuaders,* filling in details of personnel, locale and genesis, the Creature Who Lost Himself emerged as a statistical probability from the file cards of the social analyst. Since then, he has regularly inhabited the unhappy hunting grounds of beatnik poets, anti-conformist preachers, anti-modern crisis-philosophers.

In contrast to this figure of the pulverized ego—whom we may nickname the Orgman—stands the four-square dynamic individualist of the 19th century, Riesman's Inner Directed Man, Whyte's Protestant Ethic Person. It is by the measure of this fleshy hero that our contemporaries are seen as mere components of the faceless hordes of "the new middle class."

The effect of its backward-looking is to denude the new social criticism of radical implications, or, for that matter, of any political or moral consequence. Its charge that *all* present-day social behavior tends towards robotization is a more extreme accusation than that of the Leftism that preceded it; it implicates everyone, without distinction as to social class, function or idea, in a single, deepening process of dehumanization. Yet by this very extremism it generates an atmosphere of relaxed acquiescence to a developing totalitarianism from which there can be no escape. Regretting the disappearance of the old, driving, uncomfortable capitalist type, *The Organization Man* places the fate of the new corporation executive, as well as of the beneficiaries of

Adapted by the author from *The Tradition of the New* (1959), pp. 280-285; printed by the permission of the author and the publisher, Horizon Press, Inc. Title supplied by the author.

"fringe benefits" farther down the line, in a shadow world where "the demands for his surrender are constant and powerful, and the more he has come to like the organization the more difficult does he find it to resist these demands, or even to recognize them."

But there is more to the conception of the Orgman than regret for an older social type. As the representative of the new post-War employed intelligentsia, the post-radical critic suffers also a nostalgia for himself as an independent individual. For his former abstract sympathy with a nominal working class, the intellectual of this decade has substituted an examination in the mirror of his own social double as insider of The Organization and The Community. It is what he sees there that has caused him to project a morbid image of society compared with which the old "class struggle" America seems not only naïf but as relatively healthy as a war with rifles and cannons.

For in regard to the misery of alienation, who is a greater victim of what Whyte calls the split "between the individual as he is and the role he is called upon to play" than the member of the intellectual caste newly enlisted *en masse* in carrying out society's functions? As writer, artist, social scientist, he is one with his talents and his education for creative work; in playing his part in the service of the organization he must eliminate any thought of functioning for himself. Through his personal inventiveness he has in the past fifteen years achieved prosperity and social prestige; yet he is the most dependent of wage earners and the most anxiously conscious of his dependence—*The Exurbanites* chronicles this dependence and anxiety to the last installment dollar. (Applying itself to the narrower spectrum of the commercialized intellectuals, *The Exurbanites* is the most realistic of the works here mentioned.)

The intellectual employee also accepts a more total identification with his role than other workers, in that the editorial director, the designer, the copywriter, etc., sells himself more completely in terms of both psychic energy expended and number of hours worked. With him the division between work and leisure, discipline and freedom, has truly been erased. If the free artist or the founder of a great enterprise builds his life exclusively out of the substance of his work, today's intellectual unbuilds his life in order to live his job.[1]

Besides being the prime victim and exemplar of self-loss in contemporary society, the "organized" professional cannot escape a conviction of guilt for his part in depriving others of their individuality. He has consented to use his capacities as a tool and to approve in practice the proposition recorded by

1. The rule quoted by Whyte for corporation executives generally, "You promote the guy who takes his problem home with him," becomes for the intellectual, "You hire the guy who takes his problem to bed with him." His job has a creative side in which his preconscious must also collaborate. Take this into account in computing his average salary, and the difference between the wage-earner of the suburb and of the company town becomes largely a matter of overtime pay. At $2.50 an hour, the totally employed intellectual would earn more than $20,000 a year.

Whyte that "all the great ideas have already been discovered." His skills tend to relate to human management, e.g., writing, image-making, program-forming; even if his specialty is in engineering or the physical sciences, the results of his work directly augment the force by which society is controlled. The intellectual cannot function as Organization Man without also functioning as Organization-Man moulder; as human object he must also affect others as objects; as manipulated act as manipulator. Thus he cannot help but feel himself to be a betrayer of humanity as of his own mind. Helpless to change anything, he is yet the chief culprit of the alienation drama, the driven "scientist," who directs the undermining of the simple human individual, whether as motivational expert, inventor of personnel tests, or as preacher of despairing acceptance.

Self-displacement through one's acts is the innermost problem of life in America as of that in all civilized countries. The Social Type has always been among us, of course, despite Riesman's and Whyte's efforts to distinguish today's other-directed man from his nineteenth-century ancestor. Tolstoy's Ivan Ilych, who decorated his house entirely according to his own original ideas only to have it turn out exactly like all other houses of his class, is as good an example of automatic "radared" taste-exchanging (Riesman) as can be found in Fairfield County. Tolstoy explicitly insisted that Ilych was a socially made up man, an "object" guided by public opinion, an example of "dead" living.

In the United States, nineteenth-century literature, whether in the popular stage-comedies of manners or in the symbolism of the romantics, centers on society's human abstractions. The hero of Poe's "The Man Who Was Made Up" owed to industry all his movable parts. A contemporary of this invention was the ubiquitous Salesman-Preacher, whom Melville, writing in a less unctuous age than ours, named The Confidence Man. Like Whyte, Spectorsky, and Packard, Melville saw in this professional supplier of things, ideas and feelings the outstanding specimen of man as social artifice, while from the silent recesses of the office files, he drew forth the white-collared tomb deity, Bartleby. And he too, set up an apposite type; "inner-directed" like Riesman's, morally absolutist like Whyte's "Protestant;" the brooding subjective Indian fighter, paranoiac Ahab of the prairies.

What is new in America is not the socially reflexive person but the presence of a self-conscious intellectual caste whose disillusionment has induced its members to volunteer to serve as tools. The predicament in which these individuals find themselves is what casts a bar sinister over their image of America. The fear-augury that the Orgman will become everyone in a quiet, unopposable totalitarianism is not a conclusion based on social analysis but a projection of the fate the intellectuals have chosen for themselves. The American landscape has by no means been re-made by the "Social Ethic" compression machine into an electrified Eden set out on porcelain grass.

Except in the new suburbs, the physical condition of America's cities, towns and villages is of itself proof enough that decay, shiftlessness, egotism and other forms of popular expressionism are more than holding their own against other-direction. Granted that the growth of the supercorporation and the absorption and standardization of small business has changed the independent operator into an agent, at the same time that mechanization has been turning the workman into a technician; granted that Whyte's notation that "the collectivization so visible in the corporation has affected almost every field of work" is indisputable; and that today Orgmen reproduce themselves like fruit flies in whatever is organized, be it a political party or a museum of advanced art—given this groundwork for the conquest of America by this "type", still the contention that the nation is, or even might be, subordinated to such a master is at least as ludicrous as it is alarming. The increasing concentration of control and the standardization of work present well-known alternatives which we need not discuss here; but for the individual, the last voice in the issue of being or not being himself is still his own.

The inhabitant of the sacred groves has, however, surrendered all choices. Having accepted self-alienation in trade for social place, the post-radical intellectual can see nothing ahead but other-direction and a corporately styled personality. For him the Orgworld has closed for good. Within these limits the deploring of "conformity" is simply an expression of self-pity. The strategy (Whyte's) of fighting the organization through secret resistance behind the outershaped mask is, by the measure of the ancient intellectual tradition of denunciation or self-exile, only a dreary professional's ruse for holding on to the best of both worlds. That such a proposal should seem relevant is another proof that the Orgman is, with necessary additions and disguise, none else than the new intellectual talking about himself. Certainly the deft management of the corporate Look which solves things for Whyte would be of no help to the farmer or to the workingman, nor would the boss need to make use of it. The "what to do about it" part of the studies of Whyte and Riesman are clearly sermons for their milieu rather than challenges to history in the name of mankind.

The critics of the new America are disheartened by a revolution won— their revolution, which can go no farther than the ending of the underground life of the American intellectual mass through economic recognition of the services it has to offer. With his own success achieved, the only issue the intellectual can see as remaining for society is "personality". Somehow, this seems unattainable in "the dehumanized collective" in the building of which he is taking a leading part. The result is depression—and it is by the power of the depression it generates, in contrast to the smugness of the old-time boosting, that the present sociology is a force against a more radical and realistic understanding of American life.

FROM ALIENATION TO CRITICAL INTEGRITY: THE VOCATION OF THE AMERICAN INTELLECTUALS

Sidney Hook

I CANNOT UNDERSTAND why American intellectuals should be apologetic about the fact that they are limited in their effective historical choice between endorsing a system of total terror and *critically* supporting our own imperfect democratic culture with all its promises and dangers. For after all within our culture they are not *compelled* to choose whereas in the Soviet world neutrality or even silence is treason. Surely, this should count for something even with those who, although dependent upon the protective security of our relatively free culture for their neutralism and cultivation of purity, regard its struggle for survival as a vulgar battle of ideologies. Nor is it clear to me why an appreciation of the values of American life is incompatible with vigorous criticism of its many deficiencies and with determined efforts to enhance both its chances of survival and the quality of its cultural experience by more enlightened domestic and foreign policies. And if there are any seers or prophets among us, let them make their visions known.

The political and moral issues of our time are no different for the intellectual classes, the writers, artists and scholars, than they are for the working classes who recognize that even under the dislocations of our mixed economy, they enjoy more bread and freedom than the working classes anywhere else in the world. If anything, one expects the intellectuals to see even more clearly that the relative autonomy of their craft is threatened by Soviet totalitarianism more completely than by any other social system in history.

I must also confess to some perplexity in understanding laments about the "alienation" of the creative artist in American culture if this means that he faces more obstacles to doing significant work or finding an appreciative audience than was the case fifty or a hundred years ago. Surely, compared with his forebears, he can have no complaint on the score of creature comforts, which he certainly deserves no less than other human beings. The

Reprinted from *Partisan Review* (September-October, 1952), pp. 569-574, by permission of the author and the periodical. Title supplied by the author.

notion circulated in some quarters that university life is the Golgotha of the intellectual spirit is absurd. It seems to me that the creative life in America suffers more from mediocrity than from frustration. Equally bewildering is the view that mass culture or the popular arts constitute a profound menace to the position of the American intellectuals. Certainly those who love cream more than their own work may drown in it. The only sense I can find in the violent garrulities of Ortega y Gasset is that the mass "kind of man" who threatens the individual, is the man who lurks inside of anyone who fears to be himself. That mass "kind of man" in one form or another has always existed. And he sometimes is present in the man who strives and strains to be different as distinct from one who genuinely feels and thinks differently from his fellows.

There are all kinds of alienations in the world and one can get startling effects by confusing them. Hegel understood by self-alienation the process of dialectical development by which the individual consciousness progresses from innocence to maturity, from the simplicity of bare perception to the richly funded comprehension of a complexly interrelated system. Remove the mystification about the Absolute Self, drop the consolatory, religious overtones about the meaningfulness of the Whole, and what we get in the language of a barbarous literary psychology is an account of the travail of spiritual growth in any culture—not only for the artist but for every human being.

Marx's notion of self-alienation is historically circumscribed and has much less sweep than Hegel's. It applies primarily to the worker who is compelled to labor at something which neither expresses nor sustains his own needs and interests as a person. The unalienated man for Marx is the creative man. It is anyone who, under an inner compulsion, is doing significant work wrestling with a problem or striving to articulate a vision. The artist for Marx is the unalienated man par excellence to the extent that he does not produce *merely* a commodity. Remove the Utopianism of believing that all work in an industrial society can make a call on man's creative capacities, and of imagining that everybody, once a market economy disappears, will be able to do creative work, and what Marx is really saying is not obscure. The more truly human a society is, the more will it arrange its institutions to afford opportunities for creative fulfillment through uncoerced work. Man humanizes himself through work, which in association with others, is the source of speech. Man is dehumanized by *forced* work. There are some echoes of Rousseauistic myth in this and by a strange un-Marxian lapse Marx refers to a society in which there is no forced labor as a more natural society. From this point of view, the workers attending a conveyor belt, feeding a machine, endlessly filing orders or names are far more alienated than those intellectuals who have chosen their vocations and enjoy some freedom in setting their own goals or selecting their tasks.

There is a third conception of alienation popular with some sociologists and Bohemians which is applied to the artist who breaks with the conventions or norms of his family, society, or class. He is pitied and sometimes pities himself because he has no market or patron or reputation on the assumption that this is a necessary consequence of his non-conformity despite the fact that other non-conformists created their own audience and following and feel unalienated in the Marxian sense even when hostile critics ignore or rage against them. This is the most popular conception of the alienated artist in America and the shallowest. Why it is so popular I do not know unless it be that many individuals mistake the indifference of the world or their private creative agonies—which may very well be due to lack of creative capacity or to an ambition altogether incommensurate to their talents—for unerring signs of election to an alienated elite. But all a free culture can do is to provide opportunities for revolt: it cannot guarantee professional success.

No one knows the secret of significant creativity. We do know it cannot be mass produced and that it cannot emerge under conditions of extreme privation. But since the material lot of American artists has improved considerably in the last few decades and since the cultural atmosphere in America is much more receptive to the notion of total dedication to a creative calling—the son's announcement that he refuses to enter business or a profession but wants to be a writer, artist or musician no longer causes a family crisis—I must confess I do not know why the American arts are more anemic than the arts abroad *if* they are. And I suspect that no one else knows. Certainly, American work in science, scholarship and medicine does not lag behind European achievements. The hypothesis that mass culture and the popular arts—the Hollywood trap!—threaten the emergence of a significant culture of vitality and integrity because they constitute a perpetual invitation to a sell-out seems very far-fetched. Unless one is an incurable snob (I am old enough to remember intense discussions by otherwise intelligent people as to whether the cinema is an art), the forms of mass culture and the popular arts should serve as a challenge to do something with them. There are "sell-outs" of course but there are two parties to every "sell-out." The writer who "sells out" to Hollywood or the slicks cannot absolve himself of responsibility on the ground that he wouldn't be able to live as plushily as if he did. Why should he? I shall be accused of saying that I am sentencing artists and writers to starvation. But if scholars can live Renan's life of "genteel poverty" and do important work so can those who don't go to Hollywood.

Finally, I see no specific virtue in the attitude of conformity or non-conformity. The important thing is that it should be voluntary, rooted in considered judgment, an authentic expression of some value or insight for which the individual is prepared to risk something. 'Conformity' or 'non-conformity' are relational terms. Before evaluating them I should like to know *to and with what* a person is conforming or not conforming and *how*. Under the Weimer Republic, Stefan George, Spengler and Hitler were non-conformists: under the Czarist regime Dostoevsky in his most fruitful years was a conformist. To the greatest of men the terms 'conformist' or 'non-conformist' have singularly little relevance—Shakespeare, Milton, Goethe, Plato, Aristotle, Kant, or Dewey.

Particularly inexplicable to me is the final question whether the American intellectual should continue the tradition of critical non-conformism. The social function of the American intellectual is to think, and to act in such a way that the results of his thinking are brought to bear upon the great issues of our time. The cardinal attribute of the life of thought—its proper virtue—is the capacity to discriminate, to make relevant distinctions. He is no more un-American when he is intelligently critical of the United States than he is chauvinistic when he is intelligently appreciative. Many American intellectuals are unaware of the extent to which the social climate and objective possibilities for a democratic welfare state have improved in the last twenty years. Some still think of socialism as a good in itself. Having made a religion of a form of economy, they are incapable of learning from experience. They comfort themselves with a superior terminological intransigence in the belief that their sincerity atones for their stupidity. Their opposite numbers now regard socialism as an evil in itself. Socialism is no longer a form of economy for them, but the principle of welfare or social control itself. Like the most orthodox of Marxists they believe that any economy uniquely entails one political way of life. Fortunately, more and more intellectuals are beginning to understand what they could have learned from John Dewey long ago, that democratic process is more important than any predetermined program, and that persons and values are the test of adequate social relations not conversely.

Outside their own immediate craft too many intellectuals are irresponsible, especially in politics. They don't know enough, don't think enough, and are the creatures of fashion. It is sufficient for the majority to believe anything, for them to oppose it. They are too conscious of "public relations." Some are exhibitionists who are always washing their hands in public, Mary Magdalenes making a cult of purity. The lowest form of intellectual life is led by left bank American expatriates who curry favor with Sartrian neutralists by giving them the lowdown on the cultural "reign of terror" (sic!) in America.

Most American intellectuals still do not understand the theory, practice, and tactics of the Communist movement. Because McCarthy has made wild and irresponsible charges, too many are inclined to dismiss the Communist danger in its total global impact as relatively unimportant. American intellectuals were more frightened of Franco in 1936 and of Hitler in 1933 than they are of Stalin today. In 1933 and 1936 they did *not* say that, after all, there were few Fascists in America, fewer Fascists than there ever were of Communists since 1919. As country after country has come under Stalin's knife, concern in the colleges, in literary circles, even scientific quarters has *not* increased. The term "anti-Communist" has not got the same overtones as "anti-Fascist." It is not enough to say that McCarthy and reactionary demagogues have ruined the term "anti-Communist." Why didn't the Communists ruin the term "anti-Fascist"? They were just as vehement in their anti-Fascism as McCarthy is in his anti-Communism and even more irresponsible, because they called men like Dewey, Kallen, and Norman Thomas "fascists."

The task of the intellectual is still to lead an intellectual life, to criticize what needs to be criticized in America, without forgetting for a moment the total threat which Communism poses to the life of the free mind. Our own vigilantes and reactionaries are much more like witches and straw scarecrows than are the paid and unpaid agents of the Kremlin who constitute the membership of the Communist Parties in all countries. They can be cleared out of the way by a little courage and a sense of humor. They have nuisance value especially because of their effects abroad.

We face grim years ahead. The democratic West will require the critical support, the dedicated energy and above all, the intelligence, of its intellectuals if it is to survive as a free culture. With the possible exception of the technical arts and their theoretical ancillaries, great creative visions, conforming or non-conforming, can today flourish only in the soil of a free culture. It was not always so. But modern totalitarianism is not the same as ancient absolutisms.

Let the neutralists of the world remember. In the West non-conformists, no matter how alienated, can always win a hearing, even if they do not win a place in the Academy or earn the Order of Merit. In the land of Purges and Brainwashing, the only thing a non-conformist can earn is a bullet in the neck. This is the historical premise of our age whose recognition is binding on all humanists whether they are democratic socialists or civil libertarian conservatives or members of the alienated avant-garde.

LIST OF CONTRIBUTORS

ARON, RAYMOND. (1905-   ). French political scientist. Professor at the Institute d'Etudes Politiques, Paris.

ASCOLI, MAX. (1898-   ). Political commentator. Born and educated in Italy. Publisher and Editor of *The Reporter*.

BARRETT, WILLIAM. (1913-   ). Literary journalist. Professor of Philosophy at New York University.

BARZUN, JACQUES. (1907-   ). Historian. Professor of History at Columbia University; Dean of Faculties and Provost of the University.

BELL, DANIEL. (1919-   ). Sociologist. Former labor editor for *Fortune*; now Associate Professor of Sociology, Columbia University.

BENDA, JULIEN. (1867-1956). French philosopher and essayist.

BERDYAEV, NICHOLAS. (1874-1948). Russian philosopher. Professor of Philosophy after the Revolution; then forced to leave Russia. Lived in Paris until his death.

BUCKLEY, WILLIAM F., JR. (1925-   ). American political commentator. Editor of *National Review*.

CAMUS, ALBERT. (1913-1960). French novelist and philosopher. In 1957 Camus was awarded the Nobel Prize for Literature.

COSER, LEWIS A. (1913-   ). Sociologist. Born in Berlin. Associate Professor of Sociology at Brandeis University, and an editor of *Dissent*.

CURTI, MERLE. (1897-   ). American historian. Professor of History at the University of Wisconsin.

DEGAS, EDGAR. (1834-1917). French artist. One of the most powerful leaders of the Impressionist school.

DOSTOEVSKY, FEODOR. (1821-1881). Russian novelist.

ELIOT, T. S. (1888-   ). Poet and playwright. Born in St. Louis, Missouri; has lived in England since 1914. Awarded the Nobel Prize for Literature in 1948.

EMERSON, RALPH WALDO. (1803-1882). American essayist.

GORKY, MAXIM. (1868-1936). Russian novelist. A supporter of the Bolshevik Revolution and chief of the Soviet propaganda bureau for a short time.

HAYEK, F. A. (1899-   ). Economist. Born in Vienna. Professor of Moral and Social Sciences, University of Chicago.

HOLTON, GERALD. (1922-   ). Physicist. Born in Austria. Professor of Physics, Harvard University. Editor-in-chief of *Daedulus,* Journal of the American Academy of Arts and Sciences.

HOOK, SIDNEY. (1902-   ). American teacher of philosophy and author. Chairman of the Graduate Division of the Philosophy and Psychology Group of the Graduate School at New York University.

JAMES, WILLIAM. (1842-1919). American philosopher. Taught philosophy at Harvard University.

JOUVENEL, BERTRAND DE. (1903-   ). French political commentator. Jouvenel has established a reputation in Europe as a writer specializing in economic questions and international relations.

KAUTSKY, KARL. (1854-1938). Born in Prague. Kautsky became a leading Marxist through the founding of a political journal, and through active participation in politics.

KIERKEGAARD, SØREN. (1813-1855). Danish philosopher and theologian.

KIRK, RUSSEL. (1918-   ). Political essayist. Formerly Research Professor of Political Science at Post College and Editor of *Modern Age.*

LAFARGUE, PAUL. (1842-1911). Historian and economist. Born in the West Indies. Married the youngest daughter of Marx, and became the leading propagandist in France for the theories of Marx and Engels. Lenin frequently referred to his works.

LASKI, HAROLD J. (1893-1950). English political scientist. Was a Professor of Political Science at the London School of Economics and a member of the National Executive Committee of the British Labor Party.

LIPSET, SEYMOUR. (1922-   ). Sociologist. Professor of Sociology at the University of California, and Research Associate at the Institute of Industrial Relations at Berkeley, California.

LÜTHY, HERBERT. (1918-   ). French political and social essayist. Author of *France Against Herself.*

LUKACS, JOHN. (1923-   ). Historian. Born in Budapest. Professor of History at Chestnut Hill College and LaSalle College.

MacLEISH, ARCHIBALD. (1892-   ). American poet and playwright. Professor of English at Harvard University.

MALLARMÉ, STÉPHANE. (1842-1898). French poet.

MANNHEIM, KARL. (1893-1947). German sociologist. From 1933 until his death, Mannheim taught at the University of London.

MANN, GOLO. (-   ). Historian. Born in Germany. Professor of History at Claremont Men's College, California.

MENCKEN, H. L. (1880-1956). American author, journalist, and philologist.

MICHELS, ROBERTO. (1876-1936). Sociologist and economist. Born in Germany. Taught economics and sociology at the University of Perugia.

MILOSZ, CZESLAW. (1911-   ). Polish poet and writer. Born in Lithuania.

MISES, LUDWIG VON. (1881-   ). Economist. Born in Austria. Visiting Professor at the Graduate School of Business Administration, New York University.

MOLNAR, THOMAS. (1921-   ). Political essayist. Teaches French literature at Brooklyn College.

MONTHERLANT, HENRY DE. (1896-   ). French novelist and playwright.

NIEBUHR, REINHOLD. (1892-   ). Theologian. Professor of Ethics at the Union Theological Seminary.

NIETZSCHE, FRIEDRICH. (1844-1900). German philosopher.

NOMAD, MAX. (-   ). Political writer. Born in Poland.

ORTEGA Y GASSET, JOSÉ. (1883-1955). Spanish philosopher. Formerly Professor of Metaphysics in Madrid.

ORWELL, GEORGE. (1903-1950). English novelist.

PADHYE, PRABHAKAR. (1909-   ). Indian writer. Secretary of the Asian Office of the Congress for Cultural Freedom.

PHILLIPS, WILLIAM. (1907-   ). American author and literary critic. An editor of *Partisan Review*.

RIESMAN, DAVID. (1909-   ). Sociologist. Henry Ford II Professor of the Social Sciences at Harvard University.

RÖPKE, WILHELM. (1899-   ). Economist. Born in Germany. Professor at the Graduate Institute of International Studies in Geneva.

ROSENBERG, HAROLD. (1906-   ). American author, literary critic, and poet.

SALOMON, ALBERT. (1891-   ). Sociologist. Born in Germany. Professor of Sociology of the Graduate Faculty, New School for Social Research, New York.

SCHOPENHAUER, ARTHUR. (1788-1860). German philosopher.

SCHÜCKING, LEVIN L. (1878-   ). Sociologist and literary critic. Born in Germany.

SCHUMPETER, JOSEPH A. (1883-1949). Economist. Born in Moravia. Taught economics at Harvard University.

SETON-WATSON, HUGH. (1916-   ). British historian. Professor of Russian History at the School of Slavonic and Eastern European Studies, London University.

SHILS, EDWARD A. (1911-   ). American sociologist. Professor of Social Sciences, Committee on Social Thought, University of Chicago.

SILONE, IGNAZIO. (1900-   ). Italian novelist.

SPENDER, STEPHEN. (1909-   ). British poet. An editor of *Encounter*.

STALIN, JOSEPH. (1879-1953). Russian political leader. After the death of Lenin, he emerged as complete master of the USSR.

STOKES, WILLIAM S. (1916-   ). Political scientist. Professor of Comparative Political Institutions at Claremont Men's College, California.

TATE, ALLEN. (1899-   ). American essayist and poet. Professor of Literature at the University of Minnesota.

TCHEKOV, ANTON. (1860-1904). Russian playwright and author of short stories.

TOCQUEVILLE, ALEXIS DE. (1805-1859). French statesman and author.

VALÉRY, PAUL. (1871-1945). French poet and essayist. Was a member of the Académie Française.

VIERECK, PETER. (1916-   ). American poet, historian, and political commentator. Professor of History at Mt. Holyoke College.

WILSON, FRANCIS G. (1901-   ). American political scientist. Professor of Political Science at the University of Illinois.

ZNANIECKI, FLORIAN. (1882-1958). Sociologist. Born in Poland. Was a Professor of Sociology at the University of Illinois.

NAME INDEX

SUBJECT INDEX

Academic freedom, 404, 495-496

Age of Reason, 9, 15, 26, 217, 517, 521-522

American Revolution, 8-10, 17, 30

Americanism, 456-457

Anarchism, 336-337

Anti-Semitism, 347-348

Aristocracy, 521

Art for Art's Sake, 38-39, 214-215, 234

Artist(s), 9-10, 32-40, 133, 162-166, 198-201, 206-211, 214-215, 245, 262, 272, 274-275, 282, 332

Bohemian(s), 9, 20-22, 24-26, 311-312, 403, 477, 486-487

Bolshevism, see Communism

Book(s), influence of, 102, 115-116, 128-131, 133, 267, 411

Bourgeois, bourgeoisie, 26, 48, 53, 63, 74, 316, 322, 324, 329, 336, 415

Capitalism, 53, 69, 71, 72, 279, 280, 282-284, 328-330, 333, 335-336, 338, 342, 343, 365-368, 385-386, 388, 390, 428

Caste, 365

Chivalry, 521

Christianity, 266, 290, 521, 523

Class, 26, 28, 52-53, 62-70, 192-193, 229, 280, 281, 328, 332, 339, 341, 343, 372-373, 400, 407-408; see also Intellectual(s) and Classes

College(s), see Education

Colonialism, 401, 430

Communism, 10, 44, 48, 50, 86-91, 235-236, 270, 279, 281, 282, 302-304, 328, 336-337, 340, 342, 355-358, 360-361, 400, 401, 404, 434-436, 438, 440, 446-447, 449, 500-503, 520, 532

Conservatism, 291

Cosmopolitanism, 227

Critic(s), 39-40, 234

Democracy, 278-279, 285-288, 290, 291, 296-301, 363, 385, 404, 405, 495, 520

Dilettante, 101, 114-115

Education, 42-43, 75-76, 103, 157-158, 259, 278, 285-288, 308, 331-332, 424-427, 430-432, 504-506

Expert(s), 103-104, 116, 126-127, 159, 163-179, 182, 194-195, 298-299, 372-375, 379, 402, 445, 514

Facts, discoverers of, 158-161, 178

Fascism, 264, 267-269, 281, 341, 342, 472

Feudalism, 338

Founding Fathers, 30-31, 102

Freedom, 382-384, 436; see also Academic freedom

French Revolution, 8-9, 12, 17, 18, 295-296, 354-355, 401

Genius, 121, 130

Humanism, 226-227, 273, 279, 292-293, 357

Humanitarianism, 226-227

Idéologues, 53, 80-86

Industrial Revolution, 386-387, 389, 427

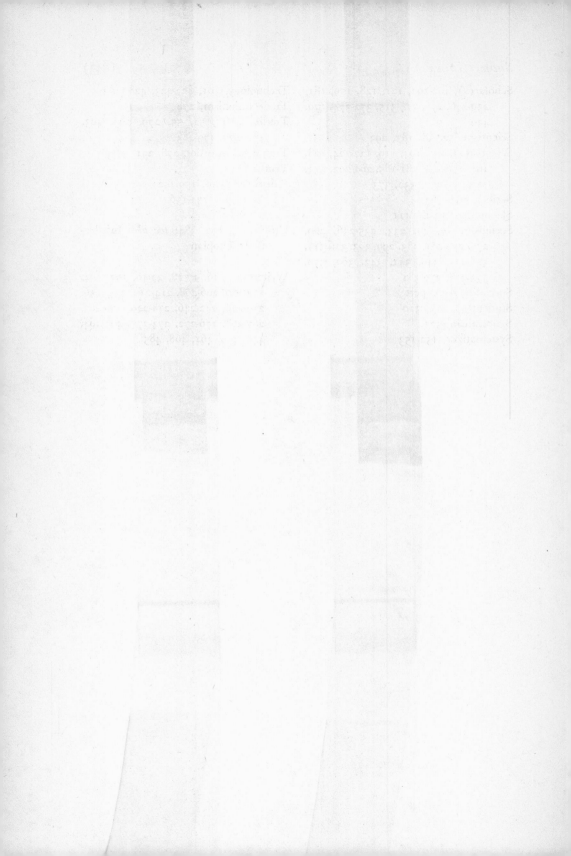